Praise for
The Most Noble Adventure

"Behrman's comprehensively researched and well-written history of the Marshall Plan—that, as much as the Allied victory, saved Europe as we know it—promises to be a definitive work."

—Dr. Henry Kissinger

"The Marshall Plan was the most creative and inspired act in modern American foreign policy. It preserved the possibility of freedom and showed the potential for great leadership. . . . Greg Behrman has captured all of this masterfully. In a beautifully researched and written narrative, he has produced a compelling tale that should be an inspiration as we face our new global challenges."

—Walter Isaacson, coauthor of *The Wise Men* and author of *Einstein*

"There is much for our times to learn from the Marshall Plan—about what common purpose can achieve and how cooperation among nations, even in dangerous times and midst high tension, can bring such great common benefit."

—Daniel Yergin, author of *The Prize*

Behrman's comprehensive study of the Marshall Plan could not arrive at a better time. . . . Behrman provides clarity, color, and one of the greatest cast of characters in America's history. . . . It's unlikely Behrman's narrative force could be surpassed. . . . [A] gripping tale."

—*Publishers Weekly* (starred review)

"A splendid narrative history of the Marshall Plan, perhaps the best foreign-policy idea America ever had. . . . Behrman's sure grasp of the geopolitics, his firm understanding of the Plan's details and his deft portrayal of the men who made it work combine to forge a remarkable story."

—*Kirkus Reviews* (starred review)

"Behrman's work will reward readers thinking beyond slogans to understand the purposes and achievements of the original. With impressively thorough research, Behrman does exactly that."

—*Booklist*

ALSO BY GREG BEHRMAN

The Invisible People:
How the U.S. Has Slept Through the Global AIDS Pandemic,
the Greatest Humanitarian Catastrophe of Our Time

★ ★ ★ ★ ★

THE MARSHALL PLAN AND HOW
AMERICA HELPED REBUILD EUROPE

★ ★ ★ ★

THE
MOST NOBLE
ADVENTURE

GREG BEHRMAN

FREE PRESS

New York   London   Toronto   Sydney

FREE PRESS
A Division of Simon & Schuster, Inc.
1230 Avenue of the Americas
New York, NY 10020

First Free Press trade paperback edition August 2008

FREE PRESS and colophon are trademarks of Simon & Schuster, Inc.

For information about special discounts for bulk purchases,
please contact Simon & Schuster Special Sales at
1-800-456-6798 or business@simonandschuster.com

Book design by Ellen R. Sasahara

Manufactured in the United States of America

1   3   5   7   9   10   8   6   4   2

The Library of Congress has cataloged the hardcover edition as follows:

Behrman, Greg.
The most noble adventure : the Marshall plan and how America helped
rebuild Europe / Greg Behrman.
p. cm.
1. Marshall Plan. 2. Economic assistance, American—Europe—History.
3. Europe—Economic conditions—1945. I. Title.
HC240.B384 2007
338.91 '730409044—dc22
2007006984

ISBN-13: 978-0-7432-8263-5
ISBN-10:   0-7432-8263-9
ISBN-13: 978-0-7432-8264-2 (pbk)
ISBN-10:   0-7432-8264-7 (pbk)

PHOTO CREDITS

Courtesy of the George C. Marshall Research Library, Lexington, Virginia:
Photos 1, 2, 4, 6, 7, 8, 9, 10, 11, 12, 14, 15, 16, 17, 22, 24, 25,
26, 27, 28, 30, 32, 33, 34, 35, 36, 37, 42, 43, 44.

National Archives Still Picture Branch (NARA):
Photos 3, 5, 13, 18, 19, 20, 21, 23, 29, 31, 38, 39, 40, 41.

To My Father,
My Hero

★ ★ ★ ★ ★

MAKE NO SMALL PLANS.

THEY HAVE NO MAGIC TO STIR MEN'S BLOOD.

—Daniel Hudson Burnham, American architect (1846–1912),
as quoted by Paul Gray Hoffman, administrator of the
Economic Cooperation Administration

★ ★ ★ ★ ★

CONTENTS

PROLOGUE

JUNE 5, 1947.

The bell tolled at 9:30 A.M. The midmorning sun made its arc in a clear blue sky, a warm salutation to the crowd of seven thousand—mostly parents of graduates, scholars and selected guests—as they filtered into the yard between Widener Library and Memorial Church. The day marked Harvard University's 286th Commencement, and the first "fully normal" graduation ceremony since the United States had entered World War II five and a half years earlier.

The war had claimed 300,000 American lives; it had cost $300 billion in treasure; and it had demanded immeasurable sacrifice. Now it was over. The crimson robes, the Latin perorations, the diplomas, the handshakes and the celebrations—all the customary features of that day were meant to mark a return to normalcy.

It was generally recognized that one man, more than any other, had delivered America victory and had made the return to peace possible. As the procession came into view, the crowd caught a glimpse of him. They sprang to their feet and offered a rousing ovation. To many, it was odd to see him without the military uniform in which they had come to know him. It was the uniform he had worn as Army chief of staff in September 1939, the month Germany invaded Poland; he wore it when he was recognized as *Time* magazine's Man of the Year in 1943, lauded as the man who transformed the United States military into the most dominant fighting force in the world; and the same one he wore when the war had ended and Winston Churchill called him the "organizer of victory."

Appointed secretary of state five months earlier, he was a civilian now. The military uniform, if not the man, had been retired. In its stead George Catlett Marshall wore a gray suit, a white shirt and a blue necktie. Old habits remained, though. As he walked past the crowd, his head moved sharply but rhythmically left to right, as if he were reviewing the troops. The lean six-foot frame was familiar, as was the short white hair, pressed back firmly and neatly; and the pale blue eyes still cut a piercing gaze.

The prolonged ovation ended only when Marshall and his fellow honorees were seated under a canopy of maple, beech and hickory trees, on a platform set up on the steps of Memorial Church. When it was his turn to receive his degree, Marshall stood to another standing ovation. When the crowd quieted, Harvard President James Conant read the citation in both Latin and English. Conant said that Marshall was "an American to whom Freedom owes an enduring debt of gratitude." He was "a soldier and statesman whose ability and character brook only one comparison in the history of the nation." The comparison was to George Washington.

It was the sort of heady stuff in which many of Marshall's subordinates—MacArthur, Patton, even Eisenhower—reveled; but not Marshall. During the war, he had refused the plentitude of awards offered him. It was unfitting, he said, to accept decorations when American men and boys were fighting and dying. It was dispositional as well. Marshall had always shunned ceremony. He had twice turned down Harvard's offer to receive the honorary degree of doctor of laws.

On this day, though, there was a purpose to Marshall's attendance. A week earlier he had written to Conant, finally accepting Harvard's offer. He would not promise a formal address, but he would be pleased to make a few remarks—and perhaps "a little more," he wrote. The content of those remarks lined seven typed and crisply folded pieces of paper in Marshall's jacket pocket. No one had seen the final draft of the speech that Marshall had come to deliver, save the general himself; not even the commander in chief, President Harry S. Truman. On that early June morning, no one in attendance knew it, but Marshall had come to give an address that would transform Europe, dramatically reconfigure the international political landscape, and launch America forward as a modern superpower with global responsibilities.

The speech was delivered not on the steps of Memorial Church, as most historical depictions suggest, but later that day, at 2 P.M. in Harvard Yard at a subsequent luncheon given for alumni, parents of alumni and select guests.

During the war, Marshall had held regular weekly press conferences in his office. He would go around the room, fielding questions from dozens of hardened, cigar-chomping reporters. His command of grand strategy and minute detail was dazzling, and the press conferences helped to fuel his legend. As it was, he much preferred to speak extemporaneously. But those wartime conferences were meant to provide reporters with background, and were strictly off-the-record affairs. When Marshall became secretary of state, however, remarks were on the record, meaning that the smallest utterance would constitute a policy pronouncement. Marshall spoke in a low and monotonal voice, and so read speeches poorly. Thus when Dean Acheson, Marshall's undersecretary, recommended that as secretary of state Marshall should deliver policy addresses strictly from texts, he found Marshall as "disappointed as a small boy," but duly in agreement.

And so it came to be that as Marshall began to speak on that early June afternoon in Cambridge, Massachusetts, he was said not to have looked up from his text once. With J. Robert Oppenheimer and T. S. Eliot both in tow as fellow honorees, Marshall adumbrated for his audience Europe's dire economic condition, its postwar dystopia—a new wasteland, dysfunctional and intensely vulnerable. The period of drift would have to end, Marshall explained, and the time for action had come. And then, it was all there, in only a few simple paragraphs. Not the details, as many would later point out—errantly suggesting that it was not even "a Plan" at all—but the elements and the contours of the Plan that would come almost immediately to bear his name.

He spoke in a soft, almost inaudible voice, "as though," it was written, "he did not care especially if they were listening." Future dignitaries in attendance that day—industrialists, acclaimed scholars, Conant himself, even future Marshall Planners—would concede that they did not comprehend the meaning or the historical salience of the Plan then unfurled. They were not alone. American networks did not broadcast it, and the American news agencies "dismissed it with a few lines." The *New York Times* and most other national papers led with other stories the next day. Even the British Embassy in Washington "did not consider it worth the cable charges to transmit to London."

But to British Foreign Secretary Ernest Bevin, the man on the other side of the Atlantic on whom its fate would most depend, perched up in his bed, listening to a broadcast of the speech on the BBC: "It was like a lifeline to sinking men. It seemed to bring hope where there was none. The generosity of it was beyond my belief." For the British foreign secretary, its significance, its need and its transformational potential were unmistakable. To Bevin—who, as a wartime Cabinet member with Churchill had heard his share of exalted orations—it was "one of the greatest speeches made in world history."

In the years to follow what Senator Arthur Vandenberg called the "electric effect of a few sentences in quiet sequence," "history wrote with a rushing pen." And the story it told was of the Marshall Plan.

• • •

HISTORIAN AND EYEWITNESS Thomas Bailey described the Marshall Plan as "the greatest act of statesmanship in the nation's history." Cold War historian Melvyn Leffler determined that it was "probably the most effective program the United States launched during the entire Cold War." Journalist Arthur Krock wrote that "it was one of the great achievements of the century, as nearly everyone eventually saw." Combined, the encomiums seem almost to elevate reality into myth, offering perhaps well-deserved paeans, but quite possibly occluding the Plan's inherent nuance and granularity, robbing it of its historic depth and true meaning.

It has been twenty years since the last comprehensive history of the Marshall Plan was written. Since then a Cold War has ended and troves of archival material have been made available from the Soviet Union and elsewhere, and much new scholarship has followed. Winston Churchill, who delighted in writing history as well as making it—especially when it was about himself—once wrote: "When the perspective of time has lengthened, all stands in a different setting." History's tides suggest this a fitting time to take another look.

The story of the Marshall Plan—and any of the Plan's success—belongs just as much to Europe as it does to the United States. Rather than a unilateral enterprise, or an initiative imposed upon one side or the other, the Marshall Plan is best viewed as a partnership in which the United States and Europe played co-leads. However, the main focus here is the story from the American side. Therein, a series of remarkable statesmen emerge. They are men like Harry S. Truman, Dean Acheson, Robert Lovett, George Kennan, Lucius Clay and David Bruce. However, as the story unfolds, six U.S. statesmen, more than the others, emerge as indispensable to the genesis, the execution and the ultimate success of the Marshall Plan. They are George Marshall, Will Clayton, Arthur Vandenberg, Richard Bissell, Paul Hoffman, and W. Averell Harriman. The story of the Marshall Plan is in large part their shared story.

FROM JUNE 1947 to its termination at the end of 1951, the Marshall Plan provided approximately $13 billion to finance the recovery and rehabilitation of war-torn and postwar weary Western Europe. In today's dollars that sum equals roughly $100 billion, and as a comparable share of U.S. Gross National Product it would be in excess of $500 billion. It was a mammoth sum, more than the United States spent to govern itself in the first fifteen years of the twentieth century. More than the provision of dollars and aid, the Marshall Plan was the cornerstone of American foreign policy for much of those formative and consequential postwar years. It was a monumental undertaking and—echoing Walt Whitman's famous lines—it contained multitudes and contradictions.

An act of unprecedented beneficence, the Marshall Plan was an unabashedly strategic enterprise framed in the shifting and perilous geopolitical context of its time. Offered in humility as a hand in partnership, it sought nothing less than to refashion Europe in fundamental and audacious ways. Aiming at transparency and astoundingly free of corruption and scandal, its dollars financed—unbeknownst even to Cabinet-level officials—some of the first covert operations in CIA history. It employed U.S. capital and a free-market ideology to prop up socialist regimes, in the name of saving them from Communism. Proposed as an altruistic program to save the world from "hunger, poverty and chaos," it helped to trigger the Cold War.

Its apparent contradictions and the enormity of its scope and ambition notwithstanding—in fact, in large part because of these things—the Marshall Plan would become one of the most successful foreign policy enterprises in the annals of U.S. history. In the post–Cold War, post-9/11 world, America has not yet responded to the challenges and opportunities of the present age with programs or efforts of comparable depth or imagination. It is my conviction that the story told here contains insights that speak to the current American moment with resonance and urgency; it is my hope that it might help to illuminate a brighter path forward.

WHEN GEORGE MARSHALL was a boy, the United States of America was little more than a hundred years old. It was a nation so young that U.S. history was not commonly taught in school. In the course of Marshall's lifetime, the Plan that was to bear his name would launch America forward into a world fraught with perils, uncertainties and anxieties in a degree of engagement once thought unimaginable. Perhaps Dean Acheson put it best. For him, the Marshall Plan was "one of the greatest and most honorable adventures in history."

And it began with a trip to Moscow.

Part One

―――――――――――❦―――――――――――

THE GENESIS

Chapter One

THE MARCH TO MOSCOW

O N MARCH 5, 1947, GEORGE CATLETT MARSHALL boarded an airplane along with a coterie of aides and bureaucrats. His destination was Moscow and the latest in a series of postwar meetings with the foreign ministers of Britain, France and the Soviet Union. Summoned from retirement by his commander in chief, Harry S. Truman, for the second, though not the last, time, Marshall had been appointed secretary of state six weeks earlier. To prepare for the upcoming conference, he spent most of his first weeks in intensive briefings getting up to speed on the latest developments in Europe, the manifold intricacies involved in the various peace treaties pending and relations with the Soviet Union. The briefings suggested that the task ahead would be daunting. In a meeting shortly before leaving for Moscow, Senator Arthur Vandenberg said to Marshall: "You are going to have one difficult time!" "I anticipate that," Marshall responded.

Away for 350 out of the 562 days of his tenure, Marshall's predecessor, James Byrnes, was said to have run the State Department out of his briefcase. A former senator and political "fixer," Byrnes, a magazine article quipped, was rumored to have laid out three hats in the morning so that he could compromise on the one in the middle. To Dean Acheson, who was asked to stay on as Marshall's undersecretary, the new appointment seemed "an act of God." In the short six weeks since Marshall had become secretary, he had already brought a new sense of order and purpose to the State Department. It would take time, though, before he would feel completely comfortable in his new civilian role. His military service had spanned forty-five years, and he was known the world over simply as "General." Subordinates noticed that when he was called "Mr. Secretary," Marshall would sometimes turn around, looking for someone else.

• • •

GEORGE CATLETT MARSHALL was born in Uniontown, Pennsylvania, on December 31, 1880. But he was anchored in the deep and rich Virginian tradition of his family's past. His ancestors included Thomas Marshall, who had fought alongside George Washington in the French and Indian War. He was of the Randolph family, celebrated Virginia aristocracy. Most notably, he was a collateral descendant of John Marshall, the former secretary of state and Supreme Court Chief Justice. Marshall's immediate ancestors were a less exalted lot. His father was a failed businessman and favored George's older brother, who bullied the younger Marshall. Bouts of illness and a slow start in his education rounded out a very difficult boyhood. By the time Marshall made it to the Virginia Military Institute, or VMI, a fire had begun to burn and a mission had come into focus: "I thought the continuing harping on the name John Marshall was kind of poor business," he later said. "It was about time for somebody else to swim for the family."

When he entered VMI, fresh from a bout with typhoid fever, Marshall was "skinny, sweaty and nervous." Even more than the other first year cadets, or "rats" as they were called, Marshall emerged a prime target for hazing. In his freshman year, upperclassmen stuck an unsheathed bayonet in wooden planks in the floor, tip up. They had Marshall squat over the weapon. He held his lanky frame above the tip, praying that they would relent. They did not, and after twenty minutes he fainted and lost consciousness. Marshall woke up with a deep gash in his buttocks. Had the angle of his fall been an inch or two in another direction, he would have died. He did not tell on the offenders. "Awed by his courage," the cadets did not bother him again.

At VMI, Marshall began to evince the talents and traits that would mark his later ascent. He had a mind of logical rigor and precision. VMI inculcated, above all, discipline and austerity. Marshall had an unusual capacity for both. His surroundings prized the Virginian code of chivalry, espousing a sense of service, gentlemanly conduct and a dignified bearing. Adhering to that code, and in part a product of the insecurity born of his youth, Marshall kept his distance from others. All of these elements converged to foment in Marshall an extraordinary self-command, the hallmark trait that would come to define his unusual brand of charisma.

In 1914, stationed in the Philippines, Marshall, then a thirty-four-year-old captain, caught the eye of his commanding officer, General Franklin Bell, who one day called twenty-six officers to lunch at his quarters and told them, "Keep your eyes on George Marshall. He is the greatest military genius of America since Stonewall Jackson." Promoted to colonel during World War I, Marshall was charged with taking a leading role in planning some of the largest and most successful U.S. operations of the war. General John J. "Black Jack" Pershing, commander in chief of the American Expeditionary Force, summarily scooped Marshall up as his aide. Pershing became in many ways a father figure to Marshall, protecting, mentoring and championing his military career.

At the end of World War I, Pershing recommended Marshall for promotion to brigadier general. Peacetime had returned, though, and Congress froze all military promotions, halting Marshall's rise and consigning him to a series of disappointing postings for the twenty years to follow. The years weathered Marshall. He lost his first wife, Lily, who was sickly, and to whom he was devoted, and married a former actress named Katherine Tupper (Pershing stood in as Marshall's best man). He grappled in bureaucratic rivalries with, among others, Douglas MacArthur. It appeared, in 1939, that at fifty-nine, George Marshall, then only a one-star general, would never have his chance. Then something happened that was without precedent in Army history. Heeding Pershing's recommendation, President Franklin Roosevelt reached past twenty major generals and fourteen senior brigadier generals and chose Brigadier General George Marshall as the Chief of Staff of the United States Army.

The timing was propitious. Eight hours before Marshall was to be sworn in, on September 1, 1939, he was woken at 3 A.M. to receive the news of Nazi Germany's invasion of Poland. Marshall had inherited the reins of an army with fewer than 200,000 men, ranked nineteenth in the world, behind Portugal and Bulgaria. Officers still practiced maneuvers on horseback, and soldiers were so underequipped that they often used cardboard cutouts of rifles for drills.

He told Roosevelt that he would accept the post on the condition that he would have the right to say, at all times, what he thought. When Roosevelt answered with a quick yes, Marshall replied, "You said yes pleasantly, but it may be unpleasant." Marshall did not visit Roosevelt's estate, Hyde Park. He made a point not to laugh at his jokes. When, on one occasion, Roosevelt called him George, Marshall said that he was George only to his wife. He insisted the president call him General Marshall. Roosevelt was famed for his charm and powers of manipulation. Marshall felt it essential for the prosecution of the task ahead that he maintain his full independence. He knew that he would have to stand apart.

• • •

AS WAR BROKE OUT, and the United States entered the conflict in December 1941, Marshall worked seven days a week. In his office chair by 7:30 every morning, wrote one of his biographers, he "worked there with a ruthless efficiency that terrified his subordinates, who were expected to enter on schedule, sit down without speaking or saluting, give him a clear presentation" and duly exit. During the darkest days of the war, in 1942, Marshall seemed to become calmer. He recalled that when Pershing appeared tired or forlorn, officers took it as a sign that things were going badly, and that it damaged morale. He would not allow himself to lose his temper or show signs of frustration. "I cannot afford the luxury of sentiment, mine must be a cold logic," he said. During those years, "it was [as] though he lived outside of himself and George Marshall was someone he was constantly appraising, advising and training to meet a situation," his wife Katherine wrote later.

Behind the iron discipline and rigor, there was an even and gracious manner, an unflagging sense of justice and a discernible humanity. He wrote thousands of personal letters to grieving widows and families of fallen soldiers. He seemed free of self-concern or vanity. On one occasion he sat for hours for a portrait. When the artist asked if he would like to see the finished painting, he said that it would not be necessary and went back to work. He was capable, at rare moments, of humor. On another occasion General Walter Bedell Smith reported to Marshall on his farm in Leesburg, Virginia, on a rainy day while Marshall was doing chores. Smith asked if it was necessary that he stand there and report in the rain. No, Marshall said, you can grab that bucket and report sitting down.

As head of the U.S. military, Marshall's responsibilities and burdens were Olympian. As the war's tide turned in 1943, and the Allies met in Tehran around Thanksgiving Day of that year, they agreed on opening the long-anticipated second front with an invasion of Nazi-occupied France. They would have to decide on a general to lead the invasion, what many considered "the most important battlefield assignment in the history of warfare." Roosevelt wanted Marshall for the command. Discussing it with Dwight Eisenhower in a military plane, flying over a battlefield in Tunisia, the president said, "Ike, you and I know who was chief of staff during the last years of the Civil War, but practically no one else knows." People remember only the field generals, Roosevelt said, and "I hate to think that fifty years from now practically nobody will know who George Marshall was. That is why I want George to have the big command. He is entitled to establish his place in history as a great general." Eisenhower did not disagree.

To make the decision easier for himself, FDR tried to get Marshall to state a preference. Marshall refused. He would serve in whatever position the president asked. By the end of the Cairo Conference, Roosevelt had decided that Eisenhower would get the command. Unlike Eisenhower, Marshall had a commanding vision of each theater of war. He was masterful with Congress, and Eisenhower had less experience. In addition, the notion of Eisenhower serving as chief of staff and commanding Marshall was, as Eisenhower's biographer wrote, "an absurd situation." So, as the Allied troops stormed the beaches of Normandy, in the battle most remembered from World War II, it was Dwight Eisenhower who had field command on D-Day. "I feel I could not sleep at night with you out of the country," Roosevelt told Marshall, who never complained or expressed regret.

As 1944 came to a close, victory on the European front appeared within reach. The year before, *Time* magazine had recognized George Marshall as Man of the Year. His record included Pearl Harbor and the decision to drop atomic bombs on Hiroshima and Nagasaki, for which he was a key voice of support. There were military retreats and delays, and notable and debilitating flare-ups with George Patton and Douglas MacArthur, and no shortage of strife with the Allies. But in the end the Allies were victorious.

On V-E Day, May 8, 1945, the day that Hitler's forces surrendered, Secretary of War Henry Stimson summoned about a dozen generals and other senior officers into his office, half on each side of Marshall, who stood at the center of the semicircle facing Stimson, seated at his desk. Stimson proceeded to speak to Marshall: "I have never seen a task of such magnitude performed by man. It is rare in life to make new friends; at my age it is a slow process but there is no one for whom I have such deep respect and I think greater affection. I have seen a great many soldiers in my lifetime and you, sir, are the finest soldier I have ever known." There were tears in the eyes of several of the generals.

Four months later, with Japan's surrender in tow, Stimson wrote a letter to President Truman, who had assumed office in April 1945, aiming to sum up Marshall's contribution: "His mind has guided the grand strategy of our campaigns . . . It was his mind and character that carried through the trans-Channel campaign against Germany . . . Similarly his views have controlled the Pacific campaign although he has been most modest, and careful in recognizing the role of the Navy. His views guided Mr. Roosevelt throughout. The construction of the American Army has been entirely the fruit of his initiative and supervision. Likewise its training . . . With this Army we have won a most difficult dual war with practically no serious setbacks and astonishingly 'according to plans.' . . . Show me any war in history which has produced a general with such a surprisingly perfect record as his in this greatest and most difficult of all wars in history."

As his commanding generals returned, Marshall ensured that each received victory parades. There was none for Marshall, though. The only reward he sought was a peaceful retirement to Dodona Manor, the estate in Leesburg that he and his wife, Katherine, had dreamed of retiring to for years. Having done his duty, he wished to return home to enjoy his remaining days, as a private citizen.

It was not to be. The day after he returned to Dodona Manor, the telephone rang. It was Truman. The president asked Marshall if he would go to mediate the civil war in China. Most considered it an impossible mission. Marshall's friends and admirers resented Truman for enlisting Marshall. After listening to the president's request, Marshall said, "Yes, Mr. President," and hung up the phone. Marshall hoped for an expeditious return to Leesburg. When Secretary of State Byrnes tendered his resignation in April 1946, Truman passed along a note through Eisenhower intimating that he would like Marshall to run the State Department. Marshall responded: "I think I fully understand the question to be discussed. My answer is affirmative if that continues to be his desire. My personal reaction is something else."

As the general and Katherine pulled into Washington on a gray and cold January morning in 1947, the nation's collective spirit seemed to lift. "Your appointment as Secretary of State has filled me with a great sense of security as far as our country is concerned," wrote Stimson, who "might have been speaking for the whole nation," according to Truman biographer David McCullough. Truman's poll numbers went up immediately. In the days to follow, Truman remarked, "The more I see and talk to him the more certain I am he's the great one of the age."

Not everyone looked upon Marshall's arrival in Washington with unalloyed enthusiasm. Republicans with designs on the White House were anxious about Marshall's national standing. Upon returning to Washington, Marshall quelled the rumors about his presidential ambitions immediately: "I will never become involved in political matters," he said, "and therefore I cannot be considered a candidate for any political office." The pronouncement was explicit, "and being Marshall he was taken at his word." Republicans could breathe a sigh of relief. On Capitol Hill, McCullough noted, Senator Vandenberg "pushed the nomination through the Senate Foreign Relations Committee without a hearing or opposition, and ran it through the Senate for unanimous approval the same day."

By January 1947, when George Marshall was sworn in as secretary of state, it had become clear that the objective for which he had helped lead America in World War II remained unrealized. To be sure, Hitler was defeated, and Germany was occupied and prostrate. But to Europe's east, a new totalitarian power had emerged. In the interstices between the war's end and Marshall's appointment, the Soviet Union had transformed, in the view of most in Washington, from a vaunted wartime ally to a threatening power with the potential to imperil the larger strategic objective for which Marshall and the United States had fought and sacrificed: preventing a totalitarian power from controlling the Eurasian landmass.

SPEAKING TO THE Maryland Historical Society in November 1945, three months after the war had ended, then Assistant Secretary of State Dean Acheson told his audience: "I can state in three sentences what the 'popular' attitude is toward foreign policy today: 1. Bring the boys home; 2. Don't be a Santa Claus; 3. Don't be pushed around." The last seemed a distant number three. Only a few weeks earlier, late in October 1945, a poll showed that Americans rated domestic concerns such as jobs and labor strife far ahead of foreign affairs. Only 7 percent rated world peace as the number one problem facing the country. Americans had fought, toiled and sacrificed. There was little popular appetite for new foreign burdens or further commitments. Ambassador to the Soviet Union Averell Harriman told his colleagues that Americans just wanted to "go to the movies and drink Coke."

The war had created seismic disruptions, though, redistributing power and reshaping the topography of the international political landscape. The United States had entered the war with a meek military and on the back end of the Depression. It was to emerge as the most powerful country in the world. U.S. gross national product had more than doubled during the span of the war. By 1945, the United States accounted for one-half of the world's economic production, two-thirds of the world's gold reserves and three-fourths of its invested capital. At the Tehran conference in 1943, even Stalin offered a toast "to American production, without which this war would have been lost." The U.S. Navy and air forces were both larger than the combined navies and air forces of the rest of the world. That, together with its monopoly on the atomic bomb, made the United States the world's dominant military power.

When, in 1944, the American political scientist William T. R. Fox coined the term *superpower,* he included the United States, Great Britain and the Soviet Union in that category. Great Britain still had great military capacity and territorial breadth, but it had lost one-quarter of its national wealth by the time the war ended. The U.S. economy was five times larger than Great Britain's. The other traditional European powers were even more eviscerated. That left the Soviet Union. The Soviets had contributed, more than any other power, to victory. Although only one-third the size of the U.S. economy, the Soviet economy was still the world's second largest. During the 1930s and then in the war, it had grown key industries at prolific rates, but more importantly, the Soviet Union had the world's greatest—and most daunting—land forces. They had stopped the Nazis and rolled them back to Germany, and by war's end had occupied half of Europe. Two years after the war, Dean Acheson said, "Not since Rome and Carthage had there been such a polarization of power on this earth."

The postwar redistribution of economic and military power suggested an emergent geopolitical rivalry. To that the United States and the Soviet Union could add the "mutually hostile ideological visions" of capitalism and communism. But it would be individual actors who would give expression and shape to the international order. And none was more important than Josef Vissarionovich Dzhugashvili.

DZHUGASHVILI WAS BORN IN GORI, Georgia, a country bordering Russia to the southwest, on December 6, 1878. His father was a cobbler who expected his son to assume that vocation. His mother doted on him, and wanted him to be a priest. He attended Gori spiritual school and then had a spell at a nearby Orthodox seminary. Thoughtful and evincing signs of sensitivity, even sentimentality—he was wont to write poetry—he was also profoundly insecure and given to violence. After joining the Bolshevik movement, his ascent up the party ladder was rapid. He married and loved his wife, Ketevan. After two years, she fell ill and died, leaving him desolate and bitter. Vladimir Lenin noticed him early on and championed his rise. A competent writer, he was appointed founder and editor, in April 1912, of the new Bolshevik daily *Pravda* ("The Truth"). Around this time, he assumed a pseudonym derived from the Russian word for steel, *stal:* Josef Stalin.

Shortly after Lenin's death in 1924, Stalin, then forty-five years old, assumed national leadership. He had a tremendous capacity for work, a genius for organization and a cunning that no Soviet official could match. Hardened by the violence of his youth, the violence that he had seen in the Bolshevik movement and the violence that seemed endemic to the great European empires of his day, he had a felicity for detachment from sentiment for human life.

The 1930s were a time of remarkable growth and transformation for the Soviet Union. The economy was planned to precision, industry flourished and much of the citizenry benefited. By 1939, it was said, 87 percent of Soviet citizens between the ages of nine and forty-nine were literate and numerate. Historian Robert Service wrote: "Schools, newspapers, libraries and radio stations proliferated. Factory apprenticeships had hugely expanded in number. The universities teemed with students." To reap this sort of transformation, though, Stalin employed a scale of ruthlessness unseen in human history. He uprooted families and entire communities, sending dissenters or undesirables by the tens of millions to the gulags. Historians both in Russia and the West now agree that the number of deaths caused by Stalin's policies before World War II numbered between 17 and 22 million. By the end of the 1930s, the Soviet Union was well on its way to modernization, but "industrialization and collectivization had thrown society into the maelstrom of hunger, migration and the Gulag." It was a relatively small price to pay to sate Stalin's rapacious desire for political control. By the end of the 1930s, Stalin had ascended to absolute power in the Soviet Union, and he directed Soviet policy thereafter with an untrammeled hand.

Having achieved that position against the backdrop of a developing, though emasculated and vulnerable, state, it was Stalin's paramount concern to avoid or at least delay as long as possible war with Nazi Germany. When Stalin signed a Non-Aggression Pact with Hitler in 1939, throwing his lot in with the Germans, it seemed to confirm the suspicions then widely shared among American foreign policy officials that Stalin was a perfidious menace. When Hitler violated the pact and invaded the Soviet Union, on June 22, 1941, Stalin was said to have been so depressed that he fled to his country home and was dysfunctional for days. Overnight the Nazi invasion threw the Soviet Union's fortune in with the Allies, who would soon include the United States. Now joined in a war that had to be won, the unnatural allies offered expressions of goodwill. The ruthless dictator enjoyed an overnight makeover, becoming "Uncle Joe." Stalin was named *Time* magazine's Man of the Year in 1942.

As the Soviets recovered from the shell shock of the Nazi invasion, its leaders adopted the slogan, "Everything for the Front!" The years to follow were among the most trying that any country has had to endure. When war broke out on the eastern front, U.S. Navy commander Admiral Ernest J. King pronounced: "Russia will do nine-tenths of the job of defeating Hitler." For much of World War II, 80 percent of the Nazi forces were engaged by Soviet forces. The United States lost 300,000 soldiers in World War II. In contrast, approximately 27 million Soviets (soldiers and civilians) died as a direct result of the war. As Churchill and the Allies temporized, refusing to invade Western Europe and create another front to relieve some of the pressure on the Soviet Union, it was said that the United States and Britain were willing to fight to the last Soviet death.

The war left Soviet territory scorched. Historian David Fromkin wrote that Nazi invaders destroyed more than 1,700 cities and towns and more than 70,000 villages and hamlets. They demolished more than 6 million buildings and more than 31,000 industrial enterprises. They dismantled 40,000 miles of railroad tracks, blew up 56,000 miles of main road and ruined 90,000 bridges. They stole and slaughtered 17 million head of cattle, 20 million hogs, 27 million sheep and goats, 110 million poultry and 7 million horses. Against the backdrop of the Soviet Union's monumental sacrifices for Allied victory, Stalin's persona emerged from the crucible of wartime partnership much enhanced in the United States, or "purified," as one leading Cold War historian put it.

Behind the well-tended façade of goodwill and bonhomie, though, by early 1945, as the U.S. and Soviet militaries rushed to meet in the middle of Europe and bring the war to an end, key officials in the United States were already expressing deep concerns about the prospects for postwar cooperation. In the Moscow embassy, senior Foreign Service officer George Kennan admonished anyone who would listen that the Soviets would be an expansionist power, and that they would have to be resisted through counterpressure. Heeding Kennan's counsel and horrified at Stalin's vicious conduct in Eastern Europe—especially his refusal to support a popular anti-Nazi uprising in Warsaw—Ambassador Averell Harriman began warning the White House that Stalin was not to be trusted and that the Soviet Union might have expansionist designs.

Roosevelt held fast to his vision of postwar collaboration and cooperation. But as the Soviets marched west, they showed little regard for the sanctity of life, the rule of law or the democratic values Roosevelt envisioned shaping the new world order. On March 24, 1945, before leaving for Warm Springs, Georgia, Roosevelt read one of Harriman's cables and pounded his fist on the arms of his wheelchair: "Averell is right; we can't do business with Stalin," he said. "He has broken every one of his promises he made at Yalta," an earlier wartime conference.

Weeks later, on April 13, 1945, Franklin Delano Roosevelt died, and was succeeded by Harry S. Truman. Truman was a failed farmer and haberdasher from Independence, Missouri. He had taken a few courses at a community college but had never completed his degree. A respected war hero later in life, Truman was selected by Tom Pendergast, boss of the Kansas City political machine, to run for local office, then for the Senate in 1935, becoming junior senator from Missouri at age fifty. Later selected as a compromise candidate to run on the ticket with Roosevelt, Truman had been vice president for eighty-three days when the president died. He had met with Roosevelt only twice, and on neither occasion discussed anything of importance. FDR did not hold Truman in particularly high regard, and did not bring him into his decision-making circle. Truman did not know about the substance of negotiations with the great powers. He did not know about the atomic bomb then in the final stages of development. Weeks after his inauguration, he said of his new office, "It is a terrible responsibility, and I am the last man fitted to handle it."

The new president and the seasoned dictator were to meet for the first and last time at Cecilienhof, a country estate set in a large park in the eastern German town of Potsdam, from July 17 to August 2, 1945. Potsdam was the last of the wartime conferences among the Allies. For those two weeks, Cecilienhof was home to more posturing and gamesmanship than substantive agreement. The Soviets would not sign on to democratic elections in the Eastern European countries they had helped to liberate. They even spoke about extending their reach to the Dardanelles and to Libya. For their part, the Soviets were confounded by the United States' unwillingness to meet their request for war reparations. Given their wartime sacrifices, the Soviets "could not understand why 'the Wall Street bankers' had to be paid first." The leaders departed Potsdam with the critical issues of reparations, Poland's borders, the political status of Eastern European countries and, all importantly, Germany's future still unresolved.

Nevertheless, the American delegation was hopeful. Truman wrote home to his wife, Bess: "I like Stalin. He is straightforward." There was nothing on record to suggest that Stalin had comparable regard for Truman. The inventory of goodwill depleted quickly. The Soviet Union continued to press its influence in Eastern Europe, and Soviet rhetoric became increasingly truculent. On a frigid winter's evening, February 9, 1946, at the fabled Bolshoi Theater, Stalin delivered a speech in which he announced a new five-year plan for the Soviet economy. He laced the oration with anticapitalist rhetoric. Analysts would later agree that it was primarily meant for domestic consumption, but many U.S. policymakers were staggered. Supreme Court Justice William O. Douglas pronounced the speech "World War III."

Around this time an editorial in the *New York Times* asked the question on everyone's mind: "What does Russia want?" Experts at State and the military chiefs alike were alarmed at the Soviet Union's expansionary moves, but also noted more auspicious signs elsewhere: free elections were held in Hungary; Soviet troops were withdrawn from Czechoslovakia; and a representative government was installed in Austria. Still the *Times* editorial listed the places "annexed" since the end of the war, territory that stretched from Eastern Europe to Manchuria and totaled 273,947 square miles. "Where does the search for security end, and where does expansion begin?" the editorial asked, digging to the core of the matter.

Also in the winter of 1946, the Soviet Union declared that it would not be joining the Bretton Woods agreements, the new set of rules and institutions, named after the town in New Hampshire in which they were negotiated, that were designed to serve as the bedrock of the new international economic order. Bretton Woods was constructed to be open, collaborative and beneficial to all of its members. The United States and its chief partners had taken particular pains to meet the Soviets' demands. When the Soviets pulled out of Bretton Woods, many U.S. policymakers were baffled, none more than those at the Treasury Department. Treasury asked the State Department for an assessment. In mid-February 1946, State sent that query to the Moscow embassy.

For eighteen months, George Kennan, chargé d'affaires at the embassy, "had done little else but pluck people's sleeves, trying to make them understand the nature" of the Soviet threat. Leaving for a trip abroad, Ambassador Averell Harriman told Kennan that he was now in charge and could send all the telegrams he liked. Consigned to bed rest with a cold, fever, sinus, and tooth trouble, Kennan received the State Department's query: "They had asked for it. Now, by God, they would have it." What followed was an eight-thousand-word exposition that Kennan dictated to his secretary from his bedside. Telegraphed to Washington in five parts, Kennan expounded on the nature of the peril at hand. Communism was only a fig leaf, Kennan explained, to mask the real mainspring of Soviet intransigence: a profound and deeply rooted national insecurity. The Soviets responded only to the logic of force. Expressions of goodwill and essays at cooperation were futile, Kennan argued. The United States would have to stand up to the Soviets.

Kennan's cable reached D.C. on George Washington's birthday. Dubbed the Long Telegram, it was widely read and celebrated. Policymakers were starving for an explanation and an accompanying road map for future policy. Kennan's Long Telegram provided both. The tide was turning. That February, Truman was fielding admonitions about the Soviet Union from all quarters. That same month he received a note: "I think it is now time for [the president] to get tough with someone." It was from his mother.

In March 1946, Winston Churchill arrived in the dry town of Fulton,

Missouri, and told the crowd at Westminster College that "from Stettin in the Baltic to Trieste in the Adriatic, an iron curtain has descended across the continent." If the West did not meet the Soviet threat with force, that iron curtain—it was a phrase he first used in a telegram to Truman in May 1945—would keep moving west. The Soviet Union refused to keep an agreement to pull out of northern Iran in mid-March 1946. When the Soviets probed again that August in Turkey, asserting their right to joint control of the Dardanelle Straits, experts and leading advisers stood behind Truman, who insisted the Soviets desist. "We might as well find out whether the Russians were bent on world conquest now, as in five or ten years," the president said, before sending a battleship. The show of force and diplomacy repelled the probe.

On March 20, in another telegram to Washington, Kennan expounded further: "Nothing short of complete disarmament, delivery of our air and naval forces to Russia and resigning of powers of government to American Communists" would mitigate Stalin's insecurity. But even then, Kennan continued, Stalin would probably "smell a trap and would continue to harbor the most baleful misgivings." Most tellingly of all, in June 1946 in Moscow CBS correspondent Richard C. Hottelet interviewed the urbane Soviet diplomat Maxim Litvinov. Hottelet asked what would happen if the West were to suddenly grant the Kremlin all the demands necessary to meet its security needs. Litvinov replied: "It would lead to the West's being faced, after a more or less short time, with the next series of demands."

Late that September, Truman's special counsel, Clark Clifford, handed the President a top-secret, hardbound document entitled, "American Relations with the Soviet Union," better known as the Clifford-Elsey Report. For months, amidst an oppressively hot Washington summer, George Elsey, another senior Truman aide, had been canvassing the administration's top-level military and diplomatic officials on their views of the Soviet Union and its intentions. The report portrayed agreement among America's senior-most officials: the Soviet Union was expansionist. If necessary, America must be prepared to act militarily to "restrain" the Soviet threat. Truman read the report that night with alarm, and phoned Clifford at seven o'clock the next morning. He ordered Clifford to deliver all the existing copies to his office immediately. If it was made public, the report would ruin any remaining chances for U.S.–Soviet accommodation, he explained.

Truman could make the report disappear. But he could not undo or reverse the emerging consensus among American officials. The Iranian and Turkish crises of 1946 seemed to confirm it: whether driven by ideological zeal or implacable insecurity, the Soviets were an expansionary power. Dean

Acheson wrote later: "The year 1946 was for the most part a year of learning that minds in the Kremlin worked very much as George F. Kennan had predicted they would."

As 1946 set, no U.S. grand strategy had been designed or proclaimed. Some still held out a figment of hope for the realization of a modus vivendi, whereby both states could inhabit the postwar world in relative cooperation and peace. But that window of possibility was closing fast.

As GEORGE MARSHALL processed his subordinates' briefings in January and February of 1947 before leaving for Moscow, it seemed as though, as one historian wrote, "a get-tough attitude had become an end in itself." Marshall listened intently. He agreed that the Soviet Union had been behaving aggressively, and was concerned. But he had a different take on Stalin. During the war, the Soviet Union was a dependable military ally, and its leader had kept his agreements. When the Allies stormed Normandy, the Soviets attacked in the East, as promised. Stalin had always done what he had said he would do on the eastern front.

Marshall had met with Stalin during the major wartime conferences (Tehran, Yalta and Potsdam). At their meetings, Stalin was unfailingly decisive and action oriented. Marshall had found the Soviet leader astute, direct and, to Marshall at least, affectionate. Marshall was also aware of his own prestige and its currency. When Stalin got ornery with Ambassador Harriman on one occasion about a certain U.S. military policy, Harriman rejoined that Marshall had made the decision and that Stalin's parry was tantamount to an attack on Marshall. Stalin replied, "I trust Marshall as I trust myself." Past experience suggested to Marshall that cooperation with Stalin was possible. And perhaps he was the one man who could achieve it. He was not prepared to let the world slide back into conflict without trying.

When Marshall's plane lifted off in Washington on March 5, 1947, the general suffered no illusions about the difficulties that lay ahead, but he was hopeful that he could get through to Stalin and reach accord with the Soviet Union on the key matters that divided the powers—most notably Germany and reparations—to preserve the peace that both countries had fought so hard to achieve.

BEFORE REACHING MOSCOW, Marshall stopped in France and Germany for several preconference meetings. The flights gave Marshall a bird's-eye view of Western Europe. Flying over Germany in July 1945, General George Patton remarked: "You who have not seen it do not know what hell looks like from the top." The war had eviscerated Europe. More than 50 percent of housing in major cities, and in some up to 80 percent, was reduced to rubble. In London 3.5 million homes in the metropolitan area had been destroyed. Forty percent, 30 percent and 20 percent of the housing stock in Germany, Great Britain and France, respectively, was laid to waste. In Berlin, 75 percent of buildings were uninhabitable. Rubble—an estimated 500 million cubic yards of it in Germany—lay stories high on the sides of cleared thoroughfares. Thousands of bridges and tens of thousands of kilometers of railroad lines had been destroyed. Ninety percent of the rail lines in Germany were not operational. Ships and merchant fleets were decimated; Greece lost two-thirds of the fleet on which its economy depended. According to one American official, by war's end Western Europe's transportation systems were defunct. One simply could not go anywhere without the aid of the occupying forces.

Still worse was the human toll. One historian estimated that 36.5 million people—roughly the prewar population of France—died from 1939 to 1945 from war-related causes. On V-E Day, there were no less than 13 million displaced persons (DPs) in Europe, and the number was growing. One historian put the estimate at 20 million. Occupying Soviet forces raped as many as 2 million German women. More people faced starvation during the year following the war than during all of the war years combined, Harry Truman wrote later. According to the United Nations, in the summer of 1946 100 million Europeans were being fed at a level of 1,500 calories per day or less, a level at which health suffers severely. Another 40 million had only a few more hundred calories. Anne O'Hare McCormick of the *New York Times* proved prophetic when she wrote on March 14, 1945, "The human problem the war will leave behind has not yet been imagined, much less faced by anybody. There has never been such destruction, such disintegration of the structure of life."

The physical destruction and the human dislocation were matched by an attendant postwar misery and dispiritedness. In Germany, much of the populace felt shamed and powerless. On one occasion, the Soviets uprooted a key optical factory along with its seven thousand skilled workers from Jena, in eastern Germany, and moved it to the Soviet Union. The workers were woken one evening and given thirty minutes to collect belongings and board a train. The occupation was less rapine in the western part of the country, but the hunger was even more acute.

Wartime France had pitted collaborators with the Vichy regime against those who fought with or abetted the Resistance, French against French. France's experience left currents of antipathy, suspicion and ambiguity in the national psyche. Material and nutritional deprivation sometimes stoked the fire. In April 1945, the population of Paris averaged 1,337 calories per day. Singing at Le Club des Cinq, Yves Montand saw a patron grind out a cigar on a half-eaten lobster. He was so angry that he jumped from the stage, pounced on the customer, and punched him.

In Great Britain, they would be forever known as years of austerity. By the end of the war, Great Britain was spending more than half of its national production on the war effort. It was said in those days that Great Britain had only two natural resources: coal and the national character. The immediate postwar years taxed both, the latter almost to the breaking point. Robert Boothby, a Conservative member of Parliament declared: "We are blitzed, run-down, cold, hungry and exhausted. Our people have to endure hardship, privation, monotony, discomfort, and a crushing burden of taxation . . . If they are asked to go on doing this indefinitely, they will not rebel. They will simply fold up."

Winston Churchill summed up the condition in Europe in a famous address in Zurich, Switzerland, in May 1946, one year after the war's termination in Europe: "What is the plight to which Europe has been reduced? Over wide areas a vast quivering mass of tormented, hungry, careworn, and bewildered human beings gape at the ruins of their cities and homes, and scan the dark horizons for the approach of some new peril, tyranny, or terror. Among the victors there is a babel of jarring voices; among the vanquished a sudden silence of despair." Henry Stimson's diary entry put it in simple terms. The war and the destruction it had sown were "worse than anything probably that ever happened in the world."

Then nature intervened. Around Christmas of 1946, a vast high-pressure area began to form near the Arctic Circle. Rolling across Norway, the front settled over Britain, bringing ferocious winds and a biting cold. By dawn on January 6, 1947, snow began falling on London, and by dusk it had crowned the dome of St. Paul's Cathedral. In the ensuing weeks and months, Western Europe experienced the most punishing weather in living memory.

In Britain, snow piled up as high as twenty feet. Machinery froze, idle. Roads and rail lines were impassable anyhow. The night of January 30, the Thames froze. Coal—desperately needed and in short supply—sat frozen in carts attached to trains rendered immobile. The *Times* of London headline read: "All Britain Freezes." A week later a number of power stations shut down. "For the first time in history," wrote British historian Alan Bullock, "British industrial production was effectively halted for three weeks—something German bombing had never been able to do." Registered unemployment skyrocketed almost sixfold during the crisis.

In Germany, more than 19,000 Berliners were treated for frostbite. On the walls of the bombed-out Reichstag, someone scrawled: "Blessed are the dead, for their hands do not freeze." In an emergency measure, German families were allowed one tree for kindling to keep themselves warm. Already hungry, worn and demoralized, Germany's industrial rehabilitation stalled further.

In France, snow fell in St. Tropez. For many the cold was worse than the hunger. Secretaries at the Quai d'Orsay (the French Foreign Ministry) could only type wearing mittens. One woman wrote her sister abroad that "every breath is like a sword." Shop windows were unlit, and surgeons often found the power cut in the middle of operations and were left with total darkness. The storm ravaged an estimated 3.2–3.8 million acres of wheat planted that autumn. In both France and Italy, farmers ceased sending supplies to markets and hoarded food for themselves, their families and their livestock. Paris "terrified" philosopher Isaiah Berlin, to whom it seemed "empty and hollow and dead, like an exquisite corpse."

Up until the storm hit, Western Europe had been staging what the United Nations' postwar survey described as "a remarkable industrial recovery." From the second half of 1945 to the last quarter of 1946, fifteen European countries had increased industrial production from 60 percent to 83 percent of 1938 levels. Against the backdrop of all the physical, human, and psychological problems, it was a great achievement, abetted in part by billions of dollars in U.S. loans and aid. But the progress, impressive as it was, masked deeper dislocation in Europe's economies. The storm tore off that mask.

Well before the fabled storm of January 1947, three main underlying problems were already at work. They were interrelated, mutually reenforcing and, despite Europe's incipient recovery, grave. The first was production, a problem that predated the war. Already during the 1930s, Great Britain and France had not been modernizing and replenishing their physical capital. From 1929 to 1938, there was no new net investment in French industry. The war, of course, further destroyed and depreciated factories, machinery and other physical capital. The human loss of skilled labor, generations of know-how and intellectual capital, sent labor productivity into sharp decline. Postwar labor productivity, the U.N. estimated, dropped to 40 to 50 percent of prewar levels.

With production low and a rebuilding effort needed, the demand for vital goods and services far exceeded their supply. Inflation followed. Widespread price controls and accompanying rationing programs did little to help. To meet people's basic needs and the rebuilding efforts, government expenditures rose; but all the government spending further fueled inflation. People had little faith in the value of currencies, so they would spend immediately, exacerbating the problem even further. Inflation was dire in France. Wholesale prices rose 80 percent during 1946. It was worse in Germany. In 1947, a carton of cigarettes, which could be purchased for fifty cents on an American military base, was worth 1,800 reichsmarks on the black market, or $180 according to the legal rate of exchange. At this rate, for four cartons of cigarettes, one could hire a German orchestra for the evening. Or for twenty-four cartons, one could purchase a 1939 Mercedes-Benz.

Perhaps the most dire and fundamental problem was that Europe's traditional patterns of trade had come undone. Before the war, trade in Europe assumed essentially a triangular pattern, with Great Britain, Germany and the rest of continental Europe as the three points. Great Britain had a large import surplus vis-à-vis Germany and continental Europe. To balance its payments, it drew on earnings from investments, shipping and insurance. With the earnings from Great Britain's purchases, continental Europe could buy manufactured goods from Germany. With the Ruhr, Germany was Europe's greatest producer. With its earnings, Germany in turn could buy raw materials needed to produce its manufactured goods from other European countries as well as their overseas colonies.

The quotas, tariffs, and protective walls erected during Europe's economic depression in the 1930s yielded dislocation even before war broke out. The war and its fallout left this delicate web irrevocably rent. To finance its war effort and at the same time maintain its overseas dependencies, Great Britain had to liquidate many of the investments accumulated over centuries. Furthermore, whereas in the past Great Britain and continental Europe depended on Germany's production and purchasing power—before the war it supplied more than 40 percent of the goods, metals and chemicals traded in Europe—the war had pulled Germany almost entirely off of its place on that triangle. At the same time, the European empires were beginning to dissolve and could no longer count on raw materials from the colonies.

European countries were not able to produce what they could not afford to buy elsewhere. When governments stepped in to finance increased production, it only helped to fuel inflation. Inflation, in turn, reduced people's incentive to save and invest. It also diminished real wages, which further intensified production problems.

Increasingly, Europe found itself looking across the Atlantic to the United States. The United States was the only power whose economy had flourished during the war. Europe needed the goods and natural resources abundant in the United States to fuel its recovery. But, at the same time, Europe was not able to offer the United States goods or resources in return, nor could it draw on stores of investments or invisible earnings (like shipping or insurance). Europe had a balance-of-payments problem with the United States: in 1946 Europe's overseas trade debt was $5 billion and growing. It was known as the "Dollar Gap." It was the key problem looming behind Europe's incipient recovery and it was becoming dire.

Some economic historians have argued that through further controls, rationing and sacrifice, Western Europe could have continued to finance its incipient recovery, Dollar Gaps and underlying economic problems, notwithstanding. Yet to Western European leaders such remedies did not seem viable. Their people were desperately fatigued; they were weak, vulnerable, insecure, and hope was among the scarcest resources that spring of 1947. As foreboding as its balance-of-payments crisis was Western Europe's crisis of confidence. Western European leaders deemed the latter too grave to be able to withstand additional sacrifice in order to alleviate the former. Wrote journalist Theodore White: "Like a whale left gasping on the sand, Europe lay rotting in the sun."

It was an accurate assessment; except that winter of 1947 there was little sun to be found in Europe. The snowfall of January was interrupted by a brief thaw, which in February turned into a merciless freeze, paralyzing much of Western European industry. The storm precipitated further economic dislocation, amplifying the structural and conditional problems already in place. The transformation was perhaps most acute in Great Britain. Manufacturing output in February was down 25 percent from the month before. That month the *Times* of London wrote: "The state of emergency through which we are now passing brings back memories of wartime." And then on February 21, the British government issued a White Paper titled "Economic Survey for 1947," which the *Times* called "the most disturbing statement ever made by a British government."

It was a fateful month for Great Britain. In mid-February Britain referred Palestine to the United Nations, ceding some of its responsibilities and clout in the Middle East. It was also the month when Britain gave up the jewel in the crown, announcing that it would hand over its responsibilities to India sometime before June 1948. That February the Cabinet also agreed that Britain would have to suspend aid to Greece and Turkey, downsizing its commitment and influence in the Mediterranean forevermore. The empire as the world had known it had dissolved.

Great Britain had pared down its commitments. But still, the growing balance-of-payments crisis raised the specter of doom. The *Observer* spoke of "bankruptcy." For centuries Great Britain and the other European empires had governed the international system, and now those empires were coming undone. *Time* magazine asked the question: "Was the U.S. ready to take [their] place?"

IN 1932 THE Cambridge Union opened debate on a motion: "This house sees more hope in Moscow than in Detroit." It was a debate that would rage throughout Europe in the fifteen years to follow. Throughout the 1930s, capitalism was seen more and more to be failing Europe. Rather than dynamic and enterprising firms and leaders, old family firms, cartels and colluding oligarchs seemed to wield all the influence in economic life in Europe. In Britain and France the system was seen as "rotten" and marked by a "freezing of the capitalist spirit." When the Depression hit, most business owners embraced protectionism and countenanced mass unemployment to protect their interests. Firms deployed scant risk or new investment to turn the tide.

When war came, many of Europe's leading financial and industrial figures and institutions collaborated with the Nazis to preserve their interests. "France has got what she deserves!" declared Gabrielle Coco Chanel at a party on the Côte d'Azur with her country under Nazi occupation. Louis Renault and his family company agreed to gear production to supply the Nazi military. British socialist leader Sir Stafford Cripps called them the "Guilty Men." In Germany, industry fed the Nazi war machine and Hitler's "warfare state."

During the Occupation in France, the capitalist establishment was lumped in with the Vichy regime and colored as collaborators. Communists, in contrast, were an important component of the Resistance. When France was liberated, they were not demure about their role. Stalin's Communist forces had fought and sacrificed more than any other peoples. As they rolled west, they were greeted as liberators.

Capitalism, most Europeans felt after the war, had produced mass unemployment in the 1930s and had fed the buildup to war and Fascism's reign over the continent. Most considered it defunct and immoral. They had heard Stalin's boasts about what Communism had achieved in the Soviet Union (some were true, many were not). But the Communists' role in the Resistance, and more importantly, the Soviet Union's role in the war, gave Communism a moral sheen, a powerful aura of progress and momentum.

These were some of the ideological dynamics at play in postwar Europe, and the Soviet-led international Communist movement deftly exploited them. Far superior to the Americans at publicity, shortly after the war the Soviet Union was spending more on informational campaigns for the Communists in France than the United States was spending on its own informational campaigns in all of Europe. The message was that Communism offered Europe's suffering masses equality, material provision, shared dignity and peace. Capitalism had failed them in the past, and it was continuing to fail to deliver them from their postwar woes.

The Communist message carried. "Nobody in Europe believes in the American way of life—that is, in private enterprise," said British scholar A. J. P. Taylor. In western and central Europe the currents of the time redounded directly to the political benefit of national Communist parties. In Czechoslovakia, elections in 1946 gave the Communists just under 40 percent of the vote and a popular front. In France's first postwar political election in October 1945, the Communist Party polled 5 million votes, the largest received by any party. A year later, in November 1946, the Communists won 29 percent of the vote, once again the greatest of any party. After the election, Communist Party leader Maurice Thorez demanded (unsuccessfully) to be prime minister. In Italy, mass unemployment and twenty years of pent-up anti-Fascist sentiment delivered close to 40 percent of the vote to the Communist Party and a collaborating Socialist Party in the June 1946 election. Communist support was strong and growing in Belgium, Holland, Greece and throughout Scandinavia.

The parties were well funded, and their capacity for organization and political opportunism were advanced and finely tuned. Each economic downturn, each ratchet in desperation or hopelessness was coal fueling Communist momentum. "There is no choice between becoming a Communist on 1,500 calories and a believer in democracy on 1,000," said U.S. military commander Lucius Clay from Germany. In 1918, watching the Bolshevik Revolution from Washington, Secretary of State Robert Lansing had said: "Empty stomachs mean Bolsheviks. Full stomachs mean no Bolsheviks."

As George Marshall flew over Europe on his way to Moscow, European stomachs were empty, hope was low and prospects were bleak.

Chapter Two

THE GENERAL'S LAST STAND

A T 3:30 P.M. ON MARCH 9, 1947, George Marshall and his delegation touched down at Moscow's General Airport. It was still cold, but the worst of the Russian winter had passed. The war had taken so many men that women could be seen assiduously shoveling snow from the streets. It was a large delegation full of generals, Foreign Service officials, economists, aides and others. When they arrived at Spaso House—the "cavernous stucco mansion built by a sugar tycoon in 1914," now the American Embassy and home to the American delegation for the duration of the conference—Walter Bedell Smith, Averell Harriman's successor as ambassador and formerly a general under Marshall during the war, ceded his bedroom to Marshall and set up desks in as many cubbyholes as he could find. The capacious embassy, normally barren, teemed with officials, working around the clock, for the duration of the conference.

Some in the delegation were concerned about Marshall. He had been going too hard for too long and appeared tired. Others felt that he did not have enough time to prepare and familiarize himself with the context and intricacies of the matters at hand. They were concerned that he would be outmaneuvered by cunning diplomats. At the request of Senator Arthur Vandenberg, Marshall had invited John Foster Dulles, an experienced international lawyer generally recognized as the senior diplomat in the Republican Party. Dulles's presence and his penchant for self-promotion at Moscow led some to question whether Marshall was in full command of his delegation. Bedell Smith, who had known Marshall the best and the longest, was not concerned: "I had seen the General under all conditions of stress and strain, and I had never seen him fail eventually to dominate every gathering by sheer force of his integrity, honesty and dignified sim-plicity."

The agenda for the conference would include a peace treaty for Austria, border issues in Eastern Europe and claims for war reparations, but the number one issue would be Germany, what French Foreign Minister Georges Bidault called "the Allies' stumbling block and the biggest obstacle to a gen-uine European peace." Shortly after the Allies defeated Germany, they assumed four-part control, with the United States, the Soviet Union, Great Britain and France all responsible for administration in one sphere, and the powers collectively responsible for administering joint national policy in the Allied Control Council, or ACC. Roosevelt had believed that relations in Germany would define America's ability to cooperate with the Soviet Union in the postwar world. Since then, repeated disagreements had emerged con-cerning reparations, Germany's level of production and other policies.

The eastern zone, administered by the Soviet Union, was rich in food-stuffs and agriculture but poor in industry. The western zone administered by Great Britain contained most of the Ruhr. With prodigious coal resources, it was Germany's industrial heartland and the core of its war-making potential. In addition to stripping resources from its own zone, the Soviets sought repa-rations from the zones controlled by Great Britain and the United States. Because these zones did not have foodstuffs, and because France insisted that Germany's industrial production remain low, lest it reemerge as a security threat, the United States and Great Britain found themselves footing huge costs, not only in financing the occupation but in feeding and caring for the German population.

The differing interests and approaches of the Soviets on one side and the Americans and British on the other led to repeated squabbles and escalating contention and mistrust. Into 1946, the prospect of four-power cooperation appeared increasingly dim. As the plight of Germany's people worsened and the financial burden on the United States increased, the U.S. occupying authority, Lucius Clay—irascible and mercurial, yet forceful and effective—simply cut off all reparations from the U.S. zone in May 1946. Meanwhile, the Soviets were consolidating their economic and political ties in the east-ern zone.

As Europe's economic woes continued into the spring of 1947, a new view was gaining traction in U.S. circles. Trumpeting a seminal report released by former President Herbert Hoover in February 1947, the War Department and other important officials like Averell Harriman, then secretary of com-merce, were coming to believe that Germany's rehabilitation was the key to Europe's economic woes. The report argued: "There is only one path to recovery in Europe. That is production. The whole economy of Europe is interlinked with the German economy . . . We can keep Germany in these economic chains but it will also keep Europe in rags."

There was a problem, however, in the concept of re-igniting Germany's economy. France had been at war with Germany three times in the last three generations, and was duly petrified at the prospect of rehabilitating the fatherland. France envisioned a postwar Europe in which it, and not Germany, would be the continent's leading economy. France wanted Germany to keep providing it with key resources; otherwise, France sought to keep German production as low as possible. Many in the U.S.—including State Department officials, and Marshall himself—had sympathy for the French position. Convinced of France's importance and the fragility of her internal politics, they took pains to meet her requests. As Marshall said, one may dispute the basis of France's fears, but one cannot dispute the fact of those fears.

Nevertheless the emerging Soviet threat was coming to overshadow the German one. In mid-1946, then Secretary of State James Byrnes sought to cut through the apprehensions and mistrust with the Soviet Union over Germany. He proposed a twenty-five-year demilitarization treaty. Germany would demilitarize, deflating the suspicions each had about harnessing German power to their interests and paving the way for economic and political cooperation. Soviet Foreign Minister Vyacheslav Molotov did not accept, sowing profound seeds of suspicion in the United States over Soviet designs in Germany. "Almost all U.S. officials agreed that there was no issue of greater importance than Germany," wrote Melvyn Leffler, and they realized that "the Ruhr/Rhineland complex must not be allowed to support the military potential of a future adversary whether it be Germany or Russia or a combination of the two."

By January 1947, the scenario most dreaded was Soviet control of Germany and its industrial capacity. In a telegram to Marshall early that month, Ambassador Bedell Smith expounded on the threat: "There are signs that the dream of happy union between Soviet resources and manpower and German technical skill and administrative ability is again hovering about pillows of Soviet leaders." The Soviet approach to Germany was based on two elements, Bedell Smith cabled the general: first, maintaining and increasing control in eastern Germany, and, second, "endeavoring to assure necessary conditions in western zones most favorable to development of Communist Party and least favorable to development of western orientation."

In laying out economic and political terms for Germany, Bedell Smith predicted, the Soviets would push for a strong and centralized government. This way, they would be ensured—as they had been at the ACC—a strong voice in all decisions, perhaps even a veto and the ability to impede recovery and reform. He also predicted that the Soviets would press for reparations, in part to meet their great financial needs but also to frustrate recovery in the West, thereby fueling discontent and disorder and laying favorable conditions for Communist influence. The "issue then is Germany and with it the future of Europe," Bedell Smith concluded: "For all of these reasons impending Conference of Foreign Ministers meeting as seen from here promises to afford long and tedious struggle. Russia will be at home and patience for them will be an easy virtue."

ON A TYPICAL DAY during the conference, Marshall read cables from Washington and memos in the early morning. Around midmorning, he met with staff in the embassy's main reception room to work out the line to be followed in the negotiations that day. After lunch he would go for some exercise, always trailed by a bevy of Soviet security men. When he left Spaso House at around 3:30 P.M., flagged by Russian cars with six security men each, in front and behind, the Russians would send forth a signal so that by the time Marshall's car reached the main street, all traffic had been cleared and no one was allowed to cross the street. Sessions began at 4 P.M. at the Aviation Industry House, near the Moscow Hotel, and generally lasted three to four hours.

The general had met each of the three other foreign ministers before. His British counterpart, Ernest Bevin, had a stout, corpulent frame; one of Marshall's aides described him as a cross between Santa Claus and a Welsh coalman. An orphan, Bevin was a laborer who, through a mix of tenacity and keen strategic judgment, had worked his way up in union politics to build Britain's largest trade union. When war broke out, Churchill brought him into his Cabinet and placed him in charge of mobilizing British manpower and much of its industry. Though he led a competing party, Churchill had great respect for Bevin. To Lady Diana Cooper, a prominent British aristocrat, Bevin was "massive, rude, and strong as a Stonehenge cromlech . . . as tilled, as fertile, and generous as his English fields. Proud of his lowliness and of his achievements, he loved his fellow-men with as much fervor as he admired himself."

Bevin was ill and so had to make the long journey via train. A few years prior, a doctor had found "not a sound organ in his body, apart from his feet." But he was determined to restore the Commonwealth's power and stature. "The British Empire," he told a newspaper columnist in March 1946, "isn't going to be either the 49th [American] state or the 17th [Soviet] Republic."

But, as the year passed, America and Great Britain's interests, particularly in Germany, had converged, and suspicion about Soviet intentions brought Bevin in line with Marshall at Moscow.

It was security, above all, that French Foreign Minister Georges Bidault sought at Moscow. French Ambassador to the United States Henri Bonnet told Marshall a month prior to the conference: "Security is still the question that most concerns France. However much the situation may have changed, the French peasant still thinks of Germany and wonders whether he will have to fight a third war." Bidault was an intellectual who had become a revered leader during the Resistance. He was charming and witty, but also "impetuous, melodramatic, and known to have a penchant for alcohol." To realize its security, France wanted, like Great Britain and the United States, a politically decentralized Germany, one that would have factions and built-in checks on power. On the economic front, France sought reparations; it sought international control—and possible detachment—of the Ruhr/Rhine industrial complex; it sought the mineral-rich Saarland for itself; it sought to keep German industry down; and it desperately needed coal.

For France, there was perhaps only one scenario worse than a reemerging Germany, and that was a reemerging Germany under Soviet control. In the past, French and Soviet security concerns seemed to dovetail, and the two hewed to similar lines in the Allied Control Council. But, Bidault, too, was becoming increasingly concerned about Soviet designs in Germany. He was coming to think of France's destiny as bound to the Western powers. The French Communists' strong domestic political influence meant that he would have to proceed with caution. Marshall and much of the State Department were sympathetic, but others at the War Department and elsewhere had come to believe that there was no time to waste in re-igniting German production, and France had to fall into line.

Marshall had met Vyacheslav Molotov, the Soviet Union's longtime foreign minister, as early as 1942 when Molotov was pushing the other Allies to open a second front. The archetypal Soviet party man, Molotov was disciplined and firm, earning one of his nicknames, "stoney-arse." He was a bureaucrat's bureaucrat; Lenin had called him "comrade filing cabinet." Bland and unfailingly loyal, he won Stalin's trust and confidence. The third nickname was the best; he was his "master's voice." Molotov was a forceful negotiator of few words, guile, persistence, and seemingly interminable patience. He was complicit in Stalin's purges in the 1930s, evincing a capacity for brutality as well.

• • •

THE CONFERENCE OPENED on March 10, in a spacious, ornate room in the Aviation Industry House. The ministers sat, with several aides to their sides, at a table covered by a green baize cloth, and rows of chairs filled by other aides spread from the table in all directions. Seating was ritualistic: to the left of the French sat the British, then the Russians, then the Americans. Speaking went in clockwise order and the chairmanship rotated in that order daily. After the first day, Bevin remarked, "There is courtesy, there are no high words being used, no tempers, but all of it is cool and calculated [and] between them the two big boys look to me to be pretty determined."

By day five, on March 14, Marshall and Molotov had begun to clash over Germany. As disagreement became more pronounced, the Soviets showed scant interest in reconciliation or proceeding expeditiously to find solutions. Marshall allowed that perhaps part of the problem was procedural. Each speech had to be translated into two languages. As such, translations took up a good portion of each three- or four-hour session. Marshall proposed that speeches be submitted in advance to save time on translation. The Soviets declined. As retribution, Marshall held up one of the meetings with a prolonged oration that seemed to leave even Molotov squirming. Marshall feigned apology and said it could be redressed if the conference took up his time-saving proposal; but it was not.

On March 17, one week into the conference, the issue of war reparations came up. Molotov claimed that the Soviet Union had been promised $10 billion in reparations at earlier wartime conferences, and given the prodigious sacrifices it had made it was entitled to the funds. At various times Churchill and Roosevelt had in fact intimated that reparations at that level could be considered, but no formal agreement had been reached. As Marshall and Bevin saw it, Europe and Germany's economic troubles and Soviet truculence had refashioned the context and placed reparations in a new light. Because the United States and Great Britain had to provide large amounts of aid to their occupation zones, reparations for the Soviet Union would effectively constitute transfer payments from the United States and Great Britain to the Soviet Union. Marshall argued that if the Soviets cooperated to achieve German economic unity, Germany could produce more, and everyone would benefit from revitalized German production. On the other hand, he said, "We cannot accept a unified Germany under a procedure which in effect would mean that the American people would pay reparations to an ally."

The powers moved on to other issues, but Molotov would not agree to anything until the Soviet demand for reparations was met. It thus became the ostensible sticking point for the next several weeks. Speech followed translated speech; recrimination followed recrimination, interspersed with the occasional plea for goodwill and progress. Molotov would sit with his hand on his chin, his elbow on the table, his head nodding slowly, "completely poker-faced," as one of Marshall's aides described him. Bevin would peer through his tortoiseshell glasses, cigarette dangling from his mouth, often peeking out from books or memos passed to him from aides. To some, Bidault appeared to play the part of the urbane intellectual, "a smoothy type," one of Marshall's aides wrote. Others felt that his excessive drinking impeded his effectiveness.

Whatever Bidault's state, though, the French line remained firm: France wanted a prior claim to German industrial production; it wanted to limit Germany's level of industry and it wanted control of as much of the Ruhr/Rhine, and particularly the Saar, as possible. France had sought to navigate a middle way, tacitly colluding with the Soviet Union on keeping Germany weak, yet cooperating with the United States, the ultimate arbiter of German policy in the western zones. But that passageway was becoming compressed, and as the fissure between the U.S. and Great Britain on one side and the Soviet Union on the other calcified, it appeared that France would have to throw in its lot with one camp. When Molotov recanted on Soviet support for French annexation of the Saar, it stung Bidault deeply. More than that, it seemed to provide confirmation of the Soviet Union's disregard for French interests, its hostile intentions, and it also seemed to provide the domestic political cover Bidault sorely needed to move closer to the United States and Great Britain.

To some in the United States, $10 billion in reparations was an eminently reasonable demand, and it was certainly a cheap price to pay for cooperation. Marshall himself was willing to consider some amount of reparations. Revisionist historians have pointed out that part of the U.S. refusal was due to popular domestic unwillingness to foot the bill. Some have gone further to suggest that if the United States had met this reasonable demand the Cold War itself might have been avoided. Marshall and his advisers did not see it that way. To them, the reparation issue was one part of the equation. Agreement on political terms and interests in the Ruhr/Rhine were still to be decided, and the Soviets would not have been likely to have given any headway on either issue. Victory on all these points would have provided the Soviet Union with an untenable amount of influence in Germany at a time when Germany and the rest of Western Europe were weak and vulnerable. Second, reparations simply masked the more fundamental divergence of objectives in Germany. As the days passed and disagreement continued, Marshall and Bevin were becoming increasingly convinced that Molotov was being dilatory on purpose, and that the Soviet Union wished to see its tentacles extended as far west as possible. If the Soviet Union was truly concerned about its security, as it claimed, then why would it not accept the demilitarization plan that Marshall continued to offer? The Soviets seemed much more interested in extracting reparations and, already having established its political hold on the east, enhancing its influence in the western zones as well.

On March 24, Bevin, whose health was recovering nicely, ventured to the Kremlin to speak with Stalin. Stalin's tone was conciliatory and assuring, if entirely noncommittal. Bevin left with a renewed confidence in the conference's prospects. But no progress followed the meeting. So little was agreed upon, in fact, that the discussions had degenerated into negotiations about what subjects would be discussed. Molotov's diatribes seemed to lengthen, meandering with no discernible aim. In a letter back home to Vandenberg, Dulles wrote: "The third week has now wended its weary way, [with the Soviets] unwilling to get to grips with the real problems, apparently feeling that the process of exhaustion has not yet gone far enough."

As March passed into April, sheets of rain washed away the winter's accumulated snow. A thaw set in. The circus was on. Vendors were selling ice cream and children took to playing in the streets. At the conference, there followed a profusion of banquets. The Soviet hosts served caviar, sturgeon, pheasant and champagne, and as custom had it, the toasts flowed. There were "sumptuous" outings to the Bolshoi Theater to see *Romeo and Juliet*, *The Nutcracker* and other ballets. As Bidault would later recall, "the politeness also became more elaborate. Yet it was purely verbal politeness and did not spring from the heart." And it could not obscure the gravity of the consequences of each day that passed without agreement on Germany.

On April 2, having achieved no meaningful agreement on economic matters, the participants moved on to Germany's political organization. The Soviet Union was alone in pressing for a strong central government. The United States and Great Britain interpreted the Soviet position as a gambit that they could confidently steer Germany in the direction of their political orbit. The U.S. could not allow for that possibility. These arguments went on for the better part of a week, when Marshall finally suggested they move on to the next question. By this time, the atmosphere had become toxic. Molotov had greeted almost every proposal with counterproposals, amendments, delay. Molotov's tactics drove Bevin to declare that as far as he was concerned he "didn't care what the Council discussed next."

Convinced that they would have to act alone, Marshall and Bevin began having lunch daily, mapping out a strategy for Germany. They would proceed immediately to raise the level of industry in their zone and press for Germany's rehabilitation. No reparations would be extracted, and to assuage French concerns, they would do their best to meet its coal needs and continue to engage it on the Ruhr/Rhine and security matters. Marshall suggested to Bevin that they wait six weeks to make public any of their agreements, lest the Soviet Union propagandize that the United States and Britain had been colluding all along, sabotaging any chance of agreement.

Marshall and Bevin agreed to try once more to get Molotov to sign on to the demilitarization proposal. When Molotov delayed and then offered crippling amendments, Bevin scolded his Soviet counterpart. They had been there for five weeks now, the old union organizer said. "If we cannot agree to the basic first step of keeping Germany disarmed and unable to wage war, we have indicated to the world a complete lack of unity of purpose in our approach to the German settlement," he said. "Since we have failed to reach agreement on the four-power treaty, I suggest we move on to the next item."

BEVIN AND BIDAULT had already had their meetings with Stalin. Well aware of Communist strength in France and Bidault's precarious position, Stalin had borne down on the French minister. Two-against-two is better than three-against-one, Stalin told Bidault, in an unveiled Realpolitik entreaty. Bidault did not bite. Stalin was charming and assuring with Bevin. Marshall had waited. He did not want to see Stalin until all the diplomatic cards were on the table and all the key fault lines had come into view. Marshall had been working around the clock, up until midnight, most nights. On April 15, after some thirty fruitless meetings, he decided that it was time to cut through the temporizing and false politesse. He knew Stalin as a man of his word. They had cooperated in war and Marshall still hoped they could achieve cooperation in peace.

In the dark of night, Marshall's limousine pulled out of the American Embassy and drove along the Arbat—what Bedell Smith felt was probably the most policed street in the world—and arrived at the gates of the Kremlin. Passing security, the car drove by imposing towers, courtyards and orthodox churches and eventually to the building that housed Stalin's offices. Passing a series of ushers and soldiers, the delegation, including Bedell Smith and Chip Bohlen, a State Department aide and Marshall's translator for the meeting, got out of the elevator on the third floor, made its way down a long, narrow corridor and walked through the high double door leading to Stalin's office. Passing a series of reception rooms, the delegation entered a paneled conference room, where Molotov, a few others and Stalin himself were waiting.

Stalin greeted Marshall: "You look the same as when I saw you last time," he said, "but I am just an old man." The two were roughly the same age. But it was true. Stalin had aged poorly under the strain of war. He seemed smaller, his trademark square-cut tunic oversized. His face was badly scarred from a near-fatal bout of smallpox as a child; his teeth were discolored and his mustache seemed thinner. He was slow, but commanding, and the scars, the wear and his yellow eyes gave the appearance of "an old battle-scarred tiger." Both delegations sat around a large table, flanked on the walls by grand portraits of Russian marshals from the Napoleonic Wars.

Marshall went first. He was trained as a soldier, not as a diplomat, he told Stalin, and he would speak as a soldier, directly and without double meaning. He was "very concerned and somewhat depressed at the extent and depth of misunderstandings and differences which had been revealed at this conference." He had studied American opinion, Marshall said, and at the end of the war no other country rivaled the degree of esteem in which the American people held the Soviet Union. But in the time since, the Soviets had broken agreements and had delayed progress on further ones. "These practices," Marshall said, "unfortunately led to accusations and inevitable suspicion, so that as a result, when they came to the conference, everyone was so filled with suspicion and distrust as to make agreement virtually impossible." Still, cooperation had been possible during the war, Marshall said, and he was certain it could be once more.

The general recounted the disagreements over Germany, reparations and the demilitarization proposal. With a clear and even tone, he explained the U.S. position on each. Marshall ended the litany with a firm declaration: "We are frankly determined to do what we can to assist those countries which are suffering from economic deterioration which, if unchecked, might lead to economic collapse and the consequent elimination of any chance of democratic survival . . . it was our intention to help, insofar as we could, to restore the economy of such countries." As Marshall spoke, Stalin sat quietly, puffing on a cigarette and doodling a wolf's head in red ink on a pad of paper. Mostly he looked down or off to the side, but at moments turned to Marshall to look him in the eyes. Marshall concluded, saying that he wished to "re-erect [the] relationship of cooperation and hope and clear away some of the suspicion." He thanked Stalin for letting him speak so long and so freely.

Of course cooperation would be possible, Stalin assured him. But there had been delays and disagreement on the U.S. side as well. Economic unity was possible, Stalin said, but meant nothing without political unity. He desired a strong central government, so that Germany would not be divided and repeat its post-Napoleonic consolidation along waves of nationalism and militarism. The issue of reparations was fundamental to the Soviet Union. "While reparations might not be popular in the United States and England, ten billion dollars of reparations was very popular in the Soviet Union," Stalin said. Ten billion dollars had been agreed to at Yalta, Stalin said, and that sum spread over twenty years did not seem unreasonable.

In brief turns Stalin and Marshall rehashed their varied interpretations of the delays and recriminations. The meeting had gone on for almost an hour and a half. Marshall had done most of the talking; half of the time had been spent with translations. It was time for Stalin's parting words. He did not share Marshall's grave concern. The situation was not so tragic, he said. He was more optimistic than Marshall. Differences had occurred before, and as a rule when both parties had exhausted themselves in dispute they would arrive at a compromise. Agreement on all the main issues was possible; there was no need for desperation. It was necessary to have patience and not become too depressed, Stalin said. He wished Marshall to be convinced that the Russians would be frank and open and that it was "impermissible to turn the problem of Germany into any sort of a game or in any way to play up to or flirt with the Germans." He appreciated the frankness of Stalin's statement, Marshall said. He was encouraged by his last words and only hoped that Generalissimo Stalin was right. Stalin assured him that his closing remarks were correct. Marshall took leave. It was 11:30 P.M.

WHAT WAS STALIN'S grand design? What was he trying to achieve at the Moscow Conference? The most definitive answer remains that it is not entirely certain. An apparatchik who knew Stalin well during his postwar reign said: "He changed. I saw at least five or six Stalins." Part of the reason was that Stalin was exhausted after the war, and as tensions escalated with the Allies immediately following the war, he grew increasingly erratic. Part of the reason also had to do with Stalin's methods. Even with his closest subordinates, Stalin kept his cards close to his vest. Deception and conspiracy were the norm within Stalin's court and have endowed the Soviet dictator with a shroud of historical inscrutability.

Nevertheless, a trove of post–Cold War scholarship on Stalin helps to distill broad but discernible contours. Stalin, it is now clear, viewed the Soviet strategic interest through the prism of a distinct ideology. Informed by Leninist doctrine, and his own personal experiences and compulsions, Stalin believed in the historic inevitability of international Communism. Divining the future and the laws that would shape it, he believed that competition over territory, resources and profit would bring capitalist countries into conflict, and eventually, Stalin was certain, a third world war. The war to come would be decisive, doing away with capitalism for good and paving the way for the spread of Communism throughout the world.

This war was inevitable according to Stalin's crystal ball, but not in the near term. As World War II ended, the Soviet Union's military was emasculated, its industry was gravely depleted and its people were exhausted. He had no capabilities to wage war against any of the "imperialist" powers, least of all the United States. To sate his febrile concern for security—his own above all, and then that of the Soviet Union—and to rest and replenish for the conflict ahead, Stalin craved peace in the near term. "We shall recover in fifteen or twenty years, and then we'll have another go at it," Stalin said.

To provide that peace and respite, Stalin sought accommodation, even cooperation, with his war-time Allies. But he sought it on his own terms. The Soviet Union's wartime sacrifices entitled it to security (which he conflated with territory), to expand its sphere of influence and to ensure autonomy within that zone. The British Empire had global reach, and the United States now did as well. Driven in part by these dynamics as well as his own personal insecurity and ambition, even as he sought peace and accommodation, Stalin would probe and pursue expansion opportunistically.

Stalin's speech to Marshall, we now know, was a negotiating tactic. He had directed Molotov not to give in to U.S. or British terms during the Moscow negotiations. The negotiations over the peace treaties concerning the smaller European Axis powers had been similarly lengthy and contentious, but eventually they reached agreement. Stalin still hoped for agreement, but on terms most advantageous to him. We now know also that the U.S. atomic monopoly, and the demonstration of its destructive capabilities at Hiroshima and Nagasaki troubled Stalin deeply. He would not let the United States wield "atomic diplomacy" to dictate the terms of the peace that his country, more than any other, had sacrificed to achieve. If the U.S. and Great Britain felt resolution was urgent, wasn't it the wiser negotiating position to delay, and press the other powers into as many concessions as possible? And if the Soviets did in fact want accommodation in the near term, albeit on better terms and a modified timetable, wasn't the right course for Marshall simply to seize what Stalin scholar Geoffrey Roberts believed was in fact "an opportunity to arrive at a postwar settlement that could have averted the cold war and avoided the ideological warfare" to follow?

The answer to this question is no. And the reason is because, for Marshall, what mattered most was not what Stalin may have wanted but what he had done, how he had acted and the strategic position that had been created as a result.

The meeting confirmed Marshall's fears. Ostensibly, Stalin's justifications for the Soviet positions were reasonable. Had the United States met these demands though, it would have provided the Soviet Union with an untenable position of power in Western Europe. Reparations would have made Germany, already in desperate straits, much weaker, and would have transferred resources from the U.S. to the Soviet Union. With Germany foundering, and Soviet influence extended in each zone of the country, political centralization would mean that Germany would be consolidated, without checks to power, and ripe for Soviet picking. Precedent in Eastern Europe, the Soviets' interest in controlling Germany to eliminate the security threat and the opportunity to gain control of the Ruhr/Rhine industrial complex all suggested that this might be the Soviets' design. We now know that in 1946 Stalin said: "All of Germany must be ours, that is Soviet, Communist."

Meanwhile, conditions in Germany were getting worse every day. Strikes and food riots had erupted. Growing shortages meant even the 1,550-calorie daily ration might not be met. U.S. diplomatic representative to Germany Robert Murphy warned that he had not seen German morale so low since the days of Germany's capitulation. Lucius Clay spoke of the "rapid penetration of Communism." If Stalin wanted peace, Marshall believed, he would have pushed for real progress. As it was, Europe was in desperate straits. With each day, conditions grew more and more favorable to Communist ascension and Soviet expansion, even Soviet domination of the continent. The real issue for Marshall was that the lack of urgency Stalin demonstrated in their meeting and the instability he seemed willing to abide, or even foment, in Western Europe, as historian William Taubman noted, was in fact "indistinguishable from the disruption Moscow might have fostered if it had high hopes for immediate revolution." That is why Stalin's dilatory posture and his casual assurances chilled Marshall so.

Marshall could not have known about Stalin's genuine desire for near-term peace and accommodation. But, even if he had, the Soviet basis for accommodation was so advantageous to Stalin that it would have placed the United States in an untenable strategic position. And even after $10 billion in reparations, political concessions on Germany's political organization and authority over the Ruhr/Rhine, it is likely that Stalin would have continued to probe opportunistically. He may even have been emboldened by the affirmation that intransigence would yield such concessions. And as the United

States waited to gauge the results of those concessions, Western Europe would have continued to deteriorate further. Marshall was not prepared to abide it. The battle lines had come into view. And time would become the new theater of war in the months to follow.

IN THE WAKE OF HIS MEETING with Stalin, Marshall effectively gave up on the prospect of any meaningful agreement. Behind the scenes, though, he agreed with Bevin to move to increase the level of production in their zones in Germany, pushing for German economic recovery in the hopes that it would drive recovery in the rest of the region. A day earlier, Bevin had sent a letter back home to Prime Minister Clement Attlee. He wrote of the four-power treaty, in particular, "If the Russians had accepted it, a bridge could have been built and the antagonism growing so fast in the U.S.A. would have been checked . . . Russia has made a bad mistake, as bad as when she linked up with Hitler in 1939." In later years, Bidault would write, "The conference in Moscow proved that the only future for us lay in a Free Europe." Bidault was disgusted by the Soviets' tactics at the conference, frightened at the possibility of its aggressive designs on Western Europe and smarted from Molotov's volte-face on French claims to the Saar. In a poignant meeting with Marshall, the French minister said: "To the American question, 'Can we rely on France?' the answer was, 'Yes.'" But the French were weak, and pushing German recovery too fast could deliver the country to the Communists. Mostly France needed "time to avoid a civil war," Bidault told Marshall.

On the afternoon of April 24, the 43rd and final session of the Moscow Conference of Foreign Ministers adjourned. That evening, as procedure and protocol dictated, the host country threw a banquet for the visiting ministers. In the ornate St. George's Room, a hall built by Catherine the Great, the ministers gathered with selected members of each delegation in tow. They were greeted by all the members of the Politburo. As they sat down, the usual swath of toasts followed. Stalin raised his glass to Marshall and Bevin but omitted Bidault in the first round, a slight that left the French foreign minister furious. Stalin seemed relaxed and assured. When Marshall's turn came, though, the subterranean tension became tangible. Stalin stopped puffing on his cigarette and turned to the American secretary. "My country is a young country," Marshall said, "and like all peoples in such a country, our people are impatient. They are impatient to see Europe back on its feet . . . healthy and productive once more . . . If I have failed at this conference in showing you that this is our object[ive]—and this only—then I have failed in my duty to this country."

Marshall's plane took off the next day. On his way back, he stopped at Tempelhof Airport in Berlin to consult with Clay, and to instruct him to move to revive Germany's industrial production without delay. Then he left for home.

He had been away for six tedious weeks. It was the longest of the foreign ministers' conferences, and no meaningful agreement had been achieved. Marshall had made progress with Bevin and Bidault, though. And he had met with Stalin, had looked him in the eye, and had taken full measure of the Soviet dictator and his intentions for Germany and Europe. If not agreement, Marshall felt he had achieved clarity. John Foster Dulles later said, "The Moscow Conference was, to those who were there, like a streak of lightning that illuminated a dark and stormy scene." Now Marshall would come home. "All the way back to Washington," Chip Bohlen recalled, "Marshall talked of the importance of finding some initiative to prevent the complete breakdown of Western Europe."

IN A NEWSPAPER INTERVIEW a few months later, Marshall told a reporter that Moscow "brought us to the important conclusion that we face the choice of quitting Europe altogether or of completing the task of European recovery . . . We had no intention of quitting." For Marshall, Moscow was decisive. In meetings with Bevin, in consultations with Dulles, Bohlen and others at the embassy, and perhaps most importantly in discussion on the flight home from Berlin, Marshall had become resolved to address Europe's problems with a bold stroke. The contours of the path ahead were not yet clear, but the direction of that path was firmly set.

Upon arriving back home in Washington, Marshall decided that he would follow Byrnes's custom of speaking to the American people following the foreign ministers' conference. On Monday, April 28, at 8:30 in the evening, the general addressed the nation via radio broadcast. He said that proceedings at Moscow suggested that the prospects for cooperation with the Soviet Union were not good. At the same time, conditions in Western Europe were dire. Europe's recovery was essential to U.S. interests. Despite continued disagreement with the Soviet Union, the United States needed to proceed at once. His tone was measured and not at all provocative. But it was purposeful. "We cannot ignore the factor of time involved. Disintegrating forces are becoming evident," he said. "I believe that action can not await compromise through exhaustion." Lest anyone miss the urgency of the moment, Marshall put it in very plain terms: "the patient is sinking while the doctors deliberate."

Chapter Three

THE DRUMBEAT AT STATE

ON THE SAME DAY that George Marshall set out for Moscow in March 1947, Will Clayton was recuperating from a streptococcus infection that had almost cost him his foot, at a ranch in Tucson, Arizona. For months now, Clayton, the undersecretary of state for Economic Affairs, was becoming increasingly alarmed at Europe's deterioration. Europe was at the tail end of its most brutal winter in recent history, so the dry Arizona heat and the comfort of his favorite ranch set an odd backdrop for the memorandum that Clayton was about to pen. Clayton anticipated that the Moscow Conference would yield little progress on the continent's future and that further deterioration and grave consequences would follow. The tocsin had to be sounded.

"I am deeply disturbed by the present world picture and its implications for our country," Clayton's March 5 memorandum began. "The reins of world leadership are fast slipping from Britain's competent but very weak hands. These reins will be picked up either by the United States or by Russia." If the United States abdicated, Clayton wrote, war would follow. The American people needed to be shocked into action. That would not be difficult, Clayton believed: "To shock them, it is only necessary . . . to tell them the truth and the whole truth."

WILLIAM LOCKHART CLAYTON was born on February 7, 1880—the same year as George Marshall—in Tupelo, Mississippi. Clayton's childhood was set in the post–Civil War South. Tupelo was a backwater, and his parents were poor. As a young teenager, Clayton spent his days in school and his afternoons working for his father's laundry business, while evenings were split between studying for exams "by the light of the only good lamp in the house." and taking typing lessons, which he hoped to parlay into typing work, for which he would be well paid. Impressed with Clayton's shorthand and typing skills, a cotton merchant passing through town offered him a position in St. Louis. When Clayton left Tupelo, he had only an eighth-grade education. His would be one of the most remarkable success stories of twentieth-century America.

After a year, he followed the merchant to New York, where he began in a remedial post at the American Cotton Company, one of the biggest cotton brokerage firms in the U.S. He worked around the clock. In what spare time he had, he read assiduously. "If you read and absorb every line on the editorial page of the New York Times, you will keep posted on all the worthwhile events at home and abroad," he counseled a younger coworker. Slowly, he moved up the ranks at American Cotton.

Then, at twenty-four, with $9,000 in borrowed capital from his wife, Sue, and his brothers-in-law, Clayton founded Anderson, Clayton and Company in Oklahoma City. Immediately Clayton implemented cutting-edge technology and innovative management techniques. He took advantage of international inefficiencies, doing away with unnecessary middlemen and brokers and opening up offices all over the world. By 1920, Anderson, Clayton had offices in Bremen, Liverpool, Le Havre and China and additional operations in Czechoslovakia, Yugoslavia, Poland, Hungary and the Baltic states. By 1936, Anderson, Clayton had annual revenues of $200 million. Clayton had built the largest cotton brokerage firm in the world. He was a multimillionaire. The cover of Time magazine dubbed him "King Cotton."

Clayton applied himself to his work with an all-consuming intensity. His powers of concentration were enormous and his energy boundless. "You've got to live the thing" you are working on, he would tell Sue. At the same time, Clayton was an acute observer of the larger currents shaping the world around him. With offices and operations around the globe, Clayton came to be a fervent believer in the power of free markets and free trade. They were the foundation upon which Clayton built his firm, and the keys, he was coming to believe, to the creation of wealth in the United States and around the world.

He began speaking out and gave addresses around the country. His national profile grew. When World War II broke out, he was brought into government to run the operation focused on procuring materials and resources that the Allies needed, and, as importantly, that the Allies did not want the Axis powers to obtain. It came to be known as the "warehouse war." Clayton prosecuted it successfully and it was one of the keys to the

Allies' victory. As the war's end came into view, the materials and equipment procured and produced—roughly $100 billion in value—had to be sold, mostly to the private sector. Clayton assumed the reins and presided over what his biographer called the "biggest garage sale in history."

Clayton refused to accept pay for his services during the war. He did not seek a position; he was sought out. He was one of a cadre of successful industrialists and financiers whose talents were summoned in the war effort and who would ask nothing in return. Clayton wrote to a friend in 1943, "No doubt the war will end someday, but the battle of Washington, never. As you know, I came without any political ambitions and having acquired none during my three years stay, I can look these fellows in the eye and tell them where to go." Will was not the only member of the Clayton household who wished to return home to Houston. His wife, Sue, despised Washington. A five-foot-tall firebrand, she was ill and felt deeply neglected as her husband's work and travel seemed endless.

Clayton's exit from the nation's capital would not be that easy. He had acquired enormous stature during the war years. A correspondent named Alan Drury wrote of Clayton at that time that he was a "big, tall, well-built Texan in his 60s, with . . . a handsome rugged face, and the smoothest manner imaginable." He had a prolific memory, and was able to call up abstruse statistics about exchange rates and budget figures on command. His voice was calm and even, and "whatever his views may be, [he] never hesitates to state them with complete frankness," such that his replies always seemed highly agreeable to senators and congressmen, even if his views or recommendations were not. Roosevelt was not about to let Clayton return to the comfort of Texan living. He offered Clayton the position of undersecretary of state for Economic Affairs in the State Department, "in charge of all economic affairs" relating to foreign policy and postwar recovery, as the president's cable read. Roosevelt knew whom to go to next. He duly cabled Sue: "I know that so far as [Will] is concerned, you are the real Commander-in-Chief, and I am writing to ask you to order him to remain here and undertake the task for which I am drafting him . . . P.S. Don't relinquish your authority over him!" Sue relented, grudgingly.

Clayton assumed the new post in December 1944. He had no doubt about what his first official act would be. "The first letter I sign on State Department stationery is to you," began Clayton's letter to former Secretary of State Cordell Hull, only recently retired, and then recuperating in Bethesda Naval Hospital. "I want to thank you for your confidence and I want to assure you that your foreign policy is so thoroughly ingrained in my system that I shall always work and fight for it."

Cordell Hull had served as secretary for twelve years, the longest tenure in that position in United States history. Hull was not a brilliant grand strategist, but he had a powerful and guiding conviction: free trade and economic cooperation were the keys both to international prosperity and to peace and security. It was a conviction very much rooted in the lessons of recent history. As the global depression broke out in the beginning of the 1930s, countries staggered to mitigate the fallout. There were two major consequences. The first was that the Depression generated conditions of despair and dislocation that helped give rise to totalitarian leaders like Hitler and Mussolini, who preyed upon the people's weakness and want. The second was that to protect their own national interests and to husband their resources, powers like Great Britain, Germany and Japan instituted protectionist measures, and came to form exclusive autarkic economic blocs. Between 1929 and 1936, for example, trade between France and Germany fell 83 percent. With walls erected to keep others out, these economic blocs jostled for materials, resources and influence, fueling competition and insecurity. A virtual economic war had preceded the outbreak of actual war.

For most of the nineteenth century, in contrast, Great Britain presided over a world economy marked by free trade and economic cooperation. It was a time of prosperity and relative peace. That order and the values that underpinned it were shattered during the 1930s, and Hull, Clayton and others witnessed it. The United States missed opportunities to help prevent the slide to autarky. A State Department official wrote: "The bit of history was as well known in Cordell Hull's State Department as the Bible's account of the Fall of the Garden of Eden. History must not be repeated!" Free trade, currency stabilization and open economic policies would best promote prosperity. Prosperous and open countries were less likely to yield to totalitarianism and more likely to work for peace. Hull liked to say that "the political lineup followed the economic lineup." Or, as a popular aphorism of the time put it, "If goods can't cross borders, soldiers will."

Hull's vision had become Clayton's. He regretted not speaking out more during the 1930s. "I was so very wrong in that judgment," he said. It was his own personal lesson from history, and he would not repeat it. "Most wars originate in economic causes," he told a group of Detroit businessmen in May 1945. "Nations which act as enemies in the marketplace cannot long be friends at the council table." The key for Clayton now was to build an open and prosperous international economic and financial order. It was the key to prosperity, the key to security and peace and the key to transcending the mistakes of the past. Hull had lit the torch, and Clayton was now determined to carry it forward.

• • •

WERE IT NOT FOR Sue Clayton, George Marshall would most likely never have been secretary of state. In the spring of 1946, when James Byrnes resigned, Truman offered the position to Will Clayton. Taking notes as Clayton briefed him on international trade negotiations only a few months after he assumed the presidency, Truman looked up, sighed and said to Clayton, "I don't know anything about these things. I certainly don't know what I'm doing about them, I need help." Truman took to Clayton immediately. He was direct, commanding and self-effacing. In short order, he became part of Truman's "inner circle." Clayton was also beloved at State. A soft-spoken and mild-mannered Southern gentleman, he worked harder than his subordinates, and was known to give them credit for successes and to assume the blame when problems arose. Clayton assembled a talented cast of young businessmen and economists in the economic affairs department. They idolized him. One of them was a successful young banker named Paul Nitze, who would go on to become the head of the Policy Planning Staff at the State Department. "Will Clayton was my boss, and he was the only one for whom I had complete respect. He was without fault either in his personal or public life," wrote Nitze.

Clayton's discipline and self-control were legendary. He abstained from alcohol until the age of fifty-eight, when he finally took up drinking sweet sherry because his son-in-law doctor insisted it would be good for his health. As an adult, his weight never fluctuated more than five pounds. In Washington, Clayton walked several miles to work every morning for exercise. Like Marshall, he was ambitious. Also like Marshall, though, he was a pragmatist, interested in efficiency, impact and solutions. After one grueling day Clayton spent testifying on Capitol Hill an aide turned to him and said, "They were mighty tough on you, Will. Why didn't you go after them?" "It wouldn't have convinced them," Clayton replied. John Chamberlain wrote of Clayton in a profile in Life magazine: "People respect him, love him, find him extremely magnetic. But they feel puzzled by the very perfection of his consistency. Where is the fallible, human Clayton?"

In the spring of 1946, Truman summoned Clayton to his office. The president intimated that he would like Clayton to become his secretary of state. "Mr. President, I can see where you are heading, but I just can't. My family . . ." It was Sue. Truman said, "I need the best man available." Clayton was sixty-six. He had promised her they would return home to Houston. "We shouldn't pursue this matter any further," Clayton told the president. He said it "reluctantly, and fast, like he was getting something out he had to say before he changed his mind," Truman later told a senator, recounting the episode. Marshall was also asked around this time. Who was asked first is not known. The general was an inspired selection, and no doubt would have been Truman's first choice. It is quite possible though, that Truman did not want to have to summon Marshall from impending retirement a second time, and sought the next-best candidate he could find in Clayton. When Clayton turned the position down, it narrowed Truman's options.

While other U.S. statesmen concerned themselves with the Soviet Union in the spring of 1946, Will Clayton was focused on Western Europe's economy. The United States had already furnished Western Europe with large infusions of aid. In January 1941, Roosevelt proposed a program of assistance in which America would lend essential material and supplies to Great Britain and eventually other Allies as well. It was tantamount to lending a neighbor whose house was on fire a garden hose, Roosevelt suggested, with his customary guileful ebullience. It became known as Lend-Lease. By the end of the war, U.S. Lend-Lease aid amounted to over $50 billion. Most was for wartime purposes. By May 1945, however, the United States was furnishing on the order of $7 billion in nonmilitary Lend-Lease. Most of this would finance postwar reconstruction. In August 1945, Truman ended Lend-Lease, in some cases recalling shipments in mid-ocean. The decision was abrupt and it was ill-conceived. The diplomatic and strategic fallout was severe. Truman would later call it one of the worst decisions of his presidency. Clayton, who dreamed of a prosperous and cooperative postwar economic order, was irate. "I was never so close to resigning," he said later.

However, there was an aid vehicle in place that was meant to supplant Lend-Lease. The United Nations Relief and Rehabilitation Administration, or UNRRA, was formed in Atlantic City in November 1943 and meant to provide humanitarian relief to people around the world suffering because of the war. The United States did not conceive of the idea; it was a multilateral enterprise. For the duration of the program the U.S. committed on the order of $4 billion, approximately $2.5 billion of which went to Europe. The United States insisted that UNRRA aid be meted out to those people most in need, and that the agency be nonpolitical. It was an idea, Dean Acheson recalled, that "amused Litvinov," the Soviet foreign minister at the time.

UNRRA disbursed an extraordinary amount of aid: in excess of 20 million tons of supplies, by one estimate. That translated to roughly 2,000 full cargoes. Were all those ships to be strung out in equal distance, from New York to Gibraltar, the ships would be too close for safe navigation. The agency was effective as a humanitarian enterprise. According to Jean Monnet, a leading figure in France, "It prevented a breakdown in supplies, which would inevitably have caused appalling famine, disease, and political disorder in Europe." The agency may have prevented Austria from starving.

By 1946, though, problems began emerging for the United States. UNRRA's policy of nonpolitical, needs-based aid provision meant that roughly two-thirds of aid went to eastern and central Europe, which included Yugoslavia, Poland and the Soviet Ukraine, among others. Though the agency was founded by forty-four nations, the United States provided about 75 percent of the funding. Yet the United States had only one out of seventeen votes, and effectively no control over how aid was distributed at the local level. With the Soviet Union fastening its grip on Eastern Europe and U.S.–Soviet tensions escalating, politics began playing out at the agency. Suspicions were strong that the Soviet Union was using UNRRA aid to compensate for supplies it had plundered from Eastern Europe. There were reports that Communist parties were appropriating supplies and doling them out to supporters to firm up their political position. There were problems in Czechoslovakia, where the U.S. ambassador insisted that political authorities were misleading local populations about the source of the aid. And there were reports that in Communist Yugoslovia, Marshal Tito's army was consuming much of the aid.

Will Clayton was one of UNRRA's greatest champions. He felt the agency was the best vehicle in existence for the humanitarian work it was doing. But as the reports filed in, he grew increasingly disgruntled. To make matters worse he had to answer for the agency to a Congress deeply hostile to expensive foreign aid programs. Subsumed in geopolitical tension and Soviet manipulation, the agency's effectiveness had waned and so had congressional support. By the summer of 1946, Clayton was taking the first steps that would shut the agency down, earning him the title, from one historian, of "Lord High Executioner" of UNRRA.

Throughout 1946, Clayton focused more and more on Western Europe's economic condition. He felt that the economic stability and viability of Great Britain and France, in particular, would be critical to the region's prospects and his own postwar vision. If Great Britain and France were healthy, their temptation to retreat into closed economic blocs would be offset. Clayton had an inherent belief in this sort of system, and he also knew well that the United States would need robust export markets to accommodate its postwar industrial production. In the spring of 1946, Clayton received Jean Monnet, a French éminence grise in Washington, and negotiated a large loan of several billion dollars in aggregate value for the French.

Clayton was also spending much time with Lord John Maynard Keynes, Great Britain's éminence grise, negotiating a loan with Great Britain.

Between Keynes and Monnet, Clayton was going head-to-head with two of history's economic giants. Clayton had warm relationships with both, whom he considered partners more than competitors. Keynes had come to Washington seeking $6 billion. Without large-scale U.S. support, Britain faced "an economic Dunkirk," he declared. Despite Clayton's sympathies, the negotiations were difficult. Most of the country disfavored the prospect of yet another loan or aid package. At an official function, Sue Clayton asked Keynes, "How are you, Lord Keynes, and when are you going home to England?" Keynes smiled. "As soon as I can get through to your stubborn husband," he replied. "Oh, Lord Keynes," she said, "I'm so glad you find him stubborn too!"

The British resented what they perceived as American parsimony. Ernest Bevin did not do Britain's prospects any favors when he said that perhaps Britain wasn't getting support because there were "too many Jews in New York." The geopolitics had laid out a new context, though. Representative Christian Herter of Massachusetts wrote to Clayton that the economic arguments in favor of the loan were much less convincing to his colleagues "than the feeling that the loan may serve us in good stead by holding up a hand of a nation whom we may need badly as a friend because of impending Russian troubles." "I'm sure you are right," Clayton wrote back to Herter.

Clayton negotiated a $3.75 billion loan at very low interest to be paid back over fifty years. It also provided a multibillion-dollar forgiveness of Lend-Lease obligations. As part of the agreement, Clayton insisted that Britain make its currency convertible within one year, which he felt would promote trade and investment in Britain. Officials in London were concerned that it could lead to a drain in its reserves. Clayton wanted to help Britain, but he also wanted to advance U.S. interests. He reported to Bernard Baruch, a prominent U.S. industrialist and elder statesman, that he had loaded the loan "with all the conditions the traffic will bear." Churchill's sojourn in the United States and his "iron curtain" speech at Fulton in March 1946 were aimed at securing U.S. support for the loan. Clayton also embarked on a public campaign, giving dozens of speeches all over the country to gin up national support. U.S.-Soviet tension, Clayton's efforts and support from key congressmen secured the loan's passage in July 1946.

As the storm clouds gathered over Europe at the end of 1946, the United States had already spent approximately $10 billion aiding Europe, and by one valid estimate, several billion dollars more than that. But it wasn't working. *Washington Post* reporter Ferdinand Kuhn called them the "Billions That Didn't Prime." Most policymakers had fixed their sights and focus on the Soviet Union. Europe seemed on the road to recovery, and large quantities of aid had been doled out. Most U.S. officials did not appreciate the fragility of the incipient recovery, or the gravity of the economic and financial weaknesses that were percolating beneath the surface. The aid supplied to date was doled out in piecemeal fashion, without strategic vision or cogency. In his article, Kuhn called it "The myopia of '46."

When the storm hit, Europe's tenuous recovery came to a grinding halt. The storm exacerbated Europe's commercial dysfunction. But there was another powerful factor at work. At the State Department in Washington, Paul Nitze, an economic official then working for Clayton, was receiving delegation after delegation, and was beginning to discern an elemental part of the problem. The United States was exporting roughly $5 billion a year more to Europe than it was importing. Europe needed U.S. goods and services to fuel its recovery, but it could not sell the United States that same amount. It could not produce enough nor did it have sufficient funds to finance its recovery. In Nitze's words, "The U.S. was eating up the rest of the world's foreign exchange reserves." It was the Dollar Gap.

Nitze drafted a memorandum to Clayton proposing a global effort on the order of $20 to 25 billion over four or five years to help other countries bridge the gap. "My suggestion was not unique," Nitze noted. Secretary of Defense James Forrestal and others had discussed the need for large-scale foreign aid. A small group of junior officials in Clayton's economic affairs department were giving the matter perhaps the most elaborate and penetrating consideration. It was around this time, also, that Clayton began to apply his formidable powers of concentration on a large vision to cure Europe's economic and financial ills.

That winter, Clayton ordered his top staff and department heads to report to him once a week on the "deteriorating situation in Europe." On February 21, while Marshall was giving an address at Princeton University, the British ambassador to the United States, Lord Inverchapel, passed along an urgent cable to the State Department informing Marshall that His Majesty's empire would have to pare down its commitments in the Mediterranean. The British Empire was relinquishing international responsibilities vital to international stability. To Clayton, as well as Marshall and Acheson, it was a clarion call for U.S. engagement.

Working from the ranch in Tucson, Clayton had time to ponder the significance of Europe's predicament and the geopolitics at work. The president was to give an address at Baylor University in early March 1947. Clayton crafted much of the speech. The focus was U.S. foreign economic leadership. In drafting the speech with Dean Acheson, Clayton jotted the following passage: "prodigious efforts on our part are going to be necessary . . . if we are going to avoid economic disaster in the years to come." It would take more than dollars: "This is a time when American security and prosperity depend upon bold and imaginative economic thinking and acting . . . I think we are going to have to begin thinking in terms of bolder measures than have ever before been advanced." The passage did not make it into the final draft of the speech, but it reflected Clayton's thinking. It also, no doubt, reflected the tone and substance of discussions that Clayton was having with Truman at this time. "Clayton is the person to whom the president turns for advice on foreign economic matters to complement Marshall on foreign political matters," wrote Lester Merkel in the *New York Times*.

While drafting the Baylor address, Clayton reached the conviction that the time had arrived to move beyond vague warnings. His March 5 memorandum marked the first high-level call for a concerted U.S. program for European recovery. He called for an appropriation of $5 billion in the first year, presumably to be followed by comparable and tapering amounts for several years to follow. This was not a humanitarian enterprise. Russia was boring from within, and the United States had to build up Europe's ailing economies. "The security and interests of the United States and of the world demand that the U.S. take prompt and effective action to assist certain of these gravely threatened countries." Piecemeal aid would no longer suffice. "We must go all out in this world game or we'd better stay at home and devote our brains and energies to preparation for the third world war." More than dollars, Europe needed structural economic reform. "Assistance should take the form not only of financial aid, but of technical and administrative assistance." The memo was not circulated widely but was read by Marshall, Acheson, Kennan and the other key players at State.

In mid-March, President Harry Truman addressed a joint session of Congress. The United States would take up the responsibility history had placed on its shoulders. It would provide military and financial aid to Greece and Turkey, assuming the role in the Mediterranean that Britain had vacated. Truman spoke in strong and sweeping rhetoric, seemingly committing the United States to support any government anywhere in the world that would stand against "Communist subversion." It was dubbed the Truman Doctrine. Marshall found the blustery language irresponsible. He agreed with Clayton, though, on the larger point that the United States had a greater role to play in the postwar world and with the need for the judicious and strategic provision of aid.

A few weeks later, on April 10, Clayton left for Europe. The ostensible purpose of the trip was another round of negotiations on the General Agreement on Tariffs and Trade, or GATT. Clayton also wanted to see firsthand what was happening in Europe. While Marshall endured the tedium of Molotov's temporizing at the Moscow Conference, Clayton was soliciting views from old business contacts, selected foreign diplomats, economists and leading industrialists. Compiling statistics and soaking up the latest reports and data, Clayton also pounded the pavement. Taking his customary long walks, he got out into the open and observed shopkeepers and quotidian happenings. It was worse than he had imagined.

ON APRIL 29, while Clayton was canvassing European capitals, Marshall had arrived back in Washington from the Moscow Conference. He had just delivered his national radio address the evening before. He summoned George Kennan into his office. Marshall had met Kennan twice during the war, and was impressed by his mind. It had been a year since Kennan had sent his "Long Telegram" from the Moscow embassy, and he was considered the State Department's leading analyst on the Soviet Union. Marshall had tapped Kennan as the inaugural head of a new group he had created at State called the Policy Planning Staff, or PPS. Its purpose was to think "beyond the vision of the operating officers caught in the smoke and crisis of current battle; far enough to see the emerging forms of things to come and outline what should be done to meet or anticipate them." Marshall had planned on letting Kennan finish a stint teaching at the War College. But that was before the Moscow Conference.

The general informed Kennan that he was determined to move on a plan to aid Europe. If he did not move quickly, Congress would begin proposing ideas. Marshall felt it essential that State lead the enterprise and did not want others framing the terms of the debate. Time was of the essence. Kennan would have to begin immediately. Marshall told him that he would have roughly two weeks to submit a report with recommendations. Marshall's instructions were clear, and his advice was brief: "Avoid trivia."

The meeting with Marshall left Kennan reeling. PPS did not yet exist. He had no office, no staff, and to compound matters, he had committed to several speaking engagements in the fortnight to follow, three of which were out of town. His assignment was not a modest one: "I was supposed to review the whole great problem of European recovery in all its complexity." Kennan had a prodigious intellect and he was a seasoned expert on the Soviet Union. He had certainly given thought to Europe's predicament and had lectured on the subject in the preceding months at the War College. But Kennan was not an economist. "Kennan had little knowledge of, or experience in, economic matters," Paul Nitze recalled later. Kennan wisely proceeded to engage the best and most experienced minds in the department in his effort. Among those Kennan recruited, in varying capacities, were Thomas Blaisdell Jr., Paul R. Porter, Theodore Geiger, Charles Kindleberger and Walt Rostow. They had something in common. They were all associated with the economic side of the State Department. They had all been highly influenced by, and all reported to, Will Clayton.

A midlevel State Department official named Joseph Jones was a participant in the group's deliberations during May 1947. In his memoir, Kennan himself gave primacy to Jones's account. Jones recounted: "The most vigorous idea currents on the subject were at the time those emanating from the economic offices of the State Department, presided over by Undersecretary Clayton." Drawing on Clayton's junior officials, and in constant consultation with the best minds from around the department, Treasury and elsewhere in the government, Kennan's PPS staff was activated on May 5, 1947.

Kennan had little time to spare. He would have to synthesize all of the views from the department's best minds into a cogent set of findings and recommendations, and then he would have to defend those recommendations "against all governmental critics, including ones unavoidably more deeply versed in the details of the subject matter than myself." Ensconced in conference rooms at the new State Department in Foggy Bottom, which journalist James Reston said had "about as much character as a chewing gum factory in Los Angeles," Kennan led interminable sessions of discussion and debate. His colleagues put forward their views with intellectual rigor and force. Together they worked, Kennan recalled, "night and day, restlessly and relentlessly." For the mercurial and sensitive Kennan, the sessions were so intense that they delivered him "into an intellectual agony more intensive than anything I had ever previously experienced." On one occasion, to relieve the strain, he excused himself, went outside and walked around the entire circumference of the building, weeping.

Within those early May sessions, two important themes emerged. The first was that the group had become convinced that German recovery was essential for Europe's recovery. "To talk about the recovery of Europe and to oppose the recovery of Germany is nonsense. People can have both or they can have neither," Kennan wrote in a memo, reflecting the group's consensus on the matter. The second was that to achieve economic self-sustainability, Europe would have to come together and integrate its disparate national economies, then still wrapped in a patchwork of bilateral trade agreements, protective barriers and uncoordinated economic policies. In January 1947, Paul Porter, one of Clayton's star junior officials, had written a memorandum espousing the need for European economic integration. This sort of "creative peace," Porter wrote, was the only alternative to "an uneconomic self-sufficiency that would raise the specter of autarky, prevent recovery and foster the kind of political instability that benefited the Communists." Porter and other officials on the economic side of State had been exploring and promoting the idea of European economic integration since at least 1946. Clayton's views on free trade and economic cooperation encouraged thinking along these lines. By the spring of 1947, the idea was floated by diplomats, members of Congress and the media. Clayton's team provided the depth and substance to propel it forward. Kennan found it persuasive.

EARLY THAT MAY, as George Kennan labored in the sterile conference rooms at Foggy Bottom, Dean Acheson boarded Secretary Marshall's DC-3 plane for the Mississippi Delta. Acheson was slated to give a foreign policy speech on May 8. Originally, Truman was supposed to give the address, a promise to dear friends from Greenville, Mississippi. But a contentious and murky fight over the succession of a fatally ill senator kept Truman away. The president enlisted Acheson, and meeting with Truman in the Oval Office, Acheson said that if it was an important foreign policy address they wanted, they would get it.

Dean Gooderham Acheson was born in Middletown, Connecticut, in 1893. His father was a minister, born in England. The family's ties to Britain were strong and reinforced in his youth every year when it flew the Union Jack in celebration of the Queen's birthday. Acheson went to Groton, then Yale, then Harvard Law School. He had a brilliant legal mind, and after practicing law for some time, he was recruited into Roosevelt's State Department. In Roosevelt, Acheson found a patrician cut from like caste, but he found Roosevelt condescending and much preferred Truman, whom he described as a Yale man in the best sense of the word. Acheson was the typecast urbane statesman. He wore finely tailored suits, often with a bow tie and a hat. His carriage was firm and stiff, as was his manner. His finely cultivated mustache was a trademark.

When Marshall came on as secretary of state, he asked Acheson, who had been assistant secretary of state under James Byrnes, to stay as his undersecretary. Acheson agreed to do so for six months. Marshall had a high opinion of Acheson, and so did Truman. The president did not hesitate before deputizing him to speak in his stead. The address was to take place at the Delta State Teachers College in the town of Cleveland, Mississippi. On his way to the college, Acheson noticed healthy, robust cattle spread out over verdant pastures. When he arrived, a crowd of 10,000 people, a progressive and serious-minded group, was there to greet him. The college gymnasium could accommodate some, but most poured out onto a tree-shaded lawn, where extended families enjoyed picnics and Coca-Colas, ready to listen to Acheson's speech on the loudspeakers set up outside. It was a typically American scene, Acheson later recalled, and the striped-pants Washingtonian diplomat embraced it. Inside, Acheson took off his jacket and rolled up his sleeves.

Europe was on "the borderline of starvation," Acheson told his audience, and was beset by economic and commercial dislocation. The punishing winter had exacerbated the continent's problems. By the end of the year, it was likely that Europe would fall into a balance-of-payments deficit of as much as $8 billion with the United States. The situation would require "further emergency funding." Speaking to the audience, a collection of farmers and small businessmen who would rely on Europe's ability to pay for their goods, he said that "there is no charity involved in this. . . . We are obliged from considerations of self-interest and humanitarianism to finance a huge deficit in the world's budget." It would take more than aid, Acheson said. A "coordinated European economy . . . was a fundamental objective."

He had come to trumpet a call to "reveille," not to offer a plan or solution but to lay out the problem with unmistakable lucidity. He did not speak from a text but from notes he had made on his flight from Washington. Acheson had a passion for Europe and its traditions, and a deep-seated conviction that it was now America's turn to accept the mantle of world leadership. More than the provision of dollars and goods, there was a human and a spiritual element to the task ahead: not only do "human beings and nations exist in narrow economic margins, but also human dignity, human freedom, and democratic institutions." America could provide breathing space and life by widening those margins. It was in the nation's interest, and it was "our duty and our privilege as human beings."

Indeed, Acheson's "trumpet did not give an uncertain sound." But the American media did not seem to pick up on it. A State Department report found that press response was generally favorable. However, the speech did not receive headline coverage in most papers. The New York Times did not print the text of the speech, as it did for addresses it deemed important. Before leaving for the Delta, though, Acheson had invited three of his British media contacts to lunch to post them on the upcoming address. The speech received greater coverage in Europe, and the text was printed in the Times of London.

If Acheson's speech did not gain wide press coverage, that was fine with

George Marshall. Marshall did not want to attract attention from Congress, lest enterprising politicians seize the initiative. He did not wish to arouse isolationist or anti–foreign aid sentiment, still very strong, particularly in the Midwest. Truman had approved the concepts in Acheson's speech. Still, Marshall was "very much put out about that." Another senior State Department official named Ben Cohen had given a similar speech in California. Those speeches "did not represent 'trial balloons' or any sort of build-up," Marshall recalled. In fact, he "gave Cohen hell" for his speech "for fear that it would reveal my plans and start the much feared 'premature debate.'"

After Acheson returned to Washington, *New York Times* reporter and consummate insider James Reston asked him, "Is this a new policy that you are enunciating or is it just a bit of private kite-flying?" Acheson was evasive: "You know this town better than I do." Policy is made at the White House, he said, so "you must ask the President." Shortly thereafter, at a White House press conference, Reston asked the president if the address represented administration policy. "Yes," Truman said, it did.

Though he posed the question at a press conference, Reston might have just as easily asked it at a dinner party at one of Georgetown's redbrick row houses, or at Acheson's home while enjoying an after-dinner drink. Much of the postwar foreign policy community inhabited a tight network in which a small group of select diplomats, politicians and journalists dined, socialized and vacationed. Journalists and official policymakers enjoyed a symbiotic relationship, and the bounds of both professions were elastic and intermingled in those years. By the middle of May 1947, State was mobilized in full force behind the formulation of a policy on European recovery. As the drumbeat rolled at State, the media began picking up the sound.

NO JOURNALIST IN THIS ERA was more influential than Walter Lippmann. When Lippmann was twenty-five years old, Theodore Roosevelt called him the most brilliant young man of his age in the entire United States. Founder of the *New Republic*, he was soon to become the "High Priest of the Journalistic Order." His writing was read all over the world. His syndicated column reported on policy, and it made it.

By February and March 1947, *Barrons* and a few other publications that were following Europe closely began trumpeting the need for greater U.S. aid. During this time, Lippmann consulted regularly with Clayton as well as Acheson and Kennan. He complemented these sessions with his own extensive travels and independent analysis. On March 20, Lippmann said that the United States would have to make a vast outlay, and that it should be parceled with large-scale aid to the Soviet Union as an overture for a political settlement. On April 5, Lippmann planted a stake on the issue. Writing in the *Washington Post*, Lippmann titled the column "Cassandra Speaking." Europe was threatened with nothing less than collapse, he told his readers. It was not outlandish. He was "saying only what responsible men say when they do not have to keep up appearances in public . . . The truth is that political and economic measures on a scale which no responsible statesman has yet ventured to hint at will be needed in the next year or so." He called for an effort "equivalent to a revival of Lend-Lease."

In a follow-up column written in the *New York Herald Tribune* on May 1, 1947, Lippmann elaborated upon the contours and objectives of a new plan for European recovery. Following the Moscow Conference it was clear to Lippmann that the Soviets would not cooperate. The United States would now have to move to support Western Europe, alone if need be. Picking up on a theme that Dulles had been promoting at Moscow, and that Clayton and the junior officials in his department had been working on for a year, Lippmann said that the plan would not yield a self-sustaining recovery if the United States continued to deal with each European country as a separate entity: "That will put them on the dole, where what is needed is a reorganization of the bankrupt economy of Europe, and then, to make the reorganization succeed, a large contribution from America of working capital."

Lippmann proposed that Europe's countries assemble to formulate a common plan for their economies. From the U.S. "point of view it would be a refreshing innovation to make our contribution not to many separate governments but to Europe . . . In some such way as this, the contribution which we must inevitably make would serve not merely to relieve suffering but as a premium and inducement to the unification of Europe." If integration was to work, and if recovery was to be sustainable, Europeans needed to assume responsibility for their own affairs, and they needed a controlling voice in the determination of their future.

Lippmann's pieces planted seeds among his wide readership. In the halls of the State Department they did more than that. Joseph Jones recalled the impact of Lippmann's columns: they made top officials feel they were on the spot and challenged or encouraged them to better thinking and to move with greater expedition; they furnished junior colleagues with a lever to advocate with senior officials; and they "enlarged at once the realm of what men are inclined to regard as possible."

Following Lippmann's pieces and Acheson's speech on May 8, the media clamor grew louder. James Reston filed an article the day after Acheson's speech in the Delta titled, "Administration Now Shifts Its Emphasis on Foreign Aid: Economic Reconstruction of Western Europe Now Held Best Bar to Soviet Expansion." The *Wall Street Journal, Washington Star,* St. *Louis Post-Dispatch* and others joined the fray. On May 5, Richard Strout wrote in the *New Republic* that "State Department strategists have now come around . . . to the point a good many visionaries have been urging all along— that one way of combating Communism is to give Europe a full dinner pail." Across the Atlantic, Raymond Aron, a leading French intellectual, picked up on the speculation and wrote in *Combat* of "the more or less genuine news of a vast 'Lend-Lease for Peace' plan that America is about to produce."

Mostly, however, the European media was awash in alarming reports of Europe's dire straits. In France, food rations dropped below those of wartime. In Germany, Lucius Clay cabled the War Department, "We do not see why you have to read the *New York Times* to know the Germans are close to starving. The crisis is now, not in July." Most immediately, Europe was running out of dollars to pay for coal, supplies and food. In May, the *Economist* wrote: "More and more as weeks succeed weeks, the whole of European life is being overshadowed by the great dollar shortage. The margin between recovery and collapse throughout western Europe is dependent at this moment upon massive imports from the U.S."

A motley assortment of prominent Americans had come to espouse their own ideas on European recovery. In early May, Dwight Eisenhower wrote in his diary, "I personally believe that the best thing we could do now would be to post $5 billion to the credit of the secretary of state" to promote economic recovery where U.S. vital interests were at stake. In mid-May, Henry Wallace, Roosevelt's former vice president, called for a plan of $10 billion per year for five years. He wanted half of the $50 billion commitment to go to the Soviet Union as an expression of goodwill, unity and conciliation. Speaking from Iowa on May 21, Republican presidential candidate Harold Stassen proposed "Production for Peace," a plan whereby 10 percent of U.S. production per year would be devoted to securing peace around the globe. The Stassen Plan translated into an astonishing proposed outlay of $200 billion. Journalist Arthur Krock endorsed it. Stassen's Republican colleagues in Congress thought that Treasury Secretary John Snyder was being kind when he called the proposal "far a-field."

The heightened interest and percolating proposals unnerved Marshall. Kennan and his working group felt the heat. They had been working furiously. Despite everyone's honorable intentions, natural discord and even some genuine pessimism rendered progress challenging. Kennan proceeded apace, though: "The instructions we had from General Marshall did not permit us, of course, to listen to these pessimistic voices. We had to come up with something, and we did."

With only a few weeks, wrote Joseph Jones, "Kennan did the only thing he could do: he confined himself to figuring out an approach to a plan for a plan." He used an earlier interdepartmental study as well as reports and memoranda from the economic side of the department. On May 23, Kennan submitted a thirteen-page memorandum to Dean Acheson, with recommendations for a plan to promote European recovery. "The ideas by which it was inspired came from many sources; the drafting was largely my own," Kennan wrote in his memoirs.

The PPS did not believe that Communism was the root of the difficulties in Europe, Kennan's memo explained. Rather the difficulties "result from the disruptive effect of the war on the economic, political and social structure of Europe and from a profound exhaustion of physical plant and of spiritual vigor." The Communists were exploiting this crisis. Further Communist success would "create serious danger to American security." U.S. aid in Europe should not be directed toward combating Communism as such, the memo followed, but to "the economic maladjustment which makes European society vulnerable to exploitation by any and all totalitarian movements and which Russian Communism is now exploiting."

The fundamental objective of the plan under consideration must be Europe's self-sustained economic recovery. The State Department could not go in good conscience to Capitol Hill with yet another aid program unless it believed that plan to be the last. But first, in the short term, the United States needed to provide hope and confidence. The psychological impact was essential, Kennan believed. In a supplementary memo, he wrote, "We must recognize that much of the value of the European recovery program will lie not so much in its direct economic effects, which are difficult to calculate with any degree of accuracy, as in its psychological and political by-products." To that end, he recommended increasing coal production in the Ruhr to meet the region's urgent needs.

The program, Kennan's memo argued, "must be a joint one, agreed to by several European nations." "We insist," the memo continued, "for the sake of clarity, for the sake of soundness of concept, and for the sake of self-respect of European peoples, that the initiative be taken in Europe and that the main burden be borne by the governments of that area." Like Lippmann, Kennan wanted the Europeans to come together as a collective entity and formulate their own plan. The United States would then support the European initiative and leverage its aid to foster European integration.

Kennan lent his prodigious intellect and his great powers of analysis and exposition to the task. No one could have better synthesized all the disparate viewpoints and notions bantered about the department and elsewhere in the government. The memo was influential and illuminating, but not decisive. In Acheson's view, it was not until Will Clayton's return from Europe that a concrete plan began to emerge. Clayton's time in Europe had convinced him of the necessity of immediate and bold action. On the plane ride home he began crafting a four-page memorandum of his own.

When Clayton returned to Washington on May 19, he immediately assembled Paul Nitze and the rest of his team for lunch at the Metropolitan Club. "Will was genuinely alarmed that Europe was on the brink of disaster," Nitze recalled. After lunch he closed the door to his office and put the finishing touches to the memo that afternoon. A heavy cold consigned Clayton to bed rest shortly following his return. On May 27, Clayton submitted his memo in finished form to Acheson, along with a request for a meeting with Marshall the next day. Acheson read the memo, passed it along to Marshall and other senior officials and set up the meeting immediately.

The memo jolted Acheson and had the same effect on Marshall. It was now obvious that U.S. policymakers had underestimated the war's toll on Europe's economy, Clayton's memo conceded. They could see the physical destruction but did not appreciate the "effects of economic dislocation on production," or the breakdown of commercial ties. "Europe is steadily deteriorating," and its political condition was doing the same, he wrote in true Hullian fashion. Clayton drew on the scenes he had surveyed to paint a vivid portrait of Europe's postwar condition. It appeared a medieval work. Millions of people starved in the cities, while farmers and peasants in the country hoarded food for themselves or even their cattle. People had no confidence in the value of their currency or the prospects for their future. The modern system of division of labor was rent. Production was sliding, and Europe's payments deficit was at $5 billion and growing. "If it should [grow], there will be revolution," Clayton wrote.

Clayton was deeply concerned about what this meant for the United States. In addition to the threat to U.S. national security, America's hope for an open and prosperous postwar economic order would be dashed, and Clayton foresaw unemployment and even depression looming. "*These things must not happen,*" Clayton wrote. The facts were well-known; what remained was for the United States to harness its production surpluses and organize its fiscal policy and its own consumption into a "sound and workable plan."

He proceeded to frame the broad strokes of such a plan. It would require six or seven billion dollars in U.S. aid per year for three years. American production was sufficient to meet the demand, but Europe had to take the initiative: the "three-year grant . . . should be based on a European plan which the principal European nations . . . should work out," he said, in agreement with Lippmann and Kennan on what was becoming an essential component of the plan. Dollars had to be leveraged to encourage the Europeans to enact structural economic reform: "Such a plan should be based on a European economic federation . . . Europe cannot recover from this war and again become independent if her economy continues to be divided into many small watertight compartments as it is today." Clayton was calling for European economic unification.

The program Clayton was devising could not withstand Soviet obstructionism, local misdirection of aid or internal propaganda wars. Europe needed to take the initiative. It would be Europe's plan; but *the United States must run this show*." Clayton's May 27 memo had adumbrated most of the key elements in the emerging plan.

Ideas, concepts, recommendations and principles—most of which had originated with Clayton and his staff in the first place—had been bandied about for months now. But "it was Clayton's disturbing report," wrote *New York Times* reporter Cabell Phillips, "that lighted a match under this intellectual broth and set it bubbling."

The next morning Marshall convened a meeting in his office. The key officials were there: Clayton, Acheson, Kennan, Bohlen and two or three others. Clayton's memo had a searing impact on Marshall, and the general turned to him at the start for remarks. Clayton summarized the memo with unmistakable conviction. When Clayton had finished, Marshall announced: It would be folly "to sit back and do nothing."

There were still a few key matters to consider before the meeting could adjourn. The first involved the machinery from which U.S. support should be offered. Already, the United Nations had created an Economic Commission for Europe. Kennan wanted the ECE to take the lead. Wary of repeating the mistakes from UNRRA, Clayton disagreed. The second matter had to do with whether the United States itself, or Europe, should take the initiative, that is, whether the U.S. should devise a plan for European recovery or cede the initiative to Europe. Here there was discord. Senior State Department officials Ben Cohen and Willard Thorp felt that Europe could not successfully come together. Clayton and Kennan both thought it essential that the plan come from Europe. Kennan argued that if the Europeans couldn't come together and devise a plan with the carrot of large-scale U.S. aid, then it meant that rigor mortis had already set in, and there was nothing that the United States could do for Europe anyway.

Marshall sat back and listened intently, directing questions and the flow of the discussion. Generally, in meetings like this, he would go around the room and ask everyone their opinions. He would not offer final judgments on the spot. After meetings adjourned he would consider the matter and then render a judgment. As discussion continued, Marshall asked the group whether the offer of U.S. support should be made to Western Europe or to all of Europe, including Russia. It was the question that concerned him most. Russian participation could very easily kill the plan before it even started. Stalin could sabotage the plan through obstructionism and delay. Furthermore, Marshall did not expect members of Congress to ask their constituents to send their tax dollars to Russia.

Acheson and Kennan were most forceful here. Acheson felt strongly that the United States could not be seen as dividing Europe. Kennan hoped for more than that. He wanted the offer to induce Eastern European countries to move closer to the United States and Western Europe, loosening the Soviet grip on the region. He wanted to make a "squeeze play" for Eastern Europe, he told British diplomats a week or so earlier. While Eastern Europe could be wooed, Kennan argued, Russia would never agree to the conditions of participation. Clandestine and deeply suspicious of the West, Russia would not open its economy to Western inspection; it would not jeopardize special trading agreements with Eastern Europe, one of its critical levers of influence in the region, and it would not risk perceived infringements on its sovereignty or autonomy to cooperate in the scheme. Calculating that Stalin would not accept the offer, Kennan wanted to invite Russia to participate. His advice: "Play it straight." Everyone in that room knew that if Russia accepted, it could sabotage any chances for a successful plan. "It was a hell of a big gamble," said Chip Bohlen.

True to form, Marshall had given everyone an opportunity to voice his views. He did not reveal his own. On May 25, Reston had written a comprehensive piece for the *New York Times* with much of the detail from Kennan's PPS memo and detail that would soon appear in Clayton's May 27 memo. It even included figures. So, as the meeting adjourned, Marshall cautioned once more against any leaks. The content of the meeting was not to be discussed, he said. Said Dean Acheson, "As one looks back on it, he left us with very little to leak."

Marshall had made up his mind during his return from Moscow at the end of April, if not in mid-April after his chilling meeting with Stalin at the Kremlin. The work done at State and Clayton's memo provided the substance he had wanted. Clayton's forceful and credible appeal in the May 28 meeting added urgency. Following the meeting, Marshall asked Acheson how he could best present a picture of the European situation to the American people. Before he could formulate a response, Acheson left for a lunch with Les Biffle, the staff director of the Senate Minority Policy Committee. At lunch, Acheson found himself besieged by a dozen senators very anxious to be told of the State Department's plans for European recovery. Senator Brien McMahon, a Democrat from Connecticut and normally a staunch administration ally, told Acheson in no uncertain terms that if he were simply presented with "a fait accompli" the administration could not count on his support. It was a shot across the bow. Acheson later reported to Marshall that it was time to begin conferring with important senators and to make a speech "which would not undertake to lay down [a] solution, but would state the problem."

Marshall fielded Acheson's counsel, but he did not heed his recommendation. Isolationist sentiment ran strong and deep in pockets of America. The isolationist press could be rabid, and Marshall had felt its sting before. On December 4, 1941, convinced that the administration was conniving to bring the United States into war, Bert McCormick's isolationist paper, the *Chicago Tribune*, managed to obtain and subsequently printed the complete secret mobilization plans prepared by the U.S. Army and Navy in the event of war. As it turned out, it was only days before Pearl Harbor. The general was not about to be outflanked, lest others begin to frame the debate.

Following the May 28 meeting, Marshall had decided to mobilize at the earliest possible date. Earlier, he had thought that the commencement at Amherst College scheduled for mid-June would be the occasion. He now wanted to move sooner. He had already accepted an invitation to attend commencement at Harvard University, having declined the previous two years. Scheduled for June 5, the timing seemed perfect. Marshall asked Acheson if he thought the Harvard commencement would be a fitting occasion to unveil the plan. Acheson counseled against it. "You know," he said, "it is reported by a fellow from the college paper who gets it all mixed up. To me this was really not the thing to do." Acheson felt it would not receive wide coverage. It was precisely the backdrop Marshall sought.

On May 30, Marshall instructed a senior aide named Marshall Carter to have a draft prepared for a speech less than ten minutes in duration to be delivered to the alumni group at Harvard. Carter selected Bohlen, who knew Marshall's views and whose lucid and direct prose suited Marshall well. Marshall forwarded Bohlen copies of the Clayton and Kennan memoranda. Bohlen is generally credited as the draftsman of the speech that followed at Harvard. But according to Marshall's recollection, he solicited drafts from both Bohlen and Kennan. They were alike in content, but disparate in style, and so, using portions of both as well as excerpts from the two memoranda, Marshall constructed his own speech.

Meanwhile, on June 2, Dean Acheson showed up for lunch at the United Nations club with three British journalists. "If these limeys offer me sherry, I shall puke," he told an aide. Acheson had arrived hung over from a festive evening the previous night. Acheson had invited the journalists—Leonard Miall of BBC, Malcolm Muggeridge of the *Daily Telegraph* and Rene Mac-Coll of the *Daily Express*—to lunch to post them on the impending U.S. Plan. Its scope would be unprecedented, he told the journalists, and it aimed to deliver European recovery. He and others had been to Capitol Hill too often, Miall remembered Acheson saying. They had requested too much aid, each time promising that it would be the last. The Republican Congress had little appetite for another U.S. aid program. But if Europe asked and came together to do so, it might constitute a different sort of proposition. Acheson emphasized that the Americans would offer the Europeans the initiative, and it would be theirs to seize. And with that, he had struck the critical chord.

On June 4, Marshall and his wife, Katherine, joined General Omar Bradley (a four-star Army general and commander in World War II who was also slated to receive an honorary degree at commencement) and Bradley's wife for the trip to Boston. That same day, the State Department made Marshall's (still incomplete) speech available to the press. It was single-spaced and with none of the trappings of an important démarche. Clayton and Acheson had had a chance to review Bohlen's draft but did not hear anything more from Marshall thereafter.

Once in Cambridge, it dawned on Marshall that he had not even shown the speech to the president. Truman's senior aide, Clark Clifford, recalled that the work being done was approved by Truman but "was almost entirely a State Department project." In his memoir, George Elsey, another influential presidential aide, wrote, "I must be clear. The White House role—even the president's—was minimal in conceiving and executing the Marshall Plan." Truman was kept abreast. He was supportive, and he knew where the effort was going from meetings with Acheson, Clayton and Marshall, as well as from continued briefings with Clifford, who was somewhat more involved. But Marshall had been directing this initiative, and State was doing the planning. It is an extraordinary commentary on both Marshall and Truman, and the relationship they shared, that Marshall felt he could proceed without Truman's direct approval.

As Marshall was putting the final touches on his address at Harvard President James Conant's home, where he and Katherine were lodging the night before commencement, Leonard Miall of the BBC received a draft of the speech from the State Department. When Miall got home that night, he read the speech, and he realized that this was it. It was the Plan that Acheson had alluded to at their luncheon. The next morning, Miall telephoned his editor in London. Marshall's speech that day would be "enormously important," he told him. He was about to come "out flatly for this great continental plan of help to Europe." Is it being broadcast? Miall's editor asked. It wasn't terribly important, Miall replied, because Marshall's "voice is so poor. He is not a good broadcaster and I doubt if it is a good idea to have it in his voice." Miall said that he would have to deliver it in his own voice. He said he would call it "Marshall's Overture."

Back in Washington at the British Embassy, Chargé d'Affaires Sir John Balfour received the State Department version of the text. He had been briefed extensively by Kennan and Acheson on various occasions in late May as to what was brewing. He had already compiled a lengthy account of what was happening at State and his views of what it meant. Marshall had considered alerting Bevin in London, or the British Embassy, but he did not want to elicit any attention beforehand, and he also wanted to ensure that his offer was perceived as fair, and to all of Europe, and so did not want to favor the British. As such, the British Embassy received no advance notice. Without such notice, Balfour, believing his report to have been sufficiently comprehensive, did not even bother to cable the speech directly to the Foreign Office in London. He sent it by surface mail.

At Cambridge, the bell tolled at 9:30 A.M. Commencement was called to order, and Marshall received his honorary degree. Marshall's "intention at all times was to spring the plan with explosive force in order not to dissipate the chances of U.S. acceptance by premature political debate." No one at Cambridge had any idea of the significance of the address Marshall was to deliver later that afternoon from Harvard Yard. Despite the State Department release the day before, few if any in the American press seemed to grasp its full meaning. And no one else—save the three British journalists who lunched with Acheson—seemed to, either. The general had maneuvered masterfully.

Marshall's staccato voice evinced little emotion. His purpose was not to rouse his crowd that June morning. The crowd's reaction meant little. His words, however, their precise meaning and reception, meant everything. He began by outlining Europe's economic condition. The war had reaped tremendous damage, but "the visible destruction was probably less serious than the dislocation of the entire fabric of [the] European economy . . . The modern system of the division of labor upon which the exchange of products is based is in danger of breaking down." Europe could not manage unassisted, Marshall said. The time for American action had come.

The general proceeded to introduce the main elements and contours of the fledgling Plan. The *objective* was "the revival of a working economy in the world so as to permit the emergence of political and social conditions in which free institutions can exist." "Such assistance," Marshall made clear, "must not be on a piecemeal basis . . . Any assistance that this Government may render in the future should provide a cure rather than a palliative." The current enterprise would break with the failed ones of the past. Revival meant self-sustainability. The *means* for achieving European recovery was to "help" Europe meet its "requirements for . . . foreign food and other essential products." The United States would provide essential aid for three or four years—a *time line*—to bridge Europe to self-sustainability. Marshall was forthright about U.S. *motives*: "The consequences to the economy of the United States should be apparent to all," he said, adding that "there can be no political stability and no assured peace" as long as Europe's economy was mired in desperation and dysfunction. The Plan was rooted in U.S. security and economic interests.

With the key elements of the Plan introduced, Marshall turned to the political lineup. "Our policy is directed not against any country or doctrine but against hunger, poverty, desperation and chaos." It was a brilliant rhetorical turn. The U.S. would not define its interests in opposition to any one country but in opposition to "hunger, poverty and desperation." The implication was that any person or any country that wasn't for the Marshall Plan was promoting "hunger, poverty and desperation." And any European state that embraced the Plan could participate. No one was excluded, not even Russia.

Marshall then said, "It would be neither fitting nor efficacious to draw up unilaterally a program designed to place Europe on its feet economically. This is the business of Europeans." The United States did not seek to dictate terms to participating countries. On the contrary, it wished to empower and embolden Europe to assume control of its own destiny. The U.S. aimed to serve as a constructive partner: "The role of this country should consist of friendly aid in the drafting of a European program and of later support of such a program so far as it may be practical for us to do so. The program," he continued, "should be a joint one, agreed to by a number, if not all European nations." It was another critical component and one of the only conditions of aid: the European request for aid would have to be a joint one. To proceed, "The initiative, I think, must come from Europe," Marshall said, in a line as important as any other in his address. It contained an invitation to Europe:

an invitation to request aid and an invitation to assume the initiative in the new program for recovery.

With characteristic brevity and lucidity—in the span of only a few short paragraphs—Marshall had introduced his Plan, and he had delivered his invitation to Europe. As he finished his prepared remarks, the general removed his eyeglasses, looked out over his audience, and with great intensity, offered a few final lines impromptu: "We are remote from the scene of these troubles. It is virtually impossible at this distance merely by reading or even seeing photographs and motion pictures to grasp at all the real significance of the situation. Yet the whole world's future hangs on a proper judgment . . . of just what . . . can best be done, what must be done."

Chapter Four

THE WORLD RESPONDS

O N THE NIGHT OF JUNE 5, Ernest Bevin was home in London, sitting up in his bed listening to a small wireless set on his nightstand. At around 10:30 P.M. Leonard Miall's radio program, *American Commentary*, came on. Miall broadcast the text of the draft of Marshall's speech that he had received from the State Department a day earlier. Half-asleep, Bevin would recall thinking that he was actually listening to a live broadcast of Marshall's speech from Harvard and that he was hearing the general's voice.

In many ways, Marshall's speech was directed at Bevin. Between 1914 and 1945, Great Britain had been at war for one day in three, twice as long as the Americans. Great Britain was in an acute economic and financial bind— " 'up against it' in a desperate way," as Bevin said—and the government was about to pass yet another round of import restrictions to dam the country's hemorrhaging reserves. Around this time, some members of Britain's Cabinet were coming to hold the view that Britain could no longer afford any foreign policy at all. For Bevin, Marshall's address was "a lifeline to sinking men. It seemed to bring hope where there was none." In what may have been, according to his biographer, "his most decisive contribution as Foreign Secretary to the history of his times," Bevin grabbed that lifeline with both hands.

The next morning at the Foreign Office, Bevin demanded a complete version of Marshall's speech. Because the embassy had sent it via surface mail, though, he had to rely on Miall's report. That same day, a senior official at the Foreign Office, Sir William Strang, asked Bevin if it would be advisable to cable Marshall or others at State to inquire about the speech and the apparent offer. Bevin had seized on Marshall's line about European initiative.

It was the chance for Bevin to grasp the mantle of leadership on behalf of Great Britain, the Commonwealth and the continent—in that order. "Bill," Bevin told Strang, "we know what he said. If you ask questions, you'll get answers you don't want. Our problem is what we do, not what he meant."

Immediately, Bevin called French Foreign Minister Georges Bidault and proposed that the two meet in Paris to discuss how to proceed. At a luncheon address that day to the National Dock Labor Corporation, the impact of the speech was evident in Bevin's tone. "I know we are in difficulties," he said, "but the sense of independence is so great in us I do not want to ask anyone for anything. I want to fight through to recovery. I beg you to rise to the occasion. You dug for victory during the war, dig for dollars now." Marshall was not offering charity. Bevin interpreted it as it was meant, as "a mutual thing . . . Try and help yourselves and we will try and see what we can do." The British were weak and demoralized, but proud. Dignity and self-respect mattered. Marshall's address, in tone and approach, paid service to that. A week later, Bevin told the Foreign Press Association, "If anyone in the world has got it into his head that Britain is down and out, please get it out." Later, Bevin would call Marshall's speech "one of the greatest in world history."

Britain's economic leaders acknowledged the opportunities at hand. Leading British economic official Sir Edwin Plowden recalled of that moment: "it was obvious that if complete breakdown in Western Europe was not to come about, something would have to be done and the only country that was in a position to do that was the United States." In Plowden's judgment, "collapse really meant that the whole of Western Europe might have gone Communist." It was a smash with the press. On June 14, 1947, the *New Statesman and Nation*, an anti-Truman publication in London, offered: "Mr. Marshall's speech at Harvard was the first sign of American statesmanship since the death of Roosevelt." The *Economist* heralded the address as a watershed moment and suggested, in a recommendation that must have heartened Clayton and the rest of the officials at State, that Europe use this aid to achieve "a full customs union of the main countries of Western Europe." Its form was to assume "something like a United States."

When Marshall's address came across the wires at the Quai d'Orsay, France was in the grip of a series of large-scale strikes. Soon France's entire railway network would come to a standstill. The Monnet Plan to modernize the economy was in paralysis due to the Dollar Gap and the related problem of chronic inflation. At the same time, France was in intense political turmoil, having just expelled the Communists from the government. Amid the tumult, Marshall's address was received mostly with gratitude and acclaim.

Though Charles de Gaulle, then out of government, chose not to acknowledge it, Bidault welcomed Marshall's initiative as "the most important postwar event." Yet the French foreign minister was also circumspect. He suspected (correctly) that the American offer of aid was also an attempt to promote German recovery. Bidault expressed gratitude and saw a profound opportunity, but he also made it clear that he could not abide any scheme that prized German recovery over France's economic and security needs. France was also particularly concerned about how the United States would deal with the Soviet Union because of its own domestic Communist threat. The perception that this new plan was dividing Europe into two spheres would arouse vitriol and, some feared, even insurrection among the Communist ranks.

The reaction in the rest of Western Europe was similar. In Germany, leadership in the western zones greeted Marshall's address with excitement. But still under a strict occupation, Germany did not know exactly how it might be included. In Norway and elsewhere, Norwegian Foreign Minister Halvard Lange remembered, "The Marshall speech, of course, was greeted as a great act of statesmanship." In the Netherlands, Foreign Minister Dirk Stikker recounted, "It is not a question of whether you were in favor of it, because it was absolutely a must—you couldn't do without it." Though grateful, these smaller powers were concerned about being dictated to by the larger powers with whom they were asked to form a collective response. They were also anxious about the Soviet response.

In most European countries, it took some time, a week in some, more in others, for the offer to penetrate the public consciousness. Some were skeptical that it would materialize at all. Many remained guarded, aware that the offer would have conditions and that it would take time for aid to arrive. Some reactions reflected wounded pride: "When they sniffed dollars," remarked one Frenchman of his countrymen, "they dropped everything and came running like cats to fresh milk."

The Communist parties, meanwhile, looked to Moscow, awaiting the Soviet response. Immediate reaction from the Soviet Union was muted. On June 9, the Soviet ambassador in Washington, Nikolai Novikov, cabled Moscow with an analysis of the speech. Novikov averred that the plan was an attempt to stave off collapse in America and Western Europe. It was an American attempt to consolidate the West into an anti-Soviet bloc. In his copy of the cable, Molotov underlined and circled these two passages with particular emphasis. How Stalin would respond was still uncertain.

Back in Washington, even Marshall was taken slightly off guard, though thoroughly delighted, at the alacrity of Bevin's response. As he had hoped, the media response back in the United States was slow. In the *New York Times*, Marshall's speech got second billing to comments Truman had made that same day about a recent Communist coup in Hungary. As State labored and Europe reacted, coverage began increasing in the fortnight following the Harvard address.

The press did not know exactly how to refer to the new proposed initiative. In the *New York Times*, Harold Callender penned an article titled, "France Is Stirred by Marshall Plan," introducing the term as early as June 6, the date of the article. Many felt that it was not a "Plan" as such. Marshall's speech contained scant detail. In the weeks and months to follow, journalists and policymakers referred to the burgeoning initiative, in turns, as an overture, an offer, an idea, a notion and a proposal. To be sure, it was all of those things. The contents of the speech did not constitute a blueprint for action. Marshall himself described it as "something between a hint and a suggestion." The speech had painted broad strokes, but, nevertheless, it contained an objective (European recovery), a time line (three or four years) for getting there, the means (aid, structural economic reform and European initiative) for achieving it and an expression of resolve and willingness to meet the commitment. Suggesting that the Europeans add flesh to the bones did not mean it was not a Plan; in fact, it was one of the key elements.

At the White House, Clark Clifford suggested to Truman that they call it the Truman Plan. The president insisted otherwise. It will be called the Marshall Plan, he said. Truman revered Marshall, and wanted to honor him. The general had taken the lead since the conference in Moscow. In addition, Truman was a shrewd politician. An election was approaching, and the Republicans had an overwhelming majority in Congress. "Anything that is sent up to the Senate and House with my name on it will quiver a couple of times and die," Truman said. The act was gracious, but mostly it was a deft political maneuver. And so the enterprise would forever be known as the Marshall Plan.

SHORTLY AFTER MARSHALL'S SPEECH, Senator Styles Bridges went to purchase a railroad ticket back to Washington from his home state of New Hampshire. He soon found himself enmeshed in discussion with a displeased ticket agent. "I don't know what the hell you think about this Marshall Plan, but I don't understand it. I don't think you understand it." The senator agreed; he did not fully understand what was meant by Marshall's speech, and he didn't claim to. "Well, I think we've done about enough for the rest of the world and Europe," said the agent. "What are we going to do, keep feeding them indefinitely? We better spend some of the money here at home." The agent's reaction was not out of step with American public thinking at the time.

From 1941 to 1945, American industry had mobilized its prodigious production capacity for the war effort. By the end of the war, thirteen rationing programs were in effect, covering scarce commodities ranging from gasoline and shoes to sugar and red meat. Consumer goods such as refrigerators and automobiles were largely unavailable. Women were asked to leave the home and enter the workforce. By one count more than a quarter of American wives worked for pay during the war. Americans were asked to save as never before. In 1940, personal savings amounted to around $4 billion. By 1945, it was $137.5 billion. All of this sacrifice was summoned after a decade-long economic depression.

The American economy boomed during wartime. National production doubled. However, after America's last war, World War I, government spending had declined, and returning soldiers had put pressures on the workforce that led to unemployment and recession. With the Depression's scars still raw and the post–World War I experience alive in recent memory, Americans were petrified that they would fall into another recession or depression. It was coming " 'as sure as God made little green apples,' fathers warned their families at the dinner table, and next time it would be 'bad enough to curl your hair.'"

To keep morale high in wartime America, politicians and corporate America laid out a vision of postwar abundance. "WHAT THIS WAR IS ALL ABOUT," explained a Royal typewriter ad, "is the right to 'once more walk into any store in the land and buy anything you want.'" Revere Copper and Brass published an advertisement that read "After total war can come total living," and pictured consumers pining over "a futuristic landscape of homes and cars." More than a way to keep morale high, it was, in fact, a concerted strategy: America was to buy its way out of the dislocation that would follow in the postwar economic conversion. The strategy would keep industry producing, and keep laborers and returning soldiers employed. Consumer purchasing was the new form of patriotism. It was no accident that Scrooge McDuck, the miserly Walt Disney character, emerged in 1947.

America had fought, labored, saved and mobilized almost entirely to defeat the Axis powers and to make the world safe for democracy. The time was ripe for a peace dividend. Attention and resources were to be redirected to Americans; just reward for their sacrifice. Americans were not averse to providing wartime assistance or postwar humanitarian aid: the nation had done so with Lend-Lease, UNRRA and loans to Britain and France in the spring and summer of 1946. With each provision, though, the appetite for foreign aid and expenditure waned. In the wake of the latest rounds of British and French loans, there was an intense national fatigue with foreign aid.

The prospects for additional foreign aid dimmed further in November 1946. The November midterm elections dealt the Truman administration a stinging defeat. Republicans gained 56 seats in the House and 13 in the Senate to take control of both houses of Congress for the first time since the 1920s. New members of the 80th Congress included Representative Richard Nixon of California and Senator Joseph McCarthy of Wisconsin. The Republican agenda included slashing taxes, cutting the federal budget and slicing defense expenditures and foreign commitments at large. The frenzy to cut back reached such heights that Henry Cabot Lodge, another newly elected senator, likened it to "a man wielding a meat ax in a dark room." Fiscal belt-tightening to reward a war-weary people was the order of the day. The election results provided a ringing mandate for the Republican Congress to advance its agenda. The election left Truman reeling, his approval rating in the low 30s. He began making overtures to Dwight Eisenhower, intimating that he would run as his vice president if Ike would run for president as a Democrat.

The administration was well aware that Congress controlled the nation's purse strings and that if any of its initiatives were to see the light of day, they would require strong bipartisan support. The hope for achieving that support rested squarely on the shoulders of a veteran senator from Michigan, a former newspaper editor named Arthur Hendrick Vandenberg.

Vandenberg, or Van as he was known, was born on March 22, 1884, in Grand Rapids, Michigan. Born to a family of means, as a young boy Vandenberg watched his family's fortune dissipate in the panic of 1893. To lend a hand, young Arthur took a series of menial jobs, including carting shoes, operating a flower stand, selling vegetables and ushering at a movie theater. In 1900, at sixteen, while working as a clerk at Sears Biscuit Company, he took leave at lunch to listen to vice presidential candidate Theodore Roosevelt. Two hours later Vandenberg returned to find himself out of a job, but with a newly acquired passion for politics. He could not continue his studies full-time, and so left the University of Michigan after his first year to become a cub reporter at the *Grand Rapids Herald*. Vandenberg had written favorably of a wealthy senatorial candidate named William Alden Smith. When Smith won, he bought the nearly bankrupt newspaper and appointed twenty-two-year-old Arthur Vandenberg its editor.

Vandenberg thrived in the hurly-burly of the news business. For years Van was a consistent supporter of Republican candidates, and when a Republican senator died in 1928, his term unexpired, Van was appointed by the governor to fill it. Immediately he gained a reputation for his "purple prose and clichés," his "boom-boom" oratorical style. A large, ruddy figure, Vandenberg wore glasses and often a bow tie. He managed to economize only a few, long strands of hair over an otherwise bare head. He affected the motions and demeanor of a parliamentary dignitary. Yet he was also hearty, vibrant and affable. A vigorous, but highly constructive critic of the New Deal, Van actually spearheaded legislation for Federal Deposit Insurance, one of the most important pieces of legislation during the New Deal era. He had grand literary pretensions: he published three books, including one about Alexander Hamilton, and wrote one hundred unpublished short stories and two published songs, one of which became a popular ballad, an ode to a movie vixen of the 1920s named Bebe Daniels, entitled, "Bebe, Bebe, Bebe—Be Mine."

By the late 1930s, Vandenberg had become a Republican leader in the Senate. In foreign affairs, he had cast off an earlier romance with Wilsonian internationalism in favor of isolationism, or as he called it, "insulationism." He was a lead sponsor for the Neutrality Laws of 1937, handcuffing Roosevelt's diplomatic latitude and keeping America disengaged from volatile international developments. On Sunday, December 7, 1941, Van was home working on his personal diary when at 4 P.M. the telephone rang. The Japanese had attacked Pearl Harbor. Vandenberg phoned the White House immediately to tell Roosevelt's secretary that the president would have the support of one of his staunchest adversaries.

On January 10, 1945, as America straddled the interregnum between war and the postwar world, Arthur Vandenberg rose in the Senate to deliver a speech. He had rewritten it a dozen times, all the while intently chomping on his cigar and clicking away at his personal typewriter. "In my own mind," he would later write, "my convictions regarding international cooperation and collective security for peace took firm form on the afternoon of the Pearl Harbor attack. That day ended isolationism for any realist." The Atlantic and Pacific were no longer impassable moats, Vandenberg explained in his speech. America would have to engage with the rest of the world, broadening the nation's range of commitments. The speech marked a clean break with the foreign policy outlook that he had not only espoused, but had come to embody. It was an intellectual about-face and a brave political act.

The reaction was extraordinary. The *Cleveland Plain Dealer* called it "a shot heard around the world." Vandenberg's longtime political opponent, Franklin Roosevelt, requested fifty copies of the speech the morning before he left for Yalta. Walter Lippmann and James Reston lauded Vandenberg.

Dean Acheson, who had a gift for condescension, called the speech the capstone in Vandenberg's "long day's journey into our times." For much of America, who had recognized the false promise of isolationism, it was cathartic, and Vandenberg's reversal seemed to absolve and welcome them, too, into the internationalist camp. If it is true that, as historian John Lewis Gaddis believes, the "critical date" marking isolationism's retreat in America "was not 1945 or 1947, but 1941," then it was so in large measure because that was the date that mattered most for Arthur Vandenberg.

When the 80th Congress won the Senate, Vandenberg assumed the chairmanship of the Senate Foreign Relations Committee. The senator's experience, legislative acuity and respect in the party made him the Republican voice on foreign policy. In the past, Vandenberg had spoken out against foreign aid. In the summer of 1943, he had opposed the UNRRA, an enterprise, he said, that "pledged our resources to whatever illimitable scheme for relief and rehabilitation all around the world our New Deal crystal-gazers might desire to pursue." In March 1947, Vandenberg greeted Truman's request for aid for Greece and Turkey with skepticism. In late May 1947, when James Reston published a detailed account of the Plan being formulated, Vandenberg was irate. After the article was published, Marshall went immediately to Vandenberg to offer his case for aid and to solicit the senator's views. Vandenberg left the meeting assured and supportive.

When Vandenberg heard Marshall's address at Harvard he described it, as had been said of his own speech in 1945, as a "shot heard round the world." Still, the Plan's realization would require navigation through turbulent and unfriendly congressional waters. In June 1947, Americans were still profoundly anxious about the economy. Instead of unemployment, inflation had become the number one concern. The Consumer Price Index had increased 8 percent in 1946, and 14 percent in 1947. During the lag in postwar industrial conversion, the supply of consumer and industrial goods could not keep up with the intense demand of a people who were prodded to purchase and had savings with which to do it. Everyone worried about inflation and its impact on the economy, and workers worried about the value of their wages as a wave of strikes—the most since 1919—presented politicians with one of the period's great challenges.

On June 13, 1947, in a speech on the Senate floor, Vandenberg supported the burgeoning Plan, but he was also insistent that "intelligent American self-interest immediately requires a sound, over-all inventory of our own resources to determine the latitudes within which we may consider these foreign needs. This comes first." Vandenberg was speaking not only for himself but for his Republican colleagues, who were greeting the inchoate Plan with a much greater degree of circumspection. If it was to have any hope of passing, Van's colleagues needed assurance that the American economy could withstand the Plan's demands against the backdrop of inflation and concern about the shortage of goods.

In a meeting with Truman, Marshall, Acheson and a few others at the White House on June 22, Vandenberg advanced the idea of forming several committees. The most important would be tasked with assessing the Plan's feasibility given the demands of the American economy, and offering recommendations for the Plan. It would be comprised of leading national figures from business, academia and public life. Truman, who had worked with Vandenberg in the Senate and got on well with him, embraced the idea immediately and gave Vandenberg full credit. Within an hour Acheson had compiled a list. Vandenberg insisted on adding Robert La Follette Jr., a well-respected former Republican senator. Truman accepted the addition and made the announcement to the press on the spot. Secretary of Commerce Averell Harriman was selected to chair the sixteen-person committee, dubbed thereafter the Harriman Committee.

Vandenberg was on board. Still, he wrote to the director of the American Association for the United Nations, "I have no illusions about this so-called 'Marshall Plan.' . . . I certainly do not take it for granted that American public opinion is ready for any such burdens as would be involved." Truman waited until more than two weeks after Marshall's address to publicly acknowledge it and put his support behind it. The press was only now beginning to grasp its significance. The bipartisan spirit upon which its congressional fate would depend was being forged, and Arthur Vandenberg was making that possible. But uncertainty framed the fledgling Marshall Plan through late June. Two questions loomed above all others: Would the Europeans be able to come together? And what would the Russians do?

A WEEK AFTER the Harvard address, Marshall discussed the speech for the first time at a press conference. He announced that Will Clayton would shortly be leaving for Europe to meet with European leaders, "not to propose a United States economic plan for Europe," Marshall said, "but to hear what the European nations have to propose about ways and means of combining to help themselves." Marshall said that there was not much for him to say. The initiative now lay with the Europeans. On that point he was clear and adamant.

It did not take long for Ernest Bevin to get going. A few days later he announced his intention to travel to Paris to discuss the Plan with Georges

Bidault. Bidault told U.S. Ambassador to France Jefferson Caffrey that he was put off at Bevin's overture, what he perceived as an "attempt to steal the show." Caffrey suspected that what really rankled Bidault was that Bevin had beaten him to the punch. Meanwhile, informed observers like the *New York Times's* Harold Callender could not help expressing skepticism at the scope of the challenge at hand: "Efforts at common action in any sphere in Europe in the recent past have not provided the best possible augury for . . . economic accord."

Bevin arrived in Paris on June 17 for two days of meetings with his French counterpart. On the two vital matters at hand, they reached expedient agreement. To meet Marshall's call for European cooperation, they agreed on the concept of forming steering committees for reconstruction. These committees would promote European cooperation and coordination in key areas such as coal, food, steel and transport. The foreign ministers also agreed that they should invite the Soviets to participate in the program. But delay was not to be permitted. Britain and France would "go ahead with full steam even if the Soviets refused to do so," Ambassador Caffrey cabled Marshall. For Bidault, who faced intense domestic political pressure from Communists, it was a brave position. He assured Bevin with a "firm verbal commitment."

Before departing for London on June 18, Bevin joined Bidault in inviting Soviet Foreign Minister Vyacheslav Molotov to three-way discussions a few days hence. Publicly, both said that after two days they could not reach a decision without consulting Molotov. Of course, that was subterfuge, and vital matters had been discussed and agreed upon. The Soviets were justifiably suspicious. Bevin and Bidault waited anxiously for a reply. Days passed, and the House of Commons wanted to know what Bevin thought the Soviets would do. "The Tsar Alexander still hasn't answered Castlereagh's questions," Bevin replied. On June 23, Molotov responded to the offer and said that the Soviet Union would indeed participate in three-way discussions, a decision the Politburo had reached two days prior. Molotov suggested Paris for a location. It was a shrewd maneuver. Soviet presence in the city would arouse French Communist interest and, if a split occurred, place pressure on Bidault.

Meanwhile, the Soviet press, which was essentially a mouthpiece for Stalin, had been noncommittal. Its rhetoric, though, was antagonistic. On June 11, *Pravda Ukraine* dubbed Marshall's offer the "Marshall Doctrine" and said that it was "evidence of even wider plans" of America's "campaign against forces of world democracy and progress." It sought "quick formation of notorious western bloc under unconditional and absolute leadership of American imperialism." A week later, on June 17, *Pravda* labeled it a "plan for political pressures with dollars and a program for interference in the internal affairs of other states." The Soviet line of attack could be discerned before Molotov set one foot in Paris. But such rhetorical bluster was not unexpected.

Following developments from Moscow, U.S. Ambassador Walter Bedell Smith cabled Washington that he was "sure that this Soviet participation will be for destructive rather than constructive purposes." Bevin and Bidault, each in his own measure, shared Bedell Smith's skepticism. The great power pessimism stood in stark contrast to reaction among some of Europe's smaller powers. Listening to the ten o'clock news on a Norwegian destroyer with Foreign Minister Halvard Lange, Czechoslovak Foreign Minister Jan Masaryk heard the news that Molotov had accepted Bevin and Bidault's invitation. "Never in my life have I seen a man so happy as Masaryk," said Lange.

Just as the Soviets decided they would go to Paris, the Soviet Foreign Ministry sent out cables to Czechoslovakia, Poland and Hungary instructing Soviet ambassadors to encourage governments in those countries to prepare to participate in the Plan. The Czechoslovaks, like the Poles, were in desperate need of aid, and they did not wish to slide behind the Soviet side of the iron curtain, locked into an Eastern orbit without any measure of independence. For Masaryk in particular, as for much of Eastern Europe, Soviet acceptance signified opportunity and hope, and they would be watching developments in Paris closely.

Bevin was highly suspicious of Soviet intentions, and set on moving forward regardless. Still, he wondered: "Perhaps they will play after all," he kept repeating after hearing of Molotov's acceptance. Back in Washington, a State Department spokesman said, "Our position in this has been repeatedly stated . . . The whole department is waiting for Europe to take the initiative. We don't want to react every five minutes. There is indication that they are getting together. Now let's let them get together and not confuse them."

That was the public line. Behind the scenes, Bevin had sensitive matters to discuss, which he felt needed clarification before arriving in Paris. To address Bevin's queries, Will Clayton flew from Geneva to London for a three-day series of meetings. It was the first direct contact between the United States and Europe on the incipient Marshall Plan. "The long road toward economic cooperation," the *New York Times* declared on June 24, "began this morning, when William L. Clayton . . . went to 10 Downing Street."

In that first meeting, British officials told Clayton that the U.S. loan, which was supposed to last several more years, would be exhausted in months at the current rate. The United Kingdom needed some interim aid to tide it over. In addition, Bevin sought a "special" privileged economic partnership with the United States. Britain's economy was more advanced, its production greater, its reach and responsibilities wider than the rest of Europe's.

Clayton was firm. There could be no more piecemeal aid, he said: "The problem must be dealt with as a whole." Nor could there be a privileged partnership. The offer was to Europe. Congress would not provide interim aid or privilege for some countries over others. Bevin hoped that "a special relationship" would, as he put it, salvage "what little dignity we have left." Pride was at stake. That evening at the Treasury Chambers, the conversation grew tense and some British officials went so far as to suggest that without interim relief or a special partnership, U.S. aid would do little good. It was a heavy-handed tactic. Great Britain needed aid desperately to plug the rapid drain in its gold and dollar reserves. Clayton didn't bite, and the talks got back on track.

The next day, June 25, Bevin asked Clayton to elaborate on what the United States expected of Britain and the process going forward. Again Clayton stressed the domestic political pressures back in the United States. It would not be easy to "sell" the Plan back at home. To that end, the U.S. needed the Europeans to explain why they had not made more progress with aid already received to date. In addition, Europe would have to outline what it would do to help itself and how long it would take. Clayton was keenly aware of the importance of European export markets for the U.S. economy, he said, but many of his countrymen were not. Congress wanted to know when Europe would be back on its feet, and wanted to see European integration as evidence that Europe was willing to enact structural economic reform to serve its needs. Bevin gently pushed back on the notion of European integration. Britain had responsibilities to the Commonwealth, with which integration might interfere. It was the first manifestation of one of the defining tensions that would mark the Marshall Plan and the shape of Europe's postwar economy.

On June 26, the final day of discussions, the dialogue turned toward the vital matter of the Soviet Union and its role in the new recovery scheme. Bevin told Clayton that one of the attributes of the Marshall Plan was that "it is the quickest way to break down the iron curtain" and draw out the Soviet's Eastern European satellites, who would be lured by the promise of large-scale aid. Clayton concurred, demonstrating that loosening the Soviets' grip on Eastern Europe was an objective, albeit a secondary one, of the Marshall Plan. He added that since Russia was not short of food, fuel or fiber, it would be expected to serve as a donor, not a recipient, in the short-term phase of the program. This was clearly not aimed at facilitating Russia's participation.

Anticipating Paris, Bevin said that the Russians would dictate terms, would demand special treatment and would attempt to "sweep all other applicants aside." If they behaved this way, Bevin asked Clayton what would be the American attitude? Clayton said he would not give a categorical answer, but in his opinion it would take a radical change in Soviet policy regarding European recovery for the American people to support any aid to Russia. If Molotov was as intransigent as he expected, Bevin asked Clayton point-blank, would the United States be supportive if the British and French moved forward without them? The realization of a program for European recovery hung, in no small measure, on the answer to the question. Clayton answered: Yes.

THE CLIMATE OUTSIDE the Quai d'Orsày on June 27 was stifling. Paris was in the midst of a heat wave. In fact, Europe's most brutal winter in memory had given way to one of its hottest and driest summers. The heat dried up fields all over the region, ruining crops and exacerbating Western Europe's balance-of-payments crisis. Molotov had arrived a day earlier, while Bevin was still meeting with Clayton in London. Upon meeting Bidault, Molotov immediately peppered him about Bevin and Bidault's earlier meeting in Paris. Molotov wanted to know what they had discussed behind his back. Bidault disingenuously told him that nothing had been decided.

By the time Molotov arrived in Paris, the Soviet line for the conference had already been worked out. It was largely forged from two separate analyses, both submitted only days before Molotov left for Paris. The first was prepared by Soviet Ambassador to the United States Nikolai Novikov, and sent to Molotov on June 24. Offering his views on the Marshall Plan, Novikov wrote: "In the final analysis, it is directed toward the establishment of a Western European bloc . . . aimed at economic and political subjugation of European countries to American capital and to the establishment of anti-Soviet groupings." Novikov concluded that Soviet participation offered the best tactical means for the Soviet Union to frustrate, and hopefully sabotage, American aims. It was exactly what Marshall, Kennan and their Western European counterparts dreaded.

Then, two days later, Yevgeny Varga, the Soviet's leading economist, sent his own report to Molotov. Varga averred that the Marshall Plan was a self-interested endeavor necessary for the United States to forestall "the imminent economic crisis" Soviet ideology had been predicting. To manage its overproduction, Varga said, the United States needed to give away part of that output to its supplicant European debtors. The plan's ambition was to establish a "bloc of bourgeois countries under U.S. domination." Since U.S. economic survival depended upon the Marshall Plan, the Soviet Union ought to participate and seek to "squeeze the maximum political advantages from this."

The takeaway from Varga's analysis was that the U.S. economy was fundamentally weak and that the Marshall Plan was an imperialist attempt to bring the even weaker Western European countries under U.S. control. Ideology was clouding the Soviets' ability to objectively assess U.S. motivation and the political and economic conditions at work. The memo was sent to Stalin and other key members of the Politburo. Echoing Stalinist ideology, Novikov's and Varga's analyses reenforced each other.

Informed by these important analyses, Molotov would attempt to frame the plan as a country-by-country, not collective, initiative. Under no circumstances would the Soviets support any grouping that could serve as an anti-Soviet coalition. Under no circumstances would the Soviets allow the Americans to woo the Eastern European countries from their orbit. And under no circumstances whatsoever would the Soviets support German rehabilitation or relinquish Soviet claims for reparations and joint control of the Ruhr/Rhine industrial complex. Molotov came to Paris highly suspicious and prepared to frustrate U.S. goals.

It was not clear to anyone how it would all play out. Bevin arrived the most assured, and despite the crippling heat and his poor health, he was in good spirits. Bidault was much more nervous. Molotov had arrived with an entourage of eighty-nine Soviet officials and experts. At best, this meant that the Soviets were serious about their participation. But many suspected that these officials had connections to the French Communist Party, and had come to stir up trouble if things did not go the Soviets' way. Bidault had pledged to Bevin and U.S. Ambassador Caffrey that he would proceed with or without the Soviets. If the latter scenario came to pass, it would mean a decisive break with the Soviet Union, with all the domestic political and national security implications that could follow. Bevin would be watching Bidault's line keenly to see if the Frenchman would come through. Bidault was taking his own "hell of a gamble."

The situation in France and Bidault's show of faith added a poignancy when he told Caffrey privately, "I devoutly hope that in case we on our side accomplish something your Congress will do its part. If they failed us it would be sheer disaster here." Even as Britain and France squared off with the Soviets in Paris, Capitol Hill was never far from anyone's mind.

As the meeting opened at 4 P.M., Molotov was unusually agreeable in tone and temperament. He began with a series of questions. What additional information had the British and French received from the United States about Marshall's Harvard speech? None, they said, disingenuously. What agreements had the French and British come to at their earlier meeting in Paris? None, they said, only that they should meet with him at a later date, again disingenuously. Two hours into the meeting, Molotov said that he wished to make a proposal. They should ask the U.S. government the exact sum it was prepared to advance for European recovery, and then for a firm determination on whether Congress would vote for such a program. Bevin pounced. First, he said, the executive branch cannot speak for the legislative; second, Marshall's speech did not discuss amounts, it expressly invited the Europeans to come together and form their own proposal; and, finally, it is not the place of debtors to lay down conditions to their potential creditors.

The three foreign ministers departed in ostensible good cheer at 8 P.M. and Bevin and Bidault wondered if the Soviets might join after all. On Saturday, June 28, disagreement continued along the same lines. That evening a wild storm erupted. Jarring claps of thunder and torrential rains swept England and France. In London, wind squalls were as strong as ninety miles per hour. Debate in the House of Commons was interrupted as rain poured through the windows and onto the chamber's benches. In Paris, the storm brought reprieve from the stifling heat, but it rang an ominous note as the meetings reconvened on the afternoon of June 30. Bevin was determined to cut through Soviet temporizing. He reduced the French proposal to its most elemental form, a one-page document which the Soviets could either support or reject, and sent it to Molotov in the morning.

As the conference opened at 4 P.M. Molotov continued his line. A common European plan would infringe upon the sovereignty of other European countries. Each country should submit its own list and receive the desired amount of aid from the United States. To Bevin and Bidault's arguments, Molotov did not say "Nyet," but "No K," which he thought was the antonym for "OK." Bidault described Molotov as *"flagrant et obstiné."* Bidault took the floor to respond to Molotov and made a strong statement in support of Bevin. At that moment, Molotov was handed a telegram that Bevin felt was certainly from Moscow (i.e., Stalin). Later Bevin would recall a swelling of a bump on Molotov's forehead, a telltale sign that Molotov was agitated.

We now know that on June 29–30, Soviet intelligence agents with sources in the British Foreign Ministry had reported back to Moscow on the

Clayton-Bevin discussions a few days prior. The telegram handed to Molotov was most probably the same one sent that day reporting that Clayton and Bevin were colluding to bring Germany into the Plan, and to keep the Soviet Union out of it. Moscow wanted Molotov to hold the line, a line, it had become clear to everyone, that would lead to stasis at best, rupture at worst.

As Molotov finished a regurgitation of his same argument, Bevin looked at him, smiled and said that in effect what he was asking for was a blank check from the United States. "If I were to go to Moscow with a blank check and ask you to sign it I wonder how far I would get with your end." Again, Bidault backed Bevin. Hope and cordiality had now disappeared. The statesmen posed their way through another dinner of empty toasts at the Quai d'Orsay that evening. And at 10 P.M., Bevin paid a call to U.S. Ambassador Jefferson Caffrey. "For all intents and purposes," he said, the conference had broken down that day. He was pleased that "all the cards have been laid out on the table," and that Moscow's obstruction had been illumined for all to see. Bidault had won Bevin's great esteem. Despite political and financial crisis, Bidault stood with Bevin "wholeheartedly and with great courage." The French needed help to weather their crises. "If they stand with us I hope you will not abandon them," Bevin said to Caffrey. "Give them something to hope for."

To provide as much internal political credibility as possible and to tar the Soviets with obstructionism and ill will, the French the next morning submitted another proposal with minor modifications. Molotov said he would have to study it. If the French were to break with the Soviets, Molotov was not about to make it easy for Bidault. A few days earlier, just as the conference was opening, the United States had announced officially that Germany would be eligible to receive Marshall aid. Molotov pointedly asked the French foreign minister if he was also willing to support U.S. plans for German reconstruction; if he was prepared to forfeit French claims for reparations; if he would support an increase in the German level of industry. It was a decisive moment for Bidault. German policy would be worked out, he said. Economic relief and recovery could not wait. Wrote historian William Hitchcock of that moment: "The days of a tacit Franco-Soviet alliance on German policy were over."

As positions crystallized in Paris, the Marshall Plan had begun to capture the continent's imagination. Returning from an extended tour in Europe, Winthrop W. Aldrich, chairman of Chase National Bank, said that the Marshall speech had given Europe "new hope which a few weeks ago did not exist . . . the effect of the speech in Europe was electrifying." In Italy, Pope

Pius had come out in favor of the Marshall Plan. Italian Communists rioted in Venice and denounced pro-American Prime Minister Alcide De Gasperi, who embraced the Plan. In Germany, Lucius Clay had personally invited Robert Moses, New York City's building coordinator, to come to western Germany to offer plans for rebuilding; Clay was hoping that the Marshall Plan would provide funds to that end. Europe was watching events in Paris closely.

Bevin and Bidault had now formed a firm axis. The way the Soviets proposed it, Bidault said, the steering committees to be set up would serve merely as "a postal service for passing on the requests of European countries for U.S. aid." Gloom descended upon the proceedings. Herbert Matthews wrote that they had become "farce." That much was clear, even to Molotov. Unbeknownst to Bevin or Bidault, on the evening of July 1 the Soviet foreign minister sent a cable to Stalin: "In view of the fact that our position is fundamentally different from the Anglo-French position, we are not counting on the possibility of any joint decisions on the substance of the issue in question." But Molotov was still in Paris, still part of the process, still obstructing its progress. Molotov had asked for more time to consider the latest French proposal. Bevin agreed for the sake of the French non-Communist government's political standing. But the Soviets needed to come back the following day with a definitive answer.

Stalin's vital security need, above all, was to maintain control over his eastern orbit. The Eastern European states held vital resources which the Soviet Union needed to fuel its economy. More essentially, they served as a buffer against German, or even American, attack. The United States had invited Eastern Europe to participate in the Marshall Plan. Kennan, Clayton and Bevin, in particular, hoped that the promise of aid and economic integration with the West might lure the Soviet satellites from Stalin's grip. At the time, the United States did not fully appreciate the fragility of political conditions in Czechoslovakia, Poland and Hungary or the tensions then brewing between Stalin and the charismatic Communist leader in Yugoslovia, Marshal Tito. Stalin's grip was tenuous, and as Varga put it, "the Marshall Plan was a dagger pointed at Moscow." Stalin would not permit Soviet participation in the Marshall Plan.

The Soviet position had been worked out in advance of the fifth and final meeting on the afternoon of July 2. As the meeting opened, Molotov's tone had become vituperative. The French proposal was unacceptable. An overall plan would limit the sovereign integrity of smaller European powers and signify American control over the region. The plan disregarded prior agreements over Germany. If Great Britain and France proceeded, it would result not in the reconstruction of Europe but its division. If the effort persisted, Molotov said ominously, "it will have grave consequences."

Bidault rebuked Molotov's accusations, most of which were made for public consumption and propaganda purposes. Bevin joined in, saying that apparently Molotov kept on repeating false accusations in the hope that if he kept doing so they would somehow become true. He was sorry that Molotov would make such a threat. However, Bevin said, "Great Britain on other occasions had been threatened with grave consequences," and had not wavered. Bevin told Molotov pointedly and directly that he and Bidault intended to cooperate with those states "as were willing in the restoration of war-shattered Europe." Later that evening, Bevin called Prime Minister Clement Attlee with a blow-by-blow account of the meeting. "Clem," Bevin said, " 'e walked out, uttering threats." The conference had ended.

As the foreign ministers and their delegations left the French Foreign Ministry building that day, they walked out into a new and ominous world. Harold Callender remarked in the *New York Times* that there was "a finality about this split . . . that had not characterized such interchanges in any of the previous Foreign Ministers' conferences." Bevin had whispered to an aide in the course of that fateful meeting, "This really is the birth of the Western bloc."

BACK IN WASHINGTON, George Marshall had been following every detail of the proceedings. During the conference, Marshall had not said a word about the developments in France, nor imposed any conditions or stipulations. It was to be Europe's plan. Bevin and Bidault had performed brilliantly. Now it was time for Marshall to assure his allies with the fortification of his word: "We realize the gravity of the problem with which you have been confronted and the difficulty of the decisions which you have been forced to take." The Soviet attitude had now been clarified once and for all, and Soviet obstructionism from within would no longer constitute a delay to recovery. "We here are prepared to do all in our power to support" European recovery, Marshall pledged.

At a press conference that day, a few minutes after the conference broke up, Marshall stated that he had just read the press reports. He would make no comment on the breakup of the conference, though. The reporters badgered him. "What would America do?" "What were the details of the Plan?" He did not flag. Journalists took his silence to mean that it was up to Great Britain and France and other countries in Western Europe to proceed. Their read was correct.

In the conference rooms and back offices at State, in the parlors of embassies around the world and at swank dinner parties in Georgetown, Western statesmen and journalists everywhere were mystified. By continuing to participate, Molotov could have achieved any number of objectives. By truly cooperating with the West, he could have diluted the aid available for Western Europe by adding Russia and Eastern Europe into the mix. Russian participation could have ruined the Plan's prospects outright in an anti-Soviet Congress. He could have delayed the plan by agreeing and then in turn delaying and temporizing; it was a familiar tactic with Molotov.

But concluding that he could not chance Eastern Europe's participation, and the loosening of his grip in the region, Stalin instructed Molotov to walk out. As Averell Harriman said, "Uncle Joe helped us again." Months later, Bidault expressed his bafflement in a conversation with James Byrnes: "If he had reaped his part of the profits, or if the enterprise had failed, [Stalin] could still have gained something by the fact that nobody would have gotten anything. By sticking with us, he could not lose, and he chose the only means of losing for certain."

However, Stalin's tactics were not as foolish as his Western contemporaries thought. British sources had informed Soviet intelligence that the U.S. and U.K. wanted to move ahead with their own plans for Germany and that they hoped to woo East European states with the carrot of aid. If Stalin's goal was to maintain a firm command over Eastern Europe, with the economic and political system he desired, then his course made some sense. Soviet participation, even if disingenuous, may have exposed Eastern Europe to the thrall of the West's economy; it may have loosened what was then still a tenuous grip. Stalin's crystal ball predicted that depression would hit in the United States and undo America's ability to aid Europe. Inevitable conflict among the capitalist imperialists would frustrate cooperation. The Marshall Plan was an undertaking that sought to defy the very laws of history, as Stalin saw them.

Stalin had misread history, though, he had misread the United States, and he had ignored one critical variable in the equation: himself. Stalin's rigid ideology conflated capitalism with imperialism. It was a critical error. In 1946, Varga explained to Soviet leaders that the Western capitalist powers had reformed their brand of capitalism. Socialism in Western Europe and the New Deal and Keynesian principles in the United States had all changed the complexion of capitalism and what it could offer to a broader cross-section of society. Stalin did not heed Varga's insight. Stalin also failed to see that the United States did not seek expansion like the empires of the past. It was not destined to clash with other imperial powers over resources and territory. In fact, its past suggested a stronger tendency toward retreat (outside of its own continent), rather than expansion. If it was an empire, the United States was "an empire by invitation," not by imposition.

Determined not to be bullied by American "atomic diplomacy" and set on expanding his international influence (what he felt was the rightful reward for Soviet wartime sacrifices), Stalin adopted an intransigent negotiating position. He pursued territorial expansion opportunistically and was content to let Western Europe slide into further distress and disarray. Unchecked, Stalin would have reaped tremendous strategic gain. The United States could not abide the combination of Western Europe's slide and Soviet temporizing any further.

Stalin had lost the near-term accommodation that he craved. Instead, he had now brought the United States and other capitalist powers together in a grand enterprise to save capitalism and liberal democracy and to prevent European domination by a single totalitarian power. The U.S. was not doomed to economic collapse; it was not doomed to fight other capitalist powers in World War III. These things would not happen. Stalin, in fact, was a catalytic force to ensure that they would not. He drove the United States to Europe's aid; he drove the United States into what was becoming a nascent economic and political bloc. Stalin was viewing it all through the distorting lens of historical determinism, and he wasn't seeing straight.

Molotov departed Paris at 4 A.M. on July 4. At 10 A.M., Bevin and Bidault got together for a two-hour meeting at the Quai d'Orsay prior to Bevin's departure back to London. The two statesmen compiled a list of European nations to be invited to a follow-up conference to devise and present a collective request for U.S. aid. As they met, Molotov's plane was still in the air, passing over Eastern Europe—and the iron curtain that had fallen behind him.

Chapter Five

"FRIENDLY AID" IN PARIS

O N JULY 4, 1947, before Bevin's departure from Paris, he and Bidault issued a joint communiqué inviting twenty-two European nations to participate in a plan for European recovery. The initiative now belonged to Great Britain and France, and both of those proud countries evinced a new spirit of hope and confidence.

In France, Premier Paul Ramadier called for a vote of confidence. Ramadier embraced the Marshall Plan as "the best hope for European reconstruction" and won a decisive victory. Despite pressure from the French Communist Party, Bidault's willingness to break with the Soviets over the Marshall Plan had paid off. In England, Ernest Bevin praised "that dear little man" whose courage had won his British counterpart's esteem and affection. Bevin was worried about France, and meeting with U.S. Ambassador to the United Kingdom Lewis Douglas, he made the case for interim aid: "If no action" was to be taken "by the United States until late fall, or winter," Bevin told Douglas, "France, and with her most of Europe, would be lost."

More than France, though, Bevin said, he was worried about the United States: Would the Marshall Plan pass Congress? Having mobilized their countries and having assumed grave risks, would aid arrive in time to arrest collapse in England and indigenous Communist designs on political control in France? But Bevin recognized that the initiative was now Europe's. He said, "I say to you Mr. Marshall: 'We take you and the American nation at your word. We do not question it. I accept your challenge. I will get on with the job.'"

To reward Bidault for his bravery, Bevin, according to his own account, suggested Paris as the host city for the Conference of European Nations. The invitation included a draft of the last French proposal for moving forward with recovery, the one that Molotov had rejected. It called for a steering committee to oversee six specialized subcommittees that would each tackle a dimension of Europe's economy. Through pooling, some planning, and reducing restrictions to trade and cooperation, Europe would first help itself, then seek the balance of resources needed from the United States. The work was to be completed by September 1, and then submitted to the United States.

Bidault made sure to send a letter to the Soviet ambassador in Paris with a copy of the invitation, and wrote that participation was still very much open to the Soviet Union were its position to change. Bidault was still waging a propaganda battle on the domestic front, and the letter was mostly for French public consumption. The invitations sent to the Soviet Union's Eastern European satellites were very real, though. The continent's political constellation was in a brief and seminal period of flux. The U.S. saw a real possibility of wooing Eastern Europe from the grip of Soviet control with the promise of aid. If the gambit worked, the Marshall Plan could drag the iron curtain east and all the way back to Russia's western border. The conference was called to open on July 12.

ON JULY 5, MOSCOW CABLED ITS AMBASSADORS in Eastern Europe that the Soviet Union had pulled out of the Marshall Plan, but it did not want its Eastern European satellites to do so. On the contrary, Molotov wanted the satellites to accept the invitation. Once there, their objective was to sabotage the Plan. The cable read: "We think it would be better not to refuse participation in this conference but to send delegations to it, in order to show at the conference itself the unacceptability of the Anglo-French plan, not to allow the unanimous adoption of this plan." The satellites were then to "withdraw from the meeting, taking with them as many delegates from other countries as possible."

Most of the Soviet satellites welcomed the directive. The following two days marked a time of unease and equivocation for Stalin and the Kremlin. On July 6, Molotov cabled ambassadors in Warsaw and Belgrade assuring them that attendance in Paris on July 12 was advisable. But only hours later, a subsequent telegram directed Soviet ambassadors in Eastern Europe to desist from encouraging governments in those countries to attend. There was pressure both from the Soviet bloc (namely, Marshal Tito in Yugoslavia) to take a harder, more radical and subversive line with the West, as well as pressure from hard-liners in the Kremlin. The satellites, particularly Czechoslovakia and Poland, had welcomed the Soviet directive to participate—perhaps too eagerly. It was pointed out to Molotov that the Czech ambassador who would represent the country had a western orientation. The Marshall Plan had already outflanked Soviet hopes to reorient parts of the West eastward. The Plan's essays in Eastern Europe—Stalin's prized sphere of influence—were too much for the Soviet ruler to countenance.

On July 7, the same day that Eastern European countries dispatched a series of notes to England and France accepting the invitation to attend at Paris, the Soviets sent another set of cables to its Eastern European satellites to inform their leaders that the Soviet Union had changed its position. Two new circumstances had emerged, the cables read. First, Great Britain and France did not intend to make any changes to ensure the sovereignty and economic independence of the smaller eastern powers. Second, European recovery was in fact a pretext for the formation of an anti-Soviet western bloc. The July 5 cable was thereby rescinded. The Soviet Union now suggested that countries not attend. Evincing the Soviet conception of sovereignty, the cable did allow that "each side may present its own reasons for its refusal."

Sensing the intensity of the Soviet Union's resolution, most Eastern European countries pulled out of the conference immediately. One did not. For both the United States and the Soviet Union, Czechoslovakia's reply was laced with geostrategic and symbolic importance. President Woodrow Wilson had helped create the state after World War I and ensured that its historical roots were grounded in a democratic tradition. A visitor might pass through Woodrow Wilson Station in Prague or find herself on Hoover Street. The creation of Czechoslovakia was a source of pride for America. But it was also the locus of one of the West's most ignominious failures. In 1938, at Munich, the West had surrendered Czechoslovakia to Hitler and the Nazis. The lesson for Czechoslovakia was that it could not depend on the West. When General George Patton desisted from the march toward the Czech capital in deference to the Soviet army, the Soviets became the Czechs' main liberators. In Prague, billboards of Stalin could be seen alongside those of its own president. The Soviet Union, Czech leaders believed, was their country's most reliable safeguard against another German invasion. A tacit agreement was struck that Czechoslovakia would support the Soviet Union in foreign affairs in return for its protection and independence in domestic matters.

From its inception, geography was unkind to Czechoslovakia. It was positioned at the "physical and strategic crossroads of Europe." German Chancellor Otto von Bismarck had said that whoever controlled Bohemia (the heart of the Czech homeland) controlled Europe. As tensions escalated between the United States and the Soviet Union in 1945 and 1946, Czechoslovakia's leaders thought of their country as a "bridge between East and West." "A bridge," though, cynics rejoined, "is something that men and horses walk over." By July 1947, Czechoslovakia had preferential trading agreements with the Soviet Union, it was surrounded (though not occupied) by the Red Army, and in its last election in May 1946, the Communists won 38 percent of the popular vote and by the following year had control of most of the major ministries.

Since the war, Czechoslovakia had received more than $200 million in American-sponsored aid. Like most of Western Europe, it appeared on the road to recovery through 1946. The winter and the spring were cruel to the republic, though. By summer, Czechoslovakia was in terrible need of agricultural goods and financial assistance. To Foreign Minister Jan Masaryk and other non-Communists, the offer to participate in the Marshall Plan was a godsend. On July 1, Masaryk informed representatives of the Soviet Union, Great Britain and France: "The Czech government has authorized me to let you know that Czechoslovakia with one voice welcomes the opportunity that the offer outlines." It promised much-needed economic and financial relief. It would also enhance economic and political ties with the West. For Stalin, this was precisely the problem.

So it was particularly unnerving to the Soviet dictator when the Czechs equivocated after the July 7 cable. Most of the Czech ministers still wanted to move forward, and the Cabinet waged an intense internal debate. Stalin wanted to make the decision a little easier for them. He summoned a key delegation including Masaryk, Czech Communist Premier Klement Gottwald and other senior officials to Moscow. Arriving at the Kremlin in the evening, the delegation sat waiting anxiously for hours for their meeting with Stalin. Masaryk and some of the others did not then know that while they were waiting, Gottwald was meeting with Stalin privately. Gottwald would later say that he had never seen Stalin so angry. When he emerged, he said, "Everything is alright. I've just come to an agreement with Stalin. We're to see him this evening."

At midnight the delegation entered Stalin's office. Stalin conceded that he had changed his position on their participation. He said that aid would come with conditions that would "endanger [Czech] political and economic sovereignty," once again evincing his own curious notion of sovereignty. Then Stalin proceeded to frame the decision as he saw it. Prague's decision to go forward was "a question of friendship." Czech participation would constitute "a break in the front" of the Slav states, and "it would show that you want to cooperate in an action aimed at isolating the Soviet Union." For effect, Stalin had international newspapers placed on the table. He pointed at the headlines: "Prague Losing Her Ties to Moscow" and "Breach in the Eastern Bloc." Masaryk tried to explain to Stalin that Czechoslovakia was trade-dependent on the West for 60 to 80 percent of its raw materials. Stalin was not moved: "We know you are friends . . . but you would demonstrate by your participation in Paris that you let yourselves be used as a tool against the USSR. Neither the Soviet Union nor its government would tolerate it."

Defeated, Masaryk then feebly requested that, to save face, Czechoslovakia be allowed to attend at Paris with the agreement that its delegates would depart after the first day. The request was denied. Masaryk then asked for large-scale aid from the Soviet Union. Stalin pledged wheat shipments and other aid provisions. Soon the notion evolved into a region-wide Soviet-led aid effort that was unimaginatively dubbed the Molotov Plan. It offered Russia's Eastern European neighbors a fraction of the aid offered in the Marshall Plan, and many of the commitments were never met. For Masaryk and other non-Communists, the relative pittance was scant consolation. The meeting adjourned at 12:30 P.M.

Poland was in a similar position. On July 10, the Polish foreign minister told the U.S. ambassador in Warsaw that Poland had to recant its prior acceptance. U.S. Ambassador Stanton Griffis recalled that the foreign minister appeared "extremely apologetic and at least apparently regretful." A day earlier the Rumanian prime minister had declined, jocularly likening the Marshall Plan to a Trojan horse that would subject Rumania to undue U.S. influence. Hungary announced on July 10 it would not attend at Paris.

On the eve of the Paris Conference, all eyes were on Czechoslovakia. In Prague, the Cabinet met for almost an entire day. At the end of the day, William Siroky, deputy head of the government, read out a statement: the government had unanimously cancelled its decision to attend the Paris Conference on the Marshall Plan. "I went to Moscow as the foreign minister of an independent sovereign state," Masaryk would say. "I returned as a lackey of the Soviet Government." The Minister of Food, a Social Democrat, said the reversal had "smashed the illusion of Czechoslovak independence to smithereens."

Hopes in the United States were high that Eastern Europe would participate and that the iron curtain across Europe would be lifted, or at least dragged farther east. After Czechoslovakia's about-face, Marshall met with the Senate Foreign Relations Committee in a closed two-hour session. Europe was now divided into two distinct blocs, organized around two poles of power. The mood in the session was somber. From Moscow, Ambassador Bedell Smith cabled Marshall that the reversal "on Soviet orders, is nothing less than a declaration of war by the Soviet Union on the immediate control of Europe." The Paris Conference would be all-important now. Bedell Smith went on: "The lines are drawn. Our response is awaited. I do not need to point out to the Department the repercussions of a failure to meet the Soviet challenge."

ON SATURDAY, JULY 12, AT 11 A.M. the Paris Conference was called to order. Of the twenty-two countries that had been invited to attend, eight had declined and fourteen had accepted: Austria, Belgium, Denmark, Greece, Iceland, Ireland, Italy, Luxembourg, the Netherlands, Norway, Portugal, Sweden, Switzerland and Turkey. The only room large enough to accommodate all sixteen delegations (the fourteen plus Great Britain and France) was a spacious, ornate dining hall in the Quai d'Orsay. The hall's table was so long that delegates seated at one end of the table could not quite hear delegates seated at the opposite end.

The conference got off to an auspicious start. Bevin and Bidault opened with impassioned speeches urging the conferees to move forward quickly and in concerted fashion. Agreement was "unanimous," and the British and French delegations were struck by the seamless order at the conference. The critical factor, it was felt, was Molotov's absence. Even the translations—which no longer had to be done in Russian, and only in English and French—moved faster. Bevin was appointed the chairman of the conference by unanimous consent. The conferees agreed to set up a steering committee (on which each country was represented) and a series of technical committees to study Europe's needs and possibilities for intra-European cooperation. And a working committee was appointed to produce a report on the rules and organization for the conference. Bevin had called for a "business-like" approach, and he got it. "It is the quickest conference I have ever presided over," he said, refreshed and pleased.

For another three days, the foreign ministers remained in Paris setting up the guidelines and machinery for the conference to proceed. With the Soviets and Americans absent, the atmosphere at times seemed to revert to an esprit of Old World diplomacy. The participants proceeded with civility and purpose. Meetings that erstwhile had taken entire days were concluded with agreement in an hour or two. On July 14—Bastille Day in France—the feisty British foreign secretary took a recess from his work to enjoy the traditional parade as it passed along the Champs-Elysées. That evening he enjoyed a festive evening tour of Paris, and when he was spotted at a café in Montmartre late that night he was called upon to rise and give a speech. He did so, and received a rousing ovation, before returning to the embassy at 2 A.M. Before departing from Paris on July 15, Bevin sent a dispatch to his embassy in Washington that Paris had passed with "great smoothness and rapidity and there is every evidence of good-will and a desire to cooperate."

The harmonious beginning masked the monumental challenges that lay ahead. The notion of sixteen states coming together in peacetime to forge a common economic program was without precedent in European history. The assemblage comprised large powers and small powers; it consisted of Allied powers and Axis powers; some countries had a gaping Dollar Gap, while others did not; some were approaching bankruptcy and economic collapse, others were doing much better; some wanted to keep Germany prostrate, while others depended on German recovery for their own recoveries; some had imperial interests, others did not; each needed different sorts of resources and materials; for some, European trade and integration would be a boon, and for others it promised to bring near-term dislocation and troubles. Interests were varied and cross-cutting, and they would be hard to align and reconcile. In the preceding decade, Europe had reverted to economic nationalism, protectionism and autarky. Now those same states were being asked to tear down all safeguards, to subsume their own near-term interests, often against steep internal domestic opinion. To make matters even more challenging, the delegates set a deadline of September 1. As foreign policy analyst William Diebold Jr. wrote, "Six weeks is a short time to outline the economy of a continent [for] four years."

There was little time to waste. To chair the steering committee, now aptly named the Committee of European Economic Cooperation, or CEEC, Bevin turned to Sir Oliver Franks, a distinguished diplomat and professor of philosophy at Oxford University. Bevin had little to offer in the way of instructions: "You go to Paris and do your best," he told Franks, before his departure. A member of the British delegation recalled, "It was clear that we believed in the general idea of European cooperation, but if you had asked Franks and the rest of us what we were going to do in Paris, we couldn't have said." Franks's mission was nothing short of laying down "the principles that should guide European cooperation."

To begin his daunting task, Franks put the delegations to work. Four technical committees were established: Food and Agriculture, Iron and Steel, Fuel and Power and, finally, Transport. These were the four major areas of Europe's economy that demanded rehabilitation. To complement the committee's work, myriad subcommittees were also created. The committees would collate and synthesize the disparate countries' resources, capacities and needs, incorporate cooperative measures and map out forecasts in each

of these areas. What this new machinery lacked in flair, it made up for in efficacy. In addition to working toward its mandate, it would serve as "the primary school for many men who would play a major role on the postwar
European scene," establishing patterns of cooperation and forging ties and
interests that extended beyond national borders.

First, though, each country had to complete questionnaires outlining its
resources and its economic and financial state of affairs. Franks gave the conference a little more than a fortnight to complete the task. Some officials
were uneasy about subjecting their own economies to international review.
Some did not want to release figures which would lay bare their weakness
and vulnerability. For many of the states, though, economic management
was so antiquated that the sort of statistics or data they sought was simply
not available. Leaving his office at 2 A.M, British official Sir Eric Roll noticed
the light on in the offices of the Greek delegation. He stopped in and spotted
the Greek officials laboriously filling in the questionnaires. Roll said, "But
this is not for you, this is to be sent home to Athens for the people there to
fill in." His Greek counterpart replied, "You don't think anybody in Athens
will know anything about this . . . I will just invent the figures myself." The
French were not in much better shape when it came to command of the
desired information.

As the offices and halls in Paris's government buildings and embassies
buzzed with economists and technocrats laboring around the clock, the
people of Europe were trying mightily to return to a semblance of normal-
ity. France was stirred that summer when the government received a visit
from Argentine first lady Eva Duarte de Peron. Her dress was cut so low
that the French minister awarding her a dinner medal did not know where
to place it. Only a few months earlier, designer Christian Dior had introduced Paris and the fashion world to his "New Look." Jean-Paul Sartre,
Albert Camus and other intellectuals enjoyed jazz, cognac and highbrow
discourse at the Café Tabou, touted as the center of Bohemian Paris that
spring and summer. France was abuzz with cultural energy but mired in
chronic inflation, a widening Dollar Gap and sometimes violent strikes and
protests by Communists aggrieved at their exclusion from the Cabinet and
the government's purported supplication to Americans and their almighty
dollar.

In Great Britain, as well, the gallantry and spectacle that had long marked
summer returned. British eyes focused on high society weddings, Ascot,
Wimbledon and the Henley regatta, all returning, though not quite in their
"pre-war glory." Meanwhile, though "the Yanks [had now] gone," Britain's
youth would never be the same. "Girls" could be seen chewing gum and

heard speaking American slang. White ties and tails were slowly reintroduced and could be noticed on the British upper crust at restaurants and theaters. Austerity meant that everyone else had to make do with much less.
One group of young Englishmen formed the "Handlebar Club," a society
that had its own way of coping with the "dreadful anonymity of civilian
dress." Members would grow elaborate mustaches, or "smashers," as they
were known. At London's Temple pub, elevator operators and parachutists
who had to manage with "upsweep" shared maintenance tips with heavy
drinkers who had to contend with "boozer's droop."

Despite the return of some familiar pomp and fun, Britain's economic and
financial woes were reaching catastrophic proportions. On July 15, as per the
provision on the $3.75 billion U.S. loan, the British government made ster-
ling convertible to dollars. When Clayton had negotiated it, he had hoped
that it would help promote trade and economic recovery. He had not
accounted for Europe's economic weakness and the region-wide Dollar Gap.
Countries eager to acquire dollars but unable to do so by selling to America
began to seek sterling, which they would be able to convert to dollars as a
means of narrowing the gap.

Speaking in the House of Commons in early July, days before the conversion, Lord President of the Council Herbert Morrison announced that
Britain's "twelfth-hour" would strike that autumn. To balance its accounts,
he said, Britain would have to cut 25 percent of its imports. Such a cut,
though, would constitute "far too great adjustments . . . in our whole standard of living," already mired in deprivation. "The whole opportunity of
building a tolerable civilization may be lost," he said. Only a U.S. program
akin to Lend-Lease, Morrison declared, could save Britain.

When July 15 came, the British kept their agreement, and converted sterling to dollars. The British government had not taken appropriate precau-
tionary measures. Of the months before the conversion, Hugh Dalton,
chancellor of the Exchequer, remarked, "We debated much but decided little." There followed a dramatic and almost dizzying run on sterling and a
frightening exacerbation of Britain's balance-of-payments deficit. Bevin had
to enter the fray and push the United States. The drain was too damaging,
he told Ambassador Lewis Douglas. Under these conditions, the United
Kingdom would be forced "to retreat from one position to another, and further and further from the concept of a multilateral world economy." Translated to U.S. strategic terms that meant a reversion to economic autarky, and
it meant vulnerability to the Soviets in pockets of the world deemed critical
to U.S. interests. In Douglas's view this was no exaggeration: "I can say that
the British position is critical," he wrote Marshall in late July. "It is my view

that we run the serious risk of losing most of Western Europe if the crisis here develops as it now seems almost certain to develop."

IN EUROPE DURING that summer of 1947, Will Clayton was doing his best to stay out of view. While European dignitaries cruised around Europe's financial capitals in limousines, Clayton would take the train and walk a few miles to his meetings. At hotels he used aliases to register: sometimes "Troutman" and sometimes "Lockhart," his middle name. Clayton was determined to place the spotlight on the Europeans, and on their initiative and what they were building together. That July Clayton moved through the corridors of power talking with leading officials and heads of state, almost exclusively in off-the-record meetings, discussions or dinners. Though he did not wish to, Will Clayton struck an unmistakable figure in Europe that summer of 1947. The *New York Times* called him the U.S. "ambassador to Europe" and "No. 1 Envoy to Europe."

Clayton shared Marshall's staunch view on European initiative and cooperation. But he was also more experienced in these European negotiations and better placed to gauge the difficulties inherent in a task of this magnitude. Throughout July leaders like Franks and Belgian Foreign Minister Paul-Henri Spaak approached Clayton and asked him what the United States expected. As late as July 27, Clayton told Franks in reply to one such query that "Europeans were quite capable of preparing an adequate report and that if they desired [the State] Department's views on special aspects, they could be obtained on a 'within the family' basis." Through early August, Clayton was reasonably impressed with Europe's efforts on the technical side and was optimistic about the conference. With prospects good, he wanted to hold fast to Marshall's line and desist as much as possible.

Clayton had close and long-standing relationships in Europe, though, and the stature at the State Department to engage in developments with a certain latitude. To contacts like Jean Monnet and Franks, Clayton pointed out some of the provisions that would be important to the United States. On July 31, Clayton met with the Executive Committee, marking the conference's first "official" contact with the U.S. administration. He stressed the importance of producing a report that would be salable to a skeptical Congress at home. Europe needed to be back on its feet again in four years. There had been too many piecemeal and failed efforts. As long as progress continued at the conference, Clayton would toe Marshall's line and leave the initiative to the Europeans.

• • •

BACK IN THE UNITED STATES, the American public had picked up on the escalating tensions with the Soviet Union, but its focus was still largely domestic. In late July, Americans considered inflation a more important problem than foreign policy or preventing war. America was transfixed that summer by the Senate's scandal-ridden investigation of a maverick businessman named Howard Hughes. While 90 percent of Americans had heard of flying saucers, only 49 percent had heard of the nascent Marshall Plan. Of those who had heard of the Plan, 41 percent said they would be willing to pay more taxes to finance it and 50 percent responded that they would be unwilling. Congress was attuned to public sentiment.

So was a new official at the State Department. On July 1, Dean Acheson, having lent his formidable intellect and support to the genesis of the Marshall Plan, left the department. His position, undersecretary of state, was duly filled by Robert Lovett. Lovett, born in Texas in 1895, took leave from Yale University during World War I to serve as a fighter pilot. He was a pioneer in aviation warfare and helped to found America's air forces. A successful partner on Wall Street, Lovett served as Henry Stimson's deputy in the War Department during World War II, where he earned Marshall's esteem. Now Marshall was drafting him back to service as his undersecretary, his "copilot" once more. Despite fragile health at fifty-one years of age, Lovett could not turn the offer down. Like Acheson, Lovett had a razor-sharp intellect. Unlike Acheson, Lovett had the sort of easy and genial manner that would be of aid in dealing with members of Congress.

After a few weeks in office, Lovett wrote, "At no time in my recollection have I ever seen a world situation which was moving so rapidly toward real trouble . . . I have a feeling that this is the last clear shot that we will have in finding a solution." After meeting with him a few weeks later, Henry Ford II, president of Ford Motor Company, reported back that Lovett felt that war could break out any day. Marshall was away at a conference in Latin America for a good portion of July and August, so Lovett spent much of that summer as acting secretary of state. To his dismay, the new undersecretary found that not everyone in the department had a clear sense of direction. Ben Moore, a midlevel official, wrote to a senior colleague, "The 'Marshall Plan' has been compared to a flying saucer—nobody knows what it looks like, how big it is, in what direction it is moving, or whether it really exists."

In late July, George Kennan's thinking was much more lucid. Conditions in Europe were even more serious than "most people know," he wrote. But there was also good news. The Marshall Plan had forced Communist parties in Europe to "show their hand." It was now clear that they were attempting to impede recovery. It was also becoming clear as to how they would deal with their "allies." Tensions escalated in the Soviet bloc, even as the West experienced a rise in pro-American sentiment as well as a much-needed surge of hope and vitality. "Events of the past weeks [constituted] the greatest blow to European Communism since termination of hostilities," Kennan declared.

For Kennan, the Plan's goals were myriad, but "our main objective," he wrote, was "to render principal European countries able to exist without outside charity." To that objective, there were two underlying motivations: "(a) So they can buy from us; (b) So that they will have enough self-confidence to withstand outside pressures." Kennan was primarily concerned with advancing U.S. economic and security interests. In the third week of July, six weeks after Marshall's speech, Kennan began a memo: "Marshall 'plan.' We have no plan." It was, of course, all part of the Plan, though. Kennan's next line read: "Europe must be made to take responsibility. We would consider [a] European plan only if it were a good one and promised to do the whole job."

That same month, the foreign policy establishment was astir with an article in the July issue of *Foreign Affairs* titled, "The Sources of Soviet Conduct." Its author was revealed only as "X." The essay offered an explanation for the Soviet Union's behavior and offered a prescription for meeting the Soviet threat. It summoned the United States to embark on "a policy of firm containment, designed to confront the Russians with unalterable counter-force at every point where they show signs of encroaching upon the interests of a peaceful and stable world." Eventually, the Soviet Union's internal contradictions would force reform from within. Reform would then lead it to seek accommodation on a basis that would be acceptable to the United States. Dubbed the "X Article," it soon became clear that its author was George Kennan. Kennan's strategic prescription was audacious and controversial. The article introduced what would become the organizing concept of U.S. grand strategy for the next forty years: the "containment" of the Soviet Union. Its animating policy was to be the Marshall Plan.

As July gave way to August in Paris and delegates prepared to move from the technical phase of the conference to the policy phase, the delicate veneer of comity that marked the opening of the proceedings was lifting. With conditions becoming increasingly desperate throughout the continent and sixteen countries with cross-cutting interests jostling for aid, the delegations in Paris reverted to what they knew: the pursuit of their national interests. The French wanted the Monnet Plan and their economy to be the engine powering Europe's recovery and wanted to keep Germany down. The Benelux countries, in contrast, depended on German prosperity and the German market to drive their economies. The Turks complained that the conference's Executive Committee included only Western Europeans. The Portuguese were displeased that they were not represented on the Food Committee. Countries would not cut back on their demands and would not lift restrictions, and each grew increasingly skeptical and protective. Cooperation yielded to bickering and distrust. Historian Michael Hogan explained that the process "worked like a super-heated crucible to agitate differences only intimated earlier." In early August, two of the tensions that had been simmering all along rose to a boil and threatened the viability of the conference.

The first impasse involved Great Britain. It was clear that the Americans favored as much European economic integration as possible. The French were pushing for integration as well. In England, Churchill had called for "a United States of Europe." Bevin and his colleagues at the Foreign Office saw political and economic virtues in integration, but the governing Labour Party was apprehensive about its implications. International planning and cooperation would interfere with British national policy. If Great Britain razed its protective barriers, it would open its labor force and industry to competition from lower-cost labor and lower-cost producers. That would lead to unemployment and pains for British industry at a time when neither could be afforded. Also, pursuing economic integration with Europe would mean that Britain would have to forfeit many of its special ties to the Commonwealth, such as preferential trade and currency arrangements. Britain did twice as much trade with the Commonwealth as it did with Europe, and all of it was done in sterling as opposed to dollars. A reorientation from the Commonwealth to the continent would set back economic recovery and exacerbate England's dollar drain. Officials at Treasury and in the Labour government would not yield to pressure from Bevin or Franks on integration.

The second impasse involved France. It was no secret that France's main preoccupation was Germany. History's wounds were deep and fresh. The Soviets and French Communists aggressively propagandized that the Marshall Plan would build Germany up and so stoked political tension in France. Before the conference even began, Bidault cautioned that if the United States or Great Britain made any public statements about German recovery, it would doom the Paris Conference and "there would be no Europe." Clayton cabled State: "Beg, repeat beg, that no further measures for German rehabilitation" be discussed until Paris had concluded.

On July 16, French diplomat René Massigli reported from London that the United States and Great Britain both agreed that German rehabilitation would be necessary to fuel Europe's economy. Bidault was furious and threatened to resign if the U.S. and Britain did not desist. Days later, on July 21, Marshall assured Bidault that France's views on Germany would receive full and due consideration, which quelled tempers in Paris. Around this time, Jean Monnet sent a series of letters to Bidault. Given the breach with the Soviets, Monnet said, France was now bound to the United States and to the Marshall Plan. America and France needed each other.

In late July, a flurry of meetings ensued between Clayton and Monnet about how to reconcile France's economic and security needs with Germany's recovery. Behind the scenes, the two men were finding a path forward. Then on August 3, U.S. Secretary of the Army Kenneth Royall publicly declared that German recovery would have to proceed, and it could do so with or without France's input. It was a boon for French Communists and the Soviets and a catastrophe for Bidault and events at Paris. On August 8, Ambassador Caffrey cabled home: "All work of technical committees of CEEC . . . has come to a stop because the French are reluctant to participate."

The stagnation continued during the second week of August. Watching events from back home, many European officials grew increasingly alarmed. Speaking from Italy, Foreign Minister Count Carlo Sforza called on the conferees to push ahead, through the uncertainty, to submit a "plan that is not only daring in appearance, but also daring in substance." If Europe failed in this hour, the United States might retreat, just as it had after World War I, into "a disconsolate and sterile isolationism." Amidst the lugubrious mid-August heat, distrust and self-doubt had brought the Paris Conference to a standstill.

As the conference stalled, Western Europe's economies continued to sink. The sweltering heat had produced the worst drought the continent had seen in a decade; in some parts of Western Europe, the worst in half a century. France's wheat crop was the smallest in 132 years. Forest fires raged throughout the continent. On the German-Dutch border, the fires set off land mines left buried from the war, killing firefighters. Without rainfall, the *New York Times* wrote, "near-famine conditions will exist over wide areas again next winter."

Continued inflation converged with the shortfalls in crops to put increasing pressure on France and Italy's dollar shortage. The threat of starvation and financial collapse—Ambassador Caffrey gave France five months—loomed, poised to embolden Communist parties to pursue even more aggressive tactics. The U.S. ambassador to Italy, James Dunn, cabled back to Washington around this time: "It can be frankly said . . . that Italy is on the verge of a dollar crisis, which if allowed to break, will cause . . . [unprecedented] political upheaval." Communist propaganda flooded Italian cities. Premier De Gasperi was caricatured as a puppet of Wall Street. In cinemas, filmgoers went to see *Shoeshine*, an Italian movie about two boys caught in a web of poverty. Stealing from American soldiers and dealing on the black market, they end up in jail, and one of the boys kills the other. Despite its fatalism, it struck a resonant chord and was popular with audiences.

In France, political tensions were high. Despite winning more votes than any other party in the 1946 elections, the Communists were kicked out of government by the ruling center coalition in May 1947. Since their expulsion and the Soviet Union's withdrawal from the Marshall Plan, Communists were becoming increasingly adversarial and violent. Propaganda flew and strikes, sabotage and riots broke out in cities. With a big election coming up that October, turmoil promised only to escalate. That summer, John Foster Dulles was sent as an emissary for the Truman administration on a secret mission to France to assess the probability of civil war. Dulles reported back that the situation was desperate and that the United States had to do something to bolster the Ramadier government.

The situation was no better in Great Britain. The empire had torn through the $3.75 billion American loan in little more than a year. After convertibility in mid-July, the dollar drain was more like a bloodletting. British Treasury officials thought that the loan might be exhausted by the end of August, leaving Britain with $11 billion in gold, unpledged assets and other international holdings. That same year, Americans spent $6 billion betting on horseracing. Britain was "hanging on by its eyelashes," reported Will Clayton.

When a British delegation went to the United States to plead for suspension of convertibility, U.S. industrialist and statesman Bernard Baruch commented on the "low grade of its leadership." There was some truth in Baruch's assessment. Many of the ministers had been in office for seven intensely trying years. Some were exhausted, others were fatally ill. Bevin, who was ailing as much as any other, was the boldest figure. During August, Hugh Dalton and Stafford Cripps, then president of the Board of Trade, ventured to 11 Downing Street to propose to the foreign minister that he take over as prime minister. Bevin was loyal to Attlee and would not hear of it.

In addition to the crisis in leadership and the punishing winter, there was also American inflation. Wholesale prices had increased steeply in the year since the U.S. loan was made. That had the effect of dramatically lowering the value of the loan and also of what Britain could import from the United States. For the Marshall Plan's prospects, it was a double-edged sword. Not only was inflation placing added strain on Britain's Dollar Gap, but it was impeding its performance with the U.S. loan, a key input in Congress's calculation of whether or not to provide more U.S. taxpayer dollars.

It was clear to Lovett and his colleagues that the United States could not let Britain slide further. In mid-August the United States waived its insistence on convertibility. On August 20, Britain suspended convertibility, a temporary plug slowing the drain of dollars. "The British have turned out to be our problem children now," Truman wrote his sister that month. "They've decided to go bankrupt and if they do that, it will end our prosperity and probably all the world's too. Then Uncle Joe Stalin can have his way." With the great European empires of yore nearing bankruptcy, with intense political upheaval and vulnerability in France and Italy, that August was a bleak and ominous month. Will Clayton determined that the time had come to redefine the concept of "friendly aid."

PRIVATELY, CLAYTON HAD TOLD his American colleagues that the Marshall Plan might require as much as $16 billion in U.S. aid. Getting congressional authority for that amount, he knew well, would be a very tall task. In mid-August, Clayton learned that the European tally was coming in at around $28 billion. It was a sum, one historian wrote, that would "have raised the Capitol dome." In part, it was a "Gaston-Alphonse" situation. The United States had insisted that the Europeans move ahead first, but the Europeans felt that they needed guidance from the U.S. to push themselves forward. Without such guidance, the Europeans each submitted their own shopping lists, adhering to the "Molotov approach."

Albeit in broad and unofficial terms, Clayton had actively been making his views known in private meetings and conversations. "His has been the voice of America" at the Paris Conference, wrote Michael Hoffman in the *New York Times*. He had been the Marshall Plan's "chief pilot." Clayton still felt it essential that Europe have the initiative. But it was now clear to him that Europe also needed a big push.

Meeting in Paris from August 4–6 with the key U.S. ambassadors on the continent, Clayton formulated a more aggressive path. The Europeans should know that the United States would expect them to make monetary and fiscal adjustments as well as take cooperative action with one another. Each country was expected to move towards the eventual elimination of exchange controls, tariffs and other trade barriers. "Failure of any country to do this" would warrant U.S. "reconsideration for aid to such country." Clayton floated the idea of a customs union. It was a prospect he cherished, and he made it clear that if Europe were to propose it, it would be viewed in a highly favorable light by Congress and the American people. Yet he did not tell his European interlocutors that it was a condition of American aid.

Clayton had also begun to push for interim aid to tide Europe over until the larger Plan could get through Congress. It would mean yet another request for funds, threatening to exhaust an aid-fatigued Congress. It also probably meant that the president would have to call a special session of Congress, spending valuable political capital. Notwithstanding, Clayton had now determined that interim aid was necessary for Western Europe's democratic survival. In Washington, Lovett had also been thinking about some form of interim aid.

Clayton met again with Franks on August 19. Again, he pushed the idea of a customs union. France and Italy were on board. Great Britain was not. Franks asked about the existence of a European organization for economic cooperation beyond the CEEC. Clayton told Franks that for the duration of the Marshall Plan, at least, there should be a European organization. The meeting ended with a warning. Franks told Clayton that he did not yet know how large the European request would be, but that it was possible that it would be so large that "pruning down would be necessary before the U.S. would find the program acceptable."

At Foggy Bottom, Lovett was no less concerned than Clayton. In a mid-August cable to Clayton and Caffrey, Lovett stressed the importance of mutual aid and self-help. "Unless they are prepared to make this adjustment, no aid from this country could be really effective . . . We are entirely serious about this and we will not be able to accept, even as a basis for recommendation to Congress, any plan which does not recognize this basic requirement." The next week only brought more of the same from Paris, and increasing alarm from Lovett, whose tone was growing more adamant.

On August 24, Lovett cabled Marshall in Brazil that the Europeans had "come out so far" only with "sixteen shopping lists," tallying an "unreasonable" sum. "We are much concerned over this . . . An itemized bill summing up prospective deficits against a background of present policies and arrangements will definitely not be sufficient." Lovett now agreed that the United States needed to push the conference forward: "Against the background of our promise to lend friendly aid in drafting, I am convinced that the time has now arrived for us to give some indications that the present plan is not acceptable and to do so promptly." The outlook was "gloomy," Lovett conceded, but "I am not one bit discouraged . . . If we can keep the conferees from getting crystallized into a bad plan, perhaps we can swing them into a good one, or at least a better one."

The State Department's new willingness to project America's voice on the Paris deliberations highlighted a schism that had developed in the preceding weeks between Lovett and Clayton. The latter had pushed the Europeans toward dramatic monetary reform, a clearing scheme and a customs union. Without such reform, Europe might simply revert to "low labor productivity and maldistribution of effort which derive from segregating 270,000,000 people into [16] uneconomic principalities." Lovett held this sort of integration as a long-term objective. However, he felt that Europe was too fragile and Great Britain too resistant to get there in the near term. The key for Lovett was to increase production, to work toward monetary and fiscal stability and to lower, though perhaps not eliminate, barriers to trade. Clayton was seeking the realization of a grander vision. Reluctant British interlocutors gave him the sobriquet "Doctrinaire Willie."

Clayton had been the voice of the State Department and the United States at Paris for months. Lovett had begun to worry, though, that his views now "diverged" from the latest State Department thinking. So, in late August, Lovett sent George Kennan and a swath of officials from the economic side of the State Department to Paris to confer with Clayton. Meeting with Kennan Friday and Saturday mornings, Clayton found "the mutual exchange of ideas . . . most helpful." The "planners," as Clayton and Kennan were featured on the cover of the New York Times Magazine the following week, had reached a concerted policy synthesis. They had little time to waste. The next morning Clayton met with Franks and the rest of the five-nation Executive Committee at the U.S. Embassy in Paris. Franks had pushed the group as far as he could, he said: "Any effort to press further would so impair national sovereignty that many countries would rebel." Europe had not gone nearly far enough, though.

In the course of the three-hour meeting, Clayton laid out the terms, in unalloyed form, he felt essential in getting the conference back on track. The preliminary estimate of $28 billion would be viewed as "much too large" in the United States. The Plan's prospects would be "enhanced," Clayton said, if Europe adhered to seven guidelines. Clayton described them as "essentials." First, Europe should achieve economic independence, or self-sustainability, within four years. Second, aid requirements should taper each successive year. Third, Europe should emphasize production, especially coal and food. Fourth, in a thinly veiled allusion to the restoration of German production, Clayton said that long-run plans should not interfere with the near-term reactivation of existing production facilities. Fifth, the Europeans should work toward internal financial and monetary stabilization. The sixth point pressed the Europeans to liberalize trade. It was clear that a customs union and any institutional arrangements facilitating integration were desirable. But, meeting Lovett's concern, this point wasn't an "essential." And finally, as Clayton had been saying for weeks, the Europeans should form an ongoing multilateral organization to promote cooperation.

This was simply "friendly aid," Clayton said. He made it clear that this was not an American dictum. He was also explicit that the adoption of these measures would not guarantee passage of the Plan. He could not speak for Congress. The initiative remained with Europe. However, the message was delivered and it was heard loud and clear. Clayton had offered what journalist Harold Callender called "strong pressure" and "severe criticisms." They were, in Clayton's view, "the essentials for winning [the] approval of the American people."

For Franks, Clayton's new line was a catalytic tonic, providing much-needed direction and focus. The Executive Committee reconvened the technical committees with the mandate to scrutinize country requests further and to cut unnecessary items altogether, if not through European mutual aid. This time around the technical committees were joined by swaths of State Department economic officials. They become known as the "Friendly Aid Boys." At times they could be heard offering their European counterparts "very blunt criticism." Europe had to reduce its aid request and the United States now assumed a vocal seat at the table.

The conference had already been extended past the September 1 deadline. As the committees labored in Paris, George Kennan reflected on his impressions. Left on its own, "No bold or original approach to Europe's problems will be forthcoming," and Europe would fail, he believed. "No startling design will emerge here for the removal of the pitiful dependence of much of this great peninsular area on overseas supplies for which it cannot pay."

Marshall's speech at Harvard had posed a question: Can the Europeans help themselves? The United States, Kennan believed, had made a good-faith effort to empower them to do so. "Today we are in a position to gauge the answer," he wrote: "Europe is only partially capable of making on her own behalf . . . the effort which the Harvard speech envisaged." Time did not permit equivocation. Conditions were "deteriorating with terrifying rapidity." Kennan offered two key prescriptions to fortify Europe's position. The first was that the CEEC's findings should not be proffered as a definitive report. Instead, Kennan wanted it to serve as a preliminary report: "Let it come to us on the understanding that it will be used only as a basis of further discussion," he proposed. This would provide the Plan's champions with greater latitude in the legislative deliberations to follow. Second, Kennan argued that the United States would not be able to formulate a cogent, long-term Plan while Europe was mired in desperation. Interim aid was necessary to fortify Europe. With Europe relieved, the U.S. could then assume the needed long-term perspective.

Clayton had been a vociferous champion of interim aid for Europe throughout August. Lovett supported it as well. With Europe reaching a political and economic precipice, interim aid was no longer viewed as extraneous, but as a key ingredient to the viability of the Marshall Plan. Talk of interim aid burgeoned the first week of September. In Washington, Lovett spoke publicly of providing near-term aid to bridge the Marshall Gap—the time lag before the Marshall Plan could go into effect. In Europe, the leader of one major delegation said that without interim aid Europe would not be able to meet the trials of the coming winter and that the Marshall Plan would likely fail because aid would arrive too late. When word of Lovett's support for interim aid spread, it was received as the best news since Marshall's announcement at Harvard. It provided a much-needed boost to the work being done at Paris.

On September 10, Ambassador Lewis Douglas suggested to the British that the conference be postponed another several weeks. The United States sought time to further push Europe toward Clayton's "essentials." The Executive Committee recoiled. A postponement was unacceptable. They were concerned that continued delay would trivialize the efforts they had made and signify that Europe had lost command of its destiny. No one was more opposed than Ernest Bevin. He said that the suggestion gave the impression that the conference was now operating under "American pressure." If the impression were allowed to persist, it would do "untold harm" to the ability of the Europeans to forge ahead in the pursuit of its recovery and stability. Bevin wasn't asking the United States to desist from the provision of "friendly aid," only to allow the conference to continue with a sense of "calm" and without any "external pressures."

The situation was not calm, though. The Americans had now lost faith in Europe's ability to draft a report that could obtain congressional approval. Friendly aid now had to be delivered with a forceful hand. Kennan outlined the U.S. tactic at this stage: the United States was "to whittle it down as much as possible by negotiation; then . . . decide unilaterally what we finally wish to present to Congress." Kennan wrote: "This would mean that we would listen to all that the Europeans had to say, but in the end we would not ask them, we would just tell them what they would get." The main U.S. decision makers all now agreed that it was the best and only chance of advancing the Plan and realizing Europe's recovery. In fact, many of the European delegates were asking for that very thing. When Kennan was in Paris, a European colleague exhorted, "You people [i.e., Americans] go ahead and cut it down. We will squawk over every cut. Never mind that. Most of your cuts will be justified, and we will squawk anyway." External pressure was in fact "what some of the more far-sighted Europeans hope we will do," Kennan later wrote.

Yet Marshall, Clayton, Lovett and even Kennan never forgot that Europe's confidence, its sense that it could and must assume command of its own destiny, was essential to the success of the Marshall Plan. In the days following Douglas's meeting and Bevin's backlash, a compromise was struck. Clayton gave in on some points, though he stuck firmly to his "essentials." The conference would not be postponed as Douglas proposed, but Bevin, Franks and the Executive Committee did agree that the report could be labeled "provisional." It was the Europeans' finished report. But the new label meant that the Europeans would continue working on the details in Washington, and it also meant that Congress was now approached with a starting point, as opposed to a fait accompli. Most importantly for Clayton, his "essentials" were accepted.

On September 16, Clayton had an informal meeting with the CEEC. Through painful mutual examination and compromise, the Europeans had reduced their request from $28 billion to $19 billion. It was still more than the State Department wanted, but it was a dramatic improvement. In their work, Clayton told the representatives of the European nations, they had "blazed a new path in the history of Europe, if not in the history of the world." Clayton stated his own personal view that the report submitted would help to make the Marshall Plan a reality.

On September 22, representatives from sixteen European nations assembled in the Quai d'Orsay in Paris. The report of the CEEC was complete. As chairman of the conference, Bevin came to Paris to sign it. The report provided a detailed history accounting for Europe's economic predicament. It included analyses explaining the figures requested and the provisions Europe would take henceforth to work toward recovery. Clayton's "essentials" were there. Most notably: Europe would focus on the restoration of production; it would focus on internal monetary and fiscal stability; Europe would form an ongoing multilateral organization to promote cooperation; and in four years, it would bring Europe to a point of economic self-sustainability, eliminating the Dollar Gap. The report did not meet

U.S. hopes for structural reform or monetary cooperation and trade liberalization. How exactly the European organization would work and what form it would take were left unclear. Big questions were left unanswered or skimmed over.

Still, it was a remarkable achievement. Each country had subsumed (if not relinquished) its self-interest and transcended steep doubts, anxieties and differences. The sixteen nations pooled their hopes, and consented to wager their future, in large part, on the United States—but mostly on one another. In the cover letter of the report, the participating countries wrote: "In presenting this Report in response to Mr. Marshall's suggestion the participating countries believe that the program of concerted action, which it sets forth, marks the advent of a new state of European economic cooperation." The Dutch delegate believed that it "formed the indispensable basis for the shape of the western world in the years to come." The Paris Conference, and the report it produced, marks the first step toward European unification, and the European Union that would follow in the decades ahead.

JUST AS BEVIN affixed his signature to the CEEC report in Paris on September 22, the Central Intelligence Agency back in Washington was putting the final touches on its own report. Without action, economic collapse was likely in France and Italy, the report noted. The political center seemed to be collapsing. This could catapult the Communists to power. After signing the report in Paris, Bevin shared some remarks. This was not an appeal for charity, he said. It was a legitimate request to bridge Europe to self-sustaining recovery. Europe was prepared to sacrifice, it was prepared to work, it was prepared to reduce national barriers and cede a measure of national sovereignty to come together. Bevin said that the moment marked nothing short of "a new state in the history of international endeavor."

The 690-page report, bound in two volumes, was placed carefully in a green manila folder, which was then tied up with a ribbon of shocking pink. The official copies—all five of them—were passed immediately to Walter Kirkwood, the royal messenger for the king of England. Without delay, Kirkwood boarded a Trans World Airlines plane from Paris to La Guardia Field in New York City before proceeding on to Washington, D.C. "Here is our report," Bevin said: "It is now for the American people and the American Congress to decide whether this program, undertaken at Secretary Marshall's initiative, should be fulfilled and whether Europe can by this means contribute to the peace and prosperity of the world."

Life magazine called it perhaps the "most important decision of the 20th Century." If it worked, "the Marshall Plan will have proved to be the D-Day of the peace." As Kirkwood arrived in Washington with the Europeans' report, the baton had been passed across the Atlantic. All eyes turned to Congress and to the American people.

Chapter Six

SELLING AMERICA

I N SEPTEMBER 1947, President Harry Truman received a handwritten note from Winston Churchill. "How much I admire the policy into which you have guided your great country. Thank you from the bottom of my heart for all you are doing to save the world from Famine and War." He was moved by Churchill's note, but no man could carry the burden by himself, Truman replied. He was fortunate to have good men around him.

On October 7, Will Clayton drafted his sixth and final letter of resignation from the State Department. This time, Truman accepted. *Newsweek* called Clayton "the principal architect of American postwar foreign policy." "Mr. Clayton has been the greatest single force operating in the direction of bringing order out of the European chaos," the *New York Times* editorialized on October 16. The *London Observer* compared him to Adam Smith and John Stuart Mill.

Harry Truman's reaction was not so fine. "I'd like to spank Sue," he said to Clark Clifford. Bidault and diplomats all over Europe shared Truman's concerns about international economic policy after Clayton. Speaking at his final press conference on October 18, Clayton received a warm reception from reporters, but focused on the importance of European recovery. He sent a strong message imploring Congress and the American people to help. Clayton had kept his promise to his wife. And he had kept his compact with his president and the American people.

Still, the edifice Clayton envisioned had not yet been built. On the same day that Walter Kirkwood departed for New York City, September 22, a quote on the front page of the *Times* of London read, "The harvest is past, the summer is ended, and we are not saved. Jeremiah viii; 20." The fate of the Marshall Plan now rested with the United States Congress.

At the time, 37 percent of Americans felt that high prices, inflation and the cost of living were the most important issues before the country; 30 percent ranked foreign policy, Russia or the danger of war the most important issues. The day the CEEC report arrived, Speaker of the House Joseph Martin, a Republican from Massachusetts, said that he would not be willing to agree to anything "remotely suggesting an early Congressional commitment to Europe." The work of the Paris Conference made the paper every day, but its work was economic and technical. Even most Parisians had forgotten about the conference by its seventh week. Washington was abuzz with speculation about the Plan and its prospects. Yet most Americans still had not even heard of the Marshall Plan.

A MONTH EARLIER, on August 28, under gray skies in New York, eighteen members of the House of Representatives boarded the *Queen Mary*. Their immediate destination was Southampton, England. The group had been assembled by Representative Christian Herter, a Republican, a scholarly and earnest internationalist from Boston. Herter put together a cross section of congressmen, diverse in their politics, geography, outlook and even disposition. Together they would travel to Europe to see for themselves what was happening and assess the merits and needs of aiding Europe.

The group, which included, among others, a representative from California named Richard Nixon, became known as the "Herter Committee." Herter believed that Europe needed aid and that the United States should furnish it. But as a Republican, he was familiar with the chorus of concerns: aid would not be effective; it would place too heavy a strain on the U.S. economy; it would bloat the federal budget—to name a few. It was Herter's hope that after the mission, returning congressmen would come to share his views. Divided into five separate subcommittees, the Herter Committee spent forty-five days in Europe. Collectively, its members visited every country in Europe, save Russia, Yugoslavia and Albania. Chairman of the House Foreign Affairs Committee Charles Eaton said that the future economic hopes of Europe rested on the committee's findings.

The Herter Committee was the most watched and the most influential American group to visit Europe that autumn, but it was not the only one. From mid-August to November, more than two hundred congressmen went to Europe to investigate conditions and to assess the need and viability of a large-scale aid program. Congressmen enjoyed some dining and sightseeing. Occasionally embassy secretaries doubled as tour guides for single or lonely congressmen. One thirty-year-old congressman, like Herter from Massachusetts, asked a family friend named Pamela Churchill, who was married to Winston Churchill's son, Randolph, to drive him out to an obscure village in Ireland. His driver was less than enthused about the five-hour car ride. But it was the first chance for the young congressman to see where his family had come from. For John F. Kennedy, it was one of the most poignant moments of his life.

Herter made it clear to members of his Committee, however, that the mission was no junket. That autumn, members of the Herter Committee and other members of Congress discussed shipping problems in the elegant offices of the French Merchant Marines, met with Cabinet members and heads of state, surveyed the supply of frogs' legs in Parisian markets, and everything in between. Said one member of Herter's Committee, "We tried to look at Europe in about the way a banker would look at a bankrupt corporation trying to get a loan." Journalist Theodore White observed that many European officials received the American congressmen "in somewhat the way villagers of medieval Europe must have received their seigneurial lords—in a mixture of tongue-tied dread and hushed servility."

When the Herter Committee returned to New York on October 10, it had amassed seventeen trunks full of data. It had also achieved a consensus that Europe was in dire straits and that a large amount of U.S. aid was necessary. Some, like Lawrence Smith of Wisconsin, had done a complete turnaround. Speaking of the need to support U.S. information programs, Smith stated, "You may recall my own reservation on this matter. I became a convert on this trip and I want to state that for the record." Before the trip many committee members grappled with the cost of aiding Europe. Returning, one of the skeptical members of Herter's Committee asked, "What would it cost us not to aid Europe?" As the waves of congressmen returned, even old-line isolationists like Everett Dirksen from Illinois and Karl Mundt from South Dakota were heard making passionate appeals for aid for Europe, or in many cases, aid to stem the "Red tide."

The trips were a boon for the Marshall Plan's prospects. "This has occasioned restrained and qualified jubilation in White House and State Department circles," wrote journalist Cabell Phillips in the *New York Times*. The Plan's supporters were no doubt pleased, but they still faced an uphill battle. Even as members of Congress returned trumpeting support for U.S. aid, others remained skeptical. Still others sought to peg infeasible conditions onto any U.S. aid. Representative Clarence Brown of Ohio, for example, threatened: "No tax relief, no European relief." There was an election coming up in one year, and Republicans were pining for control of the White House. Members of Congress were still asking, What happened to the $3.75 billion loan? Why would even larger-scale aid now make any difference?

WHILE CONGRESSMEN MOVED ABOUT Europe's cities and countryside and journalists opined on the Marshall Plan's prospects, the Soviet Union had called a meeting of nine European Communist parties at an old hunting lodge at Szklarska Poreba in southwest Poland. The meeting was presided over by Andrei Zhdanov, the general who had held Leningrad in one of the greatest battles of World War II. Zhdanov was short, with a clipped brown mustache and a sharp, hard face. He was considered a Politburo intellectual, but he was loyal to Stalin, who had called for the meeting and directed its affairs via telephone from Russia. Ostensibly, the Communist parties were summoned for a mutual exchange of ideas. Stalin's animating intent was something different: to establish the Cominform, a new organization designed to chart a path forward for the international Communist movement. As one historian put it, the Cominform was "the institutional expression" of the shift in Soviet policy engendered by the Marshall Plan.

Stalin's new line was revealed to the delegates at Szklarska Poreba when Zhdanov delivered his report "On the International Situation." The Marshall Plan was part of a broader United States plan, Zhdanov explained, "a policy of preparing new military adventures" aimed at nothing less than "global expansion." The Americans were imperialists and would use economic aid to subjugate Europe to its political will. Western Europe would become America's "forty-ninth state" and then serve as a "jumping-off place for attacking Soviet Russia."

Accordingly, the first step for Stalin was to assert and secure control of his sphere of influence. Whereas before the Marshall Plan, Stalin had tolerated governing coalitions in Eastern Europe, he would now assert his unchallenged authority: the Sovietization of Eastern Europe. For the French and Italian Communist leaders, Szklarska Poreba was an intensely humiliating experience. The Western European Communist leaders had preferred to collaborate with their country's non-Communist governing coalitions. Yielding in part to pressure from countries like Yugoslavia, which took an even harder line than Stalin on this, Zhdanov made it clear that the policies of collaboration were over. "While you are fighting to stay in the Government," Zhdanov chided Jacques Duclos, the French Communist leader, "they throw you out." To the Italian party head, Zhdanov taunted, "You Italian comrades are bigger parliamentarians than De Gasperi himself. You are the biggest political party, and yet they throw you out of Government."

Duclos was so humiliated by his treatment and disturbed at Zhdanov's orders that after the meeting he sat by himself in a park, swinging his legs, crying in a rage.

When Zhdanov's report and many of the remarks made in that late September meeting were published in *Pravda* weeks later, the West was alarmed. In the United States it became known as the "two camps" speech. With the Cominform, the West and East were both now organized institutionally, and in strategic design, in political opposition to the other. When Walter Lippmann published a collection of essays that fall—largely in rebuttal to George Kennan's "X" article—the title of his book seemed an apt description of the contest that had gripped the United States, the Soviet Union and the world. Lippmann's book was called *The Cold War*. He did not conceive of the term. Bernard Baruch had used it in a speech, and George Orwell had penned the term decades before. But now it resonated and stuck.

The United States had sought to destabilize Stalin's sphere of influence with the Marshall Plan and the offer of aid to Eastern Europe. Now Stalin would retaliate and attempt to destabilize the West. The days of national Communism and political collaboration were over. Western European Communist parties were to fall in line with Soviet policy. That meant employing whatever means—propaganda, political sabotage, violence— to carry out what Zhdanov made clear was now the paramount objective of the Soviet Union: putting "all effort into seeing that the Marshall Plan is not realized."

Into October and November 1947, Western Europe's economic situation continued to deteriorate. In England, the average food ration had fallen below the caloric minimum deemed necessary to keep an unemployed worker in good health in 1933, during the darkest days of Britain's Depression. Coal strikes in Yorkshire and elsewhere further exacerbated matters. Still hemorrhaging dollars, Britain came dangerously close to bankruptcy. By December, though, Britain had turned a corner in production. The hopeful data combined with the prospect of large-scale American aid generated some optimism among the British.

Despite its economic and financial woes, Britain was stable politically. It was a different story altogether in France and Italy during that autumn. When Jacques Duclos returned from Szklarska Poreba, he told subordinates that the Kremlin no longer cared whether the Communists were in or out of government: "The only objective is to destroy the capitalist economy," to "fight against economic aid from the U.S." and to "destabilize the government." Within weeks, French Communists and the labor unions they controlled had set off a wave of strikes in cities, at ports and in the country. The

French people feared a coup or civil war. The political instability together with the country's economic predicament sank France into a collective state of despair. In mid-October, less than 1 percent of the French public thought things were going "well" in France; 93 percent believed things were going "rather badly" or "badly."

On October 19, in municipal elections, the French spoke with their ballots. Both the socialists and the Communists lost ground to de Gaulle's rightist party. It was a stinging defeat for Duclos and the Communists. With a weakening political position and increased pressure from the new Soviet hard line, Duclos found recourse in violence and sabotage. In late October, ten thousand Communists launched a violent attack on an anti-Communist meeting around Salle Wagram near Place de l'Etoile. Within the next few weeks, the Communists sought to bring the French economy to its knees. Virtually all the coal mines in the country were shut down. Metalworkers, auto workers, dockworkers and most other groups of laborers went on strike. Public transport was shut down in fits throughout October and November. Mail was not delivered, refuse went uncollected and power was not available. Cooking was impossible, and Parisians were lucky if they could get water from their taps. Throughout November, the government feared that France would be confronted with a general strike, a total shutdown. The Communists controlled much of the country's media, which blamed France's economic troubles on the government, on American imperialism and on capitalism in general. For the Communists, economic collapse would mean victory.

It was not enough for workers to go on strike; departing workers were instructed by union leaders to destroy machinery and depart with equipment and tools. That way, replacement workers would not be able to do their jobs. All of this was meant to leave the impression with the Americans that economic aid would be futile, because there would be no labor or functioning economy to aid. Toward the end of November, the Ramadier government fell apart, and the *New York Times* wrote that France was now in the throes of its "greatest crisis . . . since the liberation." "People talk only of imminence of war!" wrote Roger Martin du Gard to André Gide, one famed French author to another.

Ramadier's replacement as premier was Robert Schuman, a mild mannered, cerebral and shrewd politician from Lorraine. Schuman faced mounting strikes—3 million workers left their jobs at the strike's apex—increasing violence and widespread panic that civil war was near. For his most important Cabinet post, Schuman appointed the socialist Jules Moch as minister of the interior. It was a judicious appointment. Schuman called a state of emergency. Moch acted forcefully, mobilizing whatever forces and arms at his disposal to quell the violence. Communist disruption continued apace, though. On Sunday, November 30, the streets of Paris were empty. "All seems quiet today," wrote the British ambassador to France, Duff Cooper. "It isn't revolutionary weather."

The ambassador did not know, however, that Duclos had just returned from a hasty meeting in Moscow with Stalin, in which the Soviet dictator instructed him to use anything short of armed force to keep up the pressure on the campaign to sow political instability and to sabotage the economy and the Marshall Plan.

Events were reaching an ominous climax that December in Italy as well. After returning from Poland, the Italian Communists, who had even greater national support than their French comrades, had "declared open political warfare against the government and the forces of moderation." Waves of strikes broke out across the country. Communist leaders enlisted the Italian workers and the rest of the population to engage in "a class war." Communist propaganda assumed a militant tone and was ubiquitous. The party's slogans were scrawled along the walls of ancient ruins. Drawings of the hammer and sickle were scribbled on buildings in the Vatican. Communist leaders rallied labor and the many poor and hungry with calls against the Marshall Plan, capitalist greed and American imperialism. The vehemence with which the Communists railed against the Plan, wrote journalist Harold Hinton, "indicates that there is more confidence of the program's success in the Kremlin than exists in certain segments of the United States economic and political life."

Throughout November Italy was rife with strikes, often accompanied by riots and economic sabotage. In mid-November, Communists began exploding military ammunition depots. In Bari, the government had to send troops to push back strikers who had stormed the police barracks. The carabinieri fired on the mob, and two people were killed. Rioters and police exchanged gunfire in southern Italy. In late November, Communist Party head Palmiro Togliatti called for "mobilization," inveighing, "It is necessary to liquidate this government of reaction." By month's end around twenty Italians had died in the violence, and more than 150 had been seriously wounded. In the United States, Americans read *Life* magazine's view that as December approached, "the fabled Italy of Julius Caesar, the Renaissance and the Roman Catholic Church is today on the brink of Communist revolution." Behind Alcide De Gasperi, the Italian government stood firm. At the same time, De Gasperi was beseeching the United States for aid. Wrote journalist Arnaldo Cortesi, "The present wave of political violence that is sweeping over Italy has made most Italians more keenly aware that their political future depends to a considerable degree on the Marshall Plan."

As the political agitation and violence rose to alarming heights, Marshall, Molotov, Bevin and Bidault gathered on November 25 at Lancaster House in London for the 5th Conference of Foreign Ministers. The focus would, once again, be Germany. Since the last foreign ministers' conference in Moscow, the Marshall Plan had drastically changed things for both sides. The United States was determined to proceed apace, and in some quarters U.S. officials privately hoped that Molotov would not complicate the Plan's prospects with Congress by attempting to compromise at London. They were not to be disappointed. The conference broke down after three weeks of acrimony and seventeen fruitless, almost absurd, sessions. The failed conference codified the division of Germany.

Behind the scenes, though, Bevin implored Marshall to provide immediate American aid for France. Bidault stressed the importance of near-term aid and expressed concern over the deliberations of Congress. Marshall agreed that Congress's deliberations were of "transcendental importance." In turn, he encouraged Bidault not to jeopardize France's prospects by opposing German recovery.

Bevin had something else on his mind as well. As the Soviet line hardened and violence erupted in France and Italy that autumn, Western Europe had come to feel increasingly vulnerable vis-à-vis the Soviet Union. And it was also becoming clear that the pathology of fear would impede Europe's recovery. As one French farmer, Lucien Bourdin, told an American scholar, "Plant an apricot orchard so the Russians and the Americans can use it as a battlefield? Thanks. Not so dumb." Visiting Bevin on December 17 at the British Foreign Office two days after the London Conference formally adjourned, Marshall barely had time to sit down before Bevin could get out the idea. Bevin proposed a transatlantic security association to complement the burgeoning economic one. Marshall approved in principle. But they would need to discuss it further, he said, and with Congress about to deliberate on the Marshall Plan, it would have to wait. They had planted the seed for an extraordinary transatlantic alliance.

MEETING WITH PRESIDENT TRUMAN early that autumn about the Marshall Plan, Representative Charles Halleck, a House leader, said, "Mr. President, you must realize there is growing resistance to these programs . . . I've been out on the hustings and I know. People don't like it." Still weary from the war, and the economic and personal sacrifices involved therein; deeply skeptical of foreign aid (which had seemed to fall short so many times before); ambivalent if not averse to aiding socialist European governments; deeply preoccupied with its own economic problems and the prevention of another U.S. postwar recession or even depression, the U.S. public was not disposed toward new and costly foreign adventures. The statesmen supporting the Marshall Plan knew that to surmount the steep obstacles ahead, extraordinary effort would be required. The Herter Committee and other members of Congress who had traveled to Europe in the summer and early autumn had returned to trumpet Europe's needs. Now, the Plan's champions sought to devise and execute a campaign to sell the Marshall Plan to the American people. It was, in the words of a Dutch diplomat who had never seen anything like it, "a Marshall Plan to sell the Marshall Plan."

The statesmen who had guided America through World War II feared that autumn that the United States would retrench into isolationism, as it had after World War I. To respond, former Secretary of War Henry Stimson wrote a stirring piece in the October 1947 edition of *Foreign Affairs*, beckoning the U.S. to assume global responsibility and to support European recovery: "The reconstruction of Western Europe is a task from which Americans can decide to stand apart only if they wish to desert every principle which they claim [dear to] life . . . We must take part in this work; we must do our full part, we must be sure that we do enough."

At the end of November, Stimson agreed to serve as the honorary president for a new organization titled the Committee for the Marshall Plan. Stimson's successor, Robert Patterson, signed on to chair the Executive Committee. The committee's membership was a bipartisan who's who of the American elite. Its membership included some three hundred luminaries from business, religion, academia, agriculture, labor and other areas of American life, including a future director of the CIA, presidents of labor unions, newspaper editors, the wife of a former Republican presidential nominee and two newly private citizens: Dean Acheson and Will Clayton. Headquartered in Washington and registered as a lobbying organization, the committee's aim was to educate and inform the American public about the Marshall Plan.

The committee labored mightily that autumn. Patterson announced that it would attempt to collect one million signatures to petition Congress to ensure the Plan's expeditious passage. The committee published various pamphlets, such as "Who is the Man Against the Marshall Plan?," "The Marshall Plan: 20 Questions and Answers," as well as "What About the Marshall Plan?," which was written by a diplomat named Alger Hiss. The committee raised more than $150,000 from some 7,500 donors and used its funds to employ workers and a full-time staff, as well as to retain the Phoenix News Bureau to obtain publicity, publish op-eds and place advertisements in major newspapers and national magazines—such as the one that read "WE MUST STOP STALIN NOW through the European Recovery Program."

More than advertisements and articles were needed, though. To arouse the public's interest and to engage people on the grassroots level, the committee launched an ambitious campaign of lectures and speaking events. Hundreds of supporters—business leaders, academics, religious and labor leaders—barnstormed the country in the nation's biggest cities and smallest towns speaking about the Marshall Plan and its importance. Young Harvard professors and unknown economists found that when it was over they had given fifty or sixty speeches extolling the Plan. Some of the speakers were local personalities. Several of America's most prominent statesmen engaged as vociferously.

Dean Acheson's efforts took him from on-air radio debates in New York City to a luncheon speech at the World Affairs Council in San Francisco to another speech before the Pacific Northwest Trade Association in Spokane, Washington. Hopping on an overnight train, Acheson soon found himself teaming up with Minneapolis Mayor Hubert Humphrey in a reception hall in Duluth, Minnesota. Busloads of miners and their families had come to hear Humphrey and Acheson. When it was his turn, each would stand up on a chair and speak about the Marshall Plan for half an hour. When they finished, they found that many more people had arrived and were still interested in hearing them speak. As the first crowd left, the hall filled up again and the two orators repeated the exercise several times over until the early hours of the morning. Acheson returned to his room exhausted. He told his audiences that the Marshall Plan was "the heart and core of our foreign policy and the best hope of this and many another land," and that at the end of the day, it depended upon their support.

As it ramped up that autumn, the committee began reaching out to American civic society. The National Association of Manufacturers stapled eleven conditions to its support, but it was in favor of the Marshall Plan. So were the American Federation of Labor and the Congress of Industrial Organizations, eager to fortify the non-Communist international labor movement as well as to keep their constituents producing for European markets. The Atlantic District of the Lutheran Women's Missionary League joined the Department of International Justice and Goodwill and the Federal Council of the Churches of Christ in America, who announced, "As Christians, we support the ERP in the conviction that it can be one of history's most momentous affirmations of faith in the curative power of freedom and in the creative capacity of free men." The American Legion was for it. Speaking from Philadelphia, a spokesman for the Quakers expressed "skepticism." They were concerned that the Plan was directed against the Soviet Union, rather than serving as a vehicle to promote U.S.–Soviet friendship.

Notable personalities from cross sections of American life spoke out offering their views of the Plan. The seventy-two-year-old Nobel laureate Thomas Mann, exiled from Germany since Hitler's rise and living in the United States, announced his support after a recent trip to Western Europe. "Uncle George" Putnam of Concord, New Hampshire, eighty-five years old, who was still running his own farm and was known as "the grand old man of New England farming," announced: "I believe in full production to meet the needs of our Government and its obligations to the starving peoples of other nations." Dwight Eisenhower supported the Marshall Plan.

On November 7, the Plan received one of its most important endorsements. Speaking before a thousand business executives at a dinner at the Waldorf-Astoria, at the thirtieth-anniversary celebration of *Forbes* magazine, presidential hopeful Thomas Dewey, the Republican governor of New York, announced that America had no other choice than to support the Marshall Plan. There was an important caveat: "The errors of the past in American aid abroad must be eliminated by providing for business like administration of the foreign aid program." Dewey offered his own six-point plan.

At the same time as members of the Committee for the Marshall Plan were stumping all over the country to drum up support, private citizens and civic organizations were putting forward unprecedented peacetime sacrifices. President Truman had called for national food-saving programs, so that there would be more available, without corresponding inflationary pressures, for Europe. Many restaurants and diners around the country agreed to meatless Tuesdays. Notre Dame agreed not to serve meals to spectators at Irish home games that fall. Days before Thanksgiving, Massachusetts Governor Robert Bradford held a ceremony at Plymouth Rock. He asked Americans to donate funds equivalent to one Thanksgiving meal to Europe.

That autumn, Attorney General Tom Clark proposed the creation of a Freedom Train. Carrying the Declaration of Independence, the Magna Carta and the Constitution, the Freedom Train traveled the country to arouse national spirit and generosity. Journalist Drew Pearson suggested a Friendship Train to raise goods and supplies to send to Europe from Americans. The country responded with fervor. The Kiwanis Club offered a carload of foodstuffs. The Seventh Masonic District announced a donation of five thousand pounds of sugar and ten thousand pounds of flour. A group of restaurants donated twenty thousand pounds of spaghetti and macaroni—to

Italy. By the time the train arrived in New York, it had almost three hundred carloads of food and supplies. To those, New York City's students added five hundred tons of food and supplies. Commercial liners waived the costs to ship the goods across the Atlantic. Parades in cities and towns across America met the train with banners that read "From the heart of the American People," "Vive la France," and "Viva l'Italia."

As the Freedom Train rumbled through the country stoking the national spirit, the State Department was quietly but feverishly at work. Truman and Marshall aimed to get the Plan before Congress that winter. They were also pushing for interim aid to tide Western Europe over until the large-scale program could be passed. That meant that State Department officials might have to produce an interim package that would be ready for Congress in little more than a month, or even weeks. Much would have to be done. Despite traveling widely and despite his preparation for the London Foreign Ministers' Conference, Marshall had begun to cultivate the support of the member of Congress who mattered most: Arthur Vandenberg.

In early autumn, before the worst of the violence and turbulence in Western Europe, Vandenberg had been ambivalent about the Marshall Plan, a tepid supporter at best. That autumn, he wrote his wife: "This seems to be the time for us to make hay. But if our friends in Western Europe are allowed to starve and freeze to death this winter, the Commies will be completely back in the saddle. On the other hand, we must keep our own feet on the ground and avoid commitments that would disrupt our own economy. Where to draw the line!" Marshall was keenly aware that Vandenberg's backing was essential in establishing broader bipartisan support, and without it the Plan would fail.

Marshall brought the senator into the most confidential details of the planning at State. He solicited his views, both on what would work best and on what would be most politically salable. "He soon became a full partner in the adventure," Marshall later said. "Van was my right-hand man and at times I was his right-hand man." As they met furtively at Blair House twice each week through the autumn and winter, the media was unaware of the extraordinary bipartisan collaboration. One journalist, in particular, began criticizing Marshall for his failure to reach out to Republicans. "He was profound in his knowledge and he didn't know a damn thing," Marshall would later say of the journalist. "Vandenberg and I were just handling this business," he said. Marshall added that the tandem "couldn't have gotten much closer together unless I sat in Van's lap or he sat in mine."

By mid-November, Marshall's exertions and the escalating turmoil in Western Europe had increased Vandenberg's support. On November 13, he wrote: "I am reserving some doubts myself regarding some phases of it—but, in the main, I do not see how we can avoid the necessity of keeping ourselves insulated against world-wide Communism by maintaining these sixteen nations of the Western Union. Evidently," he added, "I am to have some degree of trouble . . . So be it!" Because Vandenberg knew better than anyone the gauntlet the Marshall Plan was to run in Congress, and because he had subjected his own head to the political chopping block, he pressed hard with Marshall to make sure that State would do its utmost to submit a comprehensive and compelling piece of legislation.

To oversee that enterprise, Marshall deputized his trusted undersecretary, Robert Lovett. Lovett, who joked to friends that dealing with Congress was like having a shave and having one's appendix taken out at the same time, did not need much prodding to realize the importance of producing authoritative legislation. During that autumn and winter, Lovett met continuously with Vandenberg, consulting openly and amicably. The two spent more waking time with each other, two historians wrote, than they did with their wives. To oversee the drafting and analysis that would go into the Plan and the interim aid's legislation, Lovett drew on the talents and energies of one of Will Clayton's most trusted subordinates, Paul Nitze, still a senior official in the economic department at State.

The Paris report received in late September was the initial basis of Nitze's work. In addition, his team had subsequent memos and analysis from Kennan's planning staff and Clayton's economic department. There were boxes and crates full of economic data and statistics. Nitze and the rest of the team on the technical and drafting side were focused on Europe's balance-of-payments deficit. Its planning also had to bake in as much European self-help and mutual cooperation as possible. Marshall provided broad, but essential and incisive guidance. He told Nitze: "The country at some time is going to return to that isolationist mood, and it is essential that these programs that you are now working on be self-liquidating." The sums requested could be large—in order to do the job they would have to be—but the program must stand Europe on its own feet after the fourth and final year, and appropriations must decline each successive year. "The country won't stand for this for long," Marshall stressed.

In addition, on October 9, Sir Oliver Franks arrived in Washington with a delegation from the CEEC. Franks wanted to ensure that the European voice was heard as the State Department reviewed the Paris Report and formulated the Plan's legislation. Franks told Lovett, "The Paris Conference has created a new hope in men's minds in Europe. They feel that the Marshall Plan offers a last chance to Western Europe to recover from the political and economic effects of the war." "A few billion dollars (and I am not suggesting that a billion dollars is a small sum)," Franks wrote to Lovett in an unofficial aide-mémoire, "may make all the difference between success and failure . . . This chance will not occur again and I am convinced it is vital that the opportunity be seized and the work begun on a scale to give it the fullest chance of success."

Franks had come to make his case to Lovett. But the month spent in Washington also provided the Europeans with a window into the political morass into which the State Department would be wading in seeking the Plan's legislative passage. "I fully recognize the combination of political circumstances in this country" that "puts the Administration in a position of real difficulty," Franks acknowledged to Lovett. The European delegates labored to provide whatever material, statistics and data they could to their American counterparts. Witnessing firsthand the political difficulties involved, the European delegation gained a heightened sense of appreciation for the sacrifice the Americans were waging in their support of the Plan. That appreciation, in turn, provided Lovett with leverage to push the Europeans further on integration. The United States was taking a calculated risk, Lovett said, and it would be beneficial for Congress and America to see Europe assume a similarly daring risk.

Meanwhile, Nitze and his team began creating "Brown Books" for each of the recipient countries. The Brown Books laid out each country's financial situation, its evolving balance of trade, its needs and the types of aid the United States would offer. It was a tedious process. To expedite the work, Nitze went to the Army and asked if his team could use new machines the Army had recently received. The Army agreed, and the "primitive devices," or computers, aided Nitze and his team enormously, saving them much time.

President Truman called a special session of Congress for November 17, in large part to press for interim aid for Europe. At a press conference around that time, Truman was asked what the United States "would get" for its aid to Europe. "We are not doing this for credit," Truman told the members of the National Conference of Editorial Writers. "We are doing it because it is right and it's necessary." Into November, with the special session looming, the pace and intensity of work picked up for Nitze and his team. Other officials were pulled from various departments and agencies, and all the hands that were needed and that Nitze requested came on deck. They worked seven days a week, around the clock.

As the legislation was being formulated, various agendas factored into the mix. Some military officials wanted military aid for Greece and Turkey included. John Hickerson, director of the Office of European Affairs, argued that if military aid were included the Soviets would inevitably propagandize that the Plan was offensive and militaristic. Lovett and Marshall agreed and ensured that the Plan would be framed in terms of economic rehabilitation only.

The urgency of Europe's predicament and the nobility of the mission—as Marshall defined it—kindled a remarkable spirit of enthusiasm and devotion among those working on the Plan at State. Leaving his office drowsy one evening, one official crashed his car on his way home. His colleagues each contributed fifty dollars for the deductible on his insurance. After working late into the evening, one of the women in the office had an accident and broke her arm. Again, her colleagues chipped in for her medical bills. Upon hearing these stories, senior officials agreed to hire cars with drivers for officials working late. One morning a midlevel economist at the department overheard a conversation between two chauffeurs in the restroom. "My God, you look terrible," one said to the other. He replied: "I have been up all night working on the Marshall Plan."

That November, junior officials convened in smoky offices and around cafeteria tables, working through meals. Talk was of dollars, of trade gaps, of steel, wheat and coal. If officials in Washington weren't working on the Marshall Plan, they were watching those who were. Lovett called that first week of November "hell week." When it was over, the legislation to be submitted to the special session of Congress was taking shape and nearing completion. As the *New York Times* wrote, the Marshall Plan "began for the first time to take on the clear-cut outlines of a genuine plan."

THE SAME WEEK that the State Department was completing the Marshall Plan legislation, Arthur Vandenberg received a report that pleased him. Back in June, only weeks after Marshall's speech at Harvard, Vandenberg, in a private White House meeting, had counseled President Truman to commission a series of committees to examine the Plan's feasibility. Truman agreed immediately.

The Nourse and Krug committees, headed by Edwin Nourse of the Council of Economic Advisers and Julius Krug, secretary of the interior, respectively, focused on the capacity of the U.S. economy and domestic production to withstand the sort of financial commitment envisioned in the Plan. The Krug Committee report, the more high-profile of the two, released on October 19, found that a large-scale foreign aid program could lead to acute domestic shortage in certain commodities as well as depletion of natural resources. Sacrifice and adjustment were necessary, the report found. However, even so, the U.S. economy had the capacity to support a large-scale foreign aid program and still preserve national security and standards of living. The Nourse report, released November 1, agreed that the program need not inflict dire short-run damage and in fact could spur long-term economic growth by strengthening Europe's ability to import U.S. goods.

The most important committee was the President's Committee on Foreign Aid. Harry Truman proposed that W. Averell Harriman, his secretary of commerce, a former diplomat and titan on Wall Street, run the committee, which was known popularly as the Harriman Committee. Despite Harriman's liberal leanings, his business background was exactly what Vandenberg was looking for. Van also added Owen Young, the chairman of General Electric, as well as Robert La Follette Jr., a former senator from Wisconsin who hailed from a prominent Midwestern family and whose former isolationist leanings gave him powerful bona fides with skeptical Republicans. The mandate for the committee was robust: to analyze the principles and policies that should guide the recovery program; to assess the capacity of the U.S. economy to support it; to estimate the volume and nature of the assistance required; and to consider matters of its financing and administration.

Vandenberg and Truman, also a seasoned operator in the Senate, knew that the committee members needed to be chosen carefully. In addition to Young, Owen and La Follette, there was the dean of Iowa State College, the president of Procter & Gamble, the secretary-treasurer of the American Federation of Labor, the president of the Federal Bank of St. Louis, and the president of B. F. Goodrich. The endorsement of its members would provide immense credibility to the Plan, and the report they were to produce would be a formidable instrument for Vandenberg and other champions to wield in the court of public opinion as well as in congressional deliberations and backroom Senate negotiations. Cosmetically, the Plan's sponsors couldn't have done better. But Vandenberg knew them and had a strong feel for where they would come out. Said one member years later, "the Committee was stacked to bring out those views."

To be sure, Vandenberg, Truman, Lovett and Acheson sought to stack the committee. But there was no way of knowing for sure how nineteen separate prominent, independent-minded men would come out. There was no way of knowing what exactly they would recommend and how effectively those recommendations would be presented. All of those questions could be answered only after months of intensive testimony, analysis and debate. Vandenberg had already announced that he would not proceed with hearings on the Marshall Plan's enabling legislation until the committee's report had been completed and presented. Harriman spent much of June and July traveling in Europe, and the committee began hearing testimony on July 23 in Harriman's office at the Commerce Department. Harriman needed someone of great intellect and ability to spearhead the work—editorial and analytical—on the committee's report. In late July, he telephoned Richard Bissell.

Richard Bissell's family arrived from England in Windsor, Connecticut, in 1636. They were an influential family, and his ancestor Sergeant Daniel Bissell was a spy for George Washington. Bissell was born in the Mark Twain House in Hartford only a few years before the outbreak of World War I. His father was president of Hartford Insurance and a prominent Connecticut Republican. Like Harriman, Bissell was sent to Groton and then to Yale University. It was a culture that valued athletic vigor and achievement. Physically, Bissell was weak, but intellectually he excelled and developed a reputation as a brilliant young thinker.

While Bissell was at Yale, the stock market crashed in 1929, and the Depression had a profound impact on him. "It is difficult to convey the severity of the Great Depression and the sense of hopelessness it induced . . . It was a feeling that almost everyone shared in the early 1930s— that the United States was on the verge of a kind of collapse." Watching Roosevelt step into the breach, Bissell cast off his Republican heritage and came to believe strongly in the "ability of an activist good government to achieve positive ends." He chose economics as his postgraduate degree. He later became one of the most popular teachers at Yale, the first at that university to teach a course on Keynesian economics. Students included Eugene and Walt Rostow and McGeorge and William Bundy.

In the spring of 1941, Bissell left the ivory tower of academia for what he anticipated would be a brief stint in government, as an economist at the Commerce Department. When Pearl Harbor came, he was recruited to join the Combined Shipping Adjustment Board. Bissell's job was to allocate all of the ships and vessels in the United States to various civilian and military programs. Without computers, with only one person from Census to help him, Bissell developed a system using note cards to track the position of every ship in the U.S. fleet. He also developed a formula for predicting when a ship in a given convoy would be back in the United States, repaired and ready to be reloaded. It was a job of tremendous importance. "I was the American merchant shipping planner," he later said. His system was crude, but it was also ingenious and highly accurate: "I could predict three months in advance with a five percent margin of error. No one else could do this."

Bissell had become one of the generals in the logistical war that helped the Allies win the larger war.

Harry Truman was famously skeptical about economists. What I would like is a one-armed economist, he said, because they keep saying on one hand, and then, on the other hand. An economist is someone with a Phi Beta Kappa pocket watch with no clock to tell the time, he once quipped. But if the United States was aiming to right Western Europe's economic condition, the services of a practical and rigorous economic mind were essential to the enterprise. To Harriman, he was "one of the most outstanding economists I've ever known." Overseeing the Lend-Lease effort from London during the war, Harriman came to know Bissell. When the war was over, Bissell had returned to a comfortable post teaching economics at the Massachusetts Institute of Technology. Harriman had not forgotten about him, though. Bissell agreed to leave the comforts of Cambridge for Washington. For the Keynesian who had a passionate belief in practical and judicious government engagement in economic problems, the Marshall Plan was a siren song.

Arriving in Washington that September, Bissell brought together a few former colleagues from the Shipping Administration Board and from Yale and began analyzing the Paris Report, documentation and statistics. Meanwhile, Harriman was focused on the rather delicate endeavor of achieving agreement among nineteen eminent leaders with varying perspectives. Debates could be heated. Some members were aghast at the sheer volume of aid being recommended. The most contentious point was the capacity of the U.S. economy to handle the demands of the aid program. With international oil supplies unstable, some committee members expressed concern about sending Europe valuable oil shipments. The "hottest fight" occurred over the availability of crude steel. Harriman knew not to instruct committee members. Rather, he sought to convince and assuage. "I was the Chairman and tried to keep people's nerves down . . . there were some people opposed to it," Harriman said. The Marshall Plan was "fantastic to them."

Some members, like George Meany, secretary-treasurer of the American Federation of Labor, were cantankerous, but Meany never really attended the sessions and did not prove troublesome. Others like Randolph Burgess, vice chairman of National City Bank, dissented from the committee's approach to dealing with monetary policy. Richard "Red" Deupree, the president of Procter & Gamble, was conservative and "plainly dissatisfied with the Committee's direction." In contrast, Robert La Follette Jr., the former Republican senator and Vandenberg's pick, emerged as one of the most supportive and productive members. Another surprise was industrialist

Paul Hoffman, president of the Studebaker Corporation and a Republican. Hoffman's finely honed people skills won him a position as one of the key "mediators" amidst debates. Hoffman believed strongly in the need for large-scale foreign aid. In fact, at the committee's final meeting in early November, Hoffman delivered an extemporaneous speech justifying the Marshall Plan that so "stirred" the committee members that they all rose to their feet in applause.

Bissell had also been working tirelessly, employing his immense technical abilities to craft the report that was to outline the U.S. strategy for European recovery. Moved by Hoffman's eloquent speech, Bissell convinced him to commit his words to paper, and as a final touch, Bissell included them, almost verbatim, as the opening remarks in the report. Beginning with Hoffman's line, very much echoing Marshall's Harvard speech, "Only the Europeans can save Europe," Bissell's report touched on all of the key facets under consideration. The objective of the Marshall Plan was not to provide relief; rather, it was to bring Europe to self-sustainability "a spark which can fire the engine." The report took the opportunity to clear up misapprehensions. The Soviets claimed, for example, that the United States needed to export or give away output to ensure its own prosperity. The notion was widely held in the U.S. but "nonsense," the report explained. In fact, with inflation and shortage the paramount concern, the program would require costly sacrifice that threatened to endanger the U.S. economy in the near term.

The United States had three "vital interests" in European recovery: humanitarian, economic and political. The third "overshadows" the others, the report made clear, because the Marshall Plan was fundamentally "an investment in the continued survival of a world economically stabilized and peacefully conducted," in which democratic principles, individual liberty and freedom of religion could continue and prosper. Weighing in on what would be one of the focal points of congressional deliberations, the report recommended a new, independent agency to administer the Marshall Plan. The Plan would demand intense national sacrifice and perhaps even reversion to wartime economic controls. The cost estimate: between $12 billion and $17 billion for the entire program.

In early November, Vandenberg suggested to Harriman and Bissell that, with the special session coming up in mid-November, the time was ripe to conclude the committee's work and to release the report. It was 4 A.M. on November 7 when Bissell put the final touches on the report and sent it to the printer. Hours later, Bissell shipped off a copy to the White House and at 10 A.M. sent off scores of copies to the press. Officially titled, "A Report on

European Recovery and American Aid," it contained lucid recommendations and, three inches thick, was backed up with a dizzying amount of analysis. "How he did it, I still don't know. On the technical side, Dick Bissell was the great figure," Paul Hoffman said.

If the committee leaned heavily on Bissell's technical contribution, the report's reception also profited from Averell Harriman's tactical savvy. Before the release of the report, committee members had all read the particular sections on which they had worked. But with Vandenberg pressuring Harriman to release it, there was no time for all of the nineteen committee members to read the entire report.

Harriman decided to append all nineteen of their names anyway. He called each and said, "We're going to issue this report. You haven't had a chance to read it, but each one of you has agreed to your segment of it." Harriman said that "if there is any aspect that any member does not approve when he reads it, he can make a minority objection." It was a great gamble. If committee members came forward in opposition, it would be a debacle and would have discredited the committee's findings.

When Arthur Vandenberg received the bulky report he couldn't imagine how he could read the whole thing in one weekend. After having read what he could, he cabled Harriman from his home in Michigan: "Only a Hollywood press agent could do justice to it." Felix Belair of the *New York Times* called it "exhaustive and eloquent." Similar acclaim poured forth from the vast majority of the press.

Harriman also had one eye on European reaction. The leading editorial in the *Times* of London said that it was now clear that the Marshall Plan would require real sacrifice from the American people and that "there is no disposition in Europe to look a gift horse in the mouth." Against the chorus of approval, none of the committee members came forward to object. Harriman's gambit had paid off, a feat of considerable legerdemain.

The report was a public relations boon. "It's all right," Vandenberg would say, brandishing a copy, "these are good people," who had endorsed the report and the Plan. The report had great traction with moderate Republicans and the public throughout congressional hearings in the months to follow. It was even more useful for its lucid recommendations and its weighty analysis. The report was of "monumental importance," recalled Hoffman.

IN THE EARLY WINTER OF 1947, remarkable happenings competed for Americans' attention. Humphrey Bogart and Lauren Bacall were in Washington protesting the House Un-American Activities Committee's investigation of suspected Communists in Hollywood. On Broadway, a thirty-three-year-old Southern playwright named Tennessee Williams looked on as the actors, including Marlon Brando, received a dozen curtain calls at opening night of his new play, *A Streetcar Named Desire*. A few blocks away, at Madison Square Garden, New Yorkers watched Joe Louis keep his crown in an epic fifteen-round battle with Jersey Joe Walcott. Weeks earlier, across the country, in Muroc, California, a twenty-four-year-old test pilot named Chuck Yeager had piloted a Bell X-1 to new speeds, becoming the first man to pierce the sound barrier.

By that winter, as well, the various efforts to examine and publicize the Marshall Plan were beginning to capture the attention of the American public. The Herter Committee, the Harriman Committee, the Committee for the Marshall Plan and officials at the State Department, though operating separately, had helped to generate an aggregate buzz. In mid-September, less than half (49 percent) of Americans had heard of the Marshall Plan. Of those who had heard of it, only one in five could define it correctly. In mid-November, roughly two-thirds—64 percent—of Americans had heard of the Plan; 56 percent had a favorable impression and 17 percent had an unfavorable impression. All of the committees, all of the work, had a resounding impact on public awareness and support.

Still, with congressional debate not yet begun, opponents of the Plan had not had a chance to make their case. When reporter William White barnstormed the country, visiting twenty-two states that fall, he noticed "a curious paradox." Regional leaders, White reported, were paying public lip service to the Plan, but privately they were skeptical or even opposed it. Because of the powerful tide of establishment support and because they did not wish to be viewed as insensitive to Europe's suffering, they chose not to express their disapproval. But many, White found, thought of the Plan as "a vast Christmas package bearing across its side a caption reading $20 billion." Wrote White in early November: "Latent hostility to the Marshall Plan is a very real fact over the country . . . Frontal attacks are neither heavy nor frequent, but there is a powerful and damaging guerilla action along the flanks . . . it is far more bitter than what would normally be considered the main field of battle."

On November 17, President Truman addressed the first special session of Congress convened since Roosevelt had summoned the 76th Congress in 1939 when war broke out in Europe. As the president read his five-thousand-word address, the chamber sat in "solemn silence." After several minutes, Truman exclaimed that the United States had achieved great power, and now it must assume great responsibility. The chamber duly applauded. "The future of free nations in Europe hangs in the balance," Truman exclaimed, urging Congress to pass interim aid and then the long-term program for European recovery. At the same time, to deal with inflation and the grave concern about prices, Truman urged consumer rationing, wage controls and other price controls. To aid Europe at its time of need, and serve the country's own long-term interests, the American people would have to sacrifice.

By late November and early December, it was becoming increasingly probable that the Marshall Plan would pass Congress—in some form. A week after the president's address, Robert Albright wrote in the *Washington Post*, "A Marshall Plan authorization in some form or other already appears as good as passed." But the doubts, "and they are big ones, are what will happen to the design in the way of legislative tinkering" when the Plan appeared before Congress. The all-important matters of how much would be appropriated, what administrative form it would take and what provisions would be attached—the central elements of the Plan—were all very much in question. With a presidential election less than one year away, in the wake of the special session and the president's call for European aid, "the dull fires of partisan strife" were set "smoldering again on Capitol Hill."

A week before hearings began on interim aid, Senator Robert Taft of Ohio, a Republican leader and presidential candidate, leveled a series of stinging attacks on the Truman administration's foreign aid program. Speaking to the Ohio Society, Taft declared: "The Marshall Plan is, of course, inflationary and means that prices will be higher than they otherwise would be," striking at Americans' most sensitive nerve. It would involve a huge tax burden, he said. Taft recited the litany of postwar aid and loans the United States had already disbursed. Each had failed in its turn, he said, and cost American taxpayers dearly.

Taft's assays had a heavy political overtone: "The Administration can't get away from the New Deal principle that Government spending is a good thing in itself." Attempting to spin the campaign to generate public support for the Plan into a shadowy enterprise, Taft said: "We have seen in the past three months the development of carefully planned propaganda for the Marshall Plan, stimulated by the State Department, by widespread publicity and by secret meetings of influential people in Washington." At its best, though, Taft's speech served the public debate well, putting forward important and eminently fair questions: "How far shall we make a present to other peoples of the fruits of our labors? Do the advantages to be gained in foreign policy outweigh the disadvantages at home? Let us have all the facts and debate them fully."

When Congress opened the hearings on interim aid, the criticisms put forward in Taft's speech served as some of the major lines of attack that would greet the procession of high-profile officials and experts who were to testify before the Senate and the House that November. Harriman and Acheson testified and, with Marshall in London, Lovett became the key administration figure, appearing before Congress almost daily throughout November. The administration framed the debate in terms of the dire need for near-term aid. It was simple: France and Italy might not make it through the winter without such aid. They were in danger of falling to Communism. Ambassador Caffrey's cables from France painted an entropic picture of the political situation and stated that interim aid was France's only hope. A CIA analysis averred, "If France is lost, Europe is lost."

For those opposed to interim aid, it was a hard case to pierce. Critics used the hearings to introduce criticism about the larger, longer-term Marshall Plan. Weeks earlier, the Bureau of the Budget released a report that estimated that the United States had spent $16.25 billion on postwar relief and aid to date. Senator Harry Byrd of Virginia put the figure at $19 billion, and many congressmen argued that if all that aid had not helped Europe, further aid would be just as ineffective and profligate. Some critics evinced a bleak fatalism about Western Europe's chances for survival and an apparent willingness to cede the region to Soviet control. The *New York Times* reported: "Why, it is being asked, if Europe is in danger of being overrun by Communist Russia should this country attempt to rebuild Western European industry when the effort would redound to Russia's benefit?" A good number of Republicans wanted to know why the administration was not doing anything to aid China, also under Communist peril. Others worried about the prospects of excessive U.S. intervention in the affairs of sovereign foreign nations and about the consequences of playing into Soviet propaganda.

Some of the lines of attack were difficult for Lovett to maneuver around. Senator Styles Bridges of New Hampshire asked Lovett what the administration would do if a country receiving aid were to fall under Communist control. He could not answer for Marshall, Lovett said, but his own view was that aid should stop immediately. Alluding to past foreign aid efforts, Wisconsin Republican Senator Alexander Wiley suggested that the U.S. had been "taken for a ride," and he wanted to know what the United States would get for its efforts. "I want to know if any effort has been made to obtain strategic bases or materials in return for our generosity. That doesn't mean we are being hard-hearted but it does mean we are through being 'Uncle Sap.'" Representative Leslie C. Arends, a Republican from Illinois, suggested a referendum in which Americans could answer whether they would accept 10 percent increases in their cost of living and a 10 percent increase in their withholding tax to finance the Marshall Plan.

The attacks were plentiful, politically adroit and in many cases not unfair. It was one thing for congressmen to punch holes in the administration's plans, though, and quite another to fail to provide interim aid to Europe at a time of acute vulnerability. The attacks were so much sword sharpening. If the contours of the debate to follow were coming into focus, so were the positions of the key players. As he had hoped, Marshall had no more effective ally than the senator from Michigan across the political aisle, Arthur Vandenberg. Van implored his colleagues to support expeditious passage of interim aid to stymie the Communist "wrecking crews" hard at work attempting to dash Western Europe's hopes for recovery.

During the debate Vandenberg wrote home to his wife that he was not well. He had intense discomfort sitting through long hearings, even getting up and down the speaker's dais. The occasional "sweat, swim and rub," and a palliative dose of lobster Newberg at the Mayflower Hotel, helped him through. Despite physical impairment, Vandenberg was extremely effective. In the Senate, in fact, the Democrats were often scarce, recessing to the upper chambers to sit and watch Vandenberg toe the administration's line with dissenting Republicans. On one occasion, wrote James Reston, in a piece entitled, "Democrats Let Van Carry Load on Aid Debate," there were all of two Democrats on the Senate floor, as Republicans fired away at Vandenberg. "If Mr. Vandenberg should break away from the Administration on any fundamental point, the Senator's opinion and not the President's might very well be decisive," concluded Reston.

Despite the partisan atmosphere and the barrage of attacks, Vandenberg managed to steer interim aid through the Senate with 83 for and only 6 against. It was a startling achievement. A highly contentious debate in the House opened on December 3, but the Senate vote sent a loud signal to France and Italy that near-term relief was on the way and that longer-term aid was increasingly probable. Privately, though, Vandenberg was less than sanguine about what was to come. In a letter back home, he wrote, "If the resistance showing up to the little short-range European relief bill . . . is any criterion, our friend Marshall is certainly going to have a helluva time down there on the Hill when he gets around to his long-range plan . . . Politics is heavy in the air." As the debate continued, Vandenberg phoned Lovett: the administration was safe on interim aid, he said, but "we're headed for the storm cellar on the Marshall Plan."

In France and Italy during early December, Communist sabotage was nearing outright insurrection and reaching its bloody climax. The strikes and turbulence had taken an extraordinary toll on France. French coal production declined by 2 million tons, auto production went down 50 percent and the country lost an estimated $16 million per day. Workers grew disconsolate at the cost to their country. France's largest Communist labor union split into Communist and non-Communist factions. On December 3, a group of Communist miners derailed the Lille-Paris line near Arras, dislodging twenty-five meters of track. They had thought that the train would be carrying riot police. Misinformed, they killed sixteen innocent people and injured another thirty seriously. The next afternoon when news reached Paris, the streets were virtually empty and armed police occupied every corner, ready for insurrection. No violence erupted, though, and when the carnage, which had been shot on film, was viewed in film houses around the country in the subsequent days, it helped to put an end to the strikes, the violence and the prospects of civil war.

The Communists had overplayed their hand. They were eviscerating France's economy, sowing instability and killing innocent people. The non-Communists, in contrast, offered a vision of recovery, of stability and, with interim aid on the way, near-term tangible relief. The Communist campaign lost momentum and a good deal of support. When the French Communist campaign fizzled, a story in *Life* magazine noted the Communist reaction: the "Reds cried, 'Watch Italy.'" After a gruesome autumnal campaign, the Italian Communists took a big gamble and called for a general strike in Rome in December. When the time came, the people of Rome did not participate. It was a humiliating failure.

The Italian Communist movement was stronger than the one in France, though. Secretly, the United States armed the Italian government and agreed that, should revolution break out, the U.S. would intervene against the Communists. U.S. Ambassador James Dunn continued to worry about the strength of the Italian Communists, who, more violent than their comrades in France, could launch a revolution any day. But as in France, Italy's Communists had overreached. The more they sought to sabotage economic recovery, the more legitimacy they lost with ther fellow Italians. One of the key elements in the equation, in both countries, was that an alternate path—a path to recovery—was on offer.

In Le Havre, France, the dockworkers returned to work just in time to unload the first shipments from the Friendship Train. The ports were decorated with American and French flags, and U.S. Ambassador Jefferson Caffrey told the crowd of several hundred that this was a gesture of generosity not from the government but from the people of the United States. Unloading the shipments etched with inscriptions reading "Friendship—Something to eat for our friends from the United States," the dockworkers—who only a week earlier had been on strike against American imperialism and the Marshall Plan—offered to work for free. The first shipments contained fifteen hundred tons of food, and filled ten trains that left immediately for regional centers of France. Seven thousand orphans and schoolchildren were on hand at the Hotel de Ville in Paris when the first shipments arrived. At the same time, liners had left Brooklyn and other ports on the East Coast for Italy's cities and towns.

On December 15, Congress passed legislation authorizing $522 million, almost $80 million less than Truman proposed, for interim aid for France, Italy and Austria. To that, Congress added roughly $20 million in relief to China and elsewhere in Asia. That same day at 10 A.M., congressional leaders from both parties (Taft was not invited) went to the White House to discuss the Marshall Plan.

On December 19, the White House submitted to Congress "A Program for the United States Support for European Recovery." It was officially titled The European Recovery Program, or ERP, but better known as the Marshall Plan. Already it was "the subject of more study, discussion and controversy than almost any other proposal in recent history," one journalist wrote. It had also already "set in motion the most comprehensive movement toward European economic integration in modern history." The president attached a nine-thousand word message to the legislation. "Our deepest concern with European recovery," the note read, "is that it is essential to the maintenance of the civilization in which the American way of life is rooted."

The message was attached to a fifty-thousand-word piece of legislation outlining the Plan. Truman requested $6.8 billion for the fifteen months from April 1948, at which point interim aid would run out, to June 1949, then $10.2 billion from July 1949 to June 30, 1952, for a total of $17 billion for a period of four years and three months. The Plan would also create an agency to administer the program. It would demand considerable sacrifice from the American people in a time of shortage and economic anxiety. The legislation also addressed U.S. objectives. First and foremost was U.S. security: "If Europe fails to recover . . . [that] turn of events would constitute a shattering blow to peace and stability in the world. It might compel us to modify our own economic system and to forgo, for the sake of our own security, the enjoyment of many of our freedoms and privileges." It was received on Capitol Hill—as indeed it was intended—foremost as a measure to prevent Communist, and thereby Soviet, expansion in Western Europe.

The Soviet Union likened it to Hitler and Goering's four-year plan, an effort to reignite the German economy and the capitalist, imperialist war-making capacity. "The essence of the two plans is the same—war," announced state-controlled Moscow Radio. "The Marshall Plan and American billions are to be used to transform Western Germany into an arsenal of American expansion."

That Christmas Eve, about ten thousand Washingtonians braved a freezing December evening to watch President Truman preside over the twenty-fifth anniversary of the White House tree lighting. The president spoke of desperation in Europe: "At this point in the world's history, the words of St. Paul have greater significance than ever before." He quoted Paul: "And now abideth faith, hope, charity, these three, but the greatest of these is charity." He said that he knew the "great heart of the American people" would rise to meet the challenge.

Chapter Seven

PUTTING IT OVER

A T MIDDAY ON JANUARY 7, 1948, President Harry Truman made his way to the podium in the House of Representatives Chamber at the U.S. Capitol to deliver his State of the Union message to the 80th Congress and the American people. There was reason for optimism. In 1947, the U.S. economy had produced what *Fortune* magazine called "the greatest productive record in the peacetime history of this or any other nation." The political violence in France and Italy had settled, the Marshall Plan had placed the Soviet Union on the defensive and, according to George Kennan, the Communist danger in Western Europe was on the wane. Truman was about to deliver a bold vision for the upcoming year, including national health insurance, an almost doubling of the minimum wage, massive increases in housing and education for the poor.

However, 1948 was an election year. The Republicans had been out of the White House for almost sixteen years. Despite the economy's unprecedented production, prices continued to soar. In early January, 25 percent of Americans still identified inflation and a danger of depression as the most important problems facing America; 19 percent identified the Marshall Plan and only 7 percent identified relations with Russia as the most important. Still, Truman chose to proceed not only with a massive program of domestic expenditure but an unprecedented program of foreign aid. As Truman read his address, one could almost hear the sharpening of political axes. Truman was vulnerable. Republicans had demolished the Democrats in the midterm election of 1946 and Truman's popularity was low. He was still looked upon as a diminutive and unworthy president. Republicans smelled blood in the water. Republican Senate Majority Leader Kenneth Wherry told reporter C. P. Trussell that Republicans would listen with an open mind to the president's address. "Then," said Wherry, "the lid will be off."

Around 1:30 P.M. that day, just before Truman began his address, the secretary of state had attempted to slip unobtrusively into a side seat in the chamber. Fellow Cabinet members noticed, though, and rushed over to shake his hand. A buzz rippled through the chamber, and members of Congress rose to their feet in a clamoring ovation. Marshall, blushing, took his seat.

Marshall did not want to show up his commander in chief, but in early 1948 it was a tactical feat the old Army general could not manage. In a thirty-two-page document titled "The Politics of 1948," a Washington lawyer named James Rowe Jr. outlined some of the themes of the political year ahead for the president. "In times of crisis the American citizen tends to back up his President. And on the issue of policy toward Russia, President Truman is comparatively invulnerable to attack because of his brilliant appointment of General Marshall." The week of the State of the Union address, Marshall appeared on the cover of *Time* magazine, honored as Man of the Year. The honor—Marshall's second in four years—was because of his role in the Marshall Plan. In the war, the article said, Marshall had led the U.S. to military victory. In 1947, again, the world needed leadership. "One man," the article continued, "symbolized U.S. action. He was Secretary of State George Marshall."

The passage of the Marshall Plan was "the number one priority of the Truman administration's national security program," wrote Melvyn Leffler. Truman believed that the fate of Western civilization hung in the balance. As he sent the legislation to Congress, though, political currents ran strong. Wrote *Life* magazine: "Anything could happen—even to the Marshall Plan—in an election year."

THAT CHRISTMAS RECESS, while most of his colleagues went back home, Arthur Vandenberg remained in his Washington apartment carefully making lists of questions and objections likely to be raised in the ensuing debate. He was determined to be prepared for the fight. On New Year's Day, the Michigan senator called the governor of his home state to declare officially that he did not want to be the Republican nominee for president. To marshal as much political currency for the contest ahead, Vandenberg put aside his presidential ambitions.

Vandenberg took Congress's temperature before the hearings. Key Republicans did not want to be bound to an extended commitment. Some argued that it was not practice to bind one Congress to another; others who were inherently skeptical of the enterprise wanted only annual commitments, allowing them to clip the program in later years. Vandenberg's reading suggested that a four-year authorization would be feasible, but commitments and appropriations would have to be presented annually. After a few days Lovett agreed. Some in the media criticized the administration for caving and showing a weak hand to Congress even before hearings had begun. Nevertheless, Vandenberg and Lovett had preemptively removed a major obstacle.

Van's public expressions of support were no less important. The Plan was indispensable from "the standpoint of intelligent American self-interest," he announced. The senator trumpeted the work of the State Department and Nitze's team as "backed by more hard work and careful research than almost any other bill to come before Congress." In the weeks before the hearings, he summoned national leaders across the spectrum—government, business, academia, labor, media, civil society—to testify. "On an issue of this importance, nobody should be satisfied merely to state his views privately," Vandenberg announced. "If a man has special knowledge, we want to hear him, and if he does not offer his information or opinion we won't hesitate to subpoena him." It was to be a great "representative national debate."

ON JANUARY 8, 1948, George Marshall made his way past a line of senators and staffers, a phalanx of reporters and the cameramen's flashing bulbs to his seat in the marble caucus room at the head of the stairway in the Senate Office Building. He was the first witness before the Senate Foreign Relations Committee's hearings. In the year he had served as secretary, Marshall had been presented with crisis after crisis; he had traveled to the Soviet Union, Brazil and London for extended conferences and extensively throughout France and Germany. He had had little chance for rest, and by late autumn 1947, Dean Acheson remarked to Supreme Court Justice Felix Frankfurter on one of their daily morning walks that the general did not seem to bring his "full force into action," that he was "a four-engine bomber going on one engine." In late December and early January, Marshall had managed a fortnight of rest at his retreat in North Carolina.

As the hearings opened, James Reston described Marshall as "looking even more relaxed and self-possessed" than he had a year earlier, evincing his legendary "quality of moral grandeur." Members of Congress had a plethora of issues and concerns. The two most pressing themes were the amount of aid requested and the setup of the agency that would administer the program. In the course of his testimony, Marshall addressed both.

Reading from his text, Marshall's delivery was "almost consciously dull."

His message, though, was forceful. On the first matter of the amount of aid, Marshall was unequivocal: "An inadequate program would involve a wastage of our resources with an ineffective result. Either undertake to meet the requirements of the problem or don't undertake it at all." The sum proposed was not "an asking figure" in a negotiation, Marshall said, it was a "realistic appraisal." On the matter of the Plan's administration, Marshall proposed that the new agency fold under the control of the State Department. European recovery was also foreign policy. The administrator needed to run the former but needed direction on the latter. There could not be "2 Secretaries of State," Marshall said. He was direct, adamant and aggressive. In closing his 5,500-word message, Marshall looked up from his text, scanned the committee members and closed his prepared remarks with conviction: "There is no doubt in my mind that if we decide to do this thing we can do it successfully."

Fielding questions following his remarks, Marshall was patient and courteous. He answered questions "Yes, sir" and "No, sir." He was flanked by Ambassador Lewis Douglas and Robert Lovett, experienced and respected businessmen. At times, Lovett would hold up a bulky binder filled with analyses, as if to stress to the senators all the work and thought that had gone into the Plan. When Marshall was interrupted in an answer to a senator's question, he said nothing. When that senator interrupted him for a second time, he flashed a glare. The senator silenced, Marshall continued.

Marshall was in command, but the war was over and so was the postwar honeymoon. Marshall was now dealing with a Congress intent on asserting itself. Some of the senators remarked that they did not appreciate Marshall's "All or nothing" approach. The constitution endowed Congress with discretion and oversight over government expenditures, and they would not be instructed on that function. Georgia Senator Walter George accused Marshall of employing "techniques of propaganda."

On the matter of the new agency's administration, several senators expressed a preference that it be independent of the State Department. Vandenberg himself felt it critical that the agency be run by people with business acumen and experience, as a results-oriented and pragmatic business enterprise. To attract the right people and achieve the best results, the agency and the administrator running it needed autonomy. In addition, if the agency was under State Department control Congress would have less direct oversight. Vandenberg said that the program would fail unless the agency was animated by "a new element of business responsibility."

Testifying a few days later, this time before the House Foreign Affairs Committee, Marshall did not give an inch. He addressed America's economic and business interests: "It is idle," he said, "to think that a Europe left to its own efforts . . . would remain open to American business in the same way that we have known it in the past." He went on to insist that the amount of aid requested was not based on "light or sentimental grounds but on the highest considerations of national interest which surely included an enduring peace and freedom for the individual." If the program was not fully funded, Marshall predicted "economic distress so intense, social discontent so violent, political confusion so widespread, and hope of the future so shattered," that "the vacuum which the war created in Western Europe will be filled by the forces of which wars are made." If the United States did not fill the breach, the region's political leadership would be "dictated by the Soviet Union." The United States would be imperiled, and, as a result, Marshall would be compelled to push for a comparable, or even greater, increase in military spending.

After the war, the government had been able to meet popular demands to scale down military costs, in large part because the United States was the only power with the atomic bomb. If the U.S. had not had a monopoly on the atomic bomb, conventional military spending would almost certainly have been much higher. With a frugal, aid-averse Congress, it would have been much harder for the administration to win support for its program for European recovery. It is one of the Marshall Plan's paradoxes: one of the United States' most destructive creations helped to underwrite one of its most beneficent.

Heeding Vandenberg's call, Marshall agreed that the program must be "administered in a business-like way," but as the keystone of America's foreign policy it ought to be under control of the State Department. Marshall was criticized in the press for holding firm to his line. Talk of a Republican Marshall Plan began swirling around Washington. If Marshall was not willing to compromise, Republicans would simply start from scratch and place their own political stamp on the initiative. Whether Marshall had overreached or preempted the sort of watering down that could cripple the program was not yet clear.

If, months earlier, Marshall had been going on one engine, as Acheson had said, the general was now refueled and firing on all cylinders. Most of his testimony complete, he would spend much of the next several months traveling the country, targeting pockets of resistance, taking the fight to the American people. He would have his work cut out for him. As testimony began, Francis Wilcox, chief of staff of the Senate Foreign Relations Committee, believed that the Plan's passage, as presented, would take nothing short of "a political miracle."

• • •

THAT JANUARY AND early February a cavalcade of government officials—leaders from industry and labor, university professors and editors from leading national publications, women's clubs, church groups, veterans' groups and plain citizens—streamed into the large marble caucus room and came before Vandenberg and the Foreign Relations Committee. "It was perhaps the most comprehensive public hearing on a foreign policy question ever undertaken," wrote a Vandenberg aide.

Bernard Baruch told Vandenberg's Committee: "Yours is one of the most momentous decisions in the history of America, indeed of the world." Security was the main objective for Baruch, and the Marshall Plan was to be "a new adventure in peace." Two days later, Averell Harriman stressed what was clearly emerging for the leading champions of the Plan as the primary aim for the program: "building a stable peace." "I believe that this program is one of the most far-reaching undertakings for peace and for human progress ever undertaken by this or any other country. It is noble in concept but is based on considerations of our own self-interest and, in my opinion, of our own self-preservation." As a prominent financier and sitting secretary of commerce, Harriman also highlighted what was emerging as the champions' second major aim for the Plan, the promotion of American economic interests and stability.

Dean Acheson had been traveling the country stumping for the Marshall Plan. Back in Washington to testify, Acheson implored Congress to meet the administration's request for funds. Much analysis and deliberation, on both sides of the Atlantic, had gone into that request. Second-guessing that work would amount to a "statistician's paradise," and decreasing that amount by several billion dollars would change the whole composition of the program, possibly meaning the difference between relief and self-sustaining recovery. Rankled by a line of questioning from one skeptical member of Congress, Acheson chided, "If you didn't talk so much and listened more, I think you would understand better what this is all about."

Some of the Plan's advocates were counting on Soviet truculence to boost support for the Plan. Stalin did not disappoint them. In late January, the British Foreign Office confirmed the authentication of the "M Protocol." The Soviet document summoned German workers and Communist sympathizers to engage in the same sort of sabotage and violence that had raged in France and Italy that past autumn. Though the violence had subdued in France and Italy, key U.S. officials expected more of the same in those two countries that upcoming spring. Now there was verifiable proof that the

Soviets were stoking the insurrectionary fires in the western zones of Germany. Increasingly, supporters of the Marshall Plan leaned on the Soviet threat, framing the Plan as the best means of meeting it.

As the testimony continued, the Plan's backers stressed another key objective. For aid to be effective, Europe would have to emerge from "the old atomized European economy into a coordinated, efficient, self-sustaining production and trading economy." In short, Congress wanted Western Europe's economies to integrate. Senator William Fulbright of Arkansas had even proposed a congressional amendment supporting European "political unification" a few months earlier. Vandenberg and others felt it would amount to too much interference in European sovereignty, and quashed it. But, as much as any matter under consideration, members of Congress agreed with Representative John Lodge of Connecticut, who argued that it would be a mistake simply to "put Humpty Dumpty together again." The vast majority of officials and experts who testified, as well as members of Congress, shared John Foster Dulles's conviction that the "moment was ripe for a really creative act in Europe." Promoting trade, cooperating to achieve stable monetary and fiscal policies and other methods of coordination and integration were keys to Europe's lasting recovery. Meaningful structural economic reform would differentiate the Marshall Plan from "giveaways" and the ineffectual aid programs of the past.

While the procession of witnesses scuttled in and out of the Senate and House, and members of Congress debated the merits and risks of the Plan, Arthur Vandenberg moved about the chambers and back rooms of the Senate, attempting to strike deals on key sticking points. As a Republican from the Midwest, and as an isolationist-cum-internationalist, Vandenberg knew the various views and perspectives jostling for influence. He declared his office open to anyone who had reservations. His modus operandi was to listen, to express understanding with his interlocutor's concerns. He endeavored to convince when possible and to broker when argument failed. He quashed support for initiation of "a Republican Marshall Plan." He did his best to quell a growing clamor among Republicans to lower the figure of aid requested.

On what he considered "the biggest single conundrum," that is, "finding a satisfactory administrative formula" for the agency that would administer the Plan, Vandenberg had taken the initiative of commissioning a report from the nonpartisan Brookings Institution. When he received the report in late January, Van riffled through it in twenty minutes before releasing it to the press. Trumpeting the report's recommendation, Vandenberg convinced Marshall and Lovett to cede State Department control of the agency. Instead, it would be autonomous, an independent agency that could attract a world-class administrator and operate free of White House or State Department control. When Marshall agreed, Vandenberg delivered a critical concession to his Republican brethren and fueled momentum behind the Plan.

There was only one other member of Congress with a comparable degree of standing to Vandenberg. That was Republican Senator Robert Alphonso Taft. Born into privilege and high expectations in Cincinnati, Ohio, Taft hailed from one of the most prominent political families in America. His grandfather, Alphonso, was secretary of war and attorney general. And his father, William Howard Taft, was the only man to serve both as Chief Justice of the Supreme Court and United States president. Finishing at the head of his class both at Yale and Harvard Law School, Taft was known for wielding a formidable and logical mind in the cause of conservative Midwestern politics. Taft's wife, Martha, was a popular Washington personality. Warm, engaging and humorous, she had coined the phrase "to err is Truman." Robert Taft was principled, persistent and had all the political ambition that his lineage suggested. Despite his presidential ambitions, Taft had none of the social attributes that one might expect of a candidate for that office. He was brusque, occasionally tart; "aloof to the point of coldness" is how one historian described him. In his trademark rimless spectacles and wearing his hat at dead center, Taft was much more comfortable arguing on the Senate floor, drafting legislation or formulating political strategy than in a social atmosphere. "Bob is not austere," said Martha, "he's just compartmentalized."

A fiscal conservative to the core, Taft wanted to do away with the massive expenditures ushered in with Roosevelt's New Deal. He wanted to tighten the budget, lower taxes and pare back foreign commitments. As congressional debate on the Marshall Plan raged, inflation and prices continued their steep climb. Since late September, prices for key commodities had increased 13 percent. Studebaker President Paul Hoffman described it as "one of the three greatest inflations in our history." Hoffman and Truman predicted "an economic crash" and "a bust," respectively, unless the alarming increase in prices was arrested. America's concern about inflation would provide Taft with powerful ammunition in his case against the Marshall Plan, as presented. It also happened that Taft was running for president.

Taft was fundamentally conservative when it came to foreign aid and its efficacy. He believed that America was better served fortifying its own economic position. He believed that the Plan's champions overestimated the effect of U.S. dollars in foreign countries. To Taft the Marshall Plan was a giant "European TVA," a vast Rooseveltian "giveaway program." "In the long run no nation can live on the bounty of another nation," he said. Given all the aid already meted out, and Europe's continued ills, Taft believed history was on his side.

Taft made it clear that he would support some well-directed aid in order to do what America could to halt the spread of Communism. But he wanted to cut the amount of aid way down. And he wanted to limit America's commitment to one year. For opponents of the Plan, Taft was a brilliant and incisive critic. For champions, his opposition was further proof that "he has the best mind in Washington," as State Department official Paul Porter said of him, "until he makes it up." Will Clayton, who had weathered Taft's attacks on Bretton Woods and GATT, had a different way of expressing the same point: "Taft always got the details, but he usually missed the big picture of what we were trying to accomplish."

Taft did not stand alone in opposition. Senator Bourke B. Hickenlooper of Iowa suggested that the same work and analysis that Vandenberg had lauded was so much "sheer guesswork." The Plan, in his view, was "a complete donation program from top to bottom." Writing from his vacation home in Florida, former President Herbert Hoover recommended that the $17 billion Plan be limited to a $4 billion, fifteen-month commitment. More and more, Republicans echoed the views of Senator Styles Bridges, who opposed the State Department's "Europe first" orientation and strategy. More focus was needed in China and Asia, Bridges argued, foreshadowing debates still to come.

Senator Homer Capehart, a Republican from Indiana, charged that the Marshall Plan was in effect "state socialism." A Republican congressman from Ohio, Frederick Smith, went further, calling it "outright communism." Capehart supported aid but wanted it all handled by the private sector. Many Republican members of Congress hewed the line expressed by Representative Ralph Gwinn of New York, when he pointed to all the aid doled out to Eastern Europe, which was now Communist. At best, Gwinn argued, the Marshall Plan would entrench the socialist element and squander American dollars. At worst, Western Europe would go the way of Eastern Europe, in which event the Marshall Plan would constitute nothing more than a wildly errant transfer of funds to the Soviet Union and a new set of Communist satellites.

Businessmen came forward to prophesy "severe shortages" in essential commodities, goods and equipment that would drive up inflation and impair the U.S. economy. "If we now add to the fantastic cost of government at home, huge sums that will be wasted through inefficient spending abroad, we can expect only one outcome," testified Ernest Weir, chairman of the National Steel Corporation: "that will be depression in the United States more serious and far-reaching than anything we have ever experienced." Other businessmen—and members of Congress—were concerned that the United States was simply building up Europe to compete with America. It would cost U.S. firms contracts and profits and it would cost the U.S. work-force jobs. Henry Hazlitt, the staunch conservative editor of *Newsweek*, joined Weir in opposition, but for a different reason. Europe's socialist economic systems were the source of its economic maladies, and without unfettered private enterprise American aid would simply subsidize Europe's flawed economic systems and prolong their demise.

Opposition ran the political and ideological spectrum. Former vice president and Progressive candidate for president Henry Wallace called it "the martial plan," and opposed it on the grounds that it was widening the rift with the Soviet Union and chances for peace. Wallace supported a $50 billion aid program administered by the United Nations and meted out to the countries attacked by Germany, which would include the Soviet Union. A small cohort of members of Congress thought similarly.

Some of the assays were barbed, as when Representative Roy Woodruff, a Republican from Michigan, admonished: "There is something so abnormal, so self-annihilating, about a program that calls upon a single nation to take care of so many other nations . . . America had better look to her own future." There were lighter moments as well. When the House took up fuel shortages in New England and the matter of what to do about them, John Rankin, a Democrat from Mississippi, had a suggestion: "Secede from the Union and get in under the Marshall Plan . . . Then you can get all the fuel you need and won't have to pay for it." The chamber erupted in laughter. For good measure, he added, "I promise you now that if you decide to take such a step we Confederates will not whip you back into the Union again—at least until the weather warms up."

Mostly, though, opponents hewed Taft's line. There were grave economic concerns in the United States. American taxpayers had sacrificed for many years now. Billions in foreign aid had failed to deliver Europe from economic prostration. There was no guarantee it would work this time. Intense political currents added charges of intensity to the opposition. In the first two months of congressional debate, more members of Congress supported the Marshall Plan than were against it. But Taft and others sought, at every turn, to clip the amount of aid and to narrow the scope of commitment on offer to Europe. The Marshall Plan was in jeopardy of dilution to a degree that might have rendered it ineffectual.

• • •

A FEW DAYS AFTER George Marshall completed his testimony before the House Foreign Affairs Committee, he set off for Pittsburgh to speak to the local chamber of commerce. It was the opening salvo in an ambitious campaign. Marshall did not enjoy stumping or appearing before large crowds. Yet in the months to follow, he traveled thousands of miles per week, venturing into hostile territory and weathering enemy fire. "Oh, Lord," he said recalling his efforts that winter: "I traveled all over the country . . . I worked on that as hard as though I was running for the Senate or the presidency."

Pittsburgh was near Marshall's boyhood home. He had friends and admirers there and was greeted congenially. Still, on the matter of European recovery, he found "strong opposition" from the crowd of businessmen. He framed the matter in business terms: would we make a capital investment that was within our means to bring long-term gains, or would we spend abundantly for immediate wants in the hope that the day of reckoning could be postponed? In Atlanta, the following week, Marshall spoke to cotton and tobacco farmers before the National Cotton Council. They were concerned that shipments to Europe would deprive them of supplies and equipment. Appealing to their self-interest, Marshall spoke of what they stood to gain from European prosperity and trade. Europe needed clothing and workers needed tobacco as an incentive to work, and the Marshall Plan would finance those expenditures. Marshall also traveled to New York, Philadelphia and elsewhere in the East.

In late January, the general took the fight to the Midwest, the region where opposition to the Plan was strongest. Marshall's nemesis, Bert McCormick of the *Chicago Tribune*, had been pummeling the Plan and its internationalist designs. Vandenberg offered Marshall words of encouragement: "You need to belittle this," he said. Remember, "I have to sit up and be called a Benedict Arnold." As he was flying to address the National Farm Institute in Des Moines, Iowa, a storm enveloped Marshall's plane, forcing him down in Knoxville, Tennessee. That flight was the closest he ever came to losing his life, Marshall said later. Undeterred, he ordered staff in Tennessee to organize a wire hookup, and his comments were delivered on time via radio in Iowa. The American people face "the greatest decision in our history," he said, a decision that will set the course of history for a long time to come.

Marshall hit the Midwest hard. Men would listen, Marshall said, but they were slow to action. Women would mobilize. So he met with many women's groups. As his campaign progressed, Marshall became increasingly impassioned. Convinced of the Plan's necessity and concerned about its vulnerability in Congress, Marshall's tone became more urgent, his rhetoric more heated and his message more anti-Soviet. Marshall's campaign was producing its desired effect, quelling dissent and arousing enthusiasm for the Plan. "It was electric what happened, just electric," Marshall said describing the responses he was getting from audiences.

At the same time, other prominent Americans were also barnstorming the country. With the Plan's legislation before Congress, the Committee for the Marshall Plan had been ratcheting up its activities. Dean Acheson promoted the Plan as "the frontline of American security" to an association of 2,500 grocers in Atlantic City, New Jersey. Financiers, academics, civic leaders, labor leaders and others stumped the country at venues ranging from the Dayton Council on World Affairs to Sarah Lawrence College. Will Clayton also managed to take leave of his wife, Sue, hopping from St. Louis to New York to Washington, giving six speeches in the course of one week in January. To galvanize leaders and draw attention to the Plan's emerging wave of popular support, the committee called a conference in Washington on March 5 that convened more than 250 delegates—prominent leaders from American life ranging from the publisher of the *Denver Post* to retired top Army and Navy brass, to presidents from institutions as diverse as Harvard, Tuskegee University, the Association of Junior Leagues of America, America's Veterans Committee and even an Alpha Kappa sorority.

Behind the public spotlight, the committee kept an itemized list entitled "Special Cultivation" of critical members of Congress. They scratched notations next to key members' names to keep track of their progress: "Practically anti-everything—pretty hopeless," "probably ok" and "Cagey—wants to separate relief and rehabilitation." It brought on six field staff to go to districts represented by legislators deemed swing votes to drum up local support. In late January it began publishing weekly fact sheets that went out to members of Congress and leaders all over America. By March, the committee had enlisted the "full support" of fifty-two prominent national organizations and, according to a survey from the Council on Foreign Relations, support from an overwhelming majority of 430 community leaders polled in twenty-one cities.

In between travel, Marshall came back to Washington. He made sure to meet with a group of Ohio farmers who had just come from a meeting with Taft. By the time the meeting was over, Marshall reported to his colleagues that they had come around, and now supported the Plan. On February 10, Marshall received another delegation. This time it was a group of seven young boys aged nine to eleven, all members of Boy Scout Troop 232 from

Bethesda, Maryland. The boys had initiated their own "Junior Marshall Plan." Securing a movie theater for a film showing, they proposed to use the funds to support eight European boys for a year. Marshall was touched and invited them to come and visit him. The boys entered Marshall's spacious office, each uniform neatly pressed and each eager face wearing a smile tailor-made for the news cameras the State Department had made sure to have on hand. The chairman, Robert Keith Linden, nine years old, said, "Mr. Secretary, we are proud and happy to have met you and want to do everything we can to help the children of Europe." "That is a fine speech," the general said, clearly enjoying himself, "You said it all in one sentence." When the Scout jumped onto Marshall's swivel chair behind his desk, Marshall laughed. "Perhaps he would like to sit there permanently," he joked.

The combined efforts of Marshall's campaign and the Committee for the Marshall Plan were eliciting fervor and engagement from all quarters of American civic life. New York State's 4-H Club organized a Marshall Plan of its own, a fund to purchase rakes, hoes and other farm tools for the people of Germany. The American Society for the Prevention of Cruelty to Animals demanded a "Marshall Plan" for the suffering dogs and cats of Europe. The Women's Action Committee for Lasting Peace put out a statement in support of the Plan and urged Congress to keep deliberations free from the "pitfalls and delays of election-year wrangling."

Members of Congress were taking note of the upswell in popular support. Yet, even as the campaign to pass the Plan picked up steam, a group of Republican "revisionists" met at Stoneleigh Court, near the Mayflower Hotel, in Washington to plot a strategy to put a Republican stamp on it. The longer Congress deliberated, the greater the Plan's vulnerability to crippling modification. At this stage, time was not on the Plan's side. With the Marshall Plan in congressional jeopardy, Marshall's chief aide, Chip Bohlen, wrote to a friend in the American Embassy in Moscow referring to the Soviet "attacks on the United States which have been most helpful in the past in regard to Congressional sentiment." He hoped that the Russians would "continue their good work and not suddenly become sweetness in life which would probably defeat the Marshall Plan." Bohlen's remarks, of course, were tongue in cheek.

MARSHALL ARRIVED BACK in Washington just in time. For the second time in a decade, the locus of the world's attention was the six-hundred-mile stretch of land, the "centerpiece of Europe," bridging East to West: Czechoslovakia. Tensions had long been simmering in the country's fragile coalition government. One key non-Communist complaint concerned the police force. The Communists already held a virtual monopoly on the media and public information. Now they were packing key positions on the force. On February 20, all non-Communist members of the government resigned in protest. They hoped that the Czech President Edvard Beneš would use the resignations to force a government realignment or perhaps even to oust the Communist Premier Klement Gottwald. It was to be a profoundly miscalculated gambit. Instead, Gottwald brilliantly used the ensuing five days and his party's control of public information to spin the resignations as treason and assume control of the streets, the police force and all key government ministries. President Beneš, who had suffered a recent stroke, was ill and proved powerless. At 4:30 P.M., on February 25, Gottwald returned from a meeting with Beneš carrying an agreement on a new government, effectively ceding Czechoslovakia to Communist control.

At the same time, the Soviets made threatening overtures to Finland, Norway and Austria. The developments sent tremors throughout Western Europe. In Britain, the $3.75 billion loan of 1946 was exhausted in May, just as the government published a White Paper predicting "drastic cuts in food and raw materials and large-scale unemployment" and further "distress and dislocation." Herbert Matthews wrote in the *New York Times* that the White Paper "demonstrates with frightening clarity that Britain's fate depends on aid this year through the European Recovery Plan." British Foreign Secretary Ernest Bevin agreed with Churchill that Europe was entering a vital window of six to eight weeks. If in that time the Marshall Plan passed, if Europe proved able to withstand further Communist takeovers and if De Gasperi defeated the Communists in Italy in the upcoming election, then Europe would have turned a corner. The period was crucial and Bevin believed perhaps the "last chance for saving the West."

Living in Paris that March, British novelist Nancy Mitford was convinced that the Soviets would invade any day. "I wake up in the night sometimes in a cold sweat," she wrote to Evelyn Waugh. "Thank goodness for having no children, I can take the pill and say goodbye." She was not alone. Almost everyone drew a parallel to Hitler and his drive for control of Czechoslovakia ten years earlier. "We are alarmed," French Foreign Minister Georges Bidault told U.S. Ambassador Jefferson Caffrey: "I know this may sound extravagant but we are sitting there under the guns and your people are on the other side of the ocean." In mid-March, de Gaulle emerged to offer himself as "a man of iron" for France, and said, for the first time, that he would be proud to accept help from the United States. In early March, Bidault told Caffrey, "If the Communists start something, and we are well aware that they have arms and are organized in a paramilitary way, armed forces will be prepared to take care of them." Caffrey's assessment: "He is a little over-confident perhaps."

The Czech coup set interesting political currents in motion in France. The United States was still pushing France to support German rehabilitation. In the wake of the coup, Bidault was afraid of stoking anti-German public sentiment that the Communists could exploit and harness to instigate a coup of their own. At the same time, the coup had forced French Communist leader Maurice Thorez's hand. Thorez's public remarks suggested that in the event of a Soviet invasion, he would support the Red Army. The coup, the Communists' failed policy of sabotage and the Plan's likely passage were all beginning to sway French public opinion. Seventy percent of the French people now felt that the United States would do more than any other country to aid France, compared to 7 percent who felt that Russia would do more. Despite French concern about Germany, it was becoming increasingly clear that the Soviet threat was greater than the German threat. France would still seek to maximize its power vis-à-vis Germany. But it was becoming reconciled to the prospect of a rehabilitated Germany as part of postwar Europe.

In early March, Bidault, Bevin and U.S. officials in the State Department were concerned, above all, with Italy. With the next election scheduled for April 18, Marshall did not believe that the Communists would accept electoral defeat without a violent backlash, possibly in the form of a coup. As the election neared, journalist Arnaldo Cortesi wrote, "American aid to Italy in general and the Marshall Plan in particular are being attacked and defended throughout the length and breadth of Italy with such intensity and fury that they clearly are the main issue capable of influencing the election results." One of Marshall's aides felt that in Communist leader Palmiro Togliatti, the non-Communists were up against "an authentic political genius." Despite the failed strikes and sabotage of the previous autumn and winter, the Communists had far outpaced their opposition in propaganda. Communist campaigners would travel the country, showing peasants maps and pointing to the land they would get if they voted Communist. Togliatti at once fumed against the Marshall Plan's "imperialist" designs and told the Italian people that Italy would receive American financial aid no matter who won the election.

Before the Czech coup, U.S. Ambassador to Italy James Dunn reported back to Washington that "the present electoral situation justifies grave concern and calls for serious U.S. consideration." Even Pope Pius was pessimistic. After the coup, the mood was grim in Italy. Senior State Department official John Hickerson worried that the coup would trigger "widespread fear and a certain band-wagon psychology" in which voters would feel Soviet or Communist control inevitable and want to align with the winning side. Italian Foreign Minister Count Sforza told Ambassador Dunn, "We must recognize we are now in a stage of Russian expansionism corresponding to Hitler's 1938 and that 1939 inevitably follows."

In high-level quarters back in Washington, it was not that some form of a Communist push for power was completely unexpected. The Communists had won the previous election in 1946, with 37 percent of the vote. George Kennan had predicted that the Soviets would attempt to tighten their grip on their sphere. Months earlier, in a top-secret Cabinet meeting, Marshall had suggested that the Soviets were likely to "clamp down completely on Czechoslovakia" in the near future. Kennan and Marshall had almost predicted the coup.

What no one could foresee was how quickly and seamlessly the Communists were able to assert their unmitigated control. Marshall had grave concerns about what the development would mean for Western Europe, its prospects, its psychological fragility and its ability to stand up to Communist subversion or insurrection. To make matters worse, the Soviet vice minister of foreign affairs, Valerian Zorin, had arrived in Prague only days before the coup. While the non-Communist Cabinet ministers had tendered their resignation of their own volition, Zorin's presence and a general fear and insecurity about Soviet designs led many in the United States and around the world to think that the Soviets were pulling the strings. French Ambassador to Czechoslovakia Maurice Dejean claimed that the coup had been planned in Moscow during December.

While Kennan and Marshall suspected that the coup was a defensive and opportunistic response to the Marshall Plan, many others worried that it was a springboard for further attempts at political control in Europe, perhaps even for a war with the United States. The analogy to Hitler and the Munich Pact of 1938 was too strong for Harry Truman to ignore. "We are faced with exactly the same situation with which Britain and France were faced in 1938–39 with Hitler," Truman wrote his daughter Margaret on March 3. *Life* magazine wrote that America was in danger of being "Munich'd or even Dunkirk'd off the European continent." No one knew what would come next.

On March 5, the occupying commander in Germany, Lucius Clay, reported to Washington that he feared that war could now come "with dramatic suddenness." The purpose of the note, Clay's biographer would later write, was not so much to give an objective assessment based on the Czech coup as it was to provide political ammunition for the military to secure more funding from Congress. Nevertheless, Clay's note amplified Washington's anxiety. Army Secretary Kenneth Royall inquired as to how long it would take to move the "eggs" (atomic bombs) to the Mediterranean, and Chief of Naval Operations Louis Denfeld suggested on March 9 that the government take certain steps "to prepare the American people for war." A general told a reporter for *Life*, off the record, "I have now accepted that war with Russia is inevitable. The only question is when and where."

On March 10, the body of Jan Masaryk, the popular non-Communist Czechoslovakian foreign minister, was found on the pavement below the open window of his third-floor office. It has never been proven whether Masaryk committed suicide or was murdered. Unlike the Soviets' other satellites, Czechoslovakia had a history of democratic traditions, and most of its trade was still with the West. Urbane and cosmopolitan, Masaryk was beloved in America, and his death had almost as powerful an impact on the American public as the coup that preceded it. At a news conference the next day Marshall said, "The situation is very, very serious."

The fever pitch kept rising. On March 13, the Joint Chiefs of Staff presented Defense Secretary James Forrestal with an emergency war plan to meet a Soviet invasion of Western Europe and the Middle East. A *Newsweek* poll showed Americans increasingly supportive of a preemptive nuclear strike against the Soviets. A Gallup poll in early March showed 73 percent of a hitherto disinterested public believing American policy toward Russia too soft. Said George Kennan: "A real war scare ensued."

Among senior officials in the government, concern was real. Marshall worried about what the Soviets would do next. He worried about Western Europe's viability and its ability to withstand similar putsches. But Marshall, Forrestal, Lovett, Kennan and other key strategic thinkers and policymakers did not expect any sort of grand Soviet offensive. The Soviets' desire to consolidate control over its sphere was a defensive response, emanating from a position of weakness. They were in no military position so soon after World War II to risk war with the United States, still in possession of the atomic monopoly. The Czech coup had two far-reaching and profound implications for U.S. foreign policy. The first was to galvanize the United States to heed Bevin's call for a Western defense association. That spring, European leaders quietly met with U.S. defense, military and diplomatic officials at the Pentagon, under Marshall's orders, exploring a framework for a new and unprecedented association for mutual defense.

American protection, though, would mean little if national Communist parties could exploit economic dislocation and misery to achieve electoral victory. So, for Marshall, the administration and the rest of the foreign policy establishment, passage of the Marshall Plan took on even greater urgency. The Czech crisis, remembered Hickerson, "scared the bejesus out of everyone." The Plan's champions had now found a powerful catalyst to dissolve obstacles to the Plan's passage, and they did not hesitate to employ it to their ends.

ON MARCH 1, 1948, Arthur Vandenberg stood behind the Senate lectern. The committee work, over which Vandenberg and Charles Eaton in the House had presided, was now complete. When published, the Senate Foreign Relations Committee's hearings amounted to 1,466 pages, and those in the House Foreign Affairs Committee totaled 2,269 pages. Vandenberg's Senate committee had heard almost one hundred witnesses and received additional recorded written statements from scores more. Now the larger debate on the Plan was to open in both houses of Congress. The Czech crisis and the attendant war scare provided a flush and dramatic backdrop for the sixty-three-year-old senator, ailing, but with bow tie neatly in place and white hair nicely combed.

The day before, Senator Joseph Ball from Minnesota had called a meeting of the twenty or so "Revisionists" in the Senate to rally opposition. The administration was requesting $5.3 billion for the first-year appropriation. Taft was recommending $4 billion. Now Ball sought to thin the request further to $3.5 billion, a decrease of one-third. It was much less than the Europeans were expecting and, the administration and Vandenberg were sure, well short of the line separating recovery from the same old piecemeal, patchwork relief provided in the past.

This would be Vandenberg's chance to frame the debate to follow. The seats were all taken; it was standing-room only in the gallery, and members of the House eager to listen to Vandenberg streamed in, lining the walls of the Senate chamber. Van had written the text of the speech himself. It had taken him more than two weeks, and he had printed out seven drafts, he told a staffer, all on his own typewriter. As Vandenberg began the nine-thousand-word address, a hush fell over the chamber. He opened by evoking the ongoing crisis in Czechoslovakia and the one that seemed to be emerging in Finland. "The exposed frontiers of hazard move almost hourly to the west," he said. America's voice was the last one still capable of preserving Europe's way of life. There was no guarantee that the Marshall Plan would work: "I understand and share the anxieties involved," he said with all the bona fides of a former isolationist. Yet, "The greatest nation on earth either justifies or surrenders its leadership. We must choose. There are no blueprints to guarantee results . . . I have no quarrel with those who disagree because we are dealing with imponderables. But I am bound to say to those who disagree that they have not escaped to safety by rejecting or subverting this plan. They have simply fled to other risks, and I fear far greater ones."

The Marshall Plan was America's best hope, the world's best hope. "It aims to preserve the victory against aggression and dictatorship which we thought we won in World War II. It strives to help stop World War III before it starts," Van said before shooting a sideways glance in the direction of Robert Taft. Anticipating Taft and other opponents, Vandenberg had ensured from day one, and now he could proclaim, that the Marshall Plan was "our voice . . . the product of eight months of more intensive study by more devoted minds than I have ever known to concentrate upon any objective in all my twenty years in Congress." The Congress must not lose sight of the big picture when considering the amount of aid to be appropriated. "This is more than a problem of mathematics; it is a problem of peace, stability and human freedoms . . . It may not work. I think it will. But if it fails let the responsibility rest elsewhere." Van's language was eloquent and evocative. He held the chamber in rapture for the eighty-minute duration of the speech, the longest of his career.

As Van concluded, those who were not already standing flouted Senate rules and sprang to their feet to join those who were in a prolonged ovation. First, Senator Tom Connally, a Democrat from Texas and ranking member of the Foreign Relations Committee, left his seat to congratulate Vandenberg; Democratic Senator Alben Barkley of Kentucky followed close behind, and before long it seemed that almost the entire membership had converged upon the senator from Michigan in a barrage of handshakes, backslaps and hollering. Marshall called the speech "a masterpiece." "Had it been possible to decide the issue at the close of his address," wrote journalist Felix Belair, "there would have been few 'nays' cast against it."

During the course of the weeks to follow, heated debate ensued in the Senate and the House. Strident opponents remained. In one of the more vituperative attacks, Senator George Malone, a representative from Nevada, charged that "Congress and the nation were punch-drunk." "European governments care nothing about hungry people. They don't look at them the same way we do." On the other end of the ideological spectrum, progressive Senator Glen Taylor of Idaho, Henry Wallace's running mate, called the Plan "vicious and stupid" and said its sponsors would "meet their Waterloo come next November."

Other critics fumed at the Committee for the Marshall Plan and the various efforts that made up the campaign to generate support for the Plan. Representative Howard Buffett of Nebraska spoke of the "barrage of propaganda that has drenched this country and been funneled into the offices and minds of Members of this House." Representative Lowell Stockman of Oregon charged, "There has never been such propaganda in the whole history of our nation as there has been for the Marshall Plan." In fact, political scientist Bernard Cohen found that many reporters and editors did systematically support the Plan with extra space and biased coverage; it was, according to Cohen's study, "a classic case where reporters went out of their way to play up the program." Another congressman alleged that he was told by a supporter that if he did not back the Plan, radio time that he had been given to communicate to his constituents would be withheld. "All the tricks of political terrorism in the book" had been used to generate support for the Plan, thundered Buffett. No official charges were ever brought forth, however. And while to the Plan's opponents the campaign for support may have been dirty, to its supporters it was an unprecedented example of leaders reaching out to educate and mobilize the broader public on a matter of far-reaching national and international import.

Opponents continued to attack the Marshall Plan for supporting Europe's socialist governments. Such support would simply facilitate their passage on the road to Communism, which would thereby deliver Western Europe into Soviet arms. Not so, testified Averell Harriman. Harriman argued that socialism was possibly the best form of government, at that time, to provide for the struggling masses in Europe, and provided the best chance to keep Western Europe from turning Communist. Republican Senator Henry Cabot Lodge weighed in that the British people could elect a government espousing free market policies in the next election. The key was that Britain was a free democracy, and that the Marshall Plan would keep it that way.

Still, other revisionists scampered to staple "emasculating amendments onto the bill" limiting the amount of aid and diluting the U.S. commitment in any number of ways. And as the vote in the Senate neared, opponents began requesting more and more time for speeches, coming up with whatever delaying tactics they could muster. Senator Olin Johnston of South Carolina was on the fence. There was popular opposition in his home state. He told an aide that he would vote for it but offer only lukewarm support, and that the aide should prepare a speech that included his reservations. When the roll was called, Johnston voted against the Plan. Afterward, the confounded aide asked him why. Johnston replied that as he was giving the speech, he found the list of reservations so compelling that he had changed his mind on the spot and voted "no."

Of those on the fence, Johnston was an exception. The Czech crisis, the war scare and Vandenberg's rousing speech all struck a deep chord. While the opposition was still "vociferous," it was thinning. Arguments about parsimony and concerns about propping up socialist governments began to appear petty measured against the threat at hand. "If we don't act fast we may lose Italy to the Communists, and if we lose Italy we may lose Austria, West Germany and possibly France," said Senator Mike Mansfield, a Democrat from Montana. Swayable revisionists and fence-sitters found Mansfield's argument compelling.

On the eve of the Senate's vote, Taft once more railed against the Plan, as presented. "If I vote for this bill it will be with the distinct understanding that we are making a one-year commitment. If we don't want to continue this program after the first year there is no commitment, moral, legal or otherwise, requiring that it be continued." Taft was asserting congressional control. The agency administering the Marshall Plan would have to go to Congress every year to secure funds. Taft had left his imprint on the debate, but on the eve of that vote on March 13, it was the senator from Michigan, "a dog tired" Arthur Vandenberg, who "was in complete control of the legislative situation." Among those joining Vandenberg in finally voting for the bill were Taft and Joseph McCarthy. Five minutes past midnight on March 14, a fortnight after Van's address, the Senate, with a vote of 69 to 17, authorized $5.3 billion for the first year of the four-year program for European recovery.

It was a triumph for Vandenberg. For some of Truman's political advisers it was, perhaps, too great a triumph for the Republican senator. Truman was struggling that March. Not only was he dealing with the Czech crisis and the Soviet threat, but the Communists were making headway in China. That winter also marked highly charged deliberations over whether or not to recognize the state of Israel in the Middle East. As Truman aide George Elsey noted, the president's prestige in foreign matters was low, and on the Marshall Plan, the administration's bright spot, Vandenberg and Marshall were getting all the credit. With popular anxiety about the Soviet threat on the rise and a campaign about to begin, the time was ripe for a speech. On March 17, Truman moved a scheduled St. Patrick's Day speech in New York to address the Congress. He pressed for the passage of the Marshall Plan, enactment of universal military training and the restoration of selective service.

As the bill entered the House and Truman entered the fray, George Marshall once again set out on the road in a last push to drum up support for the Plan. Traversing the country, Marshall spoke at the University of California at Berkeley on March 19, then the University of California at Los Angeles the next day. With the Czech crisis still smoldering and the Italian election looming, Marshall spoke with force and urgency: "This is a world-wide struggle between freedom and tyranny, between the self-rule of the many as opposed to the dictatorship of the ruthless few." He spoke more directly then ever before about the Soviet threat. The general wielded the bludgeon of Munich and appeasement in urging the passage of the ERP. Heeding Ambassador Dunn's request, Marshall took on Togliatti and the Italian Communists, making it clear that if Italy voted Communist they would receive no American aid. The remarks were reported widely in the Italian press and proved a lacerating blow to the Communists. Marshall's words "now carried a hint of ruthlessness," wrote his biographer Forrest Pogue. He would later express regret for his tone. His sense of urgency was real, though, and his message carried.

Back in Washington, Marshall took his case to the House Foreign Affairs Committee. With Lovett and Douglas in tow, he urged committee members to streamline the bill's passage without unnecessary amendments or dilatory tactics. Chairman Charles Eaton heeded Marshall's call. The bill passed the committee by a vote of 11 to 8, and the seventy-nine-year-old Eaton stated that nothing less than "the very survival of the United States" was at stake.

When the bill reached the floor, it met a flurry of proposed amendments and objections from Republican leaders. Karl Mundt of South Dakota proposed an amendment to forbid funds to countries that sold goods to Communist countries. Walter Judd of Minnesota wanted an amendment pledging support for countries resisting subjugation by armed minorities or external forces. Some wanted to include Spain in the program. Special interests had flooded Washington, and several representatives tried to win concessions for local industry or companies. The bill could not escape without some concessions to U.S. shipping and wheat interests. The Knowland amendment made sure that 50 percent of goods were to be transferred on U.S. ships and the Reed amendment stipulated that not less than 25 percent of wheat shipments from the United States were to be in the form of flour. But these concessions were scant. Vandenberg and Eaton had done a remarkable job fending off special interests, even as they kept them "in it and for it," as Acheson said.

Other amendments, like the George amendment stipulating that the

ERP's administrator would use private channels of trade whenever possible and the Aiken amendment stressing the use of agricultural surpluses to alleviate food shortages, were more sound, and stapled to the bill as well. Many Republican members were adamant about support for the Chinese Nationalists and wanted funds made available in a larger omnibus bill. The White House's April 1 deadline and the election in Italy later that month were looming. Even as the House wrangled over amendments, the momentum was moving in favor of passage.

Then on March 25, Republican Representative from Ohio John Vorys took to the floor of the House to read a letter from Herbert Hoover, the last Republican to serve as president. Hoover had done an about-face and now endorsed the Marshall Plan, essentially, as presented: "as a major dam against Russian aggression." The letter was a tipping point, and in the days to follow ambivalent lawmakers made "a stampede for the bandwagon." On March 30 the House authorized an unprecedented $6.2 billion ($5.3 billion for the European program and additional aid for China, Greece, Turkey and international emergency child relief) by the surprisingly large margin of 329 to 74.

On April 3, 1948, Harry Truman returned to the capital aboard his presidential yacht to affix his signature to the Foreign Assistance Act of 1948. "This measure," the president said, "is America's answer to the free world." It was "perhaps the greatest venture in constructive statesmanship that any nation has undertaken." Truman used a dozen pens to complete his signature, so that he could give a pen to each of the officials—those who were particularly instrumental in guiding the Act through to passage—present, and flanking him in his office as he signed.

AS THE PRESIDENT SIGNED the foreign aid bill into law on April 3, one person was noticeably absent. George Marshall had left days before for a conference in South America. On the day of the signing, Marshall cabled his thoughts from Bogotá: "The decision of the U.S. Government . . . is, I think, an historic step in the foreign policy of this country." Marshall said later: "It was just a struggle from start to finish, and that's what I'm proudest of, that we actually . . . put it over." Bert McCormick's *Chicago Tribune* railed against the passage of the "Marshall slush fund." Paul Hoffman, a key member of the Harriman Committee, estimated, "It was probably as well conceived a piece of legislation as was ever put on the books in the U.S."

Though passage meant the legislative birth of the Marshall Plan, George Kennan saw it through a different lens. Years later Kennan said, "The psychological success at the outset was so amazing that we felt that the psychological effect was four-fifths accomplished before the first supplies arrived." For Kennan, the Marshall Plan's date of birth was not April 3 but June 5, ten months earlier, when Marshall had extended America's hand in offering aid to a beleaguered continent. Already the Marshall Plan had halted the Soviet Union's march west; it had brought the democratic Western European states together; it helped France and Italy weather seminal and—it would prove—decisive Communist probes; it helped turn public opinion in Western Europe away from the Soviet Union and toward the United States; it forced the Soviets' hand, illuminating Stalin's true colors and triggering the Cominform and Stalin's totalitarian reign in Eastern Europe. In the ten months since Marshall's speech, the Marshall Plan was alive in the hearts and minds of Europeans, and it may have been the decisive psychological bridge keeping economies afloat and Western Europe free.

In Western Europe, leaders were jubilant. British Prime Minister Clement Attlee wrote to Truman to express "our deep gratification at this act of unparalleled generosity and statesmanship." According to Herbert Matthews of the *New York Times*, Attlee had good cause to be grateful. Matthews wrote, "What the Marshall Plan means to the British can metaphorically be put this way: It saves their lives. This is obvious to anyone knowing Britain's economic position." One could almost detect the stiffening of the spines of Europe's leaders as they complemented expressions of gratitude with calls for self-reliance and results. Bevin said that the bill would "give new courage to the free peoples of the world." He said that Britain must aim "to stand on its own two feet and cease to be a claimant on the taxpayers of any other country." In France, Bidault's reaction struck a similar note of gratitude and purpose. Fifty-nine percent of Dutch men and women believed that Holland should cooperate with the Marshall Plan and only 9 percent believed it should not.

Italy's Count Sforza echoed that call, exclaiming, "Either we save ourselves together or else together we go to wrack and ruin." At a Communist rally attended by twenty thousand on April 1, Communist leader Palmiro Togliatti denounced American aid and said that Italy could get aid from the Soviet Union. The audience proceeded to unleash boos and catcalls, silencing Togliatti for five minutes. The Communists then began chanting for the United States. They marched off chanting, "Long live the United States," and the Communist leader finished his address to a crowd that was smaller than when he began.

• • •

FOR MONTHS, the Marshall Plan had been subject to the parries and thrusts of its opponents. When it was signed into law, though, the Plan had remained intact, essentially what Marshall and the White House had requested. The ERP authorized—in a "moral" commitment—up to $17 billion from April 1948 to June 1952 for European recovery. It set up a separate and innovative new entity called the Economic Cooperation Administration, or ECA, to administer the Plan. ECA was to be run by an eminent American with an outstanding business background with Cabinet-level status. Its objective was to underwrite European recovery and help Europe achieve economic self-sustainability by the end of the commitment period. Its larger objective, it was clear, was to keep Western Europe free and democratic and secure from Soviet or national Communist Party control.

Famously, Vandenberg brandished a sign on his desk that read: "This too shall pass." The proverb helped him through inclement political weather. It also grounded him in times of triumph. It had been ten months since Marshall stood on the steps of Harvard's Memorial Church and delivered his address. Now the Marshall Plan had passed Congress. But steep and profound challenges remained: Would Congress meet its four-year "moral commitment," or would it renege? Could this newfangled and untried agency effectively administer the largest peacetime foreign policy enterprise in U.S. history? Who would run it? Would the aid be well spent? Could America meet its economic commitment with a similarly far-reaching and assuring security commitment? What would happen to America's commitment in seven months time if—as almost everyone expected—Truman was voted out of office and the Republicans won the White House?

Across the Atlantic, where the Plan would play out, another series of equally daunting questions loomed: Could De Gasperi fend off the Communists in the Italian election in a fortnight's time? Could the Europeans cooperate and integrate their economies? Would U.S. aid be enough to help Europe fight its way out of its economic doldrums? Would the French work to reconcile German rehabilitation and discover a modus vivendi capable of transcending the most destructive interstate relationship in world history? Would the British hazard a reorientation from Empire and Commonwealth toward an integrated Europe? And, of course, what would the Soviets do next?

The fate of the Marshall Plan, of Western Europe and of the democratic free world hinged—in large part—on the answers to these questions. No one knew the answers. And there were no guarantees that the Plan would work. Marshall had not offered any such guarantee and neither had Vandenberg.

Like Marshall, though, Arthur Vandenberg was willing to place his hopes and energies—and those of his country—behind the Marshall Plan. Van had outlined the opportunity, as he saw it, in the coda of his March 1 address: "It can be the turning point in history for 100 years to come. If it fails, we will have done our best. If it succeeds, our children and our children's children will call us blessed. May God grant his benediction upon the ultimate event."

Part Two

———————⟨∞⟩———————

THE PLAN IN
ACTION

Chapter Eight

AID FLOWS

O N APRIL 3, 1948, Paul Hoffman was in Honolulu, Hawaii, when the telephone rang. Hoffman was returning to the United States from Asia, where he had been a member of a commission inspecting Japan and Korea's economies. At the other end of the telephone was John Steelman, a White House aide, calling from Washington. The president wanted to speak with Hoffman as soon as possible, Steelman said. "Would you mind telling me what it is about?" Hoffman asked.

Leaving for a conference a few days earlier, George Marshall indicated to journalist James Reston that the Truman administration was "looking favorably" on the appointment of former Undersecretary of State William Clayton as European Recovery Program (ERP) administrator. The legislation endowed the position with a unique degree of autonomy over a $17 billion budget. No one since Harry Hopkins would wield "statutory power[s] similar to those of the ERP administrator," wrote Reston. Truman told aides in the Oval Office that "what is needed is a good hard-boiled man" for the position.

To many, Will Clayton seemed a logical selection. Arthur Vandenberg had other ideas, though. When the *Washington Post* ran a front-page story suggesting that Clayton was slated to run the ERP, Vandenberg wrote to Marshall: "I have had very unhappy repercussions today on the Hill from the story." Van assured Marshall that it was no reflection on Clayton, for whom he had the "greatest respect and affection." But, while Clayton fit the bill as far as business experience, Republican colleagues in the Senate felt it imperative that the administrator not come via the State Department. "I think it is seriously necessary—for the sake of ERP—to keep that in mind," Van wrote to Marshall. If the administrator was affiliated too closely with the

White House, he could mete out funds to curry political favor for Truman and the Democrats. Republicans were not prepared to take any risks in an election year.

With Clayton's candidacy scuttled, Truman called Dean Acheson. Acheson reminded Truman that the legislation that had just passed Congress was simply an authorization. The battle for funds was not over. Truman would need as much congressional support as he could muster to obtain the actual appropriations. Vandenberg's support was essential to that end. Acheson said that he did not expect Vandenberg to approve of his selection, for much the same reason that he had disapproved of Clayton. If Vandenberg did, though, Acheson would duly serve. Acheson suggested that Truman meet with Vandenberg to bring him into the decision-making process. He predicted that Vandenberg would propose Paul Hoffman for the position. And that is precisely what the senator did.

PAUL GRAY HOFFMAN was born in Chicago, Illinois, in 1891 into a prosperous family. His father, George, had eccentric tastes and a penchant for all things modern. One day he purchased an automobile, a Pope-Toledo, one of the first in town. As a boy, Paul became fascinated with the contraption and eventually became familiar with its intricacies and would make all the repairs. Hoffman was a fine student, but found himself uninterested in his courses at the University of Chicago. He was "encouraged" by his professors not to return after his first year. At eighteen Hoffman took his first job as a car salesman with a Studebaker dealership in Chicago. The position allowed Hoffman to indulge his passion for automobiles. And he soon discovered that he also had something of an aptitude for sales.

Hoffman noticed that salesmen were clustered in Chicago, but none seemed to focus on the rural counties. Venturing outside the city, Hoffman found untapped markets. He also refined his sales methods. The young salesman would drive to the local bank in one of the showroom's finest cars and offer the bank president a ride home for lunch. Hoffman would inquire about people who lived in the area. By the time the ride was finished, Hoffman had a detailed canvass of the community and knew who would make the best sales prospects. At twenty-one, Paul Hoffman was awarded the company prize for selling more Studebakers than anyone else in the country.

At that time an enterprising salesman could earn better commissions out west, so Hoffman moved to Los Angeles. He served in the military during World War I, and when he returned home he bought his own Studebaker dealership. Exciting things were happening in Hoffman's new city. The burgeoning movie industry was fueling rapid demographic and economic growth. The trends helped Hoffman set new sales records. The growth also meant that there were more cars on the road—and more accidents. In 1922, the mayor of Los Angeles appointed Hoffman chairman of a traffic commission. At thirty-one, Hoffman devised a highway plan for the city of Los Angeles, and he also introduced the first pedestrian crossing lights used in America. Hoffman's work helped Los Angeles decrease its automobile death rate by 30 percent. The safer the roads, Hoffman found, the more people wanted to buy cars. It was an interesting lesson: with intelligent reforms, all could benefit and an industry—or a system—could flourish. By thirty-four, Hoffman had become a millionaire.

From there, Hoffman's rise was steep. He moved to South Bend, Indiana, with his wife and six children to assume a senior executive position at Studebaker. Just shy of five foot ten, with a firm chin, dark blue eyes and a warm and affable countenance, Hoffman described himself as "Middle Western to the very marrow of my bones—and proud of it." He played gin rummy, poker and bridge, and on a good day he shot in the low eighties on the golf course. Hoffman's best friend was the town dentist. He dressed in smart but understated double-breasted suits, with light shirts, dark ties and a gray, felt-rimmed hat, slightly wrinkled along the edges. In conversation, Hoffman's tone was earnest and kind but authoritative. Humble, he prefaced remarks with phrases like "as I see it," "from our point of view" and "in my opinion." As a listener, he was masterful. His eyes were expressive and engaged and he almost always seemed to wear a genuine smile that made people feel comfortable, considered and special.

During the Depression, Hoffman was appointed the first president of the Automobile Safety Foundation and dubbed an "apostle of safety." By one estimate his leadership on auto safety saved twenty thousand lives a year. He was also named president of Studebaker, and he led the fabled American company out of receivership and back to profitability; for that he was dubbed "the Miracle Man of Motors." He ensured that labor received good wages, good work conditions and a say in management and operations. Even in a time of mass national strikes, Studebaker's workers never went on strike under Hoffman's stewardship, and *Life* magazine lauded the company's "glass-smooth labor relations."

Hoffman's work on auto safety and at Studebaker came to inform his larger economic ideology. "If you are a capitalist who is seeking exorbitant profits," he told an audience of businessmen, "you are sabotaging the free enterprise system." Tempering self-interest to ensure that others were provided for and enfranchised was not just humanitarian: when workers were provided for and included, it would eventually redound to the company's benefit, the owner's benefit and the very viability of the economic system upon which success depended. It was enlightened self-interest.

As for all Americans, the Great Depression was a searing experience for Hoffman. He was a Republican and an ardent believer in the free-enterprise system. Yet during the Depression that system seemed to fail America, and Hoffman did not understand entirely why. When the University of Chicago freshman who was "encouraged" not to return after his first year became a trustee of that institution, it brought Hoffman in contact with some of the world's leading economists. By the time World War II broke out, he had become convinced that in order to avoid another Depression, industry needed to come together with the best economic thinking to formulate a postwar vision for America's economy.

In 1942, Hoffman started the Committee for Economic Development, or CED. He brought in hundreds of economists and leading industrialists like Charles Wilson, chairman of General Electric, and Henry Ford II. CED produced a flurry of studies and reports, and reached business and labor leaders in three thousand communities across America. It became the engine for the best thinking on America's postwar economic path forward.

Through analysis and deliberation, the committee discovered a revitalized faith and sense of possibility in America's economic system. Free enterprise was still the cornerstone of that system. But at the same time, the economy had to provide sufficient security, welfare and opportunity for those who remained vulnerable, those for whom unbridled free enterprise did not provide. A renascent free enterprise industrialist, Hoffman emerged from his work with CED as a "responsible Republican," or "Republican and responsible," as he preferred to say.

Nineteen forty-seven was a golden age in sales in America. Government and industry agreed that the United States would buy its way out of a postwar economic recession. It was to be a "consumer's republic" and the country needed salesmen to sell. The United States had more salesmen per capita than the rest of the world. A young playwright named Arthur Miller wrote a tragedy called *Death of a Salesman* around this time. "If you don't get the facts," a mentor had told Hoffman, "the facts will get you." He was honest, forthright and not at all slick. Journalist Walter Lippmann (a Studebaker driver) said of him that "the outside and the inside are all the same stuff." "Selling," Hoffman said, "in my opinion, is the process of transferring a conviction from the mind of the seller into that of a buyer." No one was better.

Hoffman's testimony on the Marshall Plan before the Senate Foreign

Relations Committee was among the best received throughout the hearings. He was a leading champion of the Plan and a key participant in the Harriman Committee. And he was a Republican. By the time Vandenberg met with Truman, he had canvassed some one hundred leading national businessmen and Paul Hoffman was the leading choice to serve as administrator for more than half of them. Marshall approved: "The position required a man of competence, particularly someone completely unselfish . . . Hoffman fit the bill." In his phone call with Truman, Acheson said that Hoffman was a good man and that the president would "do well to accept him"—"and, by doing so, [would] irrevocably commit Vandenberg to the support of an adequately financed program." Truman heeded Acheson's counsel.

It seemed that everyone was behind Hoffman's appointment, save Hoffman himself. Speaking to John Steelman from Hawaii, Hoffman agreed to meet with Truman in Washington. Heading home, Hoffman was reluctant. He had plans for Studebaker and promised his wife that they would spend more time on their avocado ranch in Pasadena, California. Vandenberg was not at all subtle: "You've got to take it!" he told Hoffman when he arrived in Washington. By the time Hoffman met with Truman, his resolve had weakened, but he still did not want the job.

When Truman formally offered him the post, Hoffman replied, "Mr. President, I am deeply appreciative of your offer, but it would be a mistake for me to accept it because I don't really want to leave Studebaker . . . May I add that it would be a mistake for you to appoint me because I have employed a good many thousand people in my day and I never knew anyone who didn't want the job that was offered to perform satisfactorily." Truman replied that the same was not true of government. Some of the best appointments (perhaps he was thinking of Marshall and Clayton here) had to be drafted. It meant that they would be less encumbered by self-interest. Hoffman agreed to talk it over with his business colleagues and his wife and left it at that.

Later that afternoon, at 4:30, Hoffman appeared at the Pentagon for a press conference on his overseas mission to Japan and Korea. One of the reporters asked, "Have you been offered the post as ECA administrator?" Hoffman dodged the question. At that moment, an announcement came over the loudspeaker stating that President Truman had just announced that Paul G. Hoffman had accepted the post of administrator of the Marshall Plan. Hoffman was livid. But, on the hook, he acquiesced. He later conceded that it was a ploy he had himself used on occasion to get someone who was 90 percent in to sign on to a deal for good. "So I found myself in a job that I had never accepted," Hoffman recalled.

Hoffman was sworn in on April 9, 1948, less than one week after the ERP was signed into law. Vandenberg pushed the appointment through his committee in less than an hour, and the affirmative voice vote took less than ten minutes. Hoffman's friend, publisher Henry Luce, cabled him: "I can think of no one who has with greater modesty tried to avoid the attention of the gods, but Destiny so often unresponsive to its postulants had clearly marked you for its own." With characteristic modesty, Hoffman offered his own comment on the appointment: "It seems that I was the least obnoxious of the Republicans."

The country's leaders had staked America's strategic objectives on the policy that he was now tasked to execute. Hoffman left a $96,000 yearly salary, a comfortable position in corporate America and his avocado ranch in Pasadena for immeasurable public scrutiny, a $20,000 salary and a barren Washington apartment. "Of course I was appalled by the job," he said. When Hoffman arrived for his first meeting with the president following his swearing-in, Truman promptly greeted him with four bulging looseleaf notebooks and instructions to get to work immediately. Within hours, Hoffman announced the first official ERP expenditures. Western Europe was waiting.

ON APRIL 14, eleven days after Harry Truman signed the Foreign Assistance Act of 1948 into law, the victory ship *John H. Quick* "crept" under massive Texan grain elevators in Galveston, Texas. By the time the pouring was complete, the ship had taken on nine thousand long tons of grain. Four other ships hovered behind and took their turns under the grain elevators. When the loading was done, the fleet of five—all American ships hired with ERP funds from the Luckenbach Steamship Company of New York—contained fifty-four thousand tons of grain, as well as fuel, various foodstuffs, feed, chemicals, fertilizers, raw materials, semifinished products, vehicles and equipment. When the ships were loaded with all the cargo they could bear, they promptly headed out across the Atlantic, the first fleet to bring official ERP aid to Europe under the European Recovery Program.

Ship after ship followed the *John H. Quick* in the days, weeks and months to follow. They were loaded in ports from Texas to New York—and many in between. The ships carried everything from wheat to horse meat to lard to mixed seeds to dry peas to construction equipment. In steady and profuse waves of succession, the ships set sail for France, then the Netherlands, then Italy, Austria, Greece, Great Britain and the rest of the sixteen Marshall Plan countries. In short order, Marshall aid was flowing.

• • •

AS THE QUICK AND THE REST of the inaugural fleet steamed across the Atlantic, the world's eyes turned to the Mediterranean. On Sunday, April 17, Italy was to have what journalist Lansing Warren described as "the most important election on the continent since the war's end." The Communist coalition had won 40 percent of the vote in the last election. Non-Communist groups felt that their organization and reach were inadequate. The *New York Times* correspondent in Rome told Secretary of Defense James Forrestal and others that he took a "gloomy view of the situation" and that the Communists might very well assume control of the government.

If the Communists were victorious it would provide them with a key strategic position in the Mediterranean and in Western Europe. In the wake of the Czech coup, a Communist victory could generate a tidal wave of Communist momentum across Europe's Atlantic seaboard. French Foreign Minister Bidault was petrified that France could fall next. Officials in the United States were similarly concerned. Weeks before the election, George Kennan wrote: "As far as Europe is concerned, Italy is obviously [the] key point . . . if the Communists were to win the election there our whole position in the Mediterranean, and possibly in Western Europe as well, would probably be undermined." Kennan floated the idea of whether the United States should encourage the Italian government to simply outlaw the Communist Party and brace for whatever violence was sure to follow.

In the month leading up to the election, the United States mobilized. Encouraged by the State Department and Italian newspapers, Italian-Americans sent ten million letters and cables to relatives in Italy urging them to vote for the Christian Democrats. The United States Post Office and TWA worked together to orchestrate "Freedom Flights" to expedite shipments. Shipments of aid via the Friendship Train and interim aid arrived in waves as well. The State Department put together a film program featuring Hollywood stars such as Frank Sinatra and Bing Crosby, who offered kind words in Italian to the Italian people. The Justice Department announced that anyone who supported the Communists would not be permitted a visa to travel to the United States. The CIA, founded less than one year earlier, bombarded the Italian public with anti-Communist, pro–Christian Democrat messages via radio, literature, pamphlets and other means. Forrestal even passed the hat around to his wealthy financier friends, funneling "East Coast money" to the Christian Democrats. Taken together, it constituted an unprecedented degree of American interference in a European country's electoral process.

In late March, Ambassador Dunn and informed observers noticed the tide turning. Italian workers were displeased with all the failed strikes that past winter. They were frightened by the Czech coup and the imposition of Soviet control. The Catholic Church rallied forcefully. The pope attacked Communism, calling it "the angel of the bottomless pit." Prime Minister Alcide De Gasperi was also deft, orchestrating military parades to demonstrate government strength and willingness to quell any Communist violence. Perhaps more than any other factor, though, the election had become a proxy vote: for or against the United States or the Soviet Union, for or against the Marshall Plan.

Also in late March, Marshall had announced that if Italy voted Communist, it would not receive Marshall aid. The message forced the Communists into an ardently anti-American line, and De Gasperi exploited the fact that if the Communists were to win, Italy would forfeit needed U.S. aid. From Rome, Ambassador Dunn wrote that "morale among Government parties has been raised, while the [Communists] at the moment appear on the defensive."

Voters now had a clear choice. De Gasperi's Christian Democrats were allied with America and hailed the Marshall Plan and its potential to drive Italian recovery. To the Communists, the Plan was "American imperialism" and interference in Italian matters. Over the next few weeks, the polarization intensified. The minister of labor exhorted Italians: "Don't spit on the plate that feeds you." Communists called De Gasperi "De Gasperi–Truman." It was hard to find a wall or post in Italian cities and even the countryside that was not blotted with propaganda posters. A popular Communist slogan said, "Every vote for [De] Gasperi is a vote for Truman." The anti-Communists countered with "Every vote for Togliatti is a vote for Stalin." As *New York Times* reporter Arnaldo Cortesi wrote, "the Communists had deliberately chosen to fight the election on the issue 'the U.S. or Russia,' " and the Christian Democrats did the same, brandishing the promise of Marshall Plan aid.

As election day, Sunday, April 17, neared, U.S. officials readied themselves for the possibility of violence or even insurrection. Weeks before, there had been shootings and bomb tossings. But the Communists agreed to a cease-fire leading up to the election and the pledge held. It did not mean that Italy was quiet, however. In the days preceding the election there were parades, speeches, last-minute political maneuvering—"a cornucopia of political activity," as one American journalist reported. When the day came, 94 percent of Italy's 26 million eligible voters cast their ballots.

Two days following the election, the rightist newspaper *Ora d'Italia* ran the headline: "No To Stalin!" De Gasperi and his coalition had won 48.5 percent of the popular vote and an absolute majority of seats in the Chamber

(305 out of 574). The Communist coalition received only 31 percent. It was a resounding victory for De Gasperi's Christian Democrats, Italy's non-Communist supporters and non-Communist governments in Western Europe. From France, Ambassador Caffrey cabled Marshall that Bidault's reaction was "one of elation coupled with relief that the Communist threat on France's southern flank has received a definite setback." U.S. officials called the victory "smashing." British historian Alan Bullock wrote of the Italian election that it was "as great a fillip for confidence in the West as Prague had been a shock." When the results came in, an American journalist in Italy wrote, "It was evident this morning that the U.S. had won."

To be sure, officials in Western Europe and the United States had not heard the last of Palmiro Togliatti and the Communist Party in Italy. The Communists still had a strong presence in the legislature. Violence and sabotage were to come, and the threat of insurrection still loomed. Nevertheless, the election fortified the U.S. strategic position in the region. And it would prove a stinging defeat from which Western European Communists would never recover.

IN WASHINGTON, Paul Hoffman was thrilled with the results of the election. He did not have much time to savor the victory, though. Upon his induction on April 9, the Economic Cooperation Administration—the subject of so much deliberation and speculation—did not even have an office. Hoffman set up shop in suite W-900 of the Statler Hotel, where he was also lodging. On his first day, Hoffman arrived to find 10,000 job applications and 500 personal letters. Everyone—from Cabinet members, to ambassadors, to job seekers, to the media, to members of Congress—wanted to get on his calendar. At Studebaker he had grown accustomed to answering his own phones. Immediately, he called over to a local Studebaker dealership for a secretary and half a dozen Studebaker employees for temporary assistance. His days began with a breakfast meeting at 7:30 at the Statler and concluded with a dinner meeting back at the hotel, usually between 9 and 10 P.M.

Newsweek called Hoffman "easily the busiest" man in Washington. Journalist Cabell Phillips dubbed him "The Man Who Will Spend $17,000,000,000." "If it had not been for what at times seemed almost a glandular inability to be ruffled," wrote journalist Claire Neikind, "he might have gone to pieces at the start." "No one had a blueprint," Hoffman recalled. "I decided first to get a group of people I could talk to—who had done some thinking." His first call was to an economist in Cambridge, Massachusetts.

It was a Wednesday when Hoffman called Richard Bissell, then a professor at the Massachusetts Institute of Technology. Hoffman and Bissell had worked together on the Harriman Committee. Hoffman was an active member and Bissell, the executive secretary, was the key technical and intellectual force. The new administrator knew that Bissell "was very sophisticated about the problems we faced," and he wanted him on board immediately. Bissell asked if he could sort out his affairs in Cambridge and leave on Monday. Hoffman said that he needed him immediately. I have nowhere to stay, Bissell replied. Hoffman told him that he could bunk in his hotel suite and suggested that he catch the next train to Washington. Bissell arrived at Hoffman's suite at the Statler at midnight. He was promptly greeted with the "unwelcome news" that the very first meeting of the ECA would be in Hoffman's hotel room at 7 A.M. the next morning. Bissell had packed for a five-day stay. He would never return to live in Cambridge.

On Friday morning, Bissell's second full day on the job, Paul Nitze came over from State with a plea to mete out the first funds. Several countries had prohibitive balance-of-payments deficits and were on the verge of having to curtail essential imports from the United States. A group that had been working on the transition had already assembled fifty or sixty procurement authorizations for specific import transactions. With Hoffman scampering to build his agency from thin air, he delegated the responsibility to Bissell. Bissell handed over the authorizations to a trusted subordinate, Samuel Van Hyning, and instructed him to parse through them, eliminating any that seemed dubious or unnecessary. Within hours Van Hyning had weeded out twenty problematic requests. Bissell examined the remaining requests, and promptly signed off on $35 million in ERP aid to Western Europe before the end of the day. "It was a helter skelter beginning," remembered Bissell. Still, the aid moved seamlessly through the system. The exercise was repeated the next day. It became, more or less, the procedure for examining aid requests for much of the program to follow.

Bissell emerged as the primary architect behind the design for how Marshall aid would be spent. After the piecemeal aid handed out in the past, Congress was insistent that taxpayers' dollars be well spent. The Plan's champions knew that the first hint of corruption or scandal would spell disaster for the program's standing in Western Europe and with the American public and Congress. As a result, the ERP broke with aid programs of the past. ECA would not simply dole out funds to aid recipients. Instead, it would implement an innovative procedure: counterpart funds.

Congress wanted the program to go through normal market channels as much as possible. Hoffman and Bissell agreed. The problem for Western Europe, though, was the Dollar Gap. Western Europeans could no longer afford to import goods and services from the United States without draining their reserves and threatening the viability of their economies. Heeding congressional demands, ECA kept the market functioning. So, economic entities—whether people, companies or nationalized industries—in Marshall Plan countries continued to purchase American goods and services, as needed, with their local currency. The ECA helped set reasonable prices and exchange rates. This meant that Marshall aid was not "a giveaway program," as some factions in Congress feared it would be. Aid recipients paid for what they received in their local currency and the market continued to function.

But this was only the first half of the process. The proceeds of the transactions—local currency used to pay for U.S. goods and services—were then deposited in the government's central bank, designated for the purpose of recovery. These funds were "counterpart funds"—the counterparts of the U.S. taxpayer dollars provided through the Marshall Plan. The ECA worked with each Marshall Plan country to devise a strategy for the deployment of these funds. In some countries, most of the funds went to pay down national debt. In others they went to finance industrial modernization.

In practice, the procedure worked as follows: A French farmer who needed a tractor manufactured by a U.S. company would go to a local dealer. He would pay for the tractor in French francs. The ECA and the French government had a clearing mechanism that established a reasonable price and exchange rate for the tractor. Instead of going from the French farmer to the American tractor manufacturer, though, the French francs went back to the French central bank. The ECA and the French government would then work together to devise a strategy for the deployment of those counterpart funds to advance France's recovery. The U.S. tractor manufacturer was paid with funds appropriated from the Marshall Plan, allowing the French farmer's francs to go to the French government. Counterpart funds thus performed a "double duty." The farmer was allowed to purchase a tractor without exacerbating the French balance-of-payments deficit. At the same time, the French government received the value of that tractor in local currency in a fund to be spent on its national recovery.

Thus, the procedure adhered to normal, private commercial practices as much as possible, fortifying rather than disrupting those channels. It also helped to ensure that corruption and scandal were kept to a minimum because Western Europeans purchasing American goods and services had to pay for them. When counterpart funds were disbursed to finance recovery, there was a strict application process, an inspection process at ECA overseen by Bissell and then an innovative procedure called "spot checking" in Marshall countries to ensure funds were being spent as represented.

There was little glamour to the procedure. But beyond the mechanics was an ingenious and elegant technical architecture. More than anyone else, Richard Bissell was its draftsman. Bissell's title of Assistant Deputy Administrator was deceptively facile. Hoffman focused on building and managing ECA. He thought big-picture, painted the vision for the Marshall Plan and then sold that vision at home and abroad. Bissell provided the economic and technical acumen that powered the agency. At press conferences or testifying before Congress, Bissell was almost always at Hoffman's side. After some time, journalists and members of Congress started bypassing Hoffman and addressing the more technical questions directly to Bissell.

One of Bissell's critical early insights was that in order for Western Europe to achieve economic self-sustainability, ECA would have to do much more than simply provide aid. Bissell's deputy remembered that he built programming "around aims with respect to national economic and financial policies—aims considered in the light of the total picture within an economy—and not primarily around what was done with our aid . . . ECA's effort to see the problem as a whole. This was Bissell's great contribution." In those early days, Bissell had not yet devised all of those policies. But the notion that aid must function as an instrument to advance the larger palette of policies necessary to set each Marshall country on its path to self-sustained recovery would frame ECA's strategy and its relationships with the Marshall countries. Historian Arthur Schlesinger recalled that Bissell provided "the economic logic of the Marshall Plan."

It was a source of relief and confidence for Hoffman to have Bissell on board early on. The plaster was barely dry on four of the five floors when Hoffman moved ECA from his hotel suite to their offices at the Miatico Building at 800 Connecticut Avenue, within sight of the White House from across Lafayette Park. Hoffman's fifteen-hour workday included an endless series of meetings and hearings. There was a prodigious influx of correspondence. Most was from position seekers. Some were from well-wishers. Hoffman was delighted to receive nineteen letters from a first-grade class at Colfax School in South Bend, Indiana. One six-year-old wrote, "My Daddy is a preacher and he said if we had more men like you, he would not have to preach so hard." Hoffman found the time to write back to all of them.

Hoffman began speaking publicly about the Plan. He had to solidify its support with Congress and the American people to secure ongoing funding. He began to give several addresses a week. Selling the plan, he was masterful. When Hoffman had finished addressing an audience of New York businessmen, the crowd erupted in applause. One of the businessmen turned to another and said, "I wish Hoffman would get out of government and get back into business." The other appeared shocked and asked, "Why?" "Well," said the first, "he's such a good salesman that I'd like to buy something from him."

That spring no one in the United States, not even Truman or Marshall, received more attention than Paul Hoffman. He was on the cover of *Newsweek, Life* and the *New York Times Magazine*. Cabell Phillips of the *New York Times* wrote that "his every sneeze is recorded with alarm everywhere west of the Iron Curtain." Highly visible and speaking all over the country, Hoffman soon brought his vision for the Marshall Plan into clear view. As he did, it became apparent that the administrator would be a faithful steward of the Plan, as Marshall had laid it out that June afternoon at Harvard one year earlier.

"The idea is to get Europe on its feet and off our back," Hoffman said. The aim was Europe's economic self-sustainability. He had provided the first phrase of the Harriman Committee report: "Only the Europeans can save Europe." Now, as administrator, he would put it into practice. "I had a strong belief that no plan imposed by a group of planners in Washington could possibly be effective," he said. Hoffman viewed ECA's role "as a kind of investment banker" for recovery. ECA would help guide Europe's recovery, and it would help finance it. But Europe would own its own recovery. "The essence of genuine leadership," he would say, "is to share power with people rather than display power over people." The *New York Times* noted that Hoffman, the surgeon who would administer the blood transfusion "to the flagging European body politic is likely to prove one of those firm but kind, I-can't-help-you-if-you-don't-help yourself medicos."

The main ingredient in the prescription for achieving economic self-sustainability and narrowing Europe's Dollar Gap was production. Production plans were "the heart of the program," said one of ECA's leaders. Immediately, Hoffman said that one of his central aims was to increase Europe's economic output by one-third by the end of the program. It was received by many in Europe and the United States as an improbable goal. If it were achieved, however, it would "bring about a reasonable degree of prosperity," Hoffman said at the time of his induction. In his first testimony before Congress as administrator, Hoffman pledged to marshall all of his energies toward "one goal . . . increased production." Boosting production also implied a focus on enhancing productivity. Hoffman also made it clear that he would focus on fiscal and monetary stabilization. All were key objectives as outlined by Clayton and adopted by Marshall.

Hoffman also embraced the concept of promoting European integration. He was an apostle of free enterprise. If Europe was to increase its production, it would need a larger, less restricted market. That would drive European producers to compete, specialize and innovate. All of this in turn would generate production and growth.

At the outset, Hoffman saw that conditions were so desperate in Europe that food and relief aid were needed in order to get workers healthy and productive. Much of the early aid provided, therefore, appeared as if it were humanitarian relief aid. Still, from day one, recovery, not relief, was Hoffman's objective. "What we are confronted with by Communism is not so much a dangerous philosophy as simply a straightforward drive for world domination," he said. For Hoffman, free enterprise and individual liberty were part and parcel. "The real objective" of the ERP, Hoffman told a congressional committee, was "to stop the spread of communism."

When Hoffman was not meeting with officials, corresponding, testifying or speaking around the country, he was back at his office, building his fledgling outfit. To help him draft talent, Hoffman enlisted his close friend and Studebaker legal counsel, Tex Moore, name partner of the white-shoe New York law firm of Cravath, Swaine and Moore. Together Hoffman and Moore set in motion what *Life* called "one of the most spectacular talent-drafting jobs in the annals of Washington agencies." "In screening, our idea was that the choices must reflect America—including government, business, labor, agriculture, education, etc.," Hoffman said. Hoffman tended toward businessmen: men with practical experience who had competed, had produced and had led others in demanding and competitive enterprises. Writing to Hoffman, C. D. Jackson, managing director of Time-Life International, characterized the ECA: "Its uniqueness lies in the fact that it is not a government relief program—not an international handout—but rather a business plan to be carried out by businessmen."

For his deputy, Hoffman brought on Maryland industrialist Howard Bruce. Bissell was below Bruce in the organization chart, as assistant deputy secretary. ECA was also to have an office in Europe, the Office of the Special Representative, or OSR. Averell Harriman was selected to run it. In addition, each Marshall Plan country was to have its own ERP mission, run by mission chiefs. To select the mission chiefs, Hoffman reached out to the very best in government, industry, labor and academia. Hoffman would poach from companies, universities, even government with what *Life* described as "an impartial zeal." He would not hear of accommodating political appointments from the White House. ECA would not be a dumping ground to advance the Democrats' electoral prospects. Hoffman made it clear that he would resign if the principle was compromised. Truman was generally good about it, but when on occasion he did inquire as to why a friend or supporter was not enlisted, Hoffman simply told the president that the person was not the finest one available. Hoffman recalled that Truman would not say another word, for which the president would earn the Republican administrator's lifelong esteem. Arthur Vandenberg called ECA "the most nonpolitical organization which has ever been put together on a government project."

Most of the draftees would take a sharp cut in salary; for many businessmen, it meant a reduction of several multiples of their salary. If they declined an offer to join, Hoffman would say, "O.K., go home and try to live with yourself." After that, Hoffman found, recruits usually turned up for work within ten days. "The way he could pick up a telephone and persuade outstanding people to serve was wonderful," recalled a senior ECA personnel officer. In less than ninety days, Hoffman and Moore had convinced four hundred people—many leading national figures—to come to Washington or move to Europe.

ECA's recruiting drive ruffled feathers in Washington. Truman chose Charles Sawyer to replace Averell Harriman as secretary of commerce. On his first visit to the Commerce Department, Sawyer literally got lost in the labyrinthine offices at Commerce. Sawyer was counting on Undersecretary of Commerce William C. Foster to assist in the transition. In short order, though, Harriman appointed Foster as his deputy in Paris. David Bruce, a very able businessman and administrator, was appointed as Foster's replacement. Only hours after Foster resigned, Hoffman selected Bruce as mission chief in France, and Bruce walked into Sawyer's office to resign. Sawyer was furious. He insisted that he would not permit any other Commerce Department officials to leave for ECA and that those who had already left would not be permitted to return once "the fun was over or when they tired of it." The phenomenon was easy to understand for Bissell: "The Marshall Plan was, after all, the hottest game in town, which the Commerce Department emphatically was not."

The Marshall Plan would be as effective as the men (there were women, but they were few)—their talents and their commitment—that Hoffman would select. British diplomat Sir Ashley Clarke commented: "The quality of personnel provided by the U.S. for this program . . . and their enthusiasm—was a most elevating spectacle." Hoffman's explanation was simple: "It started with the Marshall speech. The concept was a noble one.

The people in the organization wanted to work for something worthwhile, and had the idea that they could contribute to keeping the world free . . . You couldn't want a better motive than that." It was well-known among government workers and Washington residents that the midnight oil on the eleventh floor of the ECA building burned seven days a week and all through the night. "The magic," Hoffman said, "was in the Marshall Plan itself."

To Hoffman, a true believer, the Marshall Plan was "the most generous act of any people, anytime, anywhere, to another people." Europe was starting to believe as well. When the *John H. Quick* pulled into Bordeaux, France, on May 10, the French Foreign Office and the Bordeaux Chamber of Commerce had organized an elaborate ceremony to mark the occasion. U.S. Ambassador Jefferson Caffrey was there to give a speech. American officials in the French embassy worried that Communists might try to sabotage the inaugural shipments and the ceremony. But, under the red, white and blue bunting that hung from scaffolding around the docks, hundreds of Frenchmen—including dockworkers who only months before had been on strike protesting "American imperialism"—received the shipments and the ceremonial addresses with wild cheers.

The receptions were equally stirring when ECA ships pulled into docks in other European port cities. The French Foreign Office produced a documentary film, *Bonne Chance*, portraying Marshall aid and emphasizing the objectives of the Plan to assist in French recovery. A similar film, *Helping Hands*, was produced and widely exhibited in the western zones of Austria. Pamphlets were produced by the tens of thousands. Marshall aid was streaming into Western Europe's ports. By June 30, ECA had approved grants for goods and services valued at $738 million.

The aid had a considerable near-term material impact. When shipments of carbon black reached Birmingham, England, home to Europe's largest tire plant, the plant was put back into production and its ten thousand workers back to work. "This Marshall aid," said one of the workers, "has got my thanks." The psychological impact was even greater. Even as the *John H. Quick* sat under grain elevators in Galveston, the *Economist* wrote, "This week it is fitting that the peoples of Western Europe should attempt to renew their capacity for wonder, so that they can return to the U.S. a gratitude in some way commensurate with the act they are about to receive." For a day or two, the magazine went on, "the Marshall Plan must be retrieved from the realm of normal day-to-day developments in international affairs and be seen for what it is—an act without peer in history." The Plan, the aid and the anticipation of what was to come stirred hope and revivified Western Europe's sense of possibility.

In the months to follow, Europeans answered that call in various ways. In April 1948, Jean Monnet wrote Prime Minister Robert Schuman that his plan for French economic recovery "has now become possible to achieve . . . thanks to the Marshall credits." Monnet and his colleagues and countrymen moved with alacrity to realize France's ambitions for national industrial modernization and economic growth and stability. In May 1948, 750 of Europe's leading statesmen and personalities assembled in the Netherlands at the Hague Conference. Winston Churchill was the honorary president, and he was joined by Schuman, Bidault, De Gasperi and others in calling for European political integration. Mostly this was a political and strategic response to the Czech coup and the sense of insecurity it elicited. America's insistence that Western Europe take bold steps toward integration was also a factor.

The Hague Conference provided momentum to European integration, but little tangible progress. In contrast, in mid-April, the Marshall Plan countries agreed upon a convention for the Organization for European Economic Cooperation, or OEEC (spawned from the CEEC), taking a substantive step toward the region's economic integration. The OEEC, the ECA's counterpart in Europe, would be based in Paris. It was responsible for monitoring the performance of participating countries and promoting cooperation among them. At its birth, it was uncertain how effective that organization would prove.

As waves of ships crossed the Atlantic, and the United States made good on its promise of large-scale aid and material provision, a new sense of hope wafted through Western Europe, increasingly willing to reconsider the economic customs and patterns that had failed it in the past decades. The winter had been punishing. Many Western Europeans were now coming to wonder if perhaps they had weathered the worst of it. As aid flowed, it seemed to breathe life into the Western European body politic—"a psychological blood transfusion," Paul Hoffman said.

ON APRIL 20, 1948, as the inaugural ERP fleet set out across the Atlantic for Western Europe's ports, Paul Hoffman found himself testifying before the House Appropriations Committee. As Acheson had cautioned Truman weeks earlier, the Foreign Assistance Act of 1948, passed on April 3, was an authorization. To actually receive the funds, ECA would have to receive approval from Congress's appropriation committees. Interim aid and other funding sources bridged ERP for the first two months or so of the program, but to obtain funding for the first year of the program, Hoffman and a few others would have to make the case to Congress yet again. That meant convincing the House Appropriations Committee and its chairman, Representative John Taber.

Taber was a small-town lawyer from upstate New York, first elected to Congress as a Republican in 1922. A House veteran and a fabled curmudgeon, Taber was a fiscal conservative with isolationist leanings and was deeply skeptical of foreign aid. Taber was a perennial and formidable roadblock for the White House in obtaining funds for many of its programs. Truman once remarked, "I saw a cartoon the other day called 'the Saber Dance' in which they showed a big man with a saber cutting off the heads of all the appropriations . . . Well, I named it the 'Taber Dance.'"

Following opening statements from Paul Hoffman and Robert Lovett, Paul Nitze, still at the State Department, was called upon to carry the mantle for much of the remaining testimony. Taber made it clear early on that Nitze's task would be arduous. Nitze and his team had compiled detailed "Brown Books" for each Marshall Plan country, outlining the level and types of aid each country needed to receive. The Brown Books—the product of months of exhaustive analysis and deliberation—were designed to help Western Europe overcome its balance-of-payments deficit. "We're not going to use your brown books," Taber said to Nitze the evening before testimony was set to begin, "I don't believe in balance of payments justifications." Taber had other ideas. He wanted Nitze to proceed with a country-by-country, item-by-item defense of the Marshall Plan. "I want you to start with the countries in alphabetical order."

The next day, Taber instructed Nitze to start with Austria. When they reached P and pulses (a type of bean), Taber's nose started to quiver. Taber came from a farming community, and he wanted to know why the United States needed to send Austria 25,000 tons of pulses when the Austrians ought to be perfectly capable of growing them there. Nitze, a Harvard-educated New Yorker and financier, had no idea. He said that if he could call in one of his experts from the Department of Agriculture he was sure it would all be easily explained. Taber blasted Nitze and refused to let him call in his experts. It seemed clear to Nitze that Taber was trying to discredit State's work in an effort to cut the Plan's appropriations. It "was an effective tactic," Nitze recalled.

After pulses, Taber moved on to tractors. When Nitze fumbled, Taber stormed out of the chamber, into his office, and called Robert Lovett at

State. Lovett let Taber fume about "the full horror" of Nitze's presentation. When enough steam had been released, Lovett said to Taber: "You know, I could ask you a question that you couldn't answer. For example, how many rivets are there in a B-29 wing?" Taber replied, "You would know that better than I because you were assistant secretary of war for air in World War II." "Well," Lovett said, "that's just the point. Some people are more knowledge-able about certain matters than other people. So why don't you let Nitze have his experts there to answer these technical questions?" Then before Taber could even answer, Lovett threw out another question: "If it takes eight yards of pink crepe paper to go around an elephant's leg, how long does it take to kill a fly with a flyswatter?" Taber replied: "That's a nonsensical question." Lovett said: "Of course! Now why don't you stop asking Nitze nonsensical questions?"

After that call with Lovett, Taber assumed a more reasonable tack. "That exchange between Taber and Lovett over the phone saved the Marshall Plan," Nitze wrote later. Nitze appeared before Taber and his committee for another forty sessions before his testimony was complete. Lean when the hearings began, Nitze lost fifteen pounds by the time he had finished testify-ing. When it was over, Taber realized he couldn't quash the plan, but if he couldn't kill it, the second-best option was to cut it. In early June, Taber pro-posed that instead of appropriating $5.3 billion for the first year, the U.S. appropriate that amount for the first fifteen months. The proposed modifica-tion would decrease the Plan's funding by almost a quarter. Taber was able to get the House Appropriations Committee behind him.

As the proceedings wore on, the Marshall Plan countries grew increas-ingly anxious. Ambassador Douglas radioed from London that the House action would yield "additional doubts concerning assurances which Western Europe can place on the reliability and consistency of the United States." Bevin warned that a cut would "aggravate" recovery and confidence in Western Europe sharply. French leaders expressed acute anxiety as well.

Arthur Vandenberg was livid and sprang into motion. He tendered an unusual request to appear before the Senate Appropriations Committee, and arrived loaded for bear. Assailing the "meat-axe approach" of Taber's com-mittee, Van said that the cut would "gut the enterprise," downgrading the program from one of recovery to relief. Taber's cut would "veto" the will of Congress, which had been through an exhaustive debate that winter and early spring. "Most desperately important of all, Mr. Chairman, it keeps the word of the promise to the ear but breaks it to the hope. I respectfully submit that it inevitably undermines the confidence and morale abroad upon which recovery, independent freedoms and peace so heavily lean . . . I beg you,"

Vandenberg concluded, "for the sake of the hopes by which free men live—that you give ECA a fair chance."

Vandenberg's intervention proved decisive. In mid-June, the Senate voted 60 to 9 to restore the original appropriation. Taber resisted when the bill reached conference between the House and the Senate. But, under pressure from Vandenberg, he relented and agreed to offer the $5.3 billion appropriation for fifteen months, unless the president or ECA administrator felt it needed more for the first twelve months, allowing Taber to save face but effectively restoring the original twelve-month appropriation. This was just days before the Republican National Convention was set to begin in Philadelphia, and another instance of political bravery on the part of Vandenberg, who chanced an intra-party fissure bleeding into an important convention. Once again, Van had come to the rescue of ERP.

With the first year of funds secured, Hoffman and ECA could enter the second quarter beginning in early July with assurance. It had been a busy three months for Hoffman and his agency. Hoffman had filled all of ECA's major positions in both the United States and Europe. He had brought on 620 employees. Almost 50,000 had applied. ECA had authorized almost $750 million in aid. Three-quarters went to the United Kingdom, France and Italy, Western Europe's largest and strategically most important countries. The major categories of aid broke down into 33 percent for food, feed and fertilizer; 20 percent for fuel; 22 percent for raw and semifinished products; 7 percent for machinery equipment; 3 percent for other products; and 15 percent for ocean freight. During the first year of the program, it appeared that ERP aid would finance about one-half of Western European dollar imports. Railing against those of his countrymen who still opposed the Plan, Bidault thundered that if France pulled out, the French standard of living would drop by half.

Speaking to his Advisory Board on July 16, 1948, Paul Hoffman rattled off what he estimated as thirty-four discrete and major ECA "responsibilities . . . and an astronomical number of headaches." But the Marshall Plan countries had mobilized and ECA had sprung to action with celerity and efficacy. "This is a unique adventure in human history," Hoffman told ECA officials at a training conference. His agency was responding, Western Europe was responding and the American public was responding.

It was only a matter of time before the Soviet Union responded as well. During the spring of 1948, the Soviet-directed propaganda machine was at full blast. The Soviets and European Communists called the Marshall Plan "an instrument of preparation for war" and "a means for the economic enslavement of Europe." Two months after the Italian election, Italy's Communist leader, Palmiro Togliatti, returned from a trip to Eastern Europe and declared that Italy's "2.5 million Communists would wage an all-out fight against the ERP." At a Communist parade in May in Vienna, one banner read: "The sun rises in the East and no Marshall Plan can change or stay it."

With Marshall Plan ships streaming into European ports, with food shipments meted out and factories being put back to work, European opinion was further turning away from the Soviets. The Marshall Plan was helping Western Europe to recover and attempting to integrate Western Europe's countries (including western Germany) in a fortified U.S.-led bloc. Stalin was witnessing his designs for Continental influence further recede. It would have been impossibly out of character for the Soviet dictator to sit idle and remain on the defensive for long. Aiming to regain momentum in Western Europe, Josef Stalin set his sights on a new target, an island 120 miles inside Soviet-occupied eastern Germany: Berlin.

Chapter Nine

SPRINGTIME IN PARIS

I N 1948, for the American tourist interested in adventure and a taste of the exotic, there was no place like Paris. That spring and summer, France was beset with grave political and economic troubles. Despite those troubles—or perhaps, in part, because of them—Paris was throbbing with cultural vitality and allure. Meandering through the city's narrow, cobbled, sloping streets winding around gray, dilapidated homes and buildings, a well-oriented American tourist might come across Albert Camus or Jean-Paul Sartre at one of the local hotels. Keeping an apartment was considered bourgeois, and cooking was not allowed in hotel rooms, so an even better bet was to survey the bustling cafés. At Deux Magots, one had an excellent chance of spotting Picasso or André Breton. Michel Foucault was working on his research into madness in the Latin Quarter, and an Irishman named Samuel Beckett was months away from completing a play titled *Waiting for Godot*.

The tourist would have heard, no doubt, that Americans were very much a part of that cultural stew. Duke Ellington, Charlie Parker and Miles Davis all came through around that time to perform at the Club Saint-Germain. Young American writers like Truman Capote, Richard Wright and James Baldwin were there. The franc had just been devalued that February. The booming American economy and the strong dollar further enticed Americans to Paris, and elsewhere abroad. At once welcome, envied and resented, Americans were all but impossible to miss in Paris that spring. None received as much attention as W. Averell Harriman.

William Averell Harriman was born on November 15, 1891, the oldest son of E. H. Harriman, the famed railroad tycoon and one of the richest men in America. He was a child of immense privilege, growing up on a lavish estate, traveling the world and attending the finest schools. But Harriman's hard-driving father instilled an insatiable work ethic and sense of service. He told his son, "Great wealth is an obligation and responsibility. Money must work for the country." As a student at Yale, Harriman was appointed to the board of the Union Pacific Railroad. Later he cast out on his own, an international financier whose investments included, among other interests, a mineral concession in Russia. In the 1920s he was one of the founders of Brown Brothers Harriman, which became in a short time one of the most prosperous financial houses on Wall Street. An advertisement in 1934 listed firm investments in forty-five different countries.

Harriman was tall, lean, with slicked jet-black hair and dark eyes. He was called a "Gary Cooper type" by one journalist and attracted a bevy of women admirers. He was extremely accomplished in athletics. Taking up polo in his thirties, he would leave Manhattan at 4 P.M. for the country to practice, eventually achieving an eight-goal handicap (out of ten). In 1928 he scored four out of his team's seven goals to lead the U.S. national polo team past Argentina and to the world championships. One newspaper wrote that the match "amounted to a personal triumph for W. Averell Harriman, the American No. 1, who played startlingly brilliant polo." In the decade to follow, Harriman would become a world-class skier and helped turn Sun Valley, Idaho, into a renowned ski resort. More than natural ability, Harriman's achievements were a by-product of an extraordinary drive and focus. "I like recreation that calls for just as much energy as work calls for," he said.

Harriman's interests, his father's admonishment to serve and his own ambition and desire to operate on the world's highest stage all turned his attention to government in the 1920s and 1930s. Born into a Republican family, Harriman grew displeased at Republican isolationists and irate at Hoover's economic stewardship during the stock market crash of 1929. He became an active Democrat, and the fellow-patrician president, Franklin Roosevelt, recruited him to help lead the National Recovery Administration, one of FDR's key New Deal programs.

Harriman was not brilliant. He was a poor speaker, awkward with the press and much more comfortable at the diplomatic conference table or in business meetings than in social settings. He had a rigorous mind, though, complemented by razor-sharp instincts and a businessman's sense of pragmatism. Mostly, he had a proven and felicitous ability to achieve an objective to which he applied his fierce drive and his prodigious powers of concentration. As an international financier and deal maker and as a Democrat, Harriman was a valued asset for FDR. When war broke out in Europe, and FDR decided to send aid to England, he summoned Harriman to run the Lend-

Lease operation. He called him an "Expediter." Harriman ran Lend-Lease for the first half of the war, a role that earned him the distinction of giving "away more money than any human being in world history."

Anticipating the importance of U.S.–Soviet relations in the final stages of the war and the postwar negotiations to follow, Roosevelt appointed Harriman ambassador to the Soviet Union late in 1943. When Harriman, who had provided the Soviet Union with billions of Lend-Lease dollars, paid his formal courtesy call on Molotov in October 1943, the Soviet foreign minister said, "We have found you a very tough man to deal with." Harriman replied, "I have come as a friend." "Oh, I know that," Molotov replied, "I intended my remarks to be complimentary." Soviet diplomat and future Foreign Minister Andrei Vishinsky said of Harriman that he was "the only capitalist I ever met who made some sense." He puzzled Soviet Ambassador Maxim Litvinov: "How can a man with a hundred million dollars look so sad?" he asked.

At the embassy, Harriman demanded long hours and offered subordinates little in the way of human warmth or effusion. He could be gruff and harsh. At a Washington dinner party he once decided that he had listened to enough from a young congressman named Richard Nixon—he reached behind his ear and turned off his hearing aid. Harriman's most prominent subordinate, George Kennan, often found himself wondering, "Why do I like this man?" But there was reason. He was unerringly loyal to those who were devoted to him; he drove himself hardest of all; he listened and considered his subordinates' views carefully and advocated for the embassy's positions forcefully and effectively.

In early 1946, Harriman left the Soviet post to become U.S. ambassador to the United Kingdom. Returning to London, Harriman would renew his intimate associations with Churchill and other leaders in Britain, such as diplomat Anthony Eden. Harriman was not a braggart, but he had a pronounced ego and craved recognition. As U.S. ambassador to the Soviet Union he spent more time with Stalin than any other American in history. Two historians wrote that Harriman collected important acquaintanceships almost as boys collect stamps. Harriman's friends said that when Hitler's name came up, Harriman would say wistfully that he had never met him, almost like a big game hunter recalling the big trophy that had escaped.

By the time Harry Truman recalled Harriman to Washington to join his Cabinet as secretary of commerce, he had already been a strong champion for European recovery. As early as April 1945, Harriman had cabled Washington from Moscow: "We must use our economic power to assist those countries that are naturally friendly to our concepts in so far as we can possibly do so." By June 1947, after returning from a comprehensive tour of Europe, Harriman also sounded a key note for German economic recovery at a formative time in the internal U.S. debate on Germany. Truman valued Harriman's experience, judgment and bona fides as a businessman and appointed him to run the President's Committee on Foreign Aid (better known as the Harriman Committee). He evinced a diplomat's fine touch, knowing when to push and when to convince. Reading a speech that had been written for his congressional testimony, he lashed out at aides, "Goddamn it, I am the secretary of commerce"—in the patrician accent that made it sound like "secretary of commus"—"How in the hell can I present this gahhhbage to the United States Congress?" The committee was universally lauded, and Harriman's role further added to his prestige.

A few weeks after agreeing to serve as administrator of ECA, Paul Hoffman met with President Truman. The legislation stipulated that a roving ambassador be appointed to represent the ERP in Europe. It would be an immensely important posting, Hoffman said. It would require not only extensive diplomatic experience but world-class business credentials as well. He felt it essential that he already know and trust the new ambassador. There were, Hoffman said, perhaps five men in all of America that could do the job. He would consider Clayton, he said. Lovett cabled Marshall that Clayton "could not accept for reasons known to you," an apparent reference to his wife, Sue. Hoffman then proposed Lewis Douglas and Harriman, in alphabetical order, he later recalled. Truman was reluctant to let Harriman leave the Cabinet, but he also made it clear that he wanted a staunch Democrat for the post, and Douglas had a more independent history. Hoffman had worked with Harriman and he certainly fit the bill.

It was well known that Averell Harriman had hoped to be administrator of the Marshall Plan. He had as much business experience as Hoffman and greater government experience and international stature. Harriman had already been ambassador to the world's two other leading capitals, London and Moscow. Hoffman told him that this new position would provide an opportunity no other American had ever had: to be the first American ambassador to Europe. He accepted and was sworn in on April 27, 1948. "I find I am an adventurer at heart," he had once said.

ARRIVING IN PARIS in late April, Harriman's first order of business was to secure a headquarters for the Office of the Special Representative. In short time, he obtained the Hotel de Talleyrand, a palatial building looking out on the Place de la Concorde and the American Embassy. Originally, Napoleon had presented the building to his foreign minister, Talleyrand, and it served as the site of the diplomat's many political intrigues and liaisons with women. After Napoleon's defeat, it was briefly occupied by the Russian Czar, and then later by Edouard de Rothschild. Stalin had coveted the building. It was a particular delight, therefore, for Harriman to set up his own office in a resplendent reception salon at the corner of the building, looking out over la Place through floor-to-ceiling windows, surrounded by stunning eighteenth-century antiques, oil paintings, burgundy silk cushions and a large bust of Benjamin Franklin, America's first representative to Paris.

The role of special ambassador was conceived originally as a roving diplomat, who would serve as the eyes and ears for headquarters in Washington. Harriman had a different conception of the role. He wanted OSR to function more like a theater command. His office would help devise and execute ECA policy; it would work with and negotiate with the Europeans; and it would be the voice of the Marshall Plan in Europe. Harriman would be the field commander. Originally, OSR was to be a small and focused outfit, and Harriman began operations with a staff of five. In little more than six months, OSR's headcount exceeded 2,000, dwarfing the Washington staff by more than double. Most of those were the mission chiefs and their staff, spread out across sixteen countries. But Harriman also brought on personnel to his own office at the Talleyrand, which grew multiples beyond what had been originally envisioned.

Harriman had carpenters come to the mansion to install "a labyrinthine maze of cubicles, pens and partitions" to accommodate the incoming waves of new staff. At the Talleyrand, old wooden floors squeaked with the hum of activity day and night, and Parisians started noticing. A Frenchwoman wrote to Harriman that she liked Americans in general, but that the fluorescent lights burning late "marred the somber beauty of the Concorde at night." Harriman ordered black curtains to dim the glare. Some Parisians took umbrage at the American presence at the Talleyrand. One cynical boulevardier quipped: "How very appropriate for our American friends to choose that building? The only other people who ever succeeded in unifying Europe lived there too—Talleyrand and the de Rothschilds."

Harriman's appointment and arrival in Paris provided fodder for Communist propaganda. *Pravda* called Harriman a plutocrat and said that he represented a ruling circle bent on "world political and economic supremacy of the United States." Harriman and his American cronies were concerned only with exploiting Europe's grave condition for their self-enrichment. The immediate hail of attacks made it clear to Harriman that part of his mission in Paris would include doing battle with the Communists on the psychological and propaganda fronts.

He also began to worry that his lavish surroundings would attract attention from enterprising journalists sniffing for scandal or alarm visiting congressmen concerned about waste. One of his first hires was Al Friendly, a popular newsman who would later become a managing editor at the *Washington Post*, to run communications. Harriman had Friendly launch a preemptive strike and alert Washington journalist Drew Pearson that Harriman's luxurious offices were a national monument and thus French property, and there was never any fuss about it in Congress or the press. On one occasion, when an OSR staffer noticed elaborate channel irons surrounding the elegant structure, Harriman ordered them removed and sent them to French officials, in a delivery of several tons of steel that never found itself in any of the official Marshall Plan statistics.

Harriman wasted no time in building his team. His deputy, William C. Foster, former president of Pressed and Welded Steel Products and former undersecretary of commerce, helped administer OSR and was Harriman's chief troubleshooter. To screen OEEC and Marshall country plans, Harriman brought on Calvin Hoover, head of the department of economics at Duke University. To screen new projects, Harriman enlisted George Perkins, executive vice president of Merck. As his chief aide and counsel, Harriman brought on Milton Katz, a prominent professor at Harvard Law School. Most of the mission chiefs, who were selected by Hoffman but reported to Harriman, had run large corporations; some were government officials and two were labor leaders.

Below them, a rivulet of outstanding Americans poured into Paris and OSR to fill midlevel and junior postings. They were a mix of personalities and had myriad motivations: some were college professors on leave, wishing to see theory turned to practice; others were in labor and despised what Communism was doing to the movement; some were government officials hoping to stick a prestigious feather in their cap and return to a better position in the United States; and finally, wrote Theodore White, many were "enlightened businessmen, seeking a burst of adventure or impelled by patriotism and convinced that, by God, American business could put the world to rights." Some of American history's colorful personalities found their way to OSR. "Liking Harriman and loving Paris," a young Harvard professor named Arthur Schlesinger came to Paris for part of the year to work with Friendly, primarily as a speechwriter for Harriman. For Schlesinger the Marshall Plan was the most important and dynamic undertaking in the world at that time, and he wanted to be a part of it.

Schlesinger recalled another midlevel Marshall Planner: a Brown graduate and published novelist named Howard Hunt. Hunt also worked on the communications side of OSR, producing a propaganda documentary promoting the Marshall Plan in Austria. At OSR, Hunt courted and then married Harriman's secretary, Dorothy Wetzel Day Goutiere. Hunt grew disconsolate at OSR, "a briar-patch of liberalism," in his view, and accepted an invitation to join the Central Intelligence Agency. Hunt would later garner infamy as one of the "plumbers" who broke into Democratic offices at the Watergate Hotel in Richard Nixon's 1972 reelection campaign.

In the first few months, chaos prevailed at the Talleyrand. Roles were ill-defined and the work load was furious. As the first months passed, senior officials found their footing, procedure was streamlined and order was established. The Talleyrand was bustling from early morning (by Parisian standards) to late into the night. At the American snack bar downstairs over a hot dog or ice cream, or in technicians' offices, cubicles and conference rooms, officials analyzed European plans, monitored the flow of U.S. aid, examined requests for counterpart funds, devised plans to counter Soviet propaganda charges, met with European counterparts, monitored the developments at OEEC and cabled back and forth with ECA in Washington.

It was customary for Marshall Planners to take leave of the Talleyrand in the evening, stroll across the Place de la Concorde, passing glistening new American automobiles, and amble into the Hotel Crillon, where over cocktails, Theodore White wrote, "Europe and the world were pulled apart, remodeled, put together again every evening in conversation by experts fresh out of Muncie, Indiana, and Knoxville, Tennessee." As a prominent American journalist in Paris for much of the Marshall Plan years, White recalled some of the conversations at the Crillon. One evening he heard a Marshall Planner explain how things worked at OSR: "They say they want to know how much wheat France is going to be able to export, so they ask how many tractors will France need to raise that much wheat . . . Well, we get to work and produce a figure and we give it to the commercial boys and they say how many of these do you think France can make herself, then somebody else says well so many and somebody else says when? And there you are."

Another followed: "You take Turkey, that's really fouled up. I figure they could raise maybe a million tons of wheat there, but somebody else says there's no water. So we figure we could irrigate the land, and somebody else says how are you going to move that million tons of wheat out there? By mule cart? Then after you get through figuring out how to put in machinery, the irrigation and the railways, you find out they've got 800,000 wooden ploughs there and if the wheat market goes down it'll squeeze those peasants out and they're liable to blow up the machinery and the railways. Every time you touch something it gets tangled up in something else and you have to spend all your time untangling it. I tell you this Europe is really a mess. Garçon, two more drys [martinis] over here . . ."

The breadth and gravity of the decisions that came across Marshall Planners' desks every day was extraordinary. Many OSR officials would recall their time in Paris as the most stimulating of their lives. Beyond work at the Talleyrand and musings at the Crillon, most of the Marshall Planners soaked up Paris. "The dollar was triumphant and the restaurants were wonderful," Schlesinger recalled of his time in Paris. Paris offered Marshall Planners adventure, the finest restaurants, the best music, culture and romance.

For their part, most Parisians were ambivalent about the Marshall Planners and the swarm of Americans who descended upon Paris during this period. The term *Americanization* originated in Britain in the early nineteenth century and was popularized by British journalist William Stead's *The Americanization of the World*, published in 1901. But, it was really during the war and its aftermath when American music, customs and language all began to morph Paris in some subtle, and some not so subtle ways. The Marshall Planners were "generally begged for," Theodore White wrote. But "when all is said," White continued, "they are, in varying degrees, hated, disliked, mistrusted, or accepted either in humiliation or restraint by the peoples of other countries."

Communists seized upon Western European anxiety to stir resentment in Paris and elsewhere. They assailed the Marshall Planners as *"La 5e Colonne americaine en France"* (the fifth column of America in France) and called America "the new occupying power." A popular ditty in the London salons followed: "Our uncle who art in America, Sam be thy name / Thy Navy come, Thy will be done . . . give us this day our Marshall aid, and forgive us our un-American activities . . ." American aid was needed, it was popular, and by and large, it was gratefully received. As Americans poured into Paris, though, reveling in their privilege and circumstance, their presence—however well meaning—sometimes added a bitter taste to the potion they were peddling for European recovery. Averell Harriman possessed what Arthur Schlesinger described as a "trained intuition, something like a musical ear," and as the Marshall Plan's ambassador in Europe Harriman made it his business to be finely keyed into this tune.

• • •

ON JUNE 5, 1948, Averell Harriman stood before the Executive Committee of the OEEC in Paris. It was a chance to mark the first anniversary of the adventure in which Western Europe and America were now jointly engaged. It was also a chance for Harriman to propose another one.

One of the cardinal tenets in Marshall's speech was the importance of European initiative, that Europe must have command, as much as possible, of its own recovery. To that end, Harriman and Hoffman had ambitious plans for the OEEC. They wanted it to serve as the machinery that would launch European integration. Sitting with David Schoenbrun, a CBS correspondent for Edward R. Murrow's radio show, at his Left Bank apartment in early June, Harriman said that his "immediate objective is furthering intra-European trade."

Examining the fledgling organization at its temporary headquarters at the Royal Monceau Hotel before it was to move to its permanent headquarters on the Quai d'Orsay near the French Foreign Ministry, Harriman was reasonably pleased. A well-regarded French economist named Robert Marjolin was appointed secretary general, and the requisite organizational framework was in place. In short order, though, Harriman grew very concerned. If the OEEC was to function effectively, he felt, it needed representation from the highest levels of the participants' governments—ideally, prominent Cabinet-level officials. Instead, the Marshall Plan countries sent civil servants. He noticed that France and Italy and some of the other countries were interested in promoting integration, but that Britain seemed reluctant. Great Britain appointed Sir Oliver Franks, one of its most prestigious diplomats, as its ambassador to the United States, suggesting that it wanted to bypass the OEEC and deal directly with America.

The key countries had varying perceptions of the function they wanted the OEEC to serve, of the powers with which they felt it should be endowed and the degree to which they wanted it to promote European integration. The new organization lacked any semblance of panache or allure. It did not help, one of Harriman's staff wrote, that the name sounded "like a pig caught under a fence . . . it didn't have that certain oomph necessary to capture anyone's imagination." The British chancellor of the Exchequer proposed an international contest to suggest a new name for the organization. William Foster, Harriman's deputy, proposed "European Cooperation Organization," abbreviated to Eureco, which seemed acceptable, until it was learned that "eureco" meant "something horrible" in one of the participant country's languages. An Irish consultant suggested "Europe's God-Given Support," the initials of which spelled "EGGS." No change was made.

A dull name was the least of the organization's problems. Harriman and

State and most U.S. officials expected much from OEEC. Integration was the key to ensuring that Europe did not revert to autarky, that it created a large market for itself to drive innovation and competition, that it liberalized its trade to propel growth, that it realized self-sustained recovery. Congress would demand progress when considering future appropriations. The Communist press had picked up on the organization's early stasis. The French Communist evening paper *Ce Soir* wrote in late May that Marjolin was merely Harriman's puppet: "After all, doesn't [Harriman] control the cash register and isn't he the boss of all these wind-bags?"

Harriman felt that European self-confidence, dignity and self-reliance were necessary ingredients in Europe's economic recovery, and in forging a Europe that could emerge as a viable and productive economic, and perhaps even a security, partner for the United States. To that end, Harriman adumbrated the key themes he wanted mission chiefs to stress when dealing with Europeans: "The success of the ERP Rests Mainly with Europe . . . Ninety-five percent of the program is European." Harriman continued: "The program will succeed only if Europe makes [its] own recovery program . . . It is a *European* recovery program . . . This is a Partnership between the United States and Europe." Each stood to benefit and each had to carry its weight. "The ERP is not a gesture from the rich to the poor, i.e., charity or relief. It is not the sort of gesture from which America demands the response of gratitude . . . No European need feel resentful at receive [*sic*] American help; each American and each European can, instead, take pride in joining in a partnership program for a goal of transcendent importance."

As Harriman spoke to the OEEC's Executive Committee in Paris on June 5, he stated: "May I repeat that it is Mr. Hoffman's confident hope that, in dealing with the annual program that you are about to embark upon, you will be able to develop a program of mutual co-operation and form judgments and make recommendations to him as to the manner in which the American aid can be most effective in furthering your programme." Every U.S. official to appear before Western Europe on the subject of ERP had said as much before. But, Harriman continued, "and that means of course the division [of aid] between the participating nations."

The special ambassador said that he and his staff would be there "to work with you and the staff of your organization in whatever way we can be helpful . . . and when you ask for guidance, and only when you ask for guidance, we will be prepared to give it to you. It is a mutual undertaking with, as I say, the initiative always coming from you—the nations of Western Europe." The proposal accorded with Hoffman's philosophy of European self-help and self-reliance, and he supported the concept, but it was Harriman who leveled the challenge: it would be Europe's responsibility—with OEEC as its institutional forum—to come together and offer a joint recommendation to the United States on how Marshall aid should be distributed amongst the Marshall Plan countries.

IT WAS AN AUDACIOUS PROPOSITION. The Marshall Plan countries were a regional grouping. They were not chosen, as one European diplomat recalled, "because their economies were complementary, nor because they constituted a natural and self-evident single economic region." Several of them had recently been at war with each other. Before that they had been enmeshed in autarkic policies resembling economic warfare. The Marshall Plan countries were desperate for aid. Most of them felt that the process of dividing aid among themselves would lead to conflict and animosity. Many even felt that the unproven organization could not weather the process. Britain's Stafford Cripps told the U.S. mission chief in England, Thomas Finletter, that the division of aid "would put too heavy a strain on OEEC," that it would amount to an "intolerable" burden. The Norwegians and other governments followed the British line and added their own reservations. Some of the Marshall Plan countries estimated that they stood to receive more aid if they dealt directly with the U.S. government. "To most delegates this news came as a shock," said Baron J.-Charles Snoy, a delegate from Belgium, "We feared it would wreck the organization."

Harriman was willing to gamble that it would do the opposite. He believed the process would foster habits of cooperation. The exercise would build European confidence that it could chart its own course and that its countries could assume command of their own shared destiny. Part of the motivation was more practical and even self-interested. "I had a horror of [sixteen] countries coming to the United States with their front teeth in the trough. I thought that the net result of that would be that we would have [sixteen] enemies of the United States and [sixteen] enemies among each other, because of the jealousy that would come." Harriman didn't see how the United States could do it: "How could you justify giving Holland twice the amount of money that you gave Belgium?"

Per Haekkerup, a Danish member of parliament, remembered that the notion of European integration did not begin with the Marshall Plan. "There had been some great talk about it; some great ideas about it. Everybody felt that if we were to overcome our difficulties, it would be necessary to establish some sort of form of European cooperation." Still, Haekkerup remembered, "no initiative had been taken, no sincere talks had been held,

and that was made possible by this [Harriman] proposal." The German delegate Gunther Harkort remembered, "European nations were not at all accustomed to such cooperation . . . all this had to be learned first." The Marshall
Plan fathered the OEEC, an institutional platform from which European
cooperation and integration could spring forward. Most Europeans, however,
felt that it was not firm enough to withstand the division of aid. They didn't
want to chance it. Harriman didn't give them a choice, insisting that the
Europeans take the initiative—and knowing full well that division of aid
could be the crucible upon which the OEEC (and perhaps the Marshall Plan
itself) might flourish or crumble.

LESS THAN TWO WEEKS AFTER Harriman's address to the OEEC at Paris,
on June 18, 1948, Lucius Clay, the military governor in the U.S.–occupied
zone of Germany, announced a currency reform in Germany. Inflation had
reached absurd proportions. Hoarding was rampant, and the mark had essentially lost efficacy as a unit of currency, declining to as much as one five-
hundredth of its official value, or more. At the official exchange rate, a
carton of Lucky Strikes that month cost $2,300. A German reporter asked
an American official if the United States planned to stabilize Germany's
economy with a loan of 50 million cartons of Luckies.

Lucius Clay was born into one of the most prominent political families in
the American South. His great-uncle was Henry Clay, the master legislator,
and his father was a senator from Georgia. He was trained as an engineer in
the Army and made his mark in the war on the production effort. By equal
measure brilliant and irascible, Clay was known at the Talleyrand as "the
Kaiser," and "sometimes seemed to run an emotional temperature of 104,"
Milton Katz remembered. "Clay is a fine fellow when he relaxes," it was said
in the Army during his tenure, "the only problem is that he never relaxes."
Perhaps the best indication of his temper is that he submitted his resignation
no less than eleven times. Perhaps the best gauge of his importance is that it
was never accepted.

Clay oversaw the American occupation of Germany after the war. He was
the most forceful and vociferous champion for German economic recovery.
The sooner Germany was on its way, the sooner occupation costs would go
down and troop commitments could be drawn down. Clay grew up in the
post–Civil War South of the Reconstruction. He knew from experience
what it felt like to be among a defeated and occupied people, and he had an
intuitive understanding of the fragility of their dignity. Clay remembered his
family's stories about what happened to them in Georgia after Confederate

money became worthless. He thus had a particular sensitivity to rampant inflation and the corrosive material and psychological effects it could have on societies.

Since 1946, Clay, along with the senior U.S. representative to Germany (the de facto U.S. ambassador), Robert Murphy, had been pushing for currency reform to stabilize Germany's economy and to promote recovery. The Soviets had used their veto on the Allied Control Council to prevent any sort of reform. As inflation continued to climb, conditions deteriorated. A German economic official recalled that the climate "of stagnation in misery, of hopelessness and despair, could not have endured much longer." In August 1947, two months after Marshall's Harvard speech, Harriman appealed to Truman for monetary reform.

The central development that gave rise to the currency reform was the Marshall Plan. The United States had determined that Western Europe's economic recovery was its paramount foreign policy priority, the best means of advancing U.S. security and economic interests. German recovery was necessary to drive European recovery. In late April, Army Secretary Kenneth Royall wrote to Henry Stimson: "We have tried to maintain an 'open door' to the Soviets in all our actions in Germany but we cannot permit continued stagnation in that country and still hope to revive Western Europe's economy in keeping with the objective of the ERP." That same month, Marshall wrote to Vandenberg explaining that the time had come to unify the British, French and U.S. zones in Germany "and make them an 'integral' part of the ERP."

That late spring, the London Conference concluded. Britain, the United States, the Benelux countries and even France (albeit reluctantly, and at the eleventh hour) all agreed to several provisions for Germany. They agreed to raise the ceiling in German steel production. They agreed to pursue currency reform in the western zones. Most importantly, they agreed to fuse their zones and to create a German Constitutional Assembly. In doing so, they agreed to allow the western Germans "those governmental responsibilities which are compatible with the minimum requirements of occupation." The logic of the Marshall Plan dictated German economic recovery, and for the economy to revive and be viable, western Germans needed a greater sense that they controlled their own destiny, a greater sense of political enfranchisement and autonomy. At the London Conference the western Allies essentially moved to construct a West German state.

For Stalin, it was an alarming turn. He wanted to keep the West weak and divided. He did not want to see a revived Germany, allied with a western capitalist bloc, in opposition to the Soviet Union. Futhermore, a prosperous

West German state could attract Germans from the Soviet zone in the East. Eventually, they could seek to throw out the Soviets and ally with the West, forming a unified Germany rehabilitated and allied against the Soviet Union. It was Stalin's strategic nightmare, and he would not allow it to happen without a fight.

All signs pointed to trouble in Berlin. Split into four zones, each occupied by the four main powers (United States, Britain, France and the Soviet Union), Berlin lay 120 miles inside the eastern, Soviet-occupied half of Germany. Murphy called it "an island in the heart of the Soviet zone" and it was said back then that Berlin "resembled four pieces of pie lying on a Red tablecloth." American access to Berlin required crossing Russian-occupied roads, rail lines and canals. As the London Conference progressed and it became clear that the West was proceeding separately to rehabilitate Germany and even move toward West German statehood, the Soviets began obstructing western passage to Berlin. Throughout late March, April and May, the Soviet military commander Vasily Sokolovsky and his subordinates told their western counterparts that various passageways were closed for repairs and furnished other such excuses. Clay cabled back to Washington that there would be trouble with the Soviets, and Berlin would be the locus of conflict.

When Clay announced the currency reform on June 18, he made it clear that it was for the western zones of Germany, excluding Berlin. Still, the Soviets proceeded immediately to escalate interruption of western passage into Berlin and introduced their own currency reform—in their zone in the east and also in all of Berlin, including the western zones (thereby asserting Soviet sovereignty in all of Berlin). On June 23, the West announced that its new marks—the deutschmark—would circulate in the western zones of Berlin, thereby asserting its counterclaim to sovereignty in western Berlin. On June 24, the same day that Governor Thomas Dewey of New York accepted the presidential nomination at the Republican convention in Philadelphia, the Soviets sealed all access via roads, rail lines, canals and also cut Soviet-generated power to the western zones of Berlin: the Berlin blockade.

There were 2,400,000 Berliners in the western zones. They had little more than a month's supply of food and coal. Without supplies from the outside, they would starve, and their industry would shut down. Clay felt it was tantamount to an act of war, and if the West did not stand up to the Soviets in Berlin, other Soviet offensives would follow. "The U.S. position would be gravely weakened," Murphy cabled Washington, "like a cat on a sloping tin roof." The Allies had 6,500 troops in Berlin, while the Russians had 18,000 and an additional 300,000 in the eastern zones of Germany. Clay wanted to break through and challenge the Soviets with military force and Murphy backed him.

There was another alternative, though. General Brian Robertson, Clay's counterpart in the British zone, suggested supplying the western zones of Berlin via air: a massive airlift. Marshall was reluctant to confront the Soviets militarily due to the Soviet advantage in land forces. Truman agreed and was also reluctant to chance war with an election coming up. Some senior officials in Washington advocated pulling out of Berlin altogether. On the morning of June 26, General Clay, in cooperation with the commander of the U.S. Air Forces in Europe, General Curtis LeMay, gave orders to begin airlifts from the western zones in Germany, over 120 miles of land occupied by the Soviets, to drop 225 tons of food, coal and other vital materials to the western zones of Berlin. As it began, few people even in the highest echelon of the American military and government estimated that it could be effective for long.

On June 26, the first western transport plane touched down at Tempelhof Airport in west Berlin. On June 27, Drew Middleton wrote in the *New York Times*, "U.S. airpower throughout Europe is being mobilized for a great shuttle service into besieged Berlin. U.S. aircraft, which four years ago brought death to the city, will bring life in the form of food and medicines to the people of the Western sectors, whose food supplies have been cut off by the Russians."

While the Americans and Soviets squared off in Berlin, Washington was gripped in yet another war scare. Lord Ismay, Churchill's wartime chief of staff, wrote to Eisenhower, then Chief of Staff of the Army: "The situation in Europe is very tense, as you may imagine . . . We are all standing on the precipice, and although all the parties concerned are determined not to slip over the edge, there may be a puff of wind or someone may get dizzy and trip up; or again, someone may be deliberately malicious." Churchill likened the atmosphere in Berlin to Munich. Marshall postponed a major kidney operation to remain at the helm at State and by Truman's side during the crisis.

Ten days after the blockade was complete, Clay visited his Russian counterpart, Sokolovsky, and asked him, "How long do you plan to keep it up?" The Soviet general replied, "Until you stop your plans for a West German government." A month later, meeting with U.S. Ambassador Walter Bedell Smith, Stalin suggested that if the West ceased its plans for West Germany and abolished "mark B" from Berlin, "then there would be no difficulties." Stalin would be pleased to kick the West out of Berlin, but more than that, it was probable that the blockade was a negotiating tactic to stymie U.S. plans for a separate, rehabilitated West German state, Western unity and recovery more broadly. These were, of course, the central and animating goals of the Marshall Plan and U.S. foreign policy.

Meanwhile, with so much hanging in the balance—not least of all the 2.4 million lives in Berlin—officials in Washington, London and Germany concentrated their efforts and harnessed their air power and the full extent of their logistical and technological prowess toward the airlift. By the third of July, British Yorks and Dakotas joined American C-47s and the newer, larger four-engine C54s (Americans supplied most of the planes and supplies, but it was a joint American-British effort) in a steady hum of flights, streaming into Tempelhof and Gatow airports in the western zones of Berlin. Most planes averaged three flights per day, and planes landed as often as every four minutes, already supplying twice what Clay had called for in his original estimate. Week after week, the number of landings, and the tonnage of supplies increased. "We were proud of our Air Force during the war," the *New York Times* wrote. "We're prouder of it today."

On July 20, Truman reiterated "a firm determination" to continue the airlift. It was a disastrous month for Stalin. The Americans refused to leave Berlin or to reconsider the London Conference program for West Germany. In Italy, there was an assassination attempt on Palmiro Togliatti. In Yugoslavia, the nationalist leader Tito split with Stalin, shattering the notion that Stalin wielded an invincible hand over a monolithic international Communist front. Stalin was forced in late June, only days after the start of the airlift, to expel Tito, Eastern Europe's strongest leader, from the Cominform. He directed the Cominform to call for a coup in Yugoslavia to oust Tito, and started a propaganda war. A sort of cold war within a cold war broke out. Stalin's grip over Eastern Europe, his sphere of power and his security buffer, was his paramount concern. Fearing further nationalist revolt, Stalin tightened his grip in the East even harder. The purges and oppression increased.

The Berlin blockade, the attendant war scare (the second in four months) and Stalin's behavior all amplified Western Europe's anxieties over its security even further. Quietly, below the radar of the media or the international community, Western European leaders were meeting with American officials at the Pentagon in early July, working on a new and unprecedented military alliance for countries in the North Atlantic. "Looked at properly," said Milton Katz, the Marshall Plan and the burgeoning alliance "were mutually supporting and, indeed, mutually indispensable efforts."

During the summer of 1948, the Berlin Airlift was defying expectations—the Soviets' most of all, but even America's. Most dramatically, the currency reform, almost overnight, yielded astonishing results. Two weeks after the currency reform, the *Economist* surveyed the picture in western Germany: "Housewives strolled down the streets gazing in astonishment at shop windows—at shoes, leather handbags, tools, perambulators, bicycles, cherries in baskets, young carrots tied in neat bundles." In other words, wrote historian David Ellwood, "confidence had returned overnight." The currency reform helped to launch one of the most dazzling economic recoveries in modern times.

In late July, Marshall shared his analysis of what was driving the Soviets. "The present tension in Berlin," the general said to the Cabinet, "is brought about by loss of face of Russia in Italy, France, Finland . . . It is caused by Russian desperation in the face of success of ERP." In a sense, the Berlin Airlift was a discrete enterprise, a bold and imaginative response to the Soviet blockade. Yet it was also an outgrowth of the Marshall Plan and the U.S. policy of driving German economic recovery and western Germany's return to viability and autonomy as part of an integrated Europe. As the summer passed, the airlift was keeping Berliners from starving, and keeping western Berlin's economy functioning. Supplying Berlin in summer was one thing, though. Late that summer, with winter in view, Clay cabled military officials in Washington: "The going is tough and it is too early to predict the outcome."

Chapter Ten

THE ROAD TO RECOVERY

Recalling his first six months as special representative in Paris, Averell Harriman said, "This was the toughest job I ever tackled." On an average day, Harriman was up and, with bulging briefcase by his bedside, reading cables from Washington and all over Western Europe by 7 A.M. A black Chrysler dropped him at the Talleyrand by 9, where he met with, on average, thirty people a day. Harriman had to build up his staff at OSR, appoint and consult with sixteen mission chiefs, help formulate ECA policy, function as ECA's spokesperson with the OEEC and Europe's press, and he had to troubleshoot and communicate constantly with ECA headquarters and Hoffman and Bissell back in Washington. Harriman had to deal with so many parties of such varying interests and perspectives that *BusinessWeek* said his position called "for more tact than any one man could possibly possess." For the first six months, he stayed on top of every detail, insisting that he read every single cable to come over OSR's transom himself.

Harriman's drive and focus elicited attention and respect. "He does everything intensely," said one official. "He tackles every Government paper that comes over his desk as though the fate of the nation hung on that one paper." Among his new European colleagues, he earned various sobriquets: "the Ambassador of Wall Street" and "the Marshall Plan's flying ambassador" were two. The *Washington Post* said that it was an "unprecedented job for [a] unique man." Harriman entertained often at his Left Bank flat. Visitors, mostly subordinates or European politicians or officials, could not help but notice the décor in Harriman's salon, which included a Renoir, a Picasso, a Van Gogh bowl of yellow tulips and a Gauguin hung from imposing walls. "God, how could I concentrate on what he was saying with those around?"

asked one visitor. Mostly, Harriman's cocktail parties were simply another forum for the special ambassador to solicit views and advance his agenda.

Harriman's position required him to spend extensive time traveling throughout Europe, visiting European politicians and businesspeople and his own mission chiefs and their staff. His travels required funds in excess of those made available to his budget, and he thought nothing of financing them personally. Among those Harriman visited in the summer of 1948 was a family living in a basement beneath the rubble of a destroyed building in Essen, Germany. After he left, Harriman's aide Vernon Walters asked if there could ever be recovery. There could be, and there would be, Harriman replied. Harriman had noticed something while he met with the family. He turned to Walters: "Any people who will, in the midst of this desolation, think of putting flowers on the table will rebuild the ruins."

The observation proved prophetic. Western Germany had turned a corner. Elsewhere in Western Europe, the other Marshall Plan countries were abuzz with activity that summer of 1948.

The ships—at any given time there were around 150 Marshall aid vessels on the Atlantic—pulled into European ports in increasing frequency as the summer passed. Shipyards were bustling. In place of the rubble that was cleared, railroad stations and office buildings were springing up. Repaved roads hummed with trucks carrying food and basic supplies. Danish children smiled as they enjoyed rice pudding, the first they had eaten in years, thanks to ECA shipments of rice. A vendor in the Netherlands sold bread out of a cart emblazoned with a sign that read: "More than half of your daily bread is baked with Marshall wheat." There were 40,000 other bakers in the Netherlands who displayed the same sign.

Iceland's fishermen labored on the docks using new equipment supplied by ECA to modernize and enlarge the nation's fishing fleet. Farmers were hard at work in Turkey, still an undeveloped country, opening up the hinterland and developing arable land for farming. Farmers in Denmark received shipments of tractors they would put to use, driving a sharp rise in agricultural output. In Greece, even as civil war raged, Marshall Planners were at work devising a new road system as well as a national power network. Before Marshall aid it was not possible to get fresh fish more than ten miles inland. Paul Porter, the mission chief in Greece, and his staff would help to change that.

Under their agreements with the United States, the Marshall Plan countries each agreed to publicize ECA aid. Events were scheduled to welcome incoming ships bearing aid at the ports. The British, the Dutch and the Italian governments all put on regular radio programs, published pamphlets and various materials, sent speakers out to local organizations promoting the impact of U.S. aid on their economies and societies. In Britain, the BBC was involved in the promotion. For European political leaders it was also a way of publicizing what they were working to secure for their people.

Marshall Plan assistance that first year comprised around 5 percent of the combined national incomes of ERP nations. However, Marshall aid had far greater value than that metric suggests. Part of the reason was that the goods and services provided were essential. Without them certain factories, companies, even industries might not have been able to function at all. To explain, Hoffman used an analogy from the car business. A few hundred dollars worth of metal, he said, when processed by machinery and labor, and when component parts were added, could be sold for $2,000. Without the metal, though, it was not possible to make that car. Hoffman called it "the multiplier effect." It was the notion that essential items had an aggregate value much greater than their cost. Since ERP enabled Western Europeans to purchase these essential items when they didn't have the hard dollars to do so, ERP was providing much greater value, even, than the dollars Congress was appropriating.

By September 1948, counterpart funds were at work, performing double duty for European recovery, further compounding the value of Marshall aid. Furthermore, since Europeans were purchasing items with their own currency, corruption and scandal were kept to a minimum. *Life* magazine wrote that ECA "has so far made a good start on the most complex economic job in history without a trace of scandal." *Life* believed the reason was that the top officials were mostly "accomplished executives, long accustomed to high administrative authority." To be sure, that was part of the reason. But much of it also had to do with the mechanics of that process and the machinery around counterpart funds in particular. On *Meet the Press,* Paul Hoffman said, "I would say that . . . probably the greatest single tool we have for recovery is those counterpart funds."

ECA was functioning at a very high level. But the fledgling program had its blemishes. While ECA pushed Europe to sell to the United States to reduce its Dollar Gap, stifling barriers to export to the U.S. remained in place, frustrating the Marshall Plan countries. The Danes, for example, claimed that they could make great progress on their Dollar Gap if they didn't have to contend with a "crippling 14-cents-a-pound duty" on butter (which was sold at 7 cents a pound).

In August 1948, a cotton company called Anderson, Clayton received an order for millions of dollars of cotton. It was Will Clayton's firm, and he stood to profit from the ERP contracts. Clayton was then out of government.

Furthermore, the contracts were vetted properly, and as the most prestigious firm in its industry Anderson, Clayton was likely to get such contracts. No accusations of scandal emerged. Still, the contracts highlight the blurry lines between the businessmen who devised and executed the Marshall Plan and their own financial interests.

Moreover, American industry continued to lobby Congress profusely for its own interests. Some, like the tobacco lobby and the shipping lobby, were successful. Somehow, two historians wrote, in one of the less defensible ERP procurements, millions of pounds of "unpalatable spaghetti" were shipped to Italy. Later, ECA learned that a few Austrian cabinet ministers had improperly diverted counterpart funds for personal purposes; it was the only recorded instance of corruption in the enterprise.

These blemishes were the exceptions to what even most Marshall Plan critics in the United States agreed was an extremely effective start. The statistics backed it up. After six months of ERP aid, at the end of September 1948, total output for factories and mines for Marshall Plan countries was up 10 percent from the same quarter the year before, nearly equal to prewar output. The food supply had increased, and, with only few exceptions, inflation was tapering. When Hoffman, Harriman and Bissell parsed the data and digested the progress, they found that much of the aid requested and provided in the first six months was for relief to meet basic human needs.

The time was now ripe, they determined, to shift ECA's emphasis from relief to recovery. In its quarterly report to Congress at the end of September, its second official quarter in operation, ECA reported that "the countries have a long way to go" but that considerable progress had been made. And it was reflected in the activity, the vigor and most importantly the renewed sense of hope and purpose that was visible in much of Western Europe during that summer of 1948.

THE MORE ERP'S LEADERS came to focus on Europe's self-sustaining recovery, the more European integration became a focal point. "Through greater unity," historian Michael Hogan wrote of ECA leaders, "they saw Western Europe emerging from the rubble and the ruin of war, arising, like Lazarus from the grave, with new life and vitality." Since self-help was a guiding concept, the United States wanted Western Europe to lead to that end. Great Britain was Europe's largest economy, a victorious power in the war and, of course, Bevin had famously called for western unity in his House of Commons speech in January 1948. The United States looked to Great Britain and its dynamic foreign minister to lead Western Europe in the enterprise, and most of Western Europe did as well.

Just as ECA began to throw its weight behind integration, though, a sea change had taken place in Great Britain. Ernest Bevin had yielded to pressure from the Cabinet and Treasury and modified his views on Britain's relationship with Western Europe and the capacity in which it was willing to participate in continental integration. Britain valued its political independence and a certain remove from the continent. It did not want to cede sovereignty or political autonomy to a supranational body. Furthermore, Great Britain had now determined decisively that it prized its ties to the Commonwealth and the sterling area (the group of countries that either used the pound sterling as their currency or pegged their currency to the pound) above its ties to Western Europe. Part of the reason was that the Commonwealth traded in sterling, which would allow Britain to protect its reserves at a time in which they were depleting at an alarming rate. Another reason was that British leadership deemed the continent more vulnerable to pressure from the Soviets and political and economic crisis, generally. Britain did not want to hitch its destiny to the continent and chance the fallout. According to one British Treasury official, "on [its] merits, there is no attraction for us in long-term economic cooperation with Europe. At best, it will be a drain on our resources. At worst, it can seriously damage our economy."

The Foreign Office had now also decided that its security and economic interests would be best served by a close association with the United States. Too great an orientation to Western Europe could impede Britain's ability to establish special ties with the U.S. While Bevin had previously championed Western European economic integration, "this kind of thinking now receded into the shadows of British diplomacy."

As the United States and Great Britain's respective positions crystallized in opposition to the other, the powers began to clash. The crash site, it turned out, was the OEEC in Paris. Harriman wanted to build a powerful secretariat composed of the participating countries' highest-ranking Cabinet officials—foreign ministers, finance ministers—who had the prestige and power to advance integration and enforce OEEC's dicta. Great Britain appointed a career civil servant named Edmund Hall-Patch and resisted attempts to forge a strong secretariat. Harriman wanted to appoint a prestigious European as director general. The British opposed the creation of that position. Harriman, as well as Hoffman and Bissell from Washington, wanted the OEEC to form a new Payments Agreement to promote intra-European trade. Gravitating toward the sterling area, Britain opposed it.

Britain also opposed Harriman on the division of aid, preferring to deal with the United States bilaterally.

The *Times* of London wrote on September 1, 1948: "Nearly all [of the] nations concerned, as well as the Americans, recognize that without resolute and wholehearted British leadership the plan is not likely to succeed." Yet Britain seemed to be working at cross-purposes with most everything the United States was aiming to do at OEEC. None of this was going over very well with Averell Harriman.

Harriman did not yet know if British stasis at the OEEC was because of "the low level" of representation or whether it was because of British national policy. In characteristic fashion, Harriman took the fight directly to Hall-Patch. He insisted that the British fall into line on every point or else, he said, Congress would reduce ERP appropriations. Harriman made his grievances public and launched a media campaign against British policy and Hall-Patch's efforts at OEEC. Hall-Patch, a seasoned conservative British civil servant, openly resented Harriman's tactics.

The conflict became personal, and it became bitter. Hall-Patch cabled London that Harriman "thinks himself to be such a swell that he cannot have any truck with anyone unless they are Ministers." The British interpreted Harriman's call for higher-level leadership at OEEC as vanity. Harriman's ego was running amok, many felt. He would not compromise, nor would he deal with anyone he deemed below his social or professional station. Nobody on Harriman's staff, Hall-Patch added in a letter, could understand why the foreign ministers of sixteen sovereign states "were not prepared to travel to Paris to have the honor of meeting Mr. Harriman." Bevin was irate. He fumed to Douglas that the special envoy, and old wartime colleague, was being "presumptuous." Bevin said that the selection of its representation at OEEC was an internal matter, and that he would not accept Harriman's interference. The British called it "the Harriman Problem."

Richard Bissell agreed that "Harriman was something of a snob about the civil service." Vanity played a part, perhaps. But, with the historical records illuminated, it is clear that the tension was rooted primarily in substance and two genuinely divergent policies that were bound to lead to collision. Harriman's main priority was Western European integration. Hall-Patch was faithfully executing his nation's policy by opposing ECA essays at integration. Indeed, had the British appointed a higher-level official, it would have been clear that national policy opposed integration. By keeping Hall-Patch, a lower-level official, Britain was able to sow seeds of doubt about its ultimate intentions, which afforded it diplomatic room to maneuver.

In the United States, Hoffman, Marshall and Lovett were strongly advocating for integration, the policies for which Harriman was pressing. Republican presidential candidate Thomas Dewey homed in on the apparent lack of progress. Senator William Fulbright, a Democrat, spoke out most forcefully: ECA "is doing nothing toward reaching political unity . . . To my mind, the real objective of the Marshall Plan is political unity, or a United States of Europe. No one is doing anything about that. I believe England should take the lead."

Harriman may not have won any friends among the British for his approach, but he was faithfully advancing his country's policy and, with little time and at a fragile and formative juncture, pushing hard to advance what he felt was the key to European recovery. And it generated results. Though Britain remained unwilling to hitch its destiny to Western Europe, it yielded to Harriman's threat about the next year's ERP appropriations. By late October, the British agreed to appoint a director general, though they vested the office with less authority than Harriman wished. They agreed to give Harriman greater access to their high-level meetings, and they worked on a compromise whereby Britain would participate in a new Intra-European Payments Agreement but would also carve out a special basis for its participation that did not infringe on its position in the Commonwealth.

The compromises were enough to keep OEEC together and moving forward, but they were meager concessions when measured against Congress's hopes and Harriman's expectations. The U.S. and British divergence in policies was one of the main tensions framing integration, and the Marshall Plan at large, that first year. Part of the problem, Ambassador Lewis Douglas suggested, was that the United States had not clearly defined what it meant by integration, what it expected of Britain and the other European states. Indeed, there was not a cogent U.S. vision for integration. But it was not a weakness. Rather it was in adherence to the overriding principle that the U.S. would state its aims, its preferences and perhaps a direction, but it was imperative that Europe chart its own path. Key decision makers recognized, however, that integration would work only if Europe itself determined how far it would go, what form it would assume and at what pace it would proceed.

IT WAS EUROPEAN SELF-HELP, the same principle that informed Harriman's decision to push the Marshall Plan countries to decide upon the division of aid. Harriman was asking sixteen separate, self-interested countries to come together, not only to divvy up aid but to expose one another's economic programs to an unprecedented degree of international disclosure and inspection. Many of the Marshall Plan countries did not want to do it, and many on both sides of the Atlantic felt that it would destroy the still-fragile OEEC and perhaps even the Marshall Plan itself. Harriman and Hoffman believed that if Western Europe succeeded, the exercise would serve as a basis for cooperation and fortify the OEEC with a raison d'être and forward momentum.

That June and July, the Marshall Plan countries formulated and presented their aid requests before the OEEC. As expected, each country's request far exceeded the aid available. Each country was acting in its own self-interest, deflating its projected exports and stoking its import needs to present a large balance-of-payments deficit, thus making a case for as much aid as possible. Milton Katz recalled the gist of the dialogue: the French would come to the meetings and say, 'We need this much.' The Norwegians would say, 'What do you mean you need that much? You need that much because you've shown a dollar deficit based on a set of assumptions about how you're allocating your resources. But you're allocating your resources in an extremely self-indulgent way. If you'd allocate your resources the way we do, you wouldn't have anything like that dollar deficit and you wouldn't need that much money.' It carried on this way throughout June and much of July. "This involved really heated disagreements," Katz recalled.

In July, several OEEC representatives approached the OSR and asked the Americans to step in. Harriman's staff was in touch with the Europeans, consulting, advising and pressing—but OSR refused to dictate, refused to decide. As progress came to a halt, instead of stepping in himself, Harriman proposed that the Marshall Plan countries appoint three Europeans, men above the fray, who had little personal interest and who had sufficient prestige to offer recommendations that would carry—"three wise men." "The procedure was designed to maintain the collectivity of the effort and emphasize their responsibility," Katz recalled. After much "backstage fighting," the Europeans appointed not three but four men to arbitrate. They were Guillaume Gundy of France, Dick Spierenburg of the Netherlands, Pietro Stoppari of Italy and Eric Roll of the United Kingdom. They became known as the Group of Four.

The Group of Four spent three weeks poring over the country proposals, calling in each country to present their requests and defend their presentations. Those who appeared before the Group "will remember," a Dutch delegate recalled, "that they entered the examination room with the special feeling of tension so well known to anyone who has gone through examinations in private life." Each knew that any weakness in his presentation could mean dollars lost for his country and apportioned to another country. It meant that each country had to tighten its proposals, to work as hard as possible to identify opportunities for intra-European cooperation to make its presentations as defensible as possible. After completing the arduous process, the Group of Four withdrew to Chantilly, where, in seclusion, they spent several days reviewing the presentations and requests to form a proposal for aid allocations.

When they returned to Paris to present their proposal to the OEEC's Executive Council on August 14, "pandemonium broke loose." Two hours of heated debate ensued on whether or not the Group of Four's report should even be presented at all. When it was presented, the delegates tore into one another. The most strident dissent came from the German delegate (represented by an American). There were two ironies here. The first was that the Americans had taken great care to let the Europeans grapple with the division and have command of the process. The second was that Germany was deprived of German representation at the OEEC, but because it was represented by an American, Germany's interests sometimes carried beyond the other European countries.

Eventually, a Group of Five was appointed to formulate another report. When it was submitted later in August, the Executive Council considered both reports. The deadlock continued. The press reported on the stasis, generating an aura of pessimism. There had been, according to a *Fortune* article, no fewer than 897 various meetings that July and August; and as August turned into September the committee found itself wracked with almost 100 different sets of bilateral negotiations.

That September, though, the tide began to turn. The Marshall Plan countries saw time passing and feared that they would lose credibility with the U.S. Congress and that ERP appropriations would be threatened. Guidance and consultation from OSR helped. But, mostly, in all the negotiations, haggling and even bickering—during tens of thousands of aggregate hours of work and negotiations—the Europeans were beginning to find a modus operandi for dealing with one another, a basis for finding common ground and accommodating one another's interests. There was a burgeoning sense that perhaps Western Europe shared an economic destiny and that there was benefit to be found in common interest.

On October 16, 1948, at a special Ministerial Meeting at the OEEC, Averell Harriman accepted the OEEC report for a cooperative Western European economic program complete with aid allocations and an intra-European payments plan. In receiving the report, Harriman addressed the OEEC: "I permit myself to share with you the pride that comes from a great accomplishment in a new economic area. As in the case of any undertaking without precedent, any concept beyond previous limits, there were those who said the task laid upon you was impossible. It was foolhardy, they held, to expect so many separate political entities to agree among themselves upon a cooperative program including the division of American aid and the reconciliation of the intricacies of each one's economic needs. There were skeptics who said the requirements were beyond the limits of human competence, not to mention human nature," Harriman continued. "I rejoice with you in having a report that proves it can be done, for it has been done."

The Italian representative to the OEEC, Attilio Cattani, recalled that the division of aid "gave to the [OEEC] both a responsibility and a test. It gave to the problem not the aspect of each trying to get all he could—as when meat is thrown to a pack of wolves—but more the aspect of trying to reach compromise and eventual agreement among friends. This was a very wise move among the Americans. We came to understand better each other and the need for each other." From Washington, Richard Bissell noticed a discernible change. European countries "became in spirit less an assemblage of national representatives than a group of Europeans."

European states were still pursuing their own national interest. But the division of aid launched a spirit of European cooperation and tied Europe's recovery plans to one another. It boosted OEEC from a shell, a hollow framework, to "the instrumentality" that would drive European cooperation and integration. Wrote historian Harry Price: "the OEEC stood out as the first organization through which the disintegration of Western Europe into autarkic islands had been checked and a reverse trend established." According to Arthur Schlesinger, writing in November 1948 in the *New Republic*, it was "perhaps the most remarkable example of international cooperation in the history of the world."

Soviet propaganda charged that the United States sought to dictate and control European affairs. For the United States, the most effective instrument in the propaganda war was the efficacy of its policies. While the Soviet Union blockaded Berlin, tightened its grip and purged democratically elected leaders in its own sphere, it was clear that it could hold its empire together only by imposition. In contrast, the United States labored to bolster Western European autonomy, and on most matters Western Europeans sought U.S. involvement in their affairs. In contrast to the Soviet "empire by imposition," the U.S. empire—if it could rightly be called that—was an "empire by invitation." The varied approaches were beginning to frame the escalating Cold War.

WHILE THE OEEC was making strides in Paris, the organization's host country was gripped by political and economic crisis. As mission chief to

France, David Bruce was in the eye of the tempest throughout the second half of 1948. Bruce, fifty years old, an urbane, courtly statesman working under Averell Harriman at the Commerce Department in early April 1948, had come home to his second wife, Evangeline, an elegant fixture in Washington society circles, to say that he had been offered the post of mission chief in either England or France. He asked which she would prefer. For Evangeline, it was no contest: Paris. The English were obsessed with rabies, and a post in London would mean that she could not take her dogs. For Bruce, the post was a dream come true.

Bruce was born into a prominent Virginian family and then married legendary industrialist Andrew Mellon's daughter. Early on, he acquired all the tastes and sensibilities of early twentieth-century Southern aristocracy. Bruce was a gourmand, a wine connoisseur and an art lover. His biography was titled *The Last American Aristocrat*. He spoke fluent French, and in Paris during World War II with the OSS—an elite intelligence unit that included people like Ernest Hemingway, David Rockefeller and Arthur Schlesinger—his affection for French culture and society grew. He remembered the jubilance during the days of the liberation, when all the alcohol hoarded during the occupation came out into full view. "In the course of the afternoon, we had beer, cider, white and red bordeaux, white and red burgundy, champagne, rum, cognac, armagnac and calvados . . . The combination was enough to wreck one's constitution." For Bruce, though, the euphoria was short-lived. Aggrieved at France's woes following the liberation, he yearned to return to be a part of the recovery effort.

Bruce had done well on Wall Street working for Averell Harriman at Brown Brothers Harriman. He had a sharp, deliberative mind and sound judgment. He was unflappable, and his composure made him a natural leader. After the war, he agreed to join Harriman once again with a senior posting at the Commerce Department, mostly because he knew that Harriman would be involved in European reconstruction and he wanted to be a part of it. The ECA mission posting in Paris was a chance for Bruce to help rebuild the nation that "has for so long nurtured the best hopes and aspirations of western culture."

When Bruce arrived in Paris in late June, like most of the other mission chiefs he did not expect his tour to be long. There was an American presidential election on the horizon in only five months. Truman was widely expected to lose, and Dewey would no doubt appoint new mission chiefs. Bruce set up the ECA Paris mission just across the Rue de Rivoli from the Tuileries Gardens, in relatively modest offices connected to the more imposing American Embassy, just barely touching the Place de la Concorde, close to the Talleyrand and Harriman, his patron three times over. He began to assemble a staff and get the mission up and running. When Bruce arrived in June 1948, France's prospects seemed reasonably good. France was increasing its economic output, and the centrist governing coalition seemed reasonably stable. In a matter of weeks, though, France plunged into a tailspin.

Some of France's problems could be traced to the country's national obsession: Germany. The Berlin blockade had the dual effect of producing heightened anxiety about Soviet aggression as well as indigenous Communist foment and, when the U.S.–British airlift developed, alarm that France's western allies were getting closer to Germany. The other major anxiety had to do with inflation. France's economy was moving along, but the government was spending promiscuously to fuel that recovery, helping to generate huge price increases that threatened the viability of its recovery. Swept away by these currents, the centrist governing coalition was toppled in late July.

The various parties and leaders scrambled to form a coalition. Charles de Gaulle called it "the ballet of the parties," and for a brief window of time it appeared likely that the self-proclaimed "man of iron" himself would step into the breach and form a government. The French worried that a de Gaulle government would incite the Communists and stoke violence or even civil war. Around this time de Gaulle pronounced defiantly that the French had managed to survive many centuries without Marshall aid; U.S. officials, particularly those at ECA, bristled at the prospect of his emergence. Paralyzed by anxiety and vulnerability, France went without a government for two months that summer.

Looking out his window across the Place de la Concorde on a beautiful day, Bruce remarked that "the trouble with the weather is that it makes France too optimistic about their [sic] economy." Rain would have offered a more fitting backdrop and would have been better for the crops. Bruce and others knew what was needed: fiscal rectitude, taxes, tightening credit— these things could quell inflation. But the political instability, the sense of vulnerability from outside (Germany, the Soviet Union) and inside (national Communists) produced stasis. No leader advancing the sort of program needed could win popular support or manage to secure a coalition. "Psychologically," Dutch Foreign Minister Dirk Stikker said, "France has no confidence in itself." The absence of confidence in France's security, its economy, its currency, meant that the French were not saving or investing but spending, further fueling inflation and exacerbating the problem.

As the summer passed, Bruce grew increasingly alarmed. On September 14, he cabled Hoffman in Washington: "Financial situation in France heading for tragic climax unless immediate steps taken to cure present distemper.

Prices still rising . . . Unless checked soon, inflation will destroy gains painfully achieved during first six months 1948." Bruce worried about civil war, about French collapse. In the context of the Marshall Plan and its objectives, as Robert Lovett wrote, "The goal of ERP is fundamentally political and France is the keystone of Continental Western Europe." ECA had to arrest France's slide.

There were two pieces to the puzzle: first, shorter-term measures to firm up France's political and economic condition and, second, a longer-term strategy for French stability, self-sustainability and prosperity. Bruce found the key to the latter piece in partnership with an extraordinary Frenchman named Jean Monnet, who had already devised and set in motion a long-term plan for France's economic growth and industrial modernization and now needed the funds to finance it.

Growing up in the French countryside, Monnet took his first job as a salesman for his family's cognac business. Traveling the world, Monnet developed a keen appreciation for diverse national interests and cultures— but more importantly, an appreciation for the fundamental interests and values that different nations and peoples had in common. Monnet spent much of World War I and the interwar years abroad, working in international finance and diplomacy. He served as deputy secretary general of the doomed League of Nations. Monnet spent most of World War II in London and Washington, drawing on, and further cultivating, international contacts in business and government, becoming an invaluable intermediary and deal maker in the war effort. In Washington, pressing the United States to enter the war, he coined the phrase "arsenal of democracy." He was asked not to use it publicly so that Roosevelt could appropriate it for his own rhetorical purposes. Monnet emerged from the war a leading figure known and respected in the highest circles of government, finance and business throughout the West.

In his youth, Monnet wanted to be a boxer. Later, he thought about politics but realized that he was not much of an orator. His defining strength lay in his ability to formulate a strategic vision and galvanize and align people of diverse backgrounds on a common path toward the realization of that vision. After World War II, Monnet could see that France's economic problems ran deeper than wartime destruction. French industry had fallen far behind and was in need of modernization. He approached de Gaulle and, with typical aplomb, told the staunch and prideful nationalist that if France wanted to be great again, it needed to modernize. He offered de Gaulle a choice: "modernization or decadence," greatness or obsolescence. The general's response might easily have been predicted.

With de Gaulle's sponsorship and a small staff of leading French economists and technocrats, Monnet began to formulate a plan for French recovery and modernization. It focused on setting production targets for France's key industries, such as steel, coal and transport. Rather than the near-term provision of consumer needs, France needed to harness its scant resources to the modernization of these basic industries, so they would serve as the platform for France's stability and prosperity. Nimbly, Monnet got government ministries and governing coalitions to buy in, yet refrained from hitching the effort to any one faction or party. So it was that during the summer of 1948, when all else in France seemed to be foundering, Monnet was a constant. His plan was ready for implementation, and he had the authority to execute it. What he did not have were the funds to finance it.

Monnet was a pragmatist, interested in action and results. Once, after listening to a meandering discourse, he said, "*Exact!* But *dites moi,* on whose table should I pound to get the decision?" During that summer of 1948, the table in question was situated in David Bruce's office at the ECA mission in Paris. Bruce and Monnet moved in the same international circles and had known each other for years. When Monnet arrived to suggest that ECA counterpart funds be spent on French modernization, Bruce and his staff recoiled. The funds ought to be used to pay down debt rather than on massive expenditure programs, which could increase inflation. Monnet assured Bruce that the government would devise a more responsible fiscal budget and insisted that modernization was imperative. It was a gamble for Bruce.

Bruce bought in to Monnet's vision, and an extraordinary collaboration was born. The two met several times a week, if not daily, Monnet in his trademark black tie and "somber, double-breasted suit," a plain style that belied one of the greatest political imaginations of his century. Bruce had immense respect for Monnet, for the fecundity of his mind, and felt his strategy and plans sound beyond reproach. Monnet respected Bruce as well, finding him the quintessential "civilized man," deliberative, thoughtful, humble and given to action.

Among Bruce's growing and able staff at the Paris mission, no one was more important than a twenty-eight-year-old economist, an erstwhile junior Treasury official from Idaho named William Tomlinson. When Monnet met him, he found that he looked like "a conscientious student." Tomlinson, or "Tommy" as he was known, was a brilliant economist, and in short order he mastered the issues framing the French economy's woes. Later, George Ball, a senior diplomat in the Kennedy administration, who was a fixture in Paris during those years, said that perhaps Bruce's wisest decision as mission chief was "in giving free rein to Tomlinson's talent." In turn, Bruce and Tomlinson offered almost unstinting support of Monnet and his plan for France. "There was in effect," Bruce's biographer wrote, "a triangular alliance between Bruce and Tomlinson [and] Monnet."

The deal struck between Monnet and Tomlinson, according to an ECA mission official in Paris named Arthur Hartman, "was that the Americans would not give their approval to any proposal which Monnet didn't feel fitted in with his plans." In turn, the French Treasury made certain that funds would be spent in a manner that would meet with ECA's approval. Some said that Tomlinson was "just a kid from Idaho." He had a serious cardiac condition, but he labored intensely. He loved France, Monnet recalled. "He trusted me completely, and I concealed none of our problems from him, because he made it his business with the U.S. Administration to help us solve them."

With Bruce and Tomlinson signed on to Monnet's agenda, the purse strings opened. Monnet wrote to Prime Minister Robert Schuman in April: "It has now become possible to achieve the Monnet Plan thanks to Marshall credits." In 1949, 90 percent of Monnet's Modernization Fund came from the Marshall Plan. Monnet wrote that the Marshall Plan assured him financing through 1952. Monnet continued, "The certainty that so prolonged an effort could be financed without fail gave a sense of confidence to the whole French economy. And the economy, at that time, was not just a matter of material well-being; it was the necessary basis for national independence and the preservation of democracy."

The Monnet Plan, though, was not a short-term fix to France's political or monetary woes. In mid-September, a country doctor turned politician, Henri Queuille, a colorless but courageous man, finally formed a government, becoming France's new prime minister. In the next few weeks, the Communists launched yet another wave of strikes. A Communist-led union summoned 300,000 coal miners to strike in early October. The act of sabotage cost France roughly 160,000 tons of coal output per day and was enough in itself, by some estimates, to offset the country's benefits from ERP. Knock-down battles ensued between soldiers, police and the Communist strikers; dozens were injured and several killed. After a failed Communist strike later in October, Queuille reported to the State Department that the worst of it was over.

Still, the strikes, violence and even some localized insurrection continued, claiming dozens of lives. Ambassador Caffrey reported that France was "at the lowest point in national morale in the last two years." The violence did not let up through November. Neither did inflation nor its crippling toll. "Even more demanding" than securing ERP financing for the Monnet Plan,

Monnet remembered, "was the battle against continuing inflation, which as I well knew would threaten our whole venture . . . the question was whether our standard of living would improve or totally collapse." In November, Harriman cabled Paul Hoffman that he had told French officials that France's financial instability was affecting the whole of European recovery, and unless serious progress was made ECA would have trouble getting appropriations through Congress. He was pleased with French output and production but pointed out "the disastrous effect of France's . . . financial instability."

In Washington that October, State Department officials Henry Labouisse and Ben Moore penned an incendiary memo titled, "The French Crisis." France was in the throes of "galloping inflation," they reported. "The unhealthiness of the French situation has undesirable economic and psychological repercussions on the other participating countries to such a degree that the success of the European recovery program as a whole is jeopardized unless a solution can be found." They suggested that ECA should threaten to withhold counterpart funds if they did not take strong measures to rectify the situation. This would mean starving Monnet's modernization plan. It also threatened to create an adversarial relationship with one of the United States' key partners and perhaps even exacerbate French anxieties about American reliability.

David Bruce came out strongly opposed to the notion of threatening the French with cutting off funds. The French position was fragile. Bruce estimated Queuille to be a prime minister of "character and determination." His new fiscal program was, in Bruce's view, "the most courageous and satisfactory proposed to meet present difficulties." Hoffman and Harriman agreed. Bruce was very popular in France, not only because he arrived bearing Marshall aid but because he had a genuine appreciation for French culture, and, respectful in tone, he was deeply mindful of France's national dignity during a difficult time. He repeatedly stymied some of the more ill-conceived ECA attempts to publicize Marshall aid, such as the time OSR suggested that the French mission attach a helium balloon to the Eiffel Tower with a sign saying "Merci, Marshall Plan." Bruce and his staff spoke of such initiatives as the "bronze plaque" policy and would have none of it. Bruce worked behind the scenes to push his reform agenda. As autumn passed, though, inflation continued to spike and none of the desired reforms had been implemented. It was clear to Bruce that the time had come to strike a more forceful note.

On December 6, Bruce arrived for a dinner in Lille, a northeastern industrial town, to address the French Association of Woolen Manufacturers and various business leaders. The press followed Bruce closely and so throngs of reporters were there. Even as he began his address, coal provided by the Marshall Plan was fueling the local steel mill and driving local industry. It was the same town where, one year before, Communist saboteurs had removed train tracks, killing twenty innocent people. The town was loaded with symbolic meaning.

Bruce listed the ERP's accomplishments to date and all the program was doing for Europe. Without Marshall Plan imports, he said, "French food rations would have been absolutely insufficient . . . Marshall aid has also made possible the importation of coal, petroleum, copper, zinc, textiles, wool and cotton," without which "many factories would have to discharge tens of thousands of workers." The aid carried a price tag for the American taxpayer: 10,000 francs per annum for each one of America's 145 million citizens. In addition, America was supplying some goods that were in short supply at home, risking shortage and inflation in the United States. With that, Bruce had departed from his preferred line of humility in which America was simply an enabling partner, proud to stand with France in its recovery. He took care to remark that the greatest contribution to France's rebirth needed to come from France herself. Still, he wanted to jolt the French. His next few lines would accomplish that. Further "substantial sacrifice" was necessary, he said. "The Congress of the United States will convene in a few weeks, and shortly thereafter will begin consideration of the question of a continued contribution by American taxpayers to the recovery of the French economy. These are fateful days." It was a thinly veiled threat.

"For once," wrote Bruce's biographer, "Bruce's measured French, spoken with that quaint Tidewater inflection, failed to charm." The French media responded with animus. *L'Humanité* chided "the insolent Mr. Bruce." Other papers said that his speech was very much against the spirit of Marshall's Harvard address and the presentation of the Marshall Plan to date. *Le Figaro*, more plaintive than angry, asked, "Is it not rather unjust to criticize the French at this time when our country is serving as a testing ground for the maneuvers of the men of the Cominform?"

Back in Washington, Richard Bissell agreed that "[Bruce's] actions may have been considered undiplomatic," but they were effective. At the end of December, France passed an austerity program with wide-reaching reforms. The government raised taxes, cut spending and for the first time in twenty years, the Bank of France lowered the ceiling of its borrowing, which tightened credit. It was not Bruce's preferred approach or tone, but it worked. Almost immediately inflation began to taper. The reforms helped the economy stabilize, paving the way for Monnet's modernization plan, increased output, increasing confidence and political stability.

Fiscal and monetary reform was not the only agenda that the United States was pushing in the second half of 1948. Bidault supported the U.S. agenda for the London Conference program and German recovery—a gambit that French flexibility would enhance its stature with the United States. The Berlin crisis, though, threw an unwelcome variable into that equation. France watched that summer as the United States and Britain mobilized to fortify western Berlin, which meant they were increasingly investing in— and *invested* in—Germany. The French were now irrevocably wedded to the U.S. orbit both for Marshall aid and military security. Finding themselves increasingly powerless to manage German recovery at a breathable pace, the French Foreign Ministry wrote in mid-1948, "we are participating, under American direction, in [Germany's] rapid reconstruction . . . We must, by all means possible, try to dam up this flood which threatens to carry everything away."

It was becoming increasingly clear to French foreign policy thinkers as well as centrist political leaders that France now had to "provide a constructive alternative" to U.S. policy on Germany. So, in the second half of 1948, the French "diplomatic-strategic requirement" fomented "an increasing emphasis on French-German cooperation," something considered unthinkable a few short years before.

Meanwhile, Jean Monnet, frustrated at the pace of integration at the OEEC, was beginning to beat the drum louder for European unification, even federalization. He did so in private correspondence with French political leaders and intimates. He extolled the virtues of integration in the halls of ECA and State in Washington. It was the key, he said, to bringing erstwhile warring countries into a unified and peaceful whole. Monnet was becoming "Washington's favorite European." Still, the notion of French-German reconciliation was not yet ripe. For most, coming to terms with Germany's reemergence was France's most vexing problem. For Monnet, it was beginning to look like the solution.

IN EARLY AUTUMN OF 1948 the White House was falling apart. Literally. Truman's daughter's sitting room, the president's own bathroom and much of the residence quarters had become dilapidated and were in need of repair. It seemed an apt metaphor for the defeat that almost everyone in the United States and around the world portended for Truman in the upcoming election. The Republicans had pummeled the Democrats in the preceding midterm elections. Ever since the Civil War, the party that won the off-year election had gone on to win the presidency. Truman's popularity that summer was still low, Dewey's was higher, and after sixteen years of Democratic control of the White House, all signs pointed toward Truman's defeat.

The journalist Marquis Childs wrote two months before the election that Truman's handicap in the election "loomed as large as the Rocky Mountains." Pollster Elmo Roper actually stopped polling on the election. The latest poll had Dewey ahead of Truman, 44 to 31 percent. "My whole inclination," Roper said, "is to predict the election of Thomas E. Dewey by a heavy margin and devote my time and efforts to other things." Across the Atlantic, ECA mission chiefs, such as David Bruce, braced for news of a Truman defeat come November. Three weeks before the election, Averell Harriman assured his European colleagues at the OEEC and elsewhere that John Foster Dulles, the presumptive secretary of state in a Dewey Cabinet, supported the Marshall Plan and was also for a strong OEEC.

If the election was already decided, someone had forgotten to tell Harry Truman. That September and October, Truman set out on a whistle-stop campaign and proceeded—with optimism, punch and astounding vigor—to traverse thousands of miles of country and shake tens of thousands of hands along the way. Most of the country still saw Truman as a meager and crude sequel to his stately predecessor. As Truman's train rolled from stop to stop, he spoke out in blunt, plain language haranguing the Republican "do nothing" 80th Congress and extolling his administration's accomplishments: a booming economy at home and the Marshall Plan and the Berlin Airlift abroad. The Plan and the Airlift had both reaped great strategic gain and had cast America as a beacon of freedom, strength and generosity. At the time of the election 82 percent of Americans had heard of the Marshall Plan and 62 percent were satisfied, while 14 percent were dissatisfied. The Marshall Plan was particularly popular with the 35 million foreign-born Americans, who composed a quarter of the population; Truman desperately needed their support to overcome the stiff odds.

Early on the morning of November 4, two days after the election, Harry S. Truman stood on the rear platform of the *Ferdinand Magellan* at a station in St. Louis, holding aloft a *Chicago Tribune* paper with the headline: "Dewey Defeats Truman." The last Gallup poll before the election had Truman behind by five points. The pollsters and the pundits had gotten it wrong. Truman was victorious. He would get a second term. "You've got to give credit to the little man," said Arthur Vandenberg. Marshall wrote him: "You have put over the greatest one man fight in American history." Two of his biggest donors, Will Clayton and Averell Harriman—who had donated $9,000 and $5,000, respectively—were thrilled, as were the mission chiefs, ECA and OSR staff. Truman's win would provide continuity to U.S. foreign policy and the Marshall Plan, the foreign program that, more than any other, helped deliver him victory.

Not everyone was as pleased. Taft and fellow Republicans ranged from disconsolate to irate. Truman had pummeled them during the campaign, and now they had let their best chance at the White House in twenty years slip through their fingers. One could almost hear Republican members of Congress sharpening their political axes as the stunning news of defeat sunk in. On August 4, a *Time* editor named Whittaker Chambers appeared before the House Un-American Activities Committee on Capitol Hill, admitted that he had been a Communist and named another: a former Roosevelt State Department official and blue-blooded Democrat, Alger Hiss. Hiss testified that autumn before Joseph McCarthy, Richard Nixon and other members of the committee and was indicted for perjury on December 15. The domestic Communist scare was growing. Truman was asked if it was real or just a "red herring." Meanwhile, from Tokyo, General Douglas MacArthur was sounding the tocsin about the imminent "fall" of China to the Communists in that civil war.

As 1948 and Truman's first term drew to a close, the Marshall Plan had helped Europe to make great progress in its recovery. More than $2 billion of cargo had already been delivered, with billions more still on its way from the first year's appropriations. Around $1.4 billion of Marshall aid took the form of food, fuel and fertilizer. More than $1 billion worth of raw materials and semifinished products was shipped, and half a billion dollars in machinery and vehicles as well as fuel were also sent. In Italy, railroads were being restored, ocean liners retrofitted, marshes drained and bridges built. In France, Marshall dollars were financing the construction of power plants, electric lines and the modernization of coal mines.

The combined effect generated a stellar report card for the Marshall Plan countries: industrial production exceeded prewar levels for the first time; steel production and electric power hit postwar peaks; exports set a postwar record at 13 percent above 1938 volumes; the Dollar Gap was narrowing.

The shift from relief to recovery brought a reapportionment from the provision of consumer goods to investment and modernization. That meant that standards of living had to be sacrificed and, in much of Europe, even lowered in the drive to achieve self-sustainability and long-term prosperity. The shift caused pain and discontent among many in the lower economic strata. Critics could not help but notice, also, that American exports to Europe were increasing, and American industry, and economic interests were benefiting handsomely.

Still, the progress was irrefutable. ECA reported at the end of 1948 that "great strides had been made in the reconstruction of the economies of Western Europe." Some of it had to do with the summer's good harvests; most of it had to do with European determination and self-help. Much of it also had to do with Marshall aid and the renewed spirit of confidence it instilled in the participating countries. The combination, the ECA said, enabled the participating countries "to avoid a threatened economic collapse and to advance along the road to recovery." "The United States today," Arthur Schlesinger wrote in the *New Republic* that autumn, "is engaged in the most staggering and portentous experiment in the entire history of our foreign policy." And it was working.

For Paul Hoffman it was not enough. He was pleased at the progress achieved, but ever more focused on Europe's integration. Hoffman made several trips to Europe throughout 1948, visiting with heads of state, business leaders, American mission chiefs, officials at OEEC and Europe's workers. That December, in England, Hoffman pulled aside Sir Stafford Cripps, the British chancellor of the Exchequer. He asked Cripps to meet with him privately. Around midnight, Hoffman told the chancellor that, indeed, Europe was making good on its first promise: maximum self-help. It had not on its second, though: maximum mutual aid. Hoffman said that it would be his responsibility to deliver that same message to Congress that February, when he was set to testify on ERP's progress. Despite progress at the OEEC and with the division of aid, the Marshall Plan countries were still enmeshed in a web of prohibitive tariffs, exchange controls and import quotas, which constricted the European market.

Exasperated, Cripps replied: "Well, what will satisfy you?" Hoffman replied, "If in February we can report to the Congress that 50 percent of the barriers to trade among the European countries have been removed, Congress would, I believe, be satisfied." That was a 50 percent reduction in volume of trade, Hoffman made clear, not in items traded, which could yield a much lower percentage in volume, depending on which items were selected. After hours of conversation, sometimes heated, Cripps said to Hoffman, at 3 A.M., "We'll have that 50 percent reduction in effect by February 1, 1949."

LATE THAT AUTUMN, George Marshall came to Europe to gauge for himself Europe's political and economic condition. Marshall was not well. Months away from his sixty-ninth birthday, he had postponed a serious kidney operation to stand next to Truman during the Berlin blockade and the airlift. He had spent more than one-third of his tenure abroad at international conferences, and that did not include his domestic campaign to sell the Marshall Plan the previous winter. With the blockade in effect and instability and inflation in France, tensions were high. But Marshall's trip was also a sort of victory lap. He was lavished with praise in France. At the Vatican, the pope thanked him for the Marshall Plan. Arriving early every day for a conference at the Hotel d'Iena, Marshall told an inquiring stenographer that he came early in order "to get a better seat."

Scheduled to check in to Walter Reed Hospital after Thanksgiving to have his kidney removed, Marshall would have served two full years that January. With the election over and Truman's electoral victory in hand, with the ERP passed, ECA and OSR set up and functioning at full steam, with Europe making giant strides in its recovery and the Communist threat in Western Europe in evanescence, Marshall deemed his duty fulfilled. He told his commander in chief that he would like to resign his post. Marshall's resignation was announced early that January and in effect on inauguration day, January 20, 1949—the end of an era, and the beginning of a new one.

Chapter Eleven

SHIFTING GEARS

A T 12:35 P.M. ON JANUARY 20, 1949, Harry S. Truman was standing at a podium on the steps of the east front of the Capitol about to deliver an inaugural address to the American people. The Marshall Plan had "brought new hope to all mankind," he said; "we must keep our full weight behind" the European Recovery Program. He listed the Plan's successes. Then he went on to propose a new one. "More than half the people of the world are living in conditions approaching misery." Beset by starvation and disease, "for the first time in history, humanity possesses the knowledge and skill to relieve the suffering of these people." Truman proposed a "bold new program" of investment and technological transfer to provide resources, opportunity and hope to all the world's peoples. It was called the Point Four Program. An outgrowth of the success and popularity of the Marshall Plan, it was featured prominently in Truman's inaugural and lauded widely as a landmark proposal in an address that many felt was the most inspiring of Truman's life.

Seated behind Truman as he outlined his aims for the next four years was his newly designated secretary of state. As Truman deliberated on who he would ask to fill the post Marshall had vacated, a few names percolated. Journalists and key officials in the Democratic Party floated Arthur Vandenberg's name, an homage to the role he had played in securing an effective bipartisan foreign policy and to the hopes that it would survive Marshall's retirement. Vandenberg told one of Truman's best friends that he felt that Republicans would resent it if he left them and that he could be more effective forging continued bipartisan cooperation in the Senate. From Paris, Averell Harriman was pining for the post. Harriman was one of the last two men on Truman's short list. "I believe it was a close call," remembered Clark Clifford, Truman's closest aide.

In late November 1948, Truman invited Dean Acheson to Blair House. "You had better be sitting down when you hear what I have to say," Truman told Acheson with a grin. "I want you to come back and be Secretary of State. Will you?" Acheson said that he did not believe he was qualified. Truman said perhaps it was true, but he could say the same of himself, and the fact remained that he was president, and he wanted Acheson to serve as his secretary of state. Acheson accepted.

That February, a month into the new administration, Vandenberg was already worried about the prospects for a continued bipartisan foreign policy. Reeling from Dewey's surprising defeat, the Republicans had also lost the Senate. A good number wanted to take a more radical line against Truman and the Democrats. Vandenberg wondered if he was detecting the seeds of a party revolt. The Democrats did not help their cause when they stacked the Senate Foreign Relations Committee with as many Democrats as law allowed. The election results also meant that Vandenberg was no longer chairman of the committee, and as such he lost some control. In addition, Acheson was not Marshall. The general was considered above Party, whereas Acheson was a Democrat, a Truman loyalist. Moreover, many Republicans shared the sentiments of their colleague Joseph McCarthy, who called the new secretary "a pompous diplomat in striped pants with a phony British accent." Lovett, the master conciliator, had also resigned with his boss. Finally, it was widely known that Truman revered Marshall and would fall into line with the general's policies. Now, Truman had been elected in his own right, and he would be more comfortable asserting himself, thus providing an opening for partisan attack.

Vandenberg said of the new appointment: "I am frank to say that Mr. Acheson would not have been my choice for Secretary of State." Still, he duly supported the nomination. But as Acheson took the oath to become the fifty-second secretary of state in U.S. history, he stepped into some very large shoes. Geopolitical tensions and political undercurrents both suggested that the next four years would bring new and intensified perils. When Acheson returned to his office on the day of his swearing-in, he recalled, "the surrounding gloom had deepened, or remained impenetrable, in most areas, but in one at least, Western Europe, the Marshall Plan had brought the dawn of a revivification unparalleled in modern history."

• • •

IN MARCH 1949, Paul Hoffman was invited to the home of one of his chief deputies for an intimate dinner party. When the host's twelve-year-old son approached him for his autograph, Hoffman was flattered and signed the boy's notebook, adding a few kind words. "Now, will you sign it five more times?" the boy asked, turning to a clean page. "Five times?" Hoffman asked. "What in the world do you want five of my signatures for?" "Oh," said the boy, "I've got a deal with a kid at school who will swap me a Joe DiMaggio for five Hoffmans!" That spring marked Hoffman's one-year anniversary on the job as ECA administrator. During that year, he had become one of the most visible and popular figures in American life. There was nary a moment, though, to sit still long enough to appreciate the progress made.

Hoffman's time was divided among several responsibilities. He spent, by one estimate, as much as a fifth of his tenure abroad surveying ERP in action and meeting with heads of state, various dignitaries and ECA and OSR officials. The prior December, with only two suits, a few shirts and other essentials, he left for a fourteen-day around-the-world trip, covering no less than twelve countries. Back home in the United States, Hoffman did not even have much time in Washington. ERP's funding depended upon congressional support. That, in turn, depended upon popular support. Although, as one journalist wrote in the *Saturday Evening Post*, "for more than a year now, the front pages of newspapers have devoted endless columns to the European Recovery Program, because this is the most gigantic project— apart from wars—that we Americans have undertaken outside our own country . . . most people confess that they can't read the news about it; they find these reports too boring." As far as Hoffman was concerned, though, Americans had to know about it, had to understand it. He made it his mission to explain the Plan's mission, its achievements and its workings in plain and compelling language.

Hoffman was a fixture on all the major television programs. Appearing on CBS on Sunday evening in early April 1949, he quoted his good friend, Knute Rockne, the legendary Notre Dame football coach: "A team that won't be beaten, can't be beat." He continued: "Now that the Europeans have recovered not only their confidence, but a will to win, they are proving they can't be beaten." He was as visible in print, his Rockwellian visage adorning the covers of *Life*, *Time* and the *New York Times* magazines. Occasionally, he would even write a piece or two himself. In *American Magazine* in April 1949, he wrote an article, "European Recovery . . . Will You Get Your Money's Worth?" Hoffman knew how to pinpoint the average American's concerns and anxieties: "What are your Marshall dollars buying?" he wrote. "They are buying peace and protection for our free way of life . . . your Marshall Plan dollars are buying future prosperity and a higher standard of living for Americans . . . Your dollars are buying the chance to export more luxuries from Europe . . . Your dollars are buying an increase in general world trade . . . Finally, your dollars are buying peace."

Hoffman was concerned that still too many Americans thought the program was a charity. They did not understand the concept of counterpart funds or how they functioned. He thanked the American Society of Newspaper Editors for their coverage of the Plan. "But you musn't get the idea that you are too perfect, because there is something you have not explained to the American public about ECA. You have not explained how counterpart funds are used." He spoke often about counterpart funds and their importance. To the National Association of Manufacturers he explained that Europeans were paying for goods with their own currency. "If gifts were being passed around, ten-ton tractors might find their way to five-acre farms," he said. But that was not happening because people in Marshall Plan countries were paying for goods themselves in local currency. The proceeds would then be deposited in countries' central banks, as counterpart funds—which, together, ECA and the recipient country would spend on that country's recovery.

At times, it seemed as if he were everywhere. Hoffman delivered as many as six or seven speeches a week. To the American Management Association he gave a mid-March address in New York, where he pledged that ECA would push Europe to "put forth a maximum effort at self-help and . . . maximum effort at mutual aid." European integration became an increasingly prominent theme for Hoffman throughout the first months of 1949. He spoke to every group from the American Institute of Mining and Metallurgical Engineers to the Delta Tau Delta brothers. A decidedly modest, Midwestern sartorial specimen, Hoffman received the Neiman Marcus "out-of-fashion" award in the good humor and spirit of bonhomie in which it was conferred—and used the occasion to extol the Marshall Plan's progress. *Life* referred to him as the man who supervised the expenditure of approximately $570,000 an hour, and when *Collier's* came out with an issue listing "The 25 Men Who Rule the World" in May 1949, Paul Hoffman was among them.

Back in Washington, Hoffman was responsible for the supervision of ECA's burgeoning operations. His deputy, Howard Bruce, and Bissell oversaw ECA's day-to-day administration and management. *Life* magazine wrote that visitors found the Miatico Building, where ECA was headquartered, "humming, not to say jumping with activity" from 8 A.M. until well into the night. The cable wires buzzed; Hoffman received twenty to thirty a day, as well as hundreds of letters and job applications. In the first year of operations, Hoffman had built an organization with three thousand specialists and technicians representing ECA in Washington and around the globe. They were some of the best and most qualified men and women from academia, media, government, labor—and most importantly, business.

Many were reluctant to accept posts that almost always paid less than their jobs and often took them from their families. Harry Martin, president of the American Newspaper Guild, was recruited to serve as a labor adviser in the Paris mission. Martin was reticent to leave his home in part because his son was a sixteen-year-old basketball star, and he hated to miss watching him play. But he cited his son as the main reason for accepting the post: "If another war breaks out," he said, "my boy will be in it. I cannot refuse any chance of helping to save him from that." Asked if he had changed his mind after being away from his family, Martin said that he did not regret his decision: "I still believe . . . it may prevent another war. So long as I believe that, I'm staying with it." It was a "great and thrilling" feeling for Hoffman to recall the thousands of ECA officials "whose almost religious energy and devotion to a cause made the word 'bureaucrat' something to be proud of." In Arthur Vandenberg's judgment: "As a whole, ECA is the best group ever put together for public service."

Hoffman's position and his achievements earned him a considerable store of political capital. When his testimony opened congressional hearings in a joint session of the Senate Foreign Relations Committee and the House Foreign Affairs Committee on February 8, the partisan temperature on Capitol Hill had risen. It was immensely important that Hoffman was a Republican and that he "was still the least vilified man in the top echelons of the capital." Even so, he was still the administrator of the program that the administration touted as its single greatest priority and success.

As Hoffman testified amid a blitzkrieg of flashing lightbulbs and jostling journalists, it was clear from the outset that he was peddling a pretty good product. In Western Europe, production was up markedly, agriculture and trade were up and the OEEC had made strides in integrating sixteen separate national economic programs. The Marshall Plan countries had taken far-reaching measures to achieve monetary and fiscal stability and those measures were working. Hoffman gave most of the credit to the Europeans. It was their recovery. But the ERP was indispensable. As important as the statistics, Hoffman said, was the renewed and revitalized sense of hope and determination that had sprouted to magnificent effect throughout the western half of the continent.

New Secretary of State Dean Acheson followed Hoffman in one of his first appearances before the House Foreign Affairs Committee. Acheson testified that ERP was still the administration's top priority. Averell Harriman had come from Paris to testify and pronounced: "I want to state my conviction that the struggle for reconstruction and freedom is being won . . . No one who has had occasion, as I have had, to see Europe in the summer of '47 and to see it again today can fail to be struck by the deeper progress in the things of the human spirit." No one better "perceived the immensely constructive potentialities earlier and more fully" than the Soviet Union, Harriman said, and it accounted for their violent campaign of opposition.

No one logged more hours in front of congressional committees, though, than Richard Bissell. When Hoffman testified, Bissell was at his side. When technical matters came up, Hoffman deferred to Bissell, whose explanations were comprehensible and compelling. "Bissell relished the complexity," said his deputy, Harold van B. Cleveland. "He'd be annoyed when a senator would act according to his own ego. He would say, 'Why is he reacting like this? The substance is so clear.'" When testifying together, Hoffman and Bissell packed an effective one-two punch. Hoffman focused on the high-level themes and knew the right strokes to paint. He also knew the right chords to strike. "You should see him operate with Congress," said one of his colleagues. "Whenever a knotty one comes up, he slaps his knee and says: 'Senator, you're entirely right. You've hit the nail on the head.' The next thing you know, the whole room is full of senators working like mad to help Paul Hoffman solve his problems."

That winter and spring it would not be quite that easy. Opposing members of Congress charged that the Plan was subsidizing socialism in Western Europe and rampant nationalization in Great Britain. The billions of dollars of expenditures would bankrupt the U.S. Treasury, killing "the goose that laid the golden egg." The lines of attack were familiar but, sprung from a new political backdrop, had now risen in intensity. In addition, Congress was now in a "Buy American" frenzy. Senator Tom Connally, the new chairman of the Senate Foreign Relations Committee, said that he had personally been approached by no fewer than 109 groups of producers importuning Congress in the hope of getting special consideration for their products. Hoffman had always fought congressional pressure to turn ERP into a dumping ground for overpriced American goods.

But, mostly, Congress demanded demonstrable progress. There were two metrics that mattered most. The first was production, and on that score Europe was delivering. The second was integration, and on that front Europe was failing to meet Congress's rather lofty expectations. Hoffman and Harriman pointed to the progress made to date. Some members were satisfied, but most were not and made it clear that they demanded further integration. What degree or mode or manner of integration was not always clear and differed from member to member, but demand for forward movement was the common denominator. Hoffman and Harriman heard the message loud and clear, and so did officials at the OEEC. A Dutch representative and scholar of the period believed, "The . . . congressional debates on the legislation of the ERP have been one of the most, if not the most, important influence from the other side of the Ocean on the development of European cooperation and integration."

In an ironic turn, the Plan's most strident opponents found its very success a convenient bludgeon. Some congressmen who only a year before had labeled the Marshall Plan "Operation Rathole" now argued that Europe's progress should exempt the United States from any further commitment. When rumors circulated that ECA had designs on extending ERP aid beyond the 1952 deadline, Congress roared in dissent. Hoffman ran interference immediately. The deadline would remain firmly fixed, he assured concerned members. The effect of such a change would only "be to damp the efforts of the people who are really trying to make a success of it. They might slow up." Hoffman believed that the deadline marshaled everyone's—ECA officials' and their European counterparts' alike—energy and commitment to achieve the objectives at hand. As Connally put it, it added to the "virility" of the endeavor.

As the testimony passed from winter into spring, the Hoffman and Bissell one-two punch had proven effective. But, that spring, the legislation was to be presented to the Senate and House appropriation committees, and John Taber. Immediately Hoffman was put on the defensive. Senators asked him why it would not be possible, given Europe's progress, to cut $1 billion from the appropriation request.

Though the total estimated ECA aid for fiscal 1950 was supposed to be on the order of 3 percent of the combined national incomes of the participating countries, that measurement strongly deflated the contribution of U.S. aid. In fact, Marshall aid constituted "the vital quantity . . . the means of getting extra production out of the economy to which it is applied." Beyond the "multiplier effect," which, Hoffman believed, rendered ERP imports worth four to six times their initial value, the Marshall dollars also performed "double duty" with the counterpart funds. For Hoffman, there was also a simpler way to make the case. World War II cost the United States hundreds of billions of dollars and hundreds of thousands of American lives. "If we are able through our aid under the European Recovery Program to make a substantial contribution to the building of peace and prosperity in the world, then the

European Recovery Program is the best bargain the American people ever bought."

It was not enough. Republican members of Congress called for further cuts in the appropriation. They proposed a host of crippling amendments. One sought to stop aid to countries that were nationalizing their industry (which would have stopped aid to Great Britain, among others); another stipulated that aid could not be provided until all of the United States' surplus commodities had been exhausted. The amendments would have changed the entire complexion of the ERP. Anti-Communist fervor rose in pitch as well. Some Republicans wanted to know why they should support an administration policy that was keeping socialist governments in power when it was "well known that there were Communists in the State Department."

To Arthur Vandenberg—now ill and in constant pain—ECA appropriations had become "just one more Pandora's box," unleashing partisan rancor and anti-Communist hysteria. During the appropriations hearing, Hoffman found himself on the receiving end of an attack. Hoffman had said that if ECA did not get the appropriations it requested, the "only honest thing" for him to do would be to resign and let someone else try to get the funds that he believed the program needed to be effective. It was the only time he threatened to resign. Senator Kenneth McKellar of Tennessee responded by hurling insults: "Other than giving away other people's money, I wonder what you are doing in Europe," he said, adding that it was fine by him if Hoffman retired. The *Washington Post*, the *Cleveland Press*, the *Philadelphia Inquirer*, the *Louisville Times* and many other papers around the nation came to Hoffman's defense immediately. McKellar was a lowly character, they all said, and "this incident bears out the fact why good men are loath to take government posts," wrote the *Louisville Courier-Journal*.

The vicious nature of McKellar's attack proved counterproductive. Still, Taber favored a cut in appropriations. At a low-key dinner that Hoffman hosted for some congressmen, Taber took Hoffman aside and the irascible congressman paid him an unexpected compliment. Hoffman was one of the few people left in Washington who still told the truth, he said. Taber would vote against the appropriations, a colleague told Bissell, "but there was all the difference in the world between casting their individual votes against us and fighting us. John Taber does not fight us, and the reason he doesn't is that he thinks we are honest."

That June, Vandenberg estimated, "I think we can save enough of the pieces to keep Hoffman going." Once again, Vandenberg proved an invaluable ally, quashing disabling amendments and deflecting attempts to slash

funds. The intense resistance foreshadowed difficulties to come, but Hoffman, Bissell and Vandenberg overcame formidable opposition and led a successful effort to secure funds for ERP's second year of operations.

BY THE EARLY SUMMER of 1949, Western Europe was recovering and Communism's hold on the region was on the wane. European integration was
proceeding slower than many in America liked, but much progress had
accrued. The Marshall Plan was succeeding, Paul Hoffman believed, on all
fronts—save one. ECA had underestimated the breadth and efficacy of the
Communists' information and propaganda campaign against the Plan. "We
had originally believed that in the ECA we would require very little informational apparatus," Hoffman wrote. He appointed a handful of information
officials in each mission. But he and his colleagues soon found that in most
of the Marshall Plan countries, the Communists outnumbered them 50 to 1.
"On the political front the visible sector is propaganda," *Fortune* magazine
wrote in February 1949. "Here ECA is weak. Americans may be the most
skillful sellers and promoters the world has ever seen, but you'd never know
it in Europe." The Communists outmanned ECA in the all-important war of
perception. Their breadth was greater, their techniques were more sophisticated, and their efforts were impeding the Marshall Plan from realizing its
political objectives.

Information officials working for Harriman at the Talleyrand did their
best to steel themselves to the Communist onslaught and even endeavored
to look upon some of the more outlandish Communist accusations with
good humor. They could laugh at the Danish Communist newspaper reports
that all the Marshall Plan had sent Denmark was toilet seats and water skis.
"We've seen them so often," one official recalled, "that we don't even get
startled to read, in the same article, in one or another Communist organ,
such double charges as (a) the Marshall Plan isn't working because Europe
grows more feeble day by day, and (b) the Marshall Plan is building up [West-
ern Europe] into a powerful aggressive military machine about to descend on
Russia." On occasion, certain accusations threw the Americans, such as
when the Moscow-published *Medical News* wrote that egg powder shipped
from America was laced with bacteria. The journal wrote that American
interests were colluding to sicken Europeans, driving them to doctors as a
means of increasing doctors' incomes.

In Norway, the secretary general of the Labor Party noted that the
more ground the recovery gained, the more conditions improved for labor,
the more the Communists lost ground, the more they ratcheted up their

attacks. The Communist propaganda effort was greatest in France. Communists played up French nativist and cultural anxieties. "Thanks largely to Russian propaganda," wrote historian Frances Stonor Saunders, "America was widely regarded as culturally barren, a nation of gum-chewing, Chevy-drinking, Dupont sheathed philistines." Using posters, pamphlets and public addresses, the French Communists warned that the Marshall Plan was a Trojan horse for American imperialism. Cajoled by Communist warnings, French wine producers began to worry that Coca-Cola would capture their market and ruin their business and joined forces with leftist parliamentarians to ban Coca-Cola from France and preempt the "Coca-Colonization" of their country. Coca-Cola, and other American companies, did not help their cause when they proposed foolhardy schemes such as placing a blazing Coca-Cola sign on the Eiffel Tower.

However outlandish their charges, the Communists' techniques were effective, and their reach was wide. Communist support remained strong, and popular opinion—though gravitating toward the Marshall Plan and America—remained more ambivalent, even oppositional, than ECA officials had hoped. ECA wanted results, stability, the provision of essential aid to be the primary yardsticks by which the Marshall Plan and America's role in Europe should be measured. To David Bruce, however, a seasoned intelligence officer in World War II: "Such a naïf belief that the truth alone will prevail and eventually will conquer does not seem justified in the light of human experience." Hoffman began to acknowledge the importance of enhancing ECA's information capability. In his view, "to run the ECA without a strong information arm would be as futile as trying to conduct a major business without sales, advertising, and customer-relations departments."

The agency brought on dozens of newsmen and public relations experts to run the various information programs. The aim was to employ "every method possible . . . to reach Giuseppe in the factory and Giovanni in the fields," or as Harriman's headquarters said, "slugging it out way down among the masses." During the first half of 1949, ECA published eighty-four pamphlets and special publications on the ERP in various languages reaching an estimated circulation of 5 million people. The ECA sponsored fairs and exhibits with discussions, posters, photographs and other displays helping to educate Europeans about the Plan and the positive impact it was having on their economies and societies. ECA estimated that at least 10 million Europeans attended or were reached by the fairs and exhibits. A veritable "poster war" ensued in France. It was difficult at times in Paris to find a bare patch of space on walls, fences or posts. In that six-month period, there were 1,272 press releases and feature stories produced by the ECA missions and OSR.

ECA sponsored dozens of radio programs and television shows; one radio program, *The Answer Man*, invited listeners to call in to ask any question they wished, like "What is the tallest mountain in the world?" ECA made sure that there were also questions about the Marshall Plan, so that the popular program informed Europeans about the Plan and its impact.

In Denmark, the Marshall Plan caravan released 70,000 brightly colored hydrogen-filled balloons with postcards that read: "With this balloon you will receive a sincere greeting from a peace-loving friend in Denmark who has visited a Marshall Plan exhibition 'Europe Builds' at Copenhagen. The balloon is a symbol of the hopes for peace and prosperity entertained by the free, democratic citizens of the . . . Marshall Plan countries." Some balloons were reported to have floated as far as five hundred miles away before dropping in eastern Germany, Poland and elsewhere behind the iron curtain. Authorities there were reported to have said that people should not touch the balloons, which they claimed contained dangerous microbes applied by "the Western imperialists." Hoffman remembered that notes arrived back from the east with responses such as: "Your balloon has blown a long way. It has blown to a part of Europe where people do not speak—or rather dare not speak—about the ideas you support and work for. But we are longing very much for the day we can live as Europeans. Don't think that Europe ends at the iron curtain."

Cinema was extremely popular throughout Western Europe in the postwar years. ECA sponsored a special unit of documentary filmmakers, and they produced a trove of films that were shown throughout Europe. A French film used cartoons to promote intra-European trade. A German film followed a miner through his daily routine to depict what the Plan meant to him in his everyday life. An Italian film focused on the rehabilitation of the railroads and the merchant marine and how American soil conservation programs were transforming arid plains into fertile land. Some of the films were short, some were long, some were entertaining, and some were tedious and dry. Some were clearly propaganda—occasionally Communists would barge into theaters to throw a brick through the screen, sabotaging the viewing—and others were well done and so subtle that they won critical acclaim and awards. All aimed to educate Europeans about the Marshall Plan or to advance one of the Plan's objectives.

The number one weapon in ECA's arsenal was still the ERP itself. But in 1949, the information effort—the radio, the television, the films, the exhibits, the pamphlets, the posters—was moving European public opinion. For many in that generation of Europeans, the information and propaganda efforts would help to form their views not only of the Marshall Plan but of

America itself. At the same time, the United States was waging another Cold War initiative entirely out of the public's view. Only a handful of administration and ECA officials knew it was being funded with Marshall Plan dollars.

EARLY IN 1949, Richard Bissell received a visitor named Frank Wisner in his office at ECA headquarters in Washington. Originally from Mississippi, Wisner was a college track champion, a former Wall Street lawyer, a fabled raconteur and a fixture on the Georgetown dinner party circuit. He was charming, relentless and given to zealotry when he attached himself to a cause. Bissell and Wisner traveled in the same social circles in Washington.

After the Czech coup in February 1948, Marshall, Forrestal, Kennan and others were alarmed at the Communists' political strength. They felt that America needed a more aggressive political component to its foreign policy—more precisely, covert operations capable of countering Soviet designs in Western Europe. The National Security Act of 1947 had created a new agency: the Central Intelligence Agency. In June 1948, a new office was created and shortly thereafter named the Office of Policy Coordination, or OPC. It was a purposefully ambiguous name for the new arm of the CIA that was to carry out the agency's first covert operations. Before it launched into action though, the OPC needed funds.

Intent on rallying adversarial elements in Congress and cost-conscious American taxpayers, Paul Hoffman was giving a lot of air time to the concept of "counterpart funds" in the spring of 1949. There was one element of the counterpart funds setup which Hoffman did not discuss. The way the provision was designed, 95 percent of counterpart funds were to be spent on European recovery. The remaining 5 percent was allocated to cover ERP administrative costs, to help the United States procure special strategic materials and for "other purposes." Five percent may have sounded slight, but given the total dollars involved, it was an extravagant amount of money—far more than was needed to finance ERP's administrative costs or could be spent on special strategic materials. According to Richard Bissell, Averell Harriman saw an opening.

Among his array of critical responsibilities, Bissell oversaw the disbursal of Marshall Plan funds. Wisner told Bissell that he was now running the OPC and that he had come to request a small amount of the counterpart funds that ECA had at its disposal. OPC was secretive, and Wisner was vague. Bissell was "very uninformed about covert operations" and so was "baffled by the request." Wisner was convincing, though. He assured him that Harriman had provided his approval. That was enough for Bissell. In parting, Wisner told his friend, "You should think about joining us."

In 1949, OPC's official budget was less than $5 million. Underneath the public radar, though, the Marshall Plan began funneling tens of millions of dollars to the covert outfit. Wisner sought to recruit "the very best men," which meant the men he knew from his social and professional circles. Most were Ivy Leaguers, former college athletes, World War II veterans, who had cut their professional teeth as lawyers and bankers on Wall Street, yet yearned for the purpose and adventure that they had experienced in wartime. A career intelligence officer described the OPCers as "a bunch of cowboys." During 1949, Wisner brought on hundreds of them. Under the rubric of OPC's four specialties—political, psychological and economic warfare and paramilitary operations—Wisner gave them enormous latitude to propose a wide variety of projects.

Wisner admired the Communists' powers of organization, their ability to strike and sabotage, "to put a mob on the street anywhere they chose, anytime they chose." Accordingly, OPC officials began making inroads with trade unions, supporting factions that split from Communist unions. "Bagmen" like Irving Brown, the European representative of the American Federation of Labor, passed along funds to workers on European docks, bribes so that they would shun Communist instructions to sabotage Marshall Plan shipments. Funds made their way into the hands of Western-leaning politicians and were used to court Communists or fence-sitting leaders.

Wisner had a predilection for psychological warfare, or psy-war. OPC channeled funding to hundreds of local newspapers, journals, magazines—all with the aim of fueling pro-American and anti-Communist sentiment. The OPC helped to fund the Hollywood production of George Orwell's anti-Communist classic, *Animal Farm*. OPC also helped fund local films, the "poster wars" and other media. The key was to place a local, native imprimatur on U.S.-supported ventures that sought to tip the political scale in America's favor.

Beyond propaganda and political payoffs, Wisner was willing to instigate and back armed violence to further political ends. He dreamed of supporting insurrection behind the iron curtain, of rolling back the tide of Communism in the East. With millions of Eastern Europeans displaced in Germany and other parts of central Europe, Wisner used OPC (Marshall Plan) funds to cultivate them. And on at least one occasion, he funded their deployment back to their native countries in the aim of achieving an American-backed insurrection.

OPC financed counter-demonstrators at Communist rallies. It also sought to counter Communism's ideological hold on Western Europe's intellectual elite. OPC employed Marshall funds to finance the Congress of Cultural Freedom, which assembled an array of Western Europe's cultural elite, scores of intellectuals and artists from more than twenty countries, to meet, deliberate, perform and offer scholarship—all under the banner of democracy and political liberty. The congress sought to debunk the Communist claim to intellectual ideological supremacy. Unbeknownst to almost all of its participants, it was organized by the CIA and funded, in part, by the Marshall Plan. To further discredit Soviet propaganda about American cultural vacuity, some of America's finest performers and minds were flown to Europe: Leonard Bernstein and George Gershwin performed and even premiered some of their work, and Eugene O'Neill, Thornton Wilder and Tennessee Williams productions were all put on in freezing European theaters—all funded with Marshall Plan dollars.

From ECA headquarters in Washington, Bissell was not inclined to question where exactly the funds were going. He trusted Wisner and suspected that his covert operations were advancing the Marshall Plan's political and strategic agenda. Harriman knew. Bissell felt that Hoffman most probably had an inkling, though he probably wanted to know as little as possible. A few officials at the Pentagon and a few at the State Department knew. Most Cabinet members did not. None of the Marshall Plan funds were vouchered, so there is no official record to track how OPC spent them. Wisner's personal style was intense, but his management style was loose. Obtaining funding was not a problem. In fact, recalled Gilbert Greenway, a CIA agent, "We couldn't spend it all. I remember once meeting with Wisner and the comptroller. My God, I said, how can we spend that? There were no limits, and nobody had to account for it. It was amazing." With tens of millions of dollars available—OPCers called the funds "candy"—hundreds of "cowboys" with their "Yale manners" and "Wall Street swagger[s]" were moving stealthily throughout Western Europe fighting the Cold War, undercover and secretly awash in funds from the Marshall Plan.

MINUTES BEFORE 5 P.M. on April 4, 1949, Secretary of State Dean Acheson sat at a gleaming walnut desk in a Washington auditorium near the White House, pen in hand. Acheson proceeded to affix his signature, along with representatives from ten Western European states and Canada, to an agreement creating a new twelve-member organization called the North Atlantic Treaty Organization, or NATO. Almost one and a half years earlier,

Ernest Bevin and George Marshall had met in Bevin's flat at 22 Carlton Terrace in London. Great Britain and Western Europe wanted the United States to enter into a military association with them to guarantee their security. Exploratory talks began at the Pentagon in the middle of 1948 and intensified with the Berlin blockade. The treaty bound all twelve member states to provide for one another's mutual protection in the event of external aggression. It pledged member states to an unprecedented degree of peacetime military cooperation and coordination—even an integrated allied command. Thomas Jefferson (not George Washington, to whom the saying is commonly attributed) cautioned America against "entangling alliances," and not since 1778 had the United States entered into a formal military alliance that committed it to go to war in defense of other nations outside the Western Hemisphere. It was tantamount to "a latter-day American revolution," "a treaty which represents the greatest formal shift in U.S. policy—and American thinking—since the promulgation in 1823 of the Monroe Doctrine," *Life* magazine announced at the time.

Speaking at the signing ceremony, President Truman called the treaty "a shield against aggression." NATO sought to bind America to Western Europe, its best means of deterring both Soviet aggression and a resurgent German military threat, a policy known as "dual containment." As Lord Ismay, NATO's first secretary general, said in 1949, NATO was founded "to keep the Russians out, the Americans in and the Germans down." However, to Ernest Bevin there was an underlying objective just as important as dual containment. Bevin, like Marshall before him and most leading U.S. officials in the spring of 1949, did not expect an outright Soviet invasion of the West or an uncontrollable German resurgence. But the people of Western Europe—still deeply shaken by the recent war, the experience of occupation and the emergence of the atomic bomb—did. Western Europeans' confidence in their future remained tenuous. Bevin believed that that lack of confidence was, in fact, still the greatest impediment to the region's economic recovery. An American military guarantee would ease fears and provide a sense of security. Bevin felt that it might very well be NATO's greatest contribution to Europe.

NATO was also another vehicle to advance European integration and mutual cooperation. Visiting Europe as a banker in the mid-1920s, Averell Harriman recalled a meeting of the board of directors of the International Chamber of Commerce. Harriman bluntly asked the assemblage of leading European businessmen and financiers why it was that America's economy was growing whereas Europe's was stagnant with seemingly built-in unemployment. Because you have a continent, a large market, with free trade, was the reply. "Well," Harriman asked the prominent Europeans, "if that's the case, why don't you with all your influence in different countries make the changes that are necessary to get freer trade in Europe?" The Europeans answered that unless there was a military understanding, freedom of trade could not exist. Without a military understanding, each country would not cede certain preferential agreements or advantages. Harriman and other U.S. officials hoped that NATO would advance integration. "The treaty," Dean Acheson recalled in his memoirs, "was more than a purely military treaty. It was a means and a vehicle for closer political, economic and security cooperation with Western Europe."

As the United States forged binding ties with Western Europe, it followed naturally that America wanted to bolster European member states' defense capacity, so that they could function as dependable and effective partners. The provision of military aid was a natural corollary to the treaty that had just been signed. Within a few hours of its ratification on July 25, 1949, President Truman sent to Congress a request for military aid authorization of almost $1.5 billion. Some wondered if military aid would now compete with economic aid for funding and priority.

The administration and ECA's senior officials all echoed Averell Harriman's assurance: "Of prime importance is the ERP. All agree that nothing should be permitted to interfere with that. But alongside of it, I earnestly believe we should help our associates in their own efforts to build up means to defend themselves." Months before, George Kennan had opined on NATO's significance: "The need for military alliances and rearmament on the part of Western Europe is primarily a subjective one, arising in their own minds as a result of their failure to understand correctly their own position. Their best . . . course of action if they are to save themselves from communist pressures, remains the struggle for economic recovery and for internal political stability."

The presentation of the Military Aid Program augured another key tension with which the Marshall Plan would have to contend. Not only did the program request a large authorization, on top of the largest peacetime budget request in the nation's history, it also provided the president with an unusual amount of executive discretion in how the funds would be allocated. Even Arthur Vandenberg found the arms bill "almost unbelievable in its grant of unlimited power to the Chief Executive." It would make Harry Truman "the number one war lord of the earth," Van said. Increasingly adversarial, cost-conscious Republicans were spoiling for a fight—and Truman had provided them an opening. Eventually, the administration modified some of the bill's farthest-reaching provisions, and contextual developments helped to secure

Brandenberg Gate in Berlin, July 7, 1945.

A typical scene in post-war Europe.

3

A rescue team searches for survivors amidst the rubble of a building in England demolished by German bombs toward the end of the war.

4

A food protest in Vienna, Austria, May 1947. Harry Truman noted that more people in Europe faced starvation in the year after the war then in all of the war years combined.

5

6

Secretary of State George C. Marshall (*left*) with his Soviet counterpart Foreign Minister Vyacheslav Molotov. Marshall went head-to-head with Molotov, most notably at the Moscow Conference of Foreign Ministers in March and April 1947.

Marshall addresses the nation via radio upon his return from the Moscow Foreign Ministers' Conference, April 28, 1947. "The patient is sinking while the doctors deliberate," Marshall said. "Action cannot await compromise through exhaustion."

7

8

George Kennan, head of the Policy Planning Staff at the State Department. Kennan's insights helped shape some of the central features of the Plan.

Will Clayton, Undersecretary of Economic Affairs at the State Department. More than any other man, Clayton was the intellectual architect of the Plan.

9

Marshall walks in the procession at Harvard University's 286th Commencement, June 5, 1947. He had come to accept an honorary degree and offer "a few remarks," perhaps "a little more." Bevin called his address "one of the greatest speeches in world history."

10

British Foreign Secretary Ernest Bevin (*left*) grabbed Marshall's offer of aid with both hands, and became the indispensable partner in the Marshall Plan, the Berlin Airlift and the formation of NATO.

In this *Pravda* cartoon "Sixteen in a Circle," the sixteen CEEC nations grovel at the feet of George Marshall and the prospect of Marshall dollars, summer 1947.

Edwin Marcus's 1947 cartoon "Can He Block It?" For Stalin, the Marshall Plan was "a dagger pointed at the heart of Moscow." He pulled his eastern European satellites out of the Plan and, once it was passed, he instructed western European Communist Parties to sabotage it.

French Foreign Minister Georges Bidault addresses the sixteen-nation Committee of European Economic Cooperation assembled in Paris in the summer of 1947.

14

With political and economic conditions in France and Italy becoming increasingly grave, Marshall and Undersecretary of State Robert Lovett appear before Congress to request interim aid to bridge the "Marshall Gap" before ERP would be passed, November 10, 1947.

15

After a ten-month campaign to secure congressional and public support for the Plan, President Harry S. Truman signs the Economic Cooperation Act on April 3, 1948. Truman is flanked by ERP supporters, including (*far left*) Senator Arthur Vandenberg.

The arrival of Marshall aid was celebrated throughout Western Europe in the spring of 1948. U.S. Ambassador Jefferson Caffrey welcomes the first shipment of ERP grain to France.

16

18

From left to right: President Harry Truman with Secretary Marshall, ECA Administrator Paul Hoffman and Special Representative for Europe W. Averell Harriman, seated around Truman's desk in the Oval Office, November 29, 1948.

Richard Bissell, the economist behind the Harriman Committee and much of the technical innovation and policymaking at ECA.

A dockworker unloading crates of Marshall Plan goods.

Much of the first shipments were for relief, for near-term needs such as food and fuel. A baby accepts a bottle of orange juice, and an elderly woman sits amidst a shipment of milk provided by the Marshall Plan.

The Netherlands receives a shipment of Marshall Plan–funded coal.

A French farming family receives a tractor.

Young men unload a shipment of grain.

Berliners labor to build a block of apartment buildings, and workers repair the road to Palermo.

27

The Plan helped to finance large-scale modernization and industrialization projects such as clearing the Corinth Canal and land reclamation in Italy.

28

29

Berliners watch as an American cargo plane delivers supplies in the airlift.

Paul Hoffman shaking hands with Italian Prime Minister Alcide De Gasperi, October 1950.

30

Chateau de la Muette, in Paris, headquarters to the Organization for European Economic Cooperation (OEEC).

ECA launched an ambitious information campaign to promote European integration. Among other activities, ECA financed and distributed documentaries, pamphlets and posters, like these shown here.

·ALL OUR COLOURS TO THE MAST·

32

Whatever the weather
We only reach welfare
together

3

Paul Hoffman (*center*) with the Greek ECA liaison at one of the many ERP exhibits set up to promote the Marshall Plan, October 1950.

34

A technical adviser teaches Turkish farmers how to use an American tractor at the Ankara Agricultural School, and Austrian electric engineers visit a General Electric plant in upstate New York under the auspices of the Technical Assistance Program.

Housing under construction in Nürnberg.

ERP packaging doubles as an apron for a Greek woman.

Secretary of State Dean Acheson with West Germany's first chancellor Konrad Adenauer. West Germany's rehabilitation was a key element of the Marshall Plan.

One of Europe's great post-war figures and "Washington's favorite European," Jean Monnet led France's economic modernization and fathered the concept that paved the way to Franco–German rapprochement, and eventually, European economic union.

French Foreign Minister Robert Schuman embodied the hope for Franco–German reconciliation, and the Schuman Plan realized it. Pooling their coal and steel under joint authority, the perennial enemies would thereafter be locked "in an embrace so close that neither could draw back far enough to hit the other."

42

The business district in
Hamburg, Germany:
1945 vs. 1950

43

A parade in honor of
the Marshall Plan in
the Netherlands.

44

its passage in September, but not before the political undercurrents and geopolitical criticisms, the sheer frustrations—and the Truman administration's overreach—all unleashed what Dean Acheson called the "subterranean fires."

That spring of 1949, the partisan rancor could not occlude the administration's realization of a series of remarkable foreign policy accomplishments. In addition to NATO, on May 12, 1949, the first truck from the western zones of Germany made its way through the eastern zone and into western Berlin. The blockade had been lifted. When Acheson and Charles Bohlen heard the news back in Washington at the State Department, they broke open a bottle of champagne.

In the late summer of 1948, even U.S. airmen themselves were skeptical about the airlift's prospects of supplying Berlin through the winter. The city's almost two and a half million inhabitants required approximately 4,000 tons of food and fuel per day. Supplying all of that via air, day in and day out, was an extraordinary logistical challenge. The prospect of winter and its attendant storms and ice appeared likely to complicate and frustrate the effort. With U.S. and British planes and airmen, with Germans working at Tempelhof and Gatow airports on the ground, with floodlights blazing to guide the planes to their runways, the airlift proceeded to gain steam that fall, and tonnage steadily increased. On September 9, hundreds of thousands of west Berliners rallied at the Brandenburg Gate against the Soviet blockade. A man climbed atop the gate, seized a red Soviet flag, flung it below, and the crowd set it aflame, as it chanted, "Back to Moscow."

If nature had pummeled Western Europe at its most fragile in the winter of 1946–47, it showed its kinder face in the winter of 1948–49. Blessed with a "meteorological miracle," a far milder winter than could have been predicted, the airlift dropped 4,500 tons of food and fuel daily—more than the minimal requirement—in western Berlin. American and British pilots flew missions around the clock, often, to their delight, dropping candy for western Berlin's children, who traced the plane's red and green wing lights in and out of Berlin, a seamless, droning procession.

German women labored through the night constructing a new airport in the western zone. German engineers and workers handled the back-end logistics and delivery. The Americans, the British and Berliners found themselves working in common cause, sharing the weight of the challenge and the thrill of the winter's successes. Journalist Theodore White recalled that when he sat down in a bar in Frankfurt or the Ruhr, when one heard an American use the pronoun "they," "they" referred to the Germans. But at a bar in Berlin when one heard "they," the speaker was usually referring to the

Russians. The Germans were included in "we." The Berlin Airlift marked a profound psychological turning point in the occupation and in U.S.-German relations.

Stalin had hoped that the blockade would sever the United States from western Berlin, but it was proving to be a bridge. Stalin's intention was to disrupt U.S. designs in Western Europe, and to steal a strategic victory in the wake of the Marshall Plan's success. Instead, the blockade cast Stalin and the Soviet Union as cruel, and as the airlift succeeded, feckless. Stalin could not deny the blockade's failure. So, in late January 1949, Stalin took the unusual step of answering a series of questions filed with the Soviet Foreign Office by a western newsman, Kingsbury Smith, European Manager of the International News Service. Smith had asked under what conditions the Soviets would remove the blockade. In the past, Stalin had always cited technical transportation difficulties or currency reform as the reasons for the blockade, his ostensible justifications. Answering Smith, he said that he would remove the blockade if the western allies agreed to halt their plans for the formation of a separate West German state, which he must have known they would not do from a position of strength. But the blockade was now doing Stalin more harm than good.

As U.S. and Soviet officials negotiated through back channels late that winter and early that spring, the airlift's output and efficiency kept climbing. By spring, the planes dropped more than double the 4,000 tonnage daily minimum of food and fuel. Western pilots flew 1,398 missions in the span of one single twenty-four-hour period. In early May, Stalin assented to lift the blockade with the condition that the western allies simply meet to discuss Germany. By May 12, 1949, when the blockade was formally lifted, the United States and Britain had registered 277,804 flights and the delivery of 2,325,809 tons of food and supplies. Lucius Clay called the blockade "the stupidest move the Russians could make." Winston Churchill proclaimed: "America has saved the world."

On the same day that the blockade was lifted, the allied powers approved the establishment of a new German federated republic. The constitution of the Federal Republic of Germany, or West Germany, was agreed upon on May 23, 1949. The new arrangement provided that the Allied High Commission could intervene in German affairs if it chose to, no doubt an important stipulation for the French, who were in accord but still profoundly anxious over German re-emergence. Save that one provision, the constitution provided the new West German state with almost complete political autonomy. It was a dramatic development in a triumphant spring for the United States and its foreign policy.

When Dean Acheson arrived in Paris late that May for the sixth and final meeting of the Council of Foreign Ministers, David Bruce took him to the Monseigneur for drinks and music. Hours into the evening, Acheson, after more than a few drinks, rose to his feet and pronounced, "I want to drink a toast to the Berlin airlift." Bruce, fearing the beginning of a diplomatic incident of catastrophic proportions, turned to Acheson's aide. "Make him sit down!" Bruce ordered. "But how?" asked Acheson's young aide. "Pull him down by the pants," Bruce said. The aide did as told, and to Acheson's surprise, he found himself seated, toast truncated, diplomatic incident avoided—but still giddy, no doubt, from that spring's foreign policy triumphs.

ON JUNE 5, 1949, a Sunday evening, a host of American officials and foreign dignitaries gathered at the Hotel Carlton in Washington, D.C., to celebrate the second anniversary of George Marshall's address at Harvard University and, recovered from kidney surgery and in attendance, the man who had delivered it. Truman could not be there, but passed along a speech to be read in honor of the occasion. "We are very happy to join . . . in this tribute to one of the greatest Americans of all time," he said. "The nations represented here owe as much to General Marshall, in war and in peace, as they owe to any one man in the world." Paul Hoffman had similarly kind words: "General Marshall—the military genius—has an enduring place in world history. But, in my opinion, it is General Marshall—the apostle of peace—through the Marshall Plan, who will live forever in the hearts of free men."

Hoffman said that whatever success ECA had realized to date was the result of "staying clearly behind two ideas" expressed in Marshall's Harvard speech. "General Marshall knew that freedom could not be maintained by bullets alone," Hoffman said. "He knew that free institutions could flourish only under conditions which give meaning and substance to freedom of all people. He pointed out that normal economic health was basic to enduring peace." Hoffman said that ECA had accepted that "policy as gospel . . . Increasingly, we have come to believe that this is the most effective way to fight the powers of darkness."

The other principle from Marshall's address to which Hoffman and ECA remained unstintingly faithful was that Europe's recovery needed to be "European in origin and operation." And "our activities have been concentrated wholly on helping our European partners": the governments that had held their coalitions together, had implemented painful austerity programs and faced Communist violence, sabotage and insurrection; the people who had endured deprivation, fear and vulnerability and had started to work, to invest, to rebuild with an increasing sense of confidence and hope. As the dignitaries gathered to recognize the anniversary—two years after Marshall's speech, and fifteen months after the ECA was formally established—all signs pointed to an extraordinarily successful European recovery.

When it was his turn to address the audience, Marshall said that "looking again at the conditions prevalent in the spring of 1947, and again considering the situation at this moment, I can only feel that one near miracle has been accomplished." In June 1949, Western Europe had emerged, already, a phoenix from the ashes of the war, a region with somber challenges ahead, to be sure, but renewed, revitalized and facing its future with a newfound sense of security and possibility.

Statistics only capture part of that picture. Before Marshall aid began, the 10,000 workers at Fort Dunlop, Europe's largest tire plant, in Birmingham, England, faced what some of them called an economic Dunkirk. They could no longer obtain carbon black, the toughening agent that comprises about 30 percent of a tire's carcass and tread, because Britain did not have the dollars to purchase it. "For days," said, Leslie Joseph Pridmore, one of the plant's workers, "our machines stood silent and we were idle. Without 'black' we couldn't go on. Black's our life. If we don't get it we are out of work . . . It was terrible, desperate. Then Marshall aid started, and black was put on the list. We've never had to worry since. Regular as clockwork the trucks have arrived, loaded with bags of black. The machines have kept on, and the men." A plant manager said, "Marshall aid saved us from catastrophe." Carbon black itself amounted to only a fraction of the value of the output of the tire plant. But, without it, the plant would have shut down. It was a perfect illustration of the "multiplier effect" at work.

The British government's official "Economic Survey" found: "These supplies have provided a general support to the whole U.K. economy, and without them it would have been impossible either to achieve the steady expansion of industrial production which took place in 1949 or to sustain so large a program of capital investment . . . There is not a single industry or district in the country which has not benefited in some way from American aid." In Great Britain, production was high, unemployment was low and the fiscal and monetary situation was stable—and Marshall aid was helping to fuel that progress.

Marshall aid was having a greater impact, still, in France, where it had accounted for 6.5 percent of the past year's gross national output and where it was, as one labor leader put it, the oxygen tank for the Monnet Plan. For

Georges Raoul Fremond, a Frenchman who farmed a flat and windy 222 acres of land southwest of Paris, it meant that he could upgrade to an American tractor, which would do the work of six horses. It was not a gift. Fremond had to order the tractor and pay for it, but without the Marshall Plan he wouldn't have had the opportunity to buy it. The francs he used to pay for it were in the country's counterpart fund, which financed the Monnet Plan, and projects such as the mechanization of coal mines, the electrification of railways, the construction of the first continuous strip-steel mill in Europe and the completion of the Genissiat Dam on the upper Rhone, to be the largest dam in Western Europe. Together with other dams being built on the Rhine and the Dordogne and smaller rivers in the Pyrenees and Alps, the dams would provide energy to fuel Western Europe's factories and homes.

That June was a glorious one in France. The Marshall Plan was fueling the country's rapidly increasing industrial production. A bountiful harvest was driving agricultural production higher. By spring, daily products were no longer rationed. Steel production was just about meeting Jean Monnet's ambitious targets, and car production at the end of 1949 reached 20,000, four times the total from 1947. Parisians did not even seem to mind the clamor on streets where cars and motor scooters had come to overtake bicycles as a primary mode of transport. It helped that they could stop in to the Folies Bergère to see Josephine Baker perform or stand beneath the Eiffel Tower, floodlit for the first time that summer.

Marshall dollars, the Queuille government's tough measures and Jean Monnet's leadership were producing remarkable results in France, where inflation was coming under control. In 1949, Monnet wrote in his memoirs, he could report to the government for the first time: "France has rejected the decadence that threatened her." The progress constituted a stinging defeat for the Communists, allaying French concerns about political violence and insurrection. The economic successes of 1949 brought political stability and calm. In the park along the Champs-Elysées, Pierre Lignes, a municipal worker who rented out public chairs, remarked: "Without Marshall aid probably very few people would be sitting down—most of them would be rioting and bashing each other over the head with my chairs." Not all Americans were entirely pleased. American journalists who had come to Paris to chronicle that city's vicissitudes wrote home to complain that they no longer had anything to write about.

No country had more distance to travel toward recovery, and no country traveled it in greater speed, than West Germany. Much of the reason for Germany's astounding economic progress in 1948–49 was that when its industry was unleashed, it was discovered that much less of its productive capacity was destroyed in the war than previously thought. Much German industrial and engineering know-how remained and officials like Economic Minister Ludwig Erhard adopted free-enterprise, market-oriented policies that served the state well. Still, U.S. aid had kept West Germans afloat during the occupation. The Marshall Plan ushered in the U.S. policy of German recovery, laying the foundation for currency reform, Germany's own policies for recovery, West German statehood and political autonomy and the airlift, all of which fueled confidence—and eventually Marshall aid itself.

One could measure the progress, remembered Theodore White, almost month to month. The Germans filled out; their clothes changed "from rumpled rags to decent garments, to neat business suits, to silk stockings." Food returned, "as the Germans love it, with whipped cream beaten thick in the coffee, on cake, with fruit." Buildings rose from the rubble and "neon signs festooned them, as their windows shone with goods." As in other countries, ECA directed its funds in Germany toward investment and recovery, as opposed to consumer goods or relief. "One reason for the recovery," offered the vice chancellor at the time, Franz Blucher, "is that there was such strict control over counterpart [funds] that the economy had been like a regiment drilling under its colonel . . . This was not always morally pleasant, but it contributed to the great effort."

West Germany's economic performance was so strong, in fact, that in relatively short order the German food ration came to eclipse the ration for British troops and their families occupying the Germans. Germany's recovery helped inspire a British film called *The Mouse That Roared,* released years later, in which Peter Sellers played the prime minister of a small, impoverished European country. In a stroke of inspiration, Seller's character decides that the best hope for his country would be to invade the United States and then reap the reward of vast aid after his country's defeat. Things take an unexpected turn and the Army of Grand Fenwick captures New York, foiling the grand plan. Happily, the film did not tempt any European (or Soviet) leader to see if life could imitate art.

Among the smaller Marshall countries, the Plan was having a similarly substantial impact. Therein, ECA continued to favor projects directed at investment, infrastructure and modernization. It financed a thermal electric plant in Naples. When Fiat asked for funds to build a new plant to develop a new model of car, ECA replied to the Italian government that it would provide the counterpart funds on the condition that the government also pursue an extensive road-building project and remove gasoline and horsepower taxes; the car, ECA added, also had to be small and cheap. ECA financed everything from malaria eradication in Sardinia (to keep workers alive) to a large reclamation of arable land in Zuider Zee in the Netherlands (to increase land that could be farmed), to vocational training for olive growers in Greece, to the provision of plows, tractors and railways in Turkey, where they were "changing an Asian way of life."

When Marshall aid was put to use at its best, it fostered mutual coopera-tion. In one instance four nations collaborated to build a ferry for a fifth (France): Dutch experts tested the models for the craft, built with Danish and English steel, and the United States provided the two giant electrically powered cranes. The economic benefit to the smaller European countries was sometimes greater and the impact more far-reaching. In 1950, for exam-ple, Marshall aid constituted half of Greece's national production.

The proportion of Marshall aid to national production in some of the smaller countries, such as Greece, provided ECA missions with formidable leverage in devising their recovery strategy, and how counterpart funds would be spent. In several recipient countries, though, ECA missions found that they had less influence than might have been expected. In France, Bruce and Tomlinson deferred to Monnet and his staff on the disbursal of most of the counterpart funds. In Italy, government officials petrified of inflation would not cede to Mission Chief James Zellerbach's call for invest-ment and expansionary policies. Instead, Italy spent most of its counterpart funds provided in the first years of the Plan retiring debt and keeping infla-tion under control. Some historians have highlighted the push-back from recipient countries to point out the limitations of America's influence in guiding the various national recoveries.

ECA's overriding aim, however, was not to micromanage national recov-eries (though it tried to do so at times and with mixed results). Self-help was the cardinal and governing principle. ECA wanted to promote recovery for political ends; to bolster the centrist governing coalitions that would keep countries politically stable and in the American bloc. As long as recipient countries worked on their recoveries adhering to those goals, and worked in concert—if not always in agreement—with ECA, then push-back and dis-agreement, Hoffman felt, was fine, even healthy. The main concern was that the Plan's larger objectives were still being advanced.

In the report to Congress for the quarter ended June 1949, ECA reported: "By June 1949 it was unmistakably evident that the flow of U.S. dollars and the efforts of the countries themselves had been effective in restoring the vitality of Western Europe. The importance to the U.S. and the world of a revived faith in the future cannot be overemphasized." The "outstanding achievement" of the ERP's first year, the agency said, was production. Production was on a sharp upward trajectory, having increased almost 20 percent already compared to prewar levels. Agricultural output, helped in large part by a favorable harvest that year, was increasing. Buoyed by France's remarkable progress on inflation—wholesale prices actually dropped by 5 percent from their peak five months earlier—the agency suggested (prematurely, it would turn out) that the period "may well have marked the end of inflation that has been troubling Western Europe since World War II." While Hoffman, Harriman and the U.S. Congress pressed European leaders for further integration, Sir Stafford Cripps put the progress to date in perspective: "In one year ECA has done more for European unity than was accomplished in the preceding 500 years." On the political ledger, the Communists suffered humiliating defeats in elections in Austria, Norway and West Germany, all around this time.

On April 3, Prime Minister Attlee wrote to President Truman: "A year has gone by," since the ERP had passed Congress, "and gave us hope and help when we most needed it. During the last year the whole economic scene in Western Europe has been transformed to a degree which must astonish all of us when we recall the uncertainties and perils of the immediately preceding years." This progress, Attlee continued, "is due to the generosity and far-sightedness of the people and the Government of the United States. Without their help the achievement of the past year would not have been possible nor would Europe have the confidence to go forward . . . On this happy anniversary," Attlee concluded, "we send to you the American people our heartfelt thanks." A week before, on his sixth peacetime visit to the United States, Winston Churchill proclaimed that the Marshall Plan constituted "a turning point in the history of the world."

In late June 1949, Arthur Vandenberg wrote: "It seems to be the rather general opinion that we are winning this 'cold war' through ECA and the North Atlantic Pact. In my opinion, if it were not for these policies, Soviet Communism would today be in the substantial control of Europe and this would pose the greatest threat to our own national security in the lifetime of the republic." "There were some who called it a grandiose experiment," Averell Harriman said when the Marshall Plan was first introduced, "but already," he said in July 1949, "it is among the most noble experiences in human affairs." No one was more optimistic than Harry Truman: "We are closer to world peace now than at any time in the last years."

• • •

IN JUNE 1949, most American officials looked back with pride at achievements registered and looked forward with buoyancy, optimism that progress would continue to accrue. On June 16, 1949, however, Ambassador Lewis Douglas cabled a disturbing report back to the State Department from London: "This is to alert you to the possibility that the UK may be confronted this summer with a major financial crisis not unlike that which developed in 1947. The economic consequences would almost certainly precipitate a political crisis as well." It was Great Britain's Dollar Gap, and it was getting worse.

One man more than any other presided over Great Britain's economic recovery: Sir Stafford Cripps. Cripps, sixty years old, was a tall, lean and decidedly left-leaning intellectual from the British upper crust. Winston Churchill appointed him ambassador to the Soviet Union in the late 1930s in the hope that he could win Stalin's allegiance. He failed at first, but after the Germans reneged on their pact with the Soviets and invaded, Cripps succeeded in securing a Soviet partnership, for which he was widely hailed at home. Cerebral and well respected, Cripps was brought into the Cabinet by Churchill. A devout Anglican, Cripps was also a vegetarian and favored a cheap meal of salad and cheese soufflé. Once when Cripps arrived late for a Cabinet meeting, Churchill barked, "Now that our colleagues have digested their beet juice, perhaps we can get to work." Cripps was a tireless worker and had formidable powers of intellect and oration. Churchill frowned on his politics and ideology. He once said of Cripps, "There but for the Grace of God goes God." Grudgingly, though, he admired the man.

Having assumed the dual role of minister of economic affairs and chancellor of the Exchequer in 1947, Cripps exercised enormous influence on Great Britain's economic policies. He pursued a socialist agenda: the nationalization of industry, tight fiscal and monetary policy, the construction of a welfare state, and perhaps above all, he geared the economy to achieve full employment. To finance all of this and to weather Britain's economic hardships, Cripps summoned his country to a period of austerity, with intense rationing and controls. Though well-to-do, Cripps led by example. He favored 45-cent lunches at his favorite restaurant, and he had refused to purchase a new suit, nor to use even one single clothes coupon, since clothes rationing began in 1941. Cripps came to embody British austerity in manner and practice.

In the summer of 1949, Cripps's economic strategy seemed to be working. With the help of Marshall aid, industrial recovery was proceeding at a brisk pace, employment was high, and a welfare state had been erected. Throughout 1948 and the first half of 1949 as conditions improved, Cripps approved "a bonfire of controls," and the most taxing and ascetic days seemed to be behind the weary nation. There was one problem, though. To fuel its increasing output, Britain was importing heavily from the United States. Its purchases still far outpaced its ability to export to the dollar area. Britain's Dollar Gap, therefore, was widening at an alarming rate, and as a result it was hemorrhaging dollar and gold reserves. Cripps passed U.S. Ambassador Lewis Douglas a secret internal economic analysis that showed that Britain's dollar drain had doubled in the quarter ending June 1949 from the previous quarter. British gold and dollar reserves were already at a perilously low level and at the current rate appeared likely to deplete at a rate of $100 million or more per month.

There were several precipitants. The first was that in the spring of 1949 there was a recession in America. The recession reduced America's imports from many Marshall Plan countries as much as 20 percent or more, and as much as 40 percent in some raw-material producing sterling countries. But there was more to it. American officials believed that Great Britain was not producing a sufficient quantity of high-quality goods at prices low enough to be attractive to buyers in American markets. ECA believed that the under-lying reason was England's continued orientation toward the Common-wealth. Great Britain was reluctant to opt in to a large European market, which would foster specialization, competition and innovation—the ingre-dients that would drive improvement and British goods' competitiveness in American markets. So long as Britain held firm to the Commonwealth, its productivity would lag, it would not be competitive, and its Dollar Gap would remain, ever vulnerable to swings in the U.S. economy. And as long as the specter of the Dollar Gap remained a structural feature of the U.S.-British relationship, Britain could not achieve economic self-sustainability. Britain's dollar problem thus threatened one of the central aims of the Mar-shall Plan.

The long-term solution for Great Britain was European integration. But there was also a short-term palliative. On March 17, Richard Bissell sent a cable to Harriman in Paris. The Marshall Plan countries had achieved a new level of stability. As State Department official Willard Thorp said, ECA had "passed out of the honey-moon phase of the . . . program." The time was now ripe, Bissell argued, to take aim at the Dollar Gap and European recovery with a recalibrated strategy. "A broad revaluation of European currencies" would lower prices, facilitating intra-European trade and European exports to America, reducing the Dollar Gap and paving the way for further European integration.

The notion of devaluation, first prominently suggested at ECA in Bissell's

March 1949 memorandum, began picking up steam internally at ECA and at State. When the American recession hit that spring and Great Britain's dollar position began to take a sharp turn for the worse in April, May and June, the concept gained traction among leading American officials. By the end of June, ECA estimated that "UK's hard currency reserves had fallen so low that drastic measures were required." Dean Acheson cabled Douglas in London: "prompt action is essential to put things straight." Publicly, Hoffman said that currency valuation was an internal matter for Great Britain and the other European governments to work out for themselves. Privately, all the major U.S. decision makers were now squarely behind it.

Stafford Cripps did not share ECA's enthusiasm for devaluation. If Great Britain lowered the value of sterling, it would make American imports more expensive. Great Britain needed those imports to continue to fuel its recovery. Furthermore, if imports were more expensive, British workers would demand higher wages. An offsetting inflation could kick in. Moreover, by this time Great Britain's reluctance to join in an economically integrated Western Europe had calcified. If devaluation was a step in that direction, then they did not want to take it.

The alternative prescription was typically Crippsian. He proposed a further reduction in American imports, which would mean further austerity—and additional U.S. aid. Hoffman and others at ECA feared that Cripps aimed to morph the Marshall Plan into something of an ongoing New Deal for the world. A global New Deal, though, was not on the menu at ECA. By now, the State Department viewed devaluation "probably an essential element in any long-term solution." Cripps resisted. As Harriman first began to press for devaluation late that June, he estimated that Cripps would remain "as rigid as ever" in holding the line.

On July 8, U.S. Treasury Secretary John Snyder met with Bevin and Cripps in London to see if, together, the three men could devise a path forward. Snyder was a fiscal conservative, very sensitive to congressional sentiment. Snyder, who "wore his faith in free enterprise like a chastity belt," blamed the crisis on British production and argued that Britain had to export more to America. Cripps held that the American recession had induced the crisis. After three days of fruitless discussions, Snyder returned to Washington to report that U.S. and British policies were in fundamental opposition and that the matter would be taken up again in talks scheduled for mid-September in Washington.

Much of the U.S.-British tensions played out that summer in Paris at the OEEC. "The months of June through August 1949," wrote Dutch delegate

Ernst van der Beugel, "were the most critical in OEEC's history." Highest among the "concentration of seemingly insoluble issues" was the wrench that Great Britain threw in the division of aid. With its Dollar Gap widening, Great Britain submitted a revised estimate in which the sterling area dollar deficit for the year 1949–50 was up more than $500 million, or 50 percent more than the one submitted six months earlier. It would now require additional Marshall aid, what amounted, in fact, to 40 percent of the total Marshall aid available. Even the Foreign Office admitted that Britain was solving its dollar problem by "putting the squeeze on Europe." The division of aid had been a Herculean task fraught with cross-cutting interests and difficulty. Great Britain's request deeply upset that balance. Great Britain and the United States had already been at odds over the institutional strength with which OEEC should be endowed. Harriman and Hall-Patch continued to do battle. Neither side could escape the tension.

As the United States and Great Britain squared off, U.S. officials once again grew alarmed about the specter of autarky. In late June, Harriman cabled Acheson in Washington: "I cannot avoid the thought that Cripps may hope to high-pressure us into acceptance of his ideas of a closed discriminatory sterling area expanded to include the continental countries as far as possible . . . Needless to say," he concluded, "I would view such a course as disastrous." Half the world's trade was still in sterling. Autarky would provide the British with shelter from America's economic vicissitudes and American pressure to integrate as well as plug the drain on its dollar reserves. Bevin told the House of Commons on July 18, "I confess that I have been tempted in that direction," and he dangled the proposition in front of his American interlocutors.

Douglas cabled Washington: "What we are facing is more than a British dollar crisis—it is an Anglo-American problem, the implications of which go far beyond the question of the exchange rate of sterling and British dollar reserves. The failure of our two governments to cooperate closely in the immediate future . . . might very well prejudice the Marshall program, the many aspects of our foreign economic and political policy which depend upon its success and might give comfort and support to Communist and Soviet designs."

"When one reads through the minutes and the reports of that period," wrote van der Beugel, "one can only conclude that it was almost a miracle that OEEC survived." The participating countries rolled up their sleeves that sweltering August in Paris, realizing "that this was the last chance for agreement." After painful deliberations, they did pull through with a revised division of aid around September 1.

While matters at OEEC stabilized, and the Washington talks scheduled for mid-September approached, Anglo-American relations continued to deteriorate. In mid-August, at a private lunch, U.S. Secretary of Defense Louis Johnson suggested to Undersecretary of State James Webb, "The UK was finished, there was no sense in trying to bolster it up through ECA" or other U.S. policies. "As the Empire disintegrated," he said, "we should write off the UK and continue co-operation with those parts of the Empire that remained useful to us." Even as Johnson suggested writing off Great Britain and the Marshall Plan's designs, the two men in the British Isles most able to get Anglo-American relations back on track were in dire straits themselves. Bevin was deeply worn out and suffered from attacks of angina. Cripps could not eat, and during the second half of July and the first half of August he spent five weeks in rest and recovery at a sanitarium in Switzerland.

On August 18 a paper prepared under Lewis Douglas at the U.S. Embassy in London averred: "the importance of the September meeting cannot be exaggerated." If the United States did not take dramatic steps to reverse course, it might render "the achievement of our ECA objective of dollar viability by 1952 . . . impossible." The embassy anticipated "a possible major break between the UK and the U.S. on economic policy, which would have far reaching effects on all our relations with the UK, as well as other countries, and require a reassessment and readjustment of our post-war foreign and defense policies."

No one in the American Embassy or in the U.S. knew about a fateful meeting the following day, on August 19. Early in August, it appeared that reserves were, in fact, depleting "at a rate that would drain the Bank of England in less than a year." British import restrictions were not working and Anglo-American relations were deteriorating. Autarky may have afforded Great Britain shelter, but it was not a viable option for Bevin, who pegged British security to her association with America. By the time of the meeting, the British Treasury had come around to devaluation. Bevin had as well, and Prime Minister Attlee had written to Cripps in Switzerland that devaluation was the best means of stemming the British reserve drain, maintaining Anglo-American ties and preserving the government's freedom to maneuver.

Cripps returned to London for the August 19 meeting, a "grueling" session among the ministers and other leading senior officials. Cripps was the last holdout. After three hours, he acquiesced. At a Cabinet meeting on August 29, it was decided that the British would devalue sterling 30 percent. It was further decided that the British would not negotiate with the Americans about devaluation in Washington. Attlee and Bevin wanted to demonstrate to the United States that they were willing to take the initiative to maintain the partnership. In return, they hoped that the U.S. would take measures to ameliorate the crisis and acknowledge Great Britain's special role in the world as "the nodal point" in three systems—the Commonwealth, Western Europe and the Atlantic community—thereby lowering pressure on Britain to fully integrate with Western Europe. Recognizing Great Britain's deep-seated reluctance to integrate with Europe, and the unique breadth of her Commonwealth commitments George Kennan had already begun to advocate for a greater measure of independence for Great Britain from the continent.

On September 6, 1949, the Cunarder RMS *Mauretania* docked in New York, completing Ernest Bevin's seven-day journey across the Atlantic Ocean. A pack of journalists were there to meet him. The newsmen jumped on board the ship and asked Bevin if he and Cripps had come in search of more dollars to bail out Britain. Refreshed and in fighting fettle, Bevin rattled off the list of accomplishments that the United States and Great Britain had orchestrated in the preceding eighteen months—the Marshall Plan, OEEC, NATO, a West German government. "I doubt whether so many impressive and far reaching political advances have been made in any other eighteen months in world history." He continued: "The worry we have now is: We are afraid that this will be frustrated if we cannot settle the economic maladjustment . . . We cannot have one democratic world politically if it is to be based upon two worlds economically. We must harmonize our economic affairs." Bevin had struck an auspicious note.

The following evening, still in New York, Dean Acheson and his wife, Alice, took Bevin to *South Pacific*, the most popular musical on Broadway at the time. The cast was informed that Bevin was in the theater, and the performers played to him. The portly, jovial foreign minister delighted in the performance, the attention and the ovations. As he departed the theater, Bevin had a heart attack. One of the guards on his detail stretched the foreign minister's prodigious frame across the aisle, sweat pouring down his face. After a towel soaked in ice water and some nitroglycerin were administered, Bevin regained his footing. Wobbling to his car, he turned to Acheson and asked, "Where are we goin' now?" "We're going back to the hotel to see that you go to bed," Acheson said. "Then what are you going to do?" Acheson said he would have a nightcap. Then "I'm comin' too," Bevin retorted, "I need a drink more than any of you."

By the time the talks began at the State Department in Washington, Bevin had regained his form. The British decision had successfully been kept a secret. Before the conference, the State Department remained in "uncertainty about what the British will say." As the talks began, both sides reiterated their respective positions, aiming to feel out the other. At one point, Paul Hoffman jumped in with an ardent appeal to the British to cut their costs, forgo the easier sterling markets and marshal their energy and concentration on promoting exports to the American markets. According to Acheson, Hoffman played the part of the "evangelist" preaching "his doctrine of salvation by exports with all the passion of an economic Savonarola."

Bevin met Hoffman's appeal with the assurance that he was most interested in selling British goods to the American markets. He explained that whenever Britain had geared its industry to that end in the past, Congress had raised protective measures. If the United States would guarantee that Congress would not do it again, he would be delighted to implement Hoffman's recommendations. Without such a guarantee, Bevin made it clear that he was "not going to flimflam [British] workers again." Of course, Hoffman could offer no such guarantee. Acheson wrote later of Bevin's stand: "He was entirely right."

The talks sputtered along fruitlessly for several sessions. The Americans were anxious about once again coming up empty. The time had come, the British delegation decided, to inform the Americans of their decision. Cripps and Bevin proceeded according to plan, and told the Americans that they would in fact devalue the sterling. In addition, they would cut costs, control inflation and redirect exports to the American markets as much as possible. Acheson, Hoffman and the other American officials were ecstatic. British Ambassador Oliver Franks cabled London that the program "was very well received." As the British had hoped, their decision "broke the dike of American resistance and released a flood of reciprocal concessions." The Americans agreed to lower tariffs and quotas on sterling goods, to import more, to promote private investment in the sterling area and to expand the range of sterling goods that could qualify for ECA financing, among other concessions. Cripps later described them as the "most frank . . . talks in which I have ever taken part."

The Washington agreements marked a seminal juncture in Anglo-American postwar relations. Devaluation and the upturn in America's economy increased British exports, plugged the British drain in reserves and narrowed its Dollar Gap, stabilizing Britain's economic position and restoring the momentum behind its recovery. More than that, the agreements arrested the slide toward a rupture in Anglo-American relations or the onset of economic autarky. Working together, the Americans and British preserved the western economic partnership and the spirit of their alliance.

To avoid a last minute run on sterling, the British kept devaluation a closely guarded secret. Code-named "rose," the British decision did not appear in the conference's formal communiqué. Outside of the Commonwealth countries, only the United States knew of the British decision to devalue its currency 30.5 percent, reducing the par value of the pound from $4.03 to $2.80 on September 18. However, devaluation was not welcome news to everyone.

A few days after the announcement, French Prime Minister Henri Queuille summoned U.S. Ambassador David Bruce to his office. Normally calm and composed, Queuille was livid, the most "disturbed and apprehensive" that Bruce had ever seen him. The prime minister rattled off his litany of grievances. First, the French had not been invited to Washington and had been kept in the dark about devaluation. It was a stinging slight to the French, who had moved so far and so painfully to accommodate U.S. and British policy on German recovery. This was on the back end of the decision to revise the division of aid conferring "most favored nation" status on Great Britain and raising its aid allocation to the detriment of the rest of Europe. It seemed that the United States was prizing its relationship with Great Britain above the other European countries, perhaps even above Europe itself. Perhaps most painfully, the British devaluation had triggered a 25 percent German devaluation. Now the French worried about the potency of German steel and coal on the world markets, even as West Germany was emerging into statehood. The combination was almost too much to bear.

French Minister of Finance Maurice Petsche called devaluation *"une décision brutale,"* and Hervé Alphand, a senior economic official, was described by a British counterpart as becoming "almost hysterical." Queuille told Bruce that "French pride [was] deeply wounded" as a result of the manner in which devaluation was handled. He felt that his government was in danger of falling. Acheson was aggrieved at the agitation stirring in France. "Where did we go wrong?" he asked. "What did we miscalculate or overlook?" He moved quickly to assure the French that there was no special Anglo-American partnership to the exclusion of other European allies, that the United States still put the full weight of its support behind European integration. It was a misunderstanding, and Acheson accepted full responsibility.

But much damage had been done. The French felt that they had consented to Germany's recovery and political autonomy, only to be left, it now seemed, alone on the continent to fend with a reemergent West German state. They felt that they had traveled on a far and painful journey to be effective and loyal partners to the United States, the British and to the aims of the Marshall Plan. And in return, they were receiving a swift "kick in the backside."

For his part, Paul Hoffman knew that America had work to do to reassure the French. In the meantime, though, he was elated. The day after the devaluation announcement, Hoffman and Harriman appeared at an afternoon press conference at 800 Connecticut Avenue in Washington. Hoffman heralded the British decision as "a bold and imaginative measure of far-reaching importance to ERP." It signified, Hoffman said, "that Great Britain has decided to compete in a free world to capture dollars which are essential to her recovery." But devaluation was only a bridge along which Europe needed to travel toward greater productivity and the other means of achieving self-sustainability: European integration.

Chapter Twelve

INTEGRATION AND SUBTERRANEAN FIRES

A T 1 P.M. ON OCTOBER 31, 1949, Paul Hoffman rose from his chair to address the Council of Ministers of the Organization for European Economic Cooperation in Paris. Hoffman was about to make the most important speech of his tenure as administrator of the Economic Cooperation Administration. For weeks, ECA had been trumpeting Hoffman's address. The press picked up on it and in the days preceding the meeting speculated widely. "All of the fanfare," wrote historian Michael Hogan, "created an air of anxious expectation."

During the first eighteen months of the European Recovery Program, Hoffman had pressed for European integration with increasing vigor and force. He was not satisfied with Europe's progress, though. Several factors converged that October to galvanize him into action.

Under Richard Bissell's stewardship, junior and midlevel ECA officials had been churning out a steady stream of policy analysis. In October, two of Bissell's star analysts, Harold van B. Cleveland and Theodore Geiger, submitted two seminal papers. The first argued that in the wake of Britain's recent dollar crisis, it was becoming clear that Western Europe would not achieve self-sustainability by 1952 at the current rate. They asserted that "fundamental alterations" would be needed in Western Europe's "economic structure as a whole." Cleveland and Geiger's next paper, "The Economic Integration of Western Europe," addressed one of the greatest strategic quandaries of the era: the German problem. "What solution is there to the German problem outside of membership in Western union?" The authors found that there was, in fact, no other solution. West German integration into

Europe was the best means of "harnessing [German] talents for management and production in a better cause than German nationalism . . . This, then," they concluded, "is the crucial and compelling reason for Western union. It provides the main hope for a regeneration of Western European civilization and for a new period of stability and growth." These were preexisting arguments. The papers and Bissell's sponsorship pointed the spotlight on them once more at a time when contextual dynamics provided particular resonance.

Hoffman had managed to shepherd ERP's second-year appropriations through the congressional gauntlet. But members of Congress were increasingly dissatisfied with Europe's progress on integration. Walter Lippmann wrote that a senior American official told him that ECA would not be able to obtain a full-third year appropriation unless Europe registered "some kind of impressive and substantial progress" toward integration.

At the same time, the currency devaluations fueled European exports and helped plug the drain on Great Britain's reserves. The special U.S.-Anglo accommodation, though, had shaken French confidence in American support of the European project. The revision of the division of aid in Great Britain's favor combined with British unwillingness to strengthen the OEEC as an institution—and now America's apparent consent to that posture—all raised French hackles. And now, on October 31, the same day of Hoffman's address, West Germany would become a full member of the OEEC, further elevating its national stature and increasing French anxiety.

For each of these reasons—but none more than that Hoffman truly believed that the path toward self-sustainability led through European integration—"the historical moment," Cleveland and Geiger's paper pronounced, "is now."

Hoffman began the address by acknowledging the great industrial and agricultural progress the Marshall countries had achieved to date. "We applaud the success of your efforts . . . We have seen anxiety give way to hope," he said. "Today I am asking you to turn hope into confidence." To that end, Hoffman said that the time had come to "devote our fullest energies to two major tasks." The first was to close Europe's Dollar Gap. The second, "and to say this is why I am here—is to move ahead on a far-reaching program to build in Western Europe a more dynamic expanding economy which will promise steady improvement in the conditions of life for all its people. This means nothing less than an integration of the Western European economy."

It was a watershed moment in the Marshall Plan. It was, as Milton Katz described it, the moment "when we began moving away from the original problem of how to organize a sensible aid program to the larger emphasis on the reorganization and the restructuring of the European economy and European society." European integration had previously been *a* priority, but with Hoffman's address it would now become ECA's *foremost* priority.

The recent devaluation "paved the way for a larger expansion of dollar earnings, but devaluation by itself is obviously not enough," Hoffman continued. Even balancing Europe's trade "will not be meaningful unless we have come to grips with . . . building an expanding economy in Western Europe through economic integration," which he defined as "the formation of a single large market within which quantitative restrictions on the movement of goods, monetary barriers to the flow of payments and eventually all tariffs are permanently swept away." Hoffman acknowledged the "difficulties" involved in the enterprise but cautioned his audience not to dismiss his clarion call "as a merely romantic possibility too remote to have any bearing on practical immediate decisions." Without integration Europe would degenerate into "various cycles of economic nationalism," markets would narrow, restrictive controls would mushroom and Europe would revert into a "primitive pattern of bilateral barter."

Marshall's "original suggestion" remained the guiding principle. "It is your job to devise and put into effect your own program to accomplish this purpose," Hoffman said. Still, "certain fundamental requirements suggest themselves," he said, treading the tightrope of "friendly aid." Trade liberalization, an end to dual pricing and currency convertibility were the three major provisions. Time was short, Hoffman said. ECA still had the funding available to help cushion the shock that these structural reforms might engender. He added that these reforms would be "essential" to Congress's continued support.

"For all these reasons," he said, "but particularly because of the urgency of the need, I do make this considered request that you have already early in 1950 a record of accomplishment and a program which together will take Europe well along the road toward economic integration." It was a tall order, but "that high hope can be realized if we the people of the free world continue to work together and stick together."

Harriman's deputy, William Foster, had said of Hoffman that he was "a sucker for a speech." He delivered the address "burning with a missionary's zeal," as one British spectator remembered it. Foreign policy analyst Richard Stebbins wrote that "seldom if ever had an American representative spoken more bluntly to a European official audience." Lincoln Gordon, a key ECA official, said years later that "the most ambitious aspect of the Marshall Plan" was not its 1947 formulation "but its 1949 reformulation" as promulgated by

Hoffman in his Paris address. So as to leave no doubt as to the crux of his message, Hoffman used the word "integration" fifteen times in his speech. When Hoffman finished the council rose to its feet in applause.

Reaction around Western Europe was mixed but not tepid. In London, the *Daily Telegraph* pronounced, "if Mr. Hoffman's speech yesterday was what the Americans call 'getting tough,' let us have more of such stimulating and constructive toughness." In Paris, *Le Monde* put its support behind integration. Italy's widest-read paper, *Corriere della Sera*, hailed Hoffman's speech as "very comforting" and "a warm appeal to Europe to unite, giving formal assurance of American support to this end."

The Communist papers reacted predictably. The Swedish Communist paper *Ny Dag* wrote: "USA Takes Over Hitler's 'New Order' Plan for Europe," and the Rome Communist paper *L'Unità* toed a familiar line: "Hoffman's Alternative Was: Either Obedience to his 'Diktat' or no Dollars." But opposition was much broader. Most came from Europeans who did in fact support integration; it was just that, as Theodore White wrote, "it has been accepted as men accept surgery performed on their bodies, not out of joy, but because they feel it necessary and can see no way, honestly, to escape it."

It did not escape informed European observers that it took nine years before the American Articles of Confederation were fused into the American Constitution. And while it took eighteen months of pregnancy to produce a baby elephant, the Marshall Plan countries now seemed to have less than three months to create an integrated European economy. As the *Tory Daily Express* declared: "Europe Given Eleven Weeks to Act . . . Britain and . . . other Marshall aid nations are tonight puzzled and bewildered by a 1,500 word ultimatum . . . It gives them 11 weeks to draw up a master plan for economic unity in Western Europe." The *Economist* supported European integration but said that it would "take a generation of planning and adaptation . . . America has the power, if it will be patient to impel Europe along the road to real integration," but an unduly "spectacular attempt" could "shatter the Marshall Plan and frustrate the whole purpose of American policy."

To some it seemed that Hoffman's talk about America's large market and American productivity and prosperity meant that the United States was trying to remake Europe in its own image. "The Americans wanted an integrated Europe looking like the United States of America—'God's own country,'" a British Treasury official wrote. Historian Michael Hogan suggested that this was one of the key aims of the Marshall Plan. In a sense, it was true. Hoffman and others at ECA believed that several of the attributes of the U.S. economy—a large, open market with minimal restrictions on trade or payments, productivity, a neocorporatist model in which labor and management worked together in relative comity—would all benefit Europe.

Yet it was Hoffman's intent only to highlight features of the American economy that had served America well and that most Europeans recognized were necessary. Hoffman wanted to encourage Europeans to incorporate these things in their own fashion, to devise their own institutions and their own approach. "I think the United States of Europe was a logical goal, but this wasn't an imitation of the American way of life," said Arthur Schlesinger. "It was very much accepted that Europe had a history, traditions and obstacles and habits organic to Europe and there was no sense—even from Bissell—that we were there to create another America." "We wanted each country to be itself," recalled Katz, noting that he and his colleagues even welcomed French "crotchetiness"—a salutary signal that France was returning to form.

On November 2, only two days after Hoffman's address, the OEEC acted. The organization called for "a single large market in Europe." To that end, it requested that each member country eliminate by December 15 quantitative restrictions on at least 50 percent of its imports from other member countries. On January 31, 1950, the OEEC raised that level to 60 percent and said that an increase to 75 percent by the end of 1950 should be considered. It also agreed that the member countries should devise a payments union to promote currency convertibility and raze payment barriers. To Dutch OEEC delegate Ernst van der Beugel, "the criticism of Hoffman's speech cannot conceal the basic fact that it was again American and not European initiative which pushed Western Europe further on the road to greater cooperation and integration."

On the morning of November 9, 1949, Paris was calm. Compared to the strikes and violence of the previous autumn, the city was placid, even. Buoyed by Marshall aid, the Monnet Plan, a government plan of austerity and a bountiful harvest, French industry was performing well, and the franc was stable. Their popularity enervated, the Communists occupied themselves with preparations for a grand celebration in honor of Josef Stalin's seventieth birthday (really his seventy-first), which would occur the following month. Thirty thousand posters and half a million pamphlets were printed to celebrate the Soviet dictator. Elsewhere in the city, Dean Acheson and his British counterpart Ernest Bevin had come to meet with French Foreign Minister Robert Schuman about Germany.

Less than two months before, the new West German state had held its first set of elections, voting in the Christian Democrats and the state's inaugural chancellor, a former Burgermeister, or "lord mayor," of Cologne, named Konrad Adenauer. The new chancellor had been imprisoned twice by the Nazis and had risen during the occupation as an effective administrator, a thoughtful and skillful man, modest in appearance and dignified in manner. Laconic and sparse in movement and expression, the seventy-three-year-old chancellor earned the nickname "Der Alte," or the old man. He was cerebral and shrewd, and his mission was to restore West Germany to a position of equality and dignity on the world stage.

To that end, Adenauer sought to include his fledgling state in an integrated Western Europe. Weeks before his election, Adenauer outlined his position in an article in *Life* magazine. "We are of the West," he wrote, "even though oppression, war and defeat have left Germany a pawn in the struggle of the western and eastern worlds. In our relationship with America we are at the receiving end. But in years to come an economically and politically healthy Germany, indebted as it will be for aid from the West, may eventually repay these commitments by contributing her share to the benefit of the Atlantic world to which we all belong."

American officials were encouraged by the chancellor's tone. In short order, however, Adenauer launched a sustained campaign against the Allied policy of dismantling German heavy industry. Dismantling had kept German production down and engendered resentment among the German people. Adenauer was not at all timid, and moved to throw off the yoke of what he felt were unjust provisions. The British felt that Adenauer's actions undermined the Allies' authority. For the French, Adenauer's election and his muscular policy on dismantling raised the specter that France feared most: that it would be left alone on the continent to fend with a resurgent, nationalist German state.

At the November 9 meeting, Bevin expressed his displeasure at the very opening of the conference. The foreign minister was ill, and Bevin worked himself into such a lather that Acheson and Schuman feared for his health. They were much relieved when he tired and his diatribe concluded. Bevin, though, had come to appreciate the illogicality of an overly oppressive German dismantling program. Schuman was under much greater strategic and political pressure. To Acheson, though, "one conclusion seemed plain beyond doubt. Western Europe and the United States could not contain the Soviet Union and suppress Germany and Japan at the same time. Our best hope was to make these former enemies willing and strong supporters of a free-world structure. Germany should be welcomed into Western Europe." If that was to be done, then integration was a necessary precondition, or as Acheson put it, " 'Western Europe' must become more than a phrase."

That fall, in the wake of the U.S.-Anglo accommodation during their talks in Washington, American officials increasingly looked to France to assume the mantle of leadership in forging ahead with Western European integration. In early October, George Kennan's seminal Policy Planning document, PPS/55, recommended a new course, summoning the French to engineer a rapprochement with the Germans. The British should encourage and facilitate it but could participate in an arrangement that allowed them to maintain their independence and their Commonwealth responsibilities.

Acheson led the charge, telling Schuman on September 15, "The best chance and hope seems to us to be under French leadership. It doesn't work for us to take the lead. We are too far away." On October 19, after Adenauer's inauguration and the anti-dismantling movement was under way, Acheson sent a cable to Schuman. Germany was "already taking a familiar and dangerous nationalist turn," he wrote. "This trend must be expected to continue unless German resources and energies can be harnessed to the security and welfare of Western Europe as a whole. The danger is that the time to arrest and reverse this trend is already very short. This consideration weighs heavily in our thinking," he added. "The key to progress towards integration is in French hands. In my opinion, France needs, in the interests of her own future, to take the initiative promptly and decisively if the character of West Germany is to be one permitting healthy development in Western Europe." Time was not on the side of this enterprise: "I believe that this may be the last chance for France to take her lead in developing a pattern of organization which is vital to her needs and to the needs of Western Europe." This was what would be needed if "Russian or German, or perhaps Russian-German domination, is to be avoided."

It was another painful turn for the French. The United States seemed to be exempting Great Britain from the pains of integration; it seemed to be four square behind building up Germany; and now the United States seemed to be putting the onus on France. The stakes were high. As French politician Jean Letourneau remarked: "If we refuse, the United States will bestow this leadership role on Germany within six months." France wanted to keep Germany down, but if it could not, the best alternative was to construct a framework in which German resurgence would redound as much to France's benefit as possible. Justice Minister René Mayer remarked, "Germany must not become the little darling [chou-chou] of the Marshall Plan."

At the Paris meeting, Schuman pressed the case that France did not want to go it alone with Germany in Europe. The French press had lambasted

Great Britain for the manner in which it had handled devaluation and its apparent willingness to leave France alone on the continent. Schuman told Bevin of the press attacks. France was willing to pursue reconciliation with Germany, Schuman said, as it had already taken pains to do, but "Europe was inconceivable without Great Britain," and Bevin and his countrymen were expected to play a leading role.

The Paris meetings lasted for three days. Sessions were back-to-back and exhausting. Couches were set up in adjacent rooms for breaks—they were particularly helpful for Bevin. Tables of tea, coffee and sandwiches were set up so the delegations would not have to leave the premises. When the meetings ended at 2 A.M. on November 11, the allies agreed to halt the dismantling of West Germany's nonmilitary industry, in what appeared to France as a foreordained outcome of the Americans' policy of supporting Germany's resurgence.

The following week, the *New York Times* reported that senior military officials of several European countries were considering a plan for raising five German divisions. This raised the alarming notion of German remilitarization. If Germany's economic resurgence were enough to simmer French anxiety, then the specter of German remilitarization would bring it to a boil. Days later, Lucius Clay, by now retired, called for a composite European force, to include German infantry. Then, in early December, Adenauer told the *Cleveland Plain Dealer* that he was still opposed to the reconstitution of a German army, but that he would support a German contingent inside a European army with a European command. The French were apoplectic. Aversion to the notion of any sort of German remilitarization was, wrote William Hitchcock, "perhaps the only topic on which French public opinion was united."

Some U.S. foreign policy officials felt that it was simply asking too much of France to shoulder most of the burden of integration. At a two-day meeting in late October, two senior officials had voiced their concern. Now U.S. Ambassador to France, David Bruce offered his own unvarnished prescription: "It should be clear to everyone," he said, "that the UK's economy is so intertwined with the European economy that no integration of Western Europe is conceivable without the full participation of the UK . . . No Frenchman . . . can conceive of the construction of a viable Western European world from which the UK would be absent." For the French "such disassociation would be fatal to the cause of European integration." Bruce went on: "We have been too tender with the British since the war: she has been the constant stumbling block in the economic organization of Europe." Ambassador to the United Kingdom Lewis Douglas agreed that the French wouldn't take the lead if the United Kingdom didn't participate.

The thinking softened Acheson's line toward the French somewhat, but he felt British reluctance was staunch and not entirely indefensible. He kept pushing in late October and at Paris in early November, but Western European self-help remained the guiding principle. And there was ambivalence among the key decision makers as to who should lead and on how hard to push.

In the aftermath of Hoffman's forceful address to the OEEC on October 31, Harriman cabled Acheson: "From the beginning, Hoffman and I recognized that development of leadership in OEEC was essential to give meaning to any other steps projected." Harriman now wanted Acheson to "face up to the situation. It seems clear to me that we can no longer tolerate this type of maneuver by the British. The OEEC organization is unsatisfactory." The time had come, Acheson suggested, to appoint "an outstanding European public personality on a full-time basis," someone with great international status and prestige, a director general to forge a bolder mission for OEEC.

Great Britain's resistance did not arise out of some sort of inherent contrariness. It sought to buy time until it was further recovered and it could once again speak with a greater voice in international affairs. One senior economic official in Britain quoted a colleague who argued, "we are being asked to join the Germans, who started two world wars, the French, who had in 1940 collapsed in the face of German aggression, the Italians, who changed sides, and the Low Countries, of whom not much was known but who seemed to have put up little resistance to Germany." Perceived as such, it seemed an uninviting proposition.

The more the United States pressed Great Britain to promote its integration agenda—the more Cripps pushed back, denouncing American interference and its "schoolboy lectures." As American fervor for integration increased that autumn, so too did British reluctance, frustrating U.S. designs and leaving Acheson, Hoffman and Harriman "exasperated."

During one of Hoffman and Bissell's visits to Europe, Cripps slipped Hoffman, the more agreeable of ECA's two leaders, a note requesting that they get together privately, skirting Harriman, with whom Cripps had had a series of epic diplomatic battles, to iron out U.S.-Anglo differences. Hoffman promptly passed the note over to Milton Katz, Harriman's loyal senior aide. Katz passed the note to Harriman. That evening, when Hoffman came to meet with Cripps, he brought along Katz, "who Cripps knew was Harriman's eyes, ears and chef troubleshooter," and so foiled Cripps's gambit to divide and conquer.

During Christmas, Hoffman wrote to Harriman with good tidings and a note of encouragement: "You have not only had to face extraordinary difficulties but have had to put up with some unpleasant maneuverings on the part of some of our friends which would have tried the patience of a saint. Despite all these difficulties," Hoffman wrote, "you have succeeded in bringing about accomplishments which I am certain will prove historic." The achievements notwithstanding, the winter of 1949–50 was a desolate one for the prospects of European integration. The picture was no more promising at home, where "subterranean fires," long festering, had finally begun to explode. Increasingly ill, Arthur Vandenberg could do little more than watch as the flames washed over the bipartisan foreign policy that had served as the Marshall Plan's foundation and lifeblood.

EVERY YEAR IN EARLY FEBRUARY, hewing to long-held tradition, Republican members of Congress would fan out across the country and visit with civic groups, offering addresses in commemoration of Abraham Lincoln's birthday. It was in keeping with this tradition that a forty-one-year-old Republican junior senator had arrived in Wheeling, West Virginia, on February 9, 1950. The senator had manufactured a record as a self-made Midwestern Horatio Alger, who had put himself through college and law school while working a variety of odd jobs, won election as a young circuit court judge and emerged from World War II as a wounded and decorated war hero. It was a record—embellished, if not fabricated—on which he had run to win a Senate seat in 1946. After years of failed forays into housing and banking, the ambitious young senator was considered likely to lose a reelection bid in 1952. He had earned a reputation for being unscrupulous. As a senate aide remarked: "Take any good Irishman, remove his conscience, and you've got McCarthy." The year before, a poll of Washington correspondents had voted Joseph McCarthy the worst member of the United States Senate.

McCarthy had come to Wheeling to address the West Virginia Republican Women's Club. But his ambitions extended well beyond the speech that day. Speaking to the crowd in Wheeling, he raised an envelope in his hand, claiming to possess a list of scores of well-known Communists presently working in the State Department. The Associated Press picked up on his remarks, and the story ran in more than thirty papers. The charges, it would become clear as time passed, were baseless, the enterprising senator having been entirely undeterred by a lack of evidence. In other circumstances, his bluff may have been readily called, but McCarthy was shrewd, and his timing was propitious.

On September 3, 1949, an American B-29 on patrol at eighteen thousand feet over the North Pacific had picked up a higher than normal radioactivity count. During the following week, as the high level winds blew over North America, it was confirmed. At 11:02 A.M. on September 23, 1949, Harry S. Truman addressed the American people: "We have evidence that within recent weeks," he said, "an atomic explosion occurred in the USSR." The explosion had indeed taken place, on August 29 in the desert outside of Semipalatinsk in Kazakhstan. The epoch of the U.S. monopoly of the atomic bomb had passed. The Soviet test had happened sooner than U.S. officials had anticipated—perhaps three years earlier, according to *Life* magazine.

American officials and citizens alike fielded the news somberly. Throughout 1949, Stalin had conducted a series of violent purges and attendant show trials in his Eastern European satellites. The atomic shield had provided the U.S. with a sense of security, but now that shield seemed to thin, and the national sense of security seemed to wane with it. In London, the famous insurance house of Lloyd's gave peace a less than even chance. Overnight, the development changed America's perception of the balance of power. Arthur Vandenberg remarked, "This is now a different world."

On October 1, one week after Truman's announcement about Soviet possession of the atomic bomb, Mao Zedong proclaimed the creation of the People's Republic of China. Mao and his Communist brethren now controlled China and its 500 million inhabitants—a fifth of the world's population. China had special value to many Americans, particularly Republicans. The U.S.-China link was forged in two of America's great pastimes: commerce and religion. China had long held allure as a large market and a special trading partner for American industry. For generations, American missionaries had been going to China spreading the Christian gospel.

With his victory, Mao had managed to overthrow China's Nationalist leader, Chiang Kai-shek, a Methodist with a Wellesley-educated wife and strong ties to the Republican lobby in Congress. During the Chinese civil war, Republicans had pressed the administration to support the Nationalists in their battle with Mao. They had pushed the administration to include hundreds of millions in economic and military aid into the omnibus foreign aid bill of April 3, 1948, in which the Marshall Plan was passed. Many key Republican members of Congress had made this aid for China quid pro quo for their support for ERP appropriations. All told, the United States had furnished China with close to $2 billion in military and economic aid since V-J

Day in August 1945. At every stage in the congressional hearings and during each round of appropriations, Republicans in the China lobby had attacked the administration and ECA on the grounds that funding would be better spent supporting the Chinese Nationalists. It was clear that the Truman administration subordinated China's aid needs to Europe's. The administration deemed the European focus a wiser strategic course.

For Republicans, in despair at having lost the election and Congress, desperate to assert their voice and their influence, eager to find an opening for attack on the country's fifth straight Democratic administration, Mao's victory—on top of the Soviets' possession of the bomb—offered a felicitous political opportunity. Republicans lacerated the perfidious Democrats who had let China fall into Communist and, presumptively, Soviet hands. It did not matter that the leading China experts in the U.S. did not think that China was America's to lose. It was a civil war, and Chiang was incompetent. It remains unclear whether the United States could have reversed the course of the war, even if the administration went all-out. Nevertheless, it was a stinging strategic loss for the United States and the Truman administration.

Events that autumn and early winter further fanned the brush fire. In January, Mao's monthlong visit to the Soviet Union ended in a Sino-Soviet alliance, conflating Mao's victory and strategic gain for Stalin. Having tightened its grip on Eastern Europe, the Soviet Union now appeared to direct a Communist monolith in possession of one-third of the world's land. With the Soviet possession of the bomb and the Sino-Soviet alliance, wrote historian John Lewis Gaddis, "it seemed, a fundamental shift in the balance of power had taken place: nearly overnight the communist world appeared almost to have doubled its extent."

The same day that Stalin consented to enter into alliance with the Chinese, January 22, 1950, a former State Department official named Alger Hiss was convicted of perjury. It was found that years earlier Hiss had been part of a Communist network and had passed secret documents to Whittaker Chambers, then an editor at *Life*. Dean Acheson had little sympathy for Communists, or American sympathizers, but he had known and worked with Hiss and his brother. Days after Hiss's trial, Acheson said that he did not intend "to turn my back on Alger Hiss." It was principled and courageous, but it was not prudent. Acheson would be pummeled for it. Republican Representative Richard Nixon—who would come to refer to the State Department as "Acheson's College of Cowardly Communist Containment"—called Acheson's statement "disgusting."

Little more than a week later, Klaus Fuchs, the British physicist who had worked on the Manhattan Project, was convicted in England for passing along secret technical information about the bomb to Soviet agents. Fuchs was German-born and had joined the Communist Party in the early 1930s as a reaction to the Nazis, who had imprisoned his father and other relatives, which, in turn, led to his mother's suicide. During the war, Fuchs felt that the Western allies were deliberately allowing the Soviets to bear the burden of the war effort and the devastation on the Eastern Front without doing as much as they could to come to the Soviets' aid. He began feeding his sister secret information on the bomb from Los Alamos, New Mexico. By the time he was found guilty, the Soviets had the bomb. Fuchs later conceded that his spying probably saved the Soviets years—"one year at least"—in developing the bomb.

By the time that McCarthy burst on the scene brandishing alleged lists of Communist traitors inside the government, there was a deep well of national anxiety about a Communist "fifth column" burrowed in America and its corridors of power, working to turn the strategic advantage to Stalin's favor. Against such a backdrop, Robert Taft and other Republican leaders encouraged McCarthy and the stream of accusations that would follow in the next several years.

In fact, during the 1930s, after the United States recognized the Soviet Union, and later, during the war effort, which brought many Soviet officials to America, the Soviets had successfully recruited spies in key places in the U.S. government. However, by the time of McCarthy's accusations, the House Un-American Activities Committee and Truman administration anti-Communist legislation had effectively destroyed the American Communist Party and its influence in American life. Communists had been all but weeded out of government, and former Communists, having watched Stalin's conduct during the early Cold War years, had changed their minds. Flailing about with unsubstantiated lists of alleged Communists, McCarthy was "whipping a dead horse." The American public did not know that, though, and McCarthy's attacks fueled the political flames in Washington and gave rise to a toxic, hysterical and, at times, dysfunctional political climate.

ON FEBRUARY 21, 1950, Paul Hoffman walked right into the fire, appearing before a joint session of the Senate Foreign Relations Committee and the House Foreign Affairs Committee to recount ECA's progress to date and to request funding for the third year of ERP's operations. Early that February, 31 percent of Americans familiar with the Marshall Plan supported the $3.1

billion appropriation Hoffman was requesting from Congress for 1950–51, while 26 percent did not. It was not necessarily support for the Plan that was waning, but willingness to continue to fund it with such large sums of taxpayer dollars.

As Hoffman spoke before the joint session, a familiar face was missing. Back in late September, Arthur Vandenberg wrote to his wife in Michigan: "How I wish I could resign this devastating job right now! The whole country is in a state of nerves . . . Nothing is right. The whole tenor of Senatorial correspondence has changed. Everybody is mad about something." As the nation's political discourse degenerated from there, so too did Vandenberg's health. That autumn Vandenberg tendered his last full-dress speech in the Senate. That winter Vandenberg left Washington, consigned to bed rest at home in Michigan.

Columnist Doris Fleeson wrote on March 22 that Vandenberg's absence was "remarked on fearfully by supporters of the present foreign policy, especially ECA." Vandenberg said he was "scrupulously careful not to 'lecture' my colleagues from behind the 'iron curtain' of my stubborn convalescence." With partisan tempers high, though, Van did write to Hoffman late that March, on the eve of the ERP's second anniversary. "The least I can do is to take advantage of this occasion to say that, in my humble opinion, you and your ECA associates, at home and abroad, have rendered [an] incalculably vital service to our country and its indispensable leadership for liberty . . . ECA was launched as an unpartisan enterprise—established by a Republican Congress in full and free cooperation with a Democratic Executive. This working unity typified our finest traditions and our greatest safety in the presence of external hazards to all Americans, regardless of Party . . . In all candor," Van went on, "can it be successfully denied that ECA has been substantially responsible for reversing the corroding gloom which threatened Western Civilization two years ago, and which might have brought the 'iron curtain' to the very rims of the Atlantic but for this brave adventure?"

Vandenberg suggested that the time was ripe to convene another bipartisan committee—as Van had originally recommended to Truman after Marshall's speech—to offer recommendations and to forge a bipartisan path forward. The historical record does not contain any evidence that Hoffman or Truman seriously explored Vandenberg's idea. Hoffman had his hands full testifying before an increasingly rabid Congress. As the testimony wore on, Truman wrote to Van, addressing his note "Dear Arthur": "I have been very disturbed about the situation as it has been developing in Congress with regard to the whole bipartisan foreign policy." Days later, Truman wrote again: "You just don't realize what a vacuum there has been in the Senate and in the operation of our foreign policy since you left."

Hoffman highlighted ECA's accomplishments but stated that "it is not good enough." It is not the score at half-time that counts, Hoffman said in speeches around this time. It "would be a cruel waste for America not to finish the task it has accepted in helping our partners in Western Europe to achieve a stable and secure recovery," he testified. There are "few headlines and little drama in the Battle of Recovery," but make no mistake, he said, it was the defining battle of the Cold War, the difference between peace and war. Hoffman said, "I wish to repeat the statement when I testified last February—that the Marshall Plan will turn out to be the greatest bargain the American people ever had."

The Plan's opponents echoed familiar lines about the Plan subsidizing socialist regimes, about fiscal profligacy and, more and more, about the need to redirect resources to Asia or to military, rather than economic, aid, but the tone was now more rancorous. As the hearings dragged on into May, it became clear that the Senate would demand a $250 million cut. Then on May 8, John Taber, chairman of the House Appropriations Committee, "delivered a speech so strongly isolationist that it would have had the full approval of the Daily Worker," Hoffman told Harriman in Paris. Taber then proceeded to suggest an additional cut of $250 million. The new proposal was voted down. By early June, after six months of tumultuous hearings, resembling, as Michael Hogan put it, "nothing so much as a spectacular electric storm—a brilliant display that lights up the sky but leaves the ground undisturbed," Hoffman pulled off his finest victory with Congress, securing $2.7 billion for ERP's third year of operations.

As Congress deliberated upon appropriations for the Marshall Plan, foreign policy officials were processing the seismic international developments of the past several months and reassessing the nation's foreign policy. On April 25, 1950, a document entitled NSC-68 was presented to President Truman at a National Security Council meeting. Written primarily by Paul Nitze at the State Department, the paper concluded that Stalin's aims were nothing short of global domination. A gain for Communism anywhere was a gain for the Soviet Union and a concomitant strategic loss for the United States. In this zero-sum global contest, however, the Soviet Union was far outspending the United States militarily: the nations' military budgets as a share of their total gross national product was around 14 percent for the Soviet Union compared to 6 or 7 percent for the United States. Such an imbalance might have been tenable as long as the U.S. possessed a monopoly on the atomic bomb. Given recent developments, NSC-68 argued, the

United States would have to recalibrate its defense expenditures by as much as three or four times to meet this all-encompassing existential challenge.

Such a severe recalibration would take some convincing. NSC-68 was deliberately prepared, as Acheson recalled, "to bludgeon the mass mind of 'top government' that" such a "decision had to be carried out." So, when Charles Murphy, Truman's counsel, took the document home with him to read the day he received it, he recalled, "What I read scared me so much that the next day I didn't go to the office at all. I sat at home and read this memorandum over and over, wondering what in the world to do about it. The gist of it," he said, "was that we were in pretty bad shape and we damn well better do something about it . . . It seemed to me to establish an altogether convincing case that we had to spend more on defense." Murphy was not alone. That spring a consensus was being forged among the highest-level administration officials that the time had come for the United States to embark on an unprecedented peacetime military buildup.

Paul Hoffman believed there need not be a tradeoff between a massive defense buildup and military aid to U.S. allies on the one hand and the ERP and economic aid on the other. And for a brief window of time, in the spring of 1950, it appeared as if there would not have to be.

ON DECEMBER 9, 1949, ECA submitted a paper to the OEEC in Paris titled, "Draft Working Paper on Intra European-Currency Transferability and Liberalization of Trade." The eye-glazing title was dense, but Richard Bissell was convinced that the paper contained insights and recommendations that could very well unlock the door to Western European economic integration.

As Hoffman stood before the Council of Ministers of the OEEC on October 31, Bissell and his colleagues in Washington agreed that Europe needed a large market to spur specialization, competition, innovation—all the necessary ingredients for advances in productivity and economic growth. The growth would enable Western Europe to lessen its need on American imports and export more—sealing Western Europe's Dollar Gap and paving the way to European economic self-sustainability and prosperity. In order for Europe to form the envisioned large, integrated market, its nation-states had to open their borders to the movement of goods and services. That meant getting rid of protectionist measures such as import quotas and tariffs and dual pricing.

In the summer of 1949, the intra-European payments system was failing the continent—and the Marshall Plan. With most European countries running up postwar balance-of-payments deficits, pressure on their reserves was a critical problem. In order to stem the drain, countries naturally erected a series of protectionist policies and negotiated various bilateral trading arrangements. If France, for example, was running a balance-of-payments deficit with Belgium, it would erect tariffs or quotas to make sure that trade with the Belgians did not drain the French reserves. If the deficit reached certain levels, the French might cease trading altogether. However, even as France might have had a trade-stifling deficit with the Belgians, she may have had a surplus with other countries. Yet, because of the systemic patchwork, France could not transfer her credits from trade surpluses with another country to relieve the deficit with Belgium.

In 1948, to address this problem, ECA initiated an Intra-European Payments Plan. Essentially, Marshall aid was used to finance Marshall countries' anticipated trade deficits, thus plugging the drain on reserves and facilitating trade. It had worked reasonably well, but it was a short-term fix. The overlapping and stifling bilateral arrangements were the real problem. To Bissell, the real solution was "a mechanism . . . that would 'recirculate' back to the deficit nations the currencies accumulated by the surplus nations." As Dutch Foreign Minister Dirk Stikker put it, "if you have no payments system, you cannot do anything on the liberalization of trade." Robert Marjolin, OEEC secretary general, said, "What really mattered was that there should be free movement of goods and services. A payments system had to be created which would make it possible for Europe to reach that objective."

The first step was in working out the technical details of the mechanism. Bissell's team of economists labored effectively to that end. They were not alone. Many of the Marshall Plan countries' best economic minds spent that autumn working on a new payments agreement, and by the end of 1949 at least six different plans had been submitted to OEEC for consideration.

The ECA paper was submitted to OEEC in early December. In January, ECA embarked on the daunting enterprise of convincing the Marshall Plan countries to agree to subject their reserves and economies to currency convertibility, with all the vulnerability the step entailed. At the OEEC in Paris, a group of financial experts labored, in consultation with a group of economists from ECA. As the new year dawned, the outlook for a payments union appeared promising. Harriman anticipated agreement "at a very early date." Then at the end of January, the British chancellor of the Exchequer, Sir Stafford Cripps, filed a dissenting memorandum. At issue once again was Britain's relationship with the Commonwealth and the sterling area and its reluctance to pin its economic policy to continental affairs.

In addition, memories about the convertibility clause in the 1946 U.S. loan and the concurrent run on British reserves "still haunted" Cripps and his colleagues, and they were anxious about rendering sterling convertible without special protective provisions. Finally, there was an election in February 1950. The Labour Party had governed Britain during five of the most tumultuous and exhausting years in the history of the Empire. Bevin and Cripps, its two strongest leaders, were seriously ill and exhausted. Entrance into a European payments union would constitute a bold adventure, one that in the winter of 1950 Britain had neither the inclination nor the political will to embark upon.

At this time, Hoffman was appearing before Congress, which was ratcheting up the pressure over Europe's progress. It was clear that, as Milton Katz recalled, "the attitude in Europe was, 'Until [a payments union] gets straightened out, we can make no further progress' " on integration. Averell Harriman was incensed. At one point he contended that the United States "should no longer tolerate interference and sabotage of Western European integration by [the] UK and should face Cripps with [a] clear statement of [the] U.S. view that the Marshall Plan is breaking down because of British opposition."

A "desperate battle" ensued between Harriman and Cripps. Hoffman raised the stakes, announcing that 25 percent of the next year's ERP aid would be allocated to the Marshall Plan countries that were most constructive in integration; it was one of ECA's most aggressive expressions of "friendly aid." Michael Hogan wrote that Hoffman's "warning hung the sword of Damocles over the heads of the negotiators in Paris." Cripps assailed the American "dollar dictatorship" and the "crass interference" in British internal affairs. Hoffman was serving up "a gift to Communist propaganda," he charged.

In late March 1949, Cripps offered a British proposal for a payments union. In the scheme, the British would be willing, on a limited basis, to pay off bilateral debts through the payments union. However, Great Britain would stand apart, maintaining its existing bilateral trade and payments arrangements. The EPU and the sterling area would coexist side by side—effectively Britain was opting out.

The United States responded immediately that Cripps's proposal was unacceptable. It was not just a matter of technical issues, which were soluble, ECA wrote, but "a basic difference of choice as between economic nationalism and economic internationalism." At the same time, as Britain held firm against transferability within an intra-European scheme, it was willing and in fact eagerly pursuing liberalization within the sterling area. Harriman believed the truth was that "Britain really wanted to get Europe to join the sterling area."

From there, the tone of the debate grew increasingly "bitter." Hoffman wrote Cripps that month that the Anglo-American relationship was in jeopardy, forcefully dispelling "the heady atmosphere" that had prevailed at the trilateral talks in Washington only six months earlier. Cripps and his colleagues were not willing to cede Britain's role in the Commonwealth and sterling area, nor its political autonomy. However, they were also unprepared to rupture the Anglo-American special relationship that had begun to take form the previous September.

As spring arrived, with the election past, the talks over the payments union started up once again, this time with a more constructive tone. Britain's budget cuts and devaluation had improved its trade balance and restocked its monetary reserves, providing it the position of strength from which it preferred to engage in negotiations.

The United States and Great Britain achieved a further accommodation on the structure of the OEEC. The British would not assent to appoint a director general. But Britain did agree to appoint Dirk Stikker, former Dutch foreign minister, a man of international stature and a well-regarded champion of European integration, to the position of Political Conciliator. Stikker was not endowed with all the political authority that Harriman might have hoped for. Still, it was, in his view, a "constructive" step in "strengthening OEEC at the political level." At a difficult time, Hoffman lauded it, the "single most hopeful move since the inception of OEEC." For the British, it preserved their standing with the Americans and advanced their negotiating position on EPU.

At 8 P.M. on May 14, Averell Harriman, after having slugged it out with Cripps and his colleagues for months, cabled Washington from London: Britain would accept the terms of the latest proposal for a European Payments Union and enter as a full member. The United States had to offer Britain concessions. Most importantly, it had to agree to ensure the maintenance of sterling as an international currency. It would consent to limit the use of accumulated sterling to members with a net deficit in trade and allow members with a net surplus to accept payment in sterling—thereby adding to sterling reserves. In the case of an unusual drain in Britain's reserves, ECA would provide special aid. In such a case, Britain also reserved the right to impose certain protective measures. These were meaningful concessions, but in return the British agreed to bring the sterling area into the payments union and its automatic and multilateral payments settlement.

The Council of Ministers of the OEEC adopted the treaty establishing EPU on August 18, and it was formally signed on September 19, then made retroactive the beginning of that July. EPU revolutionized European trade. The union provided a clearing mechanism in which trade between members could be made in any European currency. Each member country was assigned a quota equal to 15 percent of intra-European exports, imports and invisible transactions in 1949. The quotas were defined in a sum of units. Expressed in units rather than individual currency, members could now use these units to offset deficits and surpluses, which EPU would finance. This effectively meant that deficits and surpluses between any two members no longer mattered. What mattered was a member country's trading position with respect to Europe. To help countries buffet the shocks and underwrite the venture, ECA provided $350 million of working capital.

In foreign affairs, George Kennan wrote, the proof is in the eating. "The most astonishing thing about the EPU," wrote Dirk Stikker in his memoirs, "was that once it was agreed upon it really worked." Upon the creation of the EPU, intra-European trade ballooned. Whereas the index of intra-European trade for 1949 stood at 90, after only six months of operation of EPU, at the end of 1950, the index had increased to 140. As intended, the increased trade promoted specialization, investment, competition and innovation and helped, among other factors, to lead to "a period of economic growth which compared favorably with, and may well have exceeded, the rate achieved in any earlier period in European history."

In Richard Bissell's view, "the EPU was the greatest achievement of the Marshall Plan since once and for all intra-European trade and payments were freed up from quantitative controls." To Averell Harriman, "the European Payments Union, I'm satisfied, was a thing which made the Marshall Plan a success and made it possible for Europe to move rapidly after the Marshall Plan was finished." Paul Hoffman believed that "of all the moves that were made, the most important was the organization of the European Payments Union . . . Once the Payments Union became available, the upturn in trade was spectacular. It was a major factor in the success of the Marshall Plan." As Hoffman said, Western Europe had done in twenty-five months what might very well have taken twenty-five years.

WITH THEIR PROGRAM of liberalization of trade and the EPU, the Marshall Plan countries had delivered a revolutionary program to advance European integration. That spring of 1950, though, Dean Acheson and his senior colleagues at State and ECA agreed that it was not enough. In early March,

Acheson had shared his vision of the world situation with his senior colleagues. The achievements of the past two years were extraordinary. However, with the events of the past autumn and winter, the West now seemed to "have lost [its] momentum and we seem to have slowed down to a point where we are on the defensive while the Soviets are apparently showing more self-confidence." Acheson was not content to remain on the defensive, for "we would slip backward." As important as it was, "The successful working out of a payments union would have no popular appeal . . . there would be no holidays or torch-light parades in celebration of a payments union." Something more was needed, a grand, perhaps even transformative step to advance European integration, to advance Western unity and the West's strategic position.

The secretary and his colleagues began to brainstorm. Acheson wondered if he should meet with UK Ambassador Sir Oliver Franks simply to ask "what he thought we could do to get started." John J. McCloy, U.S. High Commissioner to Germany, said it was essential to make progress in the political field. He recommended venturing a "drastic step towards political unity such as the establishing of articles of confederation for Europe." The conversation meandered for some time. In the course of the conversation, Acheson had posed a question to his colleagues: "Were there any views on the strength and vitality of the French? Were they merely existing under the protective tent which ERP had erected over them?" That tent had provided the French much-needed succor. No one on the other side of the Atlantic yet knew that underneath its protective canopy, Jean Monnet was stirring with a bold new idea.

Chapter Thirteen

EUROPE REFASHIONED

O N SUNDAY MORNING, MAY 7, 1950, a limousine cruised through the streets of Paris on the way to the American Embassy, just off the Place de la Concorde. Secretary of State Dean Acheson had arrived the night before from Washington. Harry Truman had insisted that he take the presidential airplane, *Independence*, named after Truman's hometown in Missouri. Acheson had come to Paris to confer with French Foreign Minister Robert Schuman and U.S. Ambassador David Bruce, en route to a ministerial meeting of the North Atlantic Treaty Council in London the next week. Bruce told Acheson upon his arrival that Schuman had requested the meeting. So, as Acheson and Bruce rode in the back of the limousine, they wondered what Schuman intended to discuss.

Later that morning, in an ornate reception room at the embassy, the French foreign minister shared an idea with Acheson and Bruce. At the time of the meeting, perhaps only ten people, all French, had been apprised. Schuman could understand English but preferred to speak through an interpreter in formal meetings. So, through his interpreter, Schuman spoke of "so breathtaking a step . . . that at first" Acheson did not grasp it. The idea would soon become a plan, and the plan would come to assume the name of the foreign minister who would champion it. It was one of the boldest and most imaginative political ideas in modern history.

JEAN MONNET DID his best thinking on his morning walks. Each morning since Monnet left Cognac, where he had run his family business as a young man, he would wake up and walk for miles. At the beginning of the walk, his head was filled with the previous day's matters or worries. After half an hour, maybe an hour, those cares would evaporate, and he would begin to notice the natural world around him. It was at that point that he would let his "thoughts find their own level." For Monnet, walking was a form of intellectual as well as physical exercise. "It's simple," said André Horre, the caretaker of Monnet's house. "Monsieur puts his idea in front of him, talks to it, and then decides."

In the early spring of 1950, the Monnet Plan was propelling the French economy toward economic growth, stability and modernization. Monnet took some measure of satisfaction in that achievement. However, that spring was a time of profound anxiety for him and his countrymen. Soviet possession of the bomb and the Sino-Soviet treaty stoked anxiety about Soviet designs for Western Europe and French vulnerability. The U.S. emphasis on a large-scale defense buildup and the strident anti-Communism of McCarthy and his cohort all raised the prospect of war. Meanwhile, West Germany was flexing its nationalist muscles. The United States seemed bent on continuing West Germany's economic resurgence and, now, even its military buildup. To Monnet, European integration had long been viewed as the key vehicle to prevent a return to European rivalry and war. But Great Britain would not lend its weight to that endeavor. That spring, Monnet wrote in his diary: "Whichever way we turn, in the present world situation we see nothing but deadlock."

In the past, Monnet had always found inspiration in his long walks through the lush woods of Montfort-l'Amaury, near his home. But that spring, those woods that he knew so well seemed "stifling." In mid-March, Monnet left for the Swiss Alps. He spent a fortnight traversing the crests and slopes of the Huez range around Roseland, going from one overnight lodge to another, walking—and thinking. Monnet thought about the Berlin blockade that had ended less than a year before. He thought about the sharp escalation in U.S.-Soviet tensions. Germany would not be the instigator of another war so soon after the last, but this time, it seemed to Monnet, it could be the prize. If France did nothing, he feared, war would come. During his time in the Alps, Monnet asked himself: what could be done?

Back in Paris in early April, it had become clear to Monnet in what direction France would have to move. It was also clear that he would have to proceed with celerity. Monnet knew of the ministerial meetings beginning in London on May 11. Acheson had been pressing Schuman on Germany ever since the talks back in Washington in September 1949. The cables, the letters, the exhortations to act followed month after month. Hardly a week passed, Monnet remembered, without Schuman pressing him with the question: "What about Germany? What do I have to do to meet the responsibility upon me?" Monnet recalled: "It became an obsession with him."

Monnet's anxious diary entries during that April trace the evolution of his thinking. "The German situation is rapidly turning into a cancer that will be dangerous to peace in the near future, and immediately to France, unless," he wrote, "its development is directed towards hope for the Germans and collaboration with free peoples." A lifetime of international business, finance and diplomatic dealings at the highest level had taught Monnet that sometimes a frontal attack on a problem was not viable. Modifying the angle of attack could change the dynamics of the problem altogether. Around this time, Monnet was beginning to realize "the full possibilities of an approach that had long been familiar" to him. He would focus on changing the "element" that was "causing the block." The element in question was, in fact, two resources: coal and steel.

For the past century, the centripetal cause of French-German tension was the abundant coal and iron ore in the Ruhr/Rhine region, straddling the French-German border. Coal and steel were, Monnet wrote, "at once the key to economic power and the raw materials for forging weapons of war. This double role gave them immense symbolic significance." Neither country felt secure unless it commanded those resources. Each erected barriers to protect the resources within their boundaries. The barriers and dueling had fueled animosity, distrust and, in France, profound anxiety about West Germany's current aspirations to raise its steel output and about the specter of German industrial domination. In contrast, "a solution which would put French industry on the same footing as German industry," Monnet felt, "would restore the economic and political preconditions for the mutual understanding so vital to Europe as a whole. It could, in fact, become the germ of European unity."

Because of the Marshall Plan and U.S. policy vis-à-vis Germany, Monnet realized, "All successive attempts to keep Germany in check, mainly at French instigation, had come to nothing." Now Germany was seeking to increase national steel production from eleven to fourteen million metric tons. Monnet played out the scenario: "We shall refuse, but the Americans will insist. Finally, we shall state our reservations, but we shall give in. At the same time, French production is leveling off." If France failed to act, Monnet believed, Germany would develop rapidly "and we shall not be able to prevent her [from] being armed. France will be trapped once more in her old Malthusianism, and this will inevitably lead to her eclipse."

There was another way. Instead of jostling over coal and steel, France and Germany could pool the resources, the very source of their past wars and current insecurity. The model of state sovereignty had led France and Germany down a path of a century of interstate rivalry. However, if each relinquished some sovereignty, "to exercise joint sovereignty over part of their joint resources—then, a solid link would be forged between them," and "the way would be wide open for further collective action, and a great example would be given to the other nations of Europe." In one stroke, Monnet proposed to pool the countries' two key industrial resources, exorcising a history of conflict and insecurity, and in its stead constructing a new economic and political union welded in coal and steel.

Inside his thatched-roof cottage in Houjarray, Monnet, along with three trusted technical experts, drafted the first version of the French declaration on Sunday, April 16. The draft called for member countries to pool their coal and steel, to ensure that both were sold on identical terms, to equalize competitive conditions and to design a supranational institutional framework to govern the enterprise. These were the building blocks. However, the draft concluded: "The proposal has an essential political objective: to make a breach in the ramparts of national sovereignty which will be narrow enough to secure consent, but deep enough to open the way towards unity that is essential to peace." Monnet and his colleagues would draft nine different versions in the next three weeks, but most of the key elements were there in that first draft.

As April gave way to May, Monnet's idea was beginning to take form. Now he needed a champion to advance the idea in the political realm. "Robert Schuman seemed to me the ideal man to do so," he wrote later. Schuman had spent his life straddling France and Germany. When Schuman was born in Lorraine, on the border of France and Germany, his birthplace was still in German territory. His first language was German, he studied in German universities, and he wore a German uniform in World War I. The Treaty of Versailles delivered Lorraine to France. In the interwar years, he represented Lorraine in the French National Assembly. He worked for the Vichy regime for some time but was removed and jailed twice during the occupation. Tall and slender, Schuman was a devout Catholic, a cerebral, honest man, also strikingly reticent for a politician. France and Germany had been at war three times in the past three generations. It had been only five years since the Nazi occupation of France had ended. The experience had been searing and humiliating for France. Now Monnet was proposing that France bind its resources, its economy and ultimately its political destiny to her former occupier and perennial enemy. If any one man personified the possibility of French-German reconciliation at that moment, it was Robert Schuman.

In late April, Monnet approached Bernard Clappier, Schuman's trusted *directeur de cabinet* at the Foreign Ministry. "M. Schuman," said Clappier, "is looking for an initiative that he can propose in London on May 10. I have the feeling that this has been his one great preoccupation since the Big Three met in New York last September." "Well," said Monnet, "I have some ideas." After a brief delay, on Friday afternoon, April 28, Clappier circled back with Monnet, who gave him a proposal for Schuman. Clappier made his way immediately to the Gare de l'Est to deliver the proposal to Schuman before the foreign minister boarded his train to his country home for a weekend of solitude. "Could you read this paper of Monnet's?" Clappier asked. "It's important." Clappier was at the Gare de l'Est on Monday morning to meet Schuman. "I've read the proposal," Schuman said. "I'll use it."

Schuman and Clappier had "joined the conspiracy," Monnet wrote later. Though the moment marks the start of Schuman's advocacy of Monnet's idea, Schuman had maneuvered painstakingly during much of the preceding year to line the Cabinet up behind the idea of French-German rapprochement. It was not the sort of step that could be taken overnight. Much groundwork had to be laid, and Schuman had done the spadework.

Schuman and Monnet were antipodal personalities: the former was cerebral and reticent and the latter a gregarious deal maker. But they shared a friendship and a collaborative partnership forged of trust, mutual respect and a common vision: French-German rapprochement as the bedrock of a united Europe. The small circle of French officials worked feverishly to finalize the proposal in time for the London Conference. First, they would need the approval of the French Cabinet, which generally met on Wednesday. But with the London Conference scheduled to begin that Wednesday, they determined that they could not wait that long, and so two of Schuman's allies in the Cabinet moved the session to Tuesday morning. Until then, Schuman and Monnet cautioned their colleagues in the know, there must be total secrecy. And "there was," Monnet recalled—"but with one exception."

It was "a curious coincidence," Monnet wrote, that that weekend Dean Acheson would be in Paris to confer with Schuman in advance of the London meetings. At the U.S. Embassy, Acheson and Bruce listened intently to Schuman describe the plan that was about to be sprung on the world. Acheson was not quick to grasp the full dimensions of the proposal. He expressed concern that such an enterprise could become a powerful cartel, and stymie free enterprise and international trade. Schuman assured him that provisions could be added to ensure that the entity would not become a cartel, treating the fear "almost as an irrelevance." Acheson was missing the big picture.

There was a much larger design for the emergent enterprise. At issue, Schuman explained, was European unity, a large and "vastly productive" integrated European market and the end of national rivalries. Henceforward, France and Germany would be locked "in an embrace so close that neither could draw back far enough to hit the other."

Acheson and Bruce began to realize that the Plan was aiming at nothing short of the "rebirth of Europe." It was what Acheson and Paul Hoffman had been driving the French toward since that previous autumn. As the meeting adjourned, Schuman and Monnet felt that they had won in Acheson and Bruce "two chance accomplices who were also very powerful allies."

There were two formidable hurdles to clear before the plan could be announced—and both would have to take place within the span of a few hours. Before presenting the plan to the French Cabinet, Schuman needed assurance that he had a partner in Konrad Adenauer and West Germany. On the evening of May 8, the night before the French Cabinet meeting, or as Monnet put it, "the eve of battle," a colleague and friend of Schuman's from Lorraine left for Bonn to deliver two letters to Adenauer. He was to inform the chancellor's aide that the letters demanded urgent attention. One outlined some of the details of the proposal, and the other was a handwritten note from Schuman.

Adenauer's election the previous autumn, which had helped jolt the French into action, was a milestone in West Germany's road toward political autonomy. But in the spring of 1950, the Allies continued to preside over much of West Germany's economic and political policy: from the permissible level of steel production to the traffic regulations on German highways to the sort of textbooks German students were allowed to read. Germans yearned for equality, autonomy and peace. Tired and demoralized—and, for many, deeply ashamed of the Nazi experience—most West Germans were willing to go to great lengths to ensure that the generations to follow would not have to endure a similar fate. These impulses led Adenauer in the direction of integration. In fact, in a newspaper interview in March, Adenauer had proposed a full French-German economic union. The French were not prepared for so audacious a step at that moment, and if they were to move along such a path they wanted it to come through their own initiative. To Monnet, however, it was an encouraging sign.

As Adenauer read Schuman's personal letter in Bonn, the French Cabinet was in session in the Elysée palace. In the letter, Schuman wrote that the aim of the proposal was not economic but highly political. There was still a fear in France, he wrote, that when Germany had recovered, it might attack again. Schuman imagined that Germany also had its own security fears.

Rearmament would begin by increasing coal, iron and steel production. If an organization were set up, though, under joint and independent authority to control production of those resources, it would provide much security—and peace—for both countries. Adenauer turned to his aide and instructed him to inform Schuman that the chancellor "agreed to his proposal with all my heart."

Meanwhile, Monnet and his colleagues huddled at their office at No. 18 rue de Martignac, waiting for word via Clappier, stationed in an office near the Cabinet meeting, then in session. "The long silence," Monnet recalled, "was agony to us: was everything going to hinge on a matter of minutes?" As the Cabinet meeting neared its end, there was still no word from Adenauer. Then Adenauer's message came. Schuman reached for his briefcase. Pulling out the proposal, he turned to his colleagues and said with a smile, "I have something here." When the Cabinet meeting adjourned, Clappier telephoned Monnet: "That's it," he said, "we can go ahead."

That evening at 6, Robert Schuman strode into the gilt and cream-colored Salon de l'Horloge at the Quai d'Orsay to address two hundred journalists. With Monnet, his wife and a few of his aides in the background, Schuman began to unveil the plan: "It is no longer a time for vain words, but for a bold, constructive act," Schuman said. "France has acted, and the consequences of her action may be immense. We hope they will. She has acted essentially in the cause of peace." Coal, steel, a new supranational organization—it all sounded somewhat technical. Monnet did not want the details to obfuscate the political meaning of the plan. Maneuvering among the journalists, he steered them toward the grander design. Schuman did the same. Still, it was difficult to grasp all of the Plan's ramifications—how it would play out, what it would mean for European life. As Schuman departed for London that evening, one of the journalists exclaimed: "In other words, it's a leap in the dark?" "That's right," Schuman responded, boarding his train to London: "a leap in the dark."

REACTION FROM THE OTHER SIDE of the Atlantic poured forth immediately. John Foster Dulles, who had pressed for European integration since the Moscow Conference of April 1947, called it "brilliantly creative." Truman called it "an act of constructive statesmanship." Upon Acheson's prompting, Truman put U.S. support squarely behind the enterprise. Acheson deemed it a "major contribution toward the resolution of the pressing political and economic problems of Europe." In time, he would come to see even more clearly that the "genius of the Schuman-Monnet plan lay in its practical, common-sense approach." It steered clear of grand reformulations of intractable political issues. "What could be more earthy than coal and steel, or more desirable than a pooling and common direction of France and Germany's coal and steel industries? This would end age-old conflicts," he wrote. ECA's senior economist in Paris, Tommy Tomlinson, having labored side by side with Bruce and Monnet for two tumultuous years, met with a French counterpart, with tears in his eyes. He was overcome, he said, because at last France had made a major decision without turning to the Americans first. Remembering the desperation of 1947 and 1948, it seemed to Tomlinson that perhaps France was now standing on its own two feet.

In London, the reaction was highly charged as well. The morning after Schuman's announcement, Acheson met with Bevin. The British foreign secretary's health was deteriorating rapidly. He was taking large doses of sedative drugs and—to Acheson's great concern—would doze off intermittently in meetings. Bevin was wide awake, however, when he met with Acheson that morning. Meeting in the Foreign Office, Bevin tore into Acheson, accusing him of cooking up the scheme with Schuman behind his back. He railed against Schuman, the Schuman Plan and the apparent cabal. "Clearly, we had managed things badly," Acheson said later, "damage had been done."

Later that day, Acheson met with Bevin again, this time at the American Embassy at Lancaster House, in a "pleasant room" looking out on a handsomely tended English garden with golden-chain trees and flowers in bloom and with Schuman in attendance as well. Bevin wasted no time in launching a full-scale attack on his two counterparts. Bevin spoke with great force, outraged that the Americans, French and Germans had failed to inform or consider the British in the wake of such a seismic development.

Acheson turned to Bevin and explained that sometimes sensitive domestic political matters require that such decisions be reached in secrecy. The British had not consulted the French, Acheson pointed out, before devaluing the pound in September. Bevin could do little more than grumble at Acheson's counterthrust. As the ministers left the room, Schuman reached for Acheson's arm, pulled him back and whispered, "You have a large deposit in my bank."

Monnet wanted very much for the British to join the venture. British leadership, resources and authority would fortify the emergent union. Clement Attlee and Sir Stafford Cripps, who were both away on holiday when they learned of Schuman's announcement, returned to London. Prime Minister Attlee announced that Britain would need further time to consider the matter before reaching a decision. Tying its coal and steel resources into an economic union would cede the Labour Party's ability to manage its socialist welfare state. And once again, Britain expressed reluctance about what the Plan would mean for its special obligations to the Commonwealth. Monnet suspected an even greater impediment. Members of the Labour Party were "opposed to the Schuman Plan because they are defeatist about continental Europe," he wrote, "which they have deliberately written off in case of war—something they regard as inevitable and very near at hand."

Opting out of the enterprise, however, would clearly limit Britain's interest in, and influence on, the continent. Monnet had been in London building support for the Schuman Plan with high-level officials. Cripps asked Monnet to meet with him in his office before he departed for France. Most continental leaders—including Monnet himself for some time—felt that British leadership would be the sine qua non of European unification. "Would you go ahead with Germany and without us?" Cripps wanted to know. "My dear friend," Monnet replied, "you know how I have felt about Britain for more than thirty years: there is no question about that. I hope with all my heart that you will join in this from the start. But if you don't, we shall go ahead without you." Bevin told the French ambassador to the United Kingdom around this time: "I think something has changed between our countries." He was right.

In late May, Monnet persuaded the French government to draft a communiqué inviting seven governments to convene to move forward with the Plan. Cripps pointed out that Great Britain produced half of the coal and a third of the steel of the interested parties. Ceding Britain's sovereign control of these resources was a step he was not willing to take. The Labour Party was not willing to give up the government's autonomy nor its ability to protect its workers. Acting Prime Minister Herbert Morrison famously announced: "It's no good . . . we cannot do it, and the Durham miners won't wear it." Monnet had tried. Wrote British historian Alan Bullock: "It took, in all, ten days, eleven notes and 4,000 words before each side accepted that the other would not give way."

When the conference to forge a common market in coal and steel opened in late June 1950 at the Quai d'Orsay in Paris, six countries were present. Britain was not one of them. Britain had declined the French communiqué of late May. In doing so, the British had declined an invitation for continental leadership. They would not frame the terms of European unification, and they would forgo the tremendous economic—and the subsequent political and geopolitical—benefits. The United States and the French were disappointed. Dean Acheson believed it was Britain's greatest mistake of the postwar period. But to Monnet, "The essential prize had been won, irrevocably. Europe was on the move."

IN LATE JUNE 1950, Dean Acheson arrived in Cambridge, Massachusetts, to receive an honorary degree at Harvard University. It had been three years since George Marshall's address had launched the Plan that bore his name. Acheson recalled that it was an intimidating experience to follow in the footsteps of his predecessor. But it was a fitting occasion for the U.S. secretary to reflect on the progress that had been made.

Even as Acheson sat that day on the steps of the Memorial Church in Harvard Yard, ships bearing Marshall aid continued to pull into Europe's ports. On one day that same month, the SS *Gordon Maersk* completed its three-week journey across the seas, docked at Rouen and unloaded Marshall Plan tractors, chemicals, synthetic resin and cellulose acetate. Sixty miles down the river at Le Havre, the *Cape Race*, also from Baltimore, had pulled in to unload a similar batch of cargo. Five hundred miles to the south, the *Gibbes Lykes* pulled into Marseilles with 3,500 tons of Gulf Coast sulfur.

In the next three days, ten more American ships arrived in France's ports. They were vessels like the *Samuel Stranger*, bringing stuffed tires, borax, aircraft parts and drilling equipment; the *Rhonda*, which unloaded farm machines, chemicals and oil. The *Shirley Lykes* brought another 2,500 tons of sulfur. And together, the *Geirulo, Delmundo, Lapland, Cotton States* and *Velma Lykes* brought enough cotton to ensure that 170,000 French textile workers could keep their jobs. By that time, more than one thousand ships had unloaded Marshall Plan cargo in France's ports.

By June 1950, Marshall aid was very much a fixture in Western European life. Dockworkers, bakers, teachers, factory workers, farmers, shop customers—all came across Marshall goods or products in the course of daily life. The Marshall shield, a red, white and blue crest with the slogan "For European Recovery: Supplied by the United States of America," was emblazoned on all of the goods sent to Europe via the Marshall Plan. The shield was ubiquitous and became a popular emblem of the Plan and what it was doing for Western Europe. Young school children in Ludwigshafen, Germany, whose families could not afford their lunch, would spring into motion upon hearing the bell of the approaching American truck bearing that Marshall shield as it pulled up to the school yard, offering soup to fill young stomachs. For Helmut Kohl, future chancellor of Germany, it was one of his formative memories of the United States.

In the spring of 1950, ECA redoubled its information activities. Each month, ECA estimated that nine out of ten of the 275 million people living in Western Europe were reached through one or more media with information on Marshall Plan activity. In June 1950, fifty different Marshall Plan documentary films were being shown to people across Western Europe through commercial and noncommercial distributors; another sixty were in production. To reach Italians in the countryside, ECA sent trucks equipped with movie projectors, loudspeakers and portable displays to tell the ERP story. ECA set up dozens of fairs and traveling exhibits, visited by tens of millions of Europeans—all to advance Marshall Plan objectives such as European cooperation and productivity. Millions of posters, pamphlets and booklets were distributed and put up throughout Western Europe to similar ends. Puppet shows were set up to entertain and educate children. In Italy, an essay competition on the meaning of the Marshall Plan attracted half a million entries.

ECA wanted the continent to know about the impact that aid was having on Western Europe's economies. In Great Britain, Marshall aid, the sterling devaluation and the U.S. program of increasing sterling area imports had all helped to radically reverse Britain's balance-of-payments problems. In dire straits, with a trading deficit of almost $550 million in the third quarter of 1949, Britain now had a surplus of almost $50 million in the first quarter of 1950 and by the end of June 1950, it achieved a quarterly surplus of almost $200 million. "There is big news," heralded *Life* magazine on May 1, 1950: "Britain is coming back fast."

Meanwhile, in France 16,000 workers labored along the Rhone River constructing a series of dams and hydroelectric plants in one of the most ambitious and important development projects in postwar Europe. It had been a dream of the French for decades to harness the vast power potential of the Rhone. The Monnet Plan sought to realize it, but did not have the funds to begin. The Marshall Plan provided 90 percent of the first year's funding, breathing life into the vast undertaking, which aimed to deliver 13 billion kilowatt hours per year—3 billion more than the Tennessee Valley Authority (the much-vaunted flagship New Deal project in the United States). Like the Schuman Plan, wrote *Life*, "the Rhone development program is demonstrating that France is strongly resurgent—a nation of greater spirit and postwar accomplishment than the world has realized." Inflation, which had plagued France during the postwar years, had come under control, and prices were even beginning to fall.

Back in the United States, the Marshall Plan had not led to an inflationary spiral, a massive economic downturn or fiscal disarray, as skeptics had claimed it would in the months after Marshall's speech three years earlier. In fact, in the summer of 1950, the United States was in the throes of an unprecedented economic expansion. Production, personal income and consumer spending were all booming. Home building was at an all-time high. Cars were rolling off Detroit's production lines at a tremendous rate. "The country has been on the upsurge in practically everything," *Life* said in an editorial, "The Boom Goes On," in April 1950. "Today by the Grace of God, we stand in a free and prosperous nation with greater possibilities for the future than any people have ever had before in the history of the world," Truman had proclaimed in his January State of the Union message.

Americans had sacrificed at home to build a free, a peaceful and a more prosperous world. All the while, the U.S. economy had roared on, supporting publishing magnate Henry Luce's conviction that he was living in "the American Century." Addressing an audience in celebration of *Fortune* magazine's twentieth anniversary around this time, Luce said: "Let us undertake this effort to build up the economies of the world . . . No happier dream capable of fulfillment on earth ever entered into the mind of a nation . . . Let us be proud that we are Americans living in this hour, able therefore to match ourselves with so great a purpose."

By the end of June, the Marshall Plan had committed close to $11 billion to Europe's economic recovery. It was reaping extraordinary dividends. At the end of June 1950, Western Europe's industrial production was at an all-time peak, 24 percent higher than prewar production and 28 percent above the first quarter of 1948. Agricultural production also was at an all-time peak. Behind the gains in production, the devaluation and trade liberalization, Western Europe's exports were 20 percent higher than their prewar volume and intra-European trade had increased to 17 percent above the prewar level. Transportation facilities and harbors that had been completely destroyed in the war had been rebuilt. The volume of rail transportation in the first half of 1950 was well above prewar levels. Unemployment in most Marshall countries was low, inflation was under control, and importantly, the Dollar Gap and Western Europe's reserve position were improving dramatically—hard currency reserves increased in the quarter ending June 1950 by about $600 million.

Most Marshall Plan countries had reached or were approaching their prewar levels of real earnings. The standard of living was much improved in Western Europe. However, the wealth created was not evenly shared. To ensure that the Marshall Plan promoted recovery, that aid was diverted to investment and growth and not charity, ECA stipulated that Marshall countries were not to exceed prewar levels of consumption. The strategy worked, and it created a platform for future growth and stability for all. But it also meant that workers and lower-income Western Europeans continued to struggle with their diets, housing and standards of living. Hoffman and Harriman both considered it unfinished business and began focusing on that dimension of the problem. Still, journalist Anne O'Hare McCormick was on point when she wrote: "Anyone who compares the picture today with that of 1947 can hardly believe that such progress could be made . . . A miracle of recovery has been performed."

Hoffman agreed. Testifying before the Senate Appropriations Committee for the next year's funding, Hoffman went over the program's record. It had been three years since Marshall's speech and ERP had passed its second year in what was supposed to be a four-year program. "I would like to state," Hoffman reported "that the Europeans, through their own valiant efforts and with our help, have accomplished what can properly be called a near-miracle of recovery." Progress was so strong, in fact, that Hoffman now felt that Congress could trim $3 billion from the original estimate of $18 billion for the entire program.

That summer, a city, Berlin, and a country, Yugoslavia, joined the ranks of Marshall aid recipients. Because of the blockade and the Stalin-Tito split, respectively, both additions were of great strategic and symbolic import. Meanwhile, in the Norwegian elections of the previous October, the Communists lost every one of their 11 seats in the National Assembly. In the West German elections, Communists won a meager 15 of 402 seats. In the last Belgian election, Communists won only 12 seats out of 212, compared with 23 out of 197 in the prior election.

Communists were to remain a force in French and Italian politics and elsewhere in Western Europe, but the apogee of their influence had passed. West Germany was now bound to Western Europe and the United States. The Schuman Plan provided Europe with the platform on which the European Union would be built. Joined in various postwar economic and military programs, institutions and arrangements, the Western world was now united behind capitalism and democracy and in opposition to the Soviet Union. And while America's latent military capacity and the atomic bomb had underwritten it, the achievement was realized "chiefly through the use of economic instruments, rather than military power."

ON JUNE 24, 1950, after a day of gardening and a pleasant dinner at Harewood, his pastoral Maryland retreat, Dean Acheson turned in to bed. At about 10 P.M. a call on a secure telephone line from the White House roused the secretary of state. It was a group of Acheson's subordinates from State.

They had received a cable from the U.S. ambassador to South Korea, John Muccio. At approximately 4:30 A.M., Korean time, heavily equipped tanks and artillery had begun to shoot their way past the 38th Parallel, meeting feeble resistance from the lightly equipped South Korean forces. Muccio believed it was an all-out offensive.

Acheson telephoned Truman, who had just finished dinner with his family in Independence, Missouri. The next evening, Saturday, June 25, Truman's senior advisers assembled at Blair House at around 7:30 P.M. All were in agreement: the U.S. would enter the conflict to repel the North Korean invasion.

Arthur Vandenberg fielded the news of the invasion from his sickbed in Michigan. The administration had refused to consult with Vandenberg and the Republicans on Asia policy, as it had done with its European policy and the Marshall Plan. Vanderberg felt that the administration had failed to act proactively and forcefully in Asia and bore culpability. For McCarthy and many of his Republican brethren, in the wake of the "loss" of China, Korea was the Democrats' soft underbelly, the perfect target to assail the administration for being soft on Communism and for a negligent and failed policy in Asia.

Ernest Bevin, too, was in the hospital the day the news came. It would be almost two weeks before he could begin to resume direction of the Foreign Office, still from his bed in a London clinic. Great Britain had aligned itself closely with the United States, for security. Attlee, Bevin and their country-men now wondered: Would the localized war in Korea bleed into China and eventually draw in the Soviet Union, giving rise to a new global, possibly nuclear, conflagration? Would the alliance struck with the United States for protection now bring Britain into World War III?

In his country home sixty kilometers from Paris, Jean Monnet was confer-ring with colleagues on the Schuman Plan negotiations then in progress. It was clear to Monnet that the United States would not allow the North Korean Communists to redraw the postwar boundaries with an act of unwar-ranted aggression. Monnet worried that panic in Europe over the possibility of a wider, nuclear war would undo the foundation of confidence, hope and recovery so painstakingly constructed during the previous three years. It was also clear to Monnet that the United States would move to shore up its Western European allies' defensive position with a renewed urgency. This would, no doubt, mean a greater role for Germany. The French would not abide too rapid a German remilitarization, and U.S. pressure could upset the delicate balance of power behind the emergent French-German rapproche-ment and the Schuman Plan. If the United States moved too quickly or too severely, it could all come undone.

U.S. Special Representative in Europe Averell Harriman was in London when he heard of the invasion. By the time he made it back to Paris on Monday, the South Korean army's defensive positions along the border had been overrun. Receiving scant information on the action at the Talleyrand, Harriman stationed himself at the Paris embassy with David Bruce, where he could follow the cables between Korea and Washington. Days later, Harriman left a dinner party to board a flight, with an assumed name, from Paris to London, where he boarded a U.S. military plane for Washington, arriving in time to join a National Security Council meeting on the Korean situation at the White House on Wednesday afternoon.

On June 25, Paul Hoffman had just entered a Washington hospital under an assumed name to have his gallbladder removed. He had decided upon the operation days earlier. Hoffman had been railing against declining congressional and public interest in the Marshall Plan and had been trumpeting the consequences should the United States fail to follow through on the entirety of its commitment to Europe. The Korean War would "make people appreciate the character of the struggle in which we are now engaged," he told a friend. Hoffman hoped the invasion would rally Congress and the American public to fortify its will to see the Plan through. Previously resistant to reallocate economic aid to military aid, or even to concede any bifurcation in aid, Hoffman now acknowledged that more would have to be done to rearm Europe—as long as it did not come at the expense of the Marshall Plan.

The political wind was not blowing in Hoffman's direction, however. Only three days after the North Korean incursion, Congress allocated an additional $4 billion to the military assistance program and cut more than $200 million from that year's appropriation for ERP. That same day, Senator Robert Taft gave a speech that assigned the Truman administration full blame for the invasion. Senator Joseph McCarthy proclaimed on July 2: "American boys are dying in Korea because a group of untouchables in the State Department sabotaged the aid program" for Asia.

A week later, on July 10, Vandenberg, from his bed in Michigan, in response to a note from George Marshall, wrote: "I loved your reminiscence—It would have been a great relaxer to sit down and have a drink with you and Bob Lovett and decide just how we were going to manage the world and then have done it. Those were truly great days. My part in them will always be my proudest record. Looking backward, it is really quite amazing how well we and the world got along together."

On July 20, 1950, the Tydings subcommittee, established to investigate McCarthy's charges of Communists in government, found the senator's accusations "fraught with falsehood from beginning to end." The "reprehensible and contemptible character" of the charges leveled "defies adequate condemnation." The findings hardly even registered as a speed bump for McCarthy. In July and August, the U.S. defense of South Korea was not going well. McCarthy and his associates stepped up their attacks on the Truman administration and the State Department for their perfidious toleration of Communist infiltration of the U.S. government. On August 7, Senator Kenneth Wherry, a Republican from Nebraska, demanded Dean Acheson's removal, then a week later demanded his resignation. On August 16, Wherry proclaimed: "the blood of our boys in Korea is on [Acheson's] shoulders, and no one else."

As McCarthy and his associates lambasted the administration for its soft and negligent foreign policy, the Marshall Plan fell squarely in their crosshairs. The charges were not new: the Plan was supporting "fellow travelers" in the British Labour Party; it was impeding Western Europe's capitalist revival and private enterprise by fortifying socialist parties throughout the continent. But Soviet gains and domestic hysteria painted the old criticisms in louder and more alarming hues.

WITH ITS CALL FOR a radically recalibrated defense buildup, NSC-68 presaged an orientation toward defense and military aid in April 1950. By the time of the North Korean invasion in late June 1950, military aid had achieved parity with economic aid. As Dean Acheson recalled, "the dispatch of two [U.S.] divisions to Korea removed the recommendations of NSC-68 from the realm of theory and made them immediate budget issues."

For many at ECA, developments appeared as if they might tilt the balance outright, and the orientation toward military aid might engulf the economic program. Senior ECA official William Foster wrote to Senator Tom Connally, then chairman of the Senate Foreign Relations Committee, on July 27, 1950. All expenses would come under scrutiny and all necessary resources would have to be husbanded, Foster wrote. But he also asked Connally to consider what ECA had accomplished in Europe. "A strong economy and stable society is the foundation of military strength," he wrote. "In the months ahead, this economic base will have to bear a far heavier load as the free nations of Western Europe build up their military strength. It is, therefore, more essential than ever that ECA assistance be continued so that the European economy can carry the load of rearmament, as well as contribute to the maintenance of a decent standard of living."

Foster's argument was sound, but it failed to conceal an air of desperation about the prospects that ECA's efforts would proceed at the desired pace and with the desired resources. Many ECA officials despaired. It appeared as if reduced funding would stem their projects and perhaps force them to renege on commitments. The agency and its missions' influence in Europe would diminish.

To Richard Bissell, it was clear in the aftermath of the North Korean invasion that the nature of the Marshall Plan was beginning to change drastically. But Bissell, like Harriman, had always believed that while Europe's economic advancement was intrinsically positive, it was not a U.S. strategic end in itself. Bissell had always, he wrote later, "understood that the Marshall Plan was never meant to be a wholly altruistic affair." Now that Western Europe was no longer under the threat of Communist takeover or economic bankruptcy, "The hope was that strengthening their economies would enhance the value of Western European countries as members of the NATO alliance, eventually enabling them to assume a defense responsibility in support of the Cold War efforts." In fact, Bissell was appointed to an ad hoc group that was created to review the assumptions and conclusions of NSC-68 and thus help design the U.S. military buildup.

On July 19, President Truman called on Congress to increase manpower levels in all armed services and asked for a radical increase in military production and foreign military aid. In August, Congress agreed to double the size of the U.S. armed forces. In September, a defense appropriation of $14.6 billion was approved, and to that another $12.6 billion was added. Despite the fiscal pressures in August, ECA still clung to the notion that it could steer a "middle course" between the "twin objectives" of recovery and rearmament.

The agency, though, was swimming upstream, and that summer the currents were furious. In South Korea, General MacArthur and the troops (from dozens of countries) under his command were struggling, pinned down well south of the 38th Parallel. McCarthy and his associates were stoking the anti-Communist hysteria and targeting—among other things—economic aid to Europe. Europe's renewed strength was taken by many to mean that the Marshall Plan had done its job. The United States had sacrificed to finance Europe's recovery. Now it was Western Europe's turn to sacrifice for the Allied cause and their common security. In July and August, at the NATO deputy meetings, U.S. officials concluded that Western Europe's economic requirements would be subordinated to its defense needs and European rearmament. From West Germany, U.S. High Commissioner John McCloy and, from Britain, U.S. Ambassador Lewis Douglas both agreed that

ECA's approach was "wishful thinking" and that the Allied military buildup would now be priority one—even if it meant turning some "old hobby horses . . . out to grass."

In its revised circular of September 16, ECA came to terms with the shift in priorities. The circular "talked about reconciling military and economic requirements" in a way that would not undo the past several years' progress, nor reduce the living standard for the "lower-income groups" that ECA had become increasingly focused on in the preceding months. "The question now," Bart Harvey, a member of the ECA mission to Italy, remarked, "is what defense the economy can support, and what aid is needed to support a given defense effort."

Adjusting their sights on the Allied defense buildup was painful for most ECA officials. With the Marshall Plan countries' economies performing so well, ECA was stripped of much of its funds, the carrots with which it pursued its policy objectives. Serving the defense effort also stripped ECA of its sense of mission. The agency's transcendent mission of building a continent and keeping it safe for democracy had helped to attract the very best, to stir their sense of duty, and to galvanize their energies. Rearming Europe had its virtues, and most felt it was necessary, but it seemed to most to lack the moral grandeur that had theretofore marked ECA's sense of purpose.

Many ECA officials, Bissell included, worried about the agency's impact on Western European economic policy going forward. With less aid to deploy, ECA refocused its efforts on productivity and continued to trumpet integration. It was clear that ECA—and the Marshall Plan, as the world had known it—was coming to an end that summer of 1950. An anonymous bard at the Hotel Talleyrand offered its epitaph:

> ERP in nineteen-fifty
> Is something spick and span and nifty,
> Brightly polished, simonized, integrated, harmonized.
> The Marshall Plan is obsolete,
> Our 1950 model's neat.
> New chrome plating strikes the eyes,
> With the legend "Harmonize."
> Nineteen nations lift their voices
> In loving chant and splendid noises
> "Bread and Guns to Harmonize."
> Reconstruction, Integration,

Dollar Shortage, Liberalization,
Off with the these old-fashioned ties!
Now's the time to harmonize.

IN MID-MAY 1950, Averell Harriman's trusted deputy at OSR, Milton Katz, left Paris for meetings in Washington. Harriman had asked Katz to stop in to visit with the president and to deliver a letter. "I am most anxious to come home and do not want to tackle another job in Europe," Harriman wrote. "I feel that things are in such shape here that I can leave with [a clear] conscience." For months, if not longer, Harriman's attention and energies had been drifting from European economic recovery to the U.S. military position and the Allied defense buildup. Senior colleagues like Al Friendly noticed that Harriman spoke more and more of military security. He looked for excuses to leave the confines of the Talleyrand to share his ideas with heads of state across Europe.

On May 1, in a letter to Harriman, expressing his own interest in returning home, Katz wrote: "In ECA terms, it seems to me, as we have so often said, that 1952 is now. The main lines of our four-year job have been substantially laid in two years, and we've got to move—as we have been moving—into a new and constructive transition." Europe's industrial and agricultural output had exceeded expectations, it had achieved fiscal and monetary stability, Stikker's appointment as chairman had "vitalized" the OEEC, and agreement on the EPU was imminent. Harriman estimated that the Marshall Plan had done what it had set out to do. With the shift in the strategic balance of power in the direction of the Soviets, and the subsequent focus on the Allied defense effort, Harriman wanted to go back to Washington.

Harriman was one of the world's most prestigious and visible diplomats. His return would be a loss for the United States abroad. It so happened, though, that he was also needed at home. Republican attacks on Acheson and the State Department were becoming more virulent with each passing day. Various branches of the military were doing battle with one another for resources and influence. And Defense Secretary Louis Johnson, with an outsized ego and designs on the presidency in 1952, was waging internecine bureaucratic warfare with what seemed like every member of the Cabinet but most of all with Dean Acheson. Biographer Robert Donovan called 1950 Truman's "savage year." It was a worse year, still, for his secretary of state. "Dean's in trouble," Truman told Harriman. "I want you to help him." On June 16, the White House announced that Harriman would come back to

Washington in early August to become Special Assistant to the President, focusing on national security and foreign affairs.

It was a position without precedent, one of many that Harriman would hold throughout his life in national service. The position was to evolve into what, in time, would be called National Security Adviser. Harriman set the mold. With Acheson under attack, and Harriman assuming a position so close to Truman, speculation about Harriman replacing Acheson as secretary of state percolated. It was well known that Harriman coveted the post. And it had been difficult for Harriman to see it go to Acheson, whom he had coached in crew at Groton. For his part, Acheson had complete faith: "My forty-five years of confidence in Averell's integrity and honor would not be undermined."

When the Korean War broke out in late June, Harriman determined he could not wait until August to return to Washington. Days after the invasion, he cabled the president: "You must be a bit short-handed. Do you want me to come home a bit earlier?" He was standing in the White House less than two days later. Milton Katz, who had served Harriman so well, agreed to remain in Paris as his replacement. Harriman's departure signified, as well as symbolized, the American reprioritization from the economic to the military realm.

PAUL HOFFMAN had a difficult convalescence from his late June operation. When he returned to work, he found a reconfigured international landscape and a reordered agenda at home. ECA had less funding; it could not speak with authority and certainty that its pledges to Marshall Plan countries would be met; and the mission was now downgraded, subsumed in the war effort and the attendant military buildup. It was a difficult summer for Hoffman. He grew increasingly disconsolate. On September 25, CBS News reported: "This evening, Mr. Paul Hoffman confirmed the regrettable news that he is stepping out of government service."

Responses poured in from all directions. His initial sponsor, Arthur Vandenberg, wrote from his sickbed: "I simply wanted to tell you that you have justified every confidence I ever placed in you and that I shall always be exceptionally proud of having had a key part not only in drafting you for this public service but also in loyally upholding your hands." CBS reported: "Paul Hoffman will long be remembered in this capital, not only because he successfully administered the enormous task of resurrecting the economic civilization of half-ruined Europe, but because he became a kind of classic example of the businessman in government." Senator Robert Taft wrote that he never did agree to the amounts of aid appropriated, but he had always had great confidence in Hoffman and his administration of ECA. Even Congressman John "Saber" Taber, Hoffman's nemesis when it came to securing appropriations, wrote the administrator, "It has been a real pleasure to work with you. I have always had confidence in your sincerity of purpose and in your capacity."

The *Chicago Sun-Times* wrote in an editorial, "As head of ECA, Mr. Hoffman saved the free society of western Europe . . . It wasn't that Paul Hoffman was blind to the danger of Western weakness in battle. But he saw very clearly how military power isn't enough to stop Communism if beneath the armor, there is an unjust, decrepit, cartel-ridden economy incapable of meeting people's legitimate demands." Yet Hoffman left office concerned that too many Americans still thought of the Marshall Plan as a great charity; they did not understand the breadth of its aims nor the strategic interests it advanced.

Vacating what had been, for the previous two years, one of the most powerful positions in the world, Hoffman embarked on a twenty-day, eleven-nation European "farewell tour." From Berlin he trumpeted Germany's "economic renaissance." In Italy he dodged acerbic questions from the Communist press. In Turkey he rode an American tractor. In England he met with Clement Attlee at 10 Downing Street and called on the king. And in France, wearing antiseptic coat and boots, he toured a pharmaceutical plant built with Marshall Plan dollars. He was met with goodwill and an outpouring of gratitude. He lapped it all up. At every opportunity, he heralded the importance of continued integration. It would be the key to expanding European production and prosperity, he said. In Paris, he cautioned the OEEC not to let the burden of rearmament and concerns about shortages and inflation lead to renewed "economic nationalism."

At home, he could rest. He wrote to a friend, in characteristic good cheer, that at last, "Starting November 15, I achieved a life-long ambition—I became unemployed."

Harriman's former deputy, William Foster, was selected to replace Hoffman as the new administrator. Foster did not bring the same heft to the role, but he inherited the reins of a very different agency. "We were like a peacetime factory converted to defense production," recalled senior ECA official Paul Porter. "In retrospect more than at the time it happened, I recognize how profoundly the Korean War changed the goals and the character of ECA." Depleted of funding and stature, it seemed the Marshall Plan's days were numbered.

• • •

As Hoffman and Harriman exited their posts, another figure reluctantly stepped back onto the world stage. In August and early September, General Douglas MacArthur's forces remained pinned well below the 38th Parallel in South Korea. The war was not going well. It fueled Republican attacks on Acheson and the administration. It also amplified the feud between Dean Acheson and Louis Johnson, and seemed, to the latter, an opportune time to wage a power play. Well aware of Harriman's desire to serve as secretary of state, Johnson intimated to Harriman that if he supported the defense secretary in getting Acheson removed, he could deliver the post to him. Harriman's loyalty—to Acheson and to Truman—was not for sale, and he duly reported the incident. Truman found Johnson's influence in the Cabinet increasingly corrosive and supported Acheson staunchly. For the president it was the last straw.

Vacationing with his wife at Huron Mountain in Michigan that August, George Marshall was summoned by a town resident to a nearby country store. Since retirement, Marshall had spent months recuperating from surgery and resting at Leesburg, before agreeing to become head of the American Red Cross, a position he enjoyed. He had been running the Red Cross for almost a full year when he picked up the telephone. It was Truman. Mindful of the locals peering at him, he was overheard to say only: "Yes, Mr. President."

In early September, Marshall formally agreed to Truman's request. At seventy years of age, he would leave Leesburg once more, this time to replace Louis Johnson and serve as secretary of defense. In one of Truman's darkest hours, Marshall was summoned to right the ship of state: to manage the war in Korea, to patch the discord in the Cabinet and to elevate the stature of the administration with Congress, the press and the American public. "Now history gives him his final challenge," wrote *Life* magazine. "The job must be done. Then songs can be sung again and new words coined to express the greatness of George Catlett Marshall."

First, though, the law had to be changed. In creating the modern Department of Defense, the National Security Act of 1947 stipulated that in order to uphold the principle of civilian control of the military, any candidate for secretary of defense must ten years removed from the military. Most senators wanted to expedite Marshall's confirmation, which was certain, and Truman did not hesitate to request the exemption for Marshall. The political climate had changed, though, since Marshall's last confirmation hearings. In the wake of Mao's victory, Republicans had begun to point back to Marshall's doomed 1946 presidential mission to mediate the Chinese civil war. They criticized Marshall for not doing enough to support Chiang. They attacked the State Department that he had run for two years. They attacked the Marshall Plan: a waste and misallocation of resources, and a boon for European Socialists.

In the House of Representatives, Dewey Short, a Republican from Missouri, called Marshall "a catspaw and a pawn" who had come back "to bail out desperate men who are in a hole." In the other chamber of Congress, Senator William Jenner of Indiana, a Republican running for reelection, began a frenzied diatribe against the Democratic Party and the Truman administration and "its bloody tracks of treason." Marshall was their front man, said Jenner. Then he said, "General Marshall is not only willing, he is eager to play the role of a front man for traitors. The truth is this is no new role for him, for General George C. Marshall is a living lie . . . Unless he himself were desperate, he could not possibly agree to continue as an errand boy, a front man, a stooge, or a conspirator for this Administration's crazy assortment of collectivist cutthroat crackpots and Communist fellow-traveling appeasers." Jenner continued that General Marshall was "not enough of a patriot" to tell the American people the whole story. Senators rose to Marshall's defense, rebuking Jenner's outrageous charges. When the general was told of the speech, he replied: "Jenner? Jenner? I do not believe I know the man."

Marshall was confirmed in the Senate, 57–11. The media heralded the appointment, which seemed overnight to provide a much-needed sense of order and authority at Defense and in the Cabinet. There was good news, also, across the Pacific.

Since the first week of August, American and South Korean troops had been dug in below the 38th Parallel, behind a line near the port of Pusan. They called it the Pusan Perimeter. Trapped, vulnerable and grappling with stifling heat, the Americans had sustained almost 15,000 casualties by mid-September, and military prospects were desperate. On September 15, Douglas MacArthur led an invasion force of 262 ships and 70,000 men in a surprise amphibious attack on a port two hundred miles northwest of Pusan, called Inchon. There was no beach along the coast there, only sea walls, and the tides offered a desperately narrow window for such a landing. Leading up to the invasion, MacArthur proclaimed: "I can almost hear the ticking of the second hand of destiny . . . We shall land at Inchon and I shall crush them." It was one of the most daring gambits in U.S. military history. And it was one of the greatest successes.

Inchon fell in a day. Seoul, South Korea's capital, was retaken in eleven days. In late September, more than half of the North Korean army was trapped in a grand pincer movement. On October 1, the MacArthur-led U.N. forces reached the 38th Parallel. The objective had been to repel the North Koreans and regain South Korea up to the 38th Parallel. Now, MacArthur was authorized to pursue the North Korean army up to the Yalu River, where North Korea bordered China, on the condition, though, that the U.N. forces did not encounter any Soviet or Chinese forces. In early October, the Chinese warned that if the United States crossed the 38th Parallel, they would enter the conflict. The Chinese statement was dismissed as a bluff.

During October, MacArthur's forces pressed north. MacArthur was given virtually untrammeled command in the field. Truman had told him explicitly, though, that he was not prepared to risk a larger regional or global conflict over Korea. Korea was not to turn into World War III. By late October, it was clear that Chinese troops had begun to cross the Yalu and into North Korea. MacArthur proceeded apace.

That November would prove perhaps the most disastrous month in Truman's presidency. On November 1, two Puerto Rican nationalists attempted to assassinate the president. Days later, the midterm elections dealt Truman and the Democrats a punishing defeat. The Democrats managed to hold on to both houses of Congress, but 52 percent of voters cast their ballots for Republicans versus 42 percent for Democrats, who lost several seats in the House and the Senate. The victory was a boon for Taft and the Republicans, as well as McCarthy, whose attacks—on the State Department, Acheson, Marshall and the Marshall Plan—featured prominently in the election.

Then, as the dreaded Korean winter set in toward late November, the Chinese proved that their warning was no bluff. On Friday, November 24, the day after Thanksgiving, roughly a quarter-million Chinese streamed over the Yalu River into North Korea. There followed a rout of MacArthur's forces, a murderous and ignominious retreat through North Korea and, into December, past the 38th Parallel. In a National Security Council meeting in the Cabinet room on November 28, Marshall made it clear that there must not be a wider war with China. "To do this," the general said, "would be to fall into a carefully laid Russian trap." It would lay Europe bare for Soviet pickings, and the Eurasian landmass would be, once again, vulnerable to the domination of a totalitarian power. Truman and Acheson were in full agreement.

Douglas MacArthur did not see it that way. For MacArthur, the Chinese invasion meant that a wider, regional war had already been launched. MacArthur wanted to meet the Chinese invasion with a full-scale nuclear assault on Manchuria and Chinese cities. China had escalated the conflict, and MacArthur humiliated at the retreat and apparently convinced of his invincibility, would accept nothing short of total victory. On December 1, MacArthur told *U.S. News & World Report* that orders forbidding him to strike at Communists north of the Yalu had put his forces under "an enormous handicap, without precedent in military history." Not to meet the challenge, in MacArthur's view, was tantamount to treason. Later, Truman would say that he should have fired MacArthur on the spot.

On the morning of November 30, 1950, Harry Truman walked into the Indian Treaty Room for a press conference with an audience of two hundred newspaper reporters and various government officials. The United States would stand up to Russo-Communist expansion and wished to "halt this aggression in Korea . . . We will take whatever steps are necessarry to meet the military situation," Truman said. A reporter wanted to know if that included using the atomic bomb. "That includes every weapon we have," Truman answered. The newsmen pressed. Was use of the bomb under "active consideration?" "Always has been," Truman replied. "It is one of our weapons." Seventeen minutes after the press conference ended, a United Press bulletin hit the wire: "President Truman said today that the United States has under consideration use of the atomic bomb in connection with the war in Korea."

In London, news spread quickly. Many misinterpreted Truman's remark to mean that MacArthur would be given authorization to use the A-bomb at his discretion. "Cries of alarm" rang out during a session of the House of Commons. When Attlee announced, hours later, that he had just cabled the State Department that he wanted to fly to Washington to meet with the president, the chamber erupted with loud cheers. When the United States responded to the North Korean invasion with the prompt invocation of collective security and then decisive action in leading U.N. forces on behalf of South Korea's defense, it validated the worth for Western Europeans of the American security guarantee. The Americans would stand up to flagrant aggression. Western Europe felt assured.

However, that sense of security quickly devolved into intense insecurity. The North Korean invasion highlighted Western Europe's own military weakness and vulnerability—its inability to deter such an invasion or repel one if launched. Western Europeans worried that the United States would get pinned down in a regional war in Asia, leaving Europe vulnerable to the Soviets. They worried that the domestic pressures, combined with Mac-Arthur's recklessness, could converge to precipitate a wider regional, or even global, war. As NATO allies, they worried that they would be enmeshed in the conflict. *Life* magazine wrote that "World War III moves ever closer."

When Attlee arrived at the White House on Monday, December 4, for two days of meetings with Truman, the president refused his request for a consensus before the atomic bomb would be used, but he assured his visitor that he would be consulted. In any case, Truman assured Attlee that he had no intention of letting the conflict spread or turn nuclear.

Meanwhile, in the three months after the outbreak of war, upswings in military spending and demand for raw materials drove Western Europe's combined industrial output to an all-time peak, 13 percent above the quarter the year before. At the end of September 1950, production had increased 33 percent over the prewar level. The growing demand together with trade liberalization and the elimination of payments barriers helped lift Western Europe's export volume and its intra-European trade to record levels, easing, in turn, balance-of-payments difficulties even further. All of these trends seemed positive, and they were.

Behind the benefits, however, less salutary developments were brewing. The demand for raw materials and commodities as well as military and industrial equipment fueled worries about shortages. Several countries embarked upon massive stockpiling efforts, unleashing a "spectacular increase in world prices." The price increases generated inflationary pressures. The concern in Western Europe was twofold. First, the shortages would lead to consumer rationing and price controls, in addition to pressure on real wages, breeding further concern about the standard of living for lower-income groups, desperation, and potential political instability. It also raised the prospect that Western Europe's exports would decrease and its balance-of-payments problems would reemerge. Those who had labored so hard to construct a sturdy foundation for European integration worried that these pressures would foster a recrudescence of economic nationalism in the Marshall Plan countries or even raise once again the specter of economic autarky.

This last concern seemed dispelled, at least in the near term, when in late October 1950 the OEEC agreed to liberalize 75 percent of import quotas on private accounts on intra-OEEC trade. During this time, ECA could still report "general agreement among the participating countries on the need for such cooperative action."

When the Chinese entered the Korean War in late November 1950,

dashing all hopes that, as MacArthur had suggested within earshot of a bevy of reporters, "the boys would be home for Christmas," Western Europe's fears loomed larger. At the same time, the United States was reallocating economic aid to support Europe's military buildup, meaning that Western Europe could no longer count on Marshall aid to buffer economic shocks, should they come. In November 1950, Richard Bissell told a gathering of OEEC officials that "recovery in Northern and Western Europe was complete and that future American aid would be channeled into defense production."

IN DECEMBER 1950, Prime Minister Clement Attlee returned from his meeting with Truman in Washington. Marshall aid, devaluation, trade liberalization, payments reform, now American stockpiling and import needs, but most of all, austerity and the British spirit, had delivered Great Britain dollars and flushed her reserves. Shortages and inflation, and the potentiality of further balance-of-payments crises continued to loom. But it had never sat well with the proud Empire to receive aid from her progeny. Upon Attlee's return in early December, Great Britain announced that it would desist from requesting Marshall aid. On December 31, 1950, Great Britain, on its own initiative, ended its status as a recipient of United States aid under the Marshall Plan.

Ernest Bevin's reply to George Marshall in 1947 had launched the Marshall Plan. So it was only fitting that the ailing foreign secretary would write the new secretary of defense: "I sat in the House of Commons yesterday and heard the chancellor announce the suspension of Marshall aid, and had you been there I should have wanted to go and say to you with a full heart 'thank you.'"

Chapter Fourteen

SHUTTING IT DOWN

A s 1951 DAWNED, America was in a collective state of national anxiety. When asked who they thought was winning the Cold War, 30 percent of Americans said Russia; 9 percent believed the United States was winning. Harry Truman was not the sort to be easily intimidated by such polls. "I wonder how far Moses would have gone if he'd taken a poll in Egypt?" he once wrote. With the United States in retreat in South Korea and hundreds of thousands of Chinese troops in pursuit, the American position in the war was near a nadir. The threat of a larger regional or even a nuclear global conflict loomed. Meanwhile, with a resounding victory in the recent midterm elections, and greater weight in Congress, Joseph McCarthy and his right-wing allies—or as Dean Acheson called them, "the primitives"—escalated their attacks on Truman, Acheson and George Marshall and the Marshall Plan.

Remilitarization had emerged as the paramount priority in the United States' European policy, and it was clear to leaders at ECA that the currents would continue to work against their ability to secure large-scale appropriations for economic aid. Without vast sums to expend and recognizing that the program was approaching its conclusion, ECA focused on what the agency believed were the two remaining keys that could open the door to European economic self-sustainability. The first was productivity.

By the end of World War II, the United States had undergone a revolution in industrial management and technology. In part it was driven by the size of the American market. The bounty it offered encouraged competition and innovation and eventually growth. In part, it emerged from the experiences of the 1920s, the New Deal and World War II, when management and

labor had learned to work together in a symbiosis of interests, and productivity flourished.

Europe's experience was different. Europe had disparate, smaller, protected markets. Producers did not have the same incentive to compete and innovate, so productivity lagged. In addition, the Depression left a searing imprint on European workers. Cartels and wealthy industrialists—Cripps called them "the Guilty Men"—abided massive unemployment and did little to generate the sort of innovation or growth that might protect workers. In America, the manager-worker relationship, though not at all perfect, was by and large flourishing, but in Western Europe that relationship was still fraught with distrust.

Driven by a fear of unemployment and a distrust of business owners and managers, the European worker resisted change. There was, for many European workers, Harry Price wrote, "a psychological abhorrence of the man with a stopwatch." One American technical expert happened upon a group of European workers digging a ditch. Noticing that the workers were using shovels, the expert suggested that with advanced machinery, they could do the job in a fraction of the time. The supervisor said, "Perhaps, but this way we can give a lot more employment." The American expert replied, "Couldn't we give still more employment if we used tablespoons?"

Hoffman knew that realizing ECA's economic goals for Europe would mean modernizing, upgrading equipment and replenishing capital stores. But Europeans would need more than physical equipment. They would need to adopt a new mind-set, one that would not only accommodate but also prize innovation, competition, change, a new relationship between management and labor; a revolution of thinking and behavior was due.

On a warm day in Paris in July 1948, the new British chancellor of the Exchequer, Sir Stafford Cripps, remarked to Paul Hoffman, "If we are to raise the standard of living in Great Britain, we must have greater productivity." Great Britain had much to learn from the United States, Cripps said, and perhaps she still had a few secrets worth knowing. "Why don't we interchange this information?" Cripps proposed. Hoffman jumped at the idea. "Why don't we set up a system of transatlantic visits?" Hoffman laid out a vision for a massive exchange program between U.S. and European managers and laborers. Cripps signed on. The Anglo-American Council on Productivity was born. Hoffman recruited Philip Reed, chairman of General Electric, and Victor Reuther, a senior official in the United Auto Workers union, two of America's most prominent figures from business and labor, respectively, to run the innovative venture on the American side. It would all be funded through ERP.

Months later a group of management and labor from the British steel industry ventured across the Atlantic for a six-week tour of America's steel industry, visiting foundries and talking with managers and workers. They found that American productivity was 50 to 90 percent higher than in British foundries. Upon their return, they produced a report with their findings and recommendations. It sold twenty-five thousand copies within a fortnight and went into three extra printings. Later, Hoffman credited this and future U.S.-Anglo exchanges with bringing about "the reorganization of the steel industry in Britain." This component of ECA's work became known as technical assistance. In the two years to follow, 1949 and 1950, the French, the Germans, the Dutch and other Marshall Plan countries joined in and benefited.

At the end of 1950, ECA reported to Congress: "It is clear that only increased productivity will make it possible for the Marshall Plan countries to make a contribution to defense production of the magnitude that is needed and at the same time maintain an acceptable standard of living for their peoples." ECA called for a new and vastly upgraded "production assistance drive" in the beginning of 1951. The technical assistance program became the centerpiece of that effort.

Between March and July 1951, almost 150 productivity teams visited the United States to glean insights into American technology, manufacturing techniques and management-labor relations. Meanwhile, America had almost 400 technical experts stationed abroad to advise European industry, management and labor on productivity. Some of these experts conducted programs called "management seminars" in which they "lectured" their European counterparts on effective industrial and management techniques.

The technical assistance program made it possible for Dutch farmers to study grain growing on Iowa farms. Norwegians came to learn about American coal mines. The Italians came to America and learned how to raise hybrid corn, and a Turkish delegation came to analyze American civil aviation and public-roads building. American experts in England held a "dollar convention," at which they recommended means of gearing businesses to increase exports to the American market to an audience of 600 British industrialists. The British motorcycle industry proved able to develop a model that the American market found more desirable than the Harley-Davidson. But on the whole, the British effort to capture the American markets met with mixed to disappointing results.

Many of the program's initiatives transformed facets of European industry and life. American experts showed the Dutch at the Doboelman Soap Works in Holland how to reduce processing time from five days to two hours with upgraded American machinery. In Sardinia and Turkey, American public health officials worked with local experts to take aim at the debilitating malaria problem. ECA paid for a group of European engineers to visit nearly all the power systems east of the Mississippi. By 1952, approximately 2,600 French workers and managers—and a comparable number of Italians—visited the United States to study American industry.

By mid-1951, ECA had spent $30 million on technical assistance. When the Plan was complete, technical assistance accounted for less than .5 percent of total ECA aid, but its contribution far outweighed its cost. Paul Hoffman wrote years later: "Even more important than what Europeans learned about lathes and plows is what they learned about America. They learned that this is the land of full shelves and bulging shops, made possible by high productivity and good wages, and that its prosperity may be emulated elsewhere by those who will work toward it."

According to one ECA official named Robert Myers, by the time ECA unwound, thanks to the technical assistance effort, productivity had in fact become "a household word," the "subject of many articles and discussed in public meetings widely." French economic officials found that the technical assistance programs had in fact "generated new attitudes toward production and productivity and toward social problems." Cripps's successor, Chancellor of the Exchequer Hugh Gaitskill, said, "It did lead to new ideas." The attitudes and ideas could be measured in advances in productivity and production.

Hoffman noticed that the European delegations visiting industry in the United States were struck by the amicable, cooperative relationship between management and labor. In Hoffman's view, it was the observation that left the greatest impression. Europeans were seeing a different model of capitalism from what they had known. Wrote historian James Cronin: "The capitalism put on display . . . was a system in which the power of owners, of capitalists, had been displaced and their role in the firm taken over by professional managers. Postwar capitalism was thus depicted . . . as 'managerial capitalism.' The idea that management was in control, or should be in control, proved extremely attractive and elicited support across Europe."

America had emerged from the crucible of the 1920s neocorporatist experience, the Great Depression and the New Deal having reformed the modalities of its economic system—its brand of capitalism. Touring America's factories, farms, showrooms and boardrooms, thousands of European representatives gained a firsthand account of a free-enterprise system that delivered tremendous productivity and production. Yet, at the same time, it provided a voice for labor in the management and in the production process;

unemployment was very low; and the New Deal had given rise to a plethora of worker protection and social welfare programs. Capitalism in America did not fit the version being peddled by Communists in Europe.

The technical assistance program was not a smash with everyone. Many U.S. businessesmen complained that it was absurd for Europeans to be paid to come to the United States only to steal the techniques and secrets that afforded America its competitive advantage. Some members of Congress voiced the same view. Indeed the programs may have accounted for some dislocation in American industry, but on the whole any such disruption was minor. Hoffman always rejoined such criticism by saying that the United States was not frightened of competition; it thrived on it. And Europe's economic self-sustainability, its ability to be a partner in security as well as a viable export market, its ability to shoulder its share of the remilitarization effort, would make the technical assistance effort a profitable venture. By 1951, when it had become a cornerstone of ECA's policy, Hoffman was watching from the sidelines. By the time it was complete, he could report that technical assistance had, in fact, "turned out to be one of the most effective innovations introduced by the Marshall Program."

IN 1951, Western Europe was swarming with Americans. Tourists joined students and returning GIs, buoyed by a strong dollar, in venturing across the Atlantic for a taste of postwar Europe. The Marshall Plan had actively encouraged tourism as one way of transferring dollars to Europe and narrowing the Dollar Gap. No Americans were more conspicuous or influential, at this time, than the American experts sent to Europe under the technical assistance program. The 2,500 American officials and employees with their wives and children created an expatriate community of as many as 7,500. Only around 150 of those were American diplomats or Foreign Service officers, trained to speak for America abroad. The rest were experts in everything from labor relations to social security, to trade and payments, to press and films, to inflation, oil and aviation. Europeans called them 'N'y-a-que's,' which, explained Theodore White, were experts who came from America wielding the phrase *Il n'y a que faire*, which meant "All we have to do."

European perception of America during the Marshall Plan years depended on the lens—the country, the political ideology, the income bracket—of the European. Even within each category, perceptions of the United States were laced with nuance. However, from George Marshall's speech in June 1947 until the outbreak of the Korean War, it is fair to say that despite ambivalence about what America stood for and what its power and presence in Europe would mean, the Marshall Plan and the American security guarantee under NATO were mostly welcomed, and Europe's feeling for America and the transatlantic bond was marked by goodwill and gratitude. White wrote that "nothing in postwar history . . . more swiftly raised American prestige in European eyes" than the Marshall Plan.

During most of the Plan, ECA had prided itself on offering friendly aid and on employing the most outstanding, most qualified and judicious Americans, from all fields, to represent America to that end. Richard Bissell noted that much of the Plan's success in those years came about because of the subtlety of the American approach. American influence was best brought to bear in private consultations, at dinner, at lunches or in offices. It was to be Europe's recovery, and the Marshall Planners' approach and tone needed to evince, at every turn, consideration for European self-confidence and dignity.

By the end of 1950, when Hoffman and Harriman had left, and the Plan's funding had tapered, many of the most able American officials had returned home to reenter private life. The quality of the Marshall Planners and the American experts abroad began to depreciate, and less able men emerged. The urgency of the Korean War and the geopolitical backdrop gave rise to stridency in some Americans' tones at a time when most Europeans felt anxious and vulnerable. State Department official Henry Labouisse lamented the change: "The number of Americans running around telling everybody what to do is now very large. We don't come in as equals—but always on a platform."

At the same time, with American production booming and European growth fueling demand for American products, American goods seemed ubiquitous in Europe. Coke, in particular, seemed to symbolize the European conversion to a mass consumer society. The French communist paper *L'Humanité* asked: "Will we be Coca-colonized?" Cinema was also a cultural flashpoint. Before television spread, cinema was extremely popular in Western Europe in the late 1940s and early 1950s. By 1951, more than 60 percent of the films showing in Western Europe were American. All of these American products and values seemed to usher in changes in the European way of life. And the changes amplified European dependency. American insensitivity combined with Europe's own insecurity to breed growing anti-Americanism.

British diplomat and historian Harold Nicolson said it was not that Europeans were anti-American, it was just that they were "frightened that the destinies of the world should be in the hands of a giant with the limbs of an undergraduate, the emotions of a spinster, and the brain of a pea-hen." Europe's perception of America was developing along many emotional fault lines: gratitude, ambivalence, resentment, admiration, dependence, envy, disapproval and insecurity.

IN ADDITION TO PRODUCTIVITY, ECA's second main objective in 1951 was Western European integration. ECA had long held that integration was the best means of propelling Western Europe to economic self-sustainability. With financial aid tapering, the imperative for structural economic reform was that much greater. Moreover, the United States now needed Western Europe to shoulder remilitarization and all of its attendant costs and dislocations. Continued integration would enhance growth and fortify the Marshall Plan countries against remilitarization's shocks.

Early in 1951, the EPU proved its mettle, facilitating intra-European trade and cooperation and providing a mechanism to help West Germany weather an alarming payments crisis. At the same time, the Marshall Plan countries adhered to the OEEC program of trade liberalization. By the middle of the year, almost all of the Marshall Plan countries, even against the economic shocks induced by remilitarization and the Korean War, moved to reduce their import quotas on 75 percent of private accounts in intra-European trade. By June, most had reached that level. The Marshall Plan had charted a course toward economic integration. Western Europeans had experienced the benefits during 1949 and 1950, and they would stay the course during 1951.

In May 1950, the announcement of the Schuman Plan had elicited a chorus of acclaim from the United States. During the winter of 1950–51, though, its realization was in jeopardy, and France was blaming the United States.

To fortify Western Europe's defense and NATO's military capability, the U.S. had been increasingly advocating for West German remilitarization. With Soviet divisions in East Germany, and the Soviet Union rearming East Germany to the hilt, it seemed absurd, now that West Germany had become sovereign and a participant in the Marshall Plan, not to harness West Germany's industrial and military potential to the cause of the West's defense. For the French, it remained their bugaboo, the one step the French public would not abide.

One of the key drivers to West Germany's participation in the Schuman Plan—an arrangement that called for it to give up sole control of its most valuable resources—was its hope for dignity, equality among nations and the prospect of shedding the last yoke of occupation and restrictions. U.S. support for a West German military role in the western military partnership seemed to free West Germany of some of that yoke, enhancing its stature and its bargaining position at the international conference table. Many of West Germany's leading industrialists had opposed the venture. They did not want to cede sovereignty over the Ruhr, nor were they willing to meet French demands to break up some of Germany's largest steel interests into smaller entities to ensure de-cartelization. Around the turn of 1951, negotiations grew divisive, they stalled and the Schuman Plan, to at least one informed observer, looked like a "dead duck."

That was bad news for the United States. At the request of the French, John McCloy, the high commissioner in Germany, intervened in the negotiations "more directly, than ever" before. France agreed to abandon its demand that West Germany limit its steel production and West Germany ceded to French demands to reorganize its steel industry, breaking the larger steel firms into smaller firms and placing limits on the amount of coal production each firm controlled. McCloy's role in the negotiations helped France and Germany reconcile their positions, and may even have been decisive.

On April 18, a collection of heads of state and foreign ministers of six European countries—France, Germany, Italy, Belgium, the Netherlands and Luxembourg—stood in the Salon de l'Horloge, the same gilded room from which Schuman had sprung the audacious plan on the world almost one year earlier. There was no public audience, but a few secretaries could be seen peeping from behind the red velvet curtains to witness the historic moment. First, Adenauer sat down to sign it; then Schuman; then the Italian foreign minister, Count Carlo Sforza; then the remaining three.

Jean Monnet was there to witness it. Unbeknownst to him, one of his colleagues on the French Planning Commissariat, André Lamy, had a surprise for each of the signatories. Lamy had prepared copies of the treaty. They had been printed by the French Stationery Office, on Dutch vellum, in German ink, bound in Belgian parchment, tied in Italian silk ribbons, and sealed with Luxembourgian glue. As the foreign ministers stood, mingling, holding their gifts and sipping champagne in the reception room after the signing, the subdued scene belied the profundity of what had just transpired. It had been six years since the end of World War II. And now France and Germany and their partners in the venture had turned the most destructive interstate feud in world history into a common partnership, creating a foundation from which, in time, a unified Europe would blossom. Historian Alan Bullock called it "as bold and imaginative an idea as any in European history."

• • •

BACK IN WASHINGTON, April was not a month for celebration. Only one week earlier, on April 11, 1951, the headline across the early morning edition of the *Washington Post* read, "Truman Fires MacArthur." It was clear late in 1950 that Douglas MacArthur wanted to wage a full-scale war against China, to expand the scope of the Korean War into an Asian war. In early 1951, under General Matthew Ridgway's command, the Eighth Army launched a successful assault on the Chinese and North Korean troops. On March 12, Ridgway and his forces recaptured Seoul, which would not be lost again. By the end of March, Ridgway had led American and allied forces back up to the 38th Parallel, and by early April they held a line, one that would become known as the Kansas line, just north of the parallel. It was a desperately needed military victory for the United States.

MacArthur was not content with the progress. On March 15, he flouted Truman's orders by giving an unauthorized interview to the American press, openly criticizing Washington for halting the Eighth Army at the 38th Parallel, short of unifying Korea. Then, on March 24, MacArthur issued a statement directly to the Chinese, threatening to expand the war and antagonizing them. This was at a time when Truman was hoping to strike a cease-fire and move toward a concurrent peace settlement. "By this act MacArthur left me no choice—I could no longer tolerate his insubordination," Truman wrote in his memoirs.

On April 5, Speaker of the House Joseph Martin made public a letter that MacArthur had sent him. MacArthur wrote: "Here we fight Europe's war with arms, while the diplomats there still fight it with words . . . if we lose this war to Communism in Asia the fall of Europe is inevitable; win it and Europe most probably would avoid war and yet preserve freedom . . . we must win. There is no substitute for victory." MacArthur had violated the president's strict orders, his very authority as commander in chief under the Constitution. With the Cabinet and the military chiefs behind him, Truman acted. On April 11, the *London Evening Standard* reported: "Mac is Sacked." Most major American newspapers supported the decision; so did Europeans, much assured that the dreaded wider war would not erupt.

The American public did not agree. Douglas MacArthur was a celebrated military hero from World War I and World War II; he had presided effectively over Japan's postwar occupation; and he had devised and executed the "miracle" at Inchon. He was a brilliant and fabled commander, and at a time when the United States feared that it was losing the initiative in the Cold War, he wanted to take on the Communist threat in a decisive contest. According to a Gallup Poll, 69 percent of the country backed MacArthur, while Truman's popularity reached an all-time low, around 26 percent. After

MacArthur's dismissal, Truman was booed while throwing out the opening pitch at a baseball game.

On Thursday, April 19, one day after the signing of the Schuman Treaty, Douglas MacArthur walked down the aisle of the House of Representatives chamber to address the U.S. Congress. During his thirty-four-minute speech, MacArthur, in full theatric splendor, held the chamber rapt. The address was interrupted thirty times by wild ovation. With a record 30 million Americans watching on television, it was clear that General MacArthur would not simply fade away. As he left the building to applause, some members were overwhelmed to the point of hysteria. Men were crying. Republican Congressman Dewey Short of Missouri said: "We heard God speak here today, God in the flesh, the voice of God!"

As MacArthur basked in some of the most dramatic ticker-tape parades in American history, the Truman administration prepared for congressional testimony on MacArthur's dismissal and on its foreign policy strategy, which was to begin that May. Acheson, Marshall and Omar Bradley, now chairman of the Joint Chiefs of Staff, who testified that MacArthur's widening of the war would "involve us in the wrong war, at the wrong place, at the wrong time, and with the wrong enemy," proved convincing. Talk of impeachment and treason quieted down. But it did little to help the administration's standing with the American public. It also inspired McCarthy and other Republican opponents to escalated heights of attack.

On June 14, 1951, Senator Joseph McCarthy stood on the Senate floor and began a lengthy address. The published version of the speech would be titled "America's Retreat from Victory: The Story of George Catlett Marshall." Beforehand, McCarthy had promoted the address with the media and encouraged fellow senators to attend. In the three-hour speech, McCarthy blamed George Marshall for everything from Pearl Harbor, to appeasing Stalin at Yalta and Potsdam, to ceding China to Mao and his Communist forces, to abiding disloyal Communists in the State Department and the high echelons of government. Marshall had "helped produce" the Korean War. Marshall refused to take the fight to Communists in Asia, as MacArthur had sought to do, and now he had helped orchestrate MacArthur's removal, espousing "a foreign policy in the Far East of craven appeasement." Marshall's "mysterious" and dark hand had been present in all these turns, accounting for America's defeat by the Communists during the preceding "twenty years of treason."

Many of his supporters had warned McCarthy not to take on Marshall. It was going too far, they cautioned. But "the complete, sinister, treacherous, traitorous picture" must be unveiled once and for all, and the way McCarthy calculated it, he was the man to do it. "If Marshall were merely stupid, the laws of probability would have dictated that at least some of his decisions would have served this country's interests." But the United States was in the midst of a precipitous six-year decline in relation to the Soviet Union, "a fall into disaster." "How can we account for our present situation unless we believe that men high in this government are concerting to deliver us to disaster? This must be the product of a great conspiracy, a conspiracy so immense and an infamy so black as to dwarf any previous such instance in the history of man." And George Marshall, "this grim and solitary man," had been at the helm all along.

Appropriating the oldest criticisms, McCarthy suggested that the Marshall Plan had done little more than prop up socialists and Communists throughout Europe, draining America of taxpayer funds and diverting the country's resources and energies from fighting the Communists in Asia and elsewhere. The Marshall Plan, this "massive and unrewarding boondoggle," had turned the United States into "the patsy of the modern world." McCarthy had, in fact, voted for it.

McCarthy would later concede that he did not write much of the address (it contained classic and scholarly allusions). In his study on McCarthyism, historian Ted Morgan wrote that "McCarthy's discussion of the Marshall Plan was particularly ludicrous." By the time he concluded the harangue, what Truman biographer David McCullough called "his most vile yet," only two senators remained in the chamber. Reaction from the press was swift. McCarthy's home newspapers, the *Milwaukee Journal* and *Madison Capital Times*, lambasted the "berserk eruption," his "new outburst of misstatements, misquotations, and vilification," and his "sickening show of demagogic smear attacks." Dean Acheson called it "one of the most disgraceful plots in American history." Republican Senator Margaret Chase Smith used the occasion to reintroduce her Declaration of Conscience, a rebuke to McCarthy and his allies in the Senate for their conduct. Both Harry Truman and Dwight Eisenhower were furious. In the wake of the speech it seemed that only George Marshall was silent. If I have to explain why I am not a traitor at this point, Marshall said of the attacks, then it would hardly be worth the trouble.

What is most remarkable about the aftermath of the attack, what Ted Morgan called McCarthy's "apex in irresponsibility," is how few members of Congress took the fight to the senator. Republicans viewed anti-Communism as the key issue to discredit the Democrats and lead the way to reclaiming the White House after twenty years in the political wilderness. McCarthy was a willing and skillful front man, and he was an energizing political force. Anti-Communist hysteria had reached such a peak in 1951 that even the vast majority of Democrats were reluctant to confront McCarthy for fear of finding themselves a new target for a hunter unbound by scruples or regard for truth. Senator Lyndon Johnson told trusted friends: "Joe McCarthy's just a loudmouthed drunk . . . But he's riding high now, he's got people scared to death some Communist will strangle 'em in their sleep, and anybody who takes him on before the fevers cool—well, you don't get in a pissing contest with a polecat."

McCarthy's rants, it turned out, carried across the Atlantic Ocean. The summer of 1951 was an acutely difficult time for the Marshall Plan countries. Relieved by MacArthur's dismissal, Western Europe's leaders still worried about events in Korea and the Pacific. They worried about the Soviet Union. Western Europe was attuned to and deeply distraught over McCarthy, the wave of anti-Communist hysteria, and the possible implications for American foreign policy and transatlantic relations. The wife of a young American diplomat living in Paris at this time wrote that "the poison blows across the Atlantic like some horrible prevailing wind."

Western Europe was also extremely anxious about the pressure the United States was exerting on its allies to remilitarize. The great concern was that the buildup would create inflationary pressures and reverse the progress realized in narrowing the Dollar Gap. Through the end of 1950, though, Western Europe continued making steady gains. An OEEC report at the end of 1950 stated: "Whatever new problems the future may hold, there can be no question that a comparison between the economic position of member countries in 1947 and that in 1950 shows a remarkable and most encouraging contrast, almost whatever aspect is considered." The report went on: "Marshall aid was the blood transfusion which sustained the weakening European economies and gave them the strength to work their own recoveries." At the same time, ECA found, "The two and one-half years since the start of the European Recovery Program has witnessed a profound change in Western Europe—from an area disorganized by war, occupation and isolation, and dominated by a mood of helplessness, into a reasonably smoothly functioning economic and political community." Production and intra-European trade were up, the fiscal and monetary situations were stabilized, and most remarkably, Western Europe's Dollar Gap, which had reached an alarming postwar high of $8.5 billion, had now narrowed to around $1 billion.

Just as the New Year turned, so too did Western Europe's economies. Since the outbreak of war in Korea, there had been a steep spike in the demand for raw materials and other goods. Countries began stockpiling aggressively. The American economic boom and Europe's recovery were already placing intense pressures on these materials and goods. As demand skyrocketed, vast shortages developed, and prices soared. Remilitarization generated another wave of demand for materials and goods, compounding the shortages and increasing prices to even greater heights. Coal, iron ore and food were among the items most in demand and most responsible for inflation. From the outbreak of war in Korea to the end of June 1951, less than the span of a full year, cost of living increased 20 percent in France and around 10 percent in Great Britain, West Germany and Italy.

The rise in prices put pressure on workers and the lower-income groups, who had benefited least from the Marshall Plan and were still vulnerable. To quell the rise in prices, governments could tax or put controls into effect, but those measures would hit workers and lower-income groups hardest—and stoke the sort of political instability Western Europe hoped to leave behind. Governments began to notice an all-too-familiar development: as the cost of imports climbed, Western Europe's reserves were draining, and the Dollar Gap was returning. By the end of June 1951, the Dollar Gap was averaging around $650 million per month, the highest level since 1947. In May 1951, OEEC Secretary General Robert Marjolin again spoke out about Western Europe's condition. Whereas five months earlier OEEC had released an optimistic assessment, now Marjolin cautioned that "inflationary pressures threatened to interrupt the economic development of Europe, endangered the progress already achieved and rendered more difficult the accomplishment of [the] defense effort from which they sprung."

In France, the fallout was severe. From 1950 to 1952, as its military expenditures tripled, prices rose 40 percent, and France's trade deficit doubled. Great Britain, which had proudly exited the Marshall Plan at the end of 1950, was thrown into yet another payments crisis. Labour, ever more exhausted, reintroduced an austerity program and a round of taxes and controls in the beginning of April. Income taxes were increased 6 pence on the pound and the Labour government placed sales tax on everything from cars to radios to domestic appliances. For the first time, charges were introduced to certain sectors of Britain's National Health Service. In May, Prime Minister Clement Attlee and his team resigned, ending an era. And in September 1951, new Chancellor of the Exchequer Hugh Gaitskill traveled to Washington to request further economic aid so that Britain would not have to restrict its dollar imports or introduce additional domestic restrictions.

Only one major Western European economy was thriving: West Germany. Recovering from a payments crisis at the end of 1950, West Germany moved rapidly to increase its steel production and found itself uniquely able

"reoriented from economic assistance for recovery purposes to economic assistance for building a military shield." But for Foster, Western Europe's economies needed to move forward, needed to be strong and stable in order to hold that shield aloft. ECA had delivered in the past. The people, the processes and the know-how were all in place. To dismantle it all, in Foster's view, would impair America's ability to continue to aid Western Europe's economies at a time when it was sorely needed. He fought vigorously to save ECA.

Various figures like Acheson, Hoffman and Bissell all expressed distinct viewpoints on what to do. Exploratory committees weighed in. It was also evident that there needed to be coordination between the provision of both types of aid. Even if it survived, it was entirely unclear as to how ECA, which had been an independent agency, would be organized.

In April, it appeared as if an agreement had been reached. "Dear Mr. President," Foster cabled Truman: "the expression of confidence in the ECA, in the assignment of further responsibilities . . . is gratifying to every member of this organization. As its Administrator, I will strive to guide the organization along the lines you have directed and to continue to merit this confidence." The Defense Department would direct the provision of military aid. ECA would remain responsible for administering economic aid. And a new agency would be created to coordinate between the two.

Then in May, the Truman administration decided that ECA would fall under the aegis of the State Department, and that the secretary of state would have discretion over how aid was allocated. The new arrangement clipped ECA's independence. Foster was pleased that ECA would survive but disconsolate that it would now be effectively reduced to the status of "a country desk" at State.

When Congress opened hearings on the Foreign Aid Bill, it had just completed several weeks of highly charged joint hearings on MacArthur's dismissal. The stench of McCarthy's attack on George Marshall and the Marshall Plan still lingered. The president had scant political coin to spend to push legislation through an increasingly rabid Congress. It was against that backdrop that the administration presented its $8.6 billion request for military and economic aid (for Europe and other regions). Of that, $2.5 billion was for economic aid.

With the hearings about to begin, in late June 1951, Acheson telephoned Foster to discuss strategy. He advised Foster that he should not fight to prevent ECA from being wound up. Foster agreed that it was important that he, as administrator, remain relatively neutral, but he also thought it important that the secretary come out in favor of ECA's continuance. Acheson expressed reluctance. That would be "the surest way of bringing [Congress] to end it," he told Foster. Foster saw the secretary's point and replied that he "was quite certain that was true."

To increase its chances with Congress, the administration dropped the term "economic cooperation," which it had used in the past as a label for foreign economic aid, and replaced it with "mutual security." It would make little difference. It was clear from the outset that the Republicans were loaded for bear. Democrats on Capitol Hill did not put up much of a fight to stop them. Watching the assault on the Marshall Plan from the White House, and the Democrats' feeble defense on the Hill, Harry Truman even wondered if maybe it wasn't a bad thing for Democrats to be out of power for a little while.

The congressional debates continued through July and August. The administration backed Foster, championed ECA's survival and fought for as much economic aid as it could obtain. In July, Acheson, under pressure, stated that "if essential, the name and functions of ECA could be changed," but that the committee would do a disservice to interrupt an effective going concern. Richard Bissell gave an address extolling the importance of economic assistance to rearmament.

In early August, Acheson wrote to Democratic Representative James Richards of South Carolina, chairman of the House Committee on Foreign Affairs, admonishing Congress not to slash the economic aid request: "this reduction would seriously affect our efforts to build military strength in Europe." Economic aid, Acheson insisted, had "a multiplying effect," so that the aid coupled with European manpower, materials and facilities "had resulted in increased output many times in excess" of the aid provided. The increase accounted for the Europeans' ability to "carry the significant burdens of rearmament that have already been undertaken," and it was essential that it be continued as the United States asked for more from its allies.

Truman lent his full support to the effort to save ECA and the Marshall Plan. He told his Cabinet that he would fight congressional "sabotage" of the Plan. However, Truman, Acheson, Foster and Bissell were fighting a losing battle. In late September, the House and Senate conferees reached agreement. Congress would meet the administration's request for military aid but slash the $2.5 billion request for economic aid by $1 billion, leaving around $1.5 billion for economic aid to Western Europe. The legislation created a new independent agency, the Mutual Security Agency, or MSA, which was to administer and coordinate all U.S. foreign aid—military and economic. Some of ECA was to remain, but it was to be moved under MSA.

William Foster resigned as the agency's administrator. His replacement was Richard Bissell, the man who had helped design the ERP, the technical mastermind behind so much of ECA's most effective and innovative thinking and policy work. It seemed fitting that Bissell should know what it would feel like to be at the helm of the Marshall Plan. As he assumed those reins, though, it seemed to the new administrator that "power was [now] simply slipping away."

On October 10, 1951, President Truman signed the Mutual Security Act of 1951. Under the legislation, the administration was to appoint a director for the Mutual Security Agency, and the MSA would commence operations no later than sixty days after the new director was named. Harry Truman asked Averell Harriman to lead it. Harriman agreed and was confirmed by the Senate days later. At the same time, Dean Acheson wrote to the chairman of the House Appropriations Committee in an attempt to stave off further cuts to economic aid in the appropriations process. "The economic aid we furnish in support of [Europe's] military effort is estimated by ECA to produce on the average at least $3 of military results for each $1 of aid."

In April 1948, when the ERP was passed, Congress had authorized a commitment of up to $17 billion to execute the Marshall Plan. At the end of 1951, ECA had administered approximately $13 billion. Originally, the European Recovery Program was scheduled to terminate on June 30, 1952. The Korean War and the political climate accelerated that terminal date. As he closed the doors at ECA on December 31, 1951—six months ahead of schedule—it also seemed to Richard Bissell that it was "ECA's success in reviving Europe that had made a reduction of its activities possible in the first place." To Robert Lovett, Marshall's copilot in the Plan's early days, the Marshall Plan "was a government program that stayed within its original cost estimates, and when it had outlived its usefulness, it ended."

Many of ECA's officials would stay on to work for their former boss, now Mutual Security Agency Director Averell Harriman. Bissell resigned early in 1952. The United States would continue to send economic aid to Europe for the next several years. But the Marshall Plan had ended.

On December 30, 1951, ECA released a closing statement to the press: "The American people tomorrow close the books on the most daring and constructive venture in peacetime international relations the world has ever seen: The Marshall Plan . . . It comes to an end tomorrow, along with the ECA, the agency which built a fact out of a plan . . . Never in human history has so much been spent by so few with such great results."

EPILOGUE

DECEMBER 31, 1951.

When the doors shut on the agency that he had helped to build, Paul Hoffman was preoccupied with two goals. The first was recruiting Dwight Eisenhower to run for president in 1952. Early that December, Hoffman had written to Eisenhower: "Whether you like it or not, you have to face the fact that you are the one and only man today who can (1) redeem the Republican party, (2) change the atmosphere of the United States from one impregnated with fear and hate to one in which there will be good will and confidence, and (3) start the world down the road to peace." Hoffman's regard for Eisenhower was returned in kind. Months earlier, after a visit from Hoffman, and with the election in mind, Eisenhower wrote to Hoffman that he was the one who should seek the Republican nomination: "If you would only get into this particular ring, you can be sure of at least one man in the front row cheering you on—I would even carry the water bottle." Ike recorded in his diary: "I'd resign to work for him." Hoffman had little interest in elected office. He was successful in recruiting Eisenhower and played a leading role behind the scenes in raising funds and getting him elected.

Hoffman had also taken a job as president of the Ford Foundation. It was a chance to harness private capital to continue what he believed was the central aim of the Marshall Plan: advancing democracy, free enterprise and global prosperity "by eradicating the social and political and economic conditions on which Communism thrives." After his time at Ford, Hoffman was recruited to start a new program at the United Nations harnessing foreign aid to boost economies and conditions in the developing world. It was called the United Nations Development Program, or UNDP. Hoffman led the program for thirteen years. Reflecting on his career in service, *Fortune* magazine dubbed him "the father of foreign aid."

Paul Hoffman had understood that the Plan's success would hinge on the quality of the people executing it. He sought to bring on the most outstanding, the most experienced and talented people from a wide cross section of American life: academia, media, labor and, most importantly, business. Milton Katz said years later that people tend to think that the success of the Marshall Plan "was due to some special luck or a concatenation of circumstances of the time. I don't think so. I think it was due [in large part] to the special quality of the personnel from top to bottom who manned the Marshall Plan organization when it was in force."

Hoffman further understood that—whether in recruiting top talent, in harnessing their best efforts or in selling the Plan to a skeptical Congress and the American people—the force of the Plan resided in the nobility of its purpose and mission. The Marshall Plan was conceived of in U.S. strategic interests; but those interests were pursued with a policy that reflected the best in America's national ideals: freedom, generosity, humility, partnership and service. The Marshall Plan offered those who worked on it, or those who supported it, the opportunity to be a part of something transcendent.

AFTER CLOSING DOWN ECA and walking out of the Miatico Building for the last time, Richard Bissell joined Hoffman—and Milton Katz—at the Ford Foundation. He found, though, that he was not able to have the same sort of impact at Ford. He grew disconsolate and took his friend Frank Wisner up on an offer to join what seemed a more dynamic organization: the Central Intelligence Agency. During the Kennedy administration, Bissell was a key champion of both the CIA's enlistment of the Mafia to assassinate Fidel Castro, as well as the failed Bay of Pigs invasion of Cuba. It is for these debacles that history would record Richard Bissell's place most prominently.

Bissell's indispensable contribution as the technical and policy genius behind much of the Marshall Plan has been less noted. Bissell helped to pioneer essential technical features. The most notable of these was counterpart funds. "I can say flatly," Hoffman wrote in 1951, "that it made the difference between the success and failure for the Marshall Plan in every nation that had a shaky government, and it helped mightily with those that had strong ones. It was, I believe, the indispensable idea—the essential catalyst."

Richard Bissell also pioneered the idea that aid was not an end in itself. The disbursal of aid would not deliver Western Europe to economic self-sustainability. Instead, Bissell viewed aid as a component of, and lever for, larger policies and reforms. Bissell's thinking helped drive ECA to promote fiscal and monetary stability and productivity; currency devaluation and a European Payments Union; far-reaching structural economic reform—nothing short of Western European economic integration. The Marshall Plan took aim at lofty, transformative objectives, and Bissell ensured that ECA offered a cogent strategic vision, and underlying policies, to meet the challenge.

WEEKS AFTER ECA SHUT DOWN, merging into the newly created Mutual Security Agency, which he now directed, Averell Harriman was flying with Truman aide George Elsey on a small military plane. "The 1952 Democratic nomination will be wide open," Harriman said. "I'm going for it." Harriman had the presidential bug. But he did not get the nomination. Two years later, in 1954, he won his only elected office, becoming governor of New York. Four years later he lost his reelection bid to Nelson Rockefeller. As the elder statesman of the Democratic Party, Harriman held a number of diplomatic positions in the Kennedy-Johnson administrations. He represented the United States at the Vietnam peace talks in Paris and served as ambassador-at-large for much of that eight-year period. When Averell Harriman died in 1986 at the age of ninety-four, it marked the end of one of the most productive and protean lives in twentieth-century America. John F. Kennedy had called him "a separate sovereignty."

In the waning days of the Marshall Plan, Paul Hoffman expressed some frustration: "people still think of it as a great charity," he lamented. Averell Harriman had made it clear that it was no such thing. The Harriman Committee report made it plain that while humanitarian interests were at stake, the Marshall Plan was a strategic enterprise. Its overriding purpose was to bring political and economic stability to Western Europe, to ensure that the region remained in the United States orbit and impervious to indigenous Communist takeover or outright Soviet domination. America would benefit from a thriving Western European export market, and so economic interests were part of the calculation as well.

The Marshall Plan's genesis and continued support, however, also depended on congressional support, which in turn rested upon popular support. Insofar as the bulk of Americans viewed the Marshall Plan as a work of charity, then altruism was in fact an animating motivation. Ultimately, then, the Marshall Plan was designed to advance U.S. strategic interests, and was undergirded by a popular sense of altruism.

As U.S. special representative in Europe, Harriman's guiding operational principle was European self-help. Recipient countries continued to pursue their national self-interest in the CEEC, OEEC and in negotiating the disbursal of counterpart funds with the ECA missions. At times, recipient countries' national policies clashed with U.S. objectives. The U.S. pressed, it cajoled; sometimes it succeeded, often it was overruled. But to Harriman and Hoffman, ultimately, it was Western Europe's recovery, and the United States was there to offer "friendly aid," a hand in partnership. They were adamant about that. It was a delicate tightrope to walk, but the principle was that for European recovery to work, Europe had to own it, it had to reclaim command of its destiny. It proved one of the keys to the Plan's success.

NINE MONTHS BEFORE the Marshall Plan met its end, on March 9, 1951, the British Foreign Office paused from its daily business to celebrate Ernest Bevin's seventieth birthday. Bevin was beloved and his colleagues were particularly pleased to have a reason to celebrate their captain. The orphan turned laborer turned union leader turned world statesman had been ill for some time and had spent more of the preceding year in bed than at the helm of the Foreign Office. Around this time, Clement Attlee called to tell Bevin that with his declining health, the time had finally come for a change at the office. "I've got the sack," he told his wife. An official present said that Bevin was "the only person I have seen with a broken heart." Little more than a month later, on April 14, Bevin's heart gave out for good. Bevin had called himself "a turn-up in a million." At Bevin's funeral, Winston Churchill said that he was "one of the greatest foreign secretaries that has ever been called upon to discharge his duties." His tombstone read, simply: "Ernest Bevin / 1881–1951 / Statesman."

Bevin's contribution to the Marshall Plan—and NATO, the Berlin Airlift and to holding the Anglo-American relationship together—speaks to the role of Western Europe and its statesmen in the Marshall Plan. They designed their own national plans for recovery; they fended off political violence, sabotage and the potential for outright insurrection and external invasion; they held strained governing coalitions together; they helped convince their citizenry—so soon after a nearly cataclysmic fratricide—not to relinquish the capacity to face their future with hope and confidence. They were foreign ministers, finance ministers, statesmen—men of vision and ability—who harnessed Europe's potential and seized upon the Marshall Plan and their partnership with America to forge a new Europe, integrated, peaceful and prosperous.

• • •

BY APRIL 1951, Arthur Vandenberg also had been ill for some time. It had been almost a year since his last speech on the Senate floor. Suffering from cancer, the senator was not to return to Washington. At around nine o'clock on April 18—the same day that the Schuman Treaty was signed, on the eve of MacArthur's speech to the House and four days after Ernest Bevin passed away—Arthur Hendrick Vandenberg passed away at his home on Morris Avenue in Grand Rapids, Michigan.

Vandenberg's intellectual and emotional journey from isolationism to internationalism was emblematic of the larger American journey that he so ably helped to steward. Pearl Harbor had catalyzed the nation's acknowledgment that the Atlantic and Pacific were no longer moats and that America's power, reach and interests demanded international engagement and leadership. The Marshall Plan constituted the substantive leap, the actual policy through which the United States put its resources, its energies and its security behind a vast international commitment—launching America forward in its postwar incarnation as a modern superpower.

The Plan required congressional passage, and in a Republican-controlled Congress it would have been impossible without bipartisan collaboration. More than any other figure, Vandenberg made possible one of the extraordinary periods of bipartisan collaboration in the history of American foreign policy. Vandenberg ushered the Plan through Congress and saved it from evisceration in the appropriations process time and again. Paul Hoffman never forgot his debt to the man who proposed and championed his appointment. Hoffman described the late senator as "the most perfect example of democratic leadership I've ever known." He dedicated his 1951 book *Peace Can Be Won*, "To Arthur H. Vandenberg, Senator from Michigan, whose words and works for peace will always be an inspiration to those who love peace."

AS THE MARSHALL PLAN came to an end, Will Clayton was home in Houston. One year after Will retired in 1948, Sue divorced him. Two months later he proposed again. She accepted. They remarried, and he promised to stay out of public life and devote himself to her—which he did, dutifully, for the rest of her life. When Sue passed away in 1960, eccentric to the end, she bequeathed half of her $2 million estate to the U.S. government, to pay off the national debt. Occasionally, Democratic presidents like John F. Kennedy called on Clayton, an éminence grise, to provide counsel on important international economic matters. For the most part, he spent his time with his business interests, civic work and his family in Houston. In

1966, at the age of eighty-six, Clayton laid down on his sofa after a walk with his daughter and passed away.

More than any other man, Will Clayton was the intellectual architect of the Marshall Plan. Influenced by the lessons of the 1930s and World War II, Clayton was convinced that free trade and an open international economic system were the pathways toward durable peace and prosperity for all. Above all, he feared a return to the sort of economic protectionism and autarky that had helped lead to World War II. Clayton and his subordinates made the most fecund contributions to the Plan's genesis; his memos and testimonials constituted the most compelling internal advocacy at State and helped galvanize Marshall.

Clayton, who knew Europe so well, who loved Europe, dreamed of prosperity for the continent. He would live to see Western Europe's economies eclipse the experts' expectations. From 1947 to 1951, the Marshall Plan countries' aggregate gross national products grew from $120 billion to almost $160 billion. By the end of the Plan, Western European industrial production was 35 percent higher than the prewar level, exceeding the lofty goal Hoffman had set at the Plan's start. In June 1950, before the outbreak of war in Korea, Western Europe had made extraordinary strides in fiscal and monetary stability, in removing trade and payments barriers and in decreasing its Dollar Gap by several multiples.

Western Europe grappled with reemerging economic challenges during 1951 and 1952. In a sense, these pressures provided a test to the Marshall Plan and its impact: had production reached a sufficient level; had productivity picked up enough steam; was there adequate fiscal and monetary stability; was confidence high enough; and was Western Europe sufficiently integrated—had the Marshall Plan helped bring Western Europe to a point where it could weather the storm?

As if to answer, in 1953 the *Economist* heralded "the remarkable, and now complete, recovery of Western Europe from Hitler's war." By 1953, and certainly by 1954, Western Europe's industrial expansion resumed its prolific climb; productivity was accelerating dramatically, and, perhaps most importantly, Western Europe sealed the Dollar Gap for the first time since the war. Acknowledging Western Europe's recovery in 1953, the United Nations' Economic Commission on Europe published a survey that year of postwar Europe and found that "this prolonged boom is seen to have been carried on waves of successive external stimuli which enabled the expansion to continue each time it was threatened." When in March 1955, the OEEC published a comprehensive study, it reported that "member countries have completed—indeed exceeded—the economic recovery which, when the

Marshall Plan began, was no more than a hope and, according to the first report of the OEEC (1948), a doubtful hope at that."

The inflation and payments problems of 1951 and 1952 revealed themselves to be temporary dislocations due to extraordinary geopolitical circumstances. U.S. military aid—and marginal amounts of economic aid—continued. But by 1953–54, if not June 1950, recovery was complete. Western Europe's economic foundation had been firmly and ably constructed. On it rose the most remarkable, prolonged economic boom in European history. Great Britain called it the "postwar miracle"; in Italy it was the economic "*miracolo*"; France celebrated thirty years of growth, "*les trentes glorieuses*"; and for West Germany—which was prostrate at war's end and would become Europe's largest and most thriving economy little more than a decade later—it was nothing short of *Wirtschaftswunder*, a real economic miracle.

In France, Georges Bidault believed: "American aid prevented the French economy from coming to a standstill. There has never been a finer, more far-sighted gesture in history than the Marshall Plan." Franz Blucher, vice chancellor in West Germany, stated: "The Marshall Plan was the first fact by which Germany was re-introduced into the family of nations . . . Without the Marshall Plan we wouldn't have been able to recover." In Great Britain, Ernest Bevin let it be known to the House of Commons in 1948 that "the fact was that the UK could not see its way through its economic difficulties alone."

Whether Western Europe's 1947 economic maladies were simply temporary dislocations that could have been redressed with self-adjustment and continued growth constitutes an unverifiable counterfactual. What mattered most was that Western Europe's leaders did not believe that they had the luxury of waiting to find out; nor did they have the strength to make those adjustments without American support.

When the multiplier effect, the double duty effect from counterpart funds and the greater value that inhered in technical assistance transfers are all taken into account, the Plan's contribution, even in strictly economic terms, must be considered more than "marginal" or even a "vital margin." The Marshall Plan provided essential goods and capital that helped to power Europe's economy, its industrial modernization and helped to launch the boom to come.

The Plan's impact on Western Europe's economy, though, cannot be measured in strictly economic terms. The Marshall Plan was meant not only to take aim at Western Europe's Balance of Payments Crisis, but another debilitating ailment: a Crisis of Confidence.

The Europeans who carried their recovery forward were not inputs or statistics in an economic model. They were people, and on the whole a deeply beleaguered, dispirited people. By and large they felt vulnerable, insecure and lacked confidence in their future. Without the U.S. commitment tendered in the Marshall Plan, the imposition of even more draconian controls and sacrifices while they grappled with the internal Communist threat, political violence and the external Soviet threat, would have fueled further desperation, insecurity and pessimism. It is possible that the Plan's most substantial contribution to Western Europe was intangible: the confidence that came with knowing that the region would not have to undergo further strident controls; that it would not be threatened with bankruptcy; that it would not descend once again into economic nationalism or even autarky; that it would not starve or freeze; that it would not be threatened with hyperinflation. The world's largest economy now stood with Western Europe and hitched its security and, in large part, its destiny to Europe's recovery and security.

The psychological boost was electric and reverberated through every facet of European life. Western Europe's recovery rested primarily in the hands of Europe's leaders and its people. To affect that recovery, they would have to invest, work, save and trade. To do those things, they had to feel confident that there was a point to all of it: that their countries would remain unoccupied, that their sons would not be sent to war, that their families would not starve.

Leading economists seem to agree that Western Europe's extraordinary postwar economic boom was due primarily to a combination of European integration and an extraordinary rise in fertility on the continent during those years. The Marshall Plan's contribution to European integration is a large part of the story told here. Regarding the rise in European fertility, historian Tony Judt wrote: "There are many explanations . . . but most of them reduce to a combination of optimism plus free milk." The Marshall Plan provided the latter for some time. It also helped Western Europe's governments to keep their welfare states intact and viable, so that they could provide "free milk"—and other social services—long past the Marshall Plan's termination. Perhaps the Plan's most lasting contribution, though, to Western Europe's economic boom was to provide confidence. During one of Western Europe's darkest and most desperate periods, the Marshall Plan delivered hope, it delivered reason for Western Europeans to envision a world into which they would want to bring children.

• • •

As 1951 CLOSED, Jean Monnet was hard at work setting up the machinery for the European Coal and Steel Community. The man who decided not to go into politics because he did not believe he was a good orator had fathered one of the most important political ideas in European history. European integration was a prominent, and eventually the paramount, priority for the Marshall Plan. Assessing the Marshall Plan's contribution to that end in 1951, Paul Hoffman wrote: "Obviously, the greatest single contribution the ECA could make to Europe's enduring prosperity was to help it toward economic integration. I wish I could say that this has been done, that as a result of ECA activities all sections of the European economy have been welded into a single market as unencumbered by trade impediments as our own American market. Unfortunately that is not true." As the Marshall Plan ended, it was not true. And, it was a disappointment to some of those in Congress and at ECA who had pushed Europe to that end. But in the decades to follow Europe would realize that vision. The Treaty of Rome and eventually the Maastricht Treaty in 1992 gave birth to the European Union and fulfilled the Marshall Plan's vision for a united European economy.

It is highly possible that without the Plan, Western Europe would have consigned itself to the same pattern of economic nationalism and autarky that had produced economic depression and conflict in the 1930s. "There was a real danger, indeed," wrote Jean Monnet, that France might have sought refuge "behind a protectionist shield. This, after all, had been a national tradition." Historian Geir Lundestad agreed that "without the American role and the Atlantic framework, it is more likely that history would have repeated itself, in the sense that the traditional rivalry among Western European states, especially between Germany and France, would have continued. Integration was something dramatically new in European history."

On the twentieth anniversary of the Marshall Plan, the Belgian ambassador to the OECD, Roger Ockrent, said that "the Marshall Plan did not only save us from evil, but laid the cornerstone upon which has been built the whole apparatus of modern international economic cooperation." Ockrent could even identify the starting point. "I am convinced," he said, "that the refusal of the United States government to deal bilaterally with each European country was the decisive fact which translated the Marshall idea into facts by forcing national interests to merge in a wider common interest. This is . . . the point at which the trend towards the unification of Europe started."

The Marshall Plan did not complete Europe's evolutionary path toward union. But it started it. The Plan reversed Europe's probable slide toward economic nationalism, and possibly autarky. More than that, it created the machinery and institutions that first gave European integration substance. Western Europe's states remained guided by their national self-interest and the CEEC and the OEEC were rife with division and acrimony. But as member-states hashed out their differences and labored on common problems in shared fora, habits of cooperation and a "spirit of integration" emerged. They achieved tangible progress: the division of Marshall aid, preliminary payments agreements and dramatic intra-European trade liberalization. These hard-earned accomplishments reaped economic gain, and they reinforced the merits of cooperation and confidence that integration on a grander scale was possible.

European leadership and courage forged the EPU, the Schuman Plan and Europe's subsequent path toward union. But it was a path that could not have been forged without the Marshall Plan and American partnership. European unification was, according to Henry Kissinger, perhaps the most revolutionary phenomenon of the postwar period. On the fiftieth anniversary of the Marshall Plan, in 1997, Germany's Chancellor Helmut Schmidt reminded America: "The United States ought not to forget that the emerging European Union is one of its own greatest achievements: it would never have happened without the Marshall Plan."

As ECA DISSOLVED into the Mutual Security Agency, Josef Stalin could take delight in the shifting geopolitical landscape. The Marshall Plan, the revival of West Germany, the Berlin Airlift, NATO, the Schuman Plan were all tremendous defeats for Stalin, whose designs for broader continental reach had been decisively contained behind an iron curtain dividing eastern from western Europe. Now, though, American lives, treasure and prestige were all being drained in the Asian theater, where Stalin had reaped greater success.

The Marshall Plan seemed not to have swayed the Soviet dictator's core beliefs. As late as 1952, with the Marshall Plan, NATO and French-German rapprochement realized, Stalin insisted, "The inevitability of wars between capitalist countries remains in force." The Marshall Plan was a response to Stalin, his policies, his temporizing and the Soviet threat in Eurasia. It is difficult to pinpoint one date on which the Cold War began. But the day in July 1947 when Molotov and his ninety-person delegation departed from Paris and participation in the Marshall Plan, intent on taking their eastern and central European satellites with them, is as good as any. For Stalin, whose most desperate fear was capitalist encirclement, the Marshall Plan and U.S.–Western European partnership was a nightmare realized.

On March 5, 1953, Josef Stalin died. The only one to eulogize comrade Stalin was his trusted acolyte of more than three decades, Vyacheslav Molotov, who also appeared to be the only one genuinely aggrieved by his death. In 1975, in a presumed moment of reflective candor, Molotov expounded on his job description as foreign minister to Stalin: "I saw my task . . . as being how to expand as much as possible the boundaries of the Fatherland. And it seems to me that me and Stalin did not cope badly with this task." The Soviet dictator did have a long-term expansionary vision.

Stalin did not seek confrontation with the United States in the near term, though. He wanted near-term accommodation, even cooperation with America. Yet, Stalin's penchant for opportunistic expansion, his intransigent negotiating position and his temporizing as Western Europe slid into calamity—all of these factors suggested to Marshall and the Americans that whatever Stalin's intentions, his actions were creating conditions in Europe that imperiled America's most vital strategic objectives.

During the Moscow Foreign Minister's Conference in March and April 1947, Stalin's strategy was simple: delay, do nothing and reap the concessions and strategic advantages. Western Europe was weak, vulnerable and deteriorating rapidly. The Western European Communist parties were well organized and ever-attuned to political opportunity, willing to sabotage and stir violence in order to seize power. To remember the alarm—and even fatalism—among some of the French and Italian people, and some of their centrist leaders during the political violence in those countries in the autumn of 1947, and in the aftermath of the Czech coup in early 1948, is to remember that France's and Italy's political fates were not determined. It would be too strong to assert that without the Marshall Plan, Western Europe would have fallen to Communism. But it might have; it was a very real possibility.

Stalin did not expect the Marshall Plan. In a bold stroke, it brought Western Europe decisively into the United States orbit. Its aim was to help "forge a configuration of power" that would preclude the Soviet Union from dominating Eurasia. Going further, it sought to entice Stalin's satellites from the dictator's grip. Stalin would not chance the loss of his buffer states, his zone of influence. The Cominform, the purges and oppression in Eastern Europe, and the Berlin blockade can be traced to the Plan and its impact on the strategic balance in Europe. The Marshall Plan was the centerpiece of America's early postwar policy of containment. The configuration of power that it brought into alignment helped allow the United States to contain, and eventually transform, the Soviet Union, delivering the United States victory in the Cold War. The Marshall Plan must, therefore, be viewed as one of the most successful foreign policy initiatives—and perhaps the most successful peacetime foreign policy—in United States history.

The Cold War was in part a war of ideology, of competing systems and ideas. The Marshall Plan was a key weapon in that battle. Stalin's economic adviser, Yevgeny Varga, tried to warn Stalin in 1946 that capitalism had undergone reforms, even transformations. But Stalin's ideology was fixed. Capitalism was degenerate; it would fail the worker at home and abroad; capitalist powers' insatiable appetites for profit and territory would lead to conflict, war and ultimately self-destruction. Varga was on to something, though, and Stalin should have listened. As it emerged from the crucible of the 1920s reforms, the New Deal and the war, the United States offered Western Europe a refashioned brand of capitalism. At home, it was better able to provide for all of its citizens and was more responsive to the needs of the vulnerable. Internationally, it was willing to sacrifice "immediate economic gains to invest in long-term geopolitical stabilization." That meant a free, open and cooperative economic system that would exact near-term costs but yield a viable arrangement of shared prosperity and, ultimately, peace.

In the U.S. orbit, a shared prosperity proved possible. In the Soviet orbit, Russia wielded an oppressive hand and drained its satellites of political autonomy, resources and economic opportunity. During the Marshall Plan years, the United States spent $13 billion on Western European recovery. During that same period, Josef Stalin extracted almost an identical amount from his Eastern European zone. Perhaps nothing better symbolizes the difference between the United States and the Soviet Union and the management of their zones of influence. And it was part of the reason why the United States won the Cold War.

THREE MONTHS BEFORE the European Cooperation Administration closed its doors, George Catlett Marshall stepped down as secretary of defense, retiring once and for all. A year later, campaigning in Wisconsin for the presidency, Dwight Eisenhower wanted to take advantage of the occasion in McCarthy's home state to refute the senator's charges about Marshall. Marshall was responsible for Eisenhower's advancement during World War II and ceded him command of Overlord, the war's most remembered invasion—and the resulting fame upon which he would ride into the White House. Ike had said of Marshall that he wouldn't trade fifty Douglas

MacArthurs for one George Marshall. On second thought, he said, that would be a rotten trade. What would one do with fifty MacArthurs?

Some of his political aides thought it bad politics for Ike to show up McCarthy in his home state. Eisenhower consented to withdraw the comments in defense of Marshall. The press had received an earlier copy, which included the comments, and so when Eisenhower did not deliver them, they knew that it was a calculated omission. Ike was also photographed shaking hands with McCarthy. The press lambasted Eisenhower. "Do I need to tell you that I am sick at heart?" *New York Times* publisher Arthur Hays Sulzberger cabled to an Eisenhower aide. Truman said that Eisenhower had surrendered to a "moral scoundrel" and that he was not fit to be trusted with controlling the bomb. Once again, it seemed that about the only public figure who did not offer a reaction was George Marshall. Ike expressed profound contrition in later years; it was one of the biggest regrets of his life.

It has been suggested by some historians that George Marshall was a figurehead of the Marshall Plan. Such portrayals are inaccurate. It was Marshall who took Stalin's measure at the Moscow Conference in March and April 1947 and returned resolved to bolster Western Europe against the internal and external Communist threat. He personally recruited Acheson and Kennan and trusted Clayton, and deputized them, and pushed the State Department to work toward a plan for European recovery. Heeding Clayton's call in late May, Marshall determined that the time had come for action. Without consulting Truman on his speech—the final contents of which he, and he alone, rendered final determination upon—Marshall selected the time and place for the address and presented it as an invitation to Europe.

In the month to follow, Marshall lent the full force of his energy and his prestige to the Plan to ensure its passage through Congress. Marshall labored diligently and adroitly to construct one of the most extraordinary bipartisan foreign policy collaborations in American history. He testified often and ably. Then, with the Plan's passage still in the balance, Marshall toured the country, trumpeting the strategic, economic and humanitarian need for the Plan. It would not have been possible without his vision, his will, his tactical dexterity, his collaboration with Vandenberg, his efforts with Congress and the American people—and his prestige. It was called the Marshall Plan because of political expedience. But it could not rightly have been called anything else.

Marshall had helped to lead America and the Allies in war. But victory in war did not achieve America's paramount strategic objective: prevention of the domination of the Eurasian landmass by a totalitarian power. By the time it ended in 1951, the Marshall Plan and NATO had decisively secured Western Europe in the U.S. orbit. The Cold War and the Soviet threat would remain for decades. But, Soviet domination of Eurasia was no longer a viable threat. The objective for which the war had been fought was achieved, and the Marshall Plan helped to realize it. To Senator Henry Cabot Lodge: "These achievements in war and peace justify the statement that General George Marshall stands out as the greatest American of the 20th century."

BY 1953, the general had fallen ill. In early December 1953, though, he left his sickbed in Leesburg to venture across the Atlantic Ocean one last time. On the afternoon of December 10, in Oslo, Norway, Marshall, outfitted in white tie and tails, arrived at a resplendent hall. He had come to receive the Nobel Peace Prize. He was the first—and the only—professional soldier ever to receive it. He was not receiving the honor for his role in war, the Nobel representative reading the citation said, but for his work in the cause of peace.

Later that evening at a formal dinner, Marshall addressed the international audience of diplomats, dignitaries and press. The address included reflections on a unique life of service and leadership. It was in some ways Marshall's last will and testament, his hopes for mankind: "The cost of war is constantly spread before me, written neatly in many ledgers of whose columns are gravestones. I am greatly moved," therefore, "to find some means or method of avoiding a calamity of war." He spoke of democracy and the moral power of freedom and self-respect for the individual. "These democratic principles," however, "do not flourish on empty stomachs," he said. When there is want and deprivation "people turn to false promises or dictators because they are hopeless for anything that promises something better than the miserable existence they endure."

Marshall spoke of history. He spoke of the importance of absorbing its teachings so that future generations might not make the same mistakes, so that they might do better.

Perhaps he felt that the Marshall Plan contained principles and insights that might be applicable or useful to successive generations of Americans as they endeavored to formulate policies to meet the threats and opportunities of their own times. Perhaps it is worth remembering a time when extraordinary men summoned their vast talents, wisdom and creative potential to design and execute a plan with a transcendent aim; when America's foreign policy was defined, at once, by its strategic interests and the very best of its ideals; when Americans were infused with a shared sense of mission and purpose—so much so that it roused the national spirit and elevated America's own conception about what it could accomplish, what it could be.

Much of what is best about America, its potential and its possibility was alive and in operation in the Marshall Plan. When he championed it in Congress, Arthur Vandenberg conceded that it was a big gamble. He did not know if it would succeed. There was much reason not to take the leap. But America did, embarking upon a shared national adventure; an adventure, ultimately, of the national will, spirit and imagination—the most noble adventure.

★ ★ ★ ★ ★

NOTES

THE HISTORICAL LITERATURE on the Marshall Plan is vast. There are several important single-volume studies of the Plan. However, there is no comprehensive single volume *narrative* history of the Marshall Plan; no volume that profiles the personalities and examines the main themes and currents shaping the enterprise, start to finish, in narrative form.* This book attempts to fill that gap.

There are many questions on the Plan that continue to stimulate scholarly inquiry and debate. I take up several of those questions here. I address them implicitly in the narrative, often elaborating upon my analysis and engaging the historiography more directly in the corresponding notes.

*Harry Price's *The Marshall Plan and Its Meaning*, Joseph Jones's *The Fifteen Weeks*, Charles Gimbel's *The Origins of the Marshall Plan*, Immanuel Wexler's *The Marshall Plan Revisited*, Michael Hogan's *The Marshall Plan*, Alan Milward's *Reconstruction of Western Europe* and Charles Mee's *The Marshall Plan: The Launching of the Pax Americana* are all single volumes primarily focused on the Marshall Plan. Of these, only Price, Wexler, Hogan and Milward take the reader from the Plan's inception to its completion, and as such could be said to be comprehensive in chronological scope. Of those mentioned, only Jones's and Mee's works could be called narrative histories, in the sense that they tell a story. Both Jones and Mee concentrate primarily on the origins of the Marshall Plan. Mee focuses on the actual execution of the Plan for a chapter or two. It is in this sense that I place this book as the first comprehensive narrative history of the Marshall Plan.

Abbreviations

ERP   European Recovery Program
FRUS   Foreign Relations of the United States
HST   Harry S. Truman
MP   Marshall Plan

Prologue

PAGE

1 *The bell tolled:* Jones, *The Fifteen Weeks*, pp. 30–32.
1 *The midmorning sun:* Pogue, *George C. Marshall: Statesman 1945–1959*, p. 211.
1 *first "fully normal" graduation:* Frank Kluckhohn, "As 'Cure' for Ills," *New York Times*, June 6, 1947.
1 *The war had claimed:* Most estimates are around 300,000, with some a few thousand higher. Gaddis, *The Cold War*, p. 8.
1 *one man, more than any other:* To President Harry Truman, George C. Marshall, "more than any other man, had been responsible for winning the war." He said there was not a decoration big enough for Marshall. McCullough, *Truman*, p. 472. Dean Acheson said he was "the great figure of the whole war period." Acheson, *Present at the Creation*, p. 252.
1 *As he walked past:* Jones, *The Fifteen Weeks*, pp. 30–32.
2 *The prolonged ovation:* The scene is described in many sources. Mee, *The Marshall Plan*; Pogue, *George C. Marshall*; Chace, *Acheson*; Acheson, *Present at the Creation*; and Isaacson and Thomas, *The Wise Men*.
2 *"a soldier and statesman":* Pogue, *George C. Marshall*, pp. 211, 212.
2 *It was unfitting:* McCullough, *Truman*, p. 472.
2 *He had twice turned down:* Pogue, *George C. Marshall*, p. 208.
2 *"a little more":* Pogue, *George C. Marshall*, p. 210.
2 *The content of those remarks:* E-mail message from Larry Bland, of the Marshall Library, to author, February 5, 2007.
2 *No one had seen:* In his memoirs, *Witness to History*, Charles Bohlen writes that he was charged with drafting the Marshall Plan speech. Subsequent histories subscribe to his account. The best and most likely account is in Pogue's *George C. Marshall*, pp. 210, 211. Pogue writes that Marshall solicited drafts both from Bohlen, then a senior State Department aide (who himself relied on papers prepared by both Undersecretary of State for Economic Affairs Will Clayton and State Department head of the Policy Planning Staff George Kennan) and George Kennan. Marshall told Pogue that he synthesized both drafts, disparate in tone and structure, if not substance, into his own language. Marshall later worked on the speech on the plane ride to Cambridge and the evening before his delivery. Clayton, Kennan and Bohlen emerge as important contributors. Marshall himself, contrary to popular depiction, deserves authorship.
2 *not even the commander in chief:* It is often intimated that Truman was privy to contents of Marshall's speech. He was certainly posted on the work developing at the State Department. However, in a revealing interview between Forrest Pogue and Marshall, Marshall asked Pogue to stop the recorder. Marshall then said, "I made the speech without telling the President. The speech was not finished when I left for Washington, so I worked with it on the plane and then at Conant's house. I realized just before making the speech that he hadn't seen it. Of course, he knew what we were doing and we were thinking along the same lines." Bland, ed., *George C. Marshall*, p. 559. It is remarkable, and very much a reflection of the trust and esteem in which Truman held Marshall, that an address of such significance would be made without the president's final approval.

2   *The speech was delivered*: Pogue, *George C. Marshall*, p. 212.
2   *the press conferences helped*: "Sometimes he would invite forty or fifty correspondents into his office, listen to a long series of questions from them, and then, without notes, deliver a half-hour monologue in which he answered each question in turn (facing the correspondent directly as he answered that correspondent's question) and at the same time wove all the answers into an overall coherent picture." Morrow, *The Best Years of Their Lives*, p. 137.
3   *"disappointed as a small boy"*: The account is from two of Dean Acheson's memoirs. See Acheson, *Present at the Creation*, p. 215, and Acheson, *Sketches from Life of Men I Have Known*, p. 155.
3   *as Marshall began to speak*: Payne, *The Marshall Story*, p. 299.
3   *He spoke in a soft*: Payne, *The Marshall Story*, p. 299.
3   *"as though," it was written*: McCullough, *Truman*, p. 562.
3   *"did not consider it"*: Leonard Miall, "How the Marshall Plan Started," *The Listener*, April 20, 1961. From the Marshall Plan Vertical File in the Harry S. Truman Library.
3   *"It was like a lifeline"*: The account appears in many histories of this time. For example, see Chace, *Acheson*, p. 179.
3   *"one of the greatest speeches"*: Bailey, *The Marshall Plan Summer*, p. 33.
3   *"electric effect of a few sentences"*: Price, *The Marshall Plan and Its Meaning*, pp. 63, 64.
4   *"the greatest act of statesmanship"*: Bailey, *The Marshall Plan Summer*, p. viii.
4   *"probably the most effective program"*: Leffler, "Inside Enemy Archives," p. 133.
4   *"it was one of the great"*: McCullough, *Truman*, p. 583.
4   *It has been twenty*: Here, I am alluding to Michael Hogan's landmark work *The Marshall Plan: America, Britain, and the Reconstruction of Western Europe, 1947–1952*. Hogan's book was published by Cambridge University Press in 1987. There have been scores of books and essays published on the Marshall Plan since Hogan's work: anthologies, volumes focused on Western European reconstruction, volumes focusing on a facet of the Plan, volumes taking a regional approach to gauging the Plan's impact and much more (see Bibliography). But Hogan's book was the last major single volume dedicated to a comprehensive examination of the Plan—its origins and execution, the economics and geopolitics—from its inception to its conclusion.
4   *"when the perspective of time"*: Reynolds, ed., *The Origins of the Cold War in Europe*, p. 20.
4   *approximately $13 billion*: There are a number of different ways to calculate this figure. The calculation used here includes $4.97 billion plus in excess of $1 billion for assistance on favorable credit terms for 1948–49; $3.78 billion for 1949–50; $2.31 billion for 1950–51; roughly half of the $1.02 billion provided for 1951–52 (half because the terminal date for the Marshall Plan used here is December 31, 1951); and approximately $500 million in interim aid provided in 1948 primarily to France, Italy and Austria. The interim aid is not included in the European Recovery Program, but it came after George Marshall's June 5, 1947, speech and, as argued, should be considered part of the Marshall Plan. The total is $13.16 billion. Any number of methodologies might justifiably be used to suggest a figure in the $12–14 billion range. Figures from Price, *The Marshall Plan and Its Meaning*, p. 162.
4   *In today's dollars*: See data from http://www.bls.gov/cpi/; http://research.stlouisfed.org/fred2/data/GNPA.txt; Machado, *In Search of a Usable Past*, p. 140.
4   *more than the United States*: White, *Fire in the Ashes*, p. 58.
5   *it contained multitudes*: Walt Whitman, *Song of Myself*, 1855.
5   *It was a nation*: It was only in the 1890s, according to David Fromkin, that "systematic American history texts came into general use in the classroom." Fromkin, *In the Time of the Americans*, p. 18.
5   *"one of the greatest"*: Isaacson and Thomas, *The Wise Men*, p. 405.

PART ONE: THE GENESIS

One: The March to Moscow

PAGE

9 *"You are going to have"*: Minutes of an Executive Session of the Committee on Foreign Relations of the United States Senate, February 14, 1947. FRUS 47, 2, p. 168.

9 *Away for 350 out:* Chace, *Acheson*, p. 130.

9 *three hats in the morning:* Yergin, *Shattered Peace*, p. 183.

9 *"an act of God"*: Chace, *Acheson*, p. 159.

9 *"Mr. Secretary"*: Payne, *The Marshall Story*, pp. 290, 291.

10 *a collateral descendant of John Marshall:* Payne, *The Marshall Story*, pp. 6–8.

10 *"I thought the continuing harping"*: McCullough, *Truman*, p. 533.

10 *"Awed by his courage"*: The account and quote are from Payne, *The Marshall Story*, pp. 18, 19.

11 *"Keep your eyes on George"*: Payne, *The Marshall Story*, p. 37.

11 *Peacetime had returned:* Stoler, *George C. Marshall*, p. 42.

11 *Heeding Pershing's recommendation:* Chace, *Acheson*, p. 161, and Stoler, *George C. Marshall*, p. 66. This is almost the exact sentence from Chace.

11 *Eight hours before:* Stoler, *George C. Marshall*, p. 68.

11 *Marshall had inherited:* Payne, *The Marshall Story*, p. 117, and Morrow, *The Best Year of Their Lives*, p. 130.

11 *When Roosevelt answered with:* Stoler, *George C. Marshall*, p. 66.

11 *He insisted the president:* McCullough, *Truman*, pp. 533–35, and Stoler, *George C. Marshall*, pp. 73, 74.

12 *"worked there with a ruthless"*: Stoler, *George C. Marshall*, p. 86.

12 *He recalled that when:* Stoler, *George C. Marshall*, p. 110.

12 *"I cannot afford"*: Payne, *The Marshall Story*, p. 327.

12 *"it was [as] though"*: Payne, *The Marshall Story*, p. 327.

12 *He wrote thousands:* Payne, *The Marshall Story*, p. 326.

12 *On another occasion General:* Both anecdotes from Acheson, *Sketches from Life of Men I Have Known*, pp. 157, 159.

12 *As head of the U.S.:* The JCS structure did not then exist, but Marshall was the de facto chairman of the (not yet existent) Joint Chiefs of Staff.

13 *"an absurd situation"*: Ambrose, *Eisenhower*, p. 114.

13 *"I feel I could not"*: The story of FDR's ultimate selection of Eisenhower for field command of OVERLORD is from Morrow, *The Best Year of Their Lives*, pp. 130–32, and Ambrose, *Eisenhower*, p. 114.

13 *"I have never seen"*: Pogue, *George C. Marshall*, pp. 26, 27, and Payne, *The Marshall Story*, p. 240.

13 *"His mind has guided"*: Pogue, *George C. Marshall*, p. 27.

14 *"Yes, Mr. President"*: Stoler, *George C. Marshall*, p. 145.

14 *"I think I fully understand"*: Pogue, *George C. Marshall*, p. 139.

14 *"Your appointment as Secretary"*: According to David McCullough, "The appointment of Marshall was one of the best, most important decisions of Truman's presidency." McCullough, *Truman*, p. 532.

14 *"The more I see"*: McCullough, *Truman*, p. 535.

14 *"I will never become"*: Pogue, *George C. Marshall*, p. 145.

14 *"and being Marshall"*: McCullough, *Truman*, p. 533.

14 *"pushed the nomination through"*: McCullough, *Truman*, pp. 532, 533.

15 *preventing a totalitarian power:* This is a central concept in Melvyn Leffler's authoritative early Cold War history, *A Preponderance of Power*.

15 *"I can state in three"*: Isaacson and Thomas, *The Wise Men*, p. 338.

15 *Only 7 percent rated world peace:* Judt, *Postwar*, p. 109; Leffler, *A Preponderance of Power*, p. 39.

15 *"go to the movies":* Yergin, *Shattered Peace*, pp. 171, 172.

15 *By 1945, the United States:* Ikenberry, *After Victory*, p. 167; Leffler, *A Preponderance of Power*, p. 2.

15 *"to American production":* Gordon, *An Empire of Wealth*, p. 354.

15 *The U.S. Navy:* Gordon, *An Empire of Wealth*, p. 362.

15 *When, in 1944:* Reynolds, ed., *The Origins of the Cold War in Europe*, p. 7.

16 *The U.S. economy:* Ikenberry, *After Victory*, p. 167; Leffler, *A Preponderance of Power*, p. 2.

16 *Although only one-third:* Leffler, *A Preponderance of Power*, p. 2.

16 *"Not since Rome":* Jones, *The Fifteen Weeks*, p. 141.

16 *The postwar redistribution:* Schlesinger, *A Life in the Twentieth Century*, p. 405. Schlesinger makes this same point.

16 *"mutually hostile ideological visions":* Gaddis, *We Now Know*, p. 6.

16 *And none was more important:* Young, *Cold War Europe*, p. 57.

16 *born in Gori, in Georgia:* Robert Service, *Stalin*, p. 13. The author dates Stalin's birth here, though his "official" biography, published in the Soviet Union during his reign, lists his birth date as December 21, 1879.

16 *He married, and loved:* Service, *Stalin*, pp. 12–16, 21, 31, 41, 45.

16 *Around this time:* Service, *Stalin*, pp. 84, 85.

16 *European empires:* Service, *Stalin*, p. 93.

17 *"Schools, newspapers, libraries":* Service, *Stalin*, p. 308.

17 *Historians both in Russia:* Gaddis, *We Now Know*, p. 8.

17 *"industrialization and collectivization":* Service, *Stalin*, pp. 312, 318, 319.

17 *By the end of the 1930s:* In later years Nikita Khrushchev remarked: "Stalin had never gone out of his way to take other people's advice into account, but this was especially true after the war. The rest of us were just errand boys, and Stalin would snarl threateningly at anyone who overstepped the mark." Talbott, ed., *Khrushchev Remembers*, p. 361. Service wrote: "the Great Terror had elevated him to an unprecedented height above the other leaders. In all but name he was a despot." Service, *Stalin*, p. 374.

17 *Now joined in a war:* The title of a World War II book, *A War to Be Won: Fighting the Second World War*, by Williamson Murray and Alan Millett.

17 *Stalin was named:* Service, *Stalin*, pp. 452, 453.

17 *"Everything for the Front!":* Service, *Stalin*, p. 420.

17 *For much of World War II:* Morgan, *Reds*, p. 223; Fromkin, *In the Time of the Americans*, p. 468.

17 *In contrast, approximately 27 million Soviets:* Gaddis, *The Cold War*, p. 9.

18 *Historian David Fromkin:* Fromkin, *In the Time of the Americans*, p. 468.

18 *Stalin's persona emerged:* Gaddis, *We Now Know*, p. 32.

18 *especially his refusal:* Yergin, *Shattered Peace*, pp. 74, 75.

18 *Roosevelt held fast:* Roosevelt envisioned "Four Policemen"—the United States, Great Britain, China, and Russia—working in concert and within the construct of international institutions, to provide and enforce order in the postwar international system.

18 *"Averell is right":* Fromkin, *In the Time of the Americans*, p. 485.

19 *He had met with Roosevelt:* McCullough, *Truman*, p. 339.

19 *He did not know:* Isaacson and Thomas, *The Wise Men*, p. 254.

19 *"It is a terrible responsibility":* Isaacson and Thomas, *The Wise Men*, p. 279.

19 *The new president:* Kissinger, *Diplomacy*, p. 433; Yergin, *Shattered Peace*, p. 118.

19 *The Soviets would not sign:* Yergin, *Shattered Peace*, pp. 114, 118; Kissinger, *Diplomacy*, p. 434.

19 *"could not understand":* Yergin, *Shattered Peace*, p. 114.

19 *"I like Stalin":* McCullough, *Truman*, p. 451.

19 *There was nothing on record:* McCullough, *Truman*, p. 452.

19   *On a frigid winter's evening:* Rothkopf, *Running the World*, p. 45.

19   *"World War III":* Yergin, *Shattered Peace*, pp. 166, 167.

19   *Experts at State:* Leffler, *A Preponderance of Power*, p. 51.

20   *"Where does the search":* The *New York Times* editorial and its details are recounted in Isaacson and Thomas, *The Wise Men*, p. 366.

20   *"had done little else":* Isaacson and Thomas, *The Wise Men*, p. 348.

20   *"They had asked for it":* Kennan, *Memoirs*, p. 295.

20   *"I think it is now":* Yergin, *Shattered Peace*, p. 185.

21   *"from Stettin in the Baltic":* The speech was officially titled "The Sinews of Peace." McCullough, *Truman*, p. 383; Reynolds, ed., *The Origins of Cold War in Europe*, p. 80.

21   *"We might as well":* Yergin, *Shattered Peace*, pp. 234, 235.

21   *"Nothing short of complete":* Gaddis, *We Now Know*, pp. 20–24.

21   *"It would lead to the West's":* Pollard, *Economic Security and the Origins of the Cold War*, p. 35.

21   *If it was made public:* Clifford, with Holbrooke, *Special Counsel to the President*, pp. 123–28. Also see Yergin, *A Shattered Peace*, pp. 241–45.

21   *Truman could make:* Clifford promptly delivered 20 copies of the report to Truman in the Oval Office, whereupon the President took them, and no one else was to see the report from there. That is, until 20 years later. Clifford had kept a copy of the draft from which the final version of the report had been printed. He shared it with journalist Arthur Krock, and Krock reprinted the entire report as a sixty-three-page appendix in his 1968 memoir. Clifford, with Holbrooke, *Special Counsel to the President*, pp. 123, 124.

22   *"The year 1946":* Rothkopf, *Running the World*, p. 46.

22   *"a get tough attitude":* Yergin, *Shattered Peace*, p. 297.

22   *Marshall had met with Stalin:* Oral interview: Averell Harriman, HST Library Collection; Stoler, *George C. Marshall*, p. 161.

22   *"I trust Marshall":* Harriman recalled that on one occasion Stalin accused the United States of collaborating with the Polish underground. Harriman said that that would be accusing Marshall. Stalin said: "No, I do not accuse General Marshall. I trust General Marshall as I would myself." Averell Harriman speech delivered at Ceremonies Commemorating the 20th Anniversary of the Marshall Plan, Lexington, Va. (Washington, D.C.: U.S. Government Printing Office, 1967). From Marshall Plan Vertical Files, HST Library.

23   *"You who have not seen":* McCullough, *Truman*, p. 406.

23   *More than 50 percent of housing:* David Ellwood, *Rebuilding Europe*, p. 50.

23   *In London 3.5 million homes:* Judt, *Postwar*, p. 82.

23   *In Berlin, 75 percent:* Judt, *Postwar*, p. 16.

23   *Rubble—an estimated 500 million:* Donovan, *The Second Victory*, p. 11.

23   *Thousands of bridges:* Judt, *Postwar*, p. 85.

23   *Ships and merchant fleets:* Judt, *Postwar*, p. 17.

23   *According to one American:* Oral interview: Milton Katz, HST Library Collection.

23   *One historian estimated:* Judt, *Postwar*, p. 18.

23   *On V-E Day:* Hitchcock, *The Struggle for Europe*, p. 16.

23   *One historian put:* Fromkin, *In the Time of the Americans*, p. 498.

23   *More people faced starvation:* Donovan, *The Second Victory*, p. 18.

23   *According to the United Nations:* Ellwood, *Rebuilding Europe*, p. 34.

23   *"The human problem":* Fromkin, *In the Time of the Americans*, p. 498.

23   *On one occasion, the Soviets:* Bailey, *The Marshall Plan Summer*, pp. 93, 94.

24   *In April 1945:* Beevor and Cooper, *Paris*, p. 264.

24   *Singing at Le Club des Cinq:* Beevor and Cooper, *Paris*, p. 267.

24   *By the end of the war:* Judt, *Postwar*, p. 14.

24   *The immediate postwar years:* "The British Crisis," *Life*, February 24, 1947.

24   *"We are blitzed, run-down":* John Osborne "Britain's Spirit," *Life*, April 28, 1947.

24 *"What is the plight"*: Ellwood, *Rebuilding Europe*, p. 57.

24 *"worse than anything probably"*: Yergin, *Shattered Peace*, p. 304.

24 *Around Christmas of 1946*: Fossedal, *Our Finest Hour*, p. 203.

24 *By dawn on January 6, 1947*: Donovan, *The Second Victory*, p. 18.

24 *"For the first time in history"*: Bullock, *Ernest Bevin*, p. 361.

25 *"Blessed are the dead"*: Isaacson and Thomas, *The Wise Men*, p. 386.

25 *In an emergency measure*: Saunders, *The Cultural Cold War*, p. 8.

25 *In France, snow*: Saunders, *The Cultural Cold War*, p. 8.

25 *For many the cold*: Beevor and Cooper, *Paris*, p. 270.

25 *"empty and hollow"*: Saunders, *The Cultural Cold War*, p. 8.

25 *"a remarkable industrial recovery"*: From Hitchcock, *France Restored*, p. 63; Jackson, "Prologue to the Marshall Plan," p. 1047.

25 *From the second half*: Pollard, *Economic Security and the Origins of the Cold War*, p. 65.

25 *From 1929 to 1938*: Hitchcock, *France Restored*, p. 64.

25 *Postwar labor productivity*: Pollard, *Economic Security and the Origins of the Cold War*, p. 64.

25 *People had little faith*: Bissell, *Reflections of a Cold Warrior*, pp. 30, 31.

26 *Wholesale prices rose*: Yergin, *Shattered Peace*, pp. 306, 307.

26 *In 1947, a carton of cigarettes*: Saunders, *The Cultural Cold War*, pp. 8, 9.

26 *Before the war, trade*: Pollard presents this schematic in *Economic Security and the Origins of the Cold War*, p. 63. Theodore White presents a similar portrayal in *Fire in the Ashes*.

26 *The quotas, tariffs*: White, *Fire in the Ashes*, pp. 51, 52.

26 *To finance its war effort*: White, *Fire in the Ashes*, pp. 52, 53.

26 *before the war it supplied*: Arkes, *Bureaucracy, the Marshall Plan, and the National Interest*, p. 47.

26 *the war had pulled Germany*: Tony Judt wrote of "the effective disappearance of Germany from the European economy" in *Postwar*, p. 87.

26 *at the same time*: Western Europe was also losing access to food and resources from Eastern Europe, as the Soviet Union brought those countries into its sphere of influence and signed a series of preferential trading agreements. Ellwood, *Rebuilding Europe*, p. 31. Also, for one of the best summations of the disconnections in Europe's postwar economic patterns, see Committee of European Economic Cooperation, vol. 1, "General Report" (Paris 1947) submitted to Washington in September 1947.

27 *Europe had a balance-of-payments*: Pollard, *Economic Security and the Origins of the Cold War*, p. 64.

27 *Some economic historians*: In a landmark history, *The Reconstruction of Western Europe, 1945–1951*, Alan Milward argued that the alleged crisis of 1947 was simply a balance-of-payments crisis. According to Milward, Western Europe's economic recovery began in 1945. Its balance-of-payments problem was not a function of its economic weaknesses but rather the strength of its recovery and its need for imports to fuel that recovery. The region's maladies—production, productivity, inflation, trade patterns—were temporary dislocations due to the war, more than structural economic problems.

Milward offers a rigorous economic examination and a forceful argument. He is convincing in his argument that Western Europe was in fact on the path to economic recovery following the war, and that rather than experiencing a tailspin its economies resumed growth after the February crisis. Milward is less convincing in averring that the region did not have a production problem. Its industry was antiquated, and its leaders—most notably, Jean Monnet—felt that modernization was urgent. Thus: "modernization or decadence." It was one thing for Western Europe to grow its economy from the depths of its economic position in 1945 but another to continue along a similar trajectory as it approached prewar levels and exceeded them. As of the spring of 1947, its production was still well below prewar levels, which, taken from 1938, was still very low—coming off of a depression. Michael Hogan makes this argument in *The*

Marshall Plan and William Diebold supports it in "The Marshall Plan in Retrospect," his review essay of Milward, Hogan and Kindleberger.

Yet, even if Milward was correct, and the region was in the midst of a strong recovery and that production would have continued to climb were it not for its balance-of-payments problem, he miscalculated one essential input in his economic model. Milward judiciously points out that Western Europeans' "amount of hope for the future" was an important economic variable. Milward, *The Reconstruction of Western Europe*, p. 18. He writes that the purpose of wartime sacrifice was the "creation of a 'better' society," and therefore, "the scope of political opportunity for governments was wider in that respect than before or later." *Ibid.*, p. 19. Milward portrays a climate of hope that would have allowed Western Europe's leaders to impose the sort of sacrifices necessary to allow them to continue their import-based recoveries.

In his review of Milward, Diebold wrote that "not the least of the problems" in Milward's contention that there was no crisis in 1947 "is why, if Milward is right, everyone thought differently at the time." Diebold, p. 430. There was in fact, as Diebold points out, a remarkable consensus among Western Europe's leaders (e.g., Monnet, Bevin, De Gasperi, Stikker) as well as leading economists both in Western Europe and the United States (e.g., Marjolin, Kindleberger, Bissell) that Western Europe was in the throes of an economic crisis. As Richard Bissell wrote in a powerful 1952 article in *Foreign Affairs*, a preemptive riposte of sorts to Milward: "It cannot be said that either economic recovery or rearmament in Europe was physically impossible without foreign aid . . . [The Western Europeans] perhaps could have rebuilt their economies. But it would have imposed greater sacrifices than most of them had to undergo in wartime. There are few experienced observers," Bissell noted, "who believe the social fabric of Europe could have stood the strain. It is in this sense that the Europeans 'needed' . . . more than they could 'afford.'" Bissell, "Foreign Aid: What Sort? How Much? How Long?" p. 22.

Perhaps one of the reasons for this disconnect was that Western Europe in the spring of 1947 was not a hopeful, stable region, easily able to endure a new round of painful rations, controls and sacrifice. In contrast, it was desperate, vulnerable, insecure; pessimistic about its prospects for peace and prosperity. For example, a poll taken in France early that autumn asked French citizens whether things were going well or badly in their country. 93 percent answered "Badly" or "Rather Badly"; less than 1 percent answered "Well." Asked whether they thought France was heading toward a more serious, or a more peaceful, political scene, 77 percent answered "More Serious"; 7 percent answered "More Peaceful." George Gallup, *The Gallup Poll: Public Opinion 1935–1971*, volume 1: 1935–48, pp. 679, 680. Set against this climate, this mood, Europe's economic predicament can be seen in a different light. And it was this environment—not a permissive one—in which Western Europe's leaders had to operate. One of Europe's leading economists of the time, Robert Marjolin, described Europe that spring "on the brink of the precipice. Its lack of everything was about to become calamitous. Its people, who had lived on little but hope throughout the war, could not understand how, two or three years after the war, their situation could still be so wretched. The Soviet danger was beginning to loom. It seemed almost inevitable that the general shortage would lead to serious internal disorders." Marjolin, *Architect of European Unity*, p. 180.

In light of Communist strength—particularly in France and Italy—a further blow to morale might have been a decisive political tipping point, leading to insurrection or even peaceful Communist ascension via the ballot box. Further political instability would have impaired Western Europe's economic condition and most probably have erased its hopes for full-fledged recovery. Even without Communist ascension, though, Western Europe's economic recovery depended upon confidence and hope; it depended on people's willingness to work, save and invest, to plant and grow, to abide by laws and engage as constructive citizens. Yet another program of wide-scale sacrifice would have been a further blow to confidence and hope, an essential ingredient to the foundation of the sort of recovery needed.

It is in this sense that Western Europe was in an economic crisis in 1947 that extended beyond a balance-of-payments crisis that might have been redressed through self-adjustment, sacrifice and patience. As Marjolin wrote, "there was visibly no way to stem this drain," to redress the balance of payments crisis, "without American aid." Marjolin, *Architect of European Unity*, p. 178. In large part, that is because of the gravity of Western Europe's crisis of confidence.

27 *"Like a whale left"*: White, *Fire in the Ashes*, p. 53.

27 *The transformation was perhaps*: Ellwood, *Rebuilding Europe*, p. 75; Bullock, *Ernest Bevin*, p. 362.

27 *"bankruptcy"*: Jones, *The Fifteen Weeks*, p. 82.

28 *"Was the U.S. ready"*: Reynolds, ed., *The Origins of the Cold War in Europe*, p. 84.

28 *"This house sees more"*: Mazower, *Dark Continent*, p. 106.

28 *"rotten" and marked*: Yergin and Stanislaw, *The Commanding Heights*, p. 10.

28 *"France has got what"*: Beevor and Cooper, *Paris*, p. 135.

28 *Louis Renault and his family*: Beevor and Cooper, *Paris*, p. 104.

28 *British socialist leader*: James Cronin, "The Marshall Plan and the Cold War Political Discourse," in Shain, ed., *The Marshall Plan*, p. 289.

28 *"warfare state"*: Yergin and Stanislaw, *The Commanding Heights*, p. 14.

28 *When France was liberated*: Beevor and Cooper convincingly argue that while the Communists were a critical force in the Resistance, they exaggerated their level of participation and casualties tolled. *Paris*, Beever and Cooper, p. 18.

28 *Stalin's Communist forces*: Yet widespread rape and plundering tainted the sheen of their military heroics.

28 *As they rolled west*: These themes are explored in Yergin and Stanislaw, *The Commanding Heights*, p. 10.

28 *Far superior to the Americans*: Bailey, *The Marshall Plan Summer*, p. 45.

29 *"Nobody in Europe believes"*: Yergin and Stanislaw, *The Commanding Heights*, p. 4.

29 *In Czechoslovakia, elections*: Price, *The Marshall Plan and Its Meaning*, pp. 33, 34.

29 *In France's first postwar*: Price, *The Marshall Plan and Its Meaning*, pp. 33, 34.

29 *A year later, in November*: Beevor and Cooper, *Paris*, p. 274.

29 *In Italy, mass unemployment*: Price, *The Marshall Plan and Its Meaning*, pp. 33, 34.

29 *Communist support was strong*: Leffler, *A Preponderance of Power*, p. 7.

29 *The parties were well funded*: See White, *Fire in the Ashes*, p. 346; Beevor and Cooper, *Paris*, p. 200.

29 *"There is no choice between"*: Ellwood, *Rebuilding Europe*, p. 54.

29 *"Empty stomachs mean Bolsheviks"*: Morgan, *Reds*, p. 91.

Two: The General's Last Stand

PAGE

30 *The war had taken*: Bidault, *Resistance*, p. 144.

30 *"cavernous stucco mansion"*: Isaacson and Thomas, *The Wise Men*, p. 159.

30 *The capacious embassy*: Pogue, *George C. Marshall*, pp. 172, 173.

30 *"I had seen the General"*: John Foster Dulles and Robert Murphy and a few other members of the U.S. delegation said that Marshall did not have time to be fully prepared or that he was not on his finest form. Daniel Yergin supports the notion in *Shattered Peace*. Marshall's colleagues, though, felt he was extremely effective. Alan Bullock, Bevin's biographer, wrote that the general made "little impact to begin with." "By the end of the Conference, however, Marshall had not only impressed everybody by the firmness which underlay his restraint of manner, but had evolved his own way of meeting the offensive style of Soviet diplomacy." Bullock, *Ernest Bevin*, pp. 375, 376.

Bidault's view of Marshall, mostly formed at the conference, followed: "No other man since 1945 approaches him in uprightness and stature. Compared to Truman's Foreign Secretary, the most brilliant reputations seem shabby." Marshall was quiet in the beginning and most likely got off to a slow start. Yet even Murphy, who felt he was not at his best, concluded "it is unlikely that any Secretary of State could have accomplished more at the 1947 Moscow Conference." Murphy, *Diplomat Among Warriors*, p. 306.

31 *"the Allies' stumbling block"*: Bidault, *Resistance*, p. 148.
31 *Roosevelt had believed that relations*: Murphy, *Diplomat Among Warriors*, p. 287.
31 *With prodigious coal resources*: Leffler, *A Preponderance of Power*, p. 152.
31 *As the plight of Germany's people*: Hitchcock, *France Restored*, p. 61.
31 *"There is only one path"*: Jackson, "Prologue to the Marshall Plan," p. 1063. A month earlier, John Foster Dulles, speaking to the National Publishers Association in New York City, made a bold suggestion. Dulles said Germany's Rhine industrial basin should be incorporated, in some integrated fashion, with Western Europe's economies. Integration, Dulles argued, could propel economic recovery in the wider region. Some form of joint control could "make it possible to develop the industrial potential of western Germany in the interest of economic life of Western Europe, including Germany, and to do so without making Germans the master of Europe." Yates, *John Foster Dulles and Bipartisanship, 1944–1952*, pp. 171–73. Junior officials in the State Department had already been working on proposals along similar lines, and the prospect of some form of European federation was a long-standing idea in Europe, bantered about in various incarnations at various times.
32 *As Marshall said*: Donovan, *The Second Victory*, p. 103.
32 *"Almost all U.S. officials"*: Leffler, *A Preponderance of Power*, pp. 151, 152.
32 *"There are signs that"*: Telegram from Ambassador Walter Bedell Smith to Secretary George C. Marshall, January 7, 1947, FRUS, 47, 2, pp. 139–42.
33 *On a typical day*: Pogue, *George C. Marshall*, pp. 173, 174.
33 *His British counterpart*: Pogue, *George C. Marshall*, p. 175.
33 *"massive, rude, and strong"*: Mee, *The Marshall Plan*, pp. 108, 109.
33 *"not a sound organ"*: Craig and Lowenheim, eds., *The Diplomats*, p. 119.
33 *"The British Empire"*: Craig and Lowenheim, eds., *The Diplomats*, p. 108.
34 *"Security is still the question"*: Memorandum of conversation by Secretary Marshall, February 12, 1947, FRUS, 47, 2, p. 157.
34 *"impetuous, melodramatic, and known"*: Hitchcock, *France Restored*, p. 57.
34 *On the economic front*: See Hitchcock, *France Restored*, pp. 69, 70; Minutes of conversation between Secretary Marshall and President of France Vincent Auriol, FRUS, 47, 2, pp. 190–95.
34 *Marshall had met Vyacheslav*: Pogue, *George C. Marshall*, p. 176.
34 *"stoney-arse"*: Craig and Lowenheim, eds., *The Diplomats*, pp. 65, 66.
34 *"comrade filing cabinet"*: Craig and Lowenheim, eds., *The Diplomats*, pp. 65, 66.
34 *"master's voice"*: From the title of Steven Merritt Miner's "His Master's Voice: Viacheslav Mikhailovich Molotov as Stalin's Foreign Commissar," in Craig and Lowenheim, eds., *The Diplomats*, p. 65.
34 *He was complicit*: Craig and Lowenheim, eds., *The Diplomats*, p. 66.
35 *The conference opened*: Pogue, *George C. Marshall*, p. 174.
35 *Seating was ritualistic*: Acheson, *Present at the Creation*, pp. 292, 293.
35 *"There is courtesy"*: Yergin, *Shattered Peace*, p. 297.
35 *Each speech had to be*: Acheson, *Present at the Creation*, p. 292.
35 *As retribution, Marshall*: United States Delegation Minutes, Conference of Foreign Ministers, Eighth Meeting, Moscow, March 18, 1947, FRUS, 47, 2, p. 259.
35 *"We cannot accept a unified"*: FRUS 47, 2, p. 256.
36 *"completely poker-faced"*: Pogue, *George C. Marshall*, p. 175.
36 *Others felt that his*: Charles Kindleberger in Stanley Hoffman and Charles Maier, eds.,

The Marshall Plan, p. 9. Edward Mason said that Bidault was "drunk a good deal of the time and obviously was an emotionally disturbed man." Oral interview: Edward Mason, HST Library Collection.

36 *When Molotov recanted:* Beevor and Cooper, *Paris*, p. 275.
37 *The Soviets seemed much more:* Leffler, *A Preponderance of Power*, p. 153.
37 *On March 24, Bevin:* Bullock, *Ernest Bevin*, pp. 380–82.
37 *"the third week has now":* Yates, *John Foster Dulles and Bipartisanship*.
37 *There were "sumptuous" outings:* "Spring Comes to Moscow," *Life*, April 14, 1947.
37 *"the politeness also became":* Bidault, *Resistance*, p. 145.
37 *The U.S. could not:* Leffler, *A Preponderance of Power*, pp. 151, 153.
37 *"didn't care what":* Telegram from Secretary Marshall to Acting Secretary Lovett, April 8, 1947, FRUS, 47, 2, p. 315.
38 *"If we cannot agree":* Telegram from Secretary Marshall to Acting Secretary Lovett, April 15, 1947, FRUS, 47, 2, pp. 335, 336.
38 *Marshall had been working:* "The U.S. Talks Up at Moscow," *Life*, March 31, 1947.
38 *In the dark of night:* Most of this detail comes from Charles Mee's vibrant account in *The Marshall Plan*, pp. 52–55.
39 *"You look the same":* Yergin, *Shattered Peace*, p. 299.
39 *"an old battle-scarred tiger":* Kennan, *Memoirs*, p. 279.
39 *Both delegations sat:* Mee, *The Marshall Plan*, p. 59.
39 *He was trained as a soldier:* He said: "I am not a diplomat. I mean exactly what I say and there is no use trying to read between the lines because there is nothing to be read there." Pogue, *George C. Marshall*, p. 171.
39 *"very concerned and somewhat depressed":* Memorandum of Conversation, April 15, 1947, FRUS 47, 2, pp. 338, 339.
39 *"we are frankly determined":* Pogue, *George C. Marshall*, p. 189; Mee, *The Marshall Plan*, p. 59.
40 *In brief turns Stalin:* The account as reported by Marshall and his staff at Moscow in FRUS, 47, 2, pp. 340–44.
40 *"He changed":* Kotkin, "A Conspiracy So Immense," p. 32.
40 *Deception and conspiracy were the norm:* Kotkin, "A Conspiracy So Immense," pp. 28, 32.
41 *To sate his febrile concern:* Gaddis, *The Cold War*, p. 11, and Zubok and Pleshakov, *Inside the Kremlin's Cold War*, pp. 277, 278.
41 *to rest and replenish:* Kuromiya, *Stalin*, pp. 183–87, and Roberts, *Stalin's Wars*, pp. 311, 314–17.
41 *"We shall recover":* Kuromiya, *Stalin*, p. 183.
41 *Stalin sought accommodation:* Gaddis, *The Cold War*, p. 12; Zubok and Pleshakov, *Inside the Kremlin's Cold War*, p. 276; and Kuromiya, *Stalin*, pp. 184, 187, 188.
41 *He would not let the United States:* Kuromiya, *Stalin*, p. 186.
41 *"an opportunity":* Roberts, *Stalin's Wars*, p. 374.
42 *"All of Germany":* Gaddis, *The Cold War*, p. 22.
42 *"rapid penetration of communism":* Leffler, *A Preponderance of Power*, pp. 154, 155.
42 *"indistinguishable from the disruption":* Taubman, *Stalin's American Policy*, pp. 130, 131.
43 *In the wake of his meeting:* Bidault echoed the views of Marshall, Dulles, Bevin and most other senior policymakers at the conference when he said, "Only the most ignorant or servile people could pretend that we did not try out every path, even the most unpleasant ones, to try and find the right solution . . . the futility of all of our attempts began to wear down our patience. By nature and training, the Soviet representatives were indefatigably stubborn . . ." Bidault, *Resistance*, p. 124.
43 *"If the Russians had accepted":* Bullock, *Ernest Bevin*, p. 388.
43 *"The conference in Moscow":* Bidault, *Resistance*, p. 149.
43 *"To the American question":* Telegram: Memorandum of Conversation by Secretary Marshall, April 20, 1947, FRUS, 47, 2, pp. 369, 370.

43 *Stalin raised his glass:* Pogue, *George C. Marshall*, p. 193.
43 *"My country is a young country":* Edward Folliard, "Marshall Plan Took Shape in the Skies: The 'Impatient' Draftsman," *Washington Post*, November 23, 1947.
44 *It was the longest:* Bullock, *Ernest Bevin*, p. 387.
44 *"The Moscow Conference was":* Quoted in Parish, "The Turn Toward Confrontation," p. 8.
44 *"All the way back":* Bohlen, *Witness to History*, p. 263.
44 *"brought us to the important":* "Marshall Ties World Trade to the Success of ERP Plan," *New York Times*, January 16, 1948.
44 *For Marshall, Moscow was decisive:* In an interview in later years, he said, "The Marshall Plan was an outgrowth of the disillusionment over the Moscow conference which proved conclusively that the Soviet Union was not negotiating in good faith and could not be induced to cooperate in achieving European recovery." From Marshall Plan Vertical Files, HST Library. In another interview he said, "On returning home from the Moscow Conference I felt we couldn't let the European problem fester any longer—the time for lancing the boil was now at hand." Oral interview: George C. Marshall, Harry Price Collection. Finally, in an interview with Forrest Pogue in 1956, Marshall said that before Moscow he "thought [the Soviets] could be negotiated with. Harriman came back and said they could not be. I decided finally at Moscow . . . that they could not be. I always thought we had to make a try to negotiate with them, and I think the American people thought that." Pogue, *George C. Marshall*, p. 196.
44 *"We cannot ignore the factor":* A summary of Marshall's radio address from Pogue, *George C. Marshall*, pp. 199, 200.

Three: The Drumbeat at State

PAGE

45 *so the dry Arizona heat:* Fossedal, *Our Finest Hour*, p. 214; Garwood, *Will Clayton*, pp. 10, 11.
45 *"I am deeply disturbed":* Fossedal, *Our Finest Hour*, pp. 216, 217.
45 *William Lockhart Clayton:* Fossedal, *Our Finest Hour*, p. 15.
46 *"by the light of the only":* Fossedal, *Our Finest Hour*, p. 17.
46 *"If you read and absorb":* Fossedal, *Our Finest Hour*, p. 22.
46 *Then, at twenty-four:* Garwood, *Will Clayton*, p. 78.
46 *By 1920, Anderson, Clayton:* Fossedal, *Our Finest Hour*, p. 37.
46 *By 1936, Anderson, Clayton:* Fossedal, *Our Finest Hour*, p. 12.
46 *"You've got to live":* John Chamberlain, "Will Clayton and His Problems," *Life*, May 19, 1947.
46 *"warehouse war":* Fossedal, *Our Finest Hour*, p. 74.
47 *"biggest garage sale in history":* Fossedal, *Our Finest Hour*, p. 104.
47 *"No doubt the war":* Fossedal, *Our Finest Hour*, p. 82.
47 *A correspondent named Alan Drury:* Fossedal, *Our Finest Hour*, p. 90.
47 *"in charge of all economic affairs":* Garwood, *Will Clayton*, p. 19.
47 *"The first letter I sign":* Fossedal, *Our Finest Hour*, p. 136.
48 *Cordell Hull had served:* Craig and Lowenheim, eds., *The Diplomats*, p. 40.
48 *Between 1929 and 1936:* Judt, *Postwar*, p. 4.
48 *The United States missed:* The Smoot-Hawley Act of 1930 erected high tariffs and quotas to protect U.S. industry, and led to a wave of protectionism in Europe and elsewhere. FDR's unwillingness to promote currency coordination and stabilization at the London Conference of 1933 constituted a second important milestone in the decade's march toward economic autarky, totalitarianism, and conflict. For a good discussion of America's role and the missed opportunities see Pollard, *Economic Security and the Origins of the Cold War*, pp. 6, 7.

48 *"The bit of history"*: Jones, *The Fifteen Weeks*, p. 93.

48 *"the political lineup followed"*: Hogan, *The Marshall Plan*, p. 26.

48 *"If goods can't cross"*: Pollard, *Economic Security and the Origins of the Cold War*, p. 14.

48 *"I was so very wrong"*: Fossedal, *Our Finest Hour*, p. 59.

48 *"Most wars originate"*: Pollard, *Economic Security and the Origins of the Cold War*, p. 2.

49 *"I don't know anything"*: Fossedal, *Our Finest Hour*, p. 152.

49 *"inner circle"*: From a *New York Times* article by Lester Merkel. Merkel named five people in the circle: Marshall, Clark Clifford, Press Secretary Harry Ross, Francis Biddle and Clayton. Quoted in Fossedal, *Our Finest Hour*, p. 201.

49 *"Will Clayton was my boss"*: Fossedal, *Our Finest Hour*, p. viii.

49 *"People respect him"*: Chamberlain, "Will Clayton and His Problem."

49 *"Mr. President, I can see"*: There is an extensive and well-documented analysis offered in Fossedal, *Our Finest Hour*, pp. 1–3, and in the corresponding footnotes.

50 *In January 1941, Roosevelt proposed:* In case it needed it, the bill was numbered 1776 for additional effect. Fromkin, *In the Time of the Americans*, p. 417.

50 *By the end of the war:* Estimate from Gordon, *An Empire of Wealth*, p. 352.

50 *By May 1945:* Pollard, *Economic Security and the Origins of the Cold War*, p. 30.

50 *"I was never so close"*: Fossedal, *Our Finest Hour*, p. 183.

50 *"amused Litvinov"*: Isaacson and Thomas, *The Wise Men*, p. 220.

50 *UNRRA disbursed an extraordinary:* UNRRA Council Meeting, August 7, 1946, p. 14. From Will Clayton Papers, HST Library Collection.

50 *"It prevented a breakdown"*: Duchene, *Jean Monnet*, p. 216.

51 *The agency may have:* Judt, *Postwar*, p. 86.

51 *UNRRA's policy of nonpolitical:* Fossedal, *Our Finest Hour*, p. 77.

51 *Though the agency was founded:* Oral interview: Charles Kindleberger, HST Library Collection.

51 *Suspicions were strong:* Fossedal, *Our Finest Hour*, p. 178.

51 *By the summer of 1946:* One *Washington Post* report quoted Clayton as saying that "the gravy train is going around for the last time." He denied making the comment. Fossedal, *Our Finest Hour*, p. 181.

51 *In the spring of 1946:* Hitchcock, *France Restored*, p. 36.

52 *Most of the country:* An early Gallup Poll showed 60 percent of Americans opposed to a loan; 27 percent supported one. Fossedal, *Our Finest Hour*, p. 192.

52 *"How are you, Lord Keynes"*: Garwood, *Will Clayton*, p. 28.

52 *"too many Jews"*: Fossedal, *Our Finest Hour*, p. 198.

52 *"than the feeling that"*: Yergin, *Shattered Peace*, p. 178.

52 *"with all the conditions"*: Fossedal, *Our Finest Hour*, p. 191.

52 *As the storm clouds gathered:* Michael Hogan puts the figure at "over $9 billion." Hogan, *The Marshall Plan*, p. 30. William Hitchcock wrote that UNRRA aid and U.S. loans and credits up to the fall of 1947 totaled $11.2 billion. Hitchcock, *The Struggle for Europe*, p. 136. The *New York Times* reported that a senior official from the Budget Bureau estimated the figure at $19 billion. Charles Hurd, "Our Post-War Aid Abroad 19 Billion Now, Byrd Reports," *New York Times*, November 1, 1947.

52 *"Billions That Didn't Prime"*: Ferdinand Kuhn, "Billions That Didn't Prime," *Washington Post*, November 23, 1947.

53 *"The U.S. was eating up"*: Nitze, *From Hiroshima to Glasnost*, p. 47.

53 *"My suggestion was not unique"*: Nitze, *From Hiroshima to Glasnost*, p. 48.

53 *"deteriorating situation in Europe"*: Fossedal, *Our Finest Hour*, p. 203.

53 *"prodigious efforts on our part"*: Fossedal, *Our Finest Hour*, p. 213.

54 *"Clayton is the person"*: Fossedal, *Our Finest Hour*, p. 201. In his memoirs, Truman considers the Baylor address seminal. Very much echoing Clayton's thinking, Truman said in that address that the "economic war of the thirties" made "the lesson in history . . . plain": political and economic freedom were "indivisible." Truman, *Memoirs, Volume 2*, pp. 111, 112.

54 *"The security and interests"*: Quoted in Fossedal, *Our Finest Hour*, pp. 216–19.

54 *In mid-March, President Harry Truman*: In an interesting exchange around the time of Truman's speech, Clayton apparently said to Senator Walter George, "I do not think that it would be wise to draw any conclusions . . . that this is just the first step in a great big program of relief." Leffler, *A Preponderance of Power*, p. 147. It would be conjecture to suggest what exactly he was thinking when he made the comment. Most likely he was considering a larger program by that point, but it had not crystallized. He would probably have wanted to manage expectations for members of Congress, bringing them along gradually, as his thinking and work advanced.

55 *He summoned George Kennan*: Pogue, *George C. Marshall*, pp. 203, 204.

55 *"beyond the vision of"*: Acheson, *Present at the Creation*, p. 214.

55 *"Avoid trivia"*: It took about a week longer than Marshall had originally given Kennan. Kennan, *Memoirs*, p. 326.

55 *"I was supposed to review"*: Kennan, *Memoirs*, p. 326.

55 *"Kennan had little knowledge of"*: Nitze, *From Hiroshima to Glasnost*, p. 51.

56 *Among those Kennan recruited*: They did not necessarily join the PPS but worked on the Foreign Aid Committee of the PPS, the group that was focused on this. Or they consulted regularly and submitted important memoranda and reports. Kennan, *Memoirs*, p. 329.

56 *A midlevel State Department official*: Kennan wrote that "the background of the conception of the Marshall Plan has been so well and accurately set forth by Mr. Jones, in his book . . . that there could be no useful purpose served by going over the same ground here." Kennan, *Memoirs*, p. 326.

56 *"The most vigorous idea currents"*: Jones, *The Fifteen Weeks*, pp. 241, 242.

56 *Drawing on Clayton's junior officials*: A good deal of thinking and work had already been done on European recovery, the most substantive of it coming from Clayton's team. The State-War-Navy Coordinating Committee, or SWNCC, had also submitted a report on April 21. Following the administration's decision to provide support to Greece and Turkey, Undersecretary of State Dean Acheson instructed the committee on March 5—the same day Clayton sent his memo from Tucson—to report on what other countries the United States should aid. It is interesting to note that the report was not geared particularly to Western Europe, citing Iran, Italy, Korea, France, Austria and Hungary as top candidates for aid. In addition, like Greece and Turkey, and because War and Navy were at the table, the report leaned toward military aid. State-War-Navy Coordinating Committee Files: Series 360; Report of the Special "Ad Hoc" Committee of the SWNCC, April 21, 1947, p. 216, also from Kennan, *Memoirs*, p. 201. It included some valuable thinking, much of which would inform Kennan's work, but it was, by the report's own admission, "a hasty analysis." Jackson, "Prologue to the Marshall Plan," p. 1056.

56 *"against all governmental critics"*: Kennan, *Memoirs*, p. 326.

56 *"about as much character"*: Chace, *Acheson*, p. 162.

56 *"night and day, restlessly"*: Isaacson and Thomas, *The Wise Men*, p. 405.

56 *On one occasion, to relieve*: Kennan, *Memoirs*, pp. 327, 328.

56 *"To talk about the recovery"*: From Mee, *The Marshall Plan*, p. 90.

57 *"creative peace"*: Hogan, *The Marshall Plan*, p. 37.

57 *important foreign policy*: Acheson, *Present at the Creation*, pp. 227, 228.

57 *The family's ties to Britain*: Isaacson and Thomas, *The Wise Men*, pp. 51, 52.

57 *In Roosevelt, Acheson*: Henry Kissinger, *Diplomacy*, p. 424.

58 *It was a typically*: Acheson, *Present at the Creation*, pp. 228, 229.

58 *"the borderline of starvation"*: Excerpts from speech and much of the detail here from Chace, *Acheson*, pp. 171, 172.

58 *"trumpet did not give"*: Chace, *Acheson*, pp. 171, 172.

58 *A State Department report*: "Initial Press and Radio Reaction to Under Secretary Acheson's Speech at Cleveland, Mississippi on May 8, 1947," May 15, 1947, Marshall Plan Vertical Files, HST Library Collection.

58 *Before leaving for the Delta:* Acheson, *Present at the Creation*, pp. 228, 229.

58 *The speech received greater coverage:* Oral interview: James Reston, Harry Price Collection.

59 *"very much put out":* Bland, ed., *George C. Marshall*, p. 560.

59 *"did not represent 'trial balloons'":* Oral Interview: George C. Marshall, Harry Price Collection.

59 *"Is this a new policy":* Chace, Acheson, p. 172.

59 *Though he posed the question:* Morrow, *The Best Year of Their Lives*, p. 181.

59 *When Lippmann was twenty-five years old:* Steel, *Walter Lippmann and the American Century*, p. xiii.

59 *"High Priest of the Journalistic Order":* Isaacson and Thomas, *The Wise Men*, p. 408.

59 *By February and March:* Jackson, "Prologue to the Marshall Plan," p. 1050.

59 *During this time, Lippmann:* Steel, *Walter Lippmann and the American Century*, p. 440.

59 *On March 20, Lippmann:* Jones, *The Fifteen Weeks*, p. 227. Lippmann felt that this could be a real chance to bring the Soviets in, to lure them with a loan. He continued to press for a diplomatic solution and reconciliation more vigorously than the foreign policymakers' consensus. Steel, *Walter Lippmann and the American Century*, pp. 440–42.

60 *"saying only what responsible":* Jones, *The Fifteen Weeks*, p. 229; Steel, *Walter Lippmann and the American Century*, pp. 440–41.

60 *"That will put them on":* Jones, *The Fifteen Weeks*, p. 231.

60 *"enlarged at once the realm":* Jones, *The Fifteen Weeks*, p. 229.

61 *"State Department strategists have":* Mee, *The Marshall Plan*, p. 93.

61 *"the more or less genuine":* Bullock, *Ernest Bevin*, pp. 402, 403.

61 *"We do not see why you":* Yergin, *Shattered Peace*, p. 310.

61 *"More and more as weeks":* Ikenberry, *After Victory*, p. 192.

61 *"I personally believe":* Ambrose, *Eisenhower*, p. 227.

61 *In mid-May, Henry Wallace:* Jones, *The Fifteen Weeks*, pp. 233, 234.

61 *The Stassen Plan translated:* Oral interview: John Snyder, HST Library Collection.

61 *Journalist Arthur Krock:* Jones, *The Fifteen Weeks*, pp. 233, 234.

61 *Stassen's Republican colleagues:* Oral interview: John Snyder, HST Library Collection.

61 *"The instructions we had":* Kennan, "The Marshall Plan and the Future of Europe." Marshall Plan Vertical Files, HST Library Collection.

62 *"Kennan did the only thing":* The SWNCC study previously referenced.

62 *On May 23, Kennan:* Jones, *The Fifteen Weeks*, p. 249.

62 *"The ideas by which":* Kennan, *Memoirs*, p. 336.

62 *"result from the disruptive effect":* Memorandum from the Director of the Policy Planning Staff George Kennan to Undersecretary of State Dean Acheson, May 23, 1947, FRUS, 47, 3, pp. 224, 225.

62 *But first, in the short term:* FRUS, 47, 3, pp. 227, 224.

62 *"We must recognize that much":* Report on "Certain Aspects of the European Recovery from the U.S. Standpoint," from Mee, *The Marshall Plan*, p. 90.

62 *"must be a joint one":* FRUS, 47, 3, p. 227.

63 *"In Acheson's view":* Acheson, *Present at the Creation*, p. 228. In his memoirs Nitze wrote, "Kennan had little knowledge of, or experience in, economic matters." Nitze, *From Hiroshima to Glasnost*, p. 51.

63 *"Will was genuinely alarmed":* Nitze, *From Hiroshima to Glasnost*, pp. 52, 53.

63 *On May 27, Clayton:* Clayton was fatigued and sick (and consigned to bed rest) and wanted to gather his thoughts upon his return, and he wanted to ensure that his memo was as compelling as possible. Garwood, *Will Clayton*, p. 14.

63 *"effects of economic dislocation":* Both Forrest Pogue and Charles Kindleberger take this line to mean that the program as proposed by Clayton would be presented as American dicta, imposed on Europe. That is not what he meant. He was referencing the UNRRA experience, wherein multilateral governance had come to impede the effort.

The program was to be run by the United States, but European initiative was a central element in the Plan for Clayton; in fact, he helped conceive of the idea and advocated for it. As he says earlier in the memo, the program "should be based on a European plan which the principal European nations . . . should work out." Pogue, *George C. Marshall*, p. 207.

64 "*the United States must run this show*": Memorandum by Undersecretary of State for Economic Affairs Will Clayton, "The European Crisis," May 27, 1947, FRUS, 47, 3, pp. 230–32.

64 "*it was Clayton's disturbing report*": Quoted in Fossedal, *Our Finest Hour*, p. 9.

64 *Clayton's memo had:* Acheson wrote in his memoirs of the "powerful effect of a second memorandum of my colleague Will Clayton, written on his flight home from Geneva, upon General Marshall's thinking and framing of his proposal." Acheson, *Present at the Creation*, pp. 230, 231. Treasury Secretary John Snyder said, "I am convinced that the report which Will Clayton submitted after his return from a survey of the economic and military conditions in Europe . . . that the statistics, the background of that report, formed the proposal from which Mr. Acheson and Secretary Marshall later developed their proposals." Oral interview: John Snyder, HST Library Collection.

64 "*to sit back and do nothing*": Acheson, *Present at the Creation*, p. 232.

64 *Kennan argued that if:* Kennan, *Memoirs*, p. 342. Kennan cites this as one of his main contributions to this effort. He was, in fact, a critical advocate and deserves much credit for Marshall's ultimate decision. Oral interview: Dean Acheson, Harry Price Collection.

65 "*squeeze play*": From Pogue, *George C. Marshall*, p. 215.

65 *Clandestine and deeply suspicious:* Oral interview: George Kennan, Harry Price Collection.

65 "*Play it straight*": Kennan, *Memoirs*, p. 342.

65 "*It was a hell of*": Oral interview: Charles Bohlen, Harry Price Collection. See FRUS, 47, 3, pp. 234–37 for much of the content—and flow—of the meeting.

65 "*As one looks back on it*": Acheson, *Present at the Creation*, p. 232.

66 "*which would not undertake*": Memorandum from Undersecretary of State Acheson to Secretary of State Marshall, May 28, 1947, FRUS, 47, 3, p. 233. Also from Pogue, *George C. Marshall*, pp. 207, 208.

66 *On December 4, 1941:* Fromkin, *In the Times of the Americans*, p. 437.

66 "*You know," he said:* Chace, *Acheson*, p. 178.

66 *On May 30, Marshall:* Pogue, *George C. Marshall*, p. 210.

66 *Carter selected Bohlen:* Pogue, *George C. Marshall*, p. 210.

66 *Bohlen is generally credited:* In his memoir, Bohlen writes that Marshall asked him to draft a speech for Harvard. He spent two days on it, and the final version "closely followed the structure of my draft and picked up much of my phrasing." The excerpt, apparently, has led some historians to conclude that Bohlen is the primary author. Bohlen, *Witness to History*, p. 263. However, in a less noted interview, Marshall elaborated: "The way the speech was built was this. I talked it over with George Kennan . . . and Chip Bohlen, and I told them to start out wholly independent of the other and give me what they thought. Then I got impatient right away, and I dictated something that I thought. And when theirs came in, they were quite apart." In the end, Marshall said, "I cut out part of Kennan's speech and part of Bohlen's speech and part of my speech and put the three together, and that was the beginning of the talk." Most likely, Marshall did not let Bohlen know how much work he himself had done independently. Bohlen's account, then, is reconcilable with Marshall's, which provides the complete picture, and suggests that Marshall, not Bohlen, was the primary author. In his memoir, Bohlen suggests that he was the primary author of the Harvard speech. Bland, ed., *George C. Marshall*, p. 559.

67 "*If these limeys offer me sherry*": Isaacson and Thomas, *The Wise Men*, p. 413.

67 *Acheson had invited the journalists:* Acheson's and Miall's accounts on the lead-up to Marshall's address differed. Whatever the hour, Acheson recalled saying, "wake Ernie Bevin up and put a copy in his hands." Isaacson and Thomas, *The Wise Men*, p. 413. Marshall did not want any attention for his speech at home, but its effect would depend on whether it was picked up abroad. In a detailed account, Miall remembered that Acheson made no explicit mention of an upcoming Harvard speech but assured his British interlocutors "how important and serious a project it was, but he explained that unless there was some dramatic initiative to formulate an agreed plan on the European side of the Atlantic, nothing would happen." When Miall read Marshall's Harvard speech, it was clear to him that the "apparently casual statement . . . was in fact an important offer." Miall, "How the Marshall Plan Started."

67 *On June 4, Marshall:* Bradley would become a five-star general in 1950.

67 *It was single-spaced:* Mee, *The Marshall Plan*, p. 100.

67 *Once in Cambridge:* When his biographer Forrest Pogue asked Marshall about Truman's involvement in and knowledge of the speech, Marshall asked Pogue to stop the recording machine. With the machine turned off, Marshall said, "I made the speech without telling the president. The speech was not finished when I left for Washington, so I worked with it on the plane and then at Conant's house. I realized just before making the speech that [Truman] hadn't seen it. Of course, he knew what we were doing and we were thinking along the same lines." Bland, ed., *George C. Marshall*, p. 559. Truman's account differed. In an oral interview, Truman said: "Gen Marshall told me about a month before, maybe more, that he was going up there [to Harvard]. They were going to give him an honorary degree, and he said to me, 'I've got to make this damn speech, and you know how I hate to make speeches. And I don't know what to talk about.' I said, 'I want you to spell out the details of this plan that's being worked out over in the State Department to save Europe from going under.' " Miller, *Plain Speaking*, p. 245. Truman's recollection (published more than 25 years after Marshall's Harvard speech, and when Truman was in his late 80s) is not reliable. Marshall did not know that he would give the Harvard speech until little more than a week before, not a month before. All other accounts suggest that Marshall proceeded purposefully and methodically. Direction did not come from Truman.

67 *"was almost entirely a State":* Clifford, *Counsel to the President*, p. 143.

67 *"I must be clear":* Elsey, *An Unplanned Life*, p. 150.

68 *"enormously important":* Mee, *The Marshall Plan*, pp. 100, 101.

68 *He sent it by surface mail:* Pogue, *George C. Marshall*, p. 215.

68 *"intention at all times":* Oral interview: George C. Marshall, Harry Price Collection.

68 *"the visible destruction was":* All excerpts from speech from Appendix in Pogue, *George C. Marshall*, pp. 525–28: "Address of Secretary of State George C. Marshall at Harvard University, June 5, 1947."

Four: The World Responds

PAGE

71 *Half-asleep, Bevin would recall:* Pogue, *George C. Marshall*, pp. 216, 217.

71 *" 'up against it' in a desperate way":* Charles Egan, "Britons Now Face New Import Curbs and Tighter Belts," *New York Times*, June 8, 1947.

71 *Around this time, some members:* Alan Bullock wrote that in March 1947, "it would not have been difficult to find a majority in the Cabinet for the view which Dalton and at times even Attlee took that Britain could no longer afford a foreign policy." Bullock, *Ernest Bevin*, p. 502.

71 *"a life-line to sinking men":* Bullock, *Ernest Bevin*, pp. 404, 405.

71 *The next morning at the Foreign Office:* Pogue, *George C. Marshall*, p. 217.

72 *"we know what he said":* Acheson, *Sketches from Life of Men I Have Known*, p. 2.

72   "I know we are in difficulties": Herbert Matthews, "Bevin Bids Britain 'Dig for Dollars,' " *New York Times*, June 6, 1947.

72   "a mutual thing": Bullock, *Ernest Bevin*, p. 405.

72   "If anyone in the world": Bullock, *Ernest Bevin*, p. 406.

72   "one of the greatest": Judt, *Postwar*, p. 91.

72   "it was obvious": Oral interview: Sir Edwin Plowden, HST Library Collection.

72   "Mr. Marshall's speech at Harvard": Bailey, *The Marshall Plan Summer*, p. 17.

72   "a full customs union": *Economist*, June 13, 1947, quoted in an editorial, "Ideas for Europe," *Life*, July 21, 1947.

72   At the same time: The U.S. in fact applied pressure on both France and Italy to do so. In early May, the State Department brandished the lever of aid to encourage France and Italy's centrist governments to form coalitions without Communists. Marshall pledged aid to De Gasperi on May 1 if his new government excluded the extreme left. And shortly thereafter Caffrey reported telling Premier Ramadier: "no Communists in gov. or else." Leffler, "Strategic Dimensions of the Marshall Plan," p. 281.

73   "the most important post-war event": Bidault, *Resistance*, p. 149.

73   Bidault expressed: Hitchcock, *France Restored*, p. 74.

73   The perception that this new: Harold Callender, "France is Stirred by MP," *New York Times*, June 6, 1947.

73   But still under a strict: "The Germans, at the end of the war, were not expecting any American aid; they could not expect it. Our hopes were much more limited." Oral interview: Gunther Harkort, HST Library Collection.

73   "The Marshall speech, of course": Oral interview: Halvard Lange, HST Library Collection.

73   "It is not a question": Oral interview: Dirk Stikker, HST Library Collection.

73   Though grateful, these smaller: van der Beugel, *From Marshall Aid to Atlantic Partnership*, p. 58.

73   "When they sniffed dollars": "ECA Can't Do Everything," *Fortune*, February 1949.

73   On June 9, the Soviet ambassador: Parish, "The Turn Toward Confrontation," pp. 13, 14.

74   "something between a hint": Ellwood, *Rebuilding Europe*, p. 86.

74   "Anything that is sent up": McCullough, *Truman*, p. 564. When asked by an interviewer why it was named the Marshall Plan, Truman replied: "It was called that because I realized that it was going down in history as a very great, very important thing, and I wanted General Marshall to get credit for it, which he did." Miller, ed., *Plain Speaking*, p. 240.

74   "I don't know what": "Ideas for Europe," *Life*.

75   From 1941 to 1945: Gordon, *An Empire of Wealth*, p. 357.

75   By one count more: Cohen, *A Consumers' Republic*, p. 75.

75   In 1940, personal savings: Gordon, *An Empire of Wealth*, p. 359.

75   " 'as sure as God' ": McCullough, *Truman*, p. 469.

75   "WHAT THIS WAR IS": Cohen, *A Consumers' Republic*, pp. 72, 73.

75   The strategy would keep: The fabled GI Bill was not only a vehicle to help returning veterans but to take care of them and keep them productively engaged yet out of the job market until industry could adjust and accommodate their return. Gordon, *An Empire of Wealth*, p. 364.

75   It was no accident: Cohen, *A Consumers' Republic*, p. 121.

76   Republicans gained 56 seats: Leffler, *A Preponderance of Power*, p. 141.

76   The frenzy to cut back: McCullough, *Truman*, p. 531.

76   "a man wielding a meat ax": Jones, *The Fifteen Weeks*, p. 91.

76   He began making overtures: McCullough, *Truman*, pp. 429, 430.

76   Vandenberg, or Van: Fromkin, *In the Time of the Americans*, p. 42.

76   When Smith won, he bought: Vandenberg, ed., *The Private Papers of Senator Vandenberg*, p. viii.

77   "purple prose and clichés": Vandenberg, ed., *The Private Papers of Senator Vandenberg*, p. xviii.

77 A *vigorous, but highly:* Fromkin, *In the Time of the Americans,* pp. 351, 352.

77 *He had grand literary pretensions:* Vandenberg, ed., *The Private Papers of Senator Vandenberg,* p. xvii; Isaacson and Thomas, *The Wise Men,* p. 399.

77 *In foreign affairs:* Vandenberg, ed., *The Private Papers of Senator Vandenberg,* p. 1.

77 *"In my own mind":* Vandenberg, ed., *The Private Papers of Senator Vandenberg,* p. 1.

77 *The Atlantic and Pacific:* Vandenberg, ed., *The Private Papers of Senator Vandenberg,* pp. 130–35.

77 *"a shot heard around the world":* Vandenberg, *The Private Papers of Senator Vandenberg,* p. 140.

77 *Walter Lippmann and James Reston:* In fact Steel wrote that they pushed Vandenberg, who was very reluctant, and then wrote much of the speech for him. After Van's speech, Lippmann found him "just like a pouter pigeon all blown up with delight at this new role in the world." Steel, *Walter Lippmann and the American Century,* p. 419.

78 *"long day's journey into":* Isaacson and Thomas, *The Wise Men,* p. 220.

78 *"critical date":* Gaddis, *We Now Know,* p. 36.

78 *"pledged our resources":* Acheson, *Sketches from Life of Men I Have Known,* p. 125. Acheson, who was often the designate at State to deal with Vandenberg, was harsh and patronizing to the senator in his memoirs. He described the process of consultation with Vandenberg as constant hand-holding. Van would first recoil and disagree, then question, then find some relatively minor flaw, seize it, and then inevitably relent and offer his support when his imprint, what Acheson called the "Vandenberg brand," had been added. Acheson, *Present at the Creation,* p. 223. His treatment in *Sketches from Life of Men I Have Known,* Acheson's less formal work (and much less read), is more measured and affords Vandenberg a place as an indispensable leader.

78 *"shot heard round the world":* Vandenberg, ed., *The Private Papers of Senator Vandenberg,* p. 375.

78 *Instead of unemployment:* In early March, the President's Council of Economic Advisers had warned Truman "that the combination of rising prices and upcoming wage negotiations could trigger a new inflationary spiral . . . New proposals for foreign assistance—dollars would certainly be used to purchase American goods, thus adding to the inflationary pressure—created great alarm among the president's economic advisors." Jackson, "Prologue to the Marshall Plan," p. 1057.

78 *The Consumer Price Index:* Cohen, *A Consumers' Republic,* p. 105.

78 *Everyone worried about inflation:* Cohen, *A Consumers' Republic,* p. 108.

78 *"intelligent American self-interest":* Vandenberg, ed., *The Private Papers of Senator Vandenberg,* p. 376.

79 *In a meeting with Truman:* Account from Acheson, *Present at the Creation,* p. 235.

79 *"I have no illusions":* Vandenberg, ed., *The Private Papers of Senator Vandenberg,* p. 381.

79 *"not to propose a United States":* James Reston, "European Self-Aid Will Be Explored by Marshall Aide," *New York Times,* June 13, 1947.

80 *"attempt to steal the show":* Telegram from Ambassador Jefferson Caffrey to Secretary Marshall, June 16, 1947, FRUS, 47, 3, pp. 256, 257.

80 *"Efforts at common action":* Harold Callender, "Bevin, Bidault Meet Tuesday to Discuss Marshall Offer," *New York Times,* June 15, 1947.

80 *"go ahead with full steam":* Telegram from Ambassador Jefferson Caffrey to Secretary Marshall, June 18, 1947, FRUS, 47, 3, pp. 259, 260.

80 *"firm verbal commitment":* Telegram from Ambassador Jefferson Caffrey to Secretary Marshall, June 19, 1947, FRUS, 47, 3, p. 262.

80 *"The Tsar Alexander":* Bullock, *Ernest Bevin,* p. 409.

80 *On June 23, Molotov:* Narinsky, "The Soviet Union and the Marshall Plan," p. 42.

80 *"Marshall Doctrine":* Highlights from K. Morozov, "Marshall Doctrine," in *Pravda Ukraine,* June 11, 1947, sent from Ambassador Walter Bedell Smith to Secretary Marshall, FRUS, 47, 3, pp. 294–95.

80 *"plan for political pressures"*: Associated Press, "Marshall's Plan Under Pravda Fire," *New York Times,* June 17, 1947.

81 *"sure that this Soviet"*: Telegram from Ambassador Bedell Smith to Secretary Marshall, FRUS 47, 3, p. 266.

81 *"Never in my life"*: Oral interview: Halvard Lange, HST Library Collection.

81 *Just as the Soviets:* Narinsky, "Soviet Foreign Policy and the Origins of the Marshall Plan," p. 108.

81 *"Perhaps they will play"*: Bevin held out hope that the Soviets would cooperate longer than Marshall. Craig and Lowenheim, eds., *The Diplomats,* p. 108.

81 *"Our position in this"*: "U.S. Is Encouraged Over Paris Meeting," *New York Times,* June 24, 1947.

81 *"The long road toward"*: *New York Times,* June 25, 1947, quoted in Fossedal, *Our Finest Hour,* p. 237.

82 *"The problem must be"*: Memorandum of Conversation: Summary of First Meeting of Undersecretary Will Clayton with British Cabinet Members, June 24, 1947, FRUS, 47, 3, pp. 269–70, 272.

82 *"a special relationship"*: Bullock, *Ernest Bevin,* p. 415.

82 *The next day, June 25:* Memorandum of Conversation: Substance of Second Meeting of Undersecretary Clayton with British Cabinet Members, June 25, 1947, FRUS, 47, 3, pp. 279–81.

82 *"it is the quickest way"*: Bevin added: "My recent experience in France shows that Russia cannot hold its satellites against the attraction of fundamental help toward economic revival in Europe." Clayton agreed: "As for Russia's satellites in Eastern Europe [Clayton] doubted with Mr. Bevin whether the USSR could hold or improve its position there, because those countries would be compelled for a long time to trade actively with the rest." Memorandum of Conversation: Summary of First Meeting of Undersecretary Will Clayton with British Cabinet Members, June 24, 1947, FRUS, 47, 3, p. 268.

82 *loosening the Soviets' grip:* This is Leffler's argument in *A Preponderance of Power* and "The United States and the Strategic Dimensions of the Marshall Plan."

82 *He added that:* Leffler, "The U.S. and the Strategic Dimensions of the Marshall Plan," p. 283.

83 *"sweep all other applicants aside"*: Memorandum of Conversation: Summary of Third Meeting of Undersecretary Clayton with British Cabinet Members, June 26, 1947, FRUS, 47, 3, p. 291. In addition, Kennan and Bohlen had met with British Ambassador to the U.S. Lord Inverchapel and told him that the United States did not expect the Soviet Union to join and that it should not be allowed to impede progress. Apparently, Inverchapel cabled the Foreign Office that the Americans were counting on the British to keep the Soviets out. Isaacson and Thomas, *The Wise Men,* p. 415. Bevin's discussion with Clayton marks the decisive exchange on the matter.

83 *"In the final analysis"*: Narinsky, "The Soviet Union and the Marshall Plan," p. 43.

83 *"the imminent economic crisis"*: Narinsky, "The Soviet Union and the Marshall Plan," pp. 42, 43.

84 *"bloc of bourgeois countries"*: Narinsky, "Soviet Foreign Policy and the Origins of the Marshall Plan," p. 109.

84 *"squeeze the maximum political"*: Narinsky, "The Soviet Union and the Marshall Plan," pp. 42, 43.

84 *Informed by these analyses:* Parish, "The Turn Toward Confrontation."

84 *Molotov had arrived:* Harold Callender, "Paris Parley to Open Today; Molotov and 89 Aides Arrive," *New York Times,* June 27, 1947.

84 *"I devoutly hope that"*: Telegram from Ambassador Caffrey to Secretary Marshall, June 27, 1947, FRUS 47, 3, p. 296.

85 *As the meeting opened:* As relayed by Caffrey based on his earlier discussions with British Ambassador to France Duff Cooper in a telegram from Caffrey to Secretary

Marshall, June 28, 1947, FRUS, 47, 3, pp. 297, 298. This was, of course, precisely what Bevin had tried to do himself just days earlier, while meeting with Clayton.

85 *That evening a wild storm:* "England Lashed by Rains," *New York Times*, June 28, 1947; Beevor and Cooper, *Paris*, p. 286.

85 *A common European plan:* Telegram from Ambassador Caffrey to Secretary Marshall, July 1, 1947, FRUS, 47, 3, p. 302.

85 *"flagrant et obstiné":* Beevor and Cooper, *Paris*, p. 286.

86 *The telegram handed to Molotov:* This telegram reported that German rehabilitation would be "the basis of any plan for the rehabilitation of the continent." See Zubok and Pleshakov, *Inside the Kremlin's Cold War*, p. 105.

86 *"If I were to go":* Telegram from Ambassador Caffrey to Secretary Marshall, July 1, 1947, FRUS, 47, 3, p. 302.

86 *"For all intents and purposes":* Telegram from Ambassador Caffrey to Secretary Marshall, July 1, 1947, FRUS, 47, 3, p. 303.

86 *A few days earlier:* Jack Raymond, "Germany Included in Recovery Plan," *New York Times*, June 27, 1947.

86 *Molotov pointedly asked:* Telegram from Ambassador Caffrey to Secretary Marshall, July 2, 1947, FRUS, 47, 3, p. 305.

86 *"The days of a tacit":* Hitchcock, *France Restored*, p. 75.

86 *"new hope which":* "Aldrich Hopeful on Marshall Plan," *New York Times*, July 1, 1947.

86 *In Italy, Pope Pius:* Camille Cianfarra, "Pope Asks End of Wide Misery; Endorses the Marshall Program," *New York Times*, July 1, 1947.

87 *In Germany, Lucius Clay:* Jack Raymond, "Moses to Shape Rebuilding Plan for Cities of West Germany," *New York Times*, July 2, 1947.

87 *"a postal service for":* Herbert Matthews, "Bevin Takes Lead in Defying Soviets," *New York Times*, July 1, 1947.

87 *"farce":* Matthews, "Bevin Takes Lead in Defying Soviets."

87 *"In view of the fact":* From Roberts, "Moscow and the Marshall Plan," p. 1376.

87 *At the time, the United States:* William Hitchcock surveyed the scene in Eastern Europe: there was a rebellion in Poland before the Soviet Union secured power in February 1947; Communists fared poorly in the 1945 election and didn't secure power until May of 1947. Hitchcock, *The Struggle for Europe*, p. 90.

87 *"the Marshall Plan was":* Service, *Stalin*, p. 504.

88 *"it will have grave":* Telegram from U.S. Ambassador to the U.K. Douglas to Secretary Marshall, July 3, 1947, FRUS, 47, 3, p. 306.

88 *"Great Britain on other":* Telegram from U.S. Ambassador to the U.K. Douglas to Secretary Marshall, July 3, 1947, FRUS, 47, 3, p. 307.

88 *"as were willing in the":* Telegram from U.S. Ambassador to the U.K. Douglas to Secretary Marshall, July 3, 1947, FRUS, 47, 3, p. 307.

88 *"Clem," Bevin said:* Lord Roll recalled it in "A Discussion," in Stanley Hoffman and Charles Maier, eds., *The Marshall Plan*, p. 22.

88 *"a finality about this":* Harold Callender, "Paris Parley Ends with Europe Split," *New York Times*, July 3, 1947.

88 *"This really is the birth":* Bullock, *Ernest Bevin*, p. 422.

88 *"We realize the gravity":* Telegram from Secretary Marshall to the American Embassy in Paris, to be delivered to Bidault and Bevin, FRUS, 47, 3, p. 308.

88 *Journalists took his silence:* Bertram Hulen, "Marshall Silent," *New York Times*, July 3, 1947.

89 *He could have delayed:* Many sources make this point, Dean Acheson among them. Oral interview: Dean Acheson, Harry Price Collection.

89 *"Uncle Joe helped":* Averell Harriman, in "A Discussion," in Hoffman and Maier, eds., *The Marshall Plan*, pp. 23, 24.

89 *"If he had reaped":* Narinsky, "Soviet Foreign Policy and the Origins of the Marshall Plan," pp. 109, 110.

89 *Stalin also failed:* Of course, the United States was expansionist on its own continent. At the end of World War II, it certainly wished to broaden its reach and power. But it did not wish to expand its direct territorial holdings.

90 *"an empire by invitation":* This is the central argument in Geir Lundestad's influential work *"Empire" by Integration: The United States and European Integration, 1945–1997.* Gaddis builds on Lundestad's work, arguing that the contrasting nature and dynamics of the United States and the Soviet empire were central in determining the outcome of the Cold War. "One empire arose, therefore, by invitation," Gaddis writes, "the other by imposition . . . Two paths diverged at the end of World War II. And that, to paraphrase an American poet, really did make all the difference." Gaddis, *We Now Know,* pp. 52, 53.

90 *Instead, he had now brought:* As John Lewis Gaddis wrote, Stalin was "singularly insensitive to the possibility that he himself—objectively speaking—was capitalism's greatest ally." Gaddis, *We Now Know,* p. 197.

90 *The two statesmen compiled:* Harold Callender, "22 European States Invited by Britain, France to Meet July 12 on MP, Bid Open to Soviet," *New York Times,* July 4, 1947.

Five: "Friendly Aid" in Paris

PAGE

91 *"the best hope for":* Lansing Warren, "Ramadier Wins Confidence Vote; Backs MP Entirely," *New York Times,* July 5, 1947.

91 *"that dear little man":* "Bevin Vows Lines to U.S. Will Stand," *New York Times,* July 5, 1947.

91 *"If no action":* Telegram from Ambassador Douglas to Secretary Marshall, July 4, 1947, FRUS, 47, 3, p. 311.

91 *"I say to you":* "Bevin Vows Lines to U.S. Will Stand."

91 *The invitation included:* "22 European States Invited by Britain, France to Meet July 12 on MP, Bid Open to Soviet."

92 *Bidault made sure:* "22 European States Invited."

92 *"We think it would":* Roberts, "Moscow and the Marshall Plan," p. 1377.

92 *But only hours later:* Narinsky, "The Soviet Union and the Marshall Plan," p. 47.

92 *There was pressure:* Roberts, "Moscow and the Marshall Plan," p. 1381.

93 *It was pointed out:* Narinsky, "The Soviet Union and the Marshall Plan," p. 47.

93 *The Marshall Plan had already:* Parish, "The Turn Toward Confrontation."

93 *"each side may present":* Narinsky, "The Soviet Union and the Marshall Plan," p. 50; Kratky, "Czechoslovakia, the Soviet Union, and the Marshall Plan," p. 17.

93 *A visitor might pass:* Bailey, *The Marshall Plan Summer,* p. 174.

93 *When General George Patton:* Bailey, *The Marshall Plan Summer,* p. 168.

93 *In Prague, billboards:* Judt, *Postwar,* p. 139.

93 *"physical and strategic crossroads":* Bailey, *The Marshall Plan Summer,* p. 166.

94 *"bridge between East and West":* Bailey, *The Marshall Plan Summer,* p. 166.

94 *By July 1947, Czechoslovakia:* Bailey, *The Marshall Plan Summer,* pp. 168, 169.

94 *Since the war, Czechoslovakia:* Bailey, *The Marshall Plan Summer,* p. 168.

94 *"The Czech government has":* Kratky, "Czechoslovakia, the Soviet Union, and the Marshall Plan," p. 13.

94 *"Everything is alright":* Parish, "The Turn Toward Confrontation," p. 29.

94 *"endanger [Czech] political":* Parish, "The Turn Toward Confrontation," p. 30.

94 *For effect, Stalin:* From Bradley Abrams's essay "The Marshall Plan and Czechoslovak Democracy," in Shain, ed., *The Marshall Plan,* p. 102.

95 *"We know you are friends":* Kratky, "Czechoslovakia, the Soviet Union, and the Marshall Plan," p. 18.

95 *Soon the notion evolved:* Yergin, *Shattered Peace,* p. 325.

95 *"extremely apologetic"*: FRUS, 47, 3, p. 322.
95 *A day earlier*: W. H. Lawrence, "Groza Fears Ruse in Marshall Plan," *New York Times*, July 10, 1947.
95 *Hungary announced*: "Czechs Withdraw Paris Acceptance to Avoid Soviet Ire," *New York Times*, July 11, 1947.
95 *At the end of the day*: Narinsky, "The Soviet Union and the Marshall Plan," p. 51.
95 *"I returned as a lackey"*: Quoted in Narinsky, "The Soviet Union and the Marshall Plan," p. 51.
95 *"smashed the illusion"*: Abrams, "The Marshall Plan and Czechoslovak Democracy," p. 104.
95 *After Czechoslovakia's about-face*: William White, "Marshall Voices U.S. Perturbation on European Split," *New York Times*, July 12, 1947.
95 *"on Soviet orders"*: Telegram from Ambassador Bedell Smith to Secretary Marshall, July 11, 1947, FRUS, 47, 3, p. 327.
96 *Of the twenty-two countries*: Western Germany would be represented shortly thereafter by a U.S. representative and would eventually achieve full status as a member and send its own representative. Price, *The Marshall Plan and Its Meaning*, p. 29.
96 *The hall's table was*: Beevor and Cooper, *Paris*, p. 288.
96 *Bevin and Bidault opened*: Bevin and Bidault once again made it clear that the door was open to Soviet participation were the Soviets to modify their position.
96 *"It is the quickest"*: Harold Callender, "Bevin Named Head," *New York Times*, July 13, 1947.
96 *With the Soviets and*: Callender, "Bevin Named Head."
96 *Meetings that erstwhile*: Beevor and Cooper, *Paris*, p. 288.
96 *That evening he enjoyed*: Bullock, *Ernest Bevin*, p. 425.
97 *"great smoothness and rapidity"*: Telegram from the British Chargé Balfour to Secretary Marshall, July 16, 1947, FRUS, 47, 3, p. 331.
97 *The assemblage comprised*: Van der Beugel, *From Marshall Aid to Atlantic Partnership*, pp. 68, 69.
97 *"Six weeks is a short"*: William Diebold Jr., *Trade and Payments in Western Europe* (New York: Harper & Bros., 1952), quoted in van der Beugel, *From Marshall Aid to Atlantic Partnership*, p. 69.
97 *"You go to Paris"*: Price, *The Marshall Plan and Its Meaning*, p. 36.
97 *"the principles"*: Oral interview: Paul Hoffman, Harry Price Collection.
98 *"the primary school"*: van der Beugel, *From Marshall Aid to Atlantic Partnership*, pp. 71, 72.
98 *"But this is not"*: Eric Roll, "The Marshall Plan as Anglo-American Response," in Shain, ed., *The Marshall Plan*, p. 43.
98 *The French were not*: Nitze, *From Hiroshima to Glasnost*, pp. 54, 55.
98 *Her dress was cut*: Beevor and Cooper, *Paris*, p. 299.
98 *Jean-Paul Sartre*: "*Life* Visits Bohemian Paris," *Life*, September 29, 1947.
98 *"Girls" could be seen*: Charles Steed, "Old London Sheds a Bit of Austerity," *New York Times*, July 6, 1947.
99 *One group of young*: "Handlebar Club," *Life*, August 11, 1947.
99 *"twelfth-hour"*: Herbert Morrison, "Britain is Warned of Crisis This Fall," *New York Times*, July 9, 1947.
99 *"We debated much"*: Bullock, *Ernest Bevin*, pp. 39, 43.
99 *"to retreat from one"*: Aide-mémoire from the British Embassy to the Department of State, July 28, 1947, FRUS 47, 3, pp. 46, 47.
99 *"I can say that"*: Telegram from Ambassador Douglas to Secretary Marshall, July 25, 1947, FRUS, 47, 3, p. 44.
100 *"Troutman"*: Fossedal, *Our Finest Hour*, p. 248.
100 *"Lockhart"*: Oral interview: Paul Porter (observation made by interviewer: Theodore Wilson), HST Library Collection.

100 "ambassador to Europe": Michael Hoffman, "No. 1 Envoy to Europe," New York Times Magazine, September 21, 1947.

100 "Europeans were quite": Telegram from Ambassador Caffrey to Secretary Marshall, July 27, 1947, FRUS, 47, 3, p. 340.

100 With prospects good: Van der Beugel writes of Clayton's "rather vague approach" engaging his European interlocutors in July. Van der Beugel, From Marshall Aid to Atlantic Partnership, p. 77.

100 On July 31, Clayton: Van der Beugel, From Marshall Aid to Atlantic Partnership, p. 78.

101 While 90 percent of Americans: Gallup, The Gallup Poll, vol. 1, pp. 661, 666.

101 Lovett, born in: Edward Lockett, "Robert Lovett—Co-Pilot of 'State,'" New York Times Magazine, August 17, 1947.

101 "At no time in": Yergin, Shattered Peace, p. 328.

101 "The 'Marshall Plan' has": Telegram from the Assistant Chief of the Division of Commercial Policy Ben Moore to the Director of the Office of International Policy Wilcox at Geneva, July 28, 1947, FRUS, 47, 3, p. 240.

101 "most people know": Memorandum Prepared by the Policy Planning Staff, from PPS Files, July [21?], 1947, FRUS, 47, 3, pp. 335, 337.

102 "Marshall 'plan.' We have no plan": Memorandum Prepared by the Policy Planning Staff, from PPS Files, July [21?], 1947, FRUS, 47, 3, p. 335. Several historians have taken the first portion of what Kennan wrote—"Marshall 'plan.' We have no plan"— to suggest that State did not have a real plan and that the department was behind the curve and struggling to move forward. In this way, Kennan is taken out of context. The next sentence follows: "Europe must be made to take responsibility. We would consider European plan only if it were a good one and promised to do the whole job." The U.S. plan was to look to Europe for a more detailed plan.

102 "The Sources of Soviet Conduct": "X," "The Sources of Soviet Conduct," Foreign Affairs, July 1947.

102 The article introduced: To this point, Gaddis wrote: "Americans managed to merge their original vision of a single international order built around common security with a second and more hastily improvised concept that sought to counter the expanding power and influence of the Soviet Union. That concept was, of course, containment, and its chief instrument was the Marshall Plan." Gaddis, We Now Know, p. 37.

103 The Benelux countries: Van der Beugel, From Marshall Aid to Atlantic Partnership, p. 73.

103 The Turks complained: Fossedal, Our Finest Hour, p. 248.

103 "worked like a super-heated": Hogan, The Marshall Plan, p. 55.

103 A reorientation from: Hogan, The Marshall Plan, pp. 66, 67.

103 "there would be no Europe": Bullock, Ernest Bevin, pp. 431, 432.

103 "beg, repeat beg": Gimbel, The Origins of the Marshall Plan, p. 231.

104 Bidault was furious: Hitchcock, France Restored, pp. 78, 79.

104 Days later, on July 21: "Royall's Remarks Upset Marshall," New York Times, August 7, 1947.

104 Given the breach: Monnet, Memoirs, p. 184; Hitchcock, France Restored, pp. 75, 76.

104 It was a boon: "Royall's Remarks Upset Marshall."

104 "All work of technical": Leffler, A Preponderance of Power, p. 187.

104 "plan that is not": James Reston, "Sforza Demands 'Daring' Plan by Europe to Aid Marshall Move," New York Times, August 15, 1947.

104 The sweltering heat: Associated Press, "Europe's Heat Wave Causes Destruction," New York Times, August 20, 1947; Associated Press, "Drought Imperils Crops of Europe," New York Times, August 25, 1947.

104 France's wheat crop: Yergin, Shattered Peace, p. 328.

104 On the German-Dutch: "Europe's Heat Wave Causes Destruction." New York Times, August 21, 1947.

104 "near-famine conditions": "Drought Imperils Crops of Europe." New York Times, August 26, 1947.

104 Ambassador Caffrey: Caffrey said, "France could not get by beyond the end of this year

without substantial aid, that her reduced harvest this year would provide bread for only five months at present low ration." Memorandum from Mr. Wesley C. Haraldson of the Office of the United States Political Adviser for Germany Robert Murphy; subject: Paris Discussions on the Marshall Plan (August 4 to August 6, 1947), August 8, 1947, FRUS, 47, 3, pp. 345, 346.

105 *"It can be frankly"*: Bailey, *The Marshall Plan Summer*, p. 112.

105 *Premier De Gasperi*: "The Problem Is: Too Little Bread, Too Much Politics," *Life*, October 6, 1947.

105 *In cinemas, filmgoers*: "New Italian Film Will Shock the World," *Life*, August 25, 1947.

105 *With a big election*: Lansing Warren, "French Right and Left Prepare for a Showdown," *New York Times*, August 24, 1947.

105 *Dulles reported back*: Vandenberg, ed., *Private Papers of Senator Vandenberg*, pp. 373, 374.

105 *British Treasury officials*: Bullock, *Ernest Bevin*, pp. 452, 453.

105 *That same year*: Editorial, "Britain Needs Help Again: And We Must Give It to Her but Not Without Some Stern Advice on How to Use It," *Life*, September 8, 1947.

105 *"hanging on by its"*: Quoted in Judt, *Postwar*, p. 111.

105 *"low grade of"*: Quoted in Hogan, *The Marshall Plan*, p. 82.

105 *Bevin was loyal*: Bullock, *Ernest Bevin*, pp. 452, 453.

105 *Wholesale prices had*: Duchene, *Jean Monnet*, p. 167.

106 *In mid-August*: As part of a deal whereby the United States also waived any further benefits of the loan to Great Britain.

106 *"The British have turned"*: Yergin, *Shattered Peace*, p. 328.

106 *"have raised the Capitol dome"*: Donovan, *The Second Victory*, p. 41.

106 *"Gaston-Alphonse"*: Meaning, the United States wanted Europe to tell them and Europe said, We can't tell you until you tell us. "Plan for Marshall," *New York Times*, August 31, 1947.

106 *"Molotov approach"*: Hogan, *The Marshall Plan*, pp. 70, 71.

106 *"His has been the voice"*: Hoffman, "No. 1 Envoy to Europe."

107 *"Failure of any country"*: Telegram from Ambassador Caffrey to Secretary Marshall, August 6, 1947, FRUS, 47, 3, pp. 343, 344.

107 *Yet he did not tell*: Van der Beugel wrote: "In response to Frank's question whether such a customs union could be considered as a condition for American aid, Clayton replied in the negative but added that such a commitment would greatly enhance the chance of Congressional approval." Van der Beugel, *From Marshall Aid to Atlantic Partnership*, p. 78.

107 *In Washington, Lovett*: Telegram from Ambassador Caffrey to Secretary Marshall, August 6, 1947, FRUS, 47, 3, p. 344. Leffler wrote that Lovett had foreseen the need for some sort of emergency relief plan as early as July 10. Leffler, *A Preponderance of Power*, p. 192.

107 *"pruning down would be"*: Telegram from Ambassador Caffrey to Secretary Marshall, August 20, 1947, FRUS, 47, 3, p. 366.

107 *"Unless they are prepared"*: Telegram from Acting Secretary of State Robert Lovett to U.S. Embassy in France, August 14, 1947, FRUS, 47, 3, p. 357.

107 *"come out so far"*: Telegram from Acting Secretary Lovett to Secretary Marshall at Petropolis, Brazil, August 24, 1947, FRUS, 47, 3, p. 373.

107 *"Against the background"*: Telegram from Acting Secretary Lovett to Secretary Marshall at Petropolis, Brazil, August 24, 1947, FRUS, 47, 3, p. 375.

108 *The latter had pushed*: Hogan, *The Marshall Plan*, pp. 73, 74.

108 *"low labor productivity"*: Ambassador Caffrey, quoted in Hogan, *The Marshall Plan*, p. 72.

108 *"Doctrinaire Willie"*: Yergin, *Shattered Peace*, p. 321.

108 *"the mutual exchange"*: Telegram from Ambassador Caffrey to Secretary Marshall, August 31, 1947, FRUS, 47, 3, p. 392.

108 *"planners"*: The cover of the *New York Times Magazine* on September 7, 1947, featured a picture of Clayton and Kennan with the title, "Planners for Europe."

108 *"Any effort to press"*: Bullock, *Ernest Bevin*, p. 459.

108 *"much too large"*: Harold Callender, "Paris Group Maps Drastic Aid Cuts At U.S. Suggestion," *New York Times*, August 31, 1947; Harold Callender, "Paris Parley Acts on U.S. Criticism," *New York Times*, September 2, 1947.

109 *"the essentials for winning"*: The "essentials" from telegram from Ambassador Caffrey to Secretary Marshall, August 31, 1947, FRUS, 47, 3, pp. 391–94.

109 *For Franks, Clayton's new*: Van der Beugel, *From Marshall Aid to Atlantic Partnership*, pp. 80, 81.

109 *"very blunt criticism"*: See Hogan, *The Marshall Plan*, pp. 71–74.

109 *"No bold or original"*: Telegram: Memorandum by the Director of the PPS Kennan; Report: Situation with Respect to European Recovery Program, September 4, 1947, FRUS, 47, 3, p. 398.

109 *"Today we are in"*: Telegram: Memorandum by the Director of the PPS Kennan; Report: Situation with Respect to European Recovery Program, September 4, 1947, FRUS, 47, 3, pp. 401–5.

110 *In Washington, Lovett*: Harold Hinton, "Congress Call Up to Truman," *New York Times*, September 6, 1947.

110 *In Europe, the leader*: Harold Callender, "Paris Parley Leaders Heartened by Lovett's Urging of Quick Aid," *New York Times*, September 4, 1947.

110 *When word of Lovett's*: Harold Callender, "Hope Grows in Europe for Early American Aid," *New York Times*, September 7, 1947.

110 *"American pressure"*: Bullock, *Ernest Bevin*, p. 459.

110 *"friendly aid"*: Telegram from Ambassador Douglas to Secretary Marshall, September 12, 1947, FRUS, 47, 3, p. 429.

110 *"to whittle it down"*: Telegram: Memorandum by the Director of the PPS Kennan; Report: Situation with Respect to European Recovery Program, September 4, 1947, FRUS, 47, 3, p. 402.

111 *"what some of the"*: The Kennan report from telegram: Memorandum by the Director of the PPS Kennan; Report: Situation with Respect to European Recovery Program, September 4, 1947, FRUS, 47, 3, pp. 397–405.

111 *"essentials"*: Hogan, *The Marshall Plan*, pp. 77, 78.

111 *"blazed a new path"*: Telegram from Ambassador Caffrey to Secretary Marshall, September 17, 1947, FRUS 47, 3, pp. 436, 437. There were still final details to iron out. The Marshall Plan negotiations were being held parallel with the GATT negotiations in Geneva. During this time there were final spurts of acrimony with the British, whom Clayton—also responsible for the GATT negotiations—was pushing hard to lower its imperial and Commonwealth preferences. At times, Clayton even went public, intimating on the radio that if Great Britain did not push further to liberalize trade, the Marshall Plan might not pass Congress; this angered Bevin immensely. Bob Dixon recorded: "A busy day in the Office, with Clayton and Douglas next door trying to blackmail E.B. and Cripps into dropping imperial preference under the threat of no help for Britain under Marshall Plan"; from Bullock, *Ernest Bevin*, p. 462. Free trade meant peace and prosperity for Clayton, and he knew that the historical moment would be fleeting. Despite Bevin's outrage, it was hard-nosed negotiating tactics, and it worked. Before September was out, GATT passed. Fossedal, *Our Finest Hour*, p. 253.

111 *The report of the CEEC*: All but two of the participating nations—Switzerland and Sweden—endorsed the report. Harold Callender, "Clayton Accepts 16-Nation Aid Plan," *New York Times*, September 17, 1947.

111 *The report provided*: The actual report was reprinted in the *New York Times*; a good summary is available in Pogue, *George C. Marshall*, p. 233.

112 *"In presenting this Report"*: van der Beugel, *From Marshall Aid to Atlantic Partnership*, pp. 81, 82.

112 *"formed the indispensable"*: Quoted in Van der Beugel, *From Marshall Aid to Atlantic Partnership*, pp. 81, 82.

112 *A collapse could catapult:* Report, "Review of the World Situation as It Relates to the Security of the United States," September 26, 1947. See Leffler, *A Preponderance of Power,* p. 189.

112 *"a new state in the":* Harold Callender, "16-Nation Aid Plan Signed As Leaders Warn of Collapse," *New York Times,* September 23, 1947.

112 *The 690-page report:* "Europe Submits Its 'Marshall Plan,'" *Life,* October 6, 1947.

112 *Without delay, Kirkwood:* Harold Callender, "Need for U.S. Aid Is Urgent, Parley Report Emphasizes," *New York Times,* September 24, 1947.

112 *"Here is our report":* Callender, "16-Nation Aid Plan Signed."

113 *"most important decision":* Editorial, "The Marshall Plan: Our Move Next," *Life,* September 22, 1947.

Six: Selling America

PAGE

114 *"How much I admire":* McCullough, *Truman,* p. 583.

114 *On October 7, Will Clayton:* Fossedal, *Our Finest Hour,* p. 256.

114 *"the principal architect":* Fossedal, *Our Finest Hour,* pp. 257, 258.

114 *"I'd like to spank Sue":* Quoted in Fossedal, *Our Finest Hour,* p. 256.

114 *Bidault and diplomats:* Lansing Warren, "Bidault Denies Serious Criticism in U.S. of Paris Report on Marshall Project," *New York Times,* October 17, 1947.

114 *"The harvest is past":* "Londoner Cites Scripture to Point Up British Crisis," *New York Times,* September 22, 1947.

115 *At the time, 37 percent:* Gallup, *The Gallup Poll,* vol. 1, p. 680.

115 *"remotely suggesting":* William White, "Congress's Leaders Reticent on U.S. Aid," *New York Times,* September 23, 1947.

115 *Even most Parisians:* "Plan for Marshall," *New York Times,* August 31, 1947.

115 *Yet most Americans:* In the last poll before the release of the report, 51 percent of the Americans responding said they had not heard of the Marshall Plan. Gallup, *The Gallup Poll,* vol. 1, p. 661.

115 *A month earlier:* "House Group Here on Way to Europe," *New York Times,* August 28, 1947.

115 *The group had been:* Cabell Phillips, "Congressional Tours Big Aid to Marshall Plan," *New York Times,* October 19, 1947.

115 *Divided into five separate:* Price, *The Marshall Plan and Its Meaning,* pp. 51–53.

115 *Chairman of the House:* "House Group Here on Way to Europe."

115 *From mid-August to:* Van der Beugel, *From Marshall Aid to Atlantic Partnership,* p. 88.

115 *to investigate conditions:* "How Much, When?: The Marshall Question," *New York Times,* October 19, 1947.

116 *For John F. Kennedy:* Dallek, *An Unfinished Life,* pp. 3, 4.

116 *That autumn, members:* "U.S. Citizens Look at Europe," *Life,* October 20, 1947; "The Visitors Pop Up Everywhere," *Life,* October 20, 1947.

116 *"We tried to look":* Phillips, "Congressional Tours Big Aid to Marshall Plan."

116 *"in somewhat the way":* White, *Fire in the Ashes,* pp. 379, 380.

116 *When the Herter Committee:* "U.S. Citizens Look at Europe," *Life.*

116 *"What would it cost":* Price, *The Marshall Plan and Its Meaning,* pp. 51–53.

116 *As the waves of:* Phillips, "Congressional Tours Big Aid to Marshall Plan."

116 *Members of Congress were:* Phillips, "Congressional Tours Big Aid to Marshall Plan."

117 *the Soviet Union had called:* Beevor and Cooper, *Paris,* pp. 291, 292.

117 *He was considered:* Djilas, *Conversations with Stalin,* p. 149; Parish, "The Turn Toward Confrontation"; Service, *Stalin,* p. 506.

117 *Ostensibly, the Communist:* Gaddis, *We Now Know,* p. 46.

117 *"the institutional expression":* Parish, "The Turn Toward Confrontation," p. 32.

117 *"a policy of preparing"*: Beevor and Cooper, *Paris*, p. 292.

117 *"forty-ninth state"*: "Communist Leader Pledges Drive to Ruin Marshall Plan," *New York Times*, October 23, 1947; Parish, "The Turn Toward Confrontation," p. 35.

117 *"While you are fighting"*: Yergin, *Shattered Peace*, p. 326.

118 The Cold War: Reynolds, ed., *The Origins of the Cold War in Europe*, p. 1.

118 *Now Stalin would*: Stalin's biographer wrote, "The purpose of the Cominform . . . was to respond to the challenge thrown down by the Marshall Plan." Service, *Stalin*, pp. 514, 515.

118 *"all effort into seeing"*: "Communist Leader Pledges Drive to Ruin Marshall Plan."

118 *The hopeful data combined*: "British Diet Drops Below 1933 Level," *New York Times*, November 11, 1947; Herbert Matthews, "British Pit Strike Gains in Gravity," *New York Times*, September 4, 1947; Charles Egan, "Statistics Give the British New Strength and Hopes," *New York Times*, December 7, 1947.

118 *"The only objective"*: Beevor and Cooper, *Paris*, p. 292.

119 *In mid-October, less*: Gallup, *The Gallup Poll*, vol. 1, pp. 679, 680.

119 *In late October, ten thousand*: Beevor and Cooper, *Paris*, p. 297.

119 *Virtually all the coal mines*: Beevor and Cooper, *Paris*, pp. 303, 304.

119 *All of this was meant*: Beevor and Cooper, *Paris*, p. 301.

119 *"greatest crisis"*: "France in Crisis," *New York Times*, November 23, 1947.

119 *"People talk only of"*: Beevor and Cooper, *Paris*, p. 296.

120 *"All seems quiet"*: Beevor and Cooper, *Paris*, p. 304.

120 *"declared open political warfare"*: Memorandum on Immediate Need for Emergency Aid to Europe, September 29, 1947, FRUS, 47, 3, p. 475.

120 *"a class war"*: Arnaldo Cortesi, "Communists Urge Italians to Enlist in a Class War," *New York Times*, October 19, 1947.

120 *Drawings of the hammer*: "Italy: An Ancient Citadel of Culture Faces a New Threat," *Life*, November 24, 1947.

120 *"indicates that there"*: Harold Hinton, "Anti-American Campaign Intensified in Europe," *New York Times*, September 21, 1947.

120 *In Bari, the government*: Arnaldo Cortesi, "Fear Rises in Italy After Arms Blast," *New York Times*, November 17, 1947; Harold Callender, "French Heads Fear a General Strike," *New York Times*, November 19, 1947.

120 *"It is necessary"*: "Trouble: From Paris to Bangkok Men Revolt and Die," *Life*, December 1, 1947.

120 *"the fabled Italy of"*: "Italy," *Life*, November 24, 1947.

120 *"The present wave"*: Arnaldo Cortesi, "One Man Is Killed, Many Hurt in Italy as Communist Riots Still Spread," *New York Times*, November 16, 1947.

121 *The United States was determined*: Bullock, *Ernest Bevin*, pp. 493–97.

121 *Behind the scenes, though*: Bullock, *Ernest Bevin*, p. 495.

121 *"Plant an apricot orchard"*: Mazower, *Dark Continent*, p. 296.

121 *Bevin proposed a transatlantic*: Craig and Lowenheim, eds., *The Diplomats*, p. 113; Bullock, *Ernest Bevin*, pp. 498, 499.

121 *"Mr. President, you must"*: Isaacson and Thomas, *The Wise Men*, p. 424.

122 *"a Marshall Plan to sell"*: Van der Beugel, *From Marshall Aid to Atlantic Partnership*, p. 83.

122 *"The reconstruction of Western Europe"*: Henry Stimson, "The Challenge to Americans," *Foreign Affairs*, October 1947. From editors James Hogue Jr. and Fareed Zakaria, *The American Encounter*, p. 148.

123 *"WE MUST STOP STALIN"*: Meeting of Committee for the Marshall Plan, at the Harvard Club in New York City, October 30, 1947. Dean Acheson Papers, HST Library Collection.

123 *Young Harvard professors*: Economist/academic Harlan Van Buren Cleveland said he gave between fifty and sixty speeches on behalf of the Marshall Plan; see "A Discussion," in Hoffman and Maier, eds., *The Marshall Plan*, pp. 25, 26.

123 *Several of America's most:* Will Clayton was one of the committee's largest donors, and spoke in passionate and forceful terms to a crowd of hundreds at the Hotel Biltmore in a widely publicized mid-December address. "Address by William Clayton at a Luncheon of the Committee for the Marshall Plan to Aid European Recovery, NY, December 18, 1947." Dean Acheson Papers, HST Library Collection.

123 *Dean Acheson's efforts:* Acheson, *Present at the Creation*, pp. 240, 241.

123 *"the heart and core":* "Diplomatic and International Significance of the European Recovery Program," Address delivered by Dean Acheson at the *Philadelphia Bulletin* Forum. Dean Acheson Papers, HST Library Collection.

123 *The National Association of Manufacturers:* "National Association of Manufacturers Supports Aid, Asks 11 Conditions," *New York Times,* November 11, 1947.

123 *So were the American:* Louis Stark, "AFL Maps Backing of Marshall Plan," *New York Times,* November 15, 1947; Morgan, *Reds,* p. 306.

123 *"As Christians, we support":* "The Churches and the European Recovery Program," a statement submitted by the Department of International Justice and Goodwill and adopted by the Executive Committee of the Federal Council of the Churches of Christ in America, January 13, 1948. Marshall Plan Vertical Files, HST Library.

124 *Speaking from Philadelphia:* "Quaker Skeptical on Marshall Plan," *New York Times,* December 7, 1947.

124 *The seventy-two-year-old Nobel laureate:* "Planned Economy Favored by Mann," *New York Times,* September 9, 1947.

124 *"I believe in full production":* William White, "New Englanders Uphold Farm Plan," *New York Times,* October 14, 1947.

124 *Dwight Eisenhower supported:* Ambrose, *Eisenhower,* p. 233.

124 *"the errors of the past":* Will Lissner, "Dewey Favors Aid in Europe and Asia on Business Basis," *New York Times,* November 6, 1947.

124 *Notre Dame:* Associated Press, "Notre Dame Crowds Hit by Food Saving Program," *New York Times,* October 18, 1947.

124 *Days before Thanksgiving:* Frank Kluckhohn, "Bradford at First Thanksgiving Site Asks Families Share with Europe," *New York Times,* November 20, 1947.

125 *By the time the train:* "Friendship Train Gets Pledges Here," *New York Times,* November 15, 1947; "Friendship Cargo Sails for France," *New York Times,* December 8, 1947.

125 *Parades in cities and towns:* Charles Grutzner, "City Hails Friendship Train; Food Total Is Put at 270 Cars," *New York Times,* November 19, 1947.

125 *"This seems to be":* Vandenberg, ed., *The Private Papers of Senator Vandenberg,* pp. 376–78.

125 *"He soon became":* Oral interview: George C. Marshall, Harry Price Collection.

125 *"He was profound":* Pogue, *George C. Marshall,* p. 238.

125 *"couldn't have gotten much":* Yergin, *Shattered Peace,* p. 327.

126 *"I am reserving some":* Vandenberg, ed., *The Private Papers of Senator Vandenberg,* pp. 378, 379.

126 *Lovett, who joked:* Isaacson and Thomas, *The Wise Men,* p. 425.

126 *The two spent more waking:* Isaacson and Thomas, *The Wise Men,* p. 424.

126 *"the country at some":* Nitze, *From Hiroshima to Glasnost,* pp. 59–62.

126 *"The Paris Conference":* Unofficial aide-mémoire from the Chairman of the CEEC Washington Delegation Sir Oliver Franks to Undersecretary Lovett, left with Lovett after conversation on evening of October 22, FRUS, 47, 3, p. 446.

127 *"A few billion dollars":* Unofficial aide-mémoire from Franks to Lovett, p. 448. "The conferences were held in the ultra-modern conference chamber of the new State Department building. The opening was not promising. Reports circulated that the State Department thought it necessary to reconvene the full CEEC to redraft parts of the report . . . In London, one official commented: 'If anything could make us pro-Russian, it's being treated like naughty school children scolded for not having done our exercises rightly and told we must stay in after school to do them over again.'" "How Much, When?," *New York Times,* October 19, 1947.

127 "I fully recognize": Unofficial aide-mémoire from Franks to Lovett, p. 448.

127 The European delegates labored: Pogue, George C. Marshall, pp. 234, 235.

127 The United States was taking: Memorandum: The CEEC Washington Delegation to the Participating Governments Not Represented in Washington, October 31, 1947, FRUS, 47, 3, pp. 459, 460.

127 The brown books laid: Nitze, From Hiroshima to Glasnost, p. 60. Despite the ardor and care that went into these calculations and estimates, they were imprecise. Charles Kindleberger spoke of a "fudge factor." Oral interview: Charles Kindleberger, HST Library Collection.

127 "primitive devices": Nitze, From Hiroshima to Glasnost, p. 59.

127 "We are not doing": Associated Press, "Wants No Credit for Aid," New York Times, October 18, 1947.

127 Into November, with: Nitze, From Hiroshima to Glasnost, p. 60.

128 Lovett and Marshall agreed: Bissell, Reflections of a Cold Warrior, p. 38.

128 "My God you look": Oral interview: Charles Kindleberger, HST Library Collection.

128 "began for the first time": "U.S.—The Plan," New York Times, November 10, 1947.

128 Back in June, only: Harriman gave Acheson credit but also said of the committee, "I have no idea how it got started." Oral interview: Averell Harriman, HST Library Collection. In Present at the Creation, Acheson essentially gives Vandenberg credit, as do most others. It appears that Vandenberg was the primary driver. Bissell, Reflections of a Cold Warrior, pp. 34, 35.

128 The Krug Committee report: Alberts, "Domestic Aspects of the Marshall Plan," p. 13.

129 The Nourse report: Price, The Marshall Plan and Its Meaning, pp. 40, 41.

129 Van also added Owen: Oral interview: Averell Harriman, HST Library Collection.

129 "the Committee was stacked": Oral interview: Edward Mason, HST Library Collection.

129 Vandenberg had already announced: Bissell, Reflections of a Cold Warrior, p. 35.

130 Physically, Bissell was weak: Bissell, Reflections of a Cold Warrior, pp. 1, 3–5, 10.

130 "It is difficult to convey": Bissell, Reflections of a Cold Warrior, pp. 10, 11.

130 "I was the American": Bissell, Reflections of a Cold Warrior, pp. 15–26; Thomas, The Very Best Men, pp. 94, 95.

131 An economist is someone: McCullough, Truman, p. 558.

131 "one of the most outstanding": Oral interview: Averell Harriman, HST Library Collection.

131 Arriving in Washington: Bissell, Reflections of a Cold Warrior, p. 37.

131 "hottest fight": Price, The Marshall Plan and Its Meaning, p. 45; Alberts, "Domestic Aspects of the Marshall Plan," p. 30.

131 Rather, he sought: Bissell, Reflections of a Cold Warrior, p. 36.

131 "I was the Chairman": Oral interview: Averell Harriman, HST Library Collection.

131 Some members, like: Bissell, Reflections of a Cold Warrior, p. 36.

132 Hoffman's finely honed people: Particularly on the point about whether aid should go to socialist governments, or pressure governments to move toward free enterprise. And as a well-regarded industrialist and Republican, Hoffman had particular credibility on this debate. Price, The Marshall Plan and Its Meaning, pp. 44, 45.

132 In fact, at the committee's: Abramson, Spanning the Century, p. 419.

132 "Only the Europeans": Oral interview: Paul Hoffman, HST Library Collection.

132 Bissell's report touched: "European Recovery and American Aid," p. 3.

132 "vital interests": "European Recovery and American Aid," pp. 18, 19.

132 Weighing in on what: "European Recovery and American Aid," p. 10.

132 The cost estimate: "European Recovery and American Aid," p. 8.

132 In early November, Vandenberg: Pisani, The CIA and the Marshall Plan, p. 61.

132 It was 4 A.M.: Abramson, Spanning the Century, p. 419.

132 "How he did it": Oral interview: Paul Hoffman, HST Library Collection.

133 "We're going to issue": Oral interview: Averell Harriman, HST Library Collection.

133 If committee members: Bissell, Reflections of a Cold Warrior, p. 37.

133 "Only a Hollywood press agent": Abramson, Spanning the Century, p. 420.

133 *"exhaustive and eloquent"*: Felix Belair, "ERP's Domestic Phases Cause Capital Concern," *New York Times*, November 16, 1947.

133 *"there is no disposition"*: "London Is Pleased by Harriman Plan," *New York Times*, November 10, 1947.

133 *"It's all right"*: Oral interview: Harold Stein. Harry Price Collection.

133 *"monumental importance"*: Oral interview: Paul Hoffman, Harry Price Collection.

133 *Humphrey Bogart and Lauren Bacall:* "The Movie Hearing Ends: Result: 10 Contempt Charges, Countless Autographs," *Life*, November 10, 1947.

134 *On Broadway, a thirty-three-year-old:* "'A Streetcar Named Desire,'" *Life*, December 15, 1947.

134 *A few blocks away:* "The Champion's Crown Totters," *Life*, December 15, 1947.

134 *Weeks earlier, across the country:* Jay Walz, "New U.S. Plane Said to Fly Faster than the Speed of Sound," *New York Times*, December 22, 1947.

134 *The Herter Committee:* They operated separately for the most part. There was a reasonable degree of cooperation and sharing of data, analysis, etc., between the Harriman Committee, the Committee for the Marshall Plan and the State Department. There was also some resentment on the part of many in the State Department for all the attention and publicity that the work of the Harriman Committee received.

134 *In mid-September, less:* Gallup, *The Gallup Poll*, vol. 1, pp. 677, 678, 691.

134 *"a vast Christmas package"*: William White, "Marshall Plan Faces Under-Cover Opposition," *New York Times*, November 2, 1947.

134 *"solemn silence"*: "Now Congress," *New York Times*, November 16, 1947; Harold Hinton, "Truman Demands Price and Pay Controls; Ties Fight on Inflation to Aid to Europe," *New York Times*, November 18, 1947.

134 *After several minutes, Truman:* "Atmosphere Is Tense and Grave as President Reports on Crisis," *New York Times*, November 18, 1947.

134 *"The future of free nations"*: Pollard, *Economic Security and the Origins of the Cold War*, p. 147.

135 *At the same time:* Hinton, "Truman Demands Price and Pay Controls."

135 *"A Marshall Plan authorization"*: Robert Albright, "Only Danger Is Tinkering," *Washington Post*, November 23, 1947.

135 *"the dull fires of partisan strife"*: Felix Belair, "Election Year Politics Held a Threat to ERP," *New York Times*, November 23, 1947.

135 *"The Marshall Plan is"*: "Text of Taft's Speech Delivered Before the Ohio Society," *New York Times*, November 11, 1947. The speech was given on November 10.

136 *"If France is lost"*: Hitchcock, *France Restored*, pp. 83, 84.

136 *Weeks earlier, the Bureau:* Charles Hurd, "Our Post-War Aid Abroad $19 Billion Now, Byrd Reports," *New York Times*, November 1, 1947.

136 *"Why, it is being asked"*: Belair, "Election Year Politics Held a Threat to ERP."

136 *A good number of Republicans:* John Vorys, Robert Lovett's old friend from Yale, was one of them. Lovett could pass China off as Marshall's specialty. Isaacson and Thomas, *The Wise Men*, p. 427.

136 *He could not answer:* Telegram from Acting Secretary Lovett to Secretary Marshall, December 4, 1947, FRUS, 47, 3, p. 483; Pogue, *George C. Marshall*, p. 236.

136 *"taken for a ride"*: Felix Belair, "Current Taxes Must Finance Marshall Plan, Says Truman," *New York Times*, November 14, 1947.

136 *Representative Leslie C. Arends:* "Referendum on the Marshall Plan Urged by Republican Whip in House," *New York Times*, November 26, 1947.

137 *"wrecking crews"*: C. P. Trussell, "Vandenberg Asks Senate to Act Fast on Aid to Block 'Wrecking Crews' in Europe," *New York Times*, November 25, 1947.

137 *"sweat, swim and rub"*: Vandenberg, ed., *The Private Papers of Senator Vandenberg*, pp. 379–81.

137 *"Democrats Let Van Carry"*: James Reston, "Democrats Let Van Carry Load in Aid Debate," *New York Times*, November 25, 1947.

137 *"If the resistance showing"*: Vandenberg, ed., *The Private Papers of Senator Vandenberg*, pp. 379, 380.

137 *"we're headed for the storm"*: Isaacson and Thomas, *The Wise Men*, pp. 427, 428.

138 *French coal production declined*: "The Cost to France: It Was Heavy, but the Republic Is Still Free," *Life*, December 15, 1947.

138 *France's largest Communist*: Noted in Bullock, *Ernest Bevin*, p. 487.

138 *The next afternoon*: Beever and Cooper, *Paris*, p. 306.

138 *"Reds cried, 'Watch Italy'"*: "Rome's Healthy Realism," *Life*, December 29, 1947.

138 *U.S. Ambassador James Dunn*: Telegram from Ambassador Dunn to Secretary Marshall, FRUS, 48, 3, pp. 740, 741.

138 *Unloading the shipments*: "Friendship Cargo Sails for France," *New York Times*, December 8, 1947; Lansing Warren, "Friendship Cargo Hailed by France," *New York Times*, December 18, 1947.

139 *On December 15, Congress*: Robert Whitney, "Truman and Party Leaders To Weigh Foreign Aid Today," *New York Times*, December 15, 1947.

139 *"the subject of more study"*: "Truman Presents ERP," *New York Times*, December 21, 1947.

139 *"Our deepest concern"*: Price, *The Marshall Plan and Its Meaning*, p. 47.

139 *"If Europe fails"*: "Truman Presents ERP."

140 *"The essence of the two"*: "Moscow Sees War in Marshall Plan," *New York Times*, December 22, 1947.

140 *"At this point"*: Anthony Leviero, "Truman Offers Hope for All As He Lights the Nation's Tree," *New York Times*, December 25, 1947.

Seven: Putting It Over

PAGE

141 *"the greatest productive record"*: McCullough, *Truman*, p. 621.

141 *The political violence*: Kennan's early 1948 report to Marshall, "Résumé of World Situation," quoted in Isaacson and Thomas, *The Wise Men*, p. 435.

141 *Truman was about*: McCullough, *Truman*, p. 586.

141 *In early January*: Gallup, *The Gallup Poll*, vol. 1, p. 710.

142 *"Then," said Wherry*: C. P. Trussell, "ERP Bill Is Offered," *New York Times*, January 7, 1948.

142 *Around 1:30 P.M. that day*: "The Presidential Year Is Off to a Noisy Start," *Life*, January 19, 1948.

142 *"In times of crisis"*: McCullough, *Truman*, p. 591.

142 *"One man"*: Pogue, *George C. Marshall*, p. 237.

142 *"the number one"*: Leffler, *A Preponderance of Power*, p. 200.

142 *"Anything could happen"*: "The Presidential Year Is Off to a Noisy Start."

142 *On New Year's Day*: James Reston, "Moves by Vandenberg Speed Marshall Plan," *New York Times*, February 22, 1948; Arthur Krock, "ERP a Ticklish Problem as 1948 Race Shapes Up," *New York Times*, January 11, 1948.

143 *Some in the media*: Arthur Krock, "ERP Retreat Damaging," *New York Times*, January 7, 1948.

143 *"the standpoint of intelligent"*: Felix Belair, "Foreign Aid Vital, Vandenberg Says," *New York Times*, December 23, 1947.

143 *"backed by more hard"*: James Reston, "Van Lauds Work Put into Framing ERP Bill," *New York Times*, January 10, 1948.

143 *"On an issue"*: James Reston, "Vandenberg Wants a National Debate on Marshall Plan," *New York Times*, December 22, 1947.

143 *"full force into action"*: Isaacson and Thomas, *The Wise Men*, p. 449.

143 *"looking even more"*: James Reston, "Marshall Always Patient, But Adamant on His Plan," *New York Times*, January 9, 1948.

143 *"almost consciously dull"*: Reston, "Marshall Always Patient, But Adamant on His Plan."

144 *"An inadequate program"*: Felix Belair, "Marshall Asks Whole Plan for Aid to Europe, or None; Confident We Can Succeed," *New York Times*, January 9, 1948.

144 *Fielding questions following*: Reston, "Marshall Always Patient, But Adamant on His Plan."

144 *"techniques of propaganda"*: Felix Belair, "Marshall Chided, 'Business' Control of ERP Demanded," *New York Times*, January 10, 1948.

144 *"a new element"*: Felix Belair, "Marshall Chided." Also, Vandenberg asked about Western German inclusion in the Plan. Marshall said Western Germany should be included and that it would be a part of the program. Felix Belair, "Marshall Asks Whole Plan for Aid to Europe."

145 *"It is idle"*: Quoted in Joyce and Gabriel Kolko, *The Limits of Power*, p. 376.

145 *"light or sentimental grounds"*: From Pogue, *George C. Marshall*, pp. 240, 243.

145 *"administered in a business-like way"*: Belair, "Marshall Asks Whole Plan for Aid to Europe."

145 *Marshall was criticized*: Arthur Krock, "Marshall's Bluntness Worries ERP's Friends," *New York Times*, January 18, 1948.

145 *"a political miracle"*: *Ceremonies Commemorating the 30th Anniversary of the Passage of the Marshall Plan Legislation*, Capital Hilton Hotel, Washington, D.C., April 4, 1978. (Washington, D.C.: United States Government Printing Office, 1978). From Marshall Plan Vertical Files, HST Library Collection.

146 *"It was perhaps"*: Vandenberg, ed., *The Private Papers of Senator Vandenberg*, pp. 384, 385. The aide was also his son and editor of his papers.

146 *"Yours is one"*: Testimony of Bernard Baruch on European Recovery Program, Senate Committee on Foreign Relations, January 19, 1948. Averell Harriman Papers, Library of Congress Collection.

146 *"building a stable peace"*: Statement of Secretary of Commerce W. Averell Harriman Before Committee on Foreign Affairs, House of Representatives, Hearing on European Recovery Plan, January 21, 1948, Averell Harriman Papers, Library of Congress Collection. Secretary of Defense James Forrestal stressed the need to fill the political vacuum that would otherwise be filled by Soviet power. Hogan, *The Marshall Plan*, p. 89. Forrestal, Royall, and other top defense officials told the Senate Foreign Relations Committee that military conscription, increases in military expenditures equal to or greater than the cost of the Marshall Plan and vulnerability to "political aggression by totalitarian nations" would result should the Congress fail to pass the Plan. Felix Belair, "Choice Is Aid Plan or Larger Army, Royall Testifies," *New York Times*, January 15, 1948; Felix Belair, "Draft, Great Costs ERP Alternatives, Say Defense Heads," *New York Times*, January 16, 1948.

146 *"statistician's paradise"*: It was a term that Acheson had used the month prior. Belair, "Foreign Aid Vital, Vandenberg Says."

146 *decreasing that amount*: Committee for the Marshall Plan, "Acheson Before House Committee," release, January 28, 1948. Clark Clifford Papers, HST Library Collection.

146 *"If you didn't talk"*: Chace, *Acheson*, p. 183.

146 *"M Protocol"*: "Text of 'Protocol M,' Alleged Plot to Wreck Marshall Plan by Strikes," *New York Times*, January 16, 1948.

147 *"the old atomized"*: James Reston, "Washington Sees Big Need for a Political ERP," *New York Times*, February 1, 1948.

147 *"political unification"*: Arkes, *Bureaucracy, the Marshall Plan, and the National Interest*, pp. 136, 137.

147 *"moment was ripe"*: Hogan, *The Marshall Plan*, pp. 89, 90.

147 *"the biggest single conundrum"*: Robert Latham, "Cooperation and Community in Europe," in Shain, ed., *The Marshall Plan*, p. 65.

148 *Instead it would be autonomous*: Felix Belair, "Independent Head for ERP Adopted by Senate Group," *New York Times*, February 11, 1948; Felix Belair, "Two Billion Margin

Over ERP Cost Hit by Harriman Group," *New York Times*, January 29, 1948. Marshall later said that he was personally content to have the agency be autonomous. He said that the pressure to keep it under State came from the White House. Bland, ed., *George C. Marshall*.

148 *Finishing at the head:* Felix Morley, "The Case for Taft," *Life*, February 9, 1948.

148 *"to err is Truman":* McCullough, *Truman*, p. 493.

148 *"aloof to the point":* Mee, *The Marshall Plan*, p. 66.

148 *"Bob is not austere":* McCullough, *Truman*, pp. 530, 531.

148 *Since late September, prices:* James Reston, "Politics Affect ERP, But Not Its Basic Aims," *New York Times*, February 8, 1948.

148 *"one of the three":* "Address by Paul G. Hoffman: Evansville Manufacturers & Employers' Association," February 10, 1948. Paul Hoffman Papers, HST Library Collection.

148 *"an economic crash":* Anthony Leviero, "Truman Predicts Crash Unless Curbs Are Enacted," *New York Times*, February 6, 1948.

149 *"European TVA":* Price, *The Marshall Plan and Its Meaning*, p. 58; Ambrose, *Eisenhower*, p. 232; Morley, "The Case for Taft."

149 *"he has the best mind":* From Schlesinger, *A Life in the Twentieth Century*, p. 426.

149 *"Taft always got":* Fossedal, *Our Finest Hour*, p. 138.

149 *"a complete donation":* Felix Belair, "Choice Is Aid Plan or Larger Army."

149 *Writing from his vacation:* Felix Belair, "Hoover for Cut to 4 Billion And 15-Month Pledge on ERP," *New York Times*, January 22, 1948.

149 *More focus was needed:* William White, "Major China Aid Program Asked at Once by Bridges," *New York Times*, January 22, 1948.

149 *"state socialism":* Felix Belair, "Agreement Is Seen on 5 1/3 Billion Aid," *New York Times*, February 27, 1948.

149 *"outright communism":* Felix Belair, "Marshall Plan Attacked by Weir," *New York Times*, February 26, 1948.

149 *At best, Gwinn argued:* Belair, "Agreement Is Seen on 5 1/3 Billion Aid."

149 *"severe shortages":* Bert Pierce, "ERP Seen Causing Road Building Lag," *New York Times*, January 29, 1948.

149 *"If we now add":* Belair, "Marshall Plan Attacked by Weir."

150 *It would cost U.S. firms:* Senator Edwin Johnson, a Democrat from Colorado, said, "it would reduce prices here all right, but it would close our workshops and our factories . . . Once European industry gets underway, it will give American industry a run for its money." Alberts, "Domestic Aspects of the Marshall Plan," p. 58.

150 *Europe's socialist economic:* Hogan, *The Marshall Plan*, pp. 95–96.

150 *Wallace supported a $50 billion:* Hogan, *The Marshall Plan*, pp. 94–95; McCullough, *Truman*, p. 595.

150 *"There is something":* Alberts, "Domestic Aspects of the Marshall Plan," p. 57.

150 *"Secede from the Union":* Associated Press, "Urges Fuel-Short States Secede, Get Marshall Aid," *New York Times*, February 6, 1948.

150 *But Taft and others:* For a good account of all the maneuvering and attempts to attach amendments and delay legislation, see Arkes, *Bureaucracy, the Marshall Plan, and the National Interest*, p. 111.

151 *"Oh, Lord":* Bland, ed., *George C. Marshall*, pp. 556, 557.

151 *Europe needed clothing:* Pogue, *George C. Marshall*, pp. 245, 246.

151 *"You need to belittle this":* Bland, ed., *George C. Marshall*, p. 557.

151 *That flight was the closest:* Bland, ed., *George C. Marshall*, p. 557, and Pogue, *George C. Marshall*, p. 247.

151 *"the greatest decision":* William Blair, "Marshall Sees 'Great Hope' in Plan for European Union," *New York Times*, February 14, 1948.

152 *"It was electric":* Bland, ed., *George C. Marshall*, p. 527.

152 *"the frontline of American security":* "Europe's Recovery Seen Based on ERP," *New York Times*, January 22, 1948. Dean Acheson Papers, HST Library Collection.

152 *Will Clayton also managed:* Will Clayton Papers, HST Library Collection.
152 *To galvanize leaders:* Conference on the European Recovery Program, called by Committee for the Marshall Plan to Aid European Recovery, at Hotel Shoreham, Washington, D.C., Friday, March 5, 1948. Dean Acheson Papers, HST Library Collection.
152 *"Practically anti-everything":* List for "Special Cultivation" of congressmen, senators, and other high-profile people, January 29, 1948. Dean Acheson Papers, HST Library Collection.
152 *In late January it began:* "Report on the Activities of the Committee for the Marshall Plan to Aid European Recovery," submitted by Executive Director, April 5, 1948. Dean Acheson Papers, HST Library Collection.
152 *"full support":* Hitchens, "Influences on the Congressional Decision to Pass the Marshall Plan," p. 54.
152 *according to a survey:* "Civic Leaders Back Plan to Aid Europe," *New York Times,* March 9, 1948.
152 *By the time the meeting:* Bland, ed., *George C. Marshall,* p. 556.
153 *"Mr. Secretary, we are proud":* Pogue, *George C. Marshall,* p. 247; "People: Mr. Secretary Meets the Cubs," *Life,* February 23, 1948; " 'ERP' of Cub Scouts Pleases Marshall," *New York Times,* February 11, 1948.
153 *New York State's 4-H Club:* "Start 'Marshall Plan,' " *New York Times,* February 22, 1948.
153 *The American Society:* "ASPCA Suggests ERP Project for Animals; Society Solicits Funds for Pets Abroad," *New York Times,* February 18, 1948.
153 *"pitfalls and delays":* "Free ERP From 'Election-Year Wrangling,' Women's Group Urges in Appeal to Congress," *New York Times,* January 26, 1948.
153 *Yet, even as the campaign:* Pogue, *George C. Marshall,* p. 246.
153 *"attacks on the United States":* Leffler, "The United States and the Strategic Dimensions of the Marshall Plan," p. 288.
154 *At 4:30 P.M.:* "Soviet Expansion," *New York Times,* February 28, 1948; "U.S. Foreign Policy Takes a Licking," *Life,* March 8, 1948.
154 *"demonstrates with frightening":* Herbert Matthews, "Britain Predicts Dire Slump Unless Congress Speeds Aid," *New York Times,* March 10, 1948.
154 *"last chance for saving":* Bullock, *Ernest Bevin,* p. 526.
154 *"I wake up":* Beevor and Cooper, *Paris,* p. 231.
154 *"We are alarmed":* Telegram from Ambassador Caffrey to Secretary Marshall, March 4, 1948, FRUS, 48, 3, p. 629.
154 *"a man of iron":* "A Man of Iron Pleads for Power in France," *Life,* March 22, 1948.
154 *"If the Communists start":* Telegram from Ambassador Caffrey to Secretary Marshall, March 4, 1948, FRUS, 48, 3, p. 629.
155 *In the wake:* Leffler, "The United States and the Strategic Dimensions of the Marshall Plan," pp. 289, 290.
155 *Thorez's public remarks:* Beevor and Cooper, *Paris,* p. 331.
155 *Seventy percent of the French:* Gallup, *The Gallup Poll,* vol. 1, pp. 718–20.
155 *France would still seek:* Hitchcock, *France Restored,* p. 73.
155 *With the next election:* Telegram: Secretary Marshall to Embassy in France, March 2, 1948, FRUS, 48, 3, p. 628.
155 *"American aid to Italy":* Arnaldo Cortesi, "Communist Test in Italy Moves Towards Climax," *New York Times,* March 14, 1948.
155 *Togliatti at once fumed:* He called the prime minister an American stooge and referred to him as "De Gasperi-Truman." Telegram from Ambassador Dunn to Secretary Marshall, March 22, 1948, FRUS, 48, 3, pp. 858, 859; "Will There Be War—Editorial," *Life,* March 29, 1948; Telegram: from Ambassador Dunn to Secretary Marshall, February 7, 1948, FRUS 48, 3, p. 829.
155 *"the present electoral":* Telegram: Ambassador Dunn to Secretary Marshall, February 7, 1948, FRUS, 48, 3, p. 827.

156 *"widespread fear"*: Memorandum from the Director of the Office of European Affairs John Hickerson to Secretary Marshall, March 8, 1948, FRUS, 48, 3, p. 40.

156 *"We must recognize"*: Telegram from Ambassador Dunn to Secretary Marshall, March 1, 1948, FRUS, 48, 3, p. 835.

156 *"clamp down completely"*: Yergin, *Shattered Peace*, pp. 346, 347.

156 *Marshall had grave concerns*: Marshall said on February 24: "In so far as international affairs are concerned, a seizure of power by the Communist Party in Czechoslovakia would not materially alter in this respect the situation which has existed in the last three years . . . However, we are concerned about the probable repercussions in Western European countries of a successful Communist coup." Yergin, *Shattered Peace*, p. 349.

156 *French Ambassador to Czechoslovakia*: Hitchcock, *France Restored*, p. 93.

156 *"We are faced with exactly"*: Isaacson and Thomas, *The Wise Men*, pp. 439–40.

156 *"Munich'd or even"*: Editorial, "The Foreign Policy Crisis," *Life*, March 22, 1948.

156 *"with dramatic suddenness"*: Isaacson and Thomas, *The Wise Men*, pp. 439–40.

157 *"to prepare the American"*: Yergin, *Shattered Peace*, pp. 351, 352.

157 *"I have now accepted"*: Editorial, "Will There Be War," *Life*, March 29, 1948.

157 *Unlike the Soviets'*: Telegram from Ambassador to Czechoslovakia Lawrence Steinhardt to Secretary Marshall, February 26, 1948, FRUS, 48, 4, p. 739.

157 *"The situation is very"*: Bertram Hulen, " 'Reign of Terror' Seen by Marshall," *New York Times*, March 11, 1948.

157 *On March 13*: Yergin, *Shattered Peace*, p. 353.

157 A *Newsweek* poll: From Pisani, *The CIA and the Marshall Plan*, p. 65.

157 A *Gallup* poll: Gallup, *The Gallup Poll*, vol. 1, p. 721.

157 *"A real war scare"*: Quoted in Yergin, *Shattered Peace*, p. 351.

157 *That spring, European*: See Leffler, *A Preponderance of Power*, p. 211, and Ikenberry, *After Victory*, p. 197.

158 *"scared the bejesus"*: Isaacson and Thomas, *The Wise Men*, p. 448.

158 *When published, the Senate*: Price, *The Marshall Plan and Its Meaning*, p. 61.

158 *The Czech crisis*: Jay Walz, "Vandenberg Faces Senate Challenge in Debate on ERP," *New York Times*, March 1, 1948.

158 *It had taken him*: According to Francis Wilcox, this is what Vandenberg told him. Price, *The Marshall Plan and Its Meaning*, pp. 64, 65.

158 *"The exposed frontiers"*: March 1, 1948, Senate speech. Vandenberg, ed. *The Private Papers of Senator Vandenberg*, p. 390.

159 *"It aims to preserve"*: Felix Belair, "Van Asks ERP Speed to Avert Third World War; Senate Gives Him Ovation," *New York Times*, March 2, 1948.

159 *First, Senator Tom Connally*: Belair, "Vandenberg Asks ERP Speed."

159 *"a masterpiece"*: Oral interview: George C. Marshall, Harry Price Collection.

159 *"Had it been possible"*: Belair, "Vandenberg Asks ERP Speed."

159 *"Congress and the nation"*: Felix Belair, "ERP Critics Force Senate Vote Delay Beyond Next Week," *New York Times*, March 6, 1948.

159 *"vicious and stupid"*: James Reston, "Changes in Thinking Show Response in Europe," *New York Times*, March 10, 1948.

160 *"barrage of propaganda"*: These quotes and positions come from Hitchens, "Influences on Congressional Decision," pp. 60, 67. Buffett was the father of famed Nebraska investor Warren Buffett.

160 *Opponents continued to attack*: Belair, "ERP Critics Force Senate Vote Delay."

160 *"emasculating amendments"*: Felix Belair, "Senate by 53 to 19 Rejects a Move to Change Aid Plan," *New York Times*, March 9, 1948.

160 *And as the vote*: Belair, "ERP Critics Force Senate Vote Delay."

160 *Johnston replied*: Hitchens, "Influences on Congressional Decision," p. 57.

161 *While the opposition*: "American Moves," *New York Times*, April 4, 1948.

161 *Arguments about parsimony:* Felix Belair, "Senators Rebuff Taft on ERP Cut," *New York Times*, March 13, 1948.

161 *"If we don't act fast":* Belair, "ERP Critics Force Senate Vote Delay."

161 *"If I vote for this bill":* Belair, "Senators Rebuff Taft on ERP Cut."

161 *"a dog tired":* "The Non-Communist World Stirs Itself," *Life*, March 22, 1948.

161 *"was in complete control":* Felix Belair, "Senate Votes $5.3 Billion for European Recovery; All Amendments Defeated," *New York Times*, March 14, 1948.

161 *Among those joining:* Morgan, *Reds*, p. 413.

161 *Five minutes past midnight:* Vandenberg, ed., *The Private Papers of Senator Vandenberg*, p. 392, and Belair, "Senate Votes $5.3 Billion for European Recovery."

161 *On March 17, Truman:* Yergin, *Shattered Peace*, pp. 351, 352, 354.

162 *"This is a world-wide":* Pogue, *George C. Marshall*, pp. 248–50.

162 *Heeding Ambassador Dunn's request:* FRUS, 48, 3, p. 829; Telegrams, from Ambassador Dunn to Secretary Marshall, March 16 and 20, FRUS, 48, 3, pp. 853, 854, 857, 858.

162 *"now carried a hint":* Pogue, *George C. Marshall*, p. 249. Pogue wrote: "Later, after the heat of battle for the Marshall Plan, Marshall apologized for strong anti-Communist blasts, remarking that it was easy to get too shrill. He did not believe at that time that the United States had the armed forces to back excessive rhetoric. When you don't have the strength, he often said, you don't hit a man across the face and call him names." Pogue, *George C. Marshall*, p. 165.

162 *With Lovett and Douglas:* Pogue, *George C. Marshall*, p. 251.

162 *"the very survival":* Felix Belair, "House Set for Debate Today on Its Global Relief Program," *New York Times*, March 23, 1948.

162 *The Knowland amendment:* Price, *The Marshall Plan and Its Meaning*, p. 67; Alberts, "Domestic Aspects of the Marshall Plan," pp. 58–60.

162 *"in it and for it":* Hitchens, "Influences on the Congressional Decision," p. 59.

162 *Other amendments:* Alberts, "Domestic Aspects of the Marshall Plan," pp. 59, 60.

163 *"a stampede":* Felix Belair, "Hoover Supports $5.3 Billion for ERP; Opposition Fading," *New York Times*, March 25, 1948.

163 *additional aid:* The "additional aid" was both military and economic.

163 *the surprisingly large margin:* Pollard, *Economic Security and the Origins of the Cold War*, p. 152.

163 *"This measure":* Harold Hinton, "Aid Bill Is Signed by Truman as Reply to Foes of Liberty," *New York Times*, April 4, 1948.

163 *"The decision of the U.S.":* Hinton, "Aid Bill Is Signed by Truman."

163 *"It was just a struggle":* Bland, ed., *George C. Marshall*, p. 556. Senior ECA official Milton Katz said, "The Marshall Plan would never have succeeded, would never have circumvented the successive crises that it ran into, without this solid underpinning of real understanding and real support—never. I can't stress that too much." Oral interview: Milton Katz, HST Library Collection.

163 *"Marshall slush fund":* Pogue, *George C. Marshall*, p. 252.

163 *"It was probably":* Oral interview: Paul Hoffman, Harry Price Collection.

163 *"The psychological success":* Oral interview: George Kennan, Harry Price Collection.

164 *Already the Marshall Plan:* The Czech coup was one of the decisive factors in pushing the legislation through at the desired levels. As the editor of the *British Daily Mail* said, "Our dear old friend Joe Stalin helped put the Marshall Plan over in a great way . . . Czechoslovakia finished it." See "British Editor Terrified by the War Scare in the U.S.," *New York Times*, April 15, 1948.

164 *"our deep gratification":* "Attlee Thanks Truman," *New York Times*, April 6, 1948.

164 *"What the Marshall Plan":* Herbert Matthews, "Britain Fairness on ERP Is Pledged," *New York Times*, April 4, 1948.

164 *"give new courage":* Lansing Warren, "Bidault and Bevin Give Pledge to U.S.," *New York Times*, April 6, 1948.

164 "to stand on its own": Lansing Warren, "Nations in Paris to Support Unity on Soviet Threat, Aid," *New York Times*, March 16, 1948.

164 *Fifty-nine percent of Dutch men*: Gallup, *The Gallup Poll*, vol. 1, p. 722.

164 "Either we save ourselves": Warren, "Nations in Paris to Support Unity on Soviet Threat, Aid."

164 "Long Live the United States": "Communist Rally in Italy Ends in 'Viva U.S.' Cries," *New York Times*, April 1, 1948.

166 "It can be the turning point": Vandenberg, ed., *The Private Papers of Senator Vandenberg*, pp. 391, 392.

PART TWO: THE PLAN IN ACTION

Eight: Aid Flows

PAGE

169 "Would you mind": Oral interview: Paul Hoffman, Harry Price Collection.

169 "looking favorably": James Reston, "Hoffman as ERP Chief Seen Giving Continuity to Plan," *New York Times*, April 6, 1948.

169 "what is needed": H. Ferrell, ed., *Truman in the White House*, p. 216.

169 "I have had very unhappy": Vandenberg, ed., *The Private Papers of Senator Vandenberg*, pp. 392, 393.

169 "I think it is": Pogue, *George C. Marshall*, p. 254.

170 *Republicans were not prepared*: That was Acheson's take in *Present at the Creation*, p. 242.

170 *With Clayton's candidacy scuttled*: Charles Wilson, head of General Electric, was also considered for the post. "But concern about Wilson's chances because he had signed the civil liberties report, which served as the basis for Truman's recommendations for Congress," disqualified him in the selection process, wrote Felix Belair in "Paul Hoffman to Head ERP," *New York Times*, April 6, 1948.

170 *He predicted that Vandenberg*: Acheson, *Present at the Creation*, p. 242. Truman's own diary entry on April 3 followed: "Arrive at WH at 10:20 and dive into unfinished business . . . Talk to Dean Ach about his running ERP. He reluctantly accepts on the condition the Senate is in the right mood. Talked to Van about Acheson. He turned thumbs down. Said the Senate wanted no one connected with State Dept. Silly idea. Want some industrialist without experience." Ferrell, ed., *Off the Record*, p. 129.

170 *At eighteen years of age*: Raucher, *Paul Hoffman*, pp. 1–5.

170 *At twenty-one, Paul Hoffman*: Bill Davidson, "Paul Hoffman: Salesman of Democracy," *Coronet Magazine*, July 1948. Paul Hoffman Papers, HST Library Collection.

171 *At thirty-one, Hoffman devised*: Davidson, "Paul Hoffman."

171 *By thirty-four years of age*: Noel F. Busch, "Paul Hoffman," *Life*, April 4, 1949; Raucher, *Paul Hoffman*, pp. 8, 9.

171 "Middle Western": Address by Paul G. Hoffman before the joint meeting of Chicago Association of Commerce and Industry and Executive Club of Chicago, November 5, 1948. Paul Hoffman Papers, HST Library Collection.

171 "as I see it": Busch, "Paul Hoffman."

171 "apostle of safety": Raucher, *Paul Hoffman*, p. 30.

171 *By one estimate*: Busch, "Paul Hoffman."

171 "the Miracle Man": Davidson, "Paul Hoffman."

171 "glass-smooth labor relations": Raucher, *Paul Hoffman*, pp. 26, 38.

171 "If you are a capitalist": Raucher, *Paul Hoffman*, p. 43.

172 *Free enterprise was*: Claire Neikind, "The Education of Paul Hoffman," *Reporter*, October 25, 1949; Raucher, *Paul Hoffman*, p. 52; "Paul Hoffman: The New Boss of ECA Is a New Type of American Businessman," *Life*, April 19, 1948.

172 *"responsible Republican"*: Felix Belair, "Hoffman Sees ERP as Fight for Peace," *New York Times*, April 7, 1948.

172 *The United States had more*: Busch, "Paul Hoffman."

172 *A young playwright*: It opened in 1949.

172 *"the outside and the inside"*: Raucher, *Paul Hoffman*, p. xi.

172 *"Selling"*: Busch, "Paul Hoffman."

173 *By the time Vandenberg*: Vandenberg, ed., *The Private Papers of Senator Vandenberg*, p. 394; Price, *The Marshall Plan and Its Meaning*, pp. 71, 72.

173 *"The position required"*: Oral interview: George C. Marshall, Harry Price Collection.

173 *"do well to accept him"*: Acheson, *Present at the Creation*, p. 242.

173 *"You've got to take it"*: Vandenberg, ed., *The Private Papers of Senator Vandenberg*, p. 394.

173 *"Have you been offered"*: Oral interview: Paul Hoffman, HST Library Collection.

174 *"I can think of no one"*: Raucher, *Paul Hoffman*, p. 62.

174 *"It seems that I"*: Oral interview: Paul Hoffman, HST Library Collection.

174 *"Of course I was appalled"*: Price, *The Marshall Plan and Its Meaning*, p. 74.

174 *Within hours, Hoffman*: Cabell Phillips, "Flow of Our ERP Aid Is off to Speedy Start," *New York Times*, April 11, 1948.

174 *On April 14*: Anthony Leviero, "First ERP Wheat Shipments Start Texas Loading Today," *New York Times*, April 14, 1948; Donovan, *The Second Victory*, p. 55.

174 *Ship after ship*: Anthony Leviero, "Hoffman Orders New Aid Spending," *New York Times*, April 16, 1948.

175 *"the most important election"*: Lansing Warren, "16 Countries Sign European Aid Pact, Set Up Machinery," *New York Times*, April 17, 1948.

175 *Non-Communist groups*: Telegram from Ambassador Dunn to Secretary Marshall, March 1, 1948, FRUS, 48, 3, p. 837.

175 *"gloomy view"*: Pisani, *The CIA and the Marshall Plan*, p. 66.

175 *"As far as Europe"*: Telegram from Director of the PPS Kennan to Secretary Marshall, March 15, 1948, FRUS, 48, 3, p. 849.

175 *"Freedom Flights"*: Ellwood, *Rebuilding Europe*, p. 116.

175 *The CIA, founded less*: Leffler, *A Preponderance of Power*, p. 214.

175 *"East Coast money"*: Pisani, *The CIA and the Marshall Plan*, p. 67.

176 *"the angel of the bottomless"*: Telegram from Ambassador Dunn to Secretary Marshall, April 7, 1948, FRUS, 48, 3, p. 868; Emmet Hughes, "Pre-Election Report on Italy," *Life*, April 12, 1948.

176 *"morale among Government"*: Telegram from Ambassador Dunn to Secretary Marshall, March 22, 1948, FRUS, 48, 3, p. 858. By April 7, Dunn reported "optimism verging on over-confidence" in non-Communist political circles. The anti-Communist surge "generally is attributed to increased popular realization of U.S. aid program," Dunn wrote. Telegram from Ambassador Dunn to Secretary Marshall, April 7, 1948, FRUS, 48, 3, p. 868.

176 *"Don't spit on the plate"*: Hughes, "Pre-Election Report on Italy."

176 *"De Gasperi–Truman"*: FRUS, 48, 3, p. 858.

176 *It was hard to find*: Arnaldo Cortesi, "Millions in Italy at Party Rallies," *New York Times*, April 12, 1948.

176 *"Every vote for [De] Gasperi"*: Warren, "16 Countries Sign Europe Aid Pact."

176 *"the Communists had deliberately"*: Arnaldo Cortesi, "Communists Lose in Italy; De Gasperi Leads by 3 to 2 and May Hold a Majority," *New York Times*, April 20, 1948. Bullock wrote of the election that it was "universally regarded as a political trial of strength between the American and the Soviet connections." Bullock, *Ernest Bevin*, p. 545.

176 *"a cornucopia"*: Hughes, "Pre-Election Report on Italy."

176 *When the day came*: Cortesi, "Communists Lose in Italy"; Hughes, "Pre-Election Report on Italy."

176 *"No To Stalin"*: Telegram from Ambassador Dunn to Secretary Marshall, April 20, 1948, FRUS, 48, 3, pp. 877, 878.

176 *De Gasperi and his coalition:* Bullock, *Ernest Bevin*, p. 545.

177 *The Communist coalition:* Arnaldo Cortesi, "De Gasperi Gets Free Hand With 48% of Votes in Italy," *New York Times,* April 21, 1948.

177 *"smashing":* Telegram from Ambassador Caffrey to Secretary Marshall, April 21, 1948, FRUS, 48, 3, p. 633.

177 *"as great a fillip":* Bullock, *Ernest Bevin*, p. 545.

177 *"It was evident":* Cortesi, "Communists Lose in Italy."

177 *To be sure:* Support for the Party would remain strong. See Machado, *In Search of a Usable Past*, pp. 51–55.

177 *His days began:* Cabell Phillips, "The Man Who Will Spend $17,000,000,000," *New York Times Magazine*, July 25, 1948.

177 *"easily the busiest":* Raucher, *Paul Hoffman*, p. 65.

177 *"The Man Who Will":* Phillips, "The Man Who Will Spend $17,000,000,000."

177 *"If it had not":* Neikind, "The Education of Paul Hoffman."

177 *"No one had a blueprint":* Price, *The Marshall Plan and Its Meaning*, p. 74; Raucher, *Paul Hoffman*, p. 66.

178 *"was very sophisticated":* Oral interview: Paul Hoffman, Harry Price Collection.

178 *"unwelcome news":* Bissell, *Reflections of a Cold Warrior*, pp. 40, 41.

178 *With Hoffman scampering:* For example, any luxury items, or any requests that might have an adverse reaction on public relations.

178 *"It was a helter skelter":* Bissell, *Reflections of a Cold Warrior*, pp. 40, 41.

179 *"counterpart funds":* For a good discussion of counterpart funds see Bissell, *Reflections of a Cold Warrior*, p. 44.

180 *"spot checking":* For more on "spot checking" see ECA's quarterly reports to Congress. For example, there is a good discussion in Fifth Report to Congress of the Economic Cooperation Administration, for the Quarter Ended June 30, 1949, p. 50.

180 *"around aims":* Oral interview: Harold Van Cleveland, Harry Price Collection.

180 *"the economic logic":* Interview: Arthur Schlesinger Jr., conducted by Author.

180 *The plaster was barely dry:* "Hoffman Moves In," *Life*, April 19, 1948.

180 *"My Daddy is a preacher":* Sterling Green, "First Graders Spell 'Cheer' for Hoffman," *South Bend Tribune*, May 13, 1948. Paul Hoffman Papers, HST Library Collection.

181 *"I wish Hoffman":* Busch, "Paul Hoffman."

181 *"his every sneeze":* Phillips, "The Man Who Will Spend $17,000,000,000."

181 *"The idea is to get Europe":* Quoted in Ikenberry, *After Victory*, p. 201.

181 *"Only the Europeans":* Oral interview: Paul Hoffman, HST Library Collection.

181 *"I had a strong belief":* Oral interview: Paul Hoffman, Harry Price Collection.

181 *"The essence of genuine leadership":* Hoffman, *Peace Can Be Won*, p. 42.

181 *"to the flagging European":* Norman Kark, "Doctor E.R.P.," *Courier* (London), May 1948.

181 *"the heart of the program":* Donovan, *The Second Victory*, p. 60.

181 *"bring about a reasonable":* Belair also reported him discussing an increase of production from $100 billion to $135 billion. Belair, "Hoffman Sees ERP as a Fight for Peace."

181 *"Immediately, Hoffman":* Felix Belair, "Hoffman Fears Aid May Top 5 Billion," *New York Times*, April 21, 1948. See also Bissell, *Reflections of a Cold Warrior*, p. 254.

182 *At the outset:* Oral interview: Paul Hoffman, Harry Price Collection.

182 *"What we are confronted":* Busch, "Paul Hoffman."

182 *"The real objective":* Raucher, *Paul Hoffman*, p. 68.

182 *"one of the most spectacular":* Busch, "Paul Hoffman."

182 *"In screening, our idea":* Oral interview: Paul Hoffman, Harry Price Collection.

182 *"Its uniqueness lies":* Letter from C. D. Jackson to Paul Hoffman, September 28, 1948. Paul Hoffman Papers, HST Library Collection.

182 *"an impartial zeal":* Busch, "Paul Hoffman."

183 *Hoffman made it clear:* Oral interview: Paul Hoffman, HST Library Collection.

183 *"the most non-political organization"*: Vandenberg, ed., *The Private Papers of Senator Vandenberg*, p. 395.

183 *"O.K., go home"*: "ECA: The Economic Cooperation Administration Is Putting the Marshall Plan in Action," *Parade*, July 18, 1948. Paul Hoffman Papers, HST Library Collection.

183 *"The way he could"*: Price, *The Marshall Plan and Its Meaning*, p. 77.

183 *In less than ninety days*: McGlade, "The American Transfer," p. 13.

183 *"the fun was over"*: Lankford, *The Last American Aristocrat*, p. 194.

183 *"The Marshall Plan was"*: Abramson, *Spanning the Century*, p. 425.

183 *"The quality of personnel"*: Oral interview: Richard W. B. "Otto" Clarke, Harry Price Collection.

183 *"It started with the Marshall"*: Oral interview: Paul Hoffman, Harry Price Collection.

184 *It was well known*: Price, *The Marshall Plan and Its Meaning*, p. 224.

184 *"The magic"*: Oral interview: Paul Hoffman, HST Library Collection.

184 *"the most generous"*: Raucher, *Paul Hoffman*, p. 69.

184 *When the* John H. Quick: First Report to Congress of the Economic Cooperation Administration, for the Quarter ended June 30, 1948, p. 54.

184 *Pamphlets were produced*: First Report to Congress of the Economic Cooperation Administration, p. 54.

184 *By June 30, ECA*: Price, *The Marshall Plan and Its Meaning*, p. 83; Donovan, *The Second Victory*, p. 55.

184 *"This Marshall aid"*: Mee, *The Marshall Plan*, p. 246.

184 *"This week it is fitting"*: *Economist*, April 10, 1948, from Van der Beugel, *From Marshall Aid to Atlantic Partnership*, p. 119.

185 *"has now become possible"*: Duchene, *Jean Monnet*, pp. 171, 172. Monnet wrote in his memoirs: "The domestic financing of the 'Monnet Plan' was thereby assured until 1952, as were its overseas supplies—thanks in both cases to the same source of credit." Monnet, *Memoirs*, p. 263.

185 *In contrast, in mid-April*: Van der Beugel, *From Marshall Aid to Atlantic Partnership*, p. 133.

185 *"a psychological blood transfusion"*: Felix Belair, "The MP 20 Years Later," *New York Times*, June 5, 1967. From Marshall Plan Vertical Files, HST Library Collection.

186 *"I saw a cartoon"*: Morgan, *Reds*, p. 379; Isaacson and Thomas, *The Wise Men*, p. 433; Nitze, *From Hiroshima to Glasnost*, p. 66.

186 *"We're not going to use"*: Nitze, *From Hiroshima to Glasnost*, p. 63.

186 *"was an effective"*: Nitze, *From Hiroshima to Glasnost*, p. 64.

187 *"You know, I could"*: Nitze, *From Hiroshima to Glasnost*, p. 65.

187 *"That exchange between Taber"*: Nitze, *From Hiroshima to Glasnost*, p. 66.

187 *"additional doubts concerning"*: Vandenberg, ed., *The Private Papers of Senator Vandenberg*, p. 396.

187 *"meat-axe approach"*: Vandenberg, ed., *The Private Papers of Senator Vandenberg*, pp. 396–98.

188 *Vandenberg's intervention*: Pogue, *George C. Marshall*, p. 254; Vandenberg, ed., *The Private Papers of Senator Vandenberg*, p. 396.

188 *Almost 50,000 had applied*: "Paul Hoffman: Remarks to Public Advisory Board," Friday, July 16, 1948. Paul Hoffman Papers, HST Library Collection.

188 *The major categories*: First Report to Congress of the Economic Cooperation Administration, pp. 27, 24, 25.

188 *Railing against those*: Harold Callender, "France to Debate U.S. Aid Agreement," *New York Times*, June 26, 1948.

188 *"This is a unique"*: Paul Hoffman, "Training Conference on ECA Objectives and Programs (for Overseas Personnel and Washington Key Staff). Basic Objectives of ECA," July 19, 1948. Paul Hoffman Papers, HST Library Collection.

188 *"an instrument of preparation"*: Price, *The Marshall Plan and Its Meaning*, pp. 85, 86.

189 *"2.5 million Communists"*: "Italian Communists to Fight Marshall Plan, Says Togliatti," *New York Times,* June 27, 1948.

189 *"The sun rises"*: John MacCormack, "U.S. Aid Denounced in Vienna Parade," *New York Times,* May 2, 1948.

Nine: Springtime in Paris

PAGE

190 *Young American writers*: Beevor and Cooper, *Paris,* pp. 310, 311, 318–320, 329, 350.

191 *An advertisement in 1934*: Isaacson and Thomas, *The Wise Men,* pp. 42, 43, 112.

191 *"Gary Cooper type"*: James Wechsler, "The Name is Harriman," *Progressive,* June 1948. Averell Harriman Papers, Library of Congress Collection.

191 *"I like recreation"*: Isaacson and Thomas, *The Wise Men,* p. 105.

192 *"Expediter"*: Isaacson and Thomas, *The Wise Men,* p. 188.

192 *"away more money"*: White, *Fire in the Ashes,* pp. 60, 61.

192 *"We have found you"*: Isaacson and Thomas, *The Wise Men,* p. 221.

192 *"the only capitalist"*: Seymour Friedin, "Marshall Plan's Watchdog," *This Week,* January 22, 1950. Averell Harriman Papers, Library of Congress Collection.

192 *"How can a man"*: Yergin, *Shattered Peace,* p. 74.

192 *At a Washington dinner*: Thomas, *The Very Best Men,* p. 27.

192 *"Why do I like this man"*: Oral interview: Arthur Schlesinger Jr., conducted by the author.

192 *As U.S. ambassador*: Yergin, *Shattered Peace,* p. 74.

192 *Harriman's friends said*: Isaacson and Thomas, *The Wise Men,* p. 103.

192 *"we must use"*: Isaacson and Thomas, *The Wise Men,* p. 248.

193 *By June 1947*: Abramson, *Spanning the Century,* p. 418.

193 *"Goddamn it"*: Abramson, *Spanning the Century,* p. 421.

193 *"could not accept"*: Telegram from Acting Secretary Lovett to Secretary Marshall, FRUS, 48, 3, pp. 425, 426.

193 *It was well known*: Bissell, *Reflections of a Cold Warrior,* p. 51.

193 *"I find I am"*: Schlesinger, *A Life in the Twentieth Century,* p. 467.

193 *It was a particular*: Abramson, *Spanning the Century,* pp. 428, 429; White, *Fire in the Ashes,* pp. 60, 61.

194 *The role of special*: Abramson, *Spanning the Century,* p. 424.

194 *In little more than*: Third Report to Congress of the Economic Cooperation Administration, for the Quarter Ended December 31, 1948, p. 71.

194 *"a labyrinthine maze"*: White, *Fire in the Ashes,* p. 60.

194 *"marred the somber beauty"*: Unmarked Article. Paul Hoffman Papers, HST Library Collection.

194 *"How very appropriate"*: Unmarked Article. Paul Hoffman Papers, HST Library Collection.

194 *Harriman and his American*: Abramson, *Spanning the Century,* pp. 428, 429.

195 *One of his first hires*: Abramson, *Spanning the Century,* p. 429; Isaacson and Thomas, *The Wise Men,* pp. 442, 443.

195 *On one occasion*: Draft Column for Leonard Lyons, July 23, 1949, in Averell Harriman Papers, Library of Congress Collection.

195 *As his chief aide*: "Harriman's Men: Architects of Recovery," *BusinessWeek,* September 4, 1948. Averell Harriman Papers, Library of Congress Collection.

195 *"enlightened businessmen"*: White, *Fire in the Ashes,* p. 62.

195 *"Liking Harriman"*: Oral Interview: Arthur Schlesinger Jr., conducted by the author; Schlesinger, *A Life in the Twentieth Century,* p. 465.

196 *"a briar-patch of liberalism"*: Hunt, *Undercover,* p. 63.

196 At the American snack bar: White, *Fire in the Ashes*, pp. 60, 61.

196 "*Europe and the world*": White, *Fire in the Ashes*, p. 61.

197 "*The dollar was triumphant*": Oral interview: Arthur Schlesinger, Jr., conducted by the author.

197 The Americanization of the World: Pells, *Not Like Us*, p. 7.

197 "*generally begged for*": White, *Fire in the Ashes*, p. 362.

197 "*the new occupying power*": Beevor and Cooper, *Paris*, pp. 354, 364.

197 "*Our uncle who art*": Isaacson and Thomas, *The Wise Men*, p. 444.

197 "*trained intuition*": Schlesinger, *A Life in the Twentieth Century*, p. 473.

198 "*immediate objective*": Dispatch sent by David Schoenbrun, CBS Paris correspondent for Ed Murrow Show, June 3, 1948. Averell Harriman Papers, Library of Congress Collection.

198 Examining the fledgling: "Europe to Study Allotments in ERP," *New York Times*, June 27, 1948.

198 He noticed that France: Memorandum of Conversation by Secretary Marshall, July 15, 1948, FRUS, 48, 3, p. 473; Hitchcock, *France Restored*, p. 108; Abramson, *Spanning the Century*, p. 427.

198 Great Britain appointed: Telegram from Acting Secretary Lovett to the Embassy in the United Kingdom, April 6, 1948, FRUS, 48, 3, p. 412.

198 "*like a pig caught*": Draft Column for Leonard Lyons, July 23, 1948, from Averell Harriman Papers, Library of Congress Collection.

199 "*After all, doesn't [Harriman]*": From article in *Ce Soir*, a French Communist paper, included in Memorandum to Harriman from Press Intelligence, May 26, 1948. Averell Harriman Papers, Library of Congress Collection.

199 "*The success of the ERP*": Memorandum, "The Office of the U.S. Special Representative in Europe has prepared the following Preliminary and Tentative Summary of Information Themes Being Stressed by the Paris Headquarters. It Should be Studied Carefully and Guide Your Public Statements," July 22, 1948. Averell Harriman Papers, Library of Congress Collection.

199 "*May I repeat*": Speech of Mr. Averell Harriman before the Council of the Organization for European Economic Cooperation on the 5th of June, 1948. Averell Harriman Papers, Library of Congress Collection.

199 "*to work with you*": Speech of Mr. Averell Harriman before the Council of the Organization for European Economic Cooperation on the 5th of June, 1948.

199 The proposal accorded: Oral interview: Paul Hoffman, Harry Price Collection.

200 "*because their economies*": Van der Beugel, *From Marshall Aid to Atlantic Partnership*, p. 167.

200 "*would put too heavy*": Telegram from Chief of Economic Cooperation Administration Mission in the UK Thomas Finletter to the United States Special Representative in Europe Averell Harriman, June 15, 1948, FRUS 48, 3, pp. 452, 453.

200 "*intolerable*": Hogan, *The Marshall Plan*, p. 162.

200 The Norwegians: Oral interview: Halvard Lange, HST Library Collection.

200 "*To most delegates*": Price, *The Marshall Plan and Its Meaning*, pp. 82, 83.

200 "*I had a horror*": Oral interview: Averell Harriman, HST Library Collection.

200 "*There had been some*": Oral interview: Per Haekkerup, HST Library Collection.

201 "*European nations were not*": Oral interview: Gunther Harkort, HST Library Collection.

201 Inflation had reached: Yergin, *Shattered Peace*, p. 368.

201 At the official exchange rate: Isaacson and Thomas, *The Wise Men*, p. 455.

201 He was trained: Murphy, *Diplomat Among Warriors*, p. 289.

201 "*the Kaiser*": Abramson, *Spanning the Century*, p. 434.

201 "*sometimes seemed*": Oral interview: Milton Katz, HST Library Collection.

201 "*Clay is a fine fellow*": Yergin, *Shattered Peace*, pp. 373–75.

201 Clay remembered: Murphy, *Diplomat Among Warriors*, p. 311.

202 Since 1946, Clay: Bullock, Ernest Bevin, p. 572.

202 "of stagnation in misery": Oral interview: Gunther Harkort, HST Library Collection.

202 In August 1947: Isaacson and Thomas, The Wise Men, p. 454.

202 "We have tried": Yergin, Shattered Peace, p. 372.

202 "and make them": Hogan, The Marshall Plan, p. 129.

202 "those governmental responsibilities": Quoted in Gaddis, We Now Know, pp. 118, 119.

203 Eventually, they could seek: See Leffler, A Preponderance of Power, p. 204.

203 "an island in the heart": Yergin, Shattered Peace, p. 330.

203 "resembled four pieces": Bailey, The Marshall Plan Summer, p. 88.

203 Throughout late March: Yergin, Shattered Peace, p. 371.

203 On June 24: For a detailed account of the timing, see Yergin, Shattered Peace, pp. 376, 377.

203 "The U.S. position": Telegram from the United States Political Adviser for Germany Robert Murphy to Secretary Marshall, June 26, 1948, FRUS, 48, 3, pp. 919, 920.

204 General Brian Robertson: The idea actually originated with a British RAF officer, Air Commodore Waite. Waite convinced Robertson that it was possible and Waite and Robertson went to put the case to Clay. Clay wanted to fight his way through, but he knew there would be steep opposition in Washington, so he accepted the airlift as a temporary measure and advocated for it. For a good account, see Bullock, Ernest Bevin, p. 576.

204 Truman agreed: Yergin wrote that domestic politics was "almost certainly the decisive check on military action to break the blockade." Yergin, Shattered Peace, p. 382.

204 On the morning of June 26: FRUS, 48, 3, p. 919.

204 "U.S. airpower throughout": Drew Middleton, "U.S. Will Mobilize Planes in Europe to Supply Berlin," New York Times, June 27, 1948.

204 "The situation in Europe": Quoted in Yergin, Shattered Peace, p. 378.

204 Churchill likened: Benjamin Welles, "Churchill Likens Berlin to Munich," New York Times, June 27, 1948.

204 Marshall postponed: Richardson Dougall, "From Hull to Acheson," in Craig and Lowenheim, eds., The Diplomats, 1939–1979, p. 53. The U.S. atomic monopoly, still in effect at that point, made it unlikely that the Soviets would risk all-out war with the United States in Berlin. The monopoly figured in U.S. policymakers' calculations.

204 "How long do you": White, Fire in the Ashes, p. 145.

204 "then there would": Telegram from Ambassador Smith to Secretary Marshall, August 3, 1948, FRUS, 48, p. 1005.

204 Stalin would be pleased: John Lewis Gaddis wrote: "The blockade was a reaction to the London Conference program in general, and to its plans for currency reform in particular. The idea, a Soviet Foreign Ministry official noted, was to 'take steps which would not only restrict separate actions of the U.S., Britain and France in Germany but also efficiently thwart their plans of knocking together a Western bloc, with Germany incorporated into it." Gaddis, We Now Know, pp. 120, 121.

205 "We were proud": McCullough, Truman, p. 648.

205 "a firm determination": Telegram from Secretary Marshall to the Embassy in the United Kingdom, July 20, 1948, FRUS, 48, 3, p. 971.

205 Stalin was forced: Yergin, Shattered Peace, p. 382. For another account see Acheson, Present at the Creation, p. 332.

205 "Looked at properly": Oral interview: Milton Katz, HST Library Collection.

206 "Housewives strolled": Ellwood, Rebuilding Europe, p. 135.

206 The currency reform: See Yergin and Stanislaw, The Commanding Heights, p. 17.

206 "The present tension in": Quoted in Leffler, A Preponderance of Power, p. 219.

206 "The going is tough": Telegram from the U.S. Military Gov. for Germany Lucius Clay to the Dept. of the Army, September 4, 1948, FRUS, 48, 3, p. 1112.

Ten: The Road to Recovery

PAGE

207 *"this was the toughest"*: Henry Wales, "Harriman Reads of Talleyrand to Woo Sleep: MP Envoy 15 Years in Service." Undated article from unknown publication in Averell Harriman Papers, Library of Congress Collection.

207 *Harriman had to build*: Seymour Freidin, "Marshall Plan's Roving Watchdog," *This Week*, January 22, 1950. Averell Harriman Papers, Library of Congress Collection.

207 *"for more tact"*: "Harriman's Men: Architects of Recovery," *BusinessWeek*, June 26, 1948. Averell Harriman Papers, Library of Congress Collection.

207 *For the first six months*: Wales, "Harriman Reads of Talleyrand to Woo Sleep."

207 *"He does everything"*: Sigrid Arne, "Unprecedented Job for Unique Man: Harriman's Been Tried for Size," *Washington Post*, May 23, 1948. Averell Harriman Papers, Library of Congress Collection.

207 *"the Ambassador of Wall Street"*: Valentino Gerratana, "Biography of Harriman, the Marshall Plan Man," *Unità*, June 12, 1948. Averell Harriman Papers, Library of Congress Collection.

207 *"an unprecedented job for [a] unique man"*: Arne, "Unprecedented Job for Unique Man: Harriman's Been Tried for Size."

207 *"God, how could I"*: Unmarked article in Paul Hoffman Papers, HST Library Collection.

208 *"Any people who will"*: Abramson, *Spanning the Century*, p. 434.

208 *The ships*: Donovan, *The Second Victory*, p. 54.

208 *"More than half"*: Second Report to congress of the Economic Cooperation Administration, for the Quarter Ended September 30, 1948, p. 93.

208 *Iceland's fishermen*: Price, *The Marshall Plan and Its Meaning*, pp. 268–73.

208 *Paul Porter, the mission chief*: Oral interview: Paul Porter, HST Library Collection.

208 *In Britain, the BBC*: Second Report to Congress of the Economic Cooperation Administration, p. 93.

208 *Marshall Plan assistance*: Fourth Report to Congress of the Economic Cooperation Administration, p. 3. Also see Killick, *The United States and European Reconstruction, 1945–1960*, p. 97.

208 *"the multiplier effect"*: Arkes, *Bureaucracy, the Marshall Plan, and the National Interest*, p. 241. Price also highlights the "multiplier effect" in *The Marshall Plan and Its Meaning*.

208 *"has so far made"*: Busch, "Paul Hoffman."

208 *"I would say that"*: *Meet the Press* interview, September 17, 1948. Paul Hoffman Papers, HST Library Collection.

208 *"crippling 14-cent-a-pound"*: The duty was charged after the first 50 million pounds sold. "ECA Can't Do Everything," *Fortune*, February, 1949. Paul Hoffman Papers, HST Collection.

208 *In August 1948*: Alberts, "Domestic Aspects of the Marshall Plan," p. 89.

210 *"unpalatable spaghetti"*: Isaacson and Thomas, *The Wise Men*, p. 444.

210 *the only recorded instance*: Machado, *In Search of a Usable Past*, p. 42.

210 *The time was now ripe*: Harriman said, "The ECA in Washington, in reviewing the second and third quarter programs, found that most of the items that were requested were in what has been considered the relief area, namely food, coal, and, particularly in the third quarter, raw materials. With regard to the ERP, great stress has been laid in the U.S. Congress and by the public in the United States on 'recovery'—the items of productive capital investment." Statement by Mr. Averell Harriman Before the Executive Committee of OEEC, 6th July, 1948. Averell Harriman Papers, Library of Congress Collection.

210 *"the countries have a long"*: Second Report to Congress of the Economic Cooperation Administration, p. 24.

210 *"Through greater unity"*: Hogan, *The Marshall Plan*, p. 135.

211 *It did not want:* Hogan, *The Marshall Plan*, p. 179.

211 *"on [its] merits"*: Quoted in Hitchcock, *France Restored*, p. 108.

211 *"this kind of thinking"*: Hogan, *The Marshall Plan*, p. 179.

212 *"Nearly all [of the] nations"*: Editorial, "Self-Help in Europe: Links Between Recovery and the Marshall Plan," *London Times*, September 1, 1948. Averell Harriman Papers, Library of Congress Collection.

212 *Yet, Britain seemed:* Bissell highlighted the "points experiencing friction in [the U.S.-U.K.] relationship: [Great Britain] (a) won't produce more strategic materials; (b) won't participate in clearance of payments—b/c a threat to Brit reserves; (c) most persistent in defending their position on the sterling area; (d) Brit representation far below the rank hoped for; (e) out of step with Brit in ECE." From Memorandum by Richard M. Bissell, Jr., Director of Program, Operations, and Supply of the Economic Cooperation Administration, September 22, 1948, FRUS, 48, 3, pp. 488, 489.

212 *"the low level"*: Cable from Harriman to Washington (marked as not sent), September 6, 1948. Averell Harriman Papers, Library of Congress Collection.

212 *"thinks himself to be"*: Abramson, *Spanning the Century*, p. 428.

212 *"presumptuous"*: Hogan, *The Marshall Plan*, pp. 158, 159.

212 *"Harriman was something"*: Bissell, *Reflections of a Cold Warrior*, p. 50.

212 *In the United States, Hoffman:* Hoffman shared Harriman's concern. In a telegram from Marshall to Ambassador Douglas in the U.K., Marshall wrote, "Since Hoffman's return from Paris we have had several conversations concerning UK relations to OEEC. Hoffman has expressed grave concern over British attitude and feels they are not entering wholeheartedly into OEEC work. He further believes that unless they exercise real leadership to initiate and push forward effective measures for economic cooperation among OEEC nations there is a good chance that ERP will fail." Telegram dated August 20, 1948. Averell Harriman Papers, Library of Congress Collection.

212 *Marshall and Lovett:* Discussed in Bullock, *Ernest Bevin*, p. 617.

213 *"is doing nothing toward"*: W. D. Sisson, "ECA Misses the Real Aim, Fulbright Declares." Undated paper from Averell Harriman Papers, Library of Congress Collection.

213 *By late October, the British:* Hogan, *The Marshall Plan*, pp. 159, 160, 173.

213 *Part of the problem:* Telegram from Ambassador Douglas to Secretary Marshall, August 31, 1948, FRUS, 48, 3, p. 486.

214 *the French would come:* Oral interview: Milton Katz, HST Library Collection.

214 *"The procedure was designed"*: Oral interview: Milton Katz, HST Library Collection.

215 *After completing the arduous process:* Van der Beugel, *From Marshall Aid to Atlantic Partnership*, pp. 149, 150.

215 *"pandemonium broke loose"*: Van der Beugel, *From Marshall Aid to Atlantic Partnership*, p. 151.

215 *897 various meetings:* "ECA Can't Do Everything," *Fortune*, February 1949.

215 *100 different sets of bilateral negotiations:* Van der Beugel, *From Marshall Aid to Atlantic Partnership*, p. 154.

215 *during tens of thousands:* Press Release #31, October 16, 1948; ECA Office of U.S. Special Representative in Paris. Averell Harriman Papers, Library of Congress Collection.

215 *On October 16, 1948:* Van der Beugel, *From Marshall Aid to Atlantic Partnership*, p. 157.

216 *"I rejoice with you"*: Press Release #31, October 16, 1948; ECA Office of U.S. Special Representative in Paris. Harriman's biographer wrote: "To Averell, the successful negotiations put the Marshall Plan over its greatest hurdle." Abramson, *Spanning the Century*, p. 433.

216 *"gave to the [OEEC]"*: Price, *The Marshall Plan and Its Meaning*, pp. 302, 303.

216 *"became in spirit"*: Bissell, *Reflections of a Cold Warrior*, p. 48.

216 *"the instrumentality"*: Bissell, *Reflections of a Cold Warrior*, p. 49.

216 *"the OEEC stood out"*: Price, *The Marshall Plan and Its Meaning*, p. 356.

216 *"perhaps the most remarkable"*: Arthur Schlesinger, Jr., "Europe Takes Hope from ECA," *New Republic*, November 8, 1948. Averell Harriman Papers, Library of Congress Collection. The magazine was sold at newsstands for fifteen cents.

216 *"empire by invitation"*: Geir Lundestad coined these terms in his seminal work on this subject, most notably *"Empire" by Integration: The United States and European Integration, 1945–1997*. Gaddis draws on Lundestad's work to inform his conclusion that the contrast between the United States and the Soviet Union in the nature of and approach to their "empires" helped dictate the outcome of the Cold War. Gaddis, *We Now Know*.

217 *The English were obsessed*: Lankford, *The Last American Aristocrat*, p. 208.

217 *"In the course of the afternoon"*: Beevor and Cooper, *Paris*, p. 53.

217 *"has for so long"*: Lankford, *The Last American Aristocrat*, pp. 191, 196, 197.

217 *Bruce set up the ECA*: Lankford, *The Last American Aristocrat*, p. 199.

218 *"the ballet of the parties"*: Lankford, *The Last American Aristocrat*, p. 199.

218 *Around this time De Gaulle*: Telegram from Acting Secretary of State Lovett to the United States Special Representative in Europe Averell Harriman, December 3, 1948, FRUS, 48, 3, p. 308.

218 *Rain would have offered*: Unmarked article in Paul Hoffman Papers, HST Library Collection.

218 *"Psychologically"*: Oral interview: Dirk Stikker, Harry Price Collection.

218 *"Financial situation in France"*: Telegram from Chief of the ECA Mission in France David Bruce to the Administrator for Economic Cooperation Paul Hoffman, September 14, 1948, FRUS, 48, 3, p. 649.

219 *Bruce worried*: Lankford, *The Last American Aristocrat*, pp. 203, 204.

219 *"The goal of ERP"*: FRUS, 48, 3, p. 306.

220 *"Exacte! But dites moi"*: Lankford, *The Last American Aristocrat*, p. 209.

220 *Monnet assured Bruce*: "ECA Can't Do Everything," *Fortune*, February 1949.

220 *"somber, double-breasted suit"*: Lankford, *The Last American Aristocrat*, p. 209.

220 *"civilized man"*: Monnet, *Memoirs*, p. 269.

221 *"There was in effect"*: Lankford, *The Last American Aristocrat*, pp. 202, 209.

221 *"was that the Americans"*: Duchene, *Jean Monnet*, p. 173.

221 *"He trusted me completely"*: Monnet, *Memoirs*, p. 270.

221 *"It has now become"*: Duchene, *Jean Monnet*, p. 171.

221 *"The certainty that"*: Monnet, *Memoirs*, p. 270. Bidault wrote that the "French economy would have been paralyzed without the Marshall Plan." Bidault, *Resistance*, p. 164.

221 *A Communist-led union*: "Reds Try to Wreck Marshall Plan," *Life*, November 1, 1948.

221 *After a failed Communist*: Telegram from the Director of the Office of European Affairs John Hickerson to the Coordinator of Foreign Aid and Assistance Henry Labouisse, October 12, 1948, FRUS, 48, 3, p. 668.

221 *"at the lowest point"*: Telegram from Ambassador Caffrey to Secretary Marshall, October 5, 1948, FRUS, 48, 3, p. 663.

221 *The violence did*: Memorandum from the Acting Director of the Office of European Affairs Reber to Acting Secretary Lovett, November 28, 1948, FRUS, 48, 3, p. 727.

221 *"Even more demanding"*: Monnet, *Memoirs*, p. 275.

222 *"the disastrous effect"*: Personal telegram from Harriman to Hoffman, November 8, 1948. Averell Harriman Papers, Library of Congress Collection.

222 *"The French Crisis"*: Telegram from Hickerson to Labouisse, October 12, 1948, FRUS, 48, 3, p. 666.

222 *"The unhealthiness"*: "The French Crisis," Memorandum by Labouisse and the Assistant Chief of the Division of Commercial Policy Moore, October 16, 1948, FRUS, 48, 3, p. 668.

222 *"character and determination"*: Lankford, *The Last American Aristocrat*, p. 204.

222 *"bronze plaque"*: Lankford, *The Last American Aristocrat*, pp. 207, 208.

223 *It was the same town*: Lankford, *The Last American Aristocrat*, pp. 205, 206.

223 *"French food rations"*: David Bruce's speech in Lille, France, December 6, 1948. In Averell Harriman Papers, Library of Congress Collection. Also see Lankford, *The Last American Aristocrat*, pp. 205, 206.

223 *"For once"*: Lankford, *The Last American Aristocrat*, p. 206.

223 *"is it not rather"*: Lankford, *The Last American Aristocrat*, p. 206.

223 *"[Bruce's] actions may"*: Bissell, *Reflections of a Cold Warrior*, p. 54.

224 *"we are participating"*: Hitchcock, *France Restored*, p. 104.

224 *"diplomatic-strategic requirement"*: Hitchcock, *France Restored*, p. 100.

224 *"Washington's favorite European"*: Lundestad, *"Empire" by Integration*, p. 32.

224 *Truman's daughter's*: See McCullough, *Truman*, p. 652.

224 *Ever since the Civil War*: McCullough, *Truman*, pp. 656, 657.

225 *"loomed as large"*: McCullough, *Truman*, pp. 656, 657.

225 *Three weeks before*: Telegram from the Ambassador in Belgium Kirk to Secretary Marshall, October 11, 1948, FRUS, 48, 3, p. 491.

225 *At the time*: Gallup, *The Gallup Poll, 1935–1971*, vol. 1, pp. 770, 771.

225 *"The Marshall Plan was particularly"*: McCullough, *Truman*, p. 683.

225 *Two of his biggest donors*: McCullough, *Truman*, pp. 703, 712, 717, 679.

226 *"red herring"*: McCullough, *Truman*, p. 652.

226 *Meanwhile, from Tokyo*: McCullough, *Truman*, p. 726.

226 *More than $2 billion*: Third Report to Congress of the Economic Cooperation Administration, for the Quarter Ended December 31, 1948, pp. 142, 143.

226 *In France, Marshall dollars*: "Address by Paul G. Hoffman before the National Foreign Trade Council," Waldorf-Astoria Hotel, New York, November 10, 1948. Paul Hoffman Papers, HST Library Collection.

226 *The combined effect*: Third Report to Congress of the Economic Cooperation Administration, p. ix.

226 *Critics could not help*: For example, see Third Report to Congress of the Economic Cooperation Administration, p. 52.

227 *"great strides had been"*: Third Report to Congress of the Economic Cooperation Administration, p. 1.

227 *"to avoid a threatened"*: Third Report to Congress of the Economic Cooperation Administration, p. 1.

227 *"The United States today"*: Schlesinger, "Europe Takes Hope from ECA."

227 *"Well, what will satisfy"*: Oral interview: Paul Hoffman, HST Library Collection.

228 *"to get a better seat"*: Payne, *The Marshall Story*, p. 311.

Eleven: Shifting Gears

PAGE

229 *"brought new hope"*: McCullough, *Truman*, pp. 730, 731.

229 *Vandenberg told one*: Vandenberg, ed., *The Private Papers of Senator Vandenberg*, pp. 462, 463.

230 *"I believe it was"*: Isaacson and Thomas, *The Wise Men*, p. 463.

230 *"You had better be"*: Acheson recounted the episode in *Present at the Creation*, p. 249.

230 *Vandenberg wondered*: Vandenberg, ed., *The Private Papers of Senator Vandenberg*, p. 551.

230 *"a pompous diplomat"*: A widely known dig, recounted, for example, in Hogan, *The Marshall Plan*, p. 262.

230 *"the surrounding gloom"*: Acheson, *Present at the Creation*, p. 257.

231 *"Now, will you sign"*: Cabell Phillips, "Hoffman Reviews a Year of ECA," *New York Times Magazine*, April 3, 1949. Paul Hoffman Papers, HST Library Collection.

231 *The prior December*: "Hoffman of ECA," *Life*, April 4, 1949.

231 *"for more than a year"*: Demaree Bess, "Does ERP Mean War or Peace?" *Saturday Evening Post*, January 29, 1949. Paul Hoffman Papers, HST Library Collection.

231 "*A team that won't*": "Peace Is Our Business," CBS broadcast, Sunday, April 4, 1949, 10:30 P.M. Paul Hoffman Papers, HST Library Collection.

231 "*European Recovery*": Paul Hoffman, "European Recovery . . . Will You Get Your Money's Worth?" *American Magazine*, April 1949. Paul Hoffman Papers, HST Library Collection.

232 "*But you mustn't get*": Paul G. Hoffman, "What ECA Has Accomplished," *Commercial and Financial Chronicle*, April 21, 1949. Paul Hoffman Papers, HST Library Collection.

232 "*If gifts were being*": Address to the National Association of Manufacturers by Paul Hoffman, New York, December 1, 1948. Paul Hoffman Papers, HST Library Collection.

232 "*put forth a maximum*": "The Effect of the European Recovery Program on Marketing Management," Before the American Management Association, Hotel Statler, New York, March 18, 1949. Paul Hoffman Papers, HST Library Collection.

232 Life *referred to him:* Paul G. Hoffman, "Youth and the Economic Co-operation Administration," March 5, 1949. Paul Hoffman Papers, HST Library Collection.

232 "*The 25 Men*": George Kent, "The 25 Men Who Rule the World," *Collier's*, May 28, 1949. Paul Hoffman Papers, HST Library Collection.

232 "*humming, not to say*": "Hoffman of ECA."

233 *In the first year:* Phillips, "Hoffman Reviews a Year of ECA."

233 "*If another war*": Bess, "Does ERP Mean War or Peace?"

233 "*great and thrilling*": Hoffman, *Peace Can Be Won*, p. 88.

233 "*As a whole, ECA*": "ECA Can't Do Everything," *Fortune*, February 1949.

233 "*was still the least*": Claire Neikind, "The Education of Paul Hoffman," *The Reporter*, October 25, 1949.

233 *As important:* Statement by Paul Gray Hoffman Before a Joint Session of the Senate Foreign Relations Committee and the House Foreign Affairs Committee, February 8, 1949. Paul Hoffman Papers, HST Library Collection.

234 "*I want to state*": Statement by W. A. Harriman Before the Committee on Foreign Relations, U.S. Senate and the Committee on Foreign Affairs, House of Representatives, February 8, 1949. Averell Harriman Papers, Library of Congress Collection.

234 "*Bissell relished the complexity*": Thomas, *The Very Best Men*, p. 96.

234 "*You should see him*": "ECA: The Economic Cooperation Administration Is Putting the Marshall Plan in Action."

234 "*the goose that laid*": Hogan, *The Marshall Plan*, p. 190.

234 "*Buy American*": Alberts, "Domestic Aspects of the Marshall Plan," p. 79.

234 *Senator Tom Connally:* Hoffman, "The Effect of the ERP on Marketing Management."

235 "*The . . . congressional debates*": Van der Beugel, *From Marshall Aid to Atlantic Partnership*, p. 178.

235 *Some congressmen:* Address of Paul Gray Hoffman before the Iron and Steel Division, American Institute of Mining and Metallurgical Engineers, Hotel Statler, New York, May 25, 1949. Paul Hoffman Papers, HST Library Collection.

235 "*virility*": Arkes, *Bureaucracy, the Marshall Plan, and the National Interest*, pp. 301, 302.

235 *Senators asked him:* Statement by Paul Gray Hoffman, Economic Cooperation Administrator, Before the Senate Appropriations Committee, June 16, 1949. Paul Hoffman Papers, HST Library Collection.

235 "*the vital quantity*": Statement by Paul Gray Hoffman, June 16, 1949.

235 "*If we are able*": Statement by Paul Gray Hoffman, Economic Cooperation Administrator, Before Appropriations Committee, House of Representatives, April 26, 1949. Paul Hoffman Papers, HST Library Collection.

236 "*just one more Pandora's box*": Vandenberg, ed., *The Private Papers of Senator Vandenberg*, p. 501.

236 "*Other than giving away*": "McKellar Is Barking up Wrong Economy Tree," *Cleveland Press*, June 13, 1949. Paul Hoffman Papers, HST Library Collection.

236 *"but there was all"*: Bissell, *Reflections of a Cold Warrior*, pp. 46, 47.

236 *"I think we can save enough"*: Vandenberg, ed., *The Private Papers of Senator Vandenberg*, p. 501.

237 *"We had originally"*: Hoffman, *Peace Can Be Won*, pp. 143, 144.

237 *"On the political front"*: "ECA Can't Do Everything."

237 On occasion, certain accusations: Draft column for Leonard Lyons, July 23, 1949.

237 In Norway, the secretary general: "Marshall Plan Working in Norway," *Railway Carmen's Journal*, March 1949.

238 *"Thanks largely to Russian"*: Saunders, *The Cultural Cold War*, p. 19.

238 *"Coca-Colonization"*: Lankford, *The Last American Aristocrat*, p. 218; Beevor and Cooper, *Paris*, pp. 359, 360.

238 *"Such a naïf belief"*: Lankford, *The Last American Aristocrat*, p. 192.

238 *"to run the ECA"*: Quoted in Price, *The Marshall Plan and Its Meaning*, p. 242.

238 *"every method possible"*: Ellwood, *Rebuilding Europe*, p. 162.

238 In that six-month period: Fifth Report to Congress of the Economic Cooperation Administration, for the Quarter Ended June 30, 1949, pp. 68–71.

239 ECA sponsored dozens: Pisani, *The CIA and the Marshall Plan*, p. 94.

239 *"Your balloon has blown"*: Hoffman, *Peace Can Be Won*, pp. 144–46.

239 An Italian film: Fifth Report to Congress of the Economic Cooperation Administration, p. 72.

239 Some were clearly propaganda: Pisani, *The CIA and the Marshall Plan*, p. 118.

240 He was charming: A theme in Thomas's portrayal of Wisner in *The Very Best Men*.

240 It was a purposefully: Thomas, *The Very Best Men*, p. 29.

240 According to Richard Bissell: Pisani wrote that at a "later interview Bissell noted that Averell Harriman had conceived of the plan and mechanism to assist the OPC with Marshall Plan funds. But," she added, "it is clear from the statements of General Marshall and the actions of [Kennan] and [Forrestal] that many contemplated 'emergency funding procedures' such as this one." Still, Harriman appears to have been the person to set the process in motion. Pisani, *The CIA and the Marshall Plan*, p. 73.

240 *"very uninformed"*: Bissell, *Reflections of a Cold Warrior*, pp. 68, 69.

241 *"You should think"*: Thomas, *The Very Best Men*, pp. 87, 88.

241 Most were Ivy Leaguers: Thomas, *The Very Best Men*, pp. 63, 41.

241 Under the rubric: Pisani, *The CIA and the Marshall Plan*, p. 75.

241 *"Bagmen"*: Quoted from Bissell in Thomas, *The Very Best Men*, p. 88, and Pisani, *The CIA and the Marshall Plan*, p. 62.

241 OPC channeled: Pisani, *The CIA and the Marshall Plan*, p. 102.

241 The OPC helped to fund: Thomas, *The Very Best Men*, p. 33.

241 And on at least one: In 1951 and 1952, one such foray into Albania went very badly. Hundreds of Albanians were captured or killed, and some were even burned alive. Thomas, *The Very Best Men*, p. 68. Thomas also cites Peter Grose's 1994 biography of former CIA director Allen Dulles. In the book, Grose claims that in 1952, Wisner explored the possibility of an OPC-backed assassination attempt on Stalin at a Four-Power Conference that was supposed to take place in Paris. By this time, the Marshall Plan had closed down, but OPC was still awash in Marshall Plan funds. Had the attempt gone forward, then, it was possible that Marshall Plan funds would have financed a U.S.-backed assassination attempt on Stalin's life.

242 OPC employed Marshall funds: The congress assembled 118 prominent intellectuals from twenty countries, including Arthur Schlesinger, and from England and France leading intellectuals like Hugh Trevor-Roper, A. J. Ayer, Raymond Aron, and André Malraux. Other supporters included Eleanor Roosevelt, Upton Sinclair, Reinhold Niebuhr. John Dewey and Bertrand Russell were among the congress's honorary presidents. Pells, *Not Like Us*, pp. 70, 71.

242 The congress sought to debunk: Schlesinger was an exception. Because of his contacts, he knew. Saunders, *The Cultural Cold War*, pp. 72, 90, 91.

242 *To further discredit Soviet:* Saunders, *The Cultural Cold War,* p. 21.

242 *all funded with Marshall:* In addition, in Italy the government agreed with U.S. officials who were concerned about a surfeit of Italian labor, which, it was felt, was contributing to Italy's alarming unemployment crisis and impeding its recovery. Unemployed and discontent, this demographic was fodder for Italy's Communist recruiters. With government support, Marshall Plan funds went toward an ambitious emigration effort. The funds helped to build ships and train workers so they could be transplanted to South America where, it was believed, they would find more gainful employment. According to ECA, Italian emigration almost tripled. In 1949, ECA reported the emigration tally at 150,000.

242 *Bissell felt that Hoffman:* Pisani, *The CIA and the Marshall Plan,* pp. 72, 73; also see Bissell, *Reflections of a Cold Warrior.*

242 *"We couldn't spend":* Thomas, *The Very Best Men,* pp. 40, 41; Saunders, *The Cultural Cold War,* p. 105.

242 *Minutes before 5 P.M.:* "The Pact is Signed," *Life,* April 18, 1949.

243 *It pledged member states:* Judt, *Postwar,* p. 151.

243 *Thomas Jefferson:* See Washington's Farewell Address and Jefferson's Inaugural Address.

243 *"entangling alliances":* Yergin, *Shattered Peace,* p. 365.

243 *"a latter-day American":* Reynolds, ed., *The Origins of the Cold War in Europe,* p. 86.

243 *"a treaty which represents":* "The Atlantic Nations Unite for Defense," *Life,* March 28, 1949.

243 *"a shield against aggression":* Quoted in Reynolds, ed., *The Origins of the Cold War in Europe,* p. 13.

243 *An American military guarantee:* Bullock elaborated: Bevin "saw the NATO pact as necessary not in order to stop a Russian armed attack, which he did not anticipate, but to reassure the peoples of Western Europe. Without a guarantee they could believe, their experience of war and occupation and their fears of a repetition would continue to inhibit their recovery of confidence. Only an association which included the USA could provide such a guarantee . . ." Bullock, *Ernest Bevin,* pp. 670, 687.

244 *"Well," Harriman asked:* Oral interview: Averell Harriman, HST Library Collection.

244 *Harriman and other:* See Ikenberry, *After Victory,* pp. 197, 198; Judt, *Postwar,* p. 151.

244 *"The treaty":* Acheson, *Present at the Creation,* p. 493.

244 *Within a few hours:* Acheson, *Present at the Creation,* p. 312.

244 *"Of prime importance":* Statement by W. Averell Harriman before the Committee on Foreign Relations, United States Senate, April 29, 1949.

244 *"The need for military":* Quoted in Bullock, *Ernest Bevin,* p. 644.

244 *"the number one war lord":* Steel, *Walter Lippman and the American Century,* p. 460.

245 *When Acheson and Charles Bohlen:* Isaacson and Thomas, *The Wise Men,* p. 473.

245 *"Back to Moscow":* "The 'Little Man' Turns on the Reds," *Life,* September 20, 1948; Murphy, *Diplomat Among Warriors,* p. 319.

245 *"meteorological miracle":* Ellwood, *Rebuilding Europe,* p. 121.

245 *Journalist Theodore White:* White, *Fire in the Ashes,* p. 146.

246 *So, in late January 1949:* Acheson, *Present at the Creation,* p. 268.

246 *Western pilots flew:* Yergin, *Shattered Peace,* pp. 395, 396.

246 *By May 12, 1949:* McCullough, *Truman,* p. 734.

246 *"the stupidest move":* Yergin, *Shattered Peace,* p. 396.

246 *On the same day:* McCullough, *Truman,* p. 734.

246 *Save that one:* Hitchcock, *France Restored,* p. 112. Hitchcock goes so far as to say "sovereignty."

247 *"I want to drink":* Beevor and Cooper, *Paris,* pp. 357, 358.

247 *"We are very happy":* Presidential Address to be Given in honor of George C. Marshall by Chiefs of Mission of the Marshall Plan Countries, at the Carlton Hotel, Washington, on Sunday Evening, June 5, 1949. Clark Clifford Papers, HST Library Collection.

248 *"looking again at the"*: "The Marshall Plan at Mid-Point," Economic Cooperation Administration, Washington, D.C. Marshall Plan Vertical Files, HST Library Collection.

248 *"For days"*: "The Best Bargain the American People Ever Bought," *Time*, April 11, 1949. From Paul Hoffman Papers, HST Library Collection.

248 *"These supplies have provided"*: Price, *The Marshall Plan and Its Meaning*, pp. 330, 331.

248 *oxygen tank*: Unmarked Article, Paul Hoffman Papers, HST Library Collection.

249 *Fremond had to order*: "ECA Helps Georges: French Farmer Gets a New Tractor Which Takes Place of Six Horses," *Life*, May 9, 1949.

249 *Together with other dams*: Ellwood, *Rebuilding Europe*, p. 175. Fourth Report to Congress of the Economic Cooperation Administration, for the Quarter Ended April 2, 1949, p. 65.

249 *That June was a glorious one*: Beevor and Cooper, *Paris*, pp. 367–71.

249 *"France has rejected"*: Monnet, *Memoirs*, p. 276.

249 *"Without Marshall aid"*: "The Best Bargain the American People Ever Bought," *Time*, April 11, 1949. From Paul Hoffman Papers, HST Library Collection.

249 *American journalists who*: Beevor and Cooper, *Paris*, p. 370.

250 *"from rumpled rags"*: White, *Fire in the Ashes*, pp. 153–55.

250 *"One reason for"*: Oral interview: Franz Blucher, Harry Price Collection.

250 *West Germany's economic*: White, *Fire in the Ashes*, pp. 153–55.

250 *The Mouse That Roared*: Noted in Reid, *The United States of Europe*, p. 40.

250 *It financed a thermal*: Fifth Report to Congress of the Economic Cooperation Administration, for the Quarter Ended June 30, 1949, p. 35.

250 *When Fiat asked*: Pisani, *The CIA and the Marshall Plan*, pp. 113, 114.

251 *"changing an Asian"*: Ellwood, *Rebuilding Europe*, p. 175; Fourth Report to Congress of the Economic Cooperation Administration, pp. 70, 71; Fifth Report to Congress of the Economic Cooperation Administration, p. 43.

251 *Dutch experts tested*: Donovan, *The Second Victory*, p. 108.

251 *In 1950, for example*: Judt, *Postwar*, p. 96.

251 *Some historians have highlighted the push-back*: Chiarella Esposito's *America's Feeble Weapon: Funding the Marshall Plan in France and Italy, 1948–1950* was one such regional study. In addition, in *The Reconstruction of Western Europe, France Restored* and *In Search of a Usable Past*, Alan Milward, William Hitchcock and Barry Machado, respectively, all highlight recipient country push-back. These studies are essential in fleshing out the role of recipient countries in the Marshall Plan and in Western European recovery. Marshall aid and the lever of counterpart funds did not mean that the U.S. determined national recovery strategies. But sometimes these studies seem to forget that ECA had larger political and geopolitical goals, and despite contention over economic strategy, ECA ultimately acknowledged national control, so long as recipient countries remained partners in those larger goals. In the end, national recovery strategies were shaped in partnership between ECA and the recipient country. In some instances, ECA had greater influence, and in some the recipient country did. But these were partnerships forged in, and directed at, a larger set of shared economic, political and geopolitical goals.

251 *"By June 1949"*: Fifth Report to Congress of the Economic Cooperation Administration, p. 3.

252 *Production was on a sharp*: Fourth Report to Congress of the Economic Cooperation Administration, pp. 5, 14; Fifth Report to Congress of the Economic Cooperation Administration, pp. viii, ix.

252 *"may well have marked"*: Fourth Report to Congress of the Economic Cooperation Administration, p. 14.

252 *"In one year ECA"*: "The Best Bargain the American People Ever Bought," *Time*, April 11, 1949. From Paul Hoffman Papers, HST Library Collection.

252 *"A year has gone by"*: Letter from Prime Minister Attlee to President Truman, First

Anniversary of Signing of ECA, Sunday, April 3, 1949. Clark Clifford Papers, HST Library Collection.

252 *"a turning point"*: Gilbert, *Churchill and America*, p. 389.

252 *"It seems to be"*: Vandenberg, ed., *The Private Papers of Senator Vandenberg*, p. 489.

252 *"There were some who"*: Draft of Statement for Harriman, for *March of Time* Television Show, July 28, 1949. Averell Harriman Papers, HST Library Collection.

252 *"We are closer"*: "Check List of Errors," *Life*, July 24, 1950.

253 *"This is to alert you"*: Telegram from Ambassador Douglas to Acting Secretary of State James Webb, June 16, 1949, FRUS, 49, 4, p. 785.

253 *"There but for the Grace"*: Noel Busch, "Sir Stafford Cripps," *Life*, March 8, 1948; "Death of a Paradox," *Time*, April 28, 1952.

253 *He favored 45-cent:* Busch, "Sir Stafford Cripps."

254 *"a bonfire of controls"*: Bullock, *Ernest Bevin*, p. 704.

254 *British gold:* FRUS, 49, 4, p. 785. Memorandum by Assistant Secretary of State for Economic Affairs Willard Thorp to Secretary of State Dean Acheson; Subject: The British Financial Predicament, June 27, 1949, FRUS, 49, 4, p. 794; Sixth Report to Congress of the Economic Cooperation Administration, for the Quarter Ended September 30, 1949, pp. 6, 7.

254 *The recession reduced:* Acheson, *Present at the Creation*, p. 325.

254 *"passed out of the honey-moon"*: Concern of the United States Over the British Financial Crisis; Devaluation of the Pound Sterling, June 9, 1949, FRUS, 49, 4, pp. 781–83.

254 *"A broad revaluation"*: Telegram from Paul Hoffman (Richard Bissell) to Averell Harriman, March 17, 1949, FRUS, 49, 4, pp. 377–80; Hogan, *The Marshall Plan*, p. 211.

255 *"UK's hard currency reserves"*: Sixth Report to Congress of the Economic Cooperation Administration, for the Quarter Ended September 30, 1949, p. 8.

255 *"prompt action"*: Telegram from Secretary Acheson to Ambassador Douglas, FRUS, 49, 4, p. 790.

255 *"probably an essential"*: Editorial note, FRUS, 49, 4, p. 799, and FRUS, 49, 4, pp. 792, 793; Memorandum by Assistant Secretary Thorp to Secretary Acheson, June 27, 1949, FRUS, 49, 4, p. 794.

255 *After three days:* Hogan, *The Marshall Plan*, pp. 262, 244.

255 *"The months of June"*: Van der Beugel, *From Marshall Aid to Atlantic Partnership*, pp. 161, 162.

256 *"putting the squeeze"*: Hogan, *The Marshall Plan*, p. 244.

256 *"I cannot avoid"*: Telegram from Harriman to Acheson, June 25, 1949, FRUS, 49, 4, pp. 792, 793.

256 *"I confess that I have"*: Bullock, *Ernest Bevin*, pp. 709, 710.

256 *"What we are facing"*: Bullock, *Ernest Bevin*, p. 707.

256 *"When one reads"*: Van der Beugel, *From Marshall Aid to Atlantic Partnership*, pp. 161–64. After months of acrimony, the organization's Executive Council entrusted Marjolin of France and Snoy of Belgium to meet with all the delegations and decide upon a course of action. The organization hung on a thread at this point, as van der Beugel recalled: "Everybody realized that this was the last chance for agreement." The tandem endured a consuming "crisis of conscience" for eight arduous days and nights. Marjolin and Snoy separated, and when they came back together, they found that their separate recommendations cohered. The delegations agreed, so did Hoffman, and all were much relieved, though considerably worse for the wear in early September when the revised division of aid was set for the Plan's second year.

257 *"The UK was finished"*: Bullock, *Ernest Bevin*, p. 701.

257 *Cripps could not eat:* Hogan, *The Marshall Plan*, p. 247.

257 *"the importance of the September"*: Paper Prepared in the United States Embassy in the United Kingdom, August 18, 1949, FRUS, 49, 4, pp. 806, 807.

257 *"at a rate that"*: Hogan, *The Marshall Plan*, p. 247.

257 *"grueling"*: Hogan, *The Marshall Plan*, pp. 249–51.

257 *At a Cabinet meeting*: Bullock, *Ernest Bevin*, pp. 714, 715.

258 *"the nodal point"*: Hogan, *The Marshall Plan*, pp. 249–51.

258 *Recognizing Great Britain's*: Hogan, *The Marshall Plan*, p. 260.

258 *"I doubt whether"*: Bullock, *Ernest Bevin*, p. 716.

258 *"Where are we goin' now?"*: Bullock, *Ernest Bevin*, p. 727.

258 *"uncertainty about what"*: Position Paper for the Discussions with the British and Canadians on Pound-Dollar Problems, Prepared by the PPS, September 3, 1949, FRUS, 49, 4, p. 822.

259 *"his doctrine of salvation"*: Acheson, *Sketches from Life of Men I Have Known*, p. 19.

259 *"not going to flimflam"*: Acheson, *Present at the Creation*, p. 324.

259 *"He was entirely right"*: Acheson, *Sketches from Life of Men I Have Known*, p. 19.

259 *"was very well received"*: Hogan, *The Marshall Plan*, p. 263.

259 *"most frank"*: Athrur Krock column of September 20, 1949, as recounted in Oral interview: John Snyder. HST Library Collection.

259 *"rose"*: Hogan, *The Marshall Plan*, p. 266.

260 *Outside of the Commonwealth*: Sixth Report to Congress of the Economic Cooperation Administration, p. 8; Bullock, *Ernest Bevin*, pp. 718, 719.

260 *"disturbed and apprehensive"*: Telegram from Ambassador David Bruce to Secretary Acheson, September 22, 1949, FRUS, 49, 4, pp. 661–63.

260 *"une décision brutale"*: Bullock, *Ernest Bevin*, p. 722.

260 *"French pride"*: FRUS, 49, 4, pp. 661, 662.

260 *"Where did we go wrong?"*: Hogan, *The Marshall Plan*, p. 268.

260 *"kick in the backside"*: From Memorandum by the Special Aide to the Executive Secretary of the Economic Commission for Europe Rostow to the Executive Secretary of the Economic Commission for Europe Myrdal, October 12, 1949; Subject: Devaluation and European Cooperation, FRUS, 49, 4, p. 848. See also Hogan, *The Marshall Plan*, p. 268.

261 *"a bold and imaginative"*: Statement by Paul Gray Hoffman at Press Conference, Monday, September 19, 1949. Paul Hoffman Papers, HST Library Collection.

Twelve: Integration and Subterranean Fires

PAGE

262 *"All of the fanfare"*: Hogan, *The Marshall Plan*, p. 274.

262 *"fundamental alterations"*: For a good discussion of these documents see Van der Beugel, *From Marshall Aid to Atlantic Partnership*, p. 180.

262 *"The Economic Integration of Western Europe"*: Price, *The Marshall Plan and Its Meaning*, p. 121.

263 *"some kind of impressive"*: Walter Lippmann, "Today and Tomorrow," *San Francisco Chronicle*, October 13, 1949.

263 *"the historical moment"*: Price, *The Marshall Plan and Its Meaning*, p. 121.

263 *"We applaud the success"*: Economic Cooperation Administration Press Conference, Board Room of the Miatico Building, Washington, D.C., November 7, 1949. Paul Hoffman Papers, HST Library Collection.

263 *"when we began"*: Oral interview: Milton Katz, HST Library Collection.

264 *European integration*: Perhaps most recently in an August 16, 1949 statement delivered in Paris at the Chateau de la Muette, where he addressed the heads of the Marshall Plan country delegations. Paul Hoffman Papers, HST Library Collection.

264 *"that high hope·can"*: Speech from Statement by Paul Gray Hoffman, Economic Cooperation Administration, Before Organization for European Economic Cooperation, Paris, France, October 31, 1949. Paul Hoffman Papers, HST Library Collection.

264 *"a sucker for"*: Oral interview: William Foster, Harry Price Collection.

264 *"burning with a missionary's"*: Hogan, *The Marshall Plan*, p. 274.

264 *"seldom if ever"*: Quoted in van der Beugel, *From Marshall Aid to Atlantic Partnership*, p. 182.

264 *"but its 1949"*: Lincoln Gordon, "Lessons from the Marshall Plan: Successes and Limits," in Hoffman and Maier, eds., *The Marshall Plan*, p. 56.

265 *"integration"*: As noted by Bissell in *Reflections of a Cold Warrior*, p. 63.

265 *"very comforting"*: As noted in "Review of European Press Reaction to Mr. Hoffman's Paris Visit to OEEC Negotiations, 25 October Thru 10 November 1949," prepared by Press Intelligence Unit Editorial Research and Analysis Section Information Division, ECA, Office of the Special Representative to Europe, December 1, 1949. Paul Hoffman Papers, HST Library Collection.

265 *"USA Takes Over Hitler's"*: "Review of European Press Reaction."

265 *"it has been accepted"*: White, *Fire in the Ashes*, p. 275.

265 *And while it took*: White, *Fire in the Ashes*, p. 283.

265 *"Europe Given Eleven Weeks"*: "Review of European Press Reaction."

265 *"take a generation"*: van der Beugel, *From Marshall Aid to Atlantic Partnership*, p. 187.

265 *"The Americans wanted"*: Hogan, *The Marshall Plan*, p. 427.

266 *"I think the United States"*: Oral interview: Arthur Schlesinger, Jr., conducted by author.

266 *"We wanted each"*: Hoffman and Maier, eds., *The Marshall Plan*, p. 47.

266 *France was returning to form*: William Diebold, a foreign policy analyst during these years shared this view in a convincing critique of Hogan. He wrote that some Marshall Planners spoke about "the American way" and some were "undoubtedly quite ideological and some were naïve about Europe." Diebold argued: "For the most part, though, it strikes me that these activities were rather pragmatic efforts to foster recovery. What could the Americans teach except what they knew? I should think that the practices were put forward less because they were American than because their proponents thought they would work." Diebold, *The Marshall Plan in Retrospect*, p. 425.

Self-help was the key principle here. Hoffman certainly put forth suggestions, and he exhorted Western Europe to act. He even tacitly wielded the lever of U.S. aid. But, he was clear in his speech. Western Europe had to design its own institutions and policies, in its own manner and mode.

266 *"a single large market"*: Hogan, *The Marshall Plan*, p. 277.

266 *On January 31, 1950*: Price, *The Marshall Plan and Its Meaning*, p. 123.

266 *"the criticism of Hoffman's"*: van der Beugel, *From Marshall Aid to Atlantic Partnership*, p. 187.

266 *(really his seventy-first)*: Kuromiya, *Stalin*, p. 191.

266 *Thirty thousand posters*: Beevor and Cooper, *Paris*, p. 371.

267 *"lord mayor"*: Acheson, *Present at the Creation*, p. 340.

267 *He was cerebral*: White, *Fire in the Ashes*, p. 149; Acheson, *Present at the Creation*, p. 341.

267 *"We are of the West"*: Dr. Konrad Adenauer, "We Are of the West," *Life*, August 29, 1949.

267 *Adenauer was not*: See Hitchcock, *France Restored*, p. 113.

267 *"one conclusion seemed plain"*: Acheson, *Present at the Creation*, pp. 337, 338.

268 *In early October, George*: See Hogan, *The Marshall Plan*, p. 269.

268 *"The best chance"*: Quoted in Chace, *Acheson*, p. 246.

268 *"already taking a familiar"*: From Meeting of U.S. Ambassador at Paris, October 21–22, to Discuss Major Developments Relating to Europe, and Telegram from Secretary Acheson to the Embassy in France, October 19, 1949, FRUS, 49, 4, pp. 470–72.

268 *"Germany must not"*: Quoted in Hitchcock, *France Restored*, p. 114.

269 *"Europe was inconceivable"*: Hogan, *The Marshall Plan*, pp. 288, 289.

269 *When the meetings ended*: Acheson, *Present at the Creation*, p. 339.

269   *"perhaps the only topic"*: Hitchcock, *France Restored*, pp. 117, 119.

269   *"It should be clear"*: Summary of a Meeting of U.S. Ambassadors at Paris, October 21–22, 1949, FRUS, 49, 4, p. 493.

269   *Ambassador to the United Kingdom:* FRUS, 49, 4, pp. 480–84.

270   *He kept pushing:* See FRUS, 49, 4, pp. 475–94, and for a good discussion, Lundestad, *"Empire" by Integration*, p. 34.

270   *"From the beginning"*: Telegram from the U.S. Special Representative in Europe Harriman to Secretary Acheson, November 6, 1949, FRUS, 49, 4, pp. 441–43.

270   *"an outstanding European"*: Telegram from Secretary Acheson to Ambassador Douglas, November 16, 1949, FRUS, 49, 4, p. 449.

270   *"we are being asked"*: Quoted in Lundestad, *"Empire" by Integration*, p. 31.

270   *"schoolboy lectures"*: Memorandum of Conversation by the United States High Commissioner for Germany John McCloy, January 20, 1950, FRUS, 50, 3, p. 1608.

270   *"exasperated"*: Hogan, *The Marshall Plan*, p. 285.

270   *"who Cripps knew"*: Recounted in Abramson, *Spanning the Century*, pp. 436, 437.

271   *"You have not only"*: Letter from Paul Hoffman to Averell Harriman, December 17, 1949. Averell Harriman Papers, Library of Congress Collection.

271   *"Take any good Irishman"*: Morgan, *Reds*, p. 373.

271   *The year before:* This has been widely noted. For example, see Johnson, *The Age of Anxiety*, p. 10. Johnson's book provides one of the most recent accounts of McCarthy and one of the best accounts of the lead-up to and the speech itself at Wheeling.

272   *During the following week:* For a good account see Yergin, *Shattered Peace*, pp. 401, 402.

272   *"We have evidence"*: "U.S. Detects Atomic Blast in Russia," *Life*, October 3, 1949.

272   *The explosion had:* Service, *Stalin*, p. 508.

272   *The Soviet test had:* "U.S. Detects Atomic Blast in Russia."

272   *"This is now"*: Isaacson and Thomas, *The Wise Men*, pp. 481, 480.

272   *Mao and his Communist:* McCullough, *Truman*, pp. 744–49.

272   *The U.S.-China link:* Chace makes this point in *Acheson*, p. 211.

272   *All told, the United States:* Chace, *Acheson*, p. 216.

273   *Having tightened its grip:* Service, *Stalin*, p. 509.

273   *"it seemed, a fundamental"*: Gaddis, *We Now Know*, p. 55.

273   *"disgusting"*: Clifford, *Counsel to the President*, p. 142; McCullough, *Truman*, pp. 760, 761.

274   *"one year at least"*: Morgan, *Reds*, pp. 277–80.

274   *In fact, during the 1930s:* We now know this through the Venona tapes—Soviet cables from the time, decoded and released in 1995. For an excellent examination of the tapes and what they demonstrate, see Morgan, *Reds*.

274   *"whipping a dead horse"*: Morgan, *Reds*, p. xiv.

274   *Early that February, 31 percent:* Gallup, *The Gallup Poll*, vol. 2, pp. 891, 892.

275   *That autumn Vandenberg:* Vandenberg, ed., *The Private Papers of Senator Vandenberg*, pp. 516, 517.

275   *"The least I can do"*: Vandenberg, ed., *The Private Papers of Senator Vandenberg*, pp. 556–58.

276   *"You just don't realize"*: Vandenberg, *The Private Papers of Senator Vandenberg*, pp. 558, 560.

276   *"it is not good enough"*: Statement by Paul Gray Hoffman. Before a Joint Session of the Senate Foreign Relations Committee and the House Foreign Affairs Committee, February 21, 1950. Paul Hoffman Papers, HST Library Collection.

276   *"delivered a speech"*: Letter from Paul Hoffman to Averell Harriman, May 12, 1950. Averell Harriman Papers, HST Library Collection.

276   *"nothing so much as"*: Hogan, *The Marshall Plan*, pp. 336, 337.

276   *Given recent developments:* Yergin, *Shattered Peace*, pp. 401–3.

277   *"to bludgeon the mass"*: Acheson, *Present at the Creation*, p. 374.

277 *"What I read scared"*: Yergin, *Shattered Peace*, p. 403.

278 *"a mechanism"*: Much of this discussion comes from Bissell, *Reflections of a Cold Warrior*, p. 59.

278 *"if you have no"*: Oral interview: Dirk Stikker, HST Library Collection.

278 *"What really mattered"*: From Van der Beugel, *From Marshall Aid to Atlantic Partnership*, p. 196.

278 Many of the Marshall Plan: Price, *The Marshall Plan and Its Meaning*, p. 124.

278 *"at a very early date"*: Hogan, *The Marshall Plan*, p. 297.

278 *Then at the end of January*: Memorandum for Secretary of State: "European Payments Union" sent from ECA, Paris, from Harriman, May 5, 1950. Averell Harriman Papers, Library of Congress Collection.

279 *"still haunted"*: Van der Beugel, *From Marshall Aid to Atlantic Partnership*, p. 191.

279 *"the attitude in Europe"*: Oral interview: Milton Katz, HST Library Collection.

279 *"should no longer tolerate"*: Hogan, *The Marshall Plan*, p. 313.

279 *"friendly aid"*: It was in fact "conditional aid." See Price, *The Marshall Plan and Its Meaning*, p. 315.

279 *"warning hung the sword"*: Hogan, *The Marshall Plan*, pp. 302, 303; telegram from Secretary Acheson to Embassy in United Kingdom, February 22, 1950, FRUS, 50, 3, pp. 632, 633; Memorandum of Conversation by Secretary Acheson, March 1, 1950, FRUS 50, 3, pp. 634–37.

279 *"a basic difference"*: Report by the Economic Cooperation Administration; Explanation of the Points at Issue with the British on the Proposed European Payments Union, April 14, 1950, FRUS, 50, 3, pp. 647, 650.

279 At the same time: Van der Beugel, *From Marshall Aid to Atlantic Partnership*, p. 200.

280 *"Britain really wanted"*: Oral interview: Averell Harriman, Harry Price Collection.

280 *"bitter"*: Oral interview: Averell Harriman, Harry Price Collection.

280 Hoffman wrote Cripps: Hogan, *The Marshall Plan*, p. 310.

280 *"the heady atmosphere"*: Hogan, *The Marshall Plan*, p. 279.

280 Britain's budget cuts: Hogan, *The Marshall Plan*, p. 320.

280 *"single most hopeful move"*: Hogan, *The Marshall Plan*, p. 331.

280 At 8 P.M. on May 14: Telegram from Special Representative Harriman to Administrator Hoffman, May 14, 1950, FRUS, 50, 3, p. 657.

280 These were meaningful concessions: Hogan, *The Marshall Plan*, p. 321.

281 The Council of Ministers: Van der Beugel, *From Marshall Aid to Atlantic Partnership*, p. 201; Stikker, *Men of Responsibility*, p. 174.

281 To help countries buffet: Van der Beugel, *From Marshall Aid to Atlantic Partnership*, p. 201.

281 *"The most astonishing thing"*: Stikker, *Men of Responsibility*, p. 174.

281 *"a period of economic"*: Bullock, *Ernest Bevin*, p. 762.

281 *"the EPU was the greatest"*: Bissell, *Reflections of a Cold Warrior*, pp. 57, 64.

281 *"the European Payments Union"*: Oral interview: Averell Harriman, HST Library Collection. The EPU was an important steppingstone in that direction and was wound up in 1958. Bullock, *Ernest Bevin*, p. 762.

281 *"of all the moves"*: Oral interview: Paul Hoffman, HST Library Collection.

281 As Hoffman said: Quoted in Bullock, *Ernest Bevin*, p. 762.

282 *"have lost [its] momentum"*: Memorandum of Conversation Between Acheson, Rusk, Nitze, Douglas, McCloy, et al. March 7, 1950, FRUS, 50, 3, p. 639.

282 *"what he thought"*: From Lundestad, *"Empire" by Integration*, p. 35.

282 *"drastic step towards"*: FRUS, 50, 3, p. 640.

282 *"Were there any views"*: FRUS, 50, 3, p. 640.

Thirteen: Europe Refashioned

283 So, as Acheson and Bruce: Acheson, *Present at the Creation*, p. 382; Acheson, *Sketches from Life of Men I Have Known*, pp. 35, 36.

283 Later that morning: Monnet, *Memoirs*, pp. 301, 302.

283 At the time of the meeting: Acheson, *Present at the Creation*, p. 271.

283 "so breathtaking a step": Acheson, *Sketches from Life of Men I Have Known*, p. 36.

284 "Whichever way we turn": Monnet, *Memoirs*, pp. 289, 290.

284 "What about Germany?": Duchene, *Jean Monnet*, p. 190.

285 "The German situation": Monnet, *Memoirs*, pp. 291–93.

285 "at once the key": Monnet, *Memoirs*, pp. 292, 293.

285 "All successive attempts": Monnet, *Memoirs*, pp. 292–94.

286 "The proposal has": Monnet, *Memoirs*, pp. 293–96.

286 Monnet and his colleagues: Monnet, *Memoirs*, pp. 295, 296.

286 "Robert Schuman seemed": Monnet, *Memoirs*, pp. 298, 299.

286 In the interwar years: White, *Fire in the Ashes*, pp. 261, 262.

287 "M. Schuman": Monnet, *Memoirs*, pp. 298, 299.

287 "Could you read": Monnet, *Memoirs*, pp. 299, 300.

287 "joined the conspiracy": Monnet, *Memoirs*, pp. 299, 300.

287 Much groundwork had: Hitchcock makes this point in his section on the Schuman Plan in *France Restored*.

287 "there was": Monnet, *Memoirs*, p. 301.

287 "a curious coincidence": Monnet, *Memoirs*, p. 301.

287 "almost as an irrelevance": Acheson, *Present at the Creation*, pp. 382, 383; Acheson, *Sketches from Life of Men I Have Known*, p. 37.

288 "in an embrace": Beevor and Cooper, *Paris*, p. 375.

288 "rebirth of Europe": Acheson, *Sketches from Life of Men I Have Known*, p. 37.

288 "two chance accomplices": Monnet, *Memoirs*, pp. 301, 302.

288 But in the spring of 1950: White, *Fire in the Ashes*, pp. 244, 245.

289 "agreed to his proposal": Adenauer's memoirs as retold in Monnet, *Memoirs*, pp. 302, 303.

289 "I have something here": "Western Europe Backs Unity," *Life*, May 29, 1950.

289 "That's it": The events and attendant detail of May 8 are as told in Monnet, *Memoirs*, pp. 302, 303.

289 "It is no longer a time": Monnet, *Memoirs*, pp. 304, 305.

289 "brilliantly creative": Hogan, *The Marshall Plan*, pp. 366, 367.

289 "genius of the Schuman-Monnet": Acheson, *Present at the Creation*, p. 384.

290 He was overcome: Duchene, *Jean Monnet*, p. 201.

290 "Clearly, we had managed": Acheson, *Present at the Creation*, pp. 384, 385.

290 "You have a large": Acheson, *Present at the Creation*, pp. 386, 387.

291 "opposed to the Schuman Plan": Monnet, *Memoirs*, pp. 316, 317.

291 "Would you go ahead": Monnet, *Memoirs*, pp. 307, 308, 305.

291 Cripps pointed out: Bullock, *Ernest Bevin*, pp. 782, 783.

291 "It's no good": Hogan, *The Marshall Plan*, p. 370.

291 "It took, in all": Bullock, *Ernest Bevin*, p. 780.

291 Britain had declined: Hogan, *The Marshall Plan*, p. 372.

291 Dean Acheson believed: Acheson, *Present at the Creation*, pp. 384, 385.

292 "The essential prize": Bullock, *Ernest Bevin*, p. 778. Great Britain had missed a critical opportunity. Bullock and Beevor and Cooper had different takes on the significance of the moment. Bullock wrote: "Some decisions are critical. This one was. It was not the last clear chance for Britain to enter Europe, but it was the first wrong choice." Bullock, *Ernest Bevin*, p. 783. Beevor and Cooper put it more starkly: "Any British preten-

sion to leadership on the Continent was finished." Beevor and Cooper, *Paris*, p. 375. Bullock's take is the more accurate one. There would be junctures throughout the succeeding generation at which time Great Britain could have reclaimed the mantle of leadership in Europe. But their decision in May 1950 was a fateful one, the "first wrong choice," as Bullock put it.

The Schuman Plan would not have been possible without the United States and it would not have been possible without the Marshall Plan. After the war, France sought to keep Germany eviscerated. The Marshall Plan changed the strategic balance and France's geopolitical calculation. U.S. officials executing the Marshall Plan, and related U.S. policies, moved—sometimes delicately, sometimes forcefully, but consistently—to build Germany up. The French resisted at every turn. The Americans proceeded apace, though. The French were dependent upon American security and Marshall aid. It was Monnet's growing recognition that the United States would continue to support Germany's economic rise—and possibly even its remilitarization—with or without French assent, and his growing concern about the Cold War and France's vulnerability, that led Monnet to take up the "German problem" in the spring of 1950 and forge ahead with a creative response.

Since the talks in Washington in September 1949, the U.S. had pressed France to take the lead on continental integration. Acheson sent a stream of cables that autumn and thereafter to Schuman. As Clappier told Monnet, Schuman was "almost obsessed" with the German problem and how to resolve it. Focused on the May London meetings, Schuman needed to present Acheson with a solution. He shared his anxiety with Clappier and Monnet and was extraordinarily receptive when Monnet proposed a solution. Journalist Theodore White, in Europe during these years, opined: "There is no doubt that without American diplomatic pressure and insistence this dream [of European integration] would still be a paper nothing or the stuff of student debating contests." White, *Fire in the Ashes*, pp. 14, 15.

Marshall aid had helped deliver France from the economic desperation, the hyperinflation, the violence, the strikes and political unrest of 1947 and 1948. The Marshall Plan helped France launch its modernization; it improved the French economy, restoring stability and a sense of confidence and purpose such that the French psyche was strong enough to take such a bold step. Furthermore, it is highly improbable that France would have entered into so broad and so binding a continental arrangement with Germany and without Great Britain's participation, without the North Atlantic Treaty and the U.S. military guarantee. Wrote historian Geir Lundestad: "Without the risk being manageable in some way, Paris still might not have agreed to the full reconstruction of Germany, much less taken the crucial first step on the road to European integration . . . the United States was clearly the ultimate guarantor in case anything should go wrong with the integration of Germany." Lundestad, *"Empire" by Integration*, pp. 138, 139.

Following World War II, intra-European suspicions and animosities ran high. Earlier habits of nationalism and protectionism still reigned on the continent. Lundestad wrote that without U.S. support, it is more probable than not that Europe would have reverted and descended into its old patterns. Lundestad, *"Empire" by Integration*, p. 153. Instead, the Marshall Plan moved Europe in the direction of integration. It summoned the Marshall Plan countries to come together to provide a common answer to Marshall's offer of aid; it called for Europe to form the OEEC; to agree together to a division of aid; to liberalize its trade and payments policies and eventually to form a European Payments Union. Each step cultivated a common European identity, a sense that mutual cooperation was possible and national differences surmountable. The shared habits, customs and confidence formed a sturdy foundation without which the Schuman Plan would have been quite improbable. As Ambassador Cattini wrote, "The most important effect of the Marshall Plan and the whole European operation has been, I think, the feeling in Europe that unity is fundamental. There was no idea [in the immediate postwar period] that drastic changes were needed. The thought was that we needed a breathing space … In my mind it's absolutely sure that the Schuman Plan … couldn't have been developed without the ground being prepared and fertilized by Marshall Plan endeavors." Price, *The Marshall Plan and Its Meaning*, p. 347.

Historian of the Schuman Plan John Gillingham wrote: "without American backing the coal-steel negotiations would not have gotten off the ground." Lundestad, *"Empire" by Integration*, p. 127. The Marshall Plan and related U.S. policy constructed a broad and robust platform from which Monnet and Schuman could launch their enterprise. From that moment forward, Ernst van der Beugel wrote, "the initiative for concrete and major steps on the road to European unity," one of the most revolutionary undertakings in postwar history, "shifted to Europe." Van der Beugel, *From Marshall Aid to Atlantic Partnership*, pp. 231, 232. That was what the Marshall Plan had aimed at all along.

292 *Acheson recalled that:* Acheson, *Present at the Creation*, p. 368.
292 *By that time:* White, *Fire in the Ashes*, pp. 58, 59.
292 *For Helmut Kohl:* www.cnn.com/ALLPOLITICS/1997/05/28/Clinton.europe/. Listening to Clinton's speech evoking those years on the Plan's 50th Anniversary, Kohl had tears in his eyes.
293 *ECA set up dozens:* Ninth Report to Congress of the Economic Cooperation Administration, for the Quarter Ended June 30, 1950, pp. 40, 41.
293 *Puppet shows:* Seventh Report to Congress of the Economic Cooperation Administration, for the Quarter Ended December 31, 1949, p. 84.
293 *In Great Britain, Marshall aid:* Bullock, *Ernest Bevin*, p. 766.
293 *"There is big news":* Editorial, "Britain Comes Back," *Life*, May 1, 1950.
293 *"the Rhone development":* "Billions of Kilowatts for France" and "Dams Are the Climax of a Cherished Plan," *Life*, June 26, 1950.
294 *"The country has been":* Editorial, "The Boom Goes On," *Life*, April, 24, 1950.
294 *"Today by the Grace":* McCullough, *Truman*, p. 758.
294 *"Let us undertake":* Henry Luce, "The Reformation of the World's Economies," *Fortune*, 20th Anniversary Issue, February 1950. Paul Hoffman Papers, HST Library Collection.
294 *By the end of June:* See note in Prologue for tabulation of funds expended.
294 *At the end of June 1950:* Ninth Report to Congress of the Economic Cooperation Administration, pp. 3–10.
294 *Most Marshall Plan:* Price, *The Marshall Plan and Its Meaning*, p. 141.
294 *But it also meant:* Price, *The Marshall Plan and Its Meaning*, p. 141. Tony Judt writes, "At the beginning of the 1950s, one Italian family in four lived in poverty and most of the rest were little better off. … But in West Germany in 1950 17 million of the country's 47 million residents were still classed as 'needy,' chiefly because they had nowhere to live … In post-war polls, 'housing' always topped the list of popular concerns; in [Vittorio] De Sica's [film] *Miracle in Milan* (1951) the homeless crowd chants, 'We want a home to live in, so we and our children can believe in tomorrow.'" Judt, *Postwar*, p. 235.
295 *Hoffman and Harriman both:* Oral interview: Averell Harriman, HST Library Collection; Oral interview: Paul Hoffman, HST Library Collection and Harry Price Collection.
295 *"Anyone who compares":* Quoted in Address by Paul Gray Hoffman before the Annual Meeting of the Association of American Colleges, Hotel Netherlands Plaza, Cincinnati, Ohio, January 10, 1950. Paul Hoffman Papers, HST Library Collection.
295 *"I would like to state":* Statement by Paul G. Hoffman. Before the Senate Appropriations Committee, May 25, 1950. Paul Hoffman Papers, HST Library Collection.
295 *That summer, a city:* Acheson, *Present at the Creation*, p. 333; Mayor Ernst Reuter, "West Berlin's Mayor Defies Reds," *Life*, May 15, 1950.
295 *Meanwhile, in the Norwegian:* As noted in Statement by Ambassador Averell Harriman

Before the House Foreign Affairs Committee, February 22, 1950. Averell Harriman Papers, Library of Congress Collection.

295 *"chiefly through the use"*: Pollard, *Economic Security and the Origins of the Cold War*, p. 167.

295 *They had received a cable*: Acheson, *Present at the Creation*, pp. 402–5; "U.S. Gets into Fight for Korea," *Life*, July 10, 1950.

296 *The next evening, Saturday*: Acheson, *Present at the Creation*, pp. 402–5.

296 *Vandenberg felt*: Vandenberg, ed., *The Private Papers of Senator Vandenberg*, p. 542.

296 *Attlee, Bevin, and their countrymen*: Bullock, *Ernest Bevin*, pp. 792, 794.

296 *If the United States moved*: Monnet, *Memoirs*, pp. 336, 337; account in George W. Ball, *The Discipline of Power* (1968), as quoted in Monnet.

297 *Days later, Harriman left*: Abramson, *Spanning the Century*, pp. 442–43.

297 *"make people appreciate"*: Raucher, *Paul Hoffman*, pp. 76, 77.

297 *Only three days after*: Hogan, *The Marshall Plan*, p. 337.

297 *That same day, Senator Robert Taft*: Acheson, *Present at the Creation*, p. 410.

297 *"American boys are dying"*: Morgan, *Reds*, p. 406.

297 *"I loved your reminiscence"*: Vandenberg, ed., *The Private Papers of Senator Vandenberg*, p. 563.

298 *"the blood of our boys"*: Acheson, *Present at the Creation*, p. 365.

298 *"fellow travelers"*: Hogan, *The Marshall Plan*, p. 382.

298 *By the time of the North*: Hogan, *The Marshall Plan*, p. 337.

298 *"the dispatch of two"*: Acheson, *Present at the Creation*, p. 420.

298 *"A strong economy"*: Letter from William Foster to Senator Tom Connally, July 27, 1950. Paul Hoffman Papers, HST Library Collection.

299 *"understood that the Marshall"*: Bissell, *Reflections of a Cold Warrior*, pp. 66, 69.

299 *In September, a defense*: Acheson, *Present at the Creation*, p. 421.

299 *"middle course"*: As "codified" in a Draft Circular from Washington to ECA's Overseas Missions. Hogan, *The Marshall Plan*, p. 340.

300 *"talked about reconciling"*: Hogan, *The Marshall Plan*, pp. 341, 342.

300 *"The question now"*: Quoted in Price, *The Marshall Plan and Its Meaning*, pp. 362, 363.

300 *"ERP in nineteen-fifty"*: From White, *Fire in the Ashes*, p. 71.

301 *"I am most anxious"*: Letter from Harriman to Truman, May 20, 1950. Averell Harriman Papers, HST Library Collection.

301 *"In ECA terms"*: Letter from Katz to Harriman, May 1, 1950. Averell Harriman Papers, HST Library Collection.

301 *"vitalized"*: Letter from Harriman to Truman, May 20, 1950. Averell Harriman Papers, HST Library Collection.

301 *"Dean's in trouble"*: Abramson, *Spanning the Century*, pp. 437, 438, 440, 446.

302 *"My forty-five years"*: Acheson, *Present at the Creation*, pp. 410, 411.

302 *"You must be"*: Abramson, *Spanning the Century*, pp. 442–43.

302 *"This evening, Mr. Paul"*: CBS News, September 25, 1950, 11 P.M., Paul Hoffman Papers, HST Library Collection.

302 *"I simply wanted"*: Vandenberg, ed., *The Private Papers of Senator Vandenberg*, p. 395.

302 *"Paul Hoffman will long"*: CBS News, September 25, 1950.

302 *Senator Robert Taft wrote*: Letter from Robert Taft to Hoffman, November 24, 1950. Paul Hoffman Papers, HST Library Collection.

303 *"It has been a real pleasure"*: Letter from John Taber to Hoffman, November 27, 1950. Paul Hoffman Papers, HST Library Collection.

303 *"As head of ECA"*: Editorial in *Chicago Sun-Times*, September 28, 1950. Paul Hoffman Papers, HST Library Collection.

303 *"farewell tour"*: "Hoffman's Farewell Tour," *Life*, November 13, 1950; Hogan, *The Marshall Plan*, pp. 348, 349.

303 *"Starting November 15"*: Letter to Marian McGovern from Hoffman, December 27, 1950. Paul Hoffman Papers, HST Library Collection.

303 *"We were like"*: Oral interview: Paul Porter, HST Library Collection.

304 *"Yes, Mr. President"*: Pogue, *George C. Marshall*, p. 420.

304 *"Now history gives him"*: Editorial, "George Catlett Marshall," *Life*, September 25, 1950.

305 *"a catspaw and a pawn"*: Pogue, *George C. Marshall*, p. 426.

305 *"General Marshall is not only"*: Pogue, *George C. Marshall*, p. 428.

305 *There was no beach*: McCullough, *Truman*, pp. 795, 798.

305 *"I can almost hear"*: Acheson, *Present at the Creation*, p. 448.

306 *The Chinese statement*: McCullough, *Truman*, pp. 798, 799.

306 *The Democrats managed*: McCullough, *Truman*, pp. 814, 815.

306 *On Friday, November 24*: McCullough, *Truman*, pp. 815.

306 *"To do this"*: McCullough, *Truman*, p. 817.

307 *"an enormous handicap"*: Acheson, *Present at the Creation*, pp. 471, 472.

307 *"halt this aggression"*: McCullough, *Truman*, pp. 820–22.

307 *When Attlee announced*: Acheson, *Present at the Creation*, p. 479.

307 *Western Europeans worried*: Tenth Report to Congress of the Economic Cooperation Administration, for the Quarter Ended September 30, 1950, p. 5.

308 *"World War III"*: From McCullough, *Truman*, p. 825.

308 *When Attlee arrived*: Bullock, *Ernest Bevin*, pp. 821, 822; McCullough, *Truman*, p. 826.

308 *The growing demand together*: Tenth Report to Congress of the Economic Cooperation Administration, pp. ix, x.

308 *"a spectacular increase"*: Tenth Report to Congress of the Economic Cooperation Administration, p. 4.

308 *First, the shortages*: Tenth Report to Congress of the Economic Cooperation Administration, p. ix.

308 *This last concern seemed*: Van de Beugel, *From Marshall Aid to Atlantic Partnership*, pp. 208, 209.

308 *"general agreement"*: Tenth Report to Congress of the Economic Cooperation Administration, p. 4.

309 *"recovery in Northern"*: Hogan, *The Marshall Plan*, p. 388.

309 *Marshall aid, devaluation*: Hogan, *The Marshall Plan*, p. 338.

309 *"I sat in the House"*: Bullock, *Ernest Bevin*, p. 824.

Fourteen: Shutting It Down

PAGE

310 *When asked who*: Gallup, *The Gallup Poll*, vol. 2, p. 963.

310 *"I wonder how far"*: McCullough, *Truman*, p. 914.

310 *The first was productivity*: Hogan, *The Marshall Plan*, p. 341.

311 *In America, the manager-worker*: This is a central theme of Hogan's in *The Marshall Plan*.

311 *"a psychological abhorrence"*: Price, *The Marshall Plan and Its Meaning*, pp. 334, 335, 339.

311 *They would need to adopt*: Or as Hoffman's deputy and successor William Foster put it, "ECA is interested in [spurring] . . . a complete mental revolution in European managers and labor." Quoted in McGlade, "The American Transfer," p. 26.

311 *"If we are to raise"*: Hoffman, *Peace Can Be Won*, p. 102.

312 *It sold twenty-five thousand copies*: Hoffman, *Peace Can Be Won*, p. 102.

312 *"the reorganization of the steel"*: Oral interview: Paul Hoffman, HST Library Collection.

312 *"It is clear that only"*: As ECA reported to Congress and is noted in Hogan, *The Marshall Plan*, p. 343.

312 *"production assistance drive"*: Price, *The Marshall Plan and Its Meaning*, p. 156.

312 *The technical assistance program became*: For further discussion see Hogan, *The Marshall Plan*, p. 341.

312 *"management seminars"*: Hogan, *The Marshall Plan*, p. 416.
312 *The technical assistance program made it*: Hoffman, *Peace Can Be Won*, p. 103.
312 *But on the whole*: Oral interview: Edwin Dibrell, Harry Price Collection.
313 *In Sardinia and Turkey*: Donovan, *The Second Victory*, pp. 59, 60.
313 *ECA paid for a group*: Fifth Report to Congress of the Economic Cooperation Administration, for the Quarter Ended June 30, 1949, p. 47.
313 *By 1952, approximately*: McGlade, "The American Transfer," p. 23.
313 *When the Plan was complete*: Price, *The Marshall Plan and Its Meaning*, p. 334.
313 *"Even more important"*: Hoffman, *Peace Can Be Won*, pp. 103, 104.
313 *"a household word"*: From Price, *The Marshall Plan and Its Meaning*, p. 344.
313 *"generated new attitudes"*: Quoted in Price, *The Marshall Plan and Its Meaning*, p. 335.
313 *"It did lead to new ideas"*: Oral interview: Hugh Gaitskill, Harry Price Collection.
313 *"The capitalism put on display"*: James Cronin, "The Marshall Plan and the Cold War Political Discourse," in Shain, ed., *The Marshall Plan*, p. 289.
314 *Some members of Congress*: McGlade, "The American Transfer," pp. 25, 26.
314 *"turned out to be"*: Oral interview: Paul Hoffman, HST Library Collection.
314 *"Il n'y a que faire"*: White, *Fire in the Ashes*, p. 366.
315 *"more swiftly raised"*: The full quote follows: "Nothing in postwar history, except the Marshall Plan, more swiftly raised American prestige in European eyes than our defense of Korea." White, *Fire in the Ashes*, pp. 389, 390.
315 *"The number of Americans"*: Oral interview: Harry Labouisse, Harry Price Collection.
315 *"Will we be Coca-colonized"*: Hitchcock, *The Struggle for Europe*, p. 160.
315 *"frightened that the destinies"*: Quoted in Hitchcock, *The Struggle for Europe*, p. 157.
316 *By the middle of the year*: Hogan, *The Marshall Plan*, pp. 359, 360, 365.
316 *For the French, it remained*: A theme throughout Hitchcock's *France Restored*.
317 *"dead duck"*: Hogan, *The Marshall Plan*, pp. 377, 378.
317 *"more directly, than ever"*: Hogan, *The Marshall Plan*, pp. 377, 378.
317 *McCloy's role*: Hitchcock, *France Restored*, p. 152.
317 *There was no public audience*: Account from White, *Fire in the Ashes*, p. 283.
317 *Jean Monnet was there*: Monnet, *Memoirs*, p. 356.
317 *"as bold and imaginative"*: Quoted in Ellwood, *Rebuilding Europe*, p. 171.
318 *"Truman Fires MacArthur"*: McCullough, *Truman*, pp. 840, 843.
318 *It was a desperately needed*: For what it meant see Acheson, *Present at the Creation*, p. 512.
318 *Then, on March 24*: Acheson, *Present at the Creation*, pp. 518, 519.
318 *"By this act MacArthur"*: Quoted in McCullough, *Truman*, pp. 836, 837.
318 *"Here we fight Europe's"*: See among other accounts, Acheson, *Present at the Creation*, p. 520.
318 *Most major American newspapers*: McCullough, *Truman*, pp. 847, 848.
318 *After MacArthur's dismissal, Truman*: McCullough, *Truman*, pp. 837, 847, 848.
319 *"We heard God speak"*: McCullough, *Truman*, pp. 850–52.
319 *"involve us in the wrong"*: McCullough, *Truman*, p. 854.
319 *"America's Retreat from Victory"*: Johnson, *The Age of Anxiety*, pp. 213, 214.
319 *"the complete, sinister, treacherous"*: Johnson, *The Age of Anxiety*, pp. 213–15; and Morgan, *Reds*, p. 413.
320 *"massive and unrewarding boondoggle"*: Morgan, *Reds*, p. 413.
320 *"McCarthy's discussion"*: Morgan, *Reds*, p. 413.
320 *"his most vile yet"*: McCullough, *Truman*, pp. 860, 861.
320 *only two senators remained*: According to Pogue's account in *George C. Marshall*, p. 489.
320 *"berserk eruption"*: Johnson, *The Age of Anxiety*, p. 216.
320 *"one of the most disgraceful"*: Acheson, *Present at the Creation*, p. 528.
320 *Republican Senator Margaret Chase Smith*: Johnson, *The Age of Anxiety*, p. 217.
320 *If I have to explain*: Morgan, *Reds*, p. 414. Taft also spoke out in displeasure at McCarthy's attack on Marshall.
320 *"apex in irresponsibility"*: Morgan, *Reds*, p. 413.

321 *"Joe McCarthy's just"*: From Robert Caro biography, recounted in Johnson, *The Age of Anxiety*, p. 220.

321 *"the poison blows"*: Saunders, *The Cultural Cold War*, p. 190.

321 *"Whatever new problems"*: Price, *The Marshall Plan and Its Meaning*, pp. 137, 139.

322 Coal, iron ore and food: Price, *The Marshall Plan and Its Meaning*, pp. 148, 149.

322 From the outbreak of war: Hogan, *The Marshall Plan*, p. 393.

322 *"inflationary pressures threatened"*: Price, *The Marshall Plan and Its Meaning*, pp. 152, 153, 157.

322 In France, the fallout: Hitchcock, *France Restored*, p. 148.

322 For the first time, charges: Ellwood, *Rebuilding Europe*, p. 184.

322 And in September 1951: Hogan, *The Marshall Plan*, pp. 419, 420.

323 At the end of 1951: Judt, *Postwar*, p. 159; White, *Fire in the Ashes*, p. 251.

323 In France's May 1951 election: Hogan, *The Marshall Plan*, p. 394.

323 *"a kind of castor oil"*: Quoted in Hogan, *The Marshall Plan*, p. 408.

323 *"If we had it"*: Oral interview: Averell Harriman, HST Library Collection.

323 *"the European Manifesto"*: Hogan, *The Marshall Plan*, p. 414.

324 Calculating American defense needs: Price, *The Marshall Plan and Its Meaning*, pp. 164, 165.

324 *"We had accomplished"*: Oral interview: Milton Katz, HST Library Collection.

325 *"reoriented from economic"*: Hogan, *The Marshall Plan*, pp. 390, 391.

325 *"Dear Mr. President"*: Cable from the Administrator of the ECA William Foster to President Truman, April 18, 1951, FRUS, 51, 1, p. 298.

325 And a new agency: FRUS, 51, 1, p. 298 and circular airgram from Secretary Acheson to Certain Diplomatic and ECA Missions, April 12, 1951, FRUS, 51, 1, pp. 290, 291; Hogan, *The Marshall Plan*, pp. 390, 391.

325 *"a country desk"*: Hogan, *The Marshall Plan*, p. 391.

325 $2.5 billion: Hogan, *The Marshall Plan*, pp. 389, 390.

326 *"the surest way"*: Memorandum of Telephone Conversation by Acheson's Personal Assistant; Between Secretary Acheson and Administrator Foster, June 27, 1951, FRUS, 51, 1, p. 335.

326 *"economic cooperation"*: Price, *The Marshall Plan and Its Meaning*, p. 161; Hogan, *The Marshall Plan*, p. 390.

326 Watching the assault: McCullough, *Truman*, p. 902.

326 *"if essential, the name"*: Paper Prepared in State Department: "Administration of Mutual Security Program," July 21, 1951, FRUS, 51, 1, p. 339.

326 Richard Bissell gave: Hogan, *The Marshall Plan*, p. 392.

326 *"this reduction would seriously"*: Telegram from Secretary Acheson to Chairman of House Committee on Foreign Affairs Richards, August 7, 1951, FRUS, 51, 1, p. 354.

326 *"sabotage"*: Quoted in Hogan, *The Marshall Plan*, p. 392.

327 *"power was [now] simply"*: Bissell, *Reflections of a Cold Warrior*, pp. 70, 71.

327 Harriman agreed: From report on "Current Economic Developments," October 15, 1951, FRUS, 51, 1, p. 427.

327 *"The economic aid we furnish"*: FRUS 51, 1, p. 429.

327 *"ECA's success in reviving"*: Bissell, *Reflections of a Cold Warrior*, pp. 70, 71.

327 *"was a government program"*: Isaacson and Thomas, *The Wise Men*, p. 444.

327 *"The American people tomorrow"*: Alberts, "Domestic Aspects of the Marshall Plan," p. 108.

Epilogue

PAGE

328 *"Whether you like it"*: Ambrose, *Eisenhower*, p. 262.

328 *"If you would only"*: Raucher, *Paul Hoffman*, p. 92.

328 *"by eradicating the social"*: Hoffman, *Peace Can Be Won*, p. 34.

328 *"the father of foreign aid"*: Raucher, *Paul Hoffman*, p. 133.

329 *"was due to some special"*: Oral interview: Milton Katz, HST Library Collection.

329 *During the Kennedy administration*: Bissell's role is well documented. Among other sources see Evan Thomas, *Robert Kennedy: His Life* (New York: Simon & Schuster, 2001). Another Robert Kennedy biographer, Arthur Schlesinger Jr., who was in many of the meetings, recalled that Bissell was the most forceful and effective advocate of hiring the mob to kill Castro and also of launching the Bay of Pigs invasion. He was "attractive and hypnotic," and he "beguiled the crowd," Schlesinger recalled. Oral interview: Arthrur Schlesinger Jr., conducted by the Author.

329 *"I can say flatly"*: Hoffman, *Peace Can Be Won*, p. 91.

330 *"The 1952 Democratic"*: Elsey, *An Unplanned Life*, p. 215.

330 *"a separate sovereignty"*: Isaacson and Thomas, *The Wise Men*, p. 49.

330 *"people still think"*: Oral interview: Paul Hoffman, Harry Price Collection.

330 *The Harriman Committee report*: The present examination makes it evident that Marshall, Clayton, Kennan, Bissel, Vandenberg, and Hoffman all held this view as well.

330 *America would benefit*: The Marshall Plan was no charity. Those Europeans who benefited least were those most in need. Marshall Planners made a conscious decision—in order to assuage Congress and to most effectively help Western Europe to recover—that the focus would be on industrial investment and modernization. The Plan was not, as some members of Congress feared it would be, a giant giveaway scheme. Europeans paid for most of what they received and the Marshall Planners purposefully held down consumer spending and the standard of living from rising much above prewar levels. Mostly, the Marshall Plan aimed at a longer-term altruism, and called on Europeans to delay near-term gratification. This would help deliver stability and economic self-sustainability, a sturdy foundation that would allow Western Europe to pursue further growth and prosperity, which would redound to the benefit of all for generations to come.

331 *"I've got the sack"*: Bullock, *Ernest Bevin*, pp. 833, 856, 857.

331 *"one of the greatest"*: Craig and Lowenheim, eds., *The Diplomats*, p. 126.

331 *"Ernest Bevin"*: Bullock, *Ernest Bevin*, p. 835.

332 *"the most perfect example"*: Vandenberg, ed., *The Private Papers of Senator Vandenberg*, p. 396.

332 *"To Arthur H. Vandenberg"*: Hoffman, *Peace Can Be Won*.

332 *When Sue passed away*: Fossedal, *Our Finest Hour*, pp. 260, 280.

333 *By the end of the Plan*: See Pollard, *Economic Security and the Origins of the Cold War*, p. 165.

333 *"the remarkable"*: From the *Economist*, quoted in Ellwood, *Rebuilding Europe*, p. 207.

333 *"this prolonged boom"*: Noted in Ellwood, *Rebuilding Europe*, pp. 210, 218, 219.

334 *"postwar miracle"*: Reid, *The United States of Europe*, p. 47; Hitchcock, *France Restored*, p. 205.

It is true that Marshall aid comprised around 7 percent of France's gross national product in its first few years, around 3 or 4 percent of Great Britain's and about the same for West Germany. Taking these figures at face value, William Hitchcock wrote: "In narrowly economic terms, the contributions of the Marshall Plan to Europe's industrial recovery were small." Hitchcock, *The Struggle for Europe*, p. 134. There is more to be taken into account here, though. The Marshall Plan financed essential goods—the machinery, tools, raw materials—without which some of Western Europe's largest companies, factories and industrial towns would have been idle. The value of the goods provided often had an aggregate value to national economies several times the simple cost of that good. It was called the "multiplier effect" and it was often as much as three or four times. Arkes, *Bureaucracy, the Marshall Plan, and the National Interest*, p. 241. Hoffman, Bissell and others at ECA understood the power of the concept, and Acheson wielded it in a last push to win economic aid for Europe in the throes of remilitarization. In addition to the multiplier effect, it must be remembered that counterpart funds worked "double duty." Europeans could buy goods they would have otherwise been unable to purchase. The proceeds were then reinvested in their national recovery. Finally, these analyses often ignore the true value of the technical assistance efforts. The budgets for the exchange visits, seminars and other projects generally covered basic expenses. Had there been a charge for the knowledge or intellectual product imparted, the cost would have been multiples higher.

In strictly economic terms, the Marshall Plan was much more than "marginal" or even a "vital margin." Its economic impact was larger and more impactful.

334 *"American aid prevented"*: Bidault, *Resistance*, p. 151.

334 *"The Marshall Plan was the first"*: Oral interview: Franz Blucher, Harry Price Collection.

334 *"the fact was that"*: Bullock, *Ernest Bevin*, p. 555.

334 *The Marshall Plan was meant:* Tony Judt made this point. He wrote: "The Marshall Plan, in short, was not just economic and political; it was also and perhaps above all psychological." The Plan offered aid "at a time when many Europeans (including many non-Communist politicians) were quite pessimistic about the prospects for their continent . . . the psychological boost provided by the Marshall Plan was much more important than the dollars themselves and was without a doubt absolutely necessary." Tony Judt, "Introduction," in Martin Schain, ed., *The Marshall Plan: Fifty Years After*, p. 7. See also Tony Judt, *Postwar*, pp. 87–99.

335 *The psychological boost was electric:* In their study of the Western German textile industry during the Marshall Plan years, Knut Borchardt and Christoph Buchheim found that Marshall aid was crucial, not so much because of the imports it provided, "but because of the confidence which it gave to entrepreneurs to acquire stocks and to commit themselves to long production runs." Discussed and quoted in Milward, "Was the Marshall Plan Necessary?," p. 240. The industry studied was a microcosm for scores of industries, thousands of companies and tens of millions of Europeans.

335 *Leading economists seem:* Judt, *Postwar*, pp. 326, 327, 330.

335 *"There are many explanations"*: Judt, *Postwar*, p. 331.

335 *During one of Western Europe's darkest:* It is conceivable—or at any rate, impossible to disprove—that as Milward asserted, "postwar Europe would have looked much the same without" the Marshall Plan. Milward, "Was the Marshall Plan Necessary?," p. 252. But viewed through a larger lens—one that refracts the economic, the political, the geopolitical, and the psychological dimensions at work—and when the full breadth of the Plan's contributions are taken into account, Milward's assessment does not sufficiently recognize the importance of the Marshall Plan to Western Europe's economies and its history. It is unlikely that Western Europe would have looked the same without it, and probable that the resilient, prosperous and peaceful region that emerged would have been a darker, more desperate place were it not for the benefits reaped from the Marshall Plan.

336 *"Obviously, the greatest single"*: Hoffman, *Peace Can Be Won*, p. 125.

336 *"There was a real danger"*: From Monnet's *Memoirs* quoted in Marjolin, *Architect of European Unity*, p. 166. A slide into economic nationalism would have cut into Western Europe's production and productivity, exacerbating its payments problems. Western Europe had been recovering before the Marshall Plan, but a return to economic nationalism could very well have placed additional pressures on Western Europe's economies that could have reversed that recovery. And without the Marshall Plan, they would not have had aid to finance their Dollar Gaps or the essential goods to fuel the output needed to continue their recovery. The Plan provided aid specifically to underwrite the formative initiatives (most importantly, the EPU) that propelled European integration.

336 *"without the American role"*: Lundestad, *"Empire" by Integration*, p. 153.

336 *"I am convinced"*: "Ceremonies Commemorating the 20th Anniversary of the Mar-

shall Plan, "Lexington, Virginia, October 24, 1967," (Washington, D.C.: U.S. Government Printing Office, 1967). Marshall Plan Vertical Files, HST Library Collection.

336 *The Marshall Plan did not:* In *The Reconstruction of Western Europe,* Alan Milward offered a forceful criticism of America's role in Western Europe's integration. Milward wrote: "The purpose of Marshall aid was, through furthering the process of economic recovery in Western Europe, to develop a bloc of states which would share similar political, social, economic and cultural values to those which the United States itself publicly valued and claimed to uphold." The vision for complete economic and political unification—a United States of Europe—was, Milward went on to say, "the chief string attached to Marshall aid." Milward, *The Reconstruction of Western Europe,* p. 123. Milward argued that the CEEC, the OEEC, the division of Marshall aid and payments agreements (prior to the creation of the EPU) were impediments rather than useful steps along the road to Western European integration, which only started, for Milward, after America backed away from imposing its own vision, allowing the Western Europeans (mostly the French and the Germans) to achieve their own alternate arrangement.

Milward is correct in pointing out that a grander vision for European integration did exist on the American side and that the Marshall Plan failed to realize it. And it is certainly true that Western European member-states remained intent on pursuing their own national self-interest and that the CEEC, the OEEC, the process of the division of aid and just about all Western European attempts at integration and cooperation from 1948–1950 were replete with strife, and at moments despair and stasis. Indeed, these difficulties are documented here, as is the failure of the *near-term* realization of loftier, grandiose visions for European unification.

Milward's argument, however, begins with an inaccurate premise. The premise is that America (as a single entity) had a cogent vision for European unification, that it wanted to create a United States of Europe; and that it sought to impose that vision on Western Europe, the main "string attached to Marshall aid." In fact, there was no such cogent American vision. In the Senate, Arthur Vandenberg shot down William Fulbright's proposal for an amendment to demand European unification. Vandenberg felt that it would go too far in infringing upon the sovereignty of Western Europe's nation-states. Hoffman's October 1949 speech calling for integration outlined several steps that the United States supported, but ultimately, he made it clear that it was up to Western Europe to find its own path forward. Following devaluation, Acheson, Douglas, Bruce and others met to discuss European integration. They wanted something more than a payments union as well as some form of progress capable of maintaining the West's geopolitical momentum. To that end, they wondered what form a more integrated Europe could take and which country might be strong enough to lead. The question, however, was not how to impose a "United States of Europe" on the region, but rather, how they could help to promote continued integration in some form, as determined by the country willing to take the lead.

There were more questions on the U.S. side than answers. That wasn't because the Americans were incapable of formulating a cogent vision. It was because that was not the challenge, as they framed it. Self-help reigned as one of the cardinal and governing principles at ECA and guided America's approach to integration. The key players were not reticent to attempt to apply pressure to Great Britain, France and others. But they never sought to impose one particular vision. They dangled the carrot of Marshall aid, they even pressed it as a lever; but they did not attach it as a string. If it was an attached string, then how could Great Britain have been, simultaneously, the country that received the most amount of Marshall aid and the biggest single obstacle in the way of America's hopes for greater Western European integration?

An informed analyst during the Marshall Plan years, William Diebold agreed that while "members of Congress spoke of European unification and even wrote such words into legislation . . . no well-informed person thought such a prospect remotely likely or within the power of the United States to effect" Diebold, *The Marshall Plan in Retrospect*, p. 433. In critiquing Milward and Hogan, Diebold wrote: "Much of the discussion in Milward and Hogan's works concerns the failure of the [American] efforts," to integrate Western Europe "but sometimes one wishes for a better estimate of how much the Americans really expected and whether any substantial progress in that direction they were pushing was not a gain." Diebold continued, "American policy in terms of *mega-designs* for the future of Europe seems to me wrong. Some people thought in these terms, but most were more skeptical." Diebold, *The Marshall Plan in Retrospect*, p. 433.

This book reinforces what Diebold offered—in the confines of a brief book review—as an impression. A more detailed portrayal of the men who devised and executed the Marshall Plan demonstrates that none held any rigid conception about a United States of Europe. While each had his own perspective, integration was primarily important to each in securing the Plan's larger strategic goals: recovery, political stability and geopolitical alignment with America. Integration was a vehicle, not an end in itself. In seeming to lose sight of these larger, overriding objectives, Milward created something of a straw man, a vision of a cogent American vision for a United States of Europe ineffectually thrust upon the Western Europeans.

It is not a hard construction to tear down. But, doing so occludes the Plan's much more measured approach to, and expectations for, integration, as well as the larger objectives behind it. It obscures the very real progress that was achieved in Western Europe's integration from 1948–1950: turning the region from a probable slide into economic nationalism and perhaps autarky toward a path of cooperation and integration; progress on payments agreements and leaps on intra-European trade liberalization; fostering habits of cooperation, a spirit of integration, and perhaps most importantly the self-confidence to pursue a sturdier foundation for integration with the European Payments Union and the Schuman Plan.

Milward also discounts the Marshall Plan's contribution to the latter two efforts. The support, security and partnership, though, that the Plan provided for Western Europe was the bedrock upon which it constructed these two extraordinary achievements. Hoffman had written it as the first line in the Harriman Committee report: "Only the Europeans can Save Europe." Diebold wrote: "Thoughtful Americans knew that whatever was to be lasting in European integration would have to be done by the Europeans themselves" Diebold, *The Marshall Plan in Retrospect*, p. 434. It was America's concerted policy to press Western Europe to integrate but it did so in adherence to the principle of self-help, and in the service of the Marshall Plan's larger strategic goals.

Western Europe launched its own integration. America's partnership—and the Marshall Plan—were essential to that end.

337 *But it was a path:* Arthur Schlesinger averred: "the European Union would not have existed without the Marshall Plan." Oral interview: Arthur Schlesinger Jr., conducted by the author.

337 *"The United States ought":* Schlesinger, *A Life in the Twentieth Century*, p. 476.

337 *Now, though, American lives:* We now know that he did green-light Kim Il-Sung's North Korean invasion of South Korea. At moments in 1950, when it appeared that China would not intervene and the U.S.-led forces marched toward the Yalu, Stalin was in fact willing to concede defeat and abide the loss of the Korean peninsula to America. But hundreds of thousands of Chinese had streamed across the Yalu in November 1950, marking the beginning of a treacherous American retreat and the beginning of the end of the Marshall Plan. We also now know that Stalin was intent on keeping the Chinese in the war and keeping the American forces pinned down in Asia, where American manpower and morale were atrophying badly. Gaddis, *The Cold War*, pp. 45, 60.

337 *"The inevitability of wars":* Quoted in Gaddis, *The Cold War*, p. 14.

338 *On March 5, 1953*: With the Soviet dictator gone, Mao and North Korea could finally engage the U.S. toward a long-desired cease-fire in Korea, which all parties agreed on three months later, in July 1953. Gaddis, *The Cold War*, p. 60.

338 *The only one to eulogize*: Service, *Stalin*, p. 590.

338 *"I saw my task"*: Craig and Lowenheim, eds. *The Diplomats*, p. 92.

338 *Western Europe was weak*: In retrospect, historian Michael Hogan could suggest that the Marshall Plan and American support at large "did not fundamentally alter the political fortunes in countries like France and Italy." Hogan, *The Marshall Plan*, p. 444. It is of course, a counterfactual that cannot be proven. However, the perils and vulnerabilities in Western Europe in 1947 and 1948 chronicled here, suggest that conditions were sufficiently extreme, and more importantly, France and Italy's confidence was sufficiently low, that without the Marshall Plan, further Western European degeneration may very possibly have brought about Communist political control.

338 *"forge a configuration"*: Leffler, *A Preponderance of Power*, p. 518.

338 *The Marshall Plan was the centerpiece*: Gaddis called the Marshall Plan the "chief instrument" of the containment policy. Gaddis, *We Now Know*, p. 37.

339 *"immediate economic gains"*: Gaddis, *We Now Know*, p. 196.

339 *During the Marshall Plan years*: The point is made in several places, for example, Judt, *Postwar*, p. 195.

339 *And it was part of the reason*: This is one of the driving themes in Gaddis, *We Now Know*.

339 *Ike had said of Marshall*: Ambrose, *Eisenhower*, p. 62.

340 *"Do I need to tell you"*: Ambrose, *Eisenhower*, p. 284.

340 *"moral scoundrel"*: Ralph Weber, *Talking with Harry*, p. 133.

341 *"These achievements in war"*: "Ceremonies Commemorating the 30th Anniversary Year of the Passage of the Marshall Plan Legislation, Capital Hilton Hotel, Washington D.C., April 4, 1978" (Washington, D.C.: U.S. Government Printing Office, 1978). Marshall Plan Vertical Files, HST Library.

341 *He was not receiving*: Pogue, *George C. Marshall*, pp. 505, 506.

341 *"The cost of war"*: Pogue, *George C. Marshall*, pp. 506, 507.

BIBLIOGRAPHY

PAPERS

Dean Acheson Papers, Harry S. Truman Presidential Library Collection.
Richard Bissell Papers, Harry S. Truman Presidential Library Collection.
Will Clayton Papers, Harry S. Truman Presidential Library Collection.
Clark Clifford Papers, Harry S. Truman Presidential Library Collection.
W. Averell Harriman Papers, Library of Congress Collection.
Paul Hoffman Papers, Harry S. Truman Presidential Library Collection.
Harry S. Truman Library Vertical Files, Harry S. Truman Presidential
   Library Collection.

GOVERNMENT DOCUMENTS

Foreign Relations of the United States: 1947, Vol. 2 (FRUS 1947, 2).
Foreign Relations of the United States: 1947, Vol. 3 (FRUS 1947, 3).
Foreign Relations of the United States: 1947, Vol. 4 (FRUS 1947, 4).
Foreign Relations of the United States: 1948, Vol. 2 (FRUS 1948, 2).
Foreign Relations of the United States: 1948, Vol. 3 (FRUS 1948, 3).
Foreign Relations of the United States: 1948, Vol. 4 (FRUS 1948, 4).
Foreign Relations of the United States: 1949, Vol. 4 (FRUS 1949, 4).
Foreign Relations of the United States: 1950, Vol. 4 (FRUS 1950, 4).
Foreign Relations of the United States: 1951, Vol. 1 (FRUS 1951, 1).
First Report to Congress of the Economic Cooperation Administration.
   For the Quarter ended June 30, 1948.
Second Report to Congress of the Economic Cooperation Administration.
   For the Quarter ended September 30, 1948.
Third Report to Congress of the Economic Cooperation Administration.
   For the Quarter ended December 31, 1948.
Fourth Report to Congress of the Economic Cooperation Administration.
   For the Quarter ended April 2, 1949.
Fifth Report to Congress of the Economic Cooperation Administration.
   For the Quarter ended June 30, 1949.

Sixth Report to Congress of the Economic Cooperation Administration. For the Quarter ended September 30, 1949.

Seventh Report to Congress of the Economic Cooperation Administration. For the Quarter ended December 31, 1949.

Eighth Report to Congress of the Economic Cooperation Administration. For the Quarter ended March 31, 1950.

Ninth Report to Congress of the Economic Cooperation Administration. For the Quarter ended June 30, 1950.

Tenth Report to Congress of the Economic Cooperation Administration. For the Quarter ended September 30, 1950.

Eleventh Report to Congress of the Economic Cooperation Administration. For the Quarter ended December 31, 1950.

Twelfth Report to Congress of the Economic Cooperation Administration. For the Quarter ended March 31, 1951.

European Recovery and American Aid. Report by the President's Committee on Foreign Aid. Washington, D.C.: U.S. Government Printing Office, 1947.

Merrill, Dennis ed. *Documentary History of the Truman Presidency*. Vol. 13, *Establishing the Marshall Plan*. Bethesda, Md.: University of America, 1996.

INTERVIEWS

Harry Price Collection

Dean Acheson, October 20, 1953

Raymond Aron, November 6, 1952

Richard Bissell Jr., September 19, 1952; October 10, 1952

Franz Blucher, December 3, 1952

Charles Bohlen, February 16, 1953

Dr. Oscar Bransky, November 3, 1952

Robert Buron, November 5, 1952

Attilio Cattani, November 18, 1952

R. W. B. "Otto" Clarke, November 10, 1952

George Clemens and Addison Foster, November 3, 1952

M. Thierry de Clermont-Tonnere, November 5, 1952

Harlan Cleveland, September 27, 1952; October 25, 1952

Edwin Dibrell, November 11, 1952

Ethel Dietrich, November 3, 1952

M. George Elgozy, November 5, 1952

William Foster, February 10, 1953

Hugh Gaitskill, November 12, 1952

Robert Hall, November 12, 1952

Averell Harriman, October 1, 1952
Paul Hertz, December 4, 1952
Etienne Hirsch, November 5, 1952
Paul Hoffman, January 28, 1953
George Kennan, February 19, 1953
Lamar King, November 7, 1952
Henry Labouisse, November 15, 1952
David Linebaugh, November 12, 1952
Robert Marjolin, November 14, 1952
Denny Marris, November 11, 1952
George C. Marshall, October 30, 1952; February 18, 1953
Donald McGrew, November 5, 1952
Jean Meynaud, December 21, 1952
Robert Myers, November 5, 1952
Paul Porter, November 4, 1952
James Reston, March 17, 1953
Eric Roll, November 18, 1952
Harold Stein, August 7, 1952
Dirk Stikker, December 22, 1952
Lane Timmons, November 6, 1952
William A. Tomlinson, November 13, 1952
Henry Tosca, November 17, 1952
Olivier Wormser, November 13, 1952

Harry S. Truman Library Oral History Collection

William P. N. Edwards, London, England, August 12, 1970
Per Haekkerup, Copenhagen, Denmark, May 19, 1964
Gunther Harkort, Bonn, Germany, November 12, 1970
Averell Harriman, Washington, D.C., 1971
Samuel Hayes, New York, July 16, 1975
Paul Hoffman, New York, October 25, 1964
Milton Katz, Cambridge, Massachusetts, July 25, 1975
Charles Kindleberger, Cambridge, Massachusetts, July 16, 1973
Thorkil Kristensen, Paris, France, April 20, 1964
Halvard Lange, Oslo, Norway, May 22, 1964
Frederick J. Lawton, Washington, D.C., June 17, 1963
Edward Mason, Cambridge, Massachusetts, July 17, 1973
Charles Murphy, Washington, D.C., June 3, 1963
Giuseppe Pella, Rome, Italy, August 13, 1964
Edwin Plowden, London, England, June 15, 1964
Paul Porter, Reston, Virginia, November 30, 1971

James Riddleberger, Washington, D.C., June 24, 1971; April 6, 1972; April 26, 1972

John Snyder, Washington, D.C., various occasions from 1967–1969.

Dirk Stikker, Paris, France, April 23, 1964

Knut Getz Wold, Oslo, Norway, May 21, 1964

Interviews Conducted by the Author

Lord Clinton Davis ·
Ambassador Lincoln Gordon
Lord Maurice Peston
Arthur Schlesinger Jr.
Sandra Schulberg

MEDIA SOURCES

American Newspapers

Chicago Sun-Times
Chicago Tribune
Cleveland Press
Kansas City Star
Louisville Courier-Journal
Louisville Times
New York Herald Tribune
New York Times
Philadelphia Inquirer
The Reporter
San Francisco Chronicle
Saturday Evening Post
Washington Post

American Magazines and Journals

BusinessWeek
Collier's
Commercial and Financial Chronicle
Coronet
Export and Import Journal of America
Fortune
Life
New Republic

Newsweek
New York Times Magazine
Parade
The Progressive
This Week
Time

American Television and Radio

CBS News
March of Time
Meet the Press
Voice of America

European Media

British Broadcasting Corporation
Daily Express (British newspaper)
Economist (British magazine)
Financial Times (British newspaper)
KRO (Dutch radio station)
La Tribune Des Nations (French newspaper)
L'Aube (French newspaper)
Le Monde (French newspaper)
L'Humanité (French newspaper)
L'Unità (Italian newspaper)
Nieuwe Rotterdamsche Courant (Dutch newspaper)
Times of London (British newspaper)

BOOKS

Abramson, Rudy. *Spanning the Century*. New York: William Morrow, 1992.

Acheson, Dean. *Present at the Creation: My Years in the State Department*. New York: Norton, 1969.

———. *Sketches from Life of Men I Have Known*. New York: Harper & Bros., 1959.

Ambrose, Stephen. *Eisenhower: Soldier and President*. New York: Simon & Schuster, 1990.

Arkes, Hadley. *Bureaucracy, the Marshall Plan, and the National Interest*. Princeton, N.J.: Princeton University Press, 1972.

Bailey, Thomas A. *The Marshall Plan Summer: An Eyewitness Report on Europe and the Russians in 1947*. Stanford, Calif.: Hoover Institution Press, 1977.

Beevor, Antony, and Artemis Cooper. *Paris: After the Liberation 1944–1949.* London: Penguin, 2004.

Beisner, Robert. *Dean Acheson: A Life in the Cold War.* Oxford, U.K.: Oxford University Press, 2006.

Bidault, Georges. *Resistance: The Political Autobiography of Georges Bidault.* New York: Praeger, 1965.

Bissell, Richard M., Jr. *Reflections of a Cold Warrior: From Yalta to the Bay of Pigs.* New Haven, Conn.: Yale University Press, 1996.

Bland, Larry I., ed. *George C. Marshall: Interviews and Reminiscences for Forrest C. Pogue.* Lexington, Va.: George C. Marshall Research Foundation, 1991.

Bohlen, Charles. *Witness to History: 1929–1969.* New York: Norton, 1973.

Bullock, Alan. *Ernest Bevin: Foreign Secretary 1945–1951.* London: Heinemann, 1983.

Carr, E. H. *The Twenty Years' Crisis: 1919–1939.* New York: Harper & Row, 1964.

——. *What Is History?* London: Penguin, 1961.

Chace, James. *Acheson: The Secretary of State Who Created the American World.* New York: Simon & Schuster, 1998.

Clay, Lucius D. *Decision in Germany.* Garden City, N.Y.: Doubleday, 1950.

Clifford, Clark, with Richard Holbrooke. *Counsel to the President.* New York: Random House, 1991.

Cohen, Lizabeth. *A Consumers' Republic: The Politics of Mass Consumption.* New York: Random House, 2003.

Conant, James B. *My Several Lives: Memoirs of a Social Inventor.* New York: Harper & Row, 1970.

Craig, Gordon A., and Francis L. Lowenheim, eds. *The Diplomats, 1939–1979.* Princeton, N.J.: Princeton University Press, 1994.

Cray, Ed. *General of the Army: George C. Marshall, Soldier and Statesman.* New York: Cooper Square, 1990.

Cunliffe, Marcus, ed. *The London Times: History of Our Times.* New York: Norton, 1971.

Dallek, Robert. *An Unfinished Life: John F. Kennedy, 1917–1963.* Boston: Little, Brown, 2003.

Deighton, Anne. *The Impossible Peace: Britain, the Division of Germany, and the Origins of the Cold War.* Oxford, U.K.: Clarendon, 1990.

Djilas, Milovan. *Conversations with Stalin.* San Diego: Harcourt, Brace & Co., 1962.

Donovan, Robert. *The Second Victory: The Marshall Plan and the Postwar Revival of Europe.* New York: Madison, 1987.

Duchene, François. *Jean Monnet: The First Statesman of Independence.* New York: Norton, 1994.

Eichengreen, Barry, ed. *Europe's Postwar Recovery.* Great Britain: Cambridge University Press, 1995.

Eisenberg, Carolyn. *Drawing the Line: The American Decision to Divide Germany, 1944–1949*. Great Britain: Cambridge University Press, 1996.

Ellwood, David. *Rebuilding Europe: Western Europe, America, and Postwar Reconstruction*. London: Longman, 1992.

Elsey, George McKee. *An Unplanned Life: A Memoir*. Columbia: University of Missouri Press, 2005.

Esposito, Chiarella. *America's Feeble Weapon: Funding the Marshall Plan in France and Italy, 1948–1950*. Westport, Conn.: Greenwood Press, 1994.

Ferrell, Robert H., ed. *Dear Bess: The Letters from Harry to Bess Truman, 1910–1959*. New York: Norton, 1983.

——, ed. *Off the Record: The Private Papers of Harry S. Truman*. New York: Harper & Row, 1980.

——, ed. *Truman in the White House: The Diary of Eben A. Ayres*. Columbia: University of Missouri Press, 1991.

Fossedal, Gregory. *Our Finest Hour: Will Clayton, the Marshall Plan, and the Triumph of Democracy*. Stanford, Calif.: Hoover Institution Press, 1993.

Freeland, Richard. *The Truman Doctrine and the Origins of McCarthyism: Foreign Policy, Domestic Politics and Internal Security, 1946–48*. New York: New York University Press. 1985.

Fromkin, David. *In the Time of the Americans: FDR, Truman, Eisenhower, Marshall, MacArthur: The Generation That Changed America's Role in the World*. New York: Knopf, 1995.

Gaddis, John Lewis. *The Cold War: A New History*. New York: Penguin, 2005.

——. *The Landscape of History: How Historians Map the Past*. New York: Oxford University Press. 2002.

——. *We Now Know: Rethinking Cold War History*. Oxford, U.K.: Oxford University Press, 1997.

Gallen, David, ed. *The Quotable Truman*. New York: Carroll & Graf, 1994.

Gallup, George. *The Gallup Poll: Public Opinion 1935–1971. Volume 1: 1935–1948*. New York: Random House, 1972.

——. *The Gallup Poll: Public Opinion 1935–1971. Volume 2: 1949–1958*. New York: Random House, 1972.

Garwood, Ellen Clayton. *Will Clayton: A Short Biography*. Austin: University of Texas Press, 1958.

Gilbert, Martin. *Churchill and America*. New York: Free Press, 2005.

Gimbel, John. *The Origins of the Marshall Plan*. Stanford, Calif: Stanford University Press, 1976.

Gordon, John Steele. *An Empire of Wealth*. New York: HarperCollins, 2005.

Gromyko, Andrei. *Memoirs*. New York: Doubleday, 1989.

Hillman, William. *Mr. President: The First Publication from the Personal Diaries, Private Letters, Papers and Revealing Interviews of Harry S. Truman*. New York: Farrar, Straus & Young, 1952.

Hitchcock, William I. *France Restored: Cold War Diplomacy and the Quest for Leadership in Europe, 1944–1954*. Chapel Hill: University of North Carolina Press, 1998.

——. *The Struggle for Europe: The Turbulent History of a Divided Continent, 1945 to the Present*. New York: Anchor, 2003.

Hixson, Walter. *Parting the Curtain: Propaganda, Culture, and the Cold War, 1945–1961*. New York: St. Martin's Griffin, 1997.

Hoffman, Paul. *Peace Can Be Won*. Garden City, N.Y.: Doubleday, 1951.

Hoffman, Stanley, and Charles Maier, eds. *The Marshall Plan: A Retrospective*. Boulder, Colo.: Westview, 1984.

Hogan, Michael J. *The Marshall Plan: America, Britain, and the Reconstruction of Western Europe, 1947–1952*. Cambridge, U.K.: Cambridge University Press, 1987.

Hoopes, Townsend. *The Devil and John Foster Dulles*. Boston: Little, Brown, 1973.

Hunt, E. Howard. *Undercover: Memoirs of an American Secret Agent*. New York: Berkeley, 1974.

Ikenberry, G. John. *After Victory: Institutions, Strategic Restraint, and the Rebuilding of Order After Major Wars*. Princeton, N.J.: Princeton University Press, 2001.

Isaacson, Walter, and Evan Thomas. *The Wise Men: Six Friends and the World They Made*. New York: Simon & Schuster, 1986.

Johnson, Haynes. *The Age of Anxiety: McCarthyism to Terrorism*. Orlando, Fla.: Harcourt, 2005.

Jones, Joseph Marion. *The Fifteen Weeks: An Inside Account of the Genesis of the Marshall Plan*. New York: Viking, 1955.

Judt, Tony. *Postwar: A History of Europe Since 1945*. New York: Penguin, 2005.

Kennan, George. *Memoirs: 1925–1950*. New York: Pantheon, 1967.

Killick, John. *The United States and European Reconstruction 1945–1960*. Chicago, Illinois: Fitzroy Dearborn Publishers, 1997.

Kindleberger, Charles. *Marshall Plan Days*. New York: Allen & Unwin, 1987.

Kissinger, Henry. *Diplomacy*. New York: Simon and Schuster, 1994.

——. *Does America Need a Foreign Policy? Toward a Diplomacy for the 21st Century*. New York: Simon & Schuster, 2001.

Kolko, Joyce, and Gabriel Kolko. *The Limits of Power: The World and United States Foreign Policy, 1945–1954*. New York: Harper & Row, 1972.

Kuromiya, Hirokai. *Stalin: Profiles in Power*. United Kingdom: Pearson, 2005.

Lankford, Nelson D. *The Last American Aristocrat: The Biography of David K. E. Bruce, 1898–1977*. Boston: Little, Brown, 1996.

Leffler, Melvyn P. *A Preponderance of Power: National Security, the Truman Administration, and the Cold War*. Stanford, Calif.: Stanford University Press, 1992.

Leffler, Melvyn and David Painter, eds. *Origins of the Cold War: An International History*. Second edition. New York: Routledge, 2005.

Levering, Ralph, Vladimir Petachnov, Verena Botzenhart-Viehe, and C. Earl Edmondson. *Debating the Origins of the Cold War: American and Russian Perspectives*. New York: Rowan & Littlefield, 2002.

Lundestad, Geir. *"Empire" by Integration: The United States and European Integration, 1945–1997*. New York: Oxford University Press, 1998.

———. *The United States and Western Europe since 1945: From "Empire" by Invitation to Transatlantic Drift*. Oxford, U.K.: Oxford University Press, 2003.

Maier, Charles. *In Search of Stability: Explorations in Historical Political Economy*. Great Britain: Cambridge University Press, 1987.

Maier, Charles S., ed., with assistance of Gunter Bishof. *The Marshall Plan and Germany: West German Development Within the Framework of the European Recovery Program*. New York: Berg, 1991.

Marjolin, Robert. *Architect of European Unity: Memoirs 1911–1986*. London: Weidenfeld and Nicolson, 1986.

Mazower, Mark. *Dark Continent: Europe's Twentieth Century*. London: Penguin, 1998.

McCullough, David. *Truman*. New York: Simon & Schuster, 1992.

McKenzie, Brian Angus. *Remaking France: Americanization, Public Diplomacy, and the Marshall Plan*. New York: Berghahn Books, 2005.

Mee, Charles, Jr. *The Marshall Plan: The Launching of the Pax Americana*. New York: Simon & Schuster, 1984.

Miller, Merle. *Plain Speaking: An Oral Biography of Harry S. Truman*. New York: G. P. Putnam Sons, 1973.

Milward, Alan. *The Reconstruction of Western Europe, 1945–1951*. London: Methuen, 1984.

Monnet, Jean. *Memoirs*. Garden City, N.Y.: Doubleday, 1978.

Montefiore, Simon Sebag. *Stalin: The Court of the Red Tsar*. New York: Alfred A. Knopf, 2004.

Morgan, Ted. *Reds: McCarthyism in Twentieth-Century America*. New York: Random House, 2003.

Morrow, Lance. *The Best Year of Their Lives: Kennedy, Johnson, and Nixon in 1948*. New York: Basic Books, 2005.

Murphy, Robert. *Diplomat Among Warriors*. Garden City, N.Y.: Doubleday, 1964.

Nitze, Paul. *From Hiroshima to Glasnost: At the Center of Decision—A Memoir*. New York: Grove Weidenfeld, 1989.

Payne, Robert. *The Marshall Story: A Biography of General George Marshall*. New York: Prentice-Hall, 1951.

Pells, Richard. *Not Like Us: How Europeans Have Loved, Hated, and Transformed American Culture Since World War II*. New York: Basic Books, 1997.

Pisani, Sallie. *The CIA and the Marshall Plan*. Lawrence: University Press of Kansas, 1991.

Pogue, Forrest C. *George C. Marshall: Statesman 1945–1959*. New York: Viking, 1987.

Pollard, Robert A. *Economic Security and the Origins of the Cold War, 1945–1950.* New York: Columbia University Press, 1985.

Price, Harry Bayard. *The Marshall Plan and Its Meaning.* Ithaca, N.Y.: Cornell University Press, 1955.

Raucher, Alan. *Paul Hoffman: Architect of Foreign Aid.* Lexington: University of Kentucky Press, 1985.

Reid, T. R. *The United States of Europe: The New Superpower and the End of American Supremacy.* New York: Penguin, 2004.

Reynolds, David, ed. *The Origins of the Cold War in Europe.* New Haven, Conn.: Yale University Press, 1994.

Roberts, Geoffrey. *Stalin's Wars: From World War to Cold War, 1939–1953.* New Haven, Conn.: Yale University Press, 2006.

Roll, Eric. *Crowded Hours.* London: Faber and Faber, 1985.

Rothkopf, David. *Running the World: The Inside Story of the National Security Council and the Architects of American Power.* New York: Public Affairs, 2005.

Saunders, Frances Stonor. *The Cultural Cold War.* New York: New Press, 1999.

Schlesinger, Arthur M. Jr. *A Life in the Twentieth Century.* New York: First Mariner Books, 2002.

Service, Robert. *Stalin: A Biography.* Cambridge: Harvard University Press, 2005.

Shain, Martin, ed. *The Marshall Plan: Fifty Years After.* New York: Palgrave, 2001.

Steel, Ronald. *Walter Lippmann and the American Century.* New York: Vintage, 1980.

Stikker, Dirk U. *Men of Responsibility.* New York: Harper & Row, 1965.

Stoler, Mark A. *George C. Marshall: Soldier-Statesman of the American Century.* New York: Twayne, 1989.

Talbott, Strobe, ed. and trans. *Khrushchev Remembers.* Boston: Little, Brown, 1970.

Taubman, William. *Stalin's American Policy: From Entente to Détente to Cold War.* New York: Norton, 1982.

Thomas, Evan. *The Very Best Men: Four Who Dared: The Early Years of the CIA.* New York: Touchstone, 1995.

Truman, Harry S. *Memoirs. Volume 2: Years of Trial and Hope.* Garden City, N.Y.: Doubleday, 1956.

Truman, Margaret. *Letters from Father.* New York: Arbor House, 1981.

Ulam, Adam. *Stalin: The Man and His Era.* New York: Viking Press, 1973.

Van der Beugel, Ernst H. *From Marshall Aid to Atlantic Partnership.* Amsterdam: Elsevier, 1966.

Wall, Irwin. *The United States and the Making of Postwar France, 1945–1954.* New York: Cambridge University Press, 1991.

Weber, Ralph. *Talking with Harry.* Wilmington, Del.: SR Books, 2001.

Wexler, Immanuel. *The Marshall Plan Revisited: The European Recovery Program in Economic Perspective.* Westport, Conn.: Greenwood, 1983.

White, Theodore. *Fire in the Ashes: Europe in Mid-Century*. New York: William Sloan Associates, 1953.

Yergin, Daniel. *Shattered Peace*. Boston: Houghton Mifflin, 1977.

Yergin, Daniel, and Joseph Stanislaw. *The Commanding Heights*. New York: Simon and Schuster, 1998.

Young, John W. *Cold War Europe, 1945–1989: A Political History*. London: Edward Arnold, 1991.

Zinn, Howard. *America: 1945–1971*. Boston: South End Press, 1973.

Zubok, Vladislav, and Constantine Pleshakov. *Inside the Kremlin's Cold War: From Stalin to Khrushchev*. Cambridge: Harvard University Press, 1996.

ESSAYS, SPEECHES, ARTICLES, SELECTED DOCUMENTS

Allen, Gordon H. "Washington from the Inside." American Farm Bureau Federation. November 1949.

Committee for the Marshall Plan to Aid European Recovery. An outpouring of documents, brochures, advertisements, including "The MP: 20 Questions + Answers," and "Who's the Man Against the MP?" "What About the MP?" by Alger Hiss.

Bissell, Richard, Jr. "Foreign Aid: What Sort? How Much? How Long?" *Foreign Affairs* 31, no. 1 (October 1952): 15–38.

"Ceremonies Commemorating the 20th Anniversary of the Marshall Plan." Washington, D.C.: U.S. Government Printing Office, 1967.

"Ceremonies Commemorating the 30th Anniversary Year of the Passage of the Marshall Plan Legislation." Washington, D.C.: U.S. Government Printing Office, 1978.

Chase, James, "An Extraordinary Partnership: Marshall and Acheson," *Foreign Affairs* 76 (May–June 1997): 191–94.

"The Churches and the European Recovery Program." Statement submitted by the Department of International Justice and Goodwill and adopted by the Executive Committee of the Federal Council of the Churches of Christ in America, January 13, 1948.

Clayton, William, "GATT, The Marshall Plan, and OECD," *Political Science Quarterly* 78, no. 4 (December 1963): 493–503.

Diebold, William, "The Marshall Plan in Retrospect: A Review of Recent Scholarship," *Journal of International Affairs* 41 (Summer 1988): 421–35.

European Community Information Services. "European 10th Community" no. 101, March 1967.

Economic Cooperation Administration. "The Marshall Plan at Mid-Point." Washington, D.C.

Fossedal, Gregory, "A Modest Magician: Will Clayton and the Rebuilding of Europe," *Foreign Affairs* 76 (May–June 1997): 195–99.

"Four Americans Discuss Aid to Europe: Illustrative Interviews from a National Survey." Survey Research Center, University of Michigan, Study no. 18, December 1947.

Gaddis, John Lewis, "The Emerging Post-Revisionist Synthesis on the Origins of the Cold War," *Diplomatic History* 7 (Summer 1983): 171–90.

——. "The Tragedy of Cold War History," *Diplomatic History* 17 (Winter 1993): 171–90.

Gordon, Lincoln, "Recollections of a Marshall Planner," *Journal of International Affairs* 41 (Summer 1988): 233–45.

Grose, Peter, "The Marshall Plan—Then and Now," *Foreign Affairs* 76 (May–June 1997).

Hitchens, Harold. "Influences on the Congressional Decision to Pass the Marshall Plan," *Western Political Quarterly* 21, no. 1 (March 1968): 51–68.

Jackson, Scott, "Prologue to the Marshall Plan: The Origins of the American Commitment for a European Recovery Plan," *Journal of American History* 65, no. 4 (March 1979): 1043–68.

Kennan, George, "The Marshall Plan and the Future of Europe," *Transatlantic Perspectives* 17 (Winter 1988).

Kotkin, Stephen, "A Conspiracy So Immense: Terror Leaves in the Kremlin," *The New Republic*, February 13, 2006.

Kratky, Karel. "Czechoslovakia, the Soviet Union, and the Marshall Plan." In Odd Arne Westad, Sven Holtsmark, and Iver Neumann, eds., *The Soviet Union in Eastern Europe, 1945–1989*. New York: St. Martin's, 1994.

Kunz, Diane, "The Marshall Plan Reconsidered," *Foreign Affairs* 76 (May–June 1997).

Leffler, Melvyn P. "Inside Enemy Archives," *Foreign Affairs* 75, no. 4 (July/August 1996): 120–35.

——. "The United States and the Strategic Dimensions of the Marshall Plan," *Diplomatic History*, 12, no. 3 (Summer 1998): 277–306.

Maier, Charles, "Review: American Visions and British Interests: Hogan's Marshall Plan," *Reviews in American History* 18, no. 1 (March 1990): 102–11.

Marjolin, Robert. "Ten Years of American Aid to E."

Mark, Eduard, "Revolution by Degrees: Stalin's National-Front Strategy for Europe, 1941–1947," Cold War International History Project, Working Paper no. 31, February 2001.

"Marshall Plan Working in Norway," *Railway Carmen's Journal* 54, no. 3 (March 1949).

Miall, Leonard, "How the Marshall Plan Started," *The Listener*, April 20, 1961.

Milward, Alan, "Was the Marshall Plan Necessary?" *Diplomatic History* 13, no. 2. (spring 1989): 231–53.

Morrow, Lance, "George C. Marshall: The Last Great American," *Smithsonian Magazine*, 1997.

Narinsky, Mikhail M., "Soviet Foreign Policy and the Origins of the Marshall Plan." In Gabriel Gorodetsky, ed., *Soviet Foreign Policy 1917–1991: A Retrospective*. London: Frank Cass, 1994.

——. "The Soviet Union and the Marshall Plan," Cold War International History Project, Working Paper No. 9, March 1994.

Parish, Scott. "The Turn Toward Confrontation: The Soviet Reaction to the Marshall Plan, 1947." Cold War International History Project, Working Paper no. 9, March 1994.

Pechatnov, Vladimir, "The Big Three After World War II: New Documents on Soviet Thinking about Post War Relations with the United States and Great Britain," Cold War International History Project, Working Paper no. 13, May 1995.

Reynolds, David, "The European Response," *Foreign Affairs* 76 (May–June 1997).

Roberts, Geoffrey, "Moscow and the Marshall Plan," *Europe-Asia Studies* 46, no. 8 (1994): 1371–86.

Rostow, Walt W., "Lessons of the Plan: Looking Forward to the Next Century," *Foreign Affairs* 76 (May–June 1997): 205–12.

Schmidt, Helmut, "Miles to Go: From American Plan to European Union," *Foreign Affairs* 76 (May–June 1997).

Takhnenko, Galina, "Anatomy of a Political Decision: Notes on the Marshall Plan," *International Affairs [Moscow]* (July 1992): 111–27.

Williams, John H., "The Marshall Plan Halfway," *Foreign Affairs*, April 1950.

UNPUBLISHED MATERIAL

Alberts, Florence Gold. "Domestic Aspects of the Marshall Plan." M.A. thesis, University of Missouri–Kansas City, 1968.

Houston, Bryan. "Review of Operations of Information Service." Economic Cooperation Administration, January 14, 1949.

Machado, Barry. *In Search of a Useable Past: The Marshall Plan and Postwar Reconstruction Today*. Lexington, Virginia: George C. Marshall Foundation, 2007.

McGlade, Jacqueline. "The American Transfer: U.S. Technical Assistance to Western Europe, 1948–1958." Paper, Loyola College of Maryland, March 26, 1993.

Williams, John H. "The Long Term Program: Report to Robert Marjolin, Secretary-General, OEEC," November 23, 1948.

Yates, Lawrence A. "John Foster Dulles and Bipartisanship, 1944–1952." Ph.D. diss., University of Kansas, 1981.

ACKNOWLEDGMENTS

THERE WERE MANY PARTNERS on this adventure. It is a pleasure to have the opportunity to acknowledge them here.

Randy Sowell and Liz Safly at the Truman Library in Missouri were particularly helpful and made for wonderful company during my many weeks in Independence. Larry Bland, Joanne Hartog and Paul Barron at the Marshall Library in Lexington, Virginia, were attentive and pointed me to sources that would have gone unnoticed. Various staff members at the Library of Congress in Washington, D.C., and the Cold War International History Project at the Woodrow Wilson Center, also in Washington, were similarly generous in making valuable materials available.

During my time working on this book I had the good fortune to hold the Henry Kissinger Fellowship for Foreign Policy at the Aspen Institute. My thanks to Sid and Mercedes Bass for their generosity. I am indebted also to Elliot Gerson for his early and continued support. Walter Isaacson has offered invaluable encouragement and counsel at every turn; I am deeply grateful. I have come to know the Institute as a special place, and it is my strong hope that I will be able to contribute to the values it promotes and the work it does long after my fellowship ends.

In asking them to read drafts of this book, I imposed on many people with very demanding schedules. Graciously, they lent their expertise and provided insights and suggestions. And the book benefited immensely. My heartfelt thanks and appreciation to: Alan Batkin, Peter Beinart, Volker Berghahn, Laura Dave, Anne Deighton, David Ellwood, William Hitchcock, Walter Isaacson, Rachel Kleinfeld, Melvyn Leffler, Princeton Lyman, Edmund and Sylvia Morris, Sandra Schulberg, Matthew Spence, Louisa Thomas, Lowell Weicker, Immanuel Wexler and Daniel Yergin. Their discerning eyes helped to save the book from errors in fact and judgment. Needless to say, responsibility for any shortcomings that remain is my own.

My wonderful friends never failed to offer a kind word of encouragement, an unexpected gesture of support or a laugh when they were needed most. Thanks so much to: Bobby, Mary and Bob Jr., Nat, Sara and Oliver, Alex and Heidi, Alan, Karen and their boys, Louisa and Justin, Alan and Jane, Glen and Lynn, Georg, Chris, Annie, Joanne, Dave and Owen, Andrew, Betsy, R.P., Kelly and Reed, Caroline, Carolyn, Adam and Laura, Charlotte, Tom, John, Matt, Rachel, Romesh, Gloria and Jim, Melinda, Edmund and Sylvia, Didi, Oscar, Alexis and Filippa, Sarah, Princeton, Erica, Laura, Sunette, Meg, Lauren and Janet, Dave, Debbie and Molly, Justin and Indré, Adrian, Steve, Julie and Rajiv, David and Glenn, Pam and Lewis, Charlie and Marily, Marquez, Lisa and Mia, Maggy, Oliver and Pia, Jill and Asif, Rick and Susan, Andy, Emily, Meredith, Scott and Franny, Illan, Priya and Calypso, Jonathan, Judi, Cindy, Renee, Macy, Nancy, Zach and Leslie, Artie and Ethan. Alan, Max and Mary have become new and valued friends.

A special thank you to Ceridwen Dovey.

My agent, Jennifer Joel at ICM, has been an unerring and committed champion. I am very grateful to Martha Levin and Dominick Anfuso of Free Press for their steadfast belief in this book, its author and this subject. Thanks also to Maris Kreizman, Leah Miller and to Tom Pitoniak and Ted Landry for wonderful copyediting. The current volume marks my second collaboration with my editor, Liz Stein. For five years now, I have benefited from her editorial acumen, her extraordinary judgment and her unstinting advocacy for my work. She is more than I could have asked for in an editor and a partner in the enterprise. It should be said also that she has one of the best laughs I've ever heard; it makes me wish I was funnier.

As I wrote this book, as with my entire life, my family has been my bedrock. My late grandfathers, Errol and Leonard, would have enjoyed this project very much. It was my great pleasure to share it with Fay, Gloria, Shelley, Doug, Kimmie, Colin, Felicia, Craig, Jeannie and Sasha and Gary.

My uncle Grant was by my side for every single step. He provided encouragement, wisdom, guidance, but above all these, friendship and faith.

My nephew and niece, Josh and Julia Zeitlin, were excellent and valued helpers—and sources of much joy. Zac Zeitlin is my brother and a deeply trusted confidant. Amanda Behrman Zeitlin is the wisest soul I know, the funniest person I know and makes me proud of her every day.

My mother, Janine Behrman, is my number one fan—and I hers. Her kindness, grace and selfless devotion to her family never cease to amaze me.

As always, my thoughts turn to my father, my hero. If I can write of nobility and adventure, it is because I had a father and best friend who embodied them. At twenty-three years of age, he emigrated from South Africa to the United States. I grew up watching him live and realize his dreams. Dad had a profound love of America, its ideals and its potential. This book is for him. But the relationship we shared stands as my proudest work.

INDEX

ABOUT THE AUTHOR

Greg Behrman is the Henry Kissinger Fellow for Foreign Policy at The Aspen Institute. He is the author of *The Invisible People: How the U.S. Has Slept Through the Global AIDS Pandemic, The Greatest Humanitarian Catastrophe of Our Time.* His writing has appeared in *Newsweek International, The Los Angeles Times* and *International Herald Tribune.* He has appeared on CNN, C-SPAN, NBC and often on NPR. He graduated *magna cum laude* with a BA in Politics and a certificate in Political Economy from Princeton University. He graduated with an M.Phil. in International Relations from Oxford University. He is a member of The Explorers Club and lives in New York City.